WITHDRAWN
UST
Libraries

a

BY THE SAME AUTHOR.

Second Edition, Demy 8vo, 12s. net.

HENRY III AND THE CHURCH
A Study of his Ecclesiastical Policy and of the Relations between England and Rome.

"It is written with no desire to defend the Papacy from the charges which were made even by the faithful at the time, and it may fairly claim to represent an unbiassed survey of the evidence. He has gone carefully through a large body of evidence which English historians have too much neglected. His book will be indispensable to the student of the reign of Henry III."—*Times.*

"This substantial book is beyond doubt a valuable study of the ecclesiastical policy of Henry III and his admirers, and of the relations between England and Rome. The whole of the chapters on this exceptionally interesting half-century of English history, when the relationships of Church and State were sorely tried, are written in a spirit of admirable calmness and fairness of citation, nothing apparently of importance being kept back on one side or the other of the questions that come under discussion. . . . A trustworthy contribution to the story of this long reign on the very points upon which most historians are either silent or provokingly brief."—*Athenæum.*

Fourth Edition, Crown 8vo, 6s. net.

THE EVE OF THE REFORMATION
Studies in the Religious Life and Thought of the English People in the period preceding the Rejection of the Roman Jurisdiction by Henry VIII

"We can only rejoice that this cheap reissue of one of the most valuable contributions (as common consent has proclaimed it) to the history of the great religious change in the sixteenth century will spread the light among numerous readers to whom it has hitherto been unknown. Of such historians as Abbot Gasquet the cause of historic truth can never have too many."—*Pall Mall Gazette.*

LONDON: G. BELL AND SONS, LTD.

HENRY VIII
AND THE
ENGLISH MONASTERIES

LONDON: G. BELL & SONS, LIMITED,
PORTUGAL STREET, KINGSWAY, W.C.
CAMBRIDGE: DEIGHTON, BELL & CO.
NEW YORK: THE MACMILLAN CO.
BOMBAY: A. H. WHEELER & CO.

HENRY VIII

AND THE

ENGLISH MONASTERIES

BY

ABBOT GASQUET, D.D., O.S.B.

AUTHOR OF "HENRY III AND THE CHURCH,"
"THE EVE OF THE REFORMATION," ETC.

LONDON

G. BELL AND SONS, LTD.

1910

First volume, three editions	. . .	1888
Second volume, three editions	. . .	1889
Illustrated (fourth) edition	. . . .	1892
Revised popular edition	. . . . .	1899
Cheaper ditto	. . . .	1906
Reprinted	. . . .	1910
German translation	. .	1891
French translation	. .	1894

PREFACE

It is satisfactory to find that another edition of *Henry VIII and the English Monasteries* is required. So far as the book itself is concerned the present issue is a reprint of the Volume published in 1899, in which the old references of previous editions to documents etc. not calendered at the time the work was written, were altered to accord with the numbers assigned them in Dr. Gairdner's monumental Calendar of Papers, Foreign and Domestic, of the Reign of Henry VIII. Beyond this I have availed myself of the opinions expressed by this exceptional authority on the documents of this period in the prefaces to the volumes of his Calendar which have appeared since the first publication of this work. Dr. Gairdner's conclusions, which naturally carry great weight, will be found to be in substantial agreement with the views I had previously expressed as to the main incidents in the drama of the suppression of the English monastic houses.

One or two assertions lately made in the pages of Magazines and Journals seem to point to the fact that some at least have misunderstood the argument I have tried to expose in the pages of this book, and it may not be without its use if I devote a small amount of space to set in the forefront of this enquiry the main features of what, in my opinion, has been established by it, as to the moral state of the religious houses at the time of their dissolution.

I do not, and indeed have never contended that in

regard to discipline the monasteries of the sixteenth century were all that could be desired. Very possibly abuses, and even grave abuses did exist here and there; but this is not the question to be considered. The point is, were the English monks and nuns generally in the reign of Henry VIII the profligate hypocrites which they were subsequently represented to be by those whose interest it was to defame the religious state or to defend the wholesale destruction of the religious houses. I readily admit that the reports of Henry's visitors were bad enough, although even they do not bear out the charges of wholesale corruption; but there are elements of the greatest suspicion on the face of these documents, which would certainly cause them to be rejected as proof in any other case, whilst if the characters of the accusers are considered, no man of honour would dream of "hanging a dog" upon their word alone.

It has of late been pointed out that other "Visitation Records" contain instances of abuses and scandals, and that this is a strong corroboration of the correctness of the scandalous reports of Henry's visitors. It is hard to see how this can be so; the only evidence afforded by such documents is, what no one would deny, that men did not leave their human faults and failings behind them when they entered the cloister; and that the Church, so far from tolerating any abuses of this kind, sternly repressed them by legislation and punishment. To make this clear I may perhaps be permitted to repeat what I have elsewhere[1] written on the subject of Visitations: That Visitations were not mere formalities, is obvious on the face of the records: they were made at regular intervals, and, considering the distances which had to be covered between the

[1] *Collectanea Anglo-Premonstratensia*, ii. Introd. xviii.

houses, they were carried out at great inconvenience to the bishop and with no little physical labour. After the formal opening of the inquiry in the chapter-house of the abbey the visitor made an address, explaining the meaning of a visitation, the intention of the Church in instituting them, and declaring the strict obligation which was incumbent on all, of making known to him anything, which might appear to them in any way to call for his correction. The visitor then assumed during the time of his visit all the authority of the local superior, and one by one the members of the community were called to him and separately questioned as to the state of the house, as to their own lives, and as to what they knew about the religious observance of the community at large. Notes of what had subsequently to be considered and if necessary corrected, were kept for the personal guidance of the visitor, and these were generally known as the *Comperta* or *Comperts* of the inquiry. In the case of any serious charge a formal and legal inquiry was held; the verdict of what was practically a jury, composed of the brethren of the religious incriminated, was taken and judgment was given by the visitor in accordance with the finding. Then followed the publication of the decrees of the visitation and their record in the register of the visitor. The inquiry was concluded, if necessary, by the punishment of those who might have been found guilty of any offence against good discipline or the statutes of the Order.

So much with regard to the formal part of the regular visitations. On the face of the documents recorded in the Episcopal Registers and elsewhere, it is impossible even for the most prejudiced mind not to admit that wrong-doing was never tolerated by the authorities, and that the punishments meted out were sufficiently drastic to prove their honesty of purpose. If wrong-doing existed, as unfortunately was the case in some instances, it took place in consequence of the degradation of human nature, which was as possible in monk and canon as in secular priest and layman, and in spite of the strengthening assistance given in the religious life, and of all the checks furnished by rules and visitations. If religious fell, as sometimes they did, it was because they were human and were carried away by their passions, notwithstanding the helps and safeguards of the cloister, just as a priest might make shipwreck, notwithstanding the grace of his ordination, or a layman in spite of the Christian Sacraments.

At the same time, it must always be remembered that the whole purpose of such visits was to detect and correct what was amiss, and not to record or praise the daily round of service according to rule. Hence ordinarily only that which was irregular and blameworthy found place in visitation documents, and the rest, if it were normal and godlike, was passed over in silence. To estimate the general state of any religious house by the "Injunctions" of a visitation, without taking anything else into consideration, is hardly less absurd than estimating the morality of the world by the existence of the Ten Commandments.

By those who know anything whatever about the matter it will be readily admitted, that it does not require much art or knowledge on the part of any would-be literary *chiffonier*, routing among the records of the past, to fill up his basket with the soiled rags of frail humanity. But no one, who did not find a peculiar delight in bending over such garbage and so obscuring his mental vision, could suppose that such a collection was history. As well might we measure the morality of the present day by the police cases and the annals of the divorce court, without other considerations which would certainly mitigate the severity of the judgment we might perhaps be inclined to pass, if we were to look only at the sordid details of modern life as revealed to us in the columns of the daily press.

It is now time to turn to the Visitation of Monasteries commanded by Henry VIII prior to the attack upon the smaller religious houses in the Parliament of 1536, and when some measure of dissolution had been already determined upon between Thomas Crumwell and his master, the King. Here I give the barest outline; the details will all be found in the pages of this volume. The Visitation opened in the summer of 1535, although the visitatorial powers of the bishops were not suspended till the 18th of September following, and preachers were commissioned to go over the country to educate public opinion against the monks. These were of three sorts apparently: (1) "railers" who orated against them as "hypocrites, sorcerers, and idle drones, etc."; (2) preachers who said the monks "made the land unprofitable"; and (3) those who told the people that, "if the abbeys went down, the King would never want any taxes again." This last was a favourite argument of Cranmer at Paul's Cross.

The men employed by Crumwell—the instruments for getting up the required evidence—were chiefly four: Layton, Legh, Ap Rice and London. They were well fitted for their work, and the charges brought against the good name of some at least of the monasteries by these chosen emissaries of Crumwell are, it must be confessed, sufficiently dreadful, although, be it always remembered, even they do not bear out the modern popular notion of wholesale corruption.

The Visitation seems to have passed through three pretty clearly defined stages. During the summer the houses in the West of England were subjected to examination; and this portion of the work came to an end in September when Layton and Legh arrived at Oxford and Cambridge respectively. In October and November the visitors changed the field of their labours to the Eastern and South-Eastern districts, and in December we find Layton advancing through the midland counties to Lichfield, where he met Legh, who had finished Huntingdon and Lincolnshire. Thence they proceeded together to the North, and York was reached on 11th, January, 1536. But with all their haste, to which they were urged by Crumwell, they had not got very far forward in their northern work before the meeting of Parliament.

From time to time whilst on their work of inspection, the visitors, and principally London and Legh, sent brief written reports to their employer. Practically all the accusations made against the good name of the monks and nuns are contained in the letters sent in this way, and in the document or documents known as the *Comperta Monastica*, drawn up at the time by the same visitors and forwarded with their letters to their chief, Crumwell. No other evidence as to the state of the monasteries is forthcoming, and the inquirer is driven back ultimately upon the worth of these visitors' words. It is easy, I know, to dismiss inconvenient witnesses as being unworthy of credit, but in this case a study of these letters and documents will be quite sufficient, I believe, to cast considerable doubt upon their testimony; and an examination into their subsequent careers will more than justify the rejection of their testimony as wholly unworthy of belief.

The general method of procedure was probably much the same in each case. The visitors were furnished with eighty-six articles of inquiry and with five-and-twenty injunctions, to which they had power to add much at their discretion. The inquiries were searching and suggestive; the injunctions minute, irritating and exacting. Framed in the spirit of three centuries before, unworkable in practice and enforced by agents such as London and his fellows, it is easy to understand, even were there no written evidence of the fact, that they must have been galling in the extreme, and even unbearable to the helpless inmates of the monasteries; whilst it is hardly rash to conjecture that those who had framed them had intended that they should be so, in order that the religious might be driven into rebellion and subsequent surrender.

The method followed by the visitors may perhaps best be understood by the account given by Dr. James Gairdner in the Preface to one of the volumes of his monumental Calendar of the State papers of this period. "The mode of procedure of Layton and his fellows," he writes, "is well illustrated in the case of Leicester. There neither the abbot (whom Layton himself believed to be an honest man), nor his canons would confess anything. Layton, consequently, as he tells Crumwell, intends to accuse some of the latter, first, of the grossest vices, and then of less heinous crimes, by degrees, until he has extorted something of a confession. If this may be taken as a sample of the proceedings," pertinently asks Dr. Gairdner, "how much might be considered as a confession by Layton, sufficient against a name? The old scandals," he adds, "universally discredited at the time, and believed in by a later generation only through prejudice and ignorance, are now dispelled for ever, and no candid writer will ever dream of resuscitating them."

To this estimate of the worth of the visitors' word, I may be allowed to add the judgment of Dr. Jessopp: "When the Inquisitors of Henry VIII and his Vicar-General,

Crumwell," he writes, "went on their tours of visitation, they were men who had no experience of the ordinary forms of inquiry which had hitherto been in use. They called themselves visitors; they were, in effect, mere hired detectives of the very vilest stamp, who came to levy blackmail, and, if possible, to find some excuse for their robberies by vilifying their victims. In all the *Comperta* which have come down to us there is not, if I remember rightly, a single instance of any report or complaint having been made to the visitors from any one outside. The enormities set down against the poor people accused of them, are said to have been confessed by themselves against themselves. In other words, the *Comperta* of 1535-1536 can only be received as the horrible inventions of the miserable men who wrote them down upon their papers, well knowing that, as in no case could the charges be supported, so, on the other hand, in no case could they be met, nor were the accused even intended to be put upon their trial."

The details of the Visitation may be read in this volume, and I pass to the second step in the dissolution of the monasteries. Parliament met on 4th February, 1536, and the chief business it was called upon to transact was the scheme of suppressing the smaller religious houses. What happened to induce it to consent to the measure is well known: or rather the account to be found in most of our history books is well known. The fact is that this tale has so often been told and retold that there is probably no incident in our history so universally accepted: even, I may perhaps be allowed to add, as there is none that rests upon so slender a basis of fact. The story, for example, as told in Green's *History of the English People*, may be taken as a fairly accurate statement of what is commonly believed to be true. "Two Royal Commissioners," he writes, "were dispatched on a general visitation of the religious houses, and their reports formed a 'black-book,' which was laid before Parliament in 1536. It was acknowledged that about a third of the houses, including the bulk of the larger abbeys, were fairly and decently conducted. The rest were charged with drunkenness, with simony, and with the foulest and most revolting crimes."

I believe I am right in taking this account as presenting a version—and a fairly moderate version—of the reasons which induced the nation to consent to perhaps the greatest piece of confiscation the world has ever seen. Yet how far does this version represent the truth—the whole truth, or any part of the truth? We have now the means of judging with certainty as to the facts, and we can say that in these sample statements, brief though they be, there are some assertions that are absolutely false, some incapable of proof and unlikely, and some distinctly misleading. It is quite certain, for instance, that before the meeting of Parliament more than two Commissioners were employed in the work of visiting the monasteries. It is quite certain, moreover, that the Commissioners never reported to Parliament at all, and even in the reports (or *Comperta*) forwarded to Crumwell, his agents do not assert that "two-thirds of the monks were leading vicious lives under cover of their cowls and hoods," nor again that Parliament declared that "about a third" of the monasteries "were fairly and decently conducted." Lastly, there is no evidence of any kind that the celebrated "black-book" ever had any existence outside the minds of writers of a later date; and distinct testimony makes it highly improbable that any such book was "laid before Parliament in 1536."

Further than this: bad as the charges made by Henry's

visitors were, "drunkenness and simony" were not among them, neither, do I think, that any one who has studied the available documents could possibly assert that two-thirds —or anything approaching two-thirds—are charged in them with being guilty of "the foulest and most revolting of crimes." Probably the only item of Mr. Green's account which has any sure foundation in fact, is the remark appended to the account just given:—"that the character of the visitors, the sweeping nature of their report, and the long debate that followed on its reception, leave little doubt that the charges were grossly exaggerated."

Let me state what we know for certain about this matter. We know that the proposal to suppress the smaller religious houses gave rise to a long debate, and that Parliament passed the measure with great reluctance. Indeed, so unwilling was the assembly to vote for the measure, that according to Sir Henry Spelman, who gave the traditional account of the event—an account which bears the stamp of substantial truth—when "the Bill had stuck so long in the Lower House," Henry sent for the Commons and declared that if they did not pass it he would "have some of their heads." Acting under such threats as these, which they had ample reason to know were no idle form of words, and seeing that public opinion was turned against the monks by public orations, and in favour of a measure which was destined to relieve taxation by devoting the confiscated monastic revenues to public purposes, the faithful Commons consented to the King's bill. It is remarkable, however, that in the Act itself Parliament is careful to throw the entire responsibility for the measure upon the King himself, and to declare, if words mean anything at all, that they took the truth of the charges against the good name of the religious, solely upon the King's "declaration" that he knew the facts to be so. It must be remembered, too, that one fact proves that the actual accusations or *Comperts*—whether in the form of the visitors' notes or of the mythical "Black-book"—could never have been placed before Parliament for its consideration in detail. We have the *Comperta* documents—the findings of the visitors, whatever they may be worth, whilst on their rounds—and we can see for ourselves that no distinction is made between the greater and lesser houses. All are "tarred with the same brush": all, that is, are equally besmirched by Layton and Legh, by London and Ap Rice. "The idea that the smaller monasteries rather than the larger were particular abodes of vice," writes Dr. Gairdner, "is not borne out by the *Comperta*." Yet the preamble of the very Act suppressing the smaller monasteries because of their vicious living declares positively that "in the great and solemn monasteries of the realm" religion was well observed, and God well served. Can anybody imagine for a moment that this assertion could have found its way into the Act, had the reports of the visitors been laid, for the inspection of the members, upon the table of the House of Commons? We are consequently compelled to accept the account of the matter given in the preamble of the Act: namely, that the measure was passed on the strength of the King's "declaration" that the charges against the smaller houses were true.

In its final shape the measure enacted that all religious houses not possessed of an income of more than £200 a year should be given to the crown, the heads of such houses receiving pensions, and the religious, despite their alleged depravity, were to be admitted to the larger and more observant monasteries, or licensed to act as secular priests. The measure of turpitude fixed by the Act was thus a pecuniary one, and all monastic establishments which fell below the £200 a year standard of "good living" were to be given to the King to be dealt with at his "pleasure, to the honour of God and the wealth of the realm." This money limit at once rendered it necessary, as a first step in the direction of dissolution, to ascertain which houses came within the operation of the Act, and as early as April, 1536 (less than a month from the passing of the measure), we find mixed commissions of officials and country gentlemen appointed to make surveys of the religious, and instructions issued for their guidance.

The returns made by these commissioners are of the highest importance in determining what the moral state of the religious houses was, at the time of their dissolution. It is now beyond dispute that the accusations of Crumwell's visitors were made prior to the passing of the Act of Suppression of 1536, and consequently before, not after (as most writers have erroneously supposed) the mixed commissions of gentry and officials. The commissioners were to be six in number for each district: three were to be officials, namely, an auditor, the receiver for each county, and a clerk, whilst the remaining three were to be nominated by the Crown from "discreet persons" of the neigbourhood. The main purpose for which these Commissioners were nominated was of course to find out what houses possessed an income of less than £200 a year, and to take these over, in the King's name, as now belonging to His Majesty. They were, however, instructed to find out and report upon "the conversation of the lives" of the religious, or in other words, to examine into the moral state of the houses visited. Unfortunately, comparatively few of the returns of these mixed commissions are now known to exist, although some have turned up, which were unknown to Dr. Gairdner when he made his Calendar of the documents of 1536. Luckily, however, the extant reports deal expressly with some of the very houses against which Layton and Legh had breathed forth their pestilential suggestions. Now that the suppression was resolved upon it mattered not to Henry or Crumwell that the inmates should be described as "evil livers," and so the new commissioners returned the inmates of these same houses as being "of good and virtuous conversation," and this not in the case of one house or district, but, as Dr. Gairdner remarks, in these reports "the characters given of the inmates are almost uniformly good."

Such is the briefest of outlines of the circumstances which led up to the first dissolutions of the English monasteries. I have set it out here in the Introduction in the hope that by so doing I may induce at least some of my readers to study the details which are given in the pages that follow. The words *Comperta Monastica*, and the story about the doings of Parliament in 1536 in regard to the monks, and, in fact, the very destruction decreed against them appears to present a black enough case against their reputation. My belief is that most men of unbiassed opinions who will read what I may call the evidence I have collected, rather than what I have written, will come in the end to my conclusions. That I may claim the greatest living authority on this period, Dr. James Gairdner, as one with me in this matter, is, I think, certain from the words he used on first reviewing this book. "The old scandals," he writes, "universally discredited at the time, and believed in by a later generation only through prejudice and ignorance, are now dispelled for ever, and no candid Protestant will ever think of reviving them."

FRANCIS A. GASQUET.

February 5th, 1906.

INTRODUCTION

MONASTIC ENGLAND

The ruined abbeys of England are evidences of a past which, however diversely it may be judged in other respects, all will agree was great. To some the crumbling wall or broken arch speaks eloquently of the rapacity of an English king and indicates the completeness of his spoliation. Alas! it is to be feared that to the minds of most Englishmen the desecrated sanctuary calls up one thought above all else—the thought of wasted, wanton or vicious lives, and of the sad necessity which compelled King Henry to proceed to drastic measures of reform. The oft-repeated story proverbially gains in strength; and for many generations anecdotes about the wickedness of monk and nun have been listened to and accepted as simple truth; whilst even well-wishers to the monastic institute have thought it best friendliness to observe or counsel silence.

Undoubtedly it is no inviting task to attack a tradition so long implanted. A horror of monk and monastery has been imparted with early knowledge at many an English mother's knee,—the teaching first imbibed and latest lost. It would almost seem that in this regard the national character of honesty and fairness had been permanently warped. Englishmen have been wont to extend consideration even to a fallen enemy. In this case, they appear to have had neither mercy nor pity for those who were among the most honoured and cherished of their own household for many centuries. The truth is, that Henry's scheme for lowering monks in the popular estimation, though it did not impose on a people who knew them by experience, has served its purpose with subsequent generations. "All that men of the stamp of John Bale," says a modern writer, "could do in the way of defiling the memory of cænobites in general has been done, and though Bale is a discredited man, he and others like him have completed a work which can now scarcely be undone, and the memory of those who indubitably preserved religion and increased learning in the land is almost hopelessly besmirched."[1]

That the state of religious life in England, as described in the letters and reports of Henry's chosen visitors, was bad, is true. But even these reports do not by any means bear out the popular impression. The real question, moreover, that needs consideration is: what is the worth of the visitors' word? Edmund Burke speaks in accord with the dictates of mere common sense when he writes:—"I rather suspect that vices are feigned or exaggerated when profit is looked for in the punishment. An enemy is a bad witness, a robber is a worse."[2]

For three centuries the only voices raised in defence of the English monasteries have been those of antiquaries, who might be supposed to have a natural sympathy for a great, a romantic past. And even these, from Camden downwards, have found it well to make excuse for their weakness, and have not failed to add the general sentence of condemnation, however incongruously it might run with the context. Burnet fixed, so far as history is concerned, what it had to say on the subject, and the "History of the Reformation" was deemed sufficient to dispense with all need for further inquiry. In the last resort the utterance of the words *Comperta* and *Black Book* was enough to warn the curious or the adventurous off dangerous ground. It is only of late

[1] *Mon. Franciscana*, ii. Pref., p. xxx.
[2] *Reflections on the French Revolution.*

years that the subject has come within the scope of ordinary historical investigation, and some earnest and truthful writers have paved the way for a juster estimate of the case. Among these, stands pre-eminent Canon Dixon, who justly claims—strange as the claim may seem in regard to a subject about which so much has been written—"to have laid before the student of history for the first time a connected and particular account of the suppression of the English monasteries." The present work is an attempt to carry the investigation yet a step farther forward; and, utilising the mass of scattered material "still unpublished and unconsulted," to treat the suppression not as an episode of a greater subject, but as an object of special inquiry.

That the monasteries in the fifteenth and sixteenth centuries were all that could be desired in discipline and vigour would be maintained by no one who has studied the subject. The circumstances of the troubled times in many instances no doubt exerted a baneful influence on the interior spirit of the cloister, as it did on the Church at large.

It must be remembered, however, that denunciations as to laxity of life, even when made about the monasteries of the fifteenth and sixteenth centuries, rest, as a rule, on a comparison with primitive fervour. Whatever may be said as to the lives of the monks at this period, it must be confessed that the common and ordinary routine of their houses raised them immeasurably above the level of life around them. The Episcopal visitations of religious houses prove conclusively that, whatever failings, or even graver delinquencies required censure and correction in the case of individuals, the method of life for the community remained the same, and that in no sense could it with truth be called a life of ease and sloth.

In the chronicles and memorials of the various abbeys

we still possess, very little information can be gleaned about the interior and domestic life of the inmates. The reason for this is obvious. To the chronicler, as he wrote his volume in the cloister of his monastery, the daily course of the monastic life was so even, uneventful and well known, that it must have appeared useless and unnecessary to enter any description of it in his pages. The saying, "Happy is the nation that has no history," applies to monasteries. Troubles, difficulties, quarrels and even scandals find a place on the parchment record of an abbey or convent, while the days and years of peaceful unobtrusive labour would pass unnoticed by the monastic scribe.

In one of his suggestive lectures Mr. Ruskin bids his hearers note well the dates A.D. 421 and A.D. 481, for they are the years of the beginning of Venetian power and of the crowning of Clovis: "Not for dark Rialto's dukedom nor for fair France's kingdom only," he adds, "are these two years to be remembered of all others in the wild fifth century, but because they are also the birth years of a great lady, and a greater lord of all future Christendom, St. Genevieve and St. Benedict."[1] If St. Benedict could claim any country as his own it is England. There is no need to dwell here on the evangelisation of our land, on the messengers he sent hence to Germany and to the North to preach the gospel, on the schools in which he gathered his disciples, and whence issued the revival of letters in the darkest days of the Middle Ages, on the slow patient labour by which his sons reclaimed the soil, nor on the men through whom our very polity and law seem to have gained their temper and moderation from his spirit of discretion. All this is acknowledged though so easily forgotten. All was done so quietly, so orderly, so naturally, that a world which has entered on the fruits of

[1] *Our fathers have told us*, ii. p. 42.

the labour may almost be excused if it does not recognise
the hand that dug the soil and planted the tree.¹

The benefits conferred by the monastic order were great.
Those who experienced them had no doubt on that score,
and were not behindhand in full and ample expression of
their gratitude. And though the religious bodies were not
as rich as they were represented to be, their wealth was
undoubtedly immense. Various orders shared it, but the
Benedictines, including in their ranks, besides the Black
monks, the Cistercian, the Cluniac, the Grandmontain and
others, had incomparably the greater part. Independently of
their wealth, what gave the Benedictines further dignity was
the possession of eight or nine cathedrals, including those of
the specially dignified sees of Winchester, Durham and
Canterbury. This placed the election of the bishops of
these dioceses in the hands of the convent. At Canterbury,
in particular, the jurisdiction of the great metropolitical
church fell, during a vacancy, into the hands of the prior
and convent. In their name ran all licenses for the consecration of bishops; they held all the archiepiscopal powers
of visitation; they could nominate the consecrating prelate
and the prelate to preside at Convocation. It may be readily
understood that these powers were not always viewed with
favour by the college of bishops; but after the thirteenth
century, with a prudent use of acknowledged rights on the
one side and benevolence on the other, they managed
to avoid disagreement. Although holding the cathedral
churches, the monks did not interfere with diocesan administration. The bishop's officials were commonly chosen
from the secular clergy, even when he himself happened to
be a monk. It is almost a commonplace, however, to dwell
on the rivalry between the clergy and the monasteries as if it

---

[1] See Cardinal Newman, *Historical Sketches*, ed. 1873, iii. p. 365, *et seq.*; J. S. Brewer, *Giraldus Camb.*, iv., Pref. xv–xvii xxx.–xxxvi., and J. M. Kemble, *Codex*, i., Pref. v.–vii.

were intensified in the later ages. Unquestionably there were lawsuits about property and other rights between them, and misunderstandings such as will happen between men of all classes; but their relations seem to have been generally good and even, and exempt from any systematic bickering.

The privileged ecclesiastical position of the monastic orders found its counterpart in parliament. Abbots formed the bulk of the spiritual peerage, which in those times was both individually more influential and corporately much larger than at present. The position held by them throughout every part of the country gave yet a further weight to their great position as noblemen and local magnates. As such they went *pari passu* with baron or earl of the noblest lineage. On the blazoned Roll of the Lords, the Lord Richard Whiting and the Lord Hugh Faringdon went hand in hand with a Howard and a Talbot. This individual ennoblement indicated by the form of title is striking. Whiting and Farringdon do not walk merely as the abbot of Glaston and the abbot of Reading, but in the rôle of English peers they still hold the name by which they were known when playing as children in the country manor-house or poor man's cottage. In the letter books of Durham priory the chiefs of the Cliffords and the Nevilles address the prior as their equal in no mere words of empty form. If on occasion the layman strikes a higher tone, to which the monk responds in gentleness, it does not affect the ring of trusty and sincere friendship which is caught throughout the whole correspondence. Nor is there anything surprising in this when the character of the monastic life is realised. The monk of Durham from his earliest years combined simplicity of life with surroundings of palatial grandeur and a state and ceremony equal to that of courts, and yet more measured. As time passed on, he grew from obedience to command, and naturally, without perceiving it, the peasant's son became the equal of the peer,

And all this was done without appeal to principles of democratic levelling. The heralds' " visitations " commence at the moment when the doom of the monasteries was already fixed. Up to that time the art of sifting out the " gentleman " from the " no-gentleman," which under the Tudors and first Stuarts grew to a pitch of perfection, was not yet evolved; and it may be safe to say that the monasteries, in ages which, if any, might seem fatal to it, kept up the idea of personal nobility.

The organisation of the various orders helped to qualify the most prominent of their members for taking part in the chief council of the realm. Besides their presence in convocation, the Benedictines and Augustinians had each a quadriennial chapter, composed of the abbots and conventual priors of the whole country, and numbering for the Benedictines as many as two or three hundred persons. On these occasions even individual monks, who might be deputed by their superior, could learn the practice of great deliberative assemblies, and how to deal with affairs of far-reaching consequence. It was thus not merely by honorific distinction that we find the commissions of the peace generally headed by some principal abbot or prior of each county. They had the practice of business, and they were in touch with men of all ranks—the country gentleman, the yeoman, the artisan, the peasant and the poor. It is no mere figure of speech when monasteries are called the common hostelries for people of all sorts and conditions, the general refuge of the poor. The daily life of the heads and officers of every monastic house must have brought them in constant and natural contact with all classes of society. The monks were not merely anchorites enclosed in narrow walls, but were affected by all the movements of public life. They were not men of war, but, like the knight and the baron, they had to provide men for the musters. As great landowners they, more than the yeoman, were concerned in the crops and the weather. They resided on the land in the midst of their people, and the barns, farmhouses and cottages were no less objects of their care than the roof which covered their own heads. Beyond this, they were more than landowners to those round about them. The advisers and teachers of all, they fulfilled the duties now undertaken by the guardian, the relieving officer, the parish doctor and the schoolmaster. Their charity did not flow from public sources, yet all men expected them, as an incident of their profession, to provide for those in want, and they were well acquainted with the circumstances of those they helped. These conditions combined to ease many of the difficulties which attend the relief of the poor. "The myth of the 'fine old English gentleman,' who had a large estate, and provided every day for the poor at his gate, was realised in the case of the monks, and in their case only."[1]

Art is a finer and truer expression of the inmost mind than even words can be. Of arts, architecture is not the least in power to reveal the soul of man. "Can the same stream send forth waters both sweet and bitter?" says the writer just quoted. "Are the higher realisations of artistic beauty . . . compatible with the disordering, vulgar, and noisy pursuits of an unscrupulous avarice or ambition? Will men that gather meanly scatter nobly? Will any magic convert the sum total of sordid actions into greatness of any kind?[2]

Though the architecture of the fifteenth century has not the type of Cistercian beauty, the builders of the tower of Canterbury, of the Lady chapel of Gloucester and the church of Bath, the re-fashioners of Winchester, Chester and Sherborne, with a host of other monastic churches, could not have been men devoid either of the sense of beauty or grandeur. It seems in this matter as though, with the close of the civil wars, men had taken fresh heart, and the half century preceding the destruction of the monasteries, so far

---

[1] J. S. Brewer, *Giraldus Camb.*, iv., Pref. xxxvi.   [2] *Ibid.*, p. xxx.

from being a time of apathy and listlessness, witnessed a great revival of architectural activity. This would have been impossible had the monastic system been commonly in a state of undue relaxation or degradation. The individual sense of ownership in the common goods is singularly slight in monastic communities. It is altogether inadequate as a spur to keep things in a proper condition. Where the general level of discipline is low, the tendency is to shift off the trouble of the day to the morrow. Each man is glad to bear his own burden at the lightest, and that which is the common concern is left to take its course to the verge of ruin. A mere feeling of personal pride or spurt of personal effort is not sufficient, so strong is the tendency to avoid trouble. The only corrective is that which is of the essence of the monastic state, a strong and vigorous community life. This can only exist where at least a reasonable amount of order and discipline prevails. Hence the activity in building prevailing in the early sixteenth century has a lesson of its own to tell to those who have the power to read it. However wealthy these great foundations may have been, they could not have undertaken works of such magnitude had not the monastic tone been healthy and vigorous.

Nor was their work achieved, as is so often implied, at the expense of the parish churches. Though instances might be multiplied, one will suffice. Within a stone's throw of the cathedral of Coventry stands the church of the Holy Trinity; within a stone's throw of that, again, stands the church of St. Michael—two of the noblest ecclesiastical buildings in the kingdom. Both were in the patronage of the cathedral priory. Had the monks chosen to indulge in unworthy jealousy, the erection of these noble edifices might easily have been prevented. In these cases, it will be understood, the buildings were not for themselves. The Augustinian canons not infrequently served the churches in their own patronage; the monks as a matter of the rarest exception only. If it be asserted that, by acting in so many instances merely as vicars for the monastic houses, a portion of the secular clergy seemed thereby placed in a position of inferiority and dependence, it must be remembered that to the monastery they often owed their enrolment in the ranks of the clergy at all. Putting aside the education they commonly received in the monastic free schools, it is striking to find in the episcopal registers how large a proportion of the secular clergy were ordained to the "title" given them by some monastery or convent. This fact is emphasised by the extraordinary diminution of candidates for the priesthood immediately subsequent to the destruction of the monasteries, which accounts for the dearth of parochial clergy so often complained of a few years later.[1]

The only specimen of a monastic chronicle of the times of the civil wars[2]—that of Croyland, a place remote from

[1] From the archiepiscopal registers of the diocese of York it appears that between 1501 and 1539 there were 6190 priests ordained. Of these 1415 were religious, 4698 were seculars presented for ordination to a *title*, furnished by some monastery or convent, and 77 to a title given by a college, or *ratione beneficii*. The yearly average of ordinations to the priesthood in the diocese of York during the 39 years was over 158. The register of Archbishop Edward Lee shows that in 1536, 92 were ordained priests; in 1537 no ordinations were recorded; in 1538 only 20; and in 1539 the ordinations had dwindled down to 8. Of these, one, in the first part of 1539, received his title from a religious house, and another in the second half of the year was made priest "to the title of £4 granted him by the king from the monastery of Worksop." After 1539 among the few ordinations are some who present "titles" founded on the promises of some nobleman or gentleman.

[2] The dearth of late monastic chronicles is very remarkable. It is, however, capable of a simple explanation. In the first place, the generation which produced a Commines, a Machiavelli and a Marin Sanudo were hardly fitted for the composition of chronicles such as those of Matthew Paris and William of Malmesbury. Secondly, there is every probability that many such monastic records were destroyed at the dissolution. The little fragment of the monk of St. Augustine's, Canterbury, shows that the cloister annalists were still at work. This is not likely to have been a solitary case. Chronicles of this kind, however, would not be like the great folios of the St. Alban's Scriptorium; written on paper, looking mean and poor, and above all having nothing to do with property and estates, they would have been little regarded by the spoilers of the religious houses, and thus lost or destroyed. Thirdly, the rule of the first

the scenes of trouble—gives us a glimpse of continued activity. Besides the free school, the choral necessities required a school of music and singing. Architecture, painting, sculpture, organ-building, bell-founding, and that which English skill had raised to the dignity of an art—embroidery—all were as actively promoted at Croyland as ever. The monks too were not so wedded to old-fashioned ways, but what they were ready to greet the latest discoveries. It must not be forgotten that in England (though not in England only) the first printing presses were set up in the monasteries.

The great religious houses, moreover, afforded to the country population a sight of those splendours now confined to the great centres of population. The rich vestments and costly plate in the monastic treasure-house were no mere personal possession. The enjoyment of them belonged to the people as a whole. As feast day succeeded feast day the treasures were brought forth to delight the hearts of all who took part in the rejoicings. Thus the monasteries sent a ray of light and gladness through the lives of the great mass of the people, whose lot at best is full of hardness, dulness and sorrow.

All that is here insisted on is, that in the sixteenth century the monasteries formed an element in English social life both popular and beneficent. For the purpose of this argument it matters little whether the *Comperta* or *Black Book* be true or false. If they were true, the case would be stronger still, for it is only an overpowering sense of the benefits which the monasteries generally diffused over the

Tudors was of such a cast, that a Matthew Paris, or even a William of Newbury, that is, men disposed to tell the truth, could hardly hope to end their days in their convent. No man can be expected to make a hero of himself merely to gratify the curiosity of posterity. It is little wonder, therefore, if the later monks neglected their annals and turned in preference to other occupations.

country that, in the presence of such a catalogue of iniquity, could have prevented their fall amid general execration. But what is the case? On the part of the secular clergy, who might be supposed to be their natural rivals, the voice of Bishop Fisher, pre-eminent amongst them all for a love of sound learning and for piety, was raised as spokesman in their defence. Of the nobility, who afterwards shared in the plunder, many a one before the event put in a plea for the preservation of the house in which he himself was interested. The popular voice was expressed in the risings in the east and north, and at a later date in the west. It is only now, when the documentary history of the time is being revealed, that we begin to understand how narrowly these movements escaped a success, which would have changed the course of English history. The voices raised against the monks were those of Crumwell's agents, of the cliques of the new men and of his hireling scribes, who formed a crew of as truculent and filthy libellers as ever disgraced a revolutionary cause. The later centuries have taken their tale in good faith, but time is showing that the monasteries, up to the day of their fall, had forfeited neither the goodwill, the veneration, nor the affection of the English people.

CONTENTS

	PAGE
PREFACE	V
INTRODUCTION—MONASTIC ENGLAND	xix

CHAPTER I

THE DAWN OF DIFFICULTIES

Disastrous effects of the "Black Death" on the Church in England—The country not recovered by sixteenth century—Influence of the "Wars of the Roses"—Destruction of the power of nobility—Increased power of the crown—Rise of the new men—The royal "official"—Condition of the people in sixteenth century—The state of the Church—The bishops—The monastic orders—Influence of the times upon the cloister—Royal and other demands upon the monasteries—Attacks upon the monks by Simon Fish and others—Moral state of the monastic orders—Authentic testimony of Episcopal registers 1–11

CHAPTER II

CARDINAL WOLSEY AND THE MONASTERIES

Rise of Wolsey—His immense power—Exceptional powers in ecclesiastical affairs as legate—He obtains faculties for visiting monasteries—*Statuta* for the Augustinian canons—Wolsey disliked by the clergy generally—His scheme for founding a college at Oxford—Permission obtained from Clement VII. by pressure—Wolsey asks to be made abbot *in commendam* of St. Albans—Permission asked from Rome for further suppression for the Oxford college—The people object to the dissolutions—Bad repute of Wolsey's agents, Dr. Allen and Thomas Crumwell—The King finds fault with Wolsey's action towards the monasteries—Further suppressions asked from the Holy See—The Cardinal's design to found a college at Ipswich—Further complaints—Henry acts on the precedent established by Wolsey, and asks the Pope's permission to suppress monasteries for the foundation of new cathedrals—The difficulties of Clement VII. in the matter—The articles of impeachment against Wolsey which relate to the monasteries 12–34

CHAPTER III

THE HOLY MAID OF KENT

Early history of Elizabeth Barton—Her great reputation for sanctity—Bishop Fisher forms a good opinion of her—The special value of his judgment—The account of his dealings with the nun—Archbishop Warham's belief in her holiness—Her opposition to the divorce makes her arrest necessary—Her confessor, Dr. Bocking, monk of Christchurch, Canterbury, and others also arrested—Endeavour on the part of Crumwell to prove a conspiracy against the state—The examinations of the accused—Refusal of the judges to convict—Public penance of the nun and her companions at St. Paul's Cross—The nun's confession and its real significance—Its evidence in favour of the other accused—No conspiracy against the state intended—Endeavour of Crumwell to include Sir Thomas More in the charges against the nun—The crown proceeds by bill of attainder—The execution of Elizabeth Barton and her companions . 35–44

CHAPTER IV

THE FRIARS OBSERVANT AND THE CARTHUSIANS

Parliament renounces the papal supremacy—The check on pulpit utterances at this time—The friars difficult to deal with—Particular boldness of the Observants—High character of the Greenwich convent—These friars staunch supporters of Queen Catherine—Friar Peto's sermon and its sequel—The Observants suspected of intercourse with the fallen Queen—Friar Forest—Friar Pocock's sermon at Winchester—Henry appoints a superior over the friars—Their convents are visited and the oath of supremacy proposed—Commencement of a "reign of terror" in the monastic houses—Franciscan Observants staunch to their old opinions—Efforts to change them—Henry foiled in his design—Dispersion of the Observants—Imprisonment and death of a great number—Friar Forest's martyrdom—Retired life of Charterhouse monks—Maurice Chauncy's account of Prior Houghton—Henry's agents endeavour to obtain the signatures of the religious to the oath of succession—The prior and procurator committed to the Tower and are persuaded to take the oath—Further attempts to obtain an unqualified submission—The three Carthusian priors sent to the Tower—Their trial and execution for rejecting the royal supremacy—Further difficulties and the execution of three more fathers of the London Charterhouse—The community placed under lay governors—Their treatment—Some sent to the North of England—Ten fathers imprisoned in Newgate—Their heroism and slow death—Two more executed at York—The rest resign their house to the king . 45-74

CHAPTER V

THE VISITATION OF MONASTERIES IN 1535-36

Henry's difficulties in 1535—Royal treasury empty—The oath of supremacy proposed to the monastic houses—Intolerable nature of the oath—Necessity of subduing the monasteries, which were special supports of the papal supremacy—"Greed of great men" a second motive for the suppression of the monasteries—Their servile dependence on Crumwell—Injunctions impossible to keep and intended to drive the religious to rebellion or surrender—The visitors complain of each other—Their treatment of the religious, and especially of the nuns—Effects of the visitation on the interior life and numbers—Difficulties of religious superiors in governing their houses at all—Crumwell appoints lecturers in some monasteries 75-94

CHAPTER VI

THE PARLIAMENT OF 1536 AND THE SUPPRESSION OF THE LESSER MONASTERIES

Henry's agents preparing for the attack on the monasteries—Rapidity of the visitation of Layton and Legh—Usual account of the passing of the Act—Character of the Parliaments of Henry VIII.—House of Commons not a representative body at all—Systematic packing of the Houses—The instance of Bishop Tunstall of Durham—Methods for passing Acts through the House—The existence of the "Black Book" extremely doubtful—The preamble of the Act of Suppression—The action of the abbots in the House of Lords—Education of public opinion by Henry and Crumwell—Pulpit attacks on the monasteries—How far the suppression was justified by the law of property . . . 95–112

CHAPTER VII

THE "COMPERTA MONASTICA" AND OTHER CHARGES AGAINST THE MONKS

The *Comperta* documents—The portion preserved in the writings of Bale—In reality the notes of the visitors—Value to be attached to the charges contained in them—Meaning of *Comperta* in episcopal visitations—Date of the document—Comparatively few religious charged with crime—Accusations vague, and the result probably of malice and idle rumour—Examples of the manufacture of these reports—*Comperta* certainly not the confessions of conscience-stricken monks and nuns—Accusations often deceptive—Visitors' reports compared with those of episcopal visitations—Their charges contradicted by other royal visitors—Story of the Prior of Crutched Friars, and that of the Abbot of Langdon examined—Evil reports as to Dover and Folkestone contradicted by subsequent evidence—Charges against the Abbot of Wigmore—Origin of many of the tales against monks and nuns—Negative testimony in favour of the monasteries—Draft petition from the Lords and Commons to the King, begging him to stay any further suppressions 113–135

CHAPTER VIII

THOMAS CRUMWELL, THE KING'S VICAR-GENERAL

Crumwell's early history—Employed by Wolsey in the work of suppression—Crumwell on Wolsey's disgrace—Rapid rise—His autocratic power in England—Places spies everywhere—Instances of the reign of terror—No pretence of justice or fair dealing—Arbitrary action of Crumwell even in private life—Large sums of money coming to him as bribes and presents—Lavish in his expenditure—The patron of the ribald writers—Crumwell's fall and execution—Letters and the spoils of the monastic houses found at his house 136-157

CHAPTER IX

THE CHIEF ACCUSERS OF THE MONKS, LAYTON, LEGH, AP RICE, AND LONDON

The visitors well understood the royal purpose—Layton's origin—His complete understanding with Crumwell—Visits with intention of making out a case against the monasteries—His manufacture of *Comperta*—Understood Crumwell's weakness for money transactions—Offers bribes to his master—His filthy mind revealed in his letters—He becomes Dean of York and pawns the Cathedral plate—Legh, as a visitor, described by his fellow, Ap Rice—His large fees shared by Crumwell—His violence dreaded—Grave charges made against his morality—The punishment of Layton and Legh demanded by the "Pilgrims of Grace"—Legh made Master of Sherburn Hospital, and makes away with the property of the poor—Ap Rice had previously been in serious trouble—His money transactions with Crumwell—London chiefly occupied as a spoiler—Was possibly in Crumwell's power—His work of destruction—Treatment of the Abbess of Godstow—His public penance for incontinence—His reputation at Oxford—Imprisoned for perjury, and there dies 158-175

CHAPTER X

THE DISSOLUTION OF THE LESSER MONASTERIES

State of affairs in the spring of 1536—Obstacles to Henry's return to obedience of Rome—Establishment of Court of Augmentation—Instructions for commencement of dissolution—General method of procedure—Monasteries refounded by Henry—Fines paid for license to continue—Number of religious expelled on dissolution of lesser monasteries—Petitions for preservation of monasteries—Re-establishment of Bisham by the King—Progress of the work of destruction—Resistance of the Hexham canons . . . 176–197

CHAPTER XI

THE RISING IN LINCOLNSHIRE

Outbreak of the rising—Causes of popular discontent—The resistance at Louth—People rose in defence of the faith—Feeling against Crumwell and some of the bishops—Statute of Uses—Story of the rising—Destruction of the registrar's books in Louth—Murder of the bishop of Lincoln's chancellor—The "articles" of popular discontent—Henry's answer to the demands—Royal anxiety as to the result and the effect of the news in foreign countries—Collapse of the movement—Part taken by the monks . . . 198–219

CHAPTER XII

THE PILGRIMAGE OF GRACE

Popular sympathy with the insurgents—Severe measures taken by Henry—Causes of the Yorkshire discontent—Aske's declaration and examinations—Story of the rising—Religious replaced in their houses—Henry's instructions to Norfolk—His "politic device"—Insurgent envoys to the King—Assembly at Pomfret—The settlement at Doncaster 220–240

CHAPTER XIII

THE SECOND NORTHERN RISING

Dispersion of the insurgents—Henry's attitude with regard to the promises made to them—Proclamation of the royal pardon—Instructions to the officials as to the reinstated religious—Aske's endeavour to restrain the people—His belief in the King's honour—The new rising and its failure—Part taken by the religious in the popular movement, and especially those of Watton, Jervaulx, Whalley, and Bridlington—The *quondam* Abbot of Fountains—Trials and executions 241–264

CHAPTER XIV

DISSOLUTION BY ATTAINDER

The royal vengeance—Attainder of a religious superior advantageous to the king—Fate of Whalley, Barlings, &c.—Abbot and monks of Furness forced to surrender—Holm Cultram—Lenton Priory—Story of the fall of Woburn—Abbot Hobbes—His examinations in the Tower—His views as to papal supremacy—His anguish of mind—His death 265–290

CHAPTER XV

THE SUPPRESSION OF CONVENTS

Hard case of disbanded nuns—Number of convents—Good repute of the English nuns—Some convents purchased a temporary respite from destruction—Many reduced to a state of destitution—Injunctions for Synningthwaite convent in 1534—Conventual life—The good done by religious ladies—Testimony of royal commissioners—Importance to the King of surrenders and royal instructions on the point—Failure as regards convents—Final suppressions—Number of nuns 291–309

CHAPTER XVI

FALL OF THE FRIARS

Fundamental principle of the mendicant orders—Numbers in England on suppression—Their troubles—Bishop Ingworth's work in dissolving the friaries—The Dominican prior of Newcastle-on-Tyne—Opposition to the royal policy—Friar Anthony Brown—Progress of the dissolution—Friar Stone—Doctor London and the friars—The surrenders—Small value of the spoils—Sites of the friaries much sought after—Special hardships to which the disbanded friars were exposed 310–330

CHAPTER XVII

PROGRESS OF THE GENERAL SUPPRESSION

Value of surrenders—Policy of Henry in hiding the scheme of total suppression—Religious anticipate the work of spoliation in some instances—Second suppression of Bisham—Destruction of Lewes—Suppression of Abingdon—Example of Vale Royal—Royal pressure to secure surrender at Hinton Charterhouse and Athelney—Abbots appointed for the purpose of surrendering their houses—Deprivation of the Abbot of St. Albans, and forced resignation of Abbot of Evesham—Romsey Abbey—Dr. Hillyard and the monks—Account of the dissolution of Roche—Total number of ejected religious 331–361

CHAPTER XVIII

THE THREE BENEDICTINE ABBOTS

Pre-eminence of Glastonbury—High position of Abbot Whiting—The oath of supremacy—Royal visitation of Glastonbury—Last glimpse of Abbot Whiting at Glastonbury—Greater monasteries not legally dissolved—Whiting removed to London—The abbey dismantled in his absence—Examinations in the Tower—Crumwell's notes—Whiting removed into Somerset "to be executed"—The final scene—Abbot Cook of Reading—His friendship with the King—His attitude to the men of "the new learning"—His adherence to papal supremacy—First troubles—Examinations in the Tower—Abbot Cook's execution at Reading—Abbot Marshall of Colchester—Early troubles—Views of the abbot as to the deaths of More and Fisher—Examination of witnesses against Abbot Marshall—His execution . . . 362–396

CHAPTER XIX

THE MONASTIC SPOILS

Estimate of total value—Amount received by the crown smaller than usually stated—The general scramble for monastic lands—Work of gathering in the spoils—Private purses made by his agents—Monastic plate—Irreverence shown to relics—Demolition of shrines—Winchester, Canterbury, Durham—Feeling of the people at the work—Total value of the plate—Ecclesiastical vestments taken for the king or sold—Destruction of books and manuscripts—"Defacing" of churches—Lead and bells—Destruction of the buildings, &c. 397–427

CHAPTER XX

THE SPENDING OF THE SPOILS

Royal promises not fulfilled—Act of Parliament in 1539 dealing with the great monasteries—How Henry spent the property—Proportion spent on national purposes . . . 428–434

CHAPTER XXI

THE EJECTED MONKS AND THEIR PENSIONS

Pensions of the ejected monks—Only a portion of the monks pensioned—Voluntary surrender a condition for receiving anything—Amount of pensions—Reasons for granting large sums in a few cases—Deductions from the sum allowed—

Many patents for pensions sold—What became of the disbanded religious—Wills of some Winchester nuns—Restoration of some monasteries in Mary's reign—Last records of disbanded religious 435-459

CHAPTER XXII

SOME RESULTS OF THE SUPPRESSION

Popular prejudice against monastic bodies—A subsequent growth—The effect of the dissolution on the poor—Associated labour and prayer the fundamental idea of conventual existence—Caricature drawn by novelists—Various kinds of regulars—What the great monastic houses did for the poor—How the poor were robbed in their dissolution—Consumption of the sources of charity—Thrift of the old monastic owners—Rack-renting by new lay owners—Contemporary account of the state of the country—Vagrant laws—Effect of the dissolution on education—Possibility of monasteries taking part in revival of letters—Conclusion . . 460-477

APPENDIX

Accounts of the Augmentation Office, &c. . 478-480

General Index 481

HENRY VIII.

AND

THE ENGLISH MONASTERIES

CHAPTER I

The Dawn of Difficulties

No just appreciation of the great social and religious revolution of the sixteenth century is possible without some knowledge of the causes which produced it. "The history of the Reformation in England," writes Lord Macaulay, "is full of strange problems."[1] That the nation, at the bidding of the sovereign and in furtherance of his whims, should acquiesce in the rejection of papal supremacy over the Church, should substitute the doctrine of the spiritual headship of the king, and should tolerate the national upheaval and disregard of the rights of property implied in the dissolution of monasteries and confiscation of their lands and goods, are "problems" to be solved only by an acquaintance with the events preceding and accompanying them.

Circumstances combined to collect in the political and social atmosphere of England in the time of Henry VIII. elements fraught with dangerous and destructive power against the Church. In the first place, it would seem to be certain that the country had not fully recovered from that terrible visitation, known as the "Black Death," which devastated Europe in the middle of the fourteenth century. Although a hundred and fifty years had elapsed before

[1] *Essay on Lord Burleigh.*

Henry VIII. mounted the throne, so great had been the ravages of the scourge, and so unsettled had been the interval, that the nation was still suffering from the effects of the great sickness.

To the Church the scourge of 1349 must have been especially disastrous. Apart from the poverty and distress occasioned by the unoccupied lands and the consequent diminution of tithes, the sudden removal of the great majority of the clergy must have broken the continuity of the best traditions of ecclesiastical usage and teaching. The monastic houses also suffered, not only in the destruction of their chief source of income by the depreciated value of their lands and the want of cultivation consequent upon the impossibility of finding labourers in place of the tenants swept off by the pestilence, but more than all by reason of the great diminution of their numbers, which rendered the proper performance of their religious duties, and the diligent discharge of their obligations as regards monastic discipline, difficult, and often almost impossible.

The long and bitter feud between the Houses of York and Lancaster must likewise be regarded as an important element in the chain of events which rendered possible the political and social changes of Henry's reign. The insecurity and instability of well-nigh half a century, as well as the ferocity of that contest, must have stamped a peculiar character upon the men of the early Tudor period.[1] When Henry VIII. succeeded his father, every man of thirty must have had within his own personal recollection some knowledge of the terrible war, whilst his parents must have lived through the whole of it.

The obvious result of a knowledge of the danger and troubles of this long civil war, whether derived from personal experience or the relation of parents, was a willingness to hazard everything rather than recur to such a period of distress and bloodshed. Periods of revolution inspire peculiar prudence, and protracted war a determination at all costs to cling "to peace and pursue it." Hence the population generally throughout England in the days of Henry had

---

[1] Those who may wish to understand this more fully would do well to read an Essay by H. W. Wilberforce on "Events Preparatory to the English Reformation," in *Essays on Religion and Literature*. Second series. Longmans, 1867.

been rendered by circumstances long-suffering, and ready to endure the dictates of his whims and desires rather than to imperil their peace by resistance.

Another indirect and still more important effect of the conflict of the "Roses" upon the times of the Tudors was the destruction of the power of the nobility. The civil war completed the work begun by the pestilences of the fourteenth century, and finally broke the power of the great nobles. The "Black Death," by altering the conditions of land tenure, and thus depriving the territorial lords of their hold upon the service and lives of their retainers, gradually sapped the strength of the ancient nobility, whilst the war swept away all the pride and flower of the great noble families. It was the deliberate policy of Warwick, the "King-maker," to cut off the chiefs of the opposite party, and thus to the aristocracy especially the war was fatal. "The indirect and silent operation of these conflicts," writes Mr. Brewer, "was much more remarkable. It reft into fragments the confederated ranks of a powerful territorial aristocracy, which had hitherto bid defiance to the king, however popular, however energetic."[1]

When Henry VIII. succeeded, although every sign of growing power was eagerly watched and speedily and effectually checked, there was little that the crown had to fear from the hitherto powerful nobility. Thus the position and authority of the Tudor monarchs was altogether different from that of their predecessors, and the Royal Supremacy passed from a theory into a fact.[2]

As a consequence, the stability which the traditions and prudent counsels of the ancient nobility gave to the ship of state was gone, when it was most needed to weather the rising storm of revolutionary ideas. The new peers, who were created in the fifteenth and sixteenth centuries to take the place of the old aristocracy, had no sympathy either by birth or inclination with the best traditions of the past. Nor was the age favourable to the production of high-minded and fearless counsellors so much as to the growth of men of quick and active talents.

[1] *Calendar*, i. preface lxxv. References will be made to the *Letters and Papers, Foreign and Domestic, of the Reign of Henry VIII.*, by Brewer and Gairdner, by this word only.
[2] *Calendar*, i. preface lxxv.

The Tudor policy of government created also the "official," who was by nature restless and discontented. Working for the most inadequate of salaries, such a man was ever on the look-out for some lucky chance of supplementing his pay. Success and worldly prosperity depended on his being able to attract to himself the notice of his royal master. "It was his interest to compete for extraordinary grants in return for his work."[1] One with the other they strove who should best work their way into his favour by anticipating his wishes, satisfying his whims, and pandering to his desires, "their promotion being wholly dependent on his good-will."

As a result of the inadequate salaries, the administration of the law appears, with honourable exceptions, to have been partial and corrupt. Complaints were frequent against the lawyers of the period. Suits were kept on from year to year unless money was forthcoming to induce the authorities to make an end of the litigation. It even passed into a proverb that "the law was ended as a man was friended," and contemporary writers declaim against the mischief which men suffered "from the facility with which an accusation could be lodged against an innocent person."[2]

The same contemporary authority speaks of the miserable state of those who were unfortunate enough to be thrown into prison. There, he says, they "are lodged like hogs and fed like dogs." Moreover they were allowed to lie in these wretched prison-houses for years without any trial, and if they had no money were left to starve. If they, or their friends, could afford to pay for their food, they were allowed in some prisons to "pay for themselves four times as much as at any best inn." By all means, says Brinklow, "if a man offend the law let him have the law," but "to imprison a man and starve him is murder."[3]

In the midst of the throes of a great social crisis much depended upon the Church. There can be little doubt that the clergy of the time were ill-fitted to cope with the forces

---

[1] P. Friedmann, *Anne Boleyn*, i. p. 27.
[2] *Complaint of Roderyck Mors*, E. Eng. Text Soc. ed., Introduction, p. 25. In Starkey's *Dialogue between Card. Pole and Lupset* the same charges are made, and the same proverb is made use of by Starkey in the "Dialogue," which was afterwards quoted by Henry Brinklow in the "Complaint." Both these authors were contemporaries of the events about which they write.
[3] *Ibid.*, p. 27.

of revolution, to calm the restless spirit of the age, or resist the rising tide of novelties. Their very character was in itself out of joint with the times. In the days when might was right, and force of arms the ruling power of the world, the occupation of peace, to which the clergy were bound by their sacred calling, naturally roused hostile and violent opposition from the party rising into power. The bishops were, with some honourable exceptions, mere court officials pensioned out of ecclesiastical revenues. Holding their high offices by royal favour rather than on account of special aptitude to look after the spiritual welfare of their dioceses, they appear, perhaps not unnaturally, to have had little heart in their work.

Too often, also, the bishop of an important see would be occupied in the management of the secular affairs of state. Perhaps, even, he was paid for these services by the emoluments of his ecclesiastical office. To the king all looked for hope of reward, and to royalty all clung as long as there remained any prospect of success. The Church had few favours to give except at the wish and by the hands of the king. "Even cardinal's hats were bestowed only on royal recommendation."[1] The episcopal see was, moreover, not infrequently looked upon as a *property* conferred for political services and out of which the most, in a temporal point of view, was to be made.

The practice followed in more than one instance of rewarding foreigners by nominating them to vacant sees and benefices in return for services rendered, or as an inducement to help on some royal scheme, was also most obviously detrimental to the well-being of the Church. At one time the three bishoprics of Salisbury, Worcester, and Llandaff were all held in this way, by those whose only interest in the dioceses appears to have been the fees they obtained out of them. The bishop of Worcester lived and died in Rome, and his predecessor and successor in the see were also foreigners.

No less detrimental to the well-being of the Church in England at this time was the crying abuse and scandal of pluralities. Some priests were proved to have as many as ten or twelve benefices, and very possibly resident on none,

---

[1] Friedmann, i. p. 137.

while there were "plenty of learned men in the universities"¹ for whom no preferment could be found. Cardinal Wolsey himself set the example. He held not only a plurality of livings, but was bishop of more than one see, whilst he farmed others. He also obtained the abbey of St. Albans *in commendam*. Although the Parliament of 1529 especially legislated against this abuse, the exceptions were so numerous as to make the Act ridiculous and nugatory. At this time also benefices were bestowed upon youths of good family, who had sufficient influence to secure these preferments. Thus, for example, Reginald Pole, the future cardinal, when only seventeen was nominated to the prebendal stall of Roscombe, and two years later to Gatcombe Secunda, both in the Salisbury diocese. At eighteen he received the deanery of Wimborne Minster.²

The non-residence of bishops in their dioceses was a fruitful source of evil. The episcopal functions were very generally relegated to suffragans, who, instead of being assistants, became practically substitutes for their principals in all the spiritual work of a diocese. Not unfrequently these suffragans were bishops of Irish sees, who resided in England to the neglect of their own cure, and undertook the supervision of more than one diocese. Upon such auxiliaries rectories or other ecclesiastical preferments were bestowed in lieu of payment for their services, and these in turn were left to the care of ill-paid curates.

The occupation of the bishops in affairs of state, besides its disastrous effect on the clergy, had another result. By it a jealous opposition to ecclesiastics was created in the minds of the new nobility. The lay lords and hungry officials not unnaturally looked with dislike upon this employment of ecclesiastics in secular concerns. The occupation of clerics in all the intrigues of party politics, and in the wiles of foreign and domestic diplomacy, conduced to keep them out of coveted preferment. Hence when occasion offered they did not need much inducement to turn against the clergy and enable Henry to carry out his coercive legislation against the Church.

This state of affairs was doubtlessly reflected in the mon-

---

¹ *Complaints against Clergy in Parl.*, 1529, No. 6.
² *Calendar*, ii. No. 3943.—*Starkey's Dialogue between Pole and Lupset*, E. Eng. Text Soc., Preface cxiii.—21 Hen. VIII., c. 13.

astic orders of England. The events of the previous century and a half must necessarily have done much to lower the tone of the religious houses and rob them of their primitive fervour. Before they could recover from the effects of the great plagues of the fourteenth century the civil disturbances of the fifteenth century intensified the evils from which they were suffering, and became to them "specially disastrous."[1]

The financial state of the monasteries at the commencement of the sixteenth century was undoubtedly deplorable. Although many of them were possessed of considerable estates, which in itself was regarded as a matter of reproach, they were yet suffering from acute poverty. Denuded of their tenants, the monastic lands became neglected and unproductive. "Debt with no chance of redemption weighed heavily upon all."[2] Claims, however, upon their charity, and the exactions of royal and other founders, increased rather than diminished, till the burden was more than the crippled resources of the religious could bear. The State papers of Henry VIII.'s reign contain abundant proof of the increasing demands made by king and courtier upon monastery and convent. Farm after farm, manor after manor, benefice after benefice, office after office were yielded up, in compliance with requests that were in reality commands. Pensions in ever-increasing numbers were charged on monastic lands at the asking of those it was impossible to refuse. "In some cases," writes Mr. Brewer, "the abbots were bound to give endowments to scholars of the king's nomination[3] or provide them with competent benefices; pensions and corrodies were granted under the privy seal to yeomen ushers of the wardrobe and the chamber, to clerks of the kitchen sewers, secretaries and gentlemen of the chapel royal;[4] and these were strictly enforced, whatever might be the other encumbrances of the house."[5]

The royal munificence was liberally exercised in grants of pensions and perquisites when others had to satisfy the

---

[1] Brewer, *Henry VIII.*, i. p. 50.
[2] *Ibid.*, p. 50.
[3] *Calendar*, i. 1235, 1360. Mr. Brewer adds: "One of the most interesting of these cases is that of a pension paid by the Prior of St. Frideswide's, Oxford, to Reginald Pole, then a student at the University of Oxford, afterwards cardinal." Note, p. 50.
[4] *Calendar*, i. 49, 60, 106, 615, 920, &c.
[5] Brewer, *Henry VIII.*, i. p. 50.

recipients of the royal generosity. By established custom every bishop, every superior of a religious house, on entering upon the emoluments of his see was bound, "*ratione novæ creationis*," to allow a fitting pension to any clerk recommended by the crown until such time as he had provided a suitable benefice for him. So, in the same way, founders and their descendants claimed and exercised the right of billeting poor relations or needy dependents for maintenance, and often for lodging, on the religious houses of which they were patrons.

In their endeavour to meet the demands upon their revenue, the abbots and superiors of the religious houses endeavoured to accommodate their farming arrangements to the requirements of the time. Like the nobles and other landowners, they tried to turn their estates to the most profitable account by forming large enclosures, and devoting land hitherto cultivated to the pasture of sheep. This was regarded with great disfavour by the people, who were no longer required in the same numbers as before to make the monastic estates profitable to their owners. In the parliament of 1529 this, and the fact that the religious kept "tan houses and sold wool and cloth," &c., were causes of complaint against them by the Commons.

It is difficult for the popular mind to resist the influence of attractive pictures presented to it. The advantages to be derived from a redistribution of the worldly wealth of the Church, and in particular of the religious bodies in England, were constantly insisted upon. And the poison instilled into the people by scurrilous tales and descriptions of clerical and monastic life, circulated by their authors for the purpose of bringing discredit upon the Church, was no doubt insidious. These generally were not indigenous, but imported, venerable stories, Eastern in their origin and adapted from Mahometan life to suit the Christian character; but even they could not deprive the religious bodies of popular respect.

The most celebrated and perhaps most dangerous attack against the religious orders made in the early sixteenth century was in the "Supplication of Beggars," written by one Simon Fish. It was answered by Sir Thomas More, step by step, in his "Supplication of Poor Souls;" but, like all such stories, the answer probably reached only a

The Dawn of Difficulties

few of those who had accepted the wild statements of Fish's fables. Although aimed chiefly against the mendicant friars, the "Supplication of Beggars" involved in one sweeping condemnation the whole of the spirituality, described as "bishops, abbots, priors, deacons, archdeacons, suffragans, priests, monks, canons, friars, pardoners, and summoners."

Still, even these and similar falsehoods, although appealing to the cupidity of the people, do not seem to have alienated from the monks the affections of the general population. The insurrections in their favour furnish some indication of the opinion of the people, in spite of all that had been said and written. Henry Brinklow, a mendicant friar who had thrown off his frock, and was therefore on two accounts little likely to favour the monasteries, bears testimony to the way in which they discharged their duties to the people. "And when they," he writes, "had gifts of any (churches) not impropriated, they gave them unto their friends, of which always some were learned; for the monks found of their friends children at school. And though they were not learned, yet they kept hospitality, and helped their poor friends. And if the parsonages were impropriated, the monks were bound to deal alms to the poor, and to keep hospitality, as the writings of the gifts of such parsonages and lands do plainly declare, in these words: '*in puram eleemosinam*.' And as touching the alms that they dealt, and the hospitality that they kept, every man knoweth that many thousands were well relieved of them, and might have been better if they had not had so many great men's horses to feed, and had not been overcharged with such idle gentlemen [1] as were never out of the abbeys. And if they had any vicarage in their hands, they set in sometimes some sufficient vicar (though it were but seldom) to preach and to teach."[2] He goes on to say that the land was given to the monastic houses for education, hospitality, and to give alms to the poor, and that they were pulled down on the "pretence" of amending what was amiss. "But see," he con-

---

[1] A curious illustration of this may be seen in a letter from the son of the Duke of Buckingham to Henry VIII. It is evidence of the services rendered by the monasteries to honourable families in reduced circumstances. "And because," the writer says, "he hath no dwelling-place meet for him to inhabit, (he was) fain to live poorly at board in an Abbey this four years day, with his wife and seven children."

[2] *Complaint of Roderyck Mors*, E. Eng. Text. Soc. ed., p. 33.

tinues, "how much that was amiss is amended, for all the godly pretence. It is amended, even as the devil amended his dame's leg (as it is in the proverb): when he should have set it right he broke it quite in pieces. The monks gave too little alms, but now, where £20 was given yearly to the poor in more than a hundred places in England, is not one meal's meat given. This is fair amendment."

It will be necessary to examine more particularly the general state of moral discipline to be found within the monasteries of England at the beginning of the sixteenth century in considering the charges brought against them by those who thus sought to justify their dissolution. It may be here stated, however, that the most authentic evidence upon the subject is to be found in the episcopal registers of the various dioceses. These contain records, more or less minute, of the visitations made by the bishops to the monasteries within the limits of their special jurisdiction. Their injunctions and other acts prove the care with which the duty of supervision was exercised. Many monasteries, and even orders, were, of course, altogether exempted from episcopal control; but such exemptions were by no means as common as is generally stated. There is no reason whatever to suppose that the condition of the exempt religious was in any way worse than the rest. On the contrary, they were, as a rule, the larger monastic houses[1] which enjoyed the privilege, and in these, as the preamble of the Act of Parliament which suppressed the lesser houses expressly declares, "thanks be to God religion is right well kept." It is not too much, therefore, to regard the evidence furnished in the pages of these episcopal registers as giving a faithful picture of the state of the religious houses.

It would be affectation to suggest that the vast regular body in England was altogether free from grosser faults and immoralities. But it is unjust to regard them as existing to any but a very limited extent. Human nature in all ages of the world is the same. The religious habit, though a safe-

---

[1] This will hold good of Cistercians and Cluniacs, with some others. But in regard to the Benedictines, who held nearly all the monasteries of the first rank, absolute exemption in practice must not be too easily assumed. To say nothing of the wealthy cathedral priories, such monasteries as Glastonbury, in the south, and St. Mary's, York, in the north, seem from the bishops' registers to have been subject to little less than ordinary episcopal visitation. These are cited as instances only.

guard, gives no absolute immunity from the taint of fallen nature. The religious of the sixteenth century had passed through many difficulties dangerous to their spiritual no less than to their temporal welfare. Yet, while their moral tone had probably been lowered by the influence of the spirit of the times, the graver falls were certainly confined to individual cases. Anything like general immorality was altogether unknown among the religious of England. This much is clearly proved by the testimony of the acts of episcopal visitations, as well as by the absence of any such sweeping charge till it became necessary for Henry and his agents to blast the fair name of the monastic houses in order the more easily to gain possession of their property.

The reports of Crumwell's visitors no doubt represented the religious houses as being in the worst possible state of moral degradation. Subsequent authors have improved upon the picture, and have drawn to a great extent upon their imagination. It is to be hoped that a better knowledge of the methods employed by Henry's agents to blacken the character of those they were about to despoil may lead to a truer appreciation of the value to be attached to their testimony.

CHAPTER II

Cardinal Wolsey and the Monasteries

ENGLAND, during some fourteen years of the reign of Henry VIII., was ruled by the counsels of Wolsey. On the king's accession, in 1509, the future lord cardinal of York had already made his way to the dignity of dean of Lincoln. Six years later pope Leo X. yielded to the earnest demands of the English king and the polite but persistent pressure of Wolsey's agents in Rome, and created him cardinal. He had already become archbishop of York, and had gained an ever-increasing influence over the mind of his royal master. On December 24, 1515, one year later, he took the oaths of office as chancellor of England, in succession to the saintly and venerable Warham. He then appeared to have reached the summit of a subject's lawful ambition.

As the highest judicial officer of the realm—the "keeper of the king's conscience"—Wolsey's power in matters temporal was then practically unlimited.

"He is in very great repute," writes a foreign ambassador in England, "seven times more so than if he were pope. He is the person who rules both the king and the entire kingdom. On my (the ambassador's) first arrival in England he used to say, 'His Majesty will do so and so.' Subsequently, by degrees, he went on forgetting himself, and commenced saying, '*We* shall do so and so.' At present he has reached such a pitch that he says, '*I* shall do so and so.'"

In addition to this almost regal authority in temporal matters, the cardinal desired great and exceptional powers in ecclesiastical concerns. For a while his appointment to a place in the august College of Cardinals seemed doubtful. He consequently directed the English agent in Rome to hint that the pope's hesitation was damaging to papal influence over Henry, and that refusal would be really dangerous. "If the king forsakes the pope," he added, "he will be in greater danger on this day two years than ever was Pope Julius."[1] A few days later he again wrote to Silvester de Gigliis, the bishop of Worcester and the king's ambassador to the pope. In this despatch he enclosed a communication, which was not to be handed to the pope till his nomination as cardinal was secure. The note thus sent made a further demand on the Holy See; it was that the Holy Father should appoint him legate as well as create him cardinal. Should this demand be refused, the agent's instructions were to press for special faculties empowering Wolsey to visit all monasteries in England; powers which were to apply even to such as were by law exempt from all except papal authority. If this last request were skilfully put, Wolsey considered that the pope could not refuse it. No pope, he added, ever had a better friend than Henry "if he comply with his desires." The letter concluded by saying that the cardinal was sending his agent 10,000 ducats *propter liberalia*, and with promises of great generosity to whomsoever brought him the cardinal's hat.[2] Leo X., however, was not to be coerced. He refused either to appoint the newly-created cardinal his legate in England, or to bestow upon him the extensive spiritual jurisdiction he desired.[3]

Two years later, in March 1518, the subject of the coveted legateship was revived. The king's secretary, Pace, informed Wolsey that his master had received a communication from the pope. To ask aid against the Turk four legates had been appointed to the European powers, and Cardinal Campeggio was accredited for that purpose to England. To this communication no reply was given for a long time. The English agent wrote to say that the pope was annoyed and astonished, and asked him "ten times a day" when he might expect an answer to his letters. At length Wolsey, after consultation with Henry, wrote to de Gigliis in an imperious tone. It was not customary in England, he said, to admit any foreign cardinal to exercise legatine powers in the country; still the king was willing, under two conditions, to receive Campeggio as papal envoy. Of these two conditions the first was that all the ordinary

---

[1] *Calendar*, ii. No. 763.   [2] *Ibid.*, No. 780, Aug. 1.
[3] *Ibid.*, Nos. 967-8.

faculties exercised by papal legates *de jure* should, in this case, be suspended, and that Campeggio should be confined to the special purpose for which he had been appointed. The second condition, coming from Wolsey himself, is even more astonishing. It was simply that the pope should associate him with Campeggio in the business and should bestow upon him equal legatine faculties. The despatch then proceeded to state that unless these conditions were complied with "the king will in no wise allow Campeggio to enter England."[1]

Leo X. surrendered to the undisguised threats of Henry and Wolsey. On May 17, 1518, the latter was nominated legate with Campeggio, who had been previously appointed. In a very short time Wolsey contrived to assume the first place, leaving the subordinate one to the Italian cardinal.[2] The latter arrived in England only after many delays purposely interposed by the king and his minister. He was at once made to feel his dependent position, for Henry and the English cardinal kept the real business in their own hands, and did not conceal their desire to get rid of the unwelcome foreign visitor.

Wolsey's diplomacy or threats, probably both, scored another triumph. He obtained not only the office of legate, but also the exceptional powers of visitation which had been previously asked for and refused. On August 27, 1518, Silvester de Gigliis wrote from Rome that he had been industrious in obtaining from the pope the deprivation of Cardinal Hadrian de Castello from the see of Bath and Wells, and had secured the custody of the diocese for his master. In fact, at the agent's suggestion, until this was secured, Campeggio had not been allowed to cross into England. The deprivation appears to have been obtained on account of the pope's desire for the success of his legate's mission. De Gigliis also informed Wolsey that he had secured for him a bull for the visitation of monasteries in the same tenor "as that obtained by the bishop of Luxemburg for France." He added that he had often been struck with the necessity of reforming the monasteries, and especially the convents of women; but he thought that the cardinal "would find those of his own diocese (Worcester) complain."[3]

---

[1] *Calendar*, ii. No. 4073.   [2] *Ibid.*, No. 4179.   [3] *Ibid.*, No. 4399.

Never before in England, or probably in Christendom, had similar powers been vested in any single individual. The high office of chancellor and the dominant influence Wolsey possessed over his royal master gave him the control of all secular authority. His legatine faculties, increased by the additional powers of visitation he had extorted from the pope, made him no less supreme in matters ecclesiastical. In the hand of one man were grasped the two swords of Church and State. One mind directed the policy of secular and ecclesiastical administration in England. Had that man been a saint, the danger of such a combination would have been considerable, but when he was a worldly and ambitious man like Wolsey, it was fatal.

No sooner had Wolsey obtained the powers of visitation so long sought than he proceeded to put them in force. On March 19, 1519, he issued *statuta* to be observed by the order of Canons Regular of St. Augustin, which were to remain in force till the feast of Holy Trinity, 1521.[1] The ordinances thus enacted are valuable evidence as to the state of the great Augustinian order at that time in England. They point to a severity of discipline and a mortified mode of life altogether incompatible with that general laxity since attributed to them in common with the other great bodies of regular clergy. The mere enactments of the primary principles of the monastic life or declarations of the unlawfulness of certain evil customs must never be considered in such injunctions as proof of the existence of evil. As well might the vigorous denunciations of sin from the pulpit, or the constant reassertion of the Ten Commandments, be held as evidence that God's law was uniformly violated by those to whom such words are addressed. The tendency of human nature is ever to fall away from any standard of excellence. Hence the necessity of unwearied iteration in setting out the ideal to be aimed at, and this is sufficient to explain why constitutions and statutes of religious orders inveigh against abuses.

It is impossible not to approve the spirit which dictated constitutions such as these. And it would have been well had Wolsey continued in the same way the work he thus begun, and by watchful care endeavoured to recall the reli-

---

[1] Wilkins, *Concilia*, iii. p. 613.

gious orders to greater fervour. Unfortunately his ambitious schemes soon involved him in a conflict with them. Those who might tolerate criticism, and even welcome wholesome correction, could hardly be expected to look with approval, or even indifference, on total extinction.

At the close of 1523 the cardinal had determined to rival other great churchmen as a founder of an Oxford college. The example of Waynfleet and Wykeham, and the more recent establishment at Cambridge, through the exertions of the venerable Bishop Fisher, impelled him to add the glory of "founder" to the titles he already possessed. At this time he was engaged on the erection of magnificent palaces, and he had as much difficulty in supplying funds for these ambitious undertakings as in keeping his master, the king, from constant beggary.

To the other emoluments, ecclesiastical and lay, which Wolsey possessed, and in addition to the pensions he received from foreign countries in 1521, he added the revenues of the abbatial office of St. Albans. He was away from England when Abbot Ramridge died in November. On the 12th of that month the monks appeared before the king at Windsor to request permission to proceed to the election of a successor. Henry made them a speech, about which, on account of "its princely and godly motion," Secretary Pace wrote to Wolsey the following day. Whilst actually engaged on this letter a communication was brought to him from the cardinal "touching the monastery of St. Albans." "And after I had perused," writes Pace, "and diligently debated with myself the contents of the same, I went straight to the king's grace, with your grace's letters, to him directed, in the same matter. And I found him ready to go out a shooting; and yet, that notwithstanding, his grace happily commanded me to go down with him by his secret way into the park; whereby I had as good commodity as I could desire to advance your grace's petition as much as the case required. And the king read your grace's letters himself, and made me privy to the contents of the same. And the few words his Highness spoke to me in this cause were these: 'By God! my lord cardinal hath sustained many charges in this his voyage and expended £10,000,' which I did affirm and show his grace of good congruence, he oweth you some recompence. Whereunto his grace answered 'that he would rather give unto your grace the abbey of St. Albans than to any monk.'"[1] Thus at the cardinal's petition the revenues of the premier abbey were given in reward for secular services.

At the commencement of the year 1524, Clerk, the cardinal's agent in Rome, wrote that he was "almost at a point with the pope about Wolsey's matters." Clement VII. was "contented to confirm the legateship," he said, "with all faculties for life, which was never heard before." Further, that "the ordering of Frideswide's in Oxford was also at Wolsey's pleasure."[2]

Later on the agents report further attempts to obtain extended powers from Clement VII. The pope appeared willing, but said, "what a business other men made" about it. They conclude their communication by a significant hint to their master. It would be well, they think, for him to secure a pension out of the revenues of the bishopric of Worcester for one of the pope's officers who has been "good to him."[3] By this time, however, Wolsey had obtained the bull which enabled him to dissolve the monastery of St. Frideswide's at Oxford and apply its property to the foundation of his college.[4] The document had been sent off from Rome by the end of April. It had been procured at the earnest request of the cardinal's agents, yet they made it appear to be the result of Clement's own desire. It was not exactly such a faculty as they had wished to obtain. Still, it contained, as they said, "the clause *motus proprii*," and they trusted that it might be made more advantageous. In fact, Clerk altered the document in this sense without asking the pope; but at the last moment he found that the enlarged faculties would not be granted. The agent again concluded his communication by saying that Ghiberto, one of the pope's officials, "openly will not be known," but he has done his best, and he thinks that he is waiting to see whether he gets the pension from the See of Worcester. This Clerk advises Wolsey not to refuse, "as he may be useful."

For the next few months great pressure was put upon the Holy Father to grant permission for further suppressions in order to help out the cardinal's design at Oxford. The

[1] *Calendar*, iii. No. 1759.
[2] *Ibid.*, iv. No. 15, Jan. 9, 1524.   [3] *Ibid.*, No. 252.
[4] The king's "inspeximus" is dated May 10, and the bull April 3, 1524.

pope appeared favourable, but Cardinal Sanctorum Quatuor was "untreatable." He apparently influenced Clement VII. against the scheme. In August 1524, Clerk wrote that the Holy Father made hardly any objection to his demands for Wolsey, "except the extinction of the monasteries and the collectorship."[1] They had been told in Rome (as the bull subsequently obtained asserts) that the need for increased facilities of study in England was at this time most pressing, and that the Oxford university "seemed likely to come to an end by reason of its slender revenues."[2] Further, that the position of St. Frideswide's in the city of Oxford was admirably adapted for the purpose of a college, and that, owing to the objection of the English people to allowing land to be held for such purposes, it was impossible to buy or procure it. Lastly, they were told that there were many religious houses in England where the numbers had diminished to five or six, and where, on this account, the divine service could not be fittingly carried out.

Urged by these motives, the pope at first granted the cardinal of York the amplified faculties for visitation so long and diligently sought. Subsequently he consented to another bull for increasing the revenues of the Oxford college by further suppressions. He warned Wolsey's agent, however, "for God's sake to use mercy with those friars," as to the matter of visitation, adding, according to Clerk (what sounds much more like the agent's sentiment than the pope's) "that they were desperate beasts, past shame, that can lose nothing by clamour."[3] The bull allowing Wolsey to suppress monasteries to the value of 3000 ducats a year for the purpose of adding to the funds of his college, left Rome on September 12, 1524.[4] It provided that the king and the various founders should give their sanction, and that the religious persons should go to other monasteries.[5]

Power having been thus obtained from Rome, the cardinal commenced early in the following year, 1525, to possess himself of the revenues of various monasteries

---

[1] *Calendar*, Nos. 511, 568.

[2] Rymer, *Fœdera*, xiv. p. 23: "*Et quod Universitas studii generalis Oxoniensis ob penuriam reddituum propemodum extinctum iri videbatur.*"

[3] *Calendar*, iv. No. 610. The bull granting the additional faculties of visitation is in Rymer, xiv. p. 18.

[4] *Calendar*, iv. No. 652.   [5] Rymer, xiv. p. 23.

besides those of St. Frideswide's in Oxford. The papal bull was ratified by the king on March 15th, and several parish churches, formerly belonging to the suppressed religious houses, were appropriated by letters patent to the new foundation.[1] But both the time and the agents Wolsey employed to effect the dissolutions conduced to render the matter most unpopular. Just at this period Henry was endeavouring to raise a large loan from his people "against the time the king should pass the sea." The amount asked was no less than "the sixth part of every man's substance," and that it "should without delay be paid in money or plate to the king for the furniture of his war."[2] Wareham warned Wolsey in the spring of the year how unpopular this "amicable grant" was in Kent.[3] The work of suppression was undoubtedly disliked by both clergy and laity.

In the July of 1525 the archbishop again wrote to the cardinal about the difficulties his policy was creating in the southern parts of England. The inhabitants of Tunbridge strongly objected to the dissolution of a monastery of Austin canons from which they had derived many advantages. Warham was commissioned to go there and endeavour to persuade them that it was much better to have "forty children of that country educated and after sent to Oxford" than to have six or seven canons living amongst them; but the people did not think so. After discussing the matter for five or six days they again met Warham, and gave him a list of those who desired the continuance of their ancient priory. The inhabitants of the neighbourhood no less than of the town "would rather have the said place not suppressed," wrote the archbishop, "if it might stand with the king's pleasure." The murmurs about the matter were very difficult to repress, and this he told Wolsey, who had a "suspicion that the bruit" was against himself.[4]

---

[1] Rot. Pat. 18 Hen. VIII. p. 1, mm. 21, 22.
[2] Hall, *Union of the Famelies of Lancastre and Yorke*, ed. 1548, fol. 138d.
[3] Ellis, *Original Letters*, 1st Series, iii. p. 367.
[4] *Calendar*, iii. 1470-1. Warham to Wolsey, July 2nd and 3rd, 1525. Hall, *ut sup.*, fol. 137, gives the following account of these suppressions:— The cardinal "suddenly entered by his commissioners into the said houses, and put out the religious and took all their goods, moveables, and scarcely gave to the poor wretches anything except it were to the heads of the house. And then he caused the escheator to sit and find the houses void, as relinquished, and found the king founder where other men were founders, and with these lands withall he endowed his colleges."

In the neighbouring county of Sussex the agitation against Wolsey's dissolution of monasteries was more serious and led to a riot. Beigham Abbey, "the which was very commodious to the country,"[1] was a monastery of Premonstratensians, and Wolsey had commissioned the bishop of Chichester to visit and inquire into certain alleged scandals there.[2] The religious, however, evidently maintained a hold on the affections of their neighbours, and on the cardinal's proceeding to dissolve the house, under the powers of Pope Clement's bull, the people assembled in "a riotous company, disguised and unknown, with painted faces" and masked. They turned out the agents engaged on the suppression and reinstated the canons. Before separating they begged the religious, if they were again molested, to ring their bell, and they pledged themselves to come in force to their assistance.[3]

Rumour, apparently, attributed to the cardinal even larger schemes of confiscation than were at the time contemplated. No sooner was the bull of Clement VII. put into force than petitions against the exercise of Wolsey's legatine powers were presented to the pope, especially by the Grey Friars and the Franciscan Observants. The latter were very powerful in Rome, and, as the cardinal's agent wrote, the pope may perhaps "give them some brief," but not one derogatory to Wolsey's honour.[4] The cardinal of York himself had also representations made to him against the work in which he was engaged. The Duke of Suffolk, for example, wrote to him in favour of the priory of Conished, in Lancashire, which by common report had been doomed to extinction. The monastery, he said, was "a great help to the people," and "the prior of good and virtuous disposition."[5]

Complaints were also carried to the king of the harsh and unjust way in which Wolsey's agents, Dr. Allen and Thomas Crumwell, were conducting the suppressions and the visitations of the religious houses upon which they were then engaged. Early in 1525 the cardinal had been informed by Sir Thomas More that complaints had been made to Henry, "touching certain misorders supposed to

---

[1] Hall, *ut sup.*, fol. 143. [2] *Calendar*, iii. 1252.
[3] Hall, *ut sup.*; Ellis, *Orig. Lett.*, 2nd Ser., iii. p. 57.
[4] *Calendar*, iii. No. 1521. [5] *Ibid.*, No. 1253.

be used by Dr. Allen and other my officers in the suppression of certain exile and small monasteries wherein neither God is served nor religion kept. These, with your gracious aid and assistance, converting the same to a far better use, I purpose," writes Wolsey to the king, "to annex unto your intended college of Oxford." He further assures Henry that he can disprove any such reports, saying, "I have not meant, intended, or gone about, nor also have willed mine officers to do anything concerning the said suppressions, but under such form and manner as is, and hath largely been, to the full satisfaction, recompense, and joyous contentation of any person, which hath had, or could pretend to have, right or interest in the same."[1]

Whatever may have been Wolsey's belief, at the time, in the integrity of his agents, there is little doubt that the reports about them were well founded. Subsequently, indeed, the cardinal practically admitted the truth of the charges suggested against those he employed in dealing with the religious. Fiddes in the "Life of Wolsey" says: "The revenues of the cardinal, from the privileges of his visitatorial power, of making abbots, of proving wills, granting faculties, licenses, and dispensations from his pensions and preferments, and other visible advantages, were thought by this time to be equal to the revenues of the crown. But in the methods of enriching him under the first article no one contributed so much as his chaplain, John Allen, LL.D., who, accompanied with a great train, and riding in a kind of perpetual progress from one religious house to another, is said to have drawn very large sums for his master's service from them."[2]

This Dr. Allen was, apparently, the object of great dread and intense dislike. He was an astute, hard man, and, like his fellow, Crumwell, had evidently been trained up in business habits to the detriment of his humanity or even honesty. He was afterwards made archbishop of Dublin, "where his imperiousness and rapacity brought him to a violent end."[3]

The courtesy and consideration which the monks were likely to receive at the hands of Crumwell may be best

[1] *State Papers*, i. p. 154.
[2] Fiddes, *Life of Wolsey*, p. 351; Hall, *ut sup.*, fol. 143.
[3] Brewer, *Henry VIII.*, vol. ii. p. 270.

understood by his subsequent dealings with them. "Of Crumwell," writes Mr. Brewer, "it is enough to say that even at this early period of his career his accessibility to bribes and presents in the disposal of monastic leases was notorious."[1] For some years before the cardinal's fall, report had spoken badly of Thomas Crumwell. "Loud outcries reached the king's ears of the exactions and peculations of Wolsey's officers, in which the name of Crumwell was most frequently repeated, and more than once the king had to express his grave displeasure at the conduct of a man who soon after was destined to occupy the highest place in his favour."[2]

"In 1527, when Wolsey was at Amiens and proposed to send Dr. Allen to England with a message to the king, Knight, who was afterwards bishop of Bath and Wells, wrote to warn the cardinal against his selection. "And, sir," he said, "in case Mr. Allen be not departed hitherwards on your message, or may be in time revoked, your grace might use better any about you for your message unto the king than him. I have heard the king and noblemen speak things incredible of the acts of Mr. Allen and Crumwell."[3]

In subsequent times the superiors of religious houses endeavoured to buy off the threatened dissolution by presents and bribes or by readily acceding to requests which were tantamount to demands. Under Wolsey they tried to purchase favour by offers of gifts to the cardinal's college. The bishop of Lincoln, who greatly aided this foundation in more ways than one, put great pressure on the abbot of Peterborough to resign, or to bestow the large sum of 2000 marks on the undertaking. He tried much the same system of blackmail on the prior of Spalding. The prior, however, would not resign, "though all legal means were tried."[4] There are also many indications of distinct bribes offered for various offices. One man promises 500 marks and other considerable presents to the college, if the cardinal will make him under-treasurer.[5] When the prior of St. Bartholomew's, Smithfield, was sick of the plague and likely to die, the friends of "William Finch, cellarer of the same," offer Wolsey "£300 to your college

---

[1] Brewer, *ut supra*.   [2] *Ibid.*, p. 394.   [3] *State Papers*, i. p. 261.
[4] *Calendar*, iv. Nos. 2378, 4708.   [5] *Ibid.*, No. 4452, also 4483.

at Oxford for your favour towards his preferment."[1]
Lastly, to allow him to illegally imprison some one who has
offended him, Henry, earl of Northumberland, offers to give
the cardinal "the chapel books of his late father," which he
has been asked to bestow on the college. To induce him
to make the bargain, the earl says he will let him have four
antiphonals and graduals, "such as were not seen a great
while," £200 in money, and a benefice of £100 for his
college.[2]

At length, on the eve of the lord cardinal's fall, the king
writes strongly as to the methods employed by Wolsey's
agents and his own condemnation of them. The letters
were called forth by a difference between Henry and his
minister as to the appointment of an abbess to Wilton.
The king had determined to favour the election, or what
might be more truly called the appointment, of Dame Elinor
Carey. She was supported by powerful friends, amongst
whom was reckoned Anne Boleyn herself. The cardinal,
probably with quite sufficient reason, and in distinct opposition to the royal wishes, approved of the choice of the former prioress, Dame Isabell Jordayn. Wolsey wrote to offer
humble apologies on being informed of Henry's displeasure,
and, in accepting the explanation, the king wrote: "As
touching the help of religious houses to the building of your
colleges, I would it were more, so it were lawfully; for my
intent is none but that it should appear so to all the world,
and the occasion of all their mumbling might be secluded
and put away. For surely there is great murmuring of it
throughout all the realm, both good and bad. They say
not that all that is ill-gotten is bestowed on the college, but
that the college is the cloak for covering all mischiefs.
This grieveth me, I assure you, to hear it spoken of him
whom I so entirely love. Wherefore methought I could do
no less than thus friendly to admonish you. One thing
more I perceive by your letter, which a little, methinks,
toucheth conscience, and that is that you have received
money of the exempts for having their old visitors. Surely
this can hardly be with good conscience. For if they were
good, why should you take money? and if they were ill, it
were a sinful act. Howbeit, your legateship herein might

[1] *Calendar*, No. 3334.   [2] *Ibid.*, No. 4603.

peradventure *apud homines* be a cloak, but not *apud Deum*."[1]

In his reply the cardinal thanks his master "for the great zeal that (he) had for the purity and cleanness of my poor conscience, coveting and desiring that nothing should be by me committed or done, by the colour of my intended college or otherwise, that should not stand with God's pleasure and good conscience, or that thereby any just occasion might be given to any person to speak or judge ill of my doings. And albeit, as is contained in my other letters, I have acknowledged to have received of divers, my old lovers and friends, and other exempt religious persons, right loving and favourable aids towards the edifying of my said college, yet your majesty may be well assured that the same extendeth not to such a sum as some men doth untruly bruit and report, or that any part thereof, to my knowledge, thought, or judgment hath been corruptly or contrary to law taken or given." He then declares that henceforth he will take nothing "from any religious person being exempt or not exempt, so that thereby I trust, nor by any other thing hereafter unlawfully taken, your poor cardinal's conscience shall not be spotted, encumbered, or entangled."[2]

Notwithstanding Wolsey's excuses, Henry seems to have had just grounds for his suspicion that the cardinal had made use of his legatine authority to serve his own purposes. Popular report had spoken of immunities purchased by presents to the cardinal's colleges which were adverse to the king's interests, and which ought not to have been granted. The archbishop of Canterbury complained that, in raising the loan known as the "amicable grant," he had no power at all over the religious houses in his district

---

[1] Lord Herbert, *Henry VIII.*, p. 164; Fiddes, *Wolsey*, p. 379. Fuller, *Church Hist.*, iii. p. 357, ed. 1845, says: "God's exemplary hand ought to be heeded in the signal fatality of such as by the cardinal were employed in this service. Five they were in number, two whereof challenging the field of each other, one was slain and the other hanged for it. A third throwing himself headlong into a well, perished wilfully. A fourth, formerly wealthy, grew so poor that he begged his bread. The fifth, Dr. Allen, one of especial note, afterwards archbishop of Dublin, was slain in Ireland. What became of the cardinal himself is notoriously known, and as for his two colleges, that in Ipswich (the emblem of its builder, soon up, soon down) presently vanished into private houses; whilst the other, Christchurch in Oxford, was fain to disclaim its founder."

[2] *State Papers*, i. p. 317.

"They must be left," he writes, "to your grace (Wolsey), and unless they contribute to the loan according to the value of their benefices the clergy will complain. Had the religious houses not been exempted, but appeared before me, the loan derived from my diocese would be much greater."[1] The king likewise complains with much bitterness that among the religious are found the most strenuous and successful opponents of this enforced benevolence. "These same religious houses," he writes to the cardinal, "would not grant to their sovereign in his necessity, not by a great deal so much as they have to you for the building of your college. These things bear shrewd appearance, for, except they were accustomed to have some benefit, they, and no other I ever heard of, have used to show that kindness, *tam enim est aliena ab eis ipsa humanitas*." He concludes by urgently requiring Wolsey to look well into the conduct of those to whom he has entrusted this "meddling with religious houses."[2]

By 1527 Wolsey had conceived a desire to further emulate the example of Bishop Wykeham and establish a school, which should feed his foundation at Oxford, as that at Winchester had fed New College. For this purpose further funds were imperatively necessary. The success of his previous scheme having been secured by the dissolution of various monasteries, his agents, who had gone to Rome on the divorce question, were instructed to seek additional powers in the same direction. The cardinal at this time appears to have hesitated at nothing to carry out his designs. In the summer of this year, 1527, he had been in France, where he made three treaties with the king. It was agreed that, during the captivity of the pope, no bull or brief should be received in either country; that, with the consent of Henry, the cardinal of York should have control of all ecclesiastical affairs in England, and that Francis I. should take the like power in his dominions. Wolsey also proposed to ask Clement VII. to make him his vicar-general, as long as he was a prisoner, and to entrust him with supreme authority. In fact, according to the tenor of the bull, written ready for the pope's seal and signature, the cardinal

---

[1] *Calendar*, iv. p. 2010.
[2] Brewer, *Henry VIII.*, ii. p. 283; Fiddes, *Collect.*, p. 139.

proposed to obtain power of dispensing even from the divine law.¹

What is more extraordinary still is, that Wolsey, before leaving France, acted as if he had obtained these full and unheard-of powers. He even ordered the chancellor of France to assume the dignity and dress of cardinal, which Clement had promised but had not bestowed.²

In December 1527, the pope escaped from Rome to Orvieto, and thither Gardiner and Foxe, Wolsey's agents, followed him. The Holy Father was powerless, and at the mercy of any who chose to exert pressure upon him. On March 23, 1528, Foxe wrote describing the miserable state in which they had found the pope on their arrival at Orvieto. He had taken up his quarters in the bishop's ruined palace. Three small chambers, "all naked and unhanged," with the ceiling fallen, and about thirty persons of the "riff-raff" standing about "for a garnishment," led to the pope's private apartment. The furniture of this, "bed and all," was not worth "twenty nobles."³

In the midst of this perplexity and difficulty a further demand was made on Wolsey's behalf. Powers were asked to suppress the priory of St. Peter's, Ipswich, and other monasteries to obtain funds for the foundation of a college at Ipswich. The pope gave way; nor could he well have refused any demand which conscience would have enabled him to grant. In the middle of May 1528 the necessary bulls were dispatched to Wolsey. Gardiner appears to have acted as unscrupulously in this matter as in the divorce question. The pope, on the first suggestion of further suppressions, had asked from the agents particulars about the cardinal's colleges. He was pleased with the account given him, and told the cardinals de Monte and Sanctorum Quatuor "what a good" work it was. "In particular it rejoiced the pope," writes Strype, "when they told him that Wolsey had taken order that, in letting the farms belonging to his college, no man should have them but such as would dwell upon them and maintain hospitality . . . and he (the pope) justified and maintained the

---

¹ Pocock, *Records of the Reformation*, i. p. 19 : "*Etiamsi ad divinæ legis relaxationem.*" See Lewis, Sanders' *Schism*, Introd., p. liii. &c.

² Lewis, Introd. lv. ; Pocock, *ut supra*, ii. p. 88.

³ *Calendar*, iv. No. 4090.

commutation and alteration of those religious places, whereof only did arise the scandal of religion as he spoke. For the cardinal, for the endowing of his college, had lately obtained of the pope a bull for the dissolving of divers monasteries wherein much vice and wickedness was harboured, as he informed the pope, to incline him thereby the easier to grant his request."[1]

In this way the convent of Pre, near St. Albans, was dissolved and united to that great abbey. The pope was told that the nuns did not keep a good rule of life, and that religious discipline was much relaxed. The revenues, therefore, were transferred to St. Alban's Abbey in order that an increased number of monks might be supported for the better celebration of the divine office.[2] It may be that the nuns of Pre merited the bad character for laxity of life given to them in the papal bull. In view, however, of Wolsey's motive in giving a bad character to monasteries whose possessions he desired, the mere fact of the statement by the pope is not proof positive. Neither does the fact that the convent was united to the abbey of St. Albans show that Wolsey had no motive in the suppression. To this arrangement the cardinal really objected, and authorised his agent to obtain another bull from Clement uniting Pre to Cardinal College, Oxford. At the same time he wished that the impropriation of a living, also obtained for St. Albans, should be changed in favour of the college at Ipswich.[3]

In the various suppressions which followed complaints were again made of the high-handed action of Wolsey's servants. The abbot of Beaulieu, who was also bishop of Bangor, wrote to the cardinal of the unjust seizure of certain lands in the parish of St. Keverans, Cornwall, belonging to his abbey. He represented that Beaulieu had possessed the property for 400 years, and that now two servants had taken it. And one "gentleman hath written to me," he said, "that the benefice there, which is impropriated to Beaulieu, he mindeth to give to the finding of scholars, and feigneth that some time there was a cell of monks there."[4]

---

[1] Strype, *Eccl. Mems.*, i. p. 168; *Calendar*, iv. No. 4120.
[2] Rymer, xiv. p. 240.   [3] *Calendar*, iv. No. 5714.
[4] Ellis, *Orig. Lett.*, Ser. 2, iii. p. 60.

The abbot of York also complains of Wolsey's seizure of Romburgh Priory, in Suffolk, which was a cell of St. Mary's Abbey. He says, that on the 11th of September 1528, certain officers of the cardinal came to the priory, read the authority of the pope and king, "entered into the same priory, and that done, took away as well the goods moveable of the said priory . . . and also certain muniments, evidences, and specialities touching and appertaining unto our monastery, which we had lately sent unto our said prior and brethren there." The cell, he says, had been given to them by Alan Niger, earl of Richmond, 400 years before, and the abbey was burdened, by reason of the gift, with masses, suffrages, and alms. Further, as the revenues of the priory do not amount to more than £30, the abbot offers "towards your special, honourable, and laudable purpose concerning the erection and foundation of the said college and school . . . 300 marks sterling, which shall be delivered" at once, if the monastery is spared.[1] The representation was of no avail, and Romburgh was annexed to the Ipswich college.

The papal permissions to alienate monastic property thus obtained only served to increase Wolsey's desire for further dissolutions. In October 1528, Clement VII. was being worried and bullied by the cardinal's agents in the matter of the divorce. In turn they were threatening, exhorting, and beseeching the pope to comply with Henry's royal will, and even if necessary permit him to have two wives[2] at once. Wolsey also instructed his agents to make further overtures to allow him to take monastic property. On behalf of the king they presented a petition that certain religious houses might be given over to support the king's colleges at Windsor and at Cambridge. These two establishments the agents represented as having been founded by the grandparents of the English king, for education and for the support in old age of court officials. The pope was informed that the foundations were now reduced to poverty, and that Henry could not finish the work through want of means. Clement VII. was, no doubt, only too willing at this critical time to give way in any possible matter to the English king. Hence, "because of all that Henry had

[1] Wright, *Suppression of Monasteries* (Camden Soc.), p. 1.
[2] *Calendar*, iv. 4897. See Lewis, *Schism*, Introd., p. cxxvi. &c.

done against heresy and for the Holy See," he granted him permission to suppress monasteries to the value of 8000 ducats, provided that there were not six religious in them and that the inmates found homes in other religious houses.[1]

At the same time also the king and cardinal told their agent, Casali, to suggest a measure of wholesale suppression, so that more cathedrals might be established with the monastic property. The question was mooted in the consistory, and, according to the agent, all present seemed ready to assent to the king's desire. "As it is a matter, however," he writes, "of the greatest importance, it should be granted with greater authority than could be done then. Power might be asked for the legates to decide which monasteries were best fitted to be erected into cathedrals, to arrange the revenues, &c., and then the whole referred to the pope for confirmation. Cardinal S. Quatuor and De Monte advise this, thinking it too important to be finally settled except in consistory, the pope being present, lest it should be thought that the legates were influenced by private interest." He concludes by asking to be informed of the exact nature of the king's requests.[2]

At the same time the writer of the above letter to the king sends another to the cardinal. He tells his master that he has "showed his Holiness the integrity of his intentions towards the Church." He has also pointed out the need of reformation in the English monasteries, "and the suitableness of the present time, when a legate had gone to England," so that Wolsey might not be suspected of acting for his own advantage. Casali thought that the pope was persuaded of the necessity of the erection of new cathedrals and the reform of monasteries; but "he considered for some time the alleged necessity of suppressing monasteries of any order." The writer added: "I am sure the matter will be managed with dexterity."[3] What this kind of "dexterity" was likely to be can be understood from a letter of Gregorio Casali, the brother of the former writer. In this he says that he "has told his brother the protonotary and Vincent (his nephew) that importunity is the only way to get anything from the pope."[4]

[1] Rymer, xiv. p. 249. [2] *Calendar*, iv. No. 4886.
[3] *Ibid.*, No. 4900. [4] *Ibid.*, No. 4956.

The result of the "importunity" soon appeared. Two bulls were issued by Clement VII. on November 14, 1528. In the first it is stated that the king had presented a petition showing that in England there were many monasteries "in which the proper number (*i.e.* twelve monks or nuns) were not to be found and which had no proper income for their support. Hence regular discipline was not kept up and the divine office not properly performed. By laxity of restraint the rule of good life was not kept by the monks and nuns therein." The petition further suggested, that if these were united to other religious houses, where the day and night office was properly performed and in which good discipline was maintained, it would be better for religion. Acting on this information and in accordance with this petition, the pope by bull granted Wolsey faculties for the suggested union.[1]

The second bull had reference to the question of the proposed cathedrals. Henry represented to Clement that monasteries had previously been suppressed in England for the purpose of establishing cathedrals. He suggested that the revenues of several more should now be granted for this purpose, and that each cathedral, so erected, should have an income of 10,000 ducats from the monastic lands. The pope, having consulted with his cardinals, desired further information, which he directed Wolsey to furnish. First, he wished to know whether any and what monasteries had previously been suppressed for such a purpose; secondly, whether there was any need of increasing the number of cathedrals; thirdly, how many monasteries would be required for the purpose, and whether the monks were to remain in the cathedrals as canons, bound by their monastic vows, but taking the dress of seculars. Lastly, he asked what would be the position of the bishop, whether he would be a suffragan of the archbishop, or immediately dependent on the Holy See. Wolsey was directed by the brief to examine witnesses as to these matters, and to send their evidence attested by oath to the pope.[2]

Even yet, the cardinal of York was not satisfied. He again asked to be allowed to suppress a few more monasteries to obtain money for his colleges. These had apparently

---

[1] Rymer, xiv. p. 272.   [2] *Ibid.*, xiv. 273.

already been dissolved on his own authority. "The cardinal further demands," writes Jacobo Salviati to Campeggio, "the union to his college of three monasteries, which are not mentioned in the other bulls. This, too, shall be granted, although his Holiness could have wished that it had not been requested of him. But as it is his most reverend lordship who makes the demand, and for such a purpose, he cannot refuse him, as the elect (bishop) of Bellun is to write to him at greater length, the elect being here and soliciting this 'expedition' with much importunity."[1]

In the beginning of the following year, 1529, Pope Clement VII. fell ill. It was reported, and for the time believed, that he was dead. Upon this the king determined once more to further, as far as he possibly could, the election of Wolsey to the popedom.[2] In this design he directed his agent to bribe the cardinals, and in his efforts he was seconded by Wolsey himself. The latter writes to Gardiner, his old secretary, on February 7th: "When all things be well considered—*absit verbum jactantiæ*—there shall be none found that can and will set remedy in the aforesaid things, but only the Cardinal Ebor." He adds, that he wishes his agent to spare no expense in this matter, but to use all his power, promises, and labour to bring it to pass.[3] It is certain also from the king's instructions that it was seriously contemplated, in the event of the electors refusing the cardinal of York, to set up an anti-pope and create a schism.[4] The emperor foresaw this, and when expressing his regret at the illness of Clement, added: "His death might create a schism in Christendom."[5]

The pope recovered. Henry and Wolsey were thus again disappointed in their plans. The bulls which had been obtained in the autumn of the previous year, through the persistent importunity of the English agents, had not been altogether according to Wolsey's liking. He desired the removal of the clause "*de consensu quorum interest*" in the permission for the union of various monasteries. The agent had deliberately, and on his own authority, changed "*less* than twelve monasteries" into "*less or more*

---

[1] *Calendar*, iv. No. 4920. [2] *Ibid.*, No. 5270. [3] *Ibid.*, No. 5272.
[4] Pocock, *Records*, ii. p. 598. See Lewis, *ut supra*, Introd., p. cxxxv. *et seq.*
[5] *Calendar*, iv. No. 5301.

than twelve monasteries," which had displeased the Cardinal S. Quatuor, and delayed the transmission of the bulls to England. The cardinal of York had neglected also to forward, as requested, copies of the bulls by which, as was asserted, monasteries had previously been turned into bishoprics.[1]

At the beginning of June 1529, the question was still being discussed. Wolsey wrote to Sir Gregory Casali that he wanted certain clauses amplified in bulls he had received. As to the union of monasteries, he desired to have the power of uniting small monasteries as well as annexing them to greater. The bull for erecting cathedrals only allowed him to inquire and report, but the king and he desired powers to act. He promised that there should be no loss of fees to the court of Rome. He desired the omission of the clause "*de consensu omnium quorum interest*," not because he thought such interests ought to be neglected, but to prevent factious and malicious opposition. No such clause, he urged, was inserted in his former bulls for the suppression of monasteries.[2]

On the 4th June 1529, the final bull, to allow Wolsey to act on the king's petition for the erection of additional cathedrals, was signed by Clement VII. It was of exactly the same nature as the previous brief, but allowed the king's suggestion to be carried into effect and put the burden of the matter upon the cardinal's conscience.[3] On the 31st of the following August the second bull for the union of monasteries, in the required form, received the pope's seal and signature. The fall of Wolsey, however, prevented any further action under the powers thus granted him.

Among the articles of impeachment which, according to the authority of Lord Herbert, were exhibited in the House of Lords against the cardinal, several relate to his action against the monasteries. These articles, forty-four in number, were signed by Sir Thomas More and many others. The 13th runs thus: "And where good hospitality hath been used to be kept in houses and places of religion of this realm, and many poor people thereby relieved, the said hospitality and relief is now decayed and not used. And it is commonly

---

[1] *Calendar*, iv. No. 5226. [2] *Ibid.*, No. 5639.
[3] Rymer, xiv. p. 291.

reported that the occasion thereof is, because the said Lord Cardinal hath taken such impositions of the rulers of the said houses, as well for his favour in making of abbots and priors as for his visitation by his authority legatine, and yet, nevertheless, taketh yearly of such religious houses such yearly and continual charges, as they be not able to keep hospitality as they were used to do, which is a great cause that there be so many vagabonds, beggars, and thieves."

The 14th article charges the cardinal with having raised the rents of the lands he received through the suppressions, and made it impossible for the tenants to farm them with profit.

The 19th says: "Also the said Lord Cardinal hath not only, by his untrue suggestion to the Pope, shamefully slandered many good religious houses and good virtuous men dwelling in them, but also suppressed, by reason thereof, above thirty houses of religion. And where, by the authority of his bull, he should not suppress any house that had more men of religion in number above the number of six or seven, he hath suppressed divers houses that had above the number, and thereupon hath caused divers offices to be found by verdict, untruly, that the religious persons so suppressed had voluntarily forsaken their said houses, which was untrue, and so hath caused open perjury to be committed, to the high displeasure of Almighty God."

In the 24th it is stated: "Also the same Lord Cardinal at many times, when any houses of religion hath been void, hath sent his officers thither, and with crafty persuasions hath induced them to 'compromit' their election in him, and before he named or confirmed any of them, he and his servants received so much great goods of them, that in a manner it hath been to the undoing of the house."

Lastly, the 25th says: "Also, by his authority legatine, the same Lord Cardinal hath visited the most part of the religious houses and colleges of this realm, and hath taken from them the twenty-fifth part of their livelihood, to the great extortion of your subjects and derogation of your laws and prerogative, and no law hath been to bear him so to do."[1]

"Here," says Lord Herbert, "certainly began the taste

---

[1] Fiddes, *Collect.*, p. 172 *et seq.*

that our king took of governing in chief the clergy, of which, therefore, as well as the dissolution of monasteries, it seems the first arguments and impressions were derived from the cardinal."[1] It is difficult to read the record of Wolsey's arbitrary action as regards the religious houses, and the account of his methods in dealing with the pope, without endorsing this opinion.

[1] *Henry VIII.*, p. 209.

CHAPTER III

The Holy Maid of Kent

THE story of Elizabeth Barton, known as the "holy maid of Kent," must form a part of any detailed account of Henry's dealings with the English monasteries.

In 1525 Elizabeth Barton[1] was a domestic servant with one Thomas Cobb, a farmer of known respectability. She lived in the parish of Aldington, some twelve miles from Canterbury. About Easter time of that year, when she would have been about eighteen years of age, she was seized with a severe illness. During the progress of the sickness, which continued for seven months and more, she appeared to have frequent ecstasies, or trances. Whilst in one of these and apparently unconscious of all around her she spoke of things taking place at a distance and foretold coming events. At a subsequent date it was declared, by those who condemned her to death, that "she was brought in such debility and weakness of brain because she could not eat nor drink for a long space, that in the violence of her infirmities she seemed to be in trances and spoke and uttered many foolish and idle words."[2] But at this period, and for years after, no such suggestion was made. Certainly those who knew her best did not look upon her sayings as "foolish and idle." Amongst other things, she is said to have foretold the death of one of her master's children, who was ill, and the event followed shortly after her prediction. In one of her trances she declared that the Blessed Virgin had directed her to go to the chapel at

---

[1] This account is from W. Lambard's *Perambulation of Kent*, written in the year 1570. The author says he took the facts from a little pamphlet "containing four-and-twenty leaves," which was written by Edward Thwaites in 1527. It was called "A miraculous work at Court of Street, in Kent, published to devout people of this time for their spiritual consolation." As all books connected with Elizabeth Barton were destroyed under a provision in the act of her attainder, the pamphlet is known only in Lambard's book.

[2] Rot. Parl., 25 Hen. VIII. (No. 142).

Court of Street, where she would be cured of her sickness. On her first visit to the shrine, according to the account given of her, she did not receive her health. That, however, did not discourage her, and she professed perfect confidence that what had been promised would in good time be granted. Meanwhile her reputation became noised abroad. Either through the parish priest of Aldington, Richard Masters, or by some other means, the rumour reached the ears of the venerable Warham, archbishop of Canterbury. He "directed thither Dr. Bocking, with masters Hadleigh and Barnes, three monks of Christ Church, Canterbury, Father Lewis and his fellow (two Observants), his official of Canterbury and the parson of Aldington, with a commission to examine the matter and to inform him of the truth." Their report was favourable. They declared to the archbishop that "they found her sound therein." So that when next she went to our Lady at Court of Street, "she entered the chapel with the '*Ave Regina Cœlorum*' in prick-song, accompanied with these commissioners, many ladies, gentlewomen and gentlemen of the best degree and three thousand persons besides of the common sort of people."

During the mass, which was celebrated at the shrine, Elizabeth Barton fell into one of her usual trances and was restored to health. She afterwards declared that our Lady desired the shrine of Court of Street to be honoured more faithfully and supported with greater generosity, and that she herself should enter some convent. Acting on this declaration, archbishop Warham obtained her reception into the Benedictine convent of St. Sepulchre's, near Canterbury. There she subsequently became a nun and continued to preserve a universal reputation for holiness. From time to time, during the seven years of her religious life, she was to all appearance wrapt in ecstasy.[1]

Little is known of the life which Elizabeth Barton led in the convent. But in this period she spoke strongly and uncompromisingly against sin, and exhorted to penance

---

[1] The account given on the Parliament Roll in the act of attainder agrees with the main facts of the story as related above, which is taken from Lambard's account of Thwaites' pamphlet. The attainder, however, declares, as will be subsequently related, that the whole matter was a deception arranged by the two priests, Richard Masters and Dr. Edward Bocking.

when chance afforded her an opportunity. If she was moved by an evil spirit, as her enemies afterwards pretended, there never was a clearer case of Satan's kingdom divided against itself. She blamed the general laxity of the age and the "corruption of manners and evil life" to be found then in England. She exhorted people to approach the sacraments, and in particular to frequent confession and other good Catholic practices.[1] Her influence over the minds and hearts of those she came in contact with, as far as is known, was a powerful incentive to their leading a better life. Henry Man, for example, a Carthusian monk and procurator of their house at Sheen, writes early in 1533 to Dr. Bocking, the confessor of the nun, in enthusiastic terms of her. "Let us praise God," he says, "who has raised up this holy virgin, a mother, indeed, to me and a daughter to thee for our salvation. She has raised a fire in some hearts that you would think like unto the operation of the Holy Spirit in the primitive Church if you saw with what frequent tears some bewailed their transgressions."[2] At a subsequent date the same monk writes, that it is only "of late it has pleased God to give me some knowledge of His secret and wonderful works, which He works daily in His special spiritual daughter. This 'accends' my heart in the love of God." I beg you, he continues in his letter to Dr. Bocking, "to accept me as your spiritual son, and ask the prayers of Elizabeth Barton to obtain grace to mortify myself and live only for Christ."[3] Another monk of the same monastery writes to the nun asking her prayers for himself, as he finds as yet but little profit to his soul by his leaving the world.[4] His letter shows what an exalted idea he had formed of her holiness of life.

Without doubt, however, the most important testimony as to the character of the "holy maid" is the opinion as to her virtues entertained by the venerable bishop Fisher. It

---

[1] Lambard, p. 148. The act of attainder seems to admit her reputation for sanctity and her influence for good. Richard Morison, the uncompromising supporter of Henry's policy, in a work printed so soon after the execution of the "Holy Maid" as 1537, admits the general opinion of her sanctity. "Tandem comparata sanctimoniæ fama, cœpit mirum in modum non plebem, non vulgus imperitum, sed magnates alioqui viros, multos preterea doctores, abbates aliquot, Warramum ipsum archiepiscopum Cantuariensem, atque adeo legatos apostolicos, deludere."—*Apomaxis Calumniarum*, fol. 72 (1537).

[2] *Calendar*, vi. No. 835.   [3] *Ibid.*, No. 1149.

[4] *Ibid.*, No. 1468.

must be remembered that the bishop of Rochester was no ordinary man. He was an ecclesiastic of extraordinary ability and learning; and, unlike so many other bishops of his age, he had not spent his life, and thus perhaps blunted his judgment as to spiritual matters, in attendance at court or by occupation in affairs of state. He was justly esteemed the most learned bishop in England, and at one time Henry thought there was no ecclesiastic equal to him in Christendom.[1] Of advanced age and possessed of practical prudence, his judgment balanced by vast and varied experience, he was hardly likely to be at fault in reading the characters of Elizabeth Barton and of her adviser and confessor, Dr. Bocking.

By the middle of 1533 Henry appears to have arranged with Crumwell to take some steps to prevent any public condemnation of his marriage with Anne, resulting from the denunciations of the royal policy which had been made by the then much respected Elizabeth Barton. Even before the death of archbishop Warham, according to Harpsfield,[2] Crumwell had contemplated the advisability of taking vigorous measures against the nun and those that believed in her. She had declared, more or less openly, that in her trances God had commissioned her to bear testimony to His displeasure at the king's proceedings. She was known to have had interviews with Wolsey and Warham, to have spoken to the legates of the pope and to have written to his holiness himself. It is hardly likely, however, that her influence had much to do with the final attitude of the archbishop or the cardinal towards the divorce. Neither is it probable that it confirmed the bishop of Rochester and the friars Observant in their persistent opposition to it; nor, still less, that it deterred the pope from giving sentence in Henry's favour. But such things were said,[3] and perhaps believed, by Henry's adherents.

The position of affairs in England at midsummer, 1533, was critical. It became, therefore, vital to the designs of

[1] "Quid quod tanta virtus viri, tanta integritas, tanta fama fuit per inimicorum ora eruperit. Nam Henricus ipse octavus (ut reverendissimus Polus Cardinalis scriptum reliquit), eum in Europæ totius theologos primas tenere multus audientibus fassus est."—B. Mus. Arund. MS., 152, f. 238 b.; MS. Life of bishop Fisher.

[2] *The Pretended Divorce* (Camd. Soc.), p. 178.

[3] *Calendar*, vii. No. 72 (1) and (3).

The Holy Maid of Kent

minister and master, and indispensable to Anne Boleyn, who now reigned supreme over the heart of Henry, that any symptom of popular discontent should be instantly repressed. Anything that might tend to stir up the latent feeling of hostility to their triple alliance must at all costs be prevented. Hence, as regards the "holy maid of Kent," so universally revered and respected, it seemed necessary to fix the stigma of hypocrisy and deceit upon her.

Cranmer consequently, acting on the orders of Crumwell, about the middle of July, 1533, ordered the prioress of St. Sepulchre's to bring Elizabeth Barton to him at Otford in order that he might examine her.[1] At this interview the archbishop was apparently unable to convict the nun of anything more than a firm belief in the reality of her visions and revelations.

A month later Dr. Bocking, "cellarer of Christchurch, Canterbury, and Hadley, one of the penitentiaries there," were arrested by the attorney-general, Christopher Hales, "as secretly as possible." At the same time a promise was sent by Hales to Crumwell that he should have the parson of Aldington and the official of Canterbury within a few days.[2] The nun herself had been in the minister's power and subjected to his examinations since her visit to Cranmer. It is worthy of note that from this time all that is known of her recantations and confessions emanate from Crumwell or his agents, who had already determined to make her out to be a "hypocrite nun."

As to the connection of the monks of Christchurch, Canterbury, with the cause of Elizabeth Barton, a good deal is to be learnt from a letter which at this time Thomas Goldwell, the prior, wrote to Crumwell on the matter. "As concerning the knowledge of such things as Elizabeth Barton, nun, has spoken," he writes, "which as she said she had knowledge of in trances and revelations, these be the things that I have heard and have knowledge of. At the beginning thereof, the which was about seven or eight years past, as I think, my lord Warham, then being archbishop of Canterbury, sent his comptroller, called Thomas Walle, of Canterbury, and caused me to send two of my brethren, which were the cellarer, Dr. Bocking, and Dom

[1] *Calendar*, vi. No. 869.
[2] *Ibid.*, No. 1149. Christ. Hales to Crumwell, Sept. 25.

William Hadley, bachelor of divinity, to a place called Court of Street, to see this woman and to see what trances she had. They went there at the beginning, as I suppose, somewhat against their minds and also against my mind except the obedience that I do owe unto my lord of Canterbury; and (if) he had not been, I would not have sent them thither. After this he caused and gave license to the cellarer to be this woman's ghostly father."

About the month of October Elizabeth Barton and her companions underwent a strict examination in the Star Chamber, and almost simultaneously it became noised abroad that she had confessed herself an impostor. On the 16th of November John Capon, abbot of Hyde, and at that time bishop-elect of Bangor, wrote to a friend that "our holy nun of Kent" had admitted "treason against God and the king;" that is, he explained, she is "not only a traitress but a heretic." She and her accomplices are "like to suffer death."[1] Lady Rutland, also writing the following day to Sir W. Paston, says she hears that the "holy woman of Kent" has been examined by the Council, "which is," she concludes, "one of the most abominablest matters that ever I heard of in my life, as shall be published to all people within three or four days at the furthest."[2]

A singular spectacle was shortly afterwards witnessed in London. On Sunday, November 23, 1533, the nun and her companions, Dr. Edward Bocking and John Dering, both benedictine monks of Christ Church, Canterbury, Hugh Rich and Richard Risby, two friars Observant, with two secular priests, Richard Masters, parson of Aldington and Henry Gold, of Aldermary, London, together with a gentleman named Edward Thwaites, were placed on a high scaffold at St. Paul's Cross to do public penance. The pulpit, over against them, was occupied by Dr. Capon, the bishop-elect of Bangor, who, as Chapuys relates, "for their vituperation repeated all the chancellor had said against them, further affirming that the nun, by her feigned superstition, had prevented the cardinal of York from proceeding to give sentence for the divorce."[3] To the companions of the nun in this public humiliation the preacher attributed "levity and superstition" in believing these revelations, and "disloyalty" for

[1] *Calendar*, vi. No. 1433.   [2] *Ibid.*, No. 1438.
[3] *Ibid.*, No. 1460. Chapuys to Chas. V., Nov. 24.

not revealing them. He specially blamed the two Observant friars, "that under the shadow of the said superstition they had suborned and seduced their companions to maintain the false opinion and wicked quarrel of the queen against the king."[1]

From this public penance, which was performed in "as great a presence as was seen there (at the Cross) this forty winters,"[2] the nun and her companions were again conducted "unto the Tower of London, and much people (were gathered) through all the streets of London"[3] to witness the sight. Before leaving the platform over against the preacher's pulpit, the nun was required to hand a form of confession to Dr. Capon, who read it to the people.

A great deal was subsequently made of this so-called confession of hypocrisy and deceit. It requires, however, very little knowledge of these times to see that, after all, it proves exceedingly little. On the face of the document it is not her own; but was written for her by those in whose power she had been for the four months previously, and its terms are exceedingly vague and general.

The fact is that some acknowledgment that Elizabeth Barton had been for years wilfully deceitful was at the time a matter of vital necessity, and, with Crumwell to manage the affair, that confession would not be difficult to procure. In fact, the draft of a letter exists, with corrections in Crumwell's own hand, by which the Marchioness of Exeter is made to ask pardon of Henry VIII. for putting such belief "in the most unworthy and deceivable woman called the holy maid of Kent."[4] What he did in this case he may, with better reason, have used every effort to do in regard to the nun herself. According to the act of attainder, indeed, the poor woman is said to have confessed her duplicity and falsehood before "divers of the king's counsel." Such evidence, however, may reasonably be suspected, more especially when it was noised abroad that the confession attributed to her was a calumny,[5] and extreme measures were taken to prevent the spread of such an unwelcome report.

[1] *Calendar*, vii. No. 72.   [2] *Ibid.*, No. 72.
[3] *Grey Friars Chronicle*, Camd. Soc., p. 37.
[4] *Calendar*, vi. No. 1464.
[5] Burnet, ed. Pocock, i. p. 251, says: "It is very probable that the reports that went abroad of her being forced or cheated into a confession made the king think it necessary to proceed more severely against her."

The day following the public penance of the nun and her companions Chapuys again refers to the difficulty experienced by the king and Crumwell to obtain a conviction for treason. "The king," he tells his master, "has not yet prevailed on the judges to make the oration against those who have practised against him with the said nun in the form that I last wrote. He is going to have the affair discussed with them on Friday (November 28, 1533), and although some of the principal judges would sooner die than make the said declaration, yet when the king comes to dispute, there is no one who will dare to contradict him unless he wishes to be reputed stupid or disloyal. So that it seems as if he had made a total divorce, not only from his wife, but from good conscience, humanity and gentleness, which he used to have."[1]

The trial, however, ended without a sentence. In the face of the opposition manifested by the judges to the course proposed by Crumwell, it may have been deemed more prudent to proceed by the surer method of attainder by act of parliament. It seems at one time, early in January, 1534, to have been contemplated to try the issue of a new trial. Crumwell notes, "to cause indictments to be drawn for the offenders in treason and misprision concerning the nun of Canterbury."[2] Shortly afterwards he abandoned this plan, however, and notes that he has to "know what the king will have done" in the matter. Finally, it was determined to present a bill of attainder to parliament, and for Crumwell this was already tantamount to a condemnation to death. Hence he notes that "Elizabeth Barton, nun, Edward Bocking, John Dering, Richard Masters, Henry Gold, Hugh Rich, and Richard Risby, these by act shall be attainted of high treason and suffer death."[3]

There are many indications that, although the existence of the bill and the general tenour of its provisions were known, the names of those implicated and against whom proceedings were to be taken were purposely concealed. "The consequence was," says an historian of this period, "that everybody who ever encouraged the nun was in no little anxiety, and, fearing that his name might be on the terrible list, was anxious to please the king. In this way

[1] *Calendar*, No. 1460, Nov. 24.
[2] *Ibid.*, vii. No. 48.   [3] *Ibid.*, No. 70.

the government bridled the opposition, and, as nearly as they could, ensured the passing of the bills of succession."[1] By this concealment also, money was wrung from those who had been associated with the nun in any way. For this both master and minister were always ready. Richard Masters, the parish priest of Aldington, who was subsequently executed, sends Crumwell two gold crowns for having expedited his pardon.[2]

The Canterbury monks also professed themselves very ready to serve the king in any way, if he would only pass over their connection with the "Maid of Kent." They even were willing, as Cranmer, then on his visitation there, writes, to offer some substantial sum of money. "Only a few," he says, "consented to these revelations, almost all being Dr. Bocking's novices." The prior, a man of no malice, "has been touched by this matter. They desire my mediation, and I think they will offer £200 or £300 for their pardon. The monastery," he adds, "is not 'aforehand,' but in debt, except the church ornaments and plate."[3] Edward Thwaites, whose guilt consisted in his belief in the nun and in having printed a small volume with an account of her early life, purchased "his pardon for 1000 marks,"[4] and subsequently Bishop Fisher had to pay £300 for his share in the matter.

On Saturday, February 21, 1534, the bill of attainder "concerning the condign punishment of Elizabeth Barton, the hypocrite nun, commonly called the holy maid of Kent," was brought into the Lords and read the first time.[5] At this sitting, and throughout the proceedings during the passage of the bill, the lay lords far outnumbered the lords spiritual. The various steps were taken between the date of its introduction and the 12th of March, when it was read for the fourth time and accepted by the house. The accused had apparently been condemned unheard, since on March 6th, at the third reading of the attainder, the lords "thought proper to inquire whether it would accord with the king's wishes (*cum Regio animo quadrare potest*) that Sir Thomas

---

[1] P. Friedmann, *Anne Boleyn*, vol. i. p. 273.
[2] *Calendar*, vi. No. 1666.   [3] *Ibid.*, No. 1519.
[4] "Which was one whole year's revenue of his bishoprick." B. Mus. Arund. MS., 152, f. 49.
[5] "Lords' Journals," p. 68.

More and the others named in the said bill (except the bishop of Rochester, now very ill, whose answer is known through his letters) should be summoned before the lords to the Star chamber in order to say what they can for themselves."

It has been said that the parties attainted "were not able to disprove a single article of the act." For such a statement there is no warrant. It is by no means easy to say what they could have done had they been allowed. "They were all attainted of high treason, and condemned without any answer making for themselves," as an old writer asserts.[1] And in this statement, history bears him out.

The nun and her companions were condemned by a tribunal which had not heard them in their defence. In the very bill reference is made for the truth of the facts to examinations not before the parliament, but before the king's council. The books and writings had been "seen and examined by the king's most honourable council," and the matters "confessed plainly before the king's most honourable council," as the bill of attainder declared. The tribunal that decided the case was not that which had examined, and the attainted persons, though at hand, were not heard for themselves.

On April 20, 1534, Elizabeth Barton and her companions were executed under this act of attainder, at Tyburn. Father Thomas Bourchier, an English Franciscan Observant, declares that the lives of his two brethren, Fathers Risby and Rich, were twice offered to them if they would accept Henry as supreme head of the English Church.[2] What was done to the Franciscans would in all probability have been done in the case of those who suffered with them, Dr. Bocking and Father Dering, the two monks of the Benedictine monastery of Christ Church, Canterbury, and the two secular priests, Richard Masters and Henry Gold. It is needless to say that the offer was rejected. The character of their deaths may be estimated accordingly.

---

[1] B. Mus. Arund. MS., 152, f. 49.
[2] "Hist. Ecc. de Martyrio FF. Ord. Min.," 1583. Bourchier is an authority. He took the Franciscan habit at Greenwich about 1557 upon the restoration of the order by queen Mary. He would thus have known some of the old Franciscan brethren of Fathers Rich and Risby.

CHAPTER IV

The Friars Observant and the Carthusians

THE session of Parliament which commenced in January, 1534, was chiefly occupied in framing measures against the exercise of papal authority in England.* The Imperial ambassador, Chapuys, always well informed as to the acts and intentions of Henry, writing the following month to Charles V. says that the commons had taken away all authority from the Holy See, and given to the crown power to nominate to vacant bishoprics. He adds that "the king is very covetous of the goods of the church, which he already considers as his patrimony."[1] Before Easter he again writes that the lords, "to the great regret of good men, who were in a minority," had been obliged, "owing to the threats and practices of the king," to ratify these enactments of the lower house.[2]

Amongst other provisions made in this parliament for cutting off England from the ancient ecclesiastical jurisdiction of Rome, was the transfer of papal authority over the religious houses to the crown. The power of archbishops and bishops to visit and control the monasteries and convents situated within the limits of their individual dioceses, had long been a subject of debate. Its exercise had often given rise to difficulties and dissensions, which were settled only by recourse to the supreme authority of the Holy See. At all times, however, except in the case of the comparatively few exempt monasteries and of the various orders of friars and others associated in congregations extending beyond the limits of the country and directed by foreign superiors, the episcopal power of visitation was exercised at regular

---

[1] *Calendar*, vii. No. 171, Feb. 11, 1534.
[2] *Ibid.*, No. 373. In speaking of the Parliament of 1536 it will be necessary to show what these "threats and practices" were. We may here note that Bishop Tunstal of Durham was prevented attending Parliament by positive orders from Crumwell and the King.

periods. The bishop or his officers also directed the canonical elections.

At the time of this Parliament the pulpit was strictly guarded, and the Easter sermons of 1534, were directed as far as could be against the pope and his authority.[1] The definite sentence of the Holy See against the divorce finally forced the king, although, as it appears, most reluctantly, to widen the breach between England and Rome. He had to make his choice between dutiful submission and active retaliation.

There were some who refused to follow the king blindly in his revolt against the Holy See. Of the whole body of the clergy, none withstood the policy of Henry with greater fearlessness and pertinacity of purpose than the Franciscan Observants.[2] Two of these friars were implicated with the "Holy maid of Kent," and, as associated in her sentence, were executed at Tyburn. Death, however, had seemingly no terrors for men who had fled from the pleasures of life as they had. "Secluded from the commerce and pleasures of the world," writes the historian Lingard, "they felt fewer temptations to sacrifice their conscience to the commands of their sovereign, and seemed more eager to court the crown than to flee from the pains of martyrdom."[3]

There were six monasteries of these Franciscan Observants in England. Of these, none bore a higher character for discipline and regularity than that of Greenwich. In 1513 Henry VIII. himself had written more than once to the pope, Leo. X., in their favour. He declares that towards them he has the most deep, devoted affection. So much does he admire their holiness of life that he finds it quite impossible to describe their merits as they deserve. They present an ideal of Christian poverty, sincerity and charity; their lives are devoted to fasting, watching, prayer; and they are occupied in "hard toil by night and day" to win sinners

---

[1] *Calendar*, vii. No. 464.
[2] Sanders, *Schism* (Lewis' trans.), p. 112. The Observant friars were a reformed branch of the great Franciscan order. They were instituted about 1400 by St. Bernardine of Sienna, and confirmed by the Council of Constance in 1414, and afterwards by Eugenius IV. and other popes. King Edward IV. is said to have brought them to England. Tanner, however, says, "I find no account of their being here till king Henry VII. built two or three houses for them." Vide *Monasticon*, vi. p. 1504.
[3] Lingard, *History of England*, vi. p. 285.

back to God.¹ The convent had been placed by Henry VII. at Greenwich, near to the court, and Queen Catherine had chosen one of the brethren, the fearless and saintly friar Forest, as her confessor.²

These friars of Greenwich were not easily silenced. "They, indeed," writes Sanders, "both in public disputations and in their sermons, most earnestly maintained that the marriage of Catherine was good and lawful." Yet even here, among so many good, there were not wanting some to go with the stream. Here, as in so many religious houses at this period, Crumwell found a spy to report to him the dispositions and intentions entertained in the cloister. In this case a lay brother, Richard Lyst, afterwards rewarded for his services by a place at Cambridge,³ was Crumwell's agent, and he kept him informed as to the feelings and doings of his brethren. Early in February, 1533, he writes to his employer that he considers the discipline of his monastery altogether too severe. The religious are corrected and "punished for nothing," and many of their fathers show themselves much against the king. Of these, the chief and leading spirits are Fathers Peto, Elstow, and Forest. Above the rest he thinks friar Forest most to be blamed in the matter, because the king had always shown him special kindness. Only the day before (Monday, February 3) Henry had conversed with him in private for more than half an hour, and had "sent him some beef from his own table."⁴

The informing lay brother quite thought that "the suspect death of brother Raynscroftys" would prevent "ours preaching against the king."⁵ Early in May, however, friar Peto, a man "of good house and family," and one specially accused by Lyst of taking a leading part against the king's designs, had to preach before Henry.⁶ He did not hesitate to speak his mind boldly.

¹ Ellis, *Orig. Letters*, 3rd Series, i. p. 165. Henry VIII. to Leo X., March 12, 1513. From B. Mus. Vatic. Transcripts, vol. xxxvii. f. 17.
² Queen Catherine, when the court was at Greenwich, is said to have risen always at midnight to be present at the friars' matins. *Collectio Anglo-Minoretica*, p. 216.
³ *Calendar*, vi. No. 1264. ⁴ *Ibid.*, vi. No. 116.
⁵ *Ibid.*, No. 168.
⁶ N. Harpsfield, *The Pretended Divorce* (Camden Soc.), p. 203; Stow, *Annals* (ed. 1615), p. 561.

48   Henry VIII. and the English Monasteries

The historian Stow relates the sequel of this bold denunciation. "The king," he says, "being thus reproved, endured it patiently and did no violence to Peto, but the next Sunday, being the 8th[1] of May, Dr. Curwin[2] preached in the same place, who sharply reprehended Peto and his preaching, and called him dog, slanderer, base, beggarly friar, closeman, rebel, and traitor, saying that no subject should speak so audaciously to princes. . . . He then, supposing to have utterly suppressed Peto and his partakers, lifted up his voice and said: 'I speak to thee, Peto, who makest thyself Micheas, that thou mayest speak evil of kings, but now thou art not to be found, being fled for fear and shame, as being unable to answer my arguments.' And whilst he thus spoke there was one Elstow, a fellow friar to Peto, standing in the rood loft, who, with a bold voice, said to Dr. Curwin: 'Good sir, you know that father Peto, as he was commanded, is now gone to a provincial council held at Canterbury, and not fled for fear of you, for to-morrow he will return again. In the meantime I am here as another Micheas, and will lay down my life to prove all those things true which he hath taught out of the holy scripture. And to this combat I challenge you before God and all equal judges. Even unto thee, Curwin, I speak, who art one of the four hundred prophets into whom the spirit of lying is entered, and seekest by adultery to establish succession, betraying the king unto endless perdition, more for thy own vain glory and hope of promotion than for discharge of your clogged conscience and the king's salvation.'"

The scene can be better imagined than described. Henry himself had attended again at the church of the Greenwich Observants to witness the discomfiture of the bold preacher of the previous Sunday. In the absence of Friar Peto, Dr. Curwin calculated to carry his audience with him by means of his vigorous denunciations. The tables were turned

---

[1] Stow, p. 559, says the sermon was on May 28. Probably both dates are wrong, as neither the 8th nor 28th was a Sunday in any year about this time. May 18th, however, was a Sunday in 1533.

[2] Curwin, or as he is called in the episcopal registers of the diocese of Hereford, "Mgr. Hugo Coren, LL.D.," was a canon of Hereford. On the death of bishop Fox he was appointed by Cranmer to administer the diocese *sede vacante* (*vide* his register). Bonner, as elect of Hereford, appointed him his commissary. Under Fox, he had held the post of Vicar-general. He was made dean of Hereford in 1541, archbishop of Dublin in 1555, and in 1567 translated by Elizabeth to the See of Oxford.

when another of the Greenwich brethren leaned over from the rood, and not alone defended his absent brother, but vehemently accused Curwin himself of acting as he did through hopes of preferment. "This Elstow," continues the chronicler, "waxed hot[1] and spake very earnestly, so that they could not make him cease his speech until the king himself bade him hold his peace."[2]

The following day, as the king had directed, the two friars Peto and Elstow were brought before the council, when Elstow again boldly replied to the threats of Henry Bourchier, earl of Essex. After the lords had "rebuked them, the E. of Essex told them, that they had deserved to be put into a sack and cast into the Thames. Whereunto Elstow, smiling, said, 'Threaten these things to rich and dainty folk who are clothed in purple, fare delicately, and have their chiefest hope in this world, for we esteem them not, but are joyful that for the discharge of our duties we are driven hence. With thanks to God we know the way to heaven, to be as ready by water as by land, and, therefore, we care not which way we go.'"[3] The two friars, Peto and Elstow, apparently escaped with a reprimand and the punishment of exile from England.

By the spring of 1534 events had progressed rapidly. Parliament, under the skilful management of Crumwell, had proved itself so pliant to Henry's will that the king could contemplate a final move against the unbending Greenwich friars. Already, according to one authority,[4] friar Forest,

---

[1] After relating Elstow's answer to "this great Golias bragge," Harpsfield (*ut sup.*, p. 204) says: "Many other things he would have then spoken, and much ado there was to stay him. At the hearing of this the king was cast into a great choler, and in a great heat commanded that these friars should be conveyed thither where he should never hear more of them." The author says he heard the whole account from Elstow himself.

[2] Harpsfield (*ut sup.*) gives much the same account. He says that Dr. Curwin preached on Palm Sunday, "the next Sunday," by the king's order. "But lord," he continues, "what a stir that Currante made against that poor friar, being absent, and what nicknames he gave him! At length, as though he had now full conquered him, he began to triumph and insult upon him, crying out 'Where is miser and micher Micheas? Where doth he now micher? He is run away, for that he would not hear what should be said unto him. Belike he is somewhat lurking and musing with himself by what means he may honestly recant.'"

[3] Stow, *ut supra*.

[4] Bourchier, *Hist. Eccl. de Mart. Fratrum*, 1583. Mr. Gairdner places friar Forest's letters in his *Calendar*, vol. vii. Nos. 129 to 134, but notes that there is no sign of Forest's imprisonment at this date, although the "complaints of

who five years later died a martyr's death, was lodged in prison, although not so closely watched as to be unable to communicate by letter with Catherine and others. To the queen he wrote begging her prayers, and telling her not to grieve for his fate. At the age of sixty-four he hoped to be constant, and as he believed he had only three days to live he sent her his rosary.[1] Again, in answer to a note from one of Catherine's ladies, who expressed the distress the queen felt for the treatment her old confessor was experiencing in prison, he begged her to tell Catherine that this want of fortitude was not what he had tried to teach her. As for himself, he said he had only to break his faith to save his life, and he concluded by urging her to accept her sufferings for Christ's sake.[2] Besides friar Forest, there were in prison at this time two other Observants, friar Rich, the warden of Richmond, and friar Risby, the warden of Canterbury, both charged in connection with the Maid of Kent.

The Greenwich Franciscan house was not the only one, which at this time produced men with the courage of their convictions. On Passion Sunday, March 22, 1534, a certain Robert Cooke, of Rye, was ordered to abjure publicly, in the cathedral church of Winchester, certain heresies he had maintained about the Blessed Sacrament. On that occasion friar Pecock, warden of the Observant convent of Franciscan friars at Southampton, was the preacher. He seized the opportunity to speak earnestly of this and "other dampned heresies." He eloquently exhorted the people to stand steadfast even to death in their ancient faith and practice. He then lamented the diversity of opinions that existed in England, especially as regarded the pope. Some, he said, declared that St. Peter had no more power given him by God than the other apostles, and others that the pope had no more power than a bishop of any other diocese, whilst others

---

friar Lyst (vol. vi. Nos. 168, 334, 512) may have led to his imprisonment." Stowe in his *Chronicle* (ed. 1580) says, 1532, "The 28th of May friar Forest was put in prison for contrarying the preacher before the king." In the list of Observants published in Mr. Gairdner's *Calendar*, vol. vii. No. 1607, is "John Foreste is there (London) in prison." Perhaps the most conclusive proof that he was probably in prison at this time is that we hear no more about him. Crumwell's "remembrances" are silent about this formidable opponent.

[1] *Calendar*, vii. No. 130.   [2] *Ibid.*, No. 132.

again taught that as a bishop was no more than a simple priest, "so, consequently, the pope had no more power than a simple curate." To prove this, he continued, people bought all kinds of books that were not to be believed. Then, taking up a volume which was beside him in the pulpit, he read to his audience five or six authorities on the Primacy of St. Peter and translated the passages into English.[1]

The better to carry out his wishes in regard to the various orders of friars, Henry conceived the ingenious plan of appointing over them a general superior upon whose faithful subservience to himself he could depend. And as by 1534 his quarrel with the pope had reached its height, and the severance of the Church in England from its ancient dependence on Rome was complete, there remained no further obstacle to prevent his dealing according to his royal pleasure with the friars. As a first step, Crumwell and his master selected two worthy instruments: John Hilsey, a Dominican friar, afterwards successor to the saintly John Fisher in the see of Rochester, and Dr. George Browne, a prior of the Augustinian hermits, and subsequently, for his services to the king and his minister, created archbishop of Dublin.[2]

The two "grand visitors" were despatched with a full commission[3] to the various orders of friars in the spring of 1534. Their instructions were precise and intended to gauge the feeling of the friars very thoroughly. The members of every convent or friary in England were to be assembled in their chapter-houses and examined separately concerning their faith and obedience to Henry. The oath of allegiance to Anne Boleyn was to be administered to them, and they were to be bound to swear solemnly that they would preach and persuade the people, to accept the royal supremacy, to confess that the bishop of Rome had no more power than any other bishop and to call him Pope no

---

[1] *Calendar*, vii. No. 449.
[2] "On Sunday last," says Chapuys (1535), "an Augustinian friar (Dr. George Brown), who has been appointed by the king general of all the mendicant orders in reward for having married the king and the Lady Anne, preached. . . . The language is so abominable that it is clear it must have been prompted by the king or Crumwell, who makes the said monk his right hand man in all things unlawful."
[3] *Calendar*, vii. No. 587 (18).

longer. Further, the sermons of each preacher were to be carefully examined, and if not orthodox they were to be burned. Every friar was to be strictly enjoined to commend the king as head of the Church, the queen, the archbishop of Canterbury and the clergy to the prayers of the faithful. Lastly, each house was "to be obliged to show its gold, silver, and other moveable goods, and deliver an inventory of them," and to take a common oath, sealed with the convent seal, to observe the above orders.[1]

From the 17th to the 20th of April, Hilsey and Brown were occupied at the various friaries of London and the neighbourhood. They then proceeded to visit others in the southern parts of England. Dr. Hilsey was occupied in visiting the friaries of the south and west of England till midsummer. On June 21st he wrote from Exeter to say that none of those he had so far visited had refused the oath to "be obedient, true, and agreeable to the king's high pleasure and will." He added, "I have found some, however, that have sworn with an evil will and slenderly have taken the oath to be obedient." Of these he promised Crumwell he would have more to say on his return.[2] His attention was specially taken up with watching the proceedings of certain Franciscan Observants. At the commencement of July, he was in pursuit of two of these friars who were endeavouring to escape to the Continent from the persecution which had already begun in England. Hilsey followed them through Bristol, Somerset, Devon, and Cornwall, and at last overtook them at Cardiff, where they were already in prison.

One of these two friars was a certain Hugh Payn, who not long before had been arrested and put in prison for having visited the dethroned queen Catherine at her house at Bugden. The other was a friar named Thomas Hayfield, and both belonged to the house of Newark. They narrowly escaped capture in Somerset, to the sheriff of which county the king had sent a special commission for their seizure. At Cardiff, after almost succeeding in eluding the keen pursuit, they were taken whilst on the point of embarking in a Breton ship, disguised in secular dress.[3]

---

[1] *Calendar*, vii. 590.   [2] *Ibid.*, No. 869.
[3] *Ibid.*, No. 1020.

The Friars and the Carthusians

The State papers of this period contain various complaints made to Crumwell about the teaching and preaching of these valiant friars. They evidently remained as firmly attached to the ancient faith and practices as they were to the cause of Catherine. One or two of their number no doubt gave way under the pressure of the threats and the seductive nature of the promises addressed to them. By becoming the accusers of their brethren they may have hoped to purchase the royal favour by their treachery. Such renegades were, however, the exceptions; as a body the friars remained staunch and fearless in their opposition to the unlawful will of the king and his minister. An instance, recorded in a document of this time, reveals to us how commonly the people applauded this attitude, and condemned the weakness of those that yielded. Friar John George of Cambridge was apparently one of the latter sort. His mother, however, was made of sterner stuff, and rated him right roundly for having given in to the influence of the times. She is grieved indeed, she writes to him, to find her son a heretic. It was not for this that he had received his education from the good nuns of Dartford. "And," she continues, "you send me word that you will come over to me this summer, but come not unless you change your condition, or you shall be as welcome 'as water into the sheep.' You shall have God's curse and mine and never a penny. I had rather give all my goods to the poor than keep you in heresy."[1]

Above all the rest, the Observants of Greenwich and Richmond were the objects of the special solicitude of Henry and his agents. Rowland Lee, one of the king's chaplains, and of late made bishop of Coventry and Lichfield, was selected, together with Thomas Bedyll, clerk of the council, to make the final attempts to influence them. Friar Rich, the warden of the Richmond friars and his companion, friar Risby of Canterbury, had been executed at Tyburn with the holy maid of Kent on the 20th April 1534, and very shortly afterwards the two commissioners reported their first move in the matter to their employer, Crumwell. They had induced the prior and convent of the Carthusians of Sheen to take the required oath, and the prior and procurator, they wrote, had been doing their best to win the consent of their

[1] *Calendar*, vii. No. 939.

neighbours, the Observants of Richmond; earnestly exhorting them to bend their minds to the king's wishes. Both the bishop and his coadjutor had also been busy at the same work, holding various conferences with the friars; but, as they are obliged to confess, without any sign of success. In fact, they had been in despair of effecting their purpose, but, with the Sheen influence at work, they had some slight shadow of hope that they might finally win the Franciscans to what the king required.[1]

The next few weeks were occupied in equally fruitless efforts to obtain the consent of the Carthusians to the oath. It was not, therefore, till Saturday, June 15th, that Lee and Bedyll followed up their attacks upon the Richmond friars. On that day Dr. George Browne, or, as Lee calls him, "the provincial of the Austin friars," delivered to the bishop and his fellow-commissioner Crumwell's orders to proceed at once to conclusions. Armed with these letters, they betook themselves directly to Richmond, which they reached "between ten and eleven o'clock at night." "In the following morning," as they report to Crumwell, "we had first communication with the warden and one of the seniors, named Sebastian, and after that with the whole convent." At first, although they made use of "all the means and policies" they could devise to obtain the oath and the signatures and convent seal to the " articles " sent by Dr. George Browne, the warden and his faithful friars absolutely refused, "and showed themselves very untoward in that behalf."

They then fell back on another plan. After some argument, they finally persuaded the convent, as a body, to trust the settlement of the matter to the discretion of four of their senior members, "otherwise called discretes," who were to be given full power to act in their behalf. Having secured this much, the commissioners arranged that the four friars, to whom the community had intrusted their honour and conscience, should meet them at the house of the Greenwich Observants, and should bring with them the convent seal, on Monday, June 17th. "And so they did."

The two commissioners, Lee and Bedyll, arrived at Greenwich somewhat elated at the success of their diplomacy at Richmond. They fortified themselves with the

[1] *Calendar*, vii. No. 622, May 7.

hope that here also they might prevail upon the friars to
walk into the same trap. If they were only pliable and
would commit the matter to the judgment of some few of
the brethren, it would, in their opinion, serve a double
purpose. It would be the means of "avoiding superfluous
words and idle reasonings," and in case the "discretes"
chosen should refuse their consent to the proposed articles,
"it were better after our minds," they say, "to strain a few
than a multitude." Their plans came to nothing, for their
advice was rejected. The Greenwich Observants absolutely
refused to leave a matter of this kind to be settled by a few
deputies, saying, "that as it concerned particularly every
one of their souls, they would answer particularly every
man for himself."

The commissioners were thus driven unwillingly to
discuss the whole matter in public. After a long debate,
and after each friar had been privately examined as to his
readiness to accept the royal desires, they found that one
and all steadily refused to subscribe any rejection of Papal
authority and jurisdiction. The friars declared that the
proposed article "was clearly against their profession and
the rule of St. Francis."[1] And from this position all the
arguments of Bedyll and the bishop were unable to move
them. They represented that the two archbishops and
most of the bishops of the country, with prelates and
learned priests, had subscribed to the declaration that the
pope had no authority according to the scriptures (*ex sacris
literis*) in England. They urged that it was obvious pre-
sumption for them to persist in a refusal which virtually
condemned what so many good and well-instructed ecclesiastics had done. This argument, no doubt, had been used
with fatal effect to secure the adhesion of many who in
their own hearts condemned the doctrine of royal supremacy
as contrary to Catholic faith; but with the friars Observant
it failed, as it subsequently failed with More and Fisher.
The baffled visitors write to their master, "All this notwith-

[1] The words of the rule which the friars pointed out to Lee are: "Ad
hæc per obedientiam injungo ministris ut petant a domino Papa unum de
Sanctæ Romanæ Ecclesiæ Cardinalibus, qui sit gubernator, protector et
corrector istius fraternitatis, ut semper subditi et subjecti pedibus Sanctæ
Ecclesiæ ejusdem stabiles in fide Catholica paupertatem et humilitatem et
secundum Evangelium Domini Nostri Jesu Christi, quod firmiter promisimus
observemus."

standing, their conclusion was they had professed St. Francis' religion, and in the observance thereof they would live and die." "Sorry we be," they conclude, "we cannot bring them to no better frame and order in this behalf, as our faithful minds was to do for the accomplishment of the king's pleasure."[1]

Henry, thus foiled in his designs, determined to strike quickly and effectually. As yet, however, there was no law by which these bold and unbending friars, who set his wishes at defiance, could be made to feel the weight of his royal displeasure. Neither was it illegal for them to refuse, however obstinately, their adherence to articles proposed to them even with the royal authority. Still the question of legality was never allowed to bar the way against the royal will, and the suppression of the entire order of Observants followed quickly upon their positive refusal to be bound by the articles proposed to them by Lee and Bedyll. "Within a few days," writes the great authority on the history of this period, "two carts of friars were seen passing through the city to the Tower."[2] These were the staunch Franciscans of Observance. By the beginning of August, Chapuys wrote to tell his master that "of the seven[3] houses of Observants, four have been already emptied of friars because they have refused to swear to the statutes made against the Pope. Those in the other two expect to be expelled."[4] Three weeks later their expectation had been fulfilled, as the Imperial ambassador again wrote "that all the Observants of the kingdom have been driven from their monasteries for refusing the oath against the Holy See, and have been distributed in several monasteries, where they were locked up in chains, and worse treated than they could be in prison."

About two hundred of the Observant friars were thus cast without trial into prison. The convents from which they were expelled were temporarily occupied by friars of

---

[1] Wright, *Supp. of Monast.*, pp. 41-44.
[2] Mr. Gairdner, vii. Preface, xxviii.
[3] These convents were said to be "houses of the foundation of Henry VII." ("Prevarication of the Church's Liberties," ch. iv., Eyston MS., quoted in Lewis' Sanders' *Schism*, p. 111). Most of them, however, existed as monasteries before, and Henry VII. only made them Observants. See Dugdale, vi. p. 1504.
[4] *Calendar*, vii. No. 1057, August 7th.

the Augustinian order.¹ Fifty of the Observants died from the hardships of their prison life; several, through the influence of Wriothesley, their secret friend and admirer, obtained leave to retire into France and Scotland,² and others possibly passed into Ireland with the permission of Crumwell, who was glad to get rid of them on any terms. To this may refer the note entered in the minister's "Remembrances:"—"Item to remember the friars of Greenwich to have licence to go into Ireland."³

No account of the suppression of the Observant friars would be complete without some reference to the story of their most renowned member, the saintly John Forest. He was some sixty-four years of age when he was imprisoned in 1534, and of these forty-three he had spent in religion. He had been warden of Greenwich and provincial of all the Observant friars in England, as well as the constant friend and confessor of Queen Catherine.

Bishop Latimer seems to have thought the treatment friar Forest received in prison too gentle. "Forest, as I hear," he writes to Crumwell, "is not duly accompanied in Newgate for his amendment with the white friars of Doncaster and the monks of the Charterhouse, in a fit chamber more like to indurate than to mollify, whether through the fault of the sheriff or of the gaoler or both, no man could sooner discern than your lordship. Some think he is rather comforted in his way than discouraged; some think he is allowed both to hear mass and also to receive the Sacrament; which, if it be so, it is enough to confirm him in his obstinacy."⁴

The depositions against Forest are clear and decisive of his real sentiments as to the matters at issue between the king and Rome, and it may be taken as certain that he died for his belief in the necessity of the Papal supremacy, and that even in the agony of his fearful death he remained constant and true to this his faith.

Like More, Fisher, and the rest who were martyred in defence of the Papal primacy, Forest fell under the law of

---

¹ Editor of Sanders' *Schism* (1587), probably on Bourchier's authority, who gives the same. *Hist. de Mart. FF. Ord. Min.*, 1583.
² Lingard, *Hist.*, vi. p. 268.
³ *Calendar*, vii. No. 49.
⁴ *Latimer's Remains* (Parker Soc.), p. 392.

treason, but for him alone was reserved the additional distinction of suffering for heresy also. Collier says he "was condemned for heresy and high treason, though by what law they could stretch his crime to heresy is hard to discover, for he was tried only for dissuading his penitents in confession from owning the king's supremacy."[1] The commission which tried the friar was presided over, most probably, by Cranmer in person. He at least writes to make arrangements with Crumwell for the examination. "The bishop of Worcester" (Hugh Latimer), he says, "and I will be tomorrow with your lordship to know your pleasure concerning friar Forest. For if we should proceed against him according to the order of the law, there must be articles devised beforehand which must be ministered unto him; and therefore it will be very well done that one draw them up against our meeting."[2] The result of the meeting was that Forest was condemned to die by fire in Smithfield on the 22nd May, 1538.

On the day appointed for the execution preparations were made in Smithfield for it. A pair of new gallows were placed over the faggots for a fire, from which friar Forest could be suspended in a "cradle of chains." The billets of wood were to a large extent composed of the chips of a desecrated image, called Darvel Gadarn, which had been held in high honour by the people of North Wales[3] and which had been removed from its ancient shrine shortly before.

[1] *Eccl. Hist.*, ed. 1714, ii. p. 149. Mr. Gairdner (*Calendar*, xiii. (i), preface, xviii.) says that the execution of friar Forest for "heresy" was a clear indication to the country generally "that there was to be no abatement in the exercise of that spiritual supremacy claimed by the crown. The idea was still a novelty, and notwithstanding the severities with which it was at first enforced might not have sunk deep into the popular mind if it had been further exemplified only by such things as a royal proclamation at the beginning of March (1538), permitting faithful subjects to eat white meat, that is to say, eggs and milk food, in Lent." . . . There were many, we may be sure, even among the laity, who declined to take advantage of it; while abroad the exercise of such a dispensing power appeared simply a thing to laugh at. "The King of England," said Francis I., "gives dispensations like his Holiness, and I believe will soon want to sing Mass." Still the king's subjects were not allowed to go beyond the limits of the royal dispensations. "To transgress the old rules of the Church, except by royal license, was as dangerous as ever."

[2] Cranmer, *Works* (Parker Soc.), vol. i. p. 239.

[3] Ellis Price to Crumwell, B. Mus. Cott. MS., Cleop. E. iv. f. 556. It was held as a tradition, says Hall, that the image should set a *Forest* on fire. Perhaps this suggested the manner of death awarded to Forest.

We can easily imagine the kind of sermon that fell from the lips of Bishop Latimer, the preacher. "It was of the usual kind," writes Froude, "the passionate language of passionate conviction," as he "confuted the friar's errors and moved him to repentance."[1] But Latimer's eloquence and vigorous denunciation of the Pope and his followers proved of no avail, for "in the end, when the bishop asked him what state he would die in, the friar with a loud voice answered and said that if an angel should come down from Heaven and teach him any other doctrine than he had received and believed from his youth, he would not now believe him. And that if his body should be cut joint after joint, or member after member burnt, hanged, or what pain soever might be done to his body, he would never turn from his old profession. Moreover, he told the bishop that seven years before he dared not have made such a sermon for his life."[2]

Delay was useless; no argument was likely to shake the constancy of the friar, and, with Crumwell and the rest looking on, Forest was slung from the gallows with chains "by the middle and armholes all quick over the flames."[3] In his mortal agony he clutched at the steps of the ladder to sway himself out of the blaze; and the pitiless chronicler who records the scene could only see in this last weakness an evidence of guilt. "So impatiently," says Hall, "he took his death as never any man that put his trust in God."[4]

Before the final dispersion of the Franciscan Observants, Crumwell had, as we have seen, commenced his conflict with the fathers of the Charterhouse. Unlike the friars, the secluded religious of St. Bruno's order had taken no active part in opposing the union of Henry and Anne Boleyn. Neither had they appeared conspicuously as the champions of queen Catherine; and although it was known that the "Holy maid of Kent" had visited them at their London house, there was nothing in the evidence collected against her to mark them out as her advisers or abettors. Still, their general influence, at this time very considerable owing to the exceptional sanctity of their lives, was exercised in opposition to the king's revolt from the holy see. Rumour even spoke of the prior of the London Charterhouse, John

---

[1] Stow, *Annales*, p. 569.   [2] *Ibid.*, p. 569.
[3] Hall, ed. 1548, f. 233.   [4] Froude, *Hist.*, vol. iii. p. 296.

Houghton, as privately exhorting his penitents to remain firm in refusing to abjure the Papal supremacy.[1]

The Charterhouse of the "Salutation of the most blessed Mother of God" in London was a model of religious observance. According to Maurice Chauncy, one of the few religious of the convent who purchased their lives by compliance with the king's wishes, all were leading the most holy lives. In the language of his penitence he alone, "the spotted and diseased sheep" of the flock, deserved "to be cast out of the fold," and to lose the crown of martyrdom.[2] Twenty of the community were not yet thirty-eight years of age, and they vied one with the other in the fervour of their observance. Even the lay brethren were remarkable for their perfect lives, and were true "*conversi*" from the world and its ways. Two of their number, brothers Roger and John, had often been seen by Chauncy raised in ecstasy from the ground whilst praying.[3]

A worthy superior presided over this saintly community. Blessed John Houghton had sprung from a good Essex family, and had gone early in life to the University of Cambridge in preparation for the honourable career in the world to which the intentions of his parents had destined him. Maurice Chauncy draws a charming picture of him as prior. In person "he was short, with a graceful figure and dignified appearance; his actions modest, his voice gentle, chaste in body, in heart humble, he was admired and sought after by all, and by his community was most beloved and esteemed. One and all revered him, and none were ever known to speak a word against him."[4]

In 1533 certain portents and wonders occurred which were thought to warn the community of impending danger. Without doubt, notwithstanding the seclusion of their lives, rumours of the gathering storm must have reached them in their cells. The thorny questions which surrounded the great matter of Henry's divorce must have been suggested to their minds, and were doubtless thought over and prayed over in their solitude. The royal agents would thus have found the simple monks of the Charterhouse not unprepared for them, and resolutely resolved to meet their demands for

---

[1] Strype, *Eccl. Mems.*, i. p. 305.
[2] *Historia aliquot nostri sæculi martyrum*, 1583, p. 41.
[3] *Ibid.*, p. 47. [4] *Ibid.*, p. 40.

a surrender of their consciences by that refusal which has made their names respected even by those who cannot appreciate their motives.

Early in April, 1534, the convent was visited by Lee and Bedyll, under a commission from the king, to obtain the signatures of the religious to the oath of succession. The royal agents first saw the prior, but could make nothing of him. To all their arguments he replied, that "it pertained not to his vocation and calling nor to that of his subjects to meddle in or discuss the king's business, neither could they or ought they to do so, and that it did not concern him whom the king wished to divorce or marry, so long as he was not asked for any opinion."[1] The visitors were not satisfied with this reply and insisted on meeting the brethren in chapter. To this demand the prior was forced to agree, but the situation only obliged him to speak more plainly in the presence of his brethren. For his part, he said, "he could not understand how it was possible that a marriage ratified by the Church and so long unquestioned should now be undone," and to this view the whole community adhered.

Such plain speaking on the part of Prior Houghton was sufficient for the commissioners. His committal to the Tower, together with the procurator of the convent, Humphrey Middlemore, quickly followed. They remained there a month, suffering, as the historian of these troubles relates, from the dirt and pestilential atmosphere of the dungeon in which they were confined, as well as from absolute want of food.

Stokesley, the bishop of London, and Lee, archbishop of York, were sent to visit Houghton and Middlemore in the Tower. They persuaded them that the question of the succession was not a cause in which to sacrifice their lives for conscience sake. After a month's space, therefore, the prior and his companion promised to comply with the king's desires and returned home to their brethren. Meeting his subjects in the chapter-house, Houghton informed them of his submission, but added that he was convinced this yielding would not avail to save them for long from the destruction he foresaw. "Our hour, dear brethren," he

[1] Chauncy, *Commentariolus de vita ratione et martyrio Cartusianorum*, ed. Gandavi, 1608, p. 46.

continued, "is not yet come. In the same night in which we were set free I had a dream that I should not escape thus. Within a year I shall be brought again to that place, and then I shall finish my course."[1] Influenced by this prediction, the monks at first resolved not to abide by the prior's promised submission, but again to refuse compliance with the royal demands. For a time they were resolute. When, however, the commissioners returned, in company with the lord mayor and his officers and threatened them with immediate imprisonment, they yielded, taking the oath under the condition "so far as it was lawful." The swearing occupied two days. On the first occasion, May 29, 1534, the commissioners were Lee and Bedyll, and fourteen subscribed, amongst whom were Houghton and Middlemore; and on the second day, June 6th, the remainder of the community conformed, in the presence of Lee and another visitor, Thomas Kytson.[2]

From the hour of their compliance the community knew but little peace. Even among the brethren of the Charterhouse some were restless under the restraints of monastic discipline, and saw in the difficulties which beset their house a possible means of escape from the bonds which kept them to the cloister. But about the real spirit of the community as a body, during the months that passed before the martyrdom of the prior and his companions, there can be no doubt. Archdeacon Bedyll, at the end of August, 1534, wrote to Crumwell about them and the religious of Sion. "I am right sorry to see the foolishness and obstinacy of diverse religious men so addicted to the bishop of Rome and his usurped power, that they contemn all counsel and likewise jeopardy their bodies and souls and the suppression of their houses as careless men and willing to die."[3] Every effort was made throughout the year to bring the Charterhouse monks into real compliance with the royal will. The prior of the Brigittines of Sion, who was sometimes known under the title of "father confessor," was apparently looked upon by Crumwell as zealous in Henry's service. To him, therefore, by direction of the minister, several of the Carthusian religious were sent for advice, in

---

[1] Chauncy, in Froude, *Hist.*, ii. 347.
[2] *Calendar*, vii. No. 728; Rymer, xiv. 491.
[3] *State Papers*, i. 423.

the hopes that his influence would tend to remove their
scruples and take away the sting of their remorse. Two of
these, both priests and professed monks, named William
Broke and Bartholomew Burgoyn, surrendered their consciences after a long argument with the prior at Sion.
Writing to him later they speak of the "great pains" he has
taken to win over two other religious of their convent, and
express their hopes that he will succeed in inducing them
to trust their souls to his guidance.[1] Maurice Chauncy
probably owes the loss of his martyr's crown, which he so
much bewails, to the perverting influence of this Brigittine
friar. In company with another religious of the Charterhouse, John Foxe, he was sent to Sion at the end of August,
1534. The letter which they took with them begged the
prior to argue with them, and "show charity to them as you
have done to others." They are scrupulous, the writer
says, "about the bishop of Rome," but are not "obstinate,"
and each of them has a "book of authorities" which must
be answered.[2]

By the beginning of 1535 any doubts which might be
entertained as to the full intentions of Henry were at an
end. On January 15th the new title of "Supreme Head"
was incorporated in the king's style by decree of council.
The rupture with Rome and the causes which led to it were
unquestionably deeply distasteful to the nation at large.
"On no other subject," writes Mr. Gairdner, "during the
whole reign have we such overt and repeated expressions of
dissatisfaction with the king and his proceedings."[3] Many
of the influential persons of the realm were even anxiously
looking for some external intervention to stop the course
upon which Henry had embarked. Chapuys asserts, that
Lord Darcy's physician had assured him "that the whole
realm was so indignant at the oppressions and enormities
now practised, that if the emperor would make the smallest
effort the king would be ruined."[4] The act of supremacy
had, indeed, added greatly to the royal power, as well as to
the kingly style, and there was no pretence that it was
framed with any scrupulous concern for civil liberty. With
an authority "to visit, repress, redress, reform, order, correct,

---

[1] *Calendar*, vii. No. 1093.   [2] *Ibid.*, No. 1150.
[3] *Ibid.*, viii. Preface on Nos. 589, 736-738, &c.
[4] *Ibid.*, No. 1.

restrain, and amend heresies, errors, abuses, offences, contempts, and enormities, whatsoever they be," to the same extent as his compliant judges might hold lawful to any spiritual authority, what might not an unscrupulous king like Henry attempt when urged on by such a minister as Crumwell! No wonder the people of England looked forward with dread to the possible development of a power which had added the spiritual to the temporal authority. No wonder if they distrusted a monarch who, according to the quaint but significant expression of "an old writer," was constituted "a king with a pope in his belly."[1]

To the fathers of the Charterhouse the act of supremacy meant destruction. By the end of 1534 it would have been abundantly clear to Crumwell, that whatever the few weaker spirits among the community, who had been seduced by promise or specious argument, might do, the Carthusians as a body would resist even to death any further demand of Henry for their rejection of papal authority. Their doom was known to be certain when it became publicly understood that those suspected of hostility or even of half-heartedness in the king's cause, and of lukewarmness or secret dislike of Henry's divorce, might be submitted to questioning on this new kingly prerogative of spiritual supremacy. The prior, no longer doubting that the end of their suspense was at hand, told his subjects to prepare for the worst.

"With unobtrusive nobleness," writes Froude, "did these poor men prepare themselves for their end; not less beautiful in their resolution, not less deserving the everlasting remembrance of mankind than those three hundred who, in the summer morning, sat combing their golden hair in the passes of Thermopylæ. We will not regret their cause; there is no cause for which any man can more nobly suffer than to witness that it is better for him to die than to speak words which he does not mean. Nor, in this their hour of trial, were they left without higher comfort."[2]

When the danger seemed imminent, Robert Laurence, the prior of the Charterhouse of Beauvale in Nottinghamshire, and Augustine Webster, prior of Axholme in Lincolnshire, came to visit and consult with their brethren of the London house. The first of these had been a member of

---

[1] Amos, *Statutes of Henry VIII.*, p. 283.
[2] *History*, ii. p. 350.

this monastery; but five years before, he had been called to succeed John Houghton in the priorship of Beauvale, when the latter was summoned to London. The second, Augustine Webster, had gone to Axholme from Shene Charterhouse in Surrey. The three priors, after consultation, determined to anticipate the coming of the king's commissioners. By a personal interview with Crumwell himself, they hoped to obtain some mitigation of the expected royal demands. Perhaps, in accordance with Houghton's determination, they desired to offer themselves in behalf of their brethren. Crumwell, on learning the purpose of their visit, refused to listen to them, and sent them forthwith from his house to the Tower as rebels and would-be traitors.[1] A week later, on April 20, 1535, the minister held an examination of Webster and Laurence at his house in the "Rolls." There were present a number of the council as witnesses. The notary, John Ap-Rice, records, that when asked whether they would take the oath of supremacy and reject the authority of any other but the king, over the *Ecclesia Anglicana*, they both stoutly refused.[2]

In prison the three fathers had been joined by Father Richard Reynolds, a Brigittine monk of Sion, who had been committed to ward for the same cause.[3] The depositions record the opinions of each of the accused in much the same language. Houghton's view about the supremacy was clear and decided. Laurence and Webster both declared that they could "not take our sovereign lord to be supreme head of the Church, but him that is by God the head of the Church, that is the bishop of Rome, as Ambrose, Jerome, and Augustine teach." Richard Reynolds declared, that though "he would spend his blood for the king, still that the pope is head of the Church, that hath been these three hundred years, and not the king;" and he also said "that he doth, as a thousand thousand that are dead" had done before in this matter.[4] As nothing was likely to change

[1] Chauncy, *Commentariolus*, p. 76.
[2] *Calendar*, viii. No. 565 (1).
[3] Reynolds was a member of Corpus Christi College, Cambridge. He took his B.D. degree in 1512, and immediately after became, with a college companion, a brother of the Sion Monastery. He was the same year elected one of the University preachers. (Camb. Reg. Grace Book, B. p. 305.)
[4] *Ibid.*, No. 566, also No. 565 (2).

the constancy of these fathers, a special commission was appointed to try them for treason under the Act of Succession. On April 24th the grand jury panel was returned, and the trial appointed for Wednesday, the 28th of the same month. Two days before, they underwent an examination in the Tower by Crumwell and a committee of the privy council. Their refusal to accept the oath of supremacy on this occasion formed the substance of the charge against them. Before the jury, on the 28th, they were indicted, in common with Father Reynolds, on the charge that they "did, on 26 April, 27 Henry VIII., at the Tower of London, in the county of Middlesex, openly declare and say, 'the king, our sovereign lord, is not supreme head in earth of the Church of England.'" They all four pleaded not guilty to this novel charge of verbal treason. The verdict of the jury was deferred till the following day.[1]

"The jury," as an old account of the trial says, "could not agree to condemn these four religious persons, because their consciences proved them they did not it maliciously. The judges hereupon resolved them, that whosoever denied the supremacy denied it maliciously, and the expressing of the word maliciously in the act was a void limit and restraint of the construction of the words and intention of the offence. The jury, for all this, could not agree to condemn them, whereupon Crumwell, in a rage, went unto the jury and threatened them if they condemned them not. And so being overcome by his threats, they found them guilty, and had great thanks, but they were afterwards ashamed to show their faces, and some of them took great (harm) for it."[2]

The verdict of "guilty" was followed by a sentence of death on all the four, to be carried out according to the form usual in cases of high treason, and they were then conducted back to the Tower to prepare for their end. Meanwhile, when Houghton lay in prison, Crumwell's agents were busy amongst his community endeavouring to win them over to compliance with the king's orders. One of these commis-

[1] Deputy Keeper, Rept. iii. App. ii. 238.
[2] B. Mus. Arund. MS., 152, f. 308. A similar account is given by Chauncy. See also Strype, *Eccl. Mems.*, i. 305. Mr. Froude (ii. 357 note) says that it is impossible Crumwell could have threatened the jury, because the verdict was given the same day as the petty jury were empanelled. The jury were returned on the 28th, whilst their verdict was given the following day. It does not seem clear whether the pleadings and verdict were on the same day.

sioners, John Whalley, who appears to have been specially appointed to guard the Charterhouse at this time, writes to Crumwell his views as to the methods most likely to succeed. "It is of no use," he says, "for one Mr. Rastall to come there. He pleads, indeed, that you (Crumwell) wished him daily to resort hither," but the monks "laugh and jest at all things he speaketh. No question of it," he continues, "they be exceedingly superstitious, ceremonious, and pharisaical, and wonderfully addict to their old *mumpsimus;* nevertheless, better and more charitable it were to convert them than to put them to the extremity of the law."[1]

The three Carthusian priors, Houghton, Webster, and Lawrence, together with the Brigittine, Father Reynolds, and his neighbour, John Hale, vicar of Isleworth, were executed at Tyburn on May 4th. The details of the execution were of a nature more horrible than usual, even in the terrible and barbarous punishment of death for treason. The fact that the religious were drawn to the place of execution in their habits made a great impression upon the people, and the whole was no doubt arranged in order to afford to religious and ecclesiastics a terrible example of Henry's power. To each, as he mounted the scaffold, a pardon was offered if he would obey the king and parliament. Each in turn rejected the offer of life at the price of a guilty conscience.

"It is altogether a new thing," writes Chapuys to the Emperor the following day (May 5th), "that the dukes of Richmond and Norfolk, the earl of Wiltshire, his son, and other lords and courtiers were present at the said execution, quite near the sufferers. People say that the king himself would have liked to see the butchery, which is very probable, seeing that nearly all the court, even those of the privy chamber, were there—his principal chamberlain, Norres, bringing with him 40 horses; and it is thought that he (the king) was of the number of five who came thither accoutred and mounted like borderers, who were armed secretly, with vizors before their faces, of which that of the duke of Norfolk's brother got detached, which has caused a great stir, together with the fact that while the five thus habited were speaking all those of the court dislodged."[2]

[1] *Calendar*, viii. No. 600.
[2] *Ibid.*, No. 666. On 23rd May Chapuys wrote to Granvelle to say: "The king was not present at the execution of the Carthusians. He (the king)

Houghton was the first to die. As he mounted beneath the gibbet, in compliance with the usual custom, he spoke briefly to the people. "I call Almighty God to witness," he said, "and all good people, and I beseech you all here present to bear witness for me in the day of judgment, that being here to die, I declare that it is from no obstinate rebellious spirit that I do not obey the king, but because I fear to offend the majesty of God. Our holy mother the Church has decreed otherwise than the king and the parliament have decreed, and therefore, rather than disobey the Church I am ready to suffer. Pray for me and have mercy on my brethren, of whom I have been the unworthy prior." Then, kneeling down, he recited a few verses of the 31st Psalm and calmly resigned himself to the hands of the executioner. The rope used was stout and heavy, in order that the martyrs might not be strangled before the rest of the barbarous butchery could be performed. It is almost impossible to credit the frenzy of diabolical cruelty which is said to have been perpetrated on this occasion in the presence of the court and, as the people believed, of the king himself. Whilst still living they were ripped up in each other's presence, their bodies dishonoured, their limbs torn off, and their hearts 'cut out and rubbed into their mouths and faces.'"[1]

"The faces of these men," writes Mr. Froude, "did not grow pale; their voices did not shake; they declared themselves liege subjects of the king, and obedient children of the Church; 'giving God thanks that they were held worthy to suffer for the truth.' All died without a murmur. The stern work was ended with quartering the bodies; and the arm of Houghton was hung up as a bloody sign over the archway of the Charterhouse to awe the remaining brothers into submission."[2]

In this there was found more difficulty than had been anticipated. Two days after the execution, the faithful Bedyll wrote to Crumwell about three of the fathers, of whom he could make nothing. On the very day of the

was very angry with Norfolk and Wiltshire for not answering one of them (Prior Houghton) when he preached a remarkably fine sermon."—*Spanish State Papers*, v. 166.

[1] *Calendar*, No. 726, Bishop of Faenza to M. Ambrogio.
[2] *History*, ii. p. 359.

martyrdom of their prior he had apparently gone to the Charterhouse, "and," he says, "had with me divers books and annotations both of mine own and others against the primacy of the bishop of Rome and also of St. Peter, declaring evidently the equality of the apostles by the law of God. And after long communication of more than an hour and a half with the vicar and procurator of the house, I left those books and annotations with them, that they should see the Holy Scriptures and doctors thereupon concerning the said matters, and thereupon conform themselves accordingly. And yesterday they sent me the said books and annotations again home to my house by a servant of theirs without any word or writing. Wherefore, I sent to the procurator to come and speak with me, seeing I kept my bed by reason of sickness and could not come to him; and at his coming I demanded of him whether he and the vicar and other of the seniors had seen or heard the said annotations, or perused the titles of the books making most for the said matters. And he answered that the vicar and he and Newdigate had spent the time upon them till nine or ten of the clock at night, and that they saw nothing in them whereby they were moved to alter their opinion. I then declared to him the danger of his opinion, which was like to be the destruction of them and their house for ever; . . . I also demanded of the procurator whether the rest of his brethren were of like opinion, and he answered he was not sure, but he thought they were all of one mind."[1] In three weeks the fathers here complained of, Humphrey Middlemore, William Exmew, and Sebastian Newdigate, were lodged in prison. On June 8, 1535, the bishop of Faenza writes "that the Carthusians, whom the king himself tried to persuade to recognise him as the head of the Church, are in prison with chains round their necks, and will certainly be put to death, but perhaps not so publicly for fear of the displeasure of the people, which was shown at the death of the others."[2] And Chapuys shortly before mentions that there were "three more Carthusians" in prison, whilst the rest were strictly guarded in their convents by the king's servants, "in whose custody are all the goods of the monasteries of the order." "It is thought," he adds, "that the

---

[1] Wright, *ut supra*, p. 40.   [2] *Calendar*, vol. viii. No. 846.

king will suppress them, as they are rich, and there is no hope of making the religious change their opinion."[1]

The fact of their being chained in prison cannot now be questioned. A memorandum in the writing of John Stow, the historian, leaves no doubt as to this particular form of cruelty having been practised upon these religious whilst in the Tower and Newgate. "Three of them (the Carthusian fathers), that is to say, Humphrey (Middlemore), William (Exmew), and Sebastian (Newdigate), first stood in prison upright, chained from the neck to the arms, and their legs fettered with locks and chains, by the space of thirteen days."[2] Two years later a similar cruelty was practised upon a number of their brethren, and under this prolonged punishment many died.

At the trial of these three fathers of the Charterhouse, before the same special commission of *Oyer and Terminer* appointed to try Bishop Fisher, they were charged with the same offence as that for which their prior had already suffered death. It was declared that on May 25th, at Stepney, each of them did say in conversation together, "I cannot nor will consent to be obedient to the king's highness as a true, lawful, and obedient subject to take and repute him to be supreme head in earth of the Church of England under Christ."[3] They pleaded "not guilty," but were condemned on June 11th, and executed at Tyburn on the 19th of the same month.

For two years no more of the Carthusians were put in prison. They were left, in the hope that arguments and restrictions as to liberty and diet would break the spirit of constancy which they displayed. A body of laymen were appointed as the governors of their house, which to all intents was thus turned into a prison. From the letters of Jasper Fyllol, one of these gaolers, to Crumwell we are afforded one or two glimpses of the state of subjection under which the monks lived during this period.

Meantime a new prior had been placed over the convent

---

[1] *Calendar*, viii. No. 751.
[2] *Ibid.*, No. 895. Sanders gives the same account of the inhuman treatment of these three fathers. "They had been," he writes, "for fourteen days before they were put to death, forced to stand upright without the possibility of stirring for any purpose whatever, held fast by iron collars on their necks, arms, and thighs."—Lewis, *Trans.*, p. 119.
[3] Deputy Keeper, Rept. iii. App. ii. 239.

in the room of the martyred Houghton. His name was
William Trafford, and he had been a monk of Beauvale. In
the beginning of the troubles he had been bold enough in
his declarations of constancy, and had even been placed under
the custody of the sheriff. "In a friendly conversation (he,
the sheriff, had) showed them that the king was of *right*
spiritual head." Upon this the procurator, William Trafford,
said, "I believe firmly that the pope of Rome is supreme
head of the Church Catholic." When the commissioners
asked whether he would abide by his words, he replied,
"*usque ad mortem.*" Moreover, he wrote his words down
and Sir John Markham carried the paper away and placed the
monk in safe custody.[1] What happened to change the heart
of this religious does not appear, but the fact of his appointment,
and that Bedyll praises him, would be sufficient to
prove the surrender of his conscience to the king, to whom
he subsequently resigned his monastery. The religious
never knew him as a father and adviser. Of the period of
his administration Chauncy says: "Being deprived of a
prior exterior to ourselves, every man's conscience was his
prior."

During this period of general probation for the martyr's
crown, Chauncy relates that every pressure that could be
imagined was brought to bear upon them in the hopes their
resolution might be shaken. Privy councillors would come
and harangue them in their chapter-house on their blindness
and perversity. Sometimes these visits would be extended
so long that they were prevented chaunting their vespers or
their matins. One Sunday four of them, who were thought
to be the most obstinate, and the leaders of the rest, were
taken by force to St. Paul's to listen to a sermon against the
pope. Indeed, had Hilsey (the unworthy successor of the
martyred Fisher in the see of Rochester) obtained his desires,
all the religious of the Charterhouse would have been marshalled
at the cross weekly to listen to the sermons.[2]

At length, on May 4, 1536, the anniversary of Houghton's
death, four, who had been regarded as the leaders in the
opposition to the king's designs, were sent to the North of
England and placed in houses, the temper of which was
thought to be true to Henry. Of the rest, eight were trans-

[1] *Calendar*, viii. No. 566.   [2] *Ibid.*, ix. No. 989.

ferred to the Brigittine convent of Sion, to which a new prior of zealous loyalty had been appointed upon whose efforts to shake their constancy Crumwell counted. A year passed by before it was deemed prudent to again demand the oath. Hardship, argument, and pressure of every kind kept up for two years had sifted the chaff from the grain. The trial had proved the true metal, had prepared the strong for victory and left the weak at last in the power of an enemy who had pursued them so relentlessly. On May 18, 1537, the royal commissioners attended in the chapter-house and received the required oath from the prior and twenty of the brethren. Ten still resolutely refused, and William Say, the public notary, having summoned them, testified to their continued obstinacy.[1]

Their fate was quickly decided. On the 29th of May, eleven days after their refusal, they were removed to Newgate. Their number consisted of three priests, D. Richard Bere,[2] D. Thomas Johnson, and D. John Green, one deacon, John Davy, and six lay brothers, William Greenwood, Thomas Scryven, Robert Salt, Walter Peerson, Thomas Reding, and William Horne. Their treatment in prison was similar to that of the three fathers of their house two years previously. A pious lady named Clement, afterwards mother Margaret Clement, has left it on record that she bribed the gaolers to allow her to visit these heroic monks in their prison. Disguised as a milkmaid, she went to them and "fed them, putting meat in their mouths, they being tied and not able to stir nor help themselves." She was thus for some days able to preserve their lives, and perform other Christian acts of charity for them. After this time the king, finding they were not yet starved to death, commanded a stricter watch to be kept over them.

After they had been in prison only sixteen days, Bedyll wrote to his master concerning them: "the monks of the Charterhouse here at London, be almost dispatched by the hand of God, as it may appear to you by this bill enclosed, whereof, considering their behaviour and the whole matter,

---

[1] Rymer, xiv. p. 588.
[2] Richard Bere was born about the year 1508. He was a nephew of Abbot Bere of Glastonbury, and was educated first in the school in that abbey and afterwards sent by his uncle to Oxford. (See *Downside Review*, vol. ix. pp. 158-163.)

I am not sorry, but would that all such as love not the king's highness and his worldly honour were in like case."[1]

The list of Carthusians which archdeacon Bedyll says he forwards to Crumwell is not printed by Wright, although it is in the same collection in the British Museum from which he published the letter itself. It is of great interest, as showing that five of the ten had already died from their prison hardships. It runs thus:—

1537. June 14.

There are departed,

    Brother William Greenwood.
    Dan. John Davy.
    Brother Robert Salt.
    Brother Walter Peerson.
    Dan. Thomas Green.

There are even at the point of death,

    Brother Thomas Scryven.
    Brother Thomas Reding.

There are sick,

    Dan. Thomas Johnson.
    Brother William Horne.

One is healed,

    Dan. (Richard) Bird (Bere).[2]

In a very short time the list of the "departed" included all but one. "Furthermore, the other nine," writes the historian Stow, "died in prison with stink and miserably smothered."[3] The one who survived the horrors of that Newgate dungeon with its slow tortures of starvation and suffocation was not the monk reported by Bedyll as "healed," but Brother William Horne. He lingered in prison till 1540, when, on Wednesday, August 4, he was hung at Tyburn.

[1] Wright, p. 162; from London, June 14, 1537.
[2] B. Mus. Cott. MS., Cleop. E. iv. f. 256 b.
[3] B. Mus. Harl. MS., 530, f. 54.

Of the four monks who had been sent to the North of England in 1536, after all the efforts of Crumwell and his agents had failed to shake their constancy, two received the martyr's palm. They had been placed in the Charterhouse at Hull, and complaints having reached Crumwell that they showed no inclination to conform, in 1537 power was granted to the royal officers of the district to enforce the decrees of parliament. The two fathers were consequently seized and brought to York, where they were condemned to death by the Duke of Norfolk. The sentence was carried out in the same city, and their bodies left to hang in chains. "Item. Two of these eighteen," writes Stow, "did remain hanging, the which were John Rochester and James Walwercke."[1]

When archdeacon Bedyll wrote his letter on June 14, 1537, the monastery of the London Charterhouse had ceased to exist. By means of the threats, or, as he calls them, the "sore" words of Crumwell, and his own persuasions and promises, the remnant of the community had been induced to surrender their house and property to the king. This was done on June 10, and according to the terms, doubtless, dictated by Crumwell's agent.[2]

For this compliance with what was thus represented to them as the king's desires, the religious were rewarded, but hardly as liberally as Bedyll appears to have led them to expect. A paper among the Augmentation Office records, headed "Monks to have pensions," and signed *T. Crumwell*, shows that £20 a year was promised to Trafford, and to fourteen of his religious £5 each. The last name on the list is that of Maurice Chauncy, to whom we are indebted for so much of our knowledge about the troubles of the Carthusian fathers at this period, and who himself so narrowly missed the crown of martyrdom gained by his braver brethren.[3]

[1] Stow, *ut supra*.
[2] Rot. Claus. 29 Hen. VIII., pars. 1. 16.
[3] R. O. Augmentation Office, Miscell. Books, No. 245, f. 83.

CHAPTER V

The Visitation of Monasteries in 1535-36

ON the 22nd of June, 1535, the feast of England's promartyr, St. Alban, the saintly and venerable bishop Fisher died for his faith. Four days before, the Carthusian fathers had preceded him to their common reward. A fortnight later, on Tuesday the octave day of St. Peter, and (as he himself remarked) the eve of the translation of St. Thomas of Canterbury, the learned Sir Thomas More laid down his life for the same cause. Thus by the close of the first week in July the axe at Tower Hill and the gallows at Tyburn had rid Henry VIII. of the foremost opponents of his concubinage with Anne Boleyn, and of his assumed ecclesiastical supremacy. There was, however, hardly any period of his reign when the king and his counsellors were more harassed than during the latter half of this year. The foreign relations of the country were becoming strained. The people at home were restless and disheartened. The longest memory could not recall a summer more unfavourable to agriculture. The corn harvest was well nigh a complete failure, the yield being scarcely more than the third part of an average crop.[1] It had rained, so said the people, ever since the execution of the Carthusians,[2] and they looked upon this as a mark of divine anger at the misdeeds of Henry.[3]

In determining to strike a blow at the monastic bodies, Crumwell had a double object—to overthrow the papal system in its strongholds,[4] and to finger some of the riches with which the piety of ten centuries had endowed them.

---

[1] Bib. Nat. MSS. Dupuy, vol. 547; quoted by P. Friedmann, *Ann Boleyn*, vol. ii. p. 120.
[2] *Ibid.*, June 18, 1535.   [3] *Calendar*, ix. No. 594.
[4] Lord Herbert, *Life of Henry VIII.*, p. 395, says: "They (the monasteries) were looked upon as a body of reserve for the pope, and always ready to appear in his quarrels."

By the middle of the year 1534 commissioners were busily journeying through England to tender the oath of supremacy to the religious. As no special form had been prescribed by parliament, Crumwell took advantage of the omission. He made his agents tender to the monks a much more stringent and explicit renunciation of the papal supremacy and jurisdiction than that rejected by More and Fisher, and already subscribed to by many of the secular clergy. The commissioners appear to have met with only partial success. The intolerable nature of the oath demanded seems to suggest that the intention of its framer was to drive the religious to refuse, and thus to create a pretext for falling upon and destroying their houses.[1] If the new system of religion was to prevail, it was impossible to allow large bodies of men and women to remain opposed at heart, if not openly, to the policy of Henry's undisguised defiance of papal authority. The royal supremacy was the touchstone of loyalty and religion in the minds of king and minister. A "strong coercion" had already done much to beat down opposition, and remorseless executions had made further individual resistance to the despotic will of the king and machiavellian policy of Thomas Crumwell all but impossible. Union, moreover, might be expected to give strength and tenacity of purpose to the monks and friars. Their direct dependence, besides, on the Holy See caused them to be regarded in a special way as the "spies of the pope."[2] The popular veneration in which they were held[3] must in these circumstances have made them particularly obnoxious, and, as far as Crumwell and his policy was concerned, dangerous.

[1] Canon Dixon, *Hist. of Church of England*, vol. i. p. 213, says that "the oath was taken in almost every chapter-house where it was tendered." This is generally stated as a fact, but as far as is known there is no proof of it. The list of "acknowledgments of royal supremacy," printed in the 7th report of the Deputy Keeper, App. II., contains all the known documents as to the religious bodies. They number only 105, a very small fraction of the whole. Of these Mr. F. Devon, the assistant keeper of public records, in making the list remarks: "I believe it contains all the original acknowledgments of supremacy deposited in the branch public record office at the chapter-house. The signatures are in my opinion not all *autographs*, but *frequently* in the same handwriting, and my impression is that the writer of the deed *often* added many of the names."

[2] R. O. Crum. Cor., vol. xv No. 7.

[3] See Harpsfield, *Treatise on the Divorce* (Camd. Soc.), pp. 296-301. The records of the Pilgrimage of Grace afford ample evidence of this popular esteem.

The Visitation of Monasteries in 1535-36

It was the opinion of more than one foreigner in England at the time that any movement of the emperor or pope against Henry would have made the nation rise against their rulers.[1] John Ap-Rice and Thomas Legh, afterwards two of the royal visitors of the monasteries, who had been throughout England on the king's business, and so had means of forming a judgment, declared that even the bishops "would refer their jurisdiction to some one else than the king *if they dared.*"[2] Hence the immediate necessity of subduing the monastic bodies, which Crumwell regarded as so many strongholds of papal power scattered throughout the country. "As many of the great men of the state and church thought," writes Von Ranke, "so thought also the pious members of the monasteries and cloistered convents. They opposed the supremacy, not, as they said, from inclination to disobedience, but because Holy Mother Church ordered otherwise than king and parliament ordained. The apology merely served to condemn them. . . . In the new order of things there was absolutely no place for the monastic system. It was necessarily sacrificed to the unity of the country, and at the same time to the greed of great men."[3]

This "greed of great men," and in the first place of the king and Crumwell, was the second motive which prompted the suppression of the religious houses. It is difficult for us to estimate at its true value the prize which Henry hoped to obtain in the estates of the religious bodies. Nearly all the wealth of the country at this time consisted of real property: the amount of personal property being comparatively insignificant. Of the whole area of England, the part owned by the monasteries was indeed large, although their wealth has been greatly exaggerated.[4] Still the prize was more than regal, and by this time Henry's appetite had been sharpened by his appropriation, as supreme ecclesiastical authority, of first fruits and other church revenues.

---

[1] *Calendar*, vol. ix. Nos. 435, &c.   [2] *Ibid.*, No. 424.
[3] *Hist. of England*, vol. i. p. 158 (ed. 1875).
[4] The revenue of the king at this time has been estimated at about £140,000 a year. Hume calculates the whole rental of the nation at £3,000,000, of which from £140,000 to £170,000 belonged to the religious bodies. (*Cf.* Lingard, Note E. vol. vi.) Besides this, Henry obtained vast sums of money from the Church plate and jewels of the monasteries, so that, taking all into account, and putting the value of the money at twelve times the present value, the property confiscated must have been worth some £50,000,000 of our money. (*Cf.* Blunt, *Reformation*, p. 371.)

Even now the breach with Rome was by no means regarded as definitive. There was still some slight hope that peace might be made. Chapuys, the imperial ambassador, told Crumwell that at all events the statutes already passed, "by which the king received inestimable profit from churchmen,[1] might be confirmed to some extent." The suggestion, however, was calculated to arouse Crumwell's fears for himself, as it opened up a possibility of the ruin of Anne Boleyn and her party, which would involve his own fall. To get rid of the religious houses would make it almost impossible to turn back along the path that had been entered on. It would, moreover, strike at the very heart of the pope's power in England, and most effectually dash the hopes entertained of its renewal.

Two years before, a parliament had transferred the right of visitation from the pope to the king.[2] Henry was empowered to issue commissions for visiting "monasteries, priories, houses, and places religious exempt." In the methods of visitation Crumwell, as commissioner for Wolsey, had been well instructed. He had gone round the country for that purpose, and gained himself a reputation "for accessibility to bribes and presents in the disposal of monastic leases."[3] Lord Herbert states that the scheme for the dissolution of monasteries was discussed at a meeting of the council, where it met with considerable opposition. From this disapproval of the measure the king saw it would be necessary to carry out his designs by degrees.[4]

The royal commissioners first visited the Charterhouse monks and the Observants of Richmond and Greenwich. Shortly after they got to work, they found their paths crossed by the bishops. The king's letter of September 18th to Cranmer suspended all episcopal authority during the progress of the commission. The bishops did not relish

---

[1] The Act of Parliament giving to the king "first fruits" and "tenths."

[2] 20th clause of an act, 1533, "Concerning Peter's pence and dispensations."

[3] Brewer's *Hen. VIII.*, vol. ii. p. 268.

[4] *Life of Hen. VIII.*, p. 424. As the council books of this period are not forthcoming, it is impossible to verify this statement. It is, however, very probable. We may note here the extraordinary gaps which exist in the journal books of the houses of lords and commons as well as in the council books at the most critical period of this reign.

this interference, and it was not till a fortnight later (October 2) that the archbishop of Canterbury issued the king's inhibition to his suffragans.¹ Almost at the same time, two of the commissioners, Legh and Ap-Rice, "supposing the bishops would be in hand with you again touching the inhibitions,"² furnished Crumwell with their reasons for thus getting the bishops suspended from using their jurisdiction.

The commissioners, the chief of whom, with Legh and Layton, were Ap-Rice, Dr. London, and Bedyll, entered on their task armed with the most complete authority. They really, however, continued to be in the most servile dependence on the chief inquisitor, Crumwell. "Having experience not long ago in myself," as Ap-Rice puts it in a letter to his master, "how grievous, yea and deadly, it is for any man to have the displeasure of such a man as you are, ... I would not wish my most enemy so great a displeasure."³

Layton also, in an abject letter to Crumwell, begged that he might be sent to visit the north part of England. He promised that no one else, "of what degree soever he be, shall do the king's highness so good service in this matter for those parts, doing all things so diligently for *your purpose* and discharge. Our desire is, therefore," he said, "now to declare unto you our true hearts and faithful minds, our fast and unfeigned service that we bear towards you and owe unto you, as ye have of right bound us."⁴ It was not till later in the year, however, that Layton had his wish granted. Meantime he and the others were busy enough. They were furnished with a set of eighty-six articles of inquiry⁵ and with twenty-five injunctions, to which they had power to add much at their discretion. The articles of inquiry were searching, the injunctions minute, irritating, and exacting. Framed in the spirit of three centuries earlier, unworkable in practice and enforced by such agents, it is easy to understand, even were there no written evidence of the fact, that they were galling and unbearable to the helpless inmates of the monasteries. We

---

¹ *Calendar*, ix. No. 517.   ² *Ibid.*, No. 424.   ³ *Ibid.*, No. 630.
⁴ Wright, p. 156. The editor puts this letter in 1537, but both internal evidence and the date, "Friday, June 4th," show that it was written in 1536.
⁵ Printed together with the injunctions in Wilkins, *Concilia*, iii. 786.

may give a passing notice to one or two of these regulations, as they show the spirit which actuated those who framed them. All religious under twenty-four years of age, or who had been professed under twenty, were to be dismissed from the religious life. Those who were left became practically prisoners in their monasteries. No one was allowed to leave the precincts (which, even in the larger monasteries, were very confined as to limit) or to visit there. In many instances porters, who were in reality gaolers, were appointed to see that this impossible regulation was kept. What was simply destructive of all discipline and order in the monasteries was an injunction that every religious who wished to complain of anything done by his superior or any of his brethren was to have a right at any time to appeal to Crumwell. To facilitate this, the superior was ordered to find any subject the money and means for prosecuting such an appeal in person, if he so desired.

Injunctions such as these could only have been intended to invite disobedience, and thus to give the king numberless opportunities of interference with the internal economy of the monasteries. His object, apparently, was to harass the monks into giving up a bootless struggle and into abandoning their houses. The visitor Ap-Rice, not so deeply in Crumwell's counsels as some of his colleagues, wrote that his companion Legh was pushing matters too fast. He remarked that it was impossible for the religious to be kept as prisoners, and that even the Carthusians had found it absolutely necessary to allow their priors to go abroad on business of their monastery.[1] Legh, however, discloses the truth as to the secret policy pursued by Crumwell. In a letter from the abbey of Denny a month or so later he writes: "By this ye may see that they shall not need to be put forth, but that they will make instance themselves, so that their doing shall be imputed to themselves and to no other." To this letter Ap-Rice adds a postscript, showing that he too now understood the object of the royal injunctions. "Although I reckon it well done that all were out," he says, "yet I think it were best that at their own instant suit they might be dismissed, to avoid calumniation and envy. And so compelling them to

[1] *Calendar*, ix. No. 139.

observe these injunctions ye shall have them all to do shortly. And the people shall know it the better that it cometh upon their suit, if they be not discharged straight while we be here, for then the people would say that we went for nothing else, even though the truth were contrary."[1]

Mere petty vexations, however, were not the chief means for carrying out the great work of destruction. Layton, Crumwell's right-hand man in this matter, saw in the supremacy question a screw to torture consciences. By inducing a cowardice resulting from actions against conviction, he prepared his victims for the final surrender of their personal rights. "I should advise you," he says, in a letter containing his first suggestion as to the visitation of the province of York, "to set forth the king's authority as supreme head by all possible means. There can be no better way to beat the king's authority into the heads of the rude people of the north than to show them that the king intends reformation and correction of religious. They are more superstitious than virtuous, long accustomed to frantic fantasies and ceremonies, which they regard more than either God or their prince.

"The Book of Articles is clear written, in the custody of Bartlett your clerk, and a commission is ready for the same. You will never know," he adds significantly, "what I can do till you try me."[2]

No sooner were the commissioners at their work than difficulties rose up amongst them. The letters in which they refer their quarrels to Crumwell are instructive, in regard as well to the character as to the methods of these chosen instruments of reform. Legh complains to Crumwell of Layton, and he in his turn is complained of by his companion Ap-Rice. Layton is inclined to be too easy in keeping the unfortunate religious strict prisoners. "He has left it more at the discretion of the head," writes Legh; "I have not, in order that they might the more know the king's supreme ecclesiastical power."[3] Moreover, he has not always dismissed those under twenty-four years of age. In reply Layton writes: "And as touching the injunctions which your mastership do take to be very slender, it may

[1] *Calendar*, xi. No. 708. [2] *Ibid.*, viii. No. 955.
[3] *Ibid.*, ix. No. 621

F

please you to understand that they be not given for injunctions, but only for summary monitions and rules to be observed until the injunctions shall hereafter come to every place under the king's seal. . . . And by your better advice I think it in no wise expedient to give injunctions forthwith, but *viva voce*, or else by some note in writing, somewhat to do for a rule and order until the injunctions shall come. Over this, when your mastership writeth that the king's grace's pleasure is that the injunctions should be absolute, it shall be I dare say well," adds the wily agent, "that when ye have known my conceit in the rules and injunctions, and what I have there done in every condition, the king shall have no less expectation of your affairs than his grace had heretofore. Praying God that rather I may be buried quick than to be the occasion why the king's highness should diminish any part of the 'affiance,' confidence, or the expectation of your assured and proved mind towards his grace."[1] This would seem to mean that Layton had schemes of his own for harrying the religious, which he did not think fit to communicate, by letter at least, even to Crumwell. The nature of his "conceit" may be gathered sufficiently from his later letters.

John Ap-Rice was not better pleased with his companion, Dr. Legh, than the latter had been with Layton. He writes to Crumwell: "I see you are not pleased because I have not told you of Dr. Legh's demeanour. I often thought I ought to have revealed certain abuses and excesses, but first, I saw how little the complaint of others, like the abbot of Bruton,[2] where he used himself, methought, very insolently, did succeed. And thinking that his demeanour at Bradstock, Stanley, and Edington, where he made no less ruffling with the heads than he did at Bruton, should of all likelihood come likewise to your knowledge, and saw nothing said unto him therefore: and also supposing that you, con-

[1] *Calendar*, viii. No. 1127

[2] This abbot had been visited by Layton about the middle of August, who complained that there "and Glastonbury . . . the brethren be so straight kept that they cannot offend" (Wright, p. 59), when on the 23rd of the same month Legh arrived, and claimed the power to visit again. No wonder "the abbot, little regarding the authority committed to him, with sharp and quick answers," said: if he "would visit them anew it should be the very undoing of all abbots and monasteries, and otherwise showed himself very haughty and obstinate" (*Calendar*, ix. No. 159). What Legh said and how he treated the abbot may be gathered from Ap-Rice's letter.

sidering how he was one of them that depraved me heretofore with your mastership, for no just cause, but for displeasure which he have towards me for certain causes which I will declare unto you more at leisure . . . I called some of my servants at London to come with me and see all his proceedings, gestures, and manner of going thence at Westminster and St. Paul's. I did not want to go with him lest he, with his bold excuse, wherein he is, I advise you, ever ready, would have overcome me, being but of small audacity, especially in accusations. . . . I am not eloquent in accusations, as some men be.

"First, in his going he is too insolent and 'pompatique,' which, because he went so in London in the face of all the world, I thought you would have known. . . . Then he handleth the fathers where he cometh very roughly, and many times for small causes, as the abbots of Bruton and Stanley, and the master of Edington for not meeting of him at the door, when they had no warning of his coming. Also, I require more modesty and affability, which would purchase him more reverence than his own setting forth and 'satrapike' countenance.

"The man is young and of intolerable elation of mind. As concerning his taking, I think it excessive in many things. First, for the election of the prior of Coventry he took £15;[1] for the election lately at Bevall, the Charterhouse, £20, besides his costs, £6, and his reward unknown to me. . . . And surely he asketh no less for every election than £20 as of duty, which in my opinion is too much, and above any duty that was ever taken heretofore.

"Also in his visitations he refuseth many times his reward, though it be competent, for that they offer him so little and maketh them to send after him such rewards as may please him, for surely religious men were never afraid so much of Dr. Allen as they be of him, he useth such rough fashion with them."

After saying that Legh always went about attended by twelve men in livery besides his brother, Ap-Rice adds a word about himself, which shows us that he had evidently been complained of. "And as for mine own dealing and

[1] This would be equal to some £180 of our money. Other sums mentioned in the letter are: "Vale Royal £15, and costs £6; Tarrent £20, and costs £4."

behaviour, I trust ye shall have no wise cause of complaint against me; one thing humbly desiring your mastership, that ye give no light credence till the matter be proved and my defence. As to the defence in the other matter, I was so abashed that I had not those things in my remembrance that was for a defence."[1]

The following day Ap-Rice seems to have become alarmed at the possible consequences of his confidences to Crumwell, and wrote again: "I have certified to you certain things touching Mr. Doctor Legh. Although they be all true, I in haste did not make use of moderation. First, having experience in myself not long ago how grievous, yea and deadly, it is for any man to have the displeasure of such a man as you are, specially having your favour before and having only of you, and what desperation or other inconvenience may ensue thereupon to the same, so that I would not wish my most enemy so great a displeasure; and also considering for your part how ye cannot suddenly and violently use any extremity towards the said Mr. Doctor, but ye shall thereby give occasion to some to reckon that ye were so quick in choosing such a one to that room as ye would so soon after disallow and reprove. Also it would be thought by some other that all his doings and proceedings in such places as he was at were reproved by you, and he for the same so handled. . . . It would be well, first, gently to admonish him to amendment, and not utterly discourage him and strike him under foot."

He concludes in words the significance of which it is impossible to mistake. "And forasmuch as the said Mr. Doctor is of such acquaintance and familiarity with many rufflers and serving-men, if he knew this matter to have proceeded of me, though it be but at your commandment, I having commonly no great assistance with me when I go abroad, might take perchance irrecoverable harm of him or his ere I were aware. Please keep secret what I have said."[2] Personal violence, and even murder, was, in the opinion of his colleague, the treatment Legh would mete out to one of the king's agents. How can it be expected that the scurrilous tongue, "eloquent in accusations," should spare and slay not the reputations of the monks and nuns

---

[1] *Calendar*, ix. No. 622.   [2] *Ibid.*, No. 630.

whose destruction was his special errand. "Quia exacuit ut gladium linguam suam, intendit rem amaram ut sagittet in occulto immaculatum."

These extracts give some idea of the instruments by which Crumwell hoped to effect the ruin of the monasteries. To those who have studied the history of these times, it is a matter of no surprise to find that these men were allowed free and unrestrained license in dealing with their unfortunate victims. Legh was written to, apparently, as to his harshness, and his reply is instructive, and no doubt was conclusive from Crumwell's point of view. "Where I have in all places that I have been at, according to mine instructions and to the king's grace's pleasure and yours, restrained as well the heads and masters of the same places as the brethren from going forth of the precincts of the said places, which I assure you grieveth the said heads not a little, as ye shall perceive by the instant suites that they shall make to the king's grace and to you."[1]

He had acknowledged in a letter previously quoted that the injunctions in this matter were impossible to keep, but would teach the monks the power of the king. The permissions for mitigation, for which there will be "instant suites," may, he hints, be a source of profit also for Crumwell himself.[2] The latter no doubt considered this point, and left the victims under the torture.

Over the sad lot of the poor nuns left to the tender mercies of such ruffians, history has, perhaps wisely, drawn a veil. Here and there we may, however, still catch a glimpse of the dreadful reality. Dr. Ortiz, writing to the empress what is reported in Rome as to the visitation of English monasteries, which in common with so many he attributes to the influence of Anne Boleyn, who hated the religious as most opposed to her union with Henry, says: "In England, Anne removed from some monasteries the most able persons and left the infirm with so little to maintain themselves that they are constrained to relinquish the state of religion. They took out of the monastery all the nuns of less than twenty-five years of age, and one of the commissioners who went for this purpose spoke immodestly to the nuns, who rebuked him, saying that their apostolic

---

[1] Wright, p. 56. [2] *Calendar*, ix. Preface xx.

privileges were being violated. The commissary replied that he held more power from the king than there was in the whole apostolic see, and referring the nuns' complaint to Master Crumwell, who is the secretary of the king, by whom comes the ordering of all these evils, told her this was only the beginning of the end."[1] Sanders, almost a contemporary, states that "Lee (Legh) indeed, in order to discharge correctly the duties laid upon him, tempted the religious to sin, and he was more ready to inquire into and speak about uncleanness of living than anything else."[2]

"The papists," writes the historian Fuller, "do heavily complain (how justly God alone knoweth) that a third sort of agents were employed to practice on the chastity of the nuns, so to surprise them into wantonness. Some young gallants were on design sent to some convents, with fair faces, flattering tongues, store of gold and good clothes, youth, wit, wantonness, and what else might work on the weaker sex."[3] He then goes on to relate a story which bears out what he has said, of two young men who went to a convent near Cambridge, and who gave out that they were able to seduce the nuns at their will, although the very contrary was the case. One of these confessed the same to Sir William Stanley, who told it to a noble catholic who was alive when Fuller wrote. Of this story a modern protestant authority writes: "The story has too much *vraisemblance* to be set aside ... and in addition to this, the tone of Layton's letters to Crumwell are of such a kind as to make one fear that some nuns were indeed thus wickedly seduced, and others not less wickedly accused falsely. Those, however, who duly appreciate the character of their countrywomen, will believe that among these evil-intreated 'innocents' there were not a few who passed through the scorching fire of temptation scatheless under the protection of their heavenly bridegroom, for the English daughters of the nineteenth century whom we see around us are sisters to the English nuns of the sixteenth, of whom we know only by vague tradition."[4]

No words of description can give so lively a picture of

---

[1] *Calendar*, ix. No. 873.
[2] *Anglican Schism*, Lewis' trans., p. 129.
[3] *Church Hist.*, ii. p. 216 (ed. 1837).
[4] *The Reformation of Church of England*, Rev. J. H. Blunt, 6th ed., 1885, vol. i. p. 316.

The Visitation of Monasteries in 1535-36

the abject poverty to which many of the religious houses were reduced under the constant exactions of the king and Crumwell during the past years, as the letters of Layton himself. These will also serve to show the rapidity with which the commissioners got over their work. They will likewise help us to appreciate at their true worth charges made in a reckless and wholesale manner, and without the possibility of even a shadow of investigation.

The following is a letter regarding Layton's Sussex visitation in October 1535: "On Friday at night I came into Sussex to an abbey called Durford. It might better be called Dirtyford; the poorest abbey that I have seen, as this bearer, the abbot thereof, can tell: far in debt and great decay. This young man for his time hath done right well, whom I have licensed to repair unto you and to declare unto you his mind concerning license and liberty of himself and other his brethren.

"An abbey or a priory of minors and a priory of canons nigh together lay towards Chichester, and because of their poverty not able to lodge us, we were compelled to ride out of our way to an abbey of Cistercians called Waverly, there to lodge on Saturday at night.... These two poor priories we will dispatch on Monday by the way, and so on Monday at night we shall be at Chichester cathedral church."[1]

Apparently the doctor did not enjoy his stay at Waverly abbey, as the following tells us. It also shows how, through the tyranny of the crown in forcing lay servants upon the abbeys, the monks were by this time powerless in their own homes.

"I have licensed this bringer, the abbot of Waverly, to repair unto you for liberty to survey his husbandry, whereupon consisteth the wealth of his monastery. The man is honest, but none of the children of Solomon. Every monk within his house is his fellow, and every servant his master Mr. Treasurer and other more gentlemen hath put servants unto him, whom the poor man dare neither command nor displease. Yesterday, early in the morning, sitting in my chamber in examination, I could neither get bread, drink, nor fire of these knaves, till I was fretished,[2] and the abbot durst not speak to them. I called them all before me, and

---

[1] *Calendar*, ix. No. 444. [2] *i.e.* numbed with cold.

forgot (*sic*) their names, and took from every man his keys of his office, and made new offices for my time here, perchance as stark knaves as the other. It shall be expedient for you to give him a lesson and tell the poor fool what he should do amongst the monks."[1]

The kind of treatment which the religious were likely to meet with at the hands of this visitor sent to lead them to a better life may be also gathered from his letters. In a letter from Bath, Layton speaks of his visit to a cell of Lewes Priory, near that city, called Farley, where he had got information as to the sub-prior from "a fair young man, a priest late sent from Lewes," and adds, "I have matter sufficient here found (as I suppose) to bring the prior of Lewes into great danger."[2] The information, whatever it might be, thus obtained, was kept ready for the visitation of Lewes some months later. Layton thus describes it: "At Lewes," he says, "I found the monks morally bad and traitors. The sub-prior confessed unto me treason in his preaching, I have caused him to subscribe his name to the same, submitting himself to the king's mercy. I have also made him confess that the prior knew the same and counselled it, and the sub-prior subscribed his name to this said confession against the prior." Upon this, the doctor summoned a chapter, and put the unfortunate prior on his knees in the middle, and "I laid unto him the concealment of the treason, and called him heinous traitor, with the worst words I could devise, he all the time kneeling upon his knees, and making intercession unto me not to utter to you the premises. I listened to him, but ordered him to appear before you to answer on All Hallows eve in court, and perhaps before the king himself, and to bring his sub-prior. You will be able to do what you like with him."[3] It does not require much imagination to see what the visitor means by Crumwell having the poor man in his power, to do what he "likes with him."

From Lewes, Layton goes to Battle Abbey, to which he gives as bad a character as he had given to Lewes. He ordered the abbot, with whom he appears to have had some disagreement, into court. He also bespeaks Crumwell's attention to his case by the following description of the

[1] *Calendar*, ix. No. 452.   [2] *Ibid.*, No. 42.   [3] *Ibid.*, No. 632.

culprit: "The abbot of Battle is the varaste hayne bette and buserde, and the arants chorle that ever I see. In all other places whereat I come, specially the black sort of devilish monks, I am sorry to know as I do. Surely I thynke they be paste amendement, and that God hath utterly wtdrawn his grace from them."

The anxiety displayed by Layton for the safety of the magnificent shrine of St. Thomas of Canterbury, endangered by a fire which occurred during his visitation, or rather for the precious stones with which it was adorned, is a manifestation of another phase of the visitation of 1535. The commissioners first endeavoured to find out at each monastery all there was of value. They next tried to get possession of it, just as the king had appropriated the jewelled cross of the church of Winchester. "I have crosses of silver and gold," writes the indefatigable Layton, "some of which I send you not now, because I have more that shall be delivered me this night by the prior of Maiden Bradley himself. To-morrow early in the morning I shall bring you the rest, when I have received all, and perchance I shall find something here" (St. Augustine's, Bristol).[1] There are reasons for suspecting a deeper meaning in this illegal spoliation of churches and monasteries. Their moveable property gone; their right to lease and sell their own put under restraint; impoverished by demands from king and courtier that it was impossible or impolitic to refuse; their resources drained by blackmail levied upon them by Crumwell and his creatures, many houses were brought face to face with the alternative of starvation or surrender. For years many of the religious houses had been on the verge of ruin. To the requests of king and minister they had replied, by humbly begging to be allowed to keep some farm or some manor demanded of them, as necessary to support themselves and the poor who depended on them. The seizure of their treasures by Crumwell's agents and the heavy fees which these visitors charged for insulting and robbing them must, in the case

---

[1] Wright, p. 59, Aug. 24, 1535. It is worthy of note that the preamble of the act passed for the dissolution of the smaller monasteries in Feb. 1536 charges them with wasting the "*ornaments of their churches.*" We may see by the above how the ornaments were wasted; the charge was made, doubtlessly, to account for their disappearance.

of many, have completed their ruin and forced them to surrender.[1]

The visitation also had a most disastrous effect upon the internal life of the monasteries. No greater blow could have been struck at the whole theory of the religious life than the interference with the vows contained in the order to dismiss those who were under twenty-four years of age, or who had been professed under the age of twenty. The visitors, it is clear, had no scruple about their power to dispense with the solemn obligations of the monastic profession. They freely extended it to any who would go, in the idea that the more they could induce to leave their convents the better pleased both the king and Crumwell would be. The order was ambiguous and led to disputes and difficulties. Legh complained of Layton "that he had not dismissed all those under the age of twenty-four," as he believed Crumwell intended. But Ap-Rice, on account of his quarrel with Legh, had a scruple as to whether the practice of the latter in the matter was right. "I thought," he writes, "that you ordered that all who were between twenty-two and twenty-four should have leave to go from the religious life if they wished, but he only applies this to men," and also he setteth a clause in his injunctions that they that will, of what age soever they be, may go abroad, which I heard not of your instructions."[2] The religious could not understand that the object aimed at was the destruction of their houses. Their simplicity excites a smile sometimes, as when "Jane Gowring, Frances Somer, Mary Pilbeam, Barbara Larke and Bridget Stravye, aged $23\frac{1}{2}$, 22, 21 and 15, the first three professed, but all put out of religion," beg that they may be allowed to stay in their beloved convent, and if this would not be allowed, at least to wait in the "cloose howse" till they were above the age of 24, when they would be professed again.[3]

[1] These facts are amply borne out by many letters of melancholy interest in the fifty-two volumes of Crumwell Correspondence in the Record Office and other MSS. of the period. It has been stated, with what amount of truth we are not prepared to say, that only 123 of the monasteries doomed for destruction were able to hold out until the act of suppression. *Cf.* Blunt, *Reformation of Church of England*, i. p. 301.
[2] *Calendar*, ix. No. 622.
[3] *Ibid.*, No. 1075. It is very remarkable how few are represented in the visitors' reports as desirous of leaving the religious life. Of their personal petitions, quite as many are to stay, as to leave.

One immediate effect, therefore, of this visitation was to thin the monasteries of their inmates. In some instances only the old and infirm were left to keep up the practices of the religious life. Poor Margaret Vernon, prioress of Little Marlow, had her house almost emptied. "Your visitors," she writes to Crumwell, "have been here of late, who hath discharged three of my sisters. The one is Dame Catherine, the other two are the young women that were last professed, which is not a little to my discomfort. . . . I most humbly beseech you to be so special good master unto me, your poor bedewoman, as to give me your best advertisement and counsel, what way shall be best for me to take, seeing there shall be none left here but myself and this poor maiden."[1] Crumwell's advice appears to have been what might be expected from him. At any rate, she soon gave up her house. She is next found in London, trying to get an interview with Crumwell at the "Rolls," in order to make him keep his promise to provide for her. His servants will not allow her to see their master, and "the multitude of suitors" is so great that she cannot get a hearing. The king, she complains, has granted away the lease of her farm at Marlow, and she is in great "trouble and unquietness."[2] Crumwell generously offers to lend her £40 to defray her expenses at Stepney, provided she gives him *good security*. In the end she becomes governess to his son Gregory, of whom she writes: "Your son is in good health, and is a very good scholar, and can construe his *Pater noster, Ave*, and *Credo*." The lot of the prioress of Little Marlow, hard though it was, must have been far easier than that of the multitude of poor nuns who were turned out into the world without support or friends.[3]

There are many examples in the papers and letters of this period, of the difficulties religious superiors experienced in governing their houses at all, during these troubled days. They not only found the restrictions hard, and even impossible to bear, but there was every inducement to their subordinates to rebel against an authority they had sworn

[1] Wright, p. 55.
[2] R. O. Crumwell, Corr., vol. xlv. Nos. 43, 44, 45, 49.
[3] It is quite untrue that *all* religious were pensioned, small though that pension might have been. It can be shown from the "pension books" that only a small number ever had pensions at all. The young received none: the condition of the grant being "tempore dissolutionis et *diu antea*."

to respect. Monks were encouraged and urged to turn informers against their brethren and superiors; malicious information, sedulously fostered, became the seed of discord and unhappiness, which disturbed the peace of the cloister.

Dan Peter, a monk of Winchcombe, wrote a letter of complaint about his abbot, the gist of which is that his superior wanted to maintain discipline and he did not. He also hinted that the abbot was a staunch supporter of the ancient faith.[1] Once before, one Andrew Saunders, curate at Winchcombe, had complained that this abbot was no friend to the new order of things. He had stopped payment to the schoolmaster of the grammar-school, and would not allow him to help him in the church.[2] The same abbot was troubled by another of his subjects, John Horwoode, otherwise Dan Placidus. This young man was very anxious "for the conversion of the people from papistical ways." He would like to see the chapter of Saint Paul ad Romanos, in which he says "*non est potestas nisi a Deo*," written on every monk's head. And he suggests that Crumwell should compel his brethren more to uphold the king's supremacy. We are not surprised to find that he asks something for himself in return: "Thanks," he says, "for excusing my getting up for matins at midnight. The abbot says this has given cause to some murmurs and grudging among the convent. The truth is, I do not like the burdens and straightness of religion, such as their accustomed abstinence, the 'frayter,'[3] and other observances of the rule."[4]

"From specimens like these," writes the best authority on the public records of the time now living, "few as the cases may be that have come to light, we may form some estimate of the discord and demoralisation created within the walls of monasteries by the proceedings of Crumwell's visitors. The wonder indeed is that the recorded cases are so few, and that, in spite of all the inducements offered under the new *régime* to appeal to the king's vicegerent or the visitors, there are not more frequent instances of such appeal being actually made—a fact which, duly considered, seems to imply that the rule in most houses was far more wholesome and more willingly submitted to than many have been hitherto disposed to believe. Only here and there

[1] *Calendar*, ix. No. 314.
[2] *Ibid.*, viii. No. 171.
[3] *i.e.* the community recreations.
[4] *Calendar*, ix. Nos. 321-2.

within the walls of some great abbey did some one or two of the more audacious monks brave the displeasure of their heads and the ill-will of their brethren by malicious tale-bearing, though undoubtedly there were many refractory members, such as there must be in all large communities, who did not love the discipline imposed upon them."[1]

Another method adopted at this time by Crumwell to worry the monks, was the appointment of teachers or divinity lecturers in the monasteries. One of these unwelcome intruders, Anthony Saunder, writes to his master in November: "Whereas you have appointed me to read the pure and sincere Word of God to the monks of Winchcombe. ... I have small favour and assistance amongst these pharisaical papists. The abbot of Hailes, a valiant soldier under Antichrist's banner, resists much, fighting with all his might to keep Christ in the sepulchre. He has hired a great Goliath, a subtle *Duns* man, yea a great clerk, as he saith a Bachelor of Divinity of Oxford, to catch me in my sermons." The writer further desires Crumwell to appoint a convenient hour in the forenoon of each day for him to deliver his lectures to the monks, who manifest a greater love for their choir duties than he, Anthony Saunder, admires. "They will not come in due time; they set so much store by their popish services."[2]

We have scanty information as to the misery and depth of anxiety, which must have prevailed in the cloisters of England during this period. Their forebodings and communings with themselves on the events that were taking place around them, must have been sad enough. It requires little stretch of the imagination to picture the dismay and consternation with which the religious must have listened to the reports of violence and injustice, which were carried to them as the visitors proceeded with their work. For years they had endeavoured to buy off the fatal day of doom by plentiful bribes to Crumwell and his master. On what was left to them, they with difficulty supported their own existence and maintained the hospitality and relief of the poor which their traditional obligations required.

The visitation of Henry's royal commissioners lasted till the meeting of Parliament in February 1536. The state-

[1] Mr. J. Gairdner, *ibid.*, Preface, p. xxiii.
[2] *Calendar*, ix. No. 747.

ments they furnished to Crumwell whilst on their journey seem to show that by no means all the religious houses were inspected and reported upon. Sufficient, however, had been done to serve the king's purpose. True or false, the tales the agents had to tell were used to induce the Parliament to confiscate the property of the lesser monasteries. How this was accomplished, what the charges were which the visitors made against the monks, how far they can be relied upon, and what the characters of the accusers were, will be discussed in subsequent chapters.

CHAPTER VI

The Parliament of 1536 and the Suppression of the Lesser Monasteries

THE year 1536 opened with the death of the unfortunate Queen Catherine. She had been poisoned, at least so thought Chapuys and others, if not at the instigation, at least with the connivance of Anne Boleyn.[1] The latter was not left long to enjoy the position which had cost her and the nation so much. Already she had in great measure lost her hold over the affections of Henry, and for purposes of public or private policy Crumwell was secretly plotting her overthrow.[2] And thus, only four months after the grave had closed on the remains of her rival, Anne Boleyn was led out to the block on Tower Hill. Meantime Henry and his agents had been making preparations since the middle of the previous year for their first attack on the monasteries. This was delivered in the session of parliament which commenced on the 4th day of February 1536.

Layton and Legh had hurried from house to house in the North of England, and had supplied their master, Crumwell, with their reports as to the religious and their property. Meeting at Lichfield on the 22nd of December, the colleagues took their way "to certain abbeys upon Trent side. And so," as they write, "to Southwell, and to be at York within a day after the 12th day we intend, and thus to make speed with diligence and true knowledge of everything, is our intent."[3] On the 11th of January, Thomas Legh informed Crumwell that they had reached York and visited the archbishop.[4] They had ordered that prelate, he wrote, to appear before the vicar-general with all the documents of his office,

---

[1] Friedmann's *Anne Boleyn*, vol. ii. cap. 14.
[2] *Ibid.*, p. 242. On a letter from Chapuys, June 6, 1536: "Il se meist a fantaise et conspira le dict affaire."
[3] Layton to Crumwell, Wright, p. 94.   [4] Dr. Edward Lee.

adding, "I do not doubt when you have read them, but that you shall see and read many things worthy reformation, by the knowledge whereof I suppose the king's highness and you will be glad."[1]

To have reached York from Lichfield in little more than a fortnight, and to have visited and examined the conventual establishments, which lay on their route, as to possessions and morals, must, indeed, have required all their "speed with diligence." Their visitation, however, had to be finished and their report sent in to Crumwell in preparation for parliament within a period of six weeks from their starting on the tour. In this brief time they had to journey over the diocese of Coventry and Lichfield, as well as through the entire province of York.[2] Hence dispatch was absolutely necessary. As their chief object, however, was to find, as in the case of the archbishop of York, "many things worthy reformation," so, to please Crumwell and his royal master, they had no need of very lengthy examinations.

The rapidity of their tour, however, as rendering investigation impossible, makes their *comperts* or reports utterly valueless as pieces of evidence. They prove, however, were proof needed, that these commissioners were ready to bring any accusation against the monks, and that the fair name of many, who possibly never heard anything of the matter, was blackened by mere reckless assertions. Just as Layton in the southern monasteries "expected to find" all that his evil imagination pictured, so from Yorkshire he wrote to Crumwell: "We find corruption amongst persons religious even like as we did in the south . . and worse, if worse may be, in kinds of knavery." He then proceeds to accuse them generally of the most revolting kind of immorality.[3] The sting of this condemnation is certainly somewhat destroyed by the knowledge that the accuser could not possibly have made any inquiry worthy of the name. By his own admission he finds only what he came to seek. "This day," he says, "we begin with St. Mary's Abbey,[4] whereat we *suppose* to find much *evil disposition*, both in the abbot and the con-

---

[1] Legh to Crumwell, Wright, 96.
[2] Comprising altogether eight counties. That this visitation was really made may be seen by the epitome of reports called "Comperta." Some eighty-eight monasteries are reported on within the fortnight.
[3] Layton to Crumwell, Wright, 97, January 13, 1536.   [4] York.

Parliament and the Lesser Monasteries

vent, *whereof, God willing, I shall certify you in my next letter.*"

The parliament, which had been adjourned from the previous November, met at Westminster on the 4th of February, 1536. The chief matter of business it had to transact, in this its last session, was the passing of an act to legalise the spoliation of monastic property, which had been already commenced in the previous autumn. The operation of this act of suppression was to be left to the interpretation of the conscience of Henry, and its provisions were to be carried out by Crumwell and his agents. 'By it, the revenues of abbeys and convents and the untold riches of their churches and shrines together with the patrimony of the poor passed, within the space of four years, into the possession of king and noble and were used as their own private property.

What is even more important is, that the act robbed the monasteries of England of their good name and affixed to them the stigma of evil repute. The transactions of this memorable session of parliament have been often appealed to, during the subsequent three and a half centuries, as proof positive that the religious houses of England had forfeited all right to protection against tyranny and spoliation, by the infamous character of the lives of their inmates. English writers have accepted, unquestioned, the story of what was done in the old Chapter house of the abbey of Westminster in the spring of 1536, at the passing of the act by which the lesser monasteries were suppressed. Like most unsavoury stories, moreover, this one has not lost in the telling. Englishmen, notwithstanding their native love of honesty and fair dealing, believe implicitly and without examination the common narrative of the events that led to the dissolution of the religious houses, and even point to the fact of the destruction of the monasteries as sufficient indication of the cause.

The story, as for instance told in the pages of Green's "History of the English People," may be taken as a fair sample of what is generally accepted as true. "Two royal commissioners," he writes, "were despatched on a general visitation of the religious houses, and their reports formed a 'black book,' which was laid before Parliament in 1536. It was acknowledged that about a third of the houses, including the bulk of the larger abbeys, were fairly and decently conducted. The rest were charged with drunkenness, with simony, and with the foulest and most revolting crimes. The character of the visitors, the sweeping nature of their report, and the long debate that followed on its reception, leaves little doubt that these charges were grossly exaggerated."

A book of another kind, intended for the use of the young, gives much the same version. "The popular complaints," says professor Seebohm, "against them [the monasteries] were not found to be baseless. Scandal had long been busy about the morals of the monks. The commissioners found them on inquiry worse even than scandal had whispered, and reported to parliament that two-thirds of the monks were leading vicious lives under cover of their cowls and hoods." [1]

The account, quoted above from the pages of Mr. Green's admirable history, may be taken as a very fair sample of what is believed on all hands to be a moderate version of the reasons, which led to the greatest confiscation of property the world has ever seen. Yet in these lines, few as they are, there are some statements which are incapable of proof and others which are distinctly false and misleading. It is quite certain, for example, that more than two commissioners were employed in the work of visitation previous to the meeting of parliament. The records that exist make it at least improbable, that "on the table of the Chapter house was placed the famous 'black book,' which sealed the fate of all the monasteries of England and sent a thrill of horror through the house of commons when they heard it." [2] Moreover, it is quite certain that the commissioners never "reported to parliament that two-thirds of the monks were leading vicious lives under cover of their cowls and hoods," and that parliament never declared, that "about a third" of the monasteries "were fairly and decently conducted."

No better picture can be given of the obsequiousness and venality of the lords and commons in Henry's reign than the words of Hallam convey. "Both houses of parliament," he writes, "yielded to every mandate of Henry's imperial

---

[1] Epochs of History; *Era of Prot. Revolution*, 1877, p. 186.
[2] Stanley, *Gleanings from Westminster Abbey*, p. 425. Froude, *Hist.*, iv. 520.

Parliament and the Lesser Monasteries 99

will; they bent with every breath of his capricious humour; they were responsible for the illegal trials, for the iniquitous attainders, for the sanguinary statutes, for the tyranny which they sanctioned by law, and for that which they permitted without law. Nor was this selfish and pusillanimous subserviency more characteristic of the minions of Henry's favour —the Crumwells, the Ryders, the Pagets, the Russells, and the Pauletts. The representatives of ancient and honourable names, such as the Norfolks, the Arundels, the Shrewsburys, were the supporters of the king's policy. We trace these noble statesmen concurring in all the inconsistencies of the reign and supporting all the changes of religion, constant only in the rapacious acquisition of estates and honours from whatever source and in adherence to the present power.[1] Henry VIII. hated all Parliaments just as much as Charles I. and his minister, Lord Strafford. The Tudor tyrant carried out his plans by a code of pains and penalties so horrible as to affright every class of society, and when the nation became reduced to this abject and cowardly condition the king imbrued his hands in the best blood of the land, and he plundered his subjects on a scale never before known in any civilized country."[2]

The parliament, carefully selected for the king's purposes in 1529, met to deal with the monasteries in their last session on February 4th, 1536. The early days of the session having been occupied with other business, the bill for the suppression of the smaller monasteries was brought up to the house about the beginning of March. Unfortunately the journals of both houses of parliament for this and the next year are missing, and we have little to rely upon, for the history of this session, but the preamble of the act itself. This is to be the more deplored, as preambles are

---

[1] Henry VIII. employed towards the nobility a different policy to his father, who had depressed them. The streams of royal favour under Henry VIII. swept countless favours to those who gained his attention, such as wealthy marriages, gifts out of royal domains or confiscated properties, and, after the monasteries were suppressed, a share in the spoils. Not the least curious of these grants to courtiers were annuities out of episcopal sees or monastic revenues. Instances of the latter are numerous; of the former an act, which confirmed to the duke of Norfolk and six others, annuities out of the see of Winchester is a well-known example. By another act, the duke of Suffolk, the earl of Sussex, and lord Fitzwalter had grants confirmed out of the see of Norwich. See Amos, "Statutes of H. VIII.," p. 4.

[2] *Constitutional Hist. of Eng.*, vol. i. p. 51.

not entirely to be trusted.¹ That the bill was a government measure is not to be doubted. In all probability it was brought up to the house by the king in person, for such bills were frequently forwarded a stage by the personal interference of the king. It is not unlikely that the following extract from a letter written at this period refers to the royal visit. "On Saturday in Ember week the king's grace came in among the burgesses of the parliament, and delivered them a bill and bade them look upon it and weigh it in conscience. He would not, he said, have them pass it, nor any other thing, because his grace giveth in the bill, but they to see it if it be for the commonweal to his subjects and have an eye thitherward. And on Wednesday ² next he will be there again to hear their minds." ³

The preamble of the act proves beyond doubt that the king did pay a visit to the House on the introduction of this "bill." It says, that the discussion was preceded by what is called a "declaration" by the king, as to the meaning and necessity of the proposed measure. It asserts that, "In consideration of (the evil lives of those in the smaller monasteries) the *king's most royal majesty* . . . *having knowledge* that the premises be true as well by the *compertes*⁴ of his late *visitation* as by sundry *credible informations*, considering also that divers and great solemn monasteries of this realm, wherein, thanks be to God, religion is right well kept and observed, be destitute of such full numbers of religious persons as they ought and may keep, hath thought good that a plain *declaration*

---

¹ "If preambles to acts of parliament were to be accepted as trustworthy evidence as to facts they recite, English history would be a very strange tale— even stranger than it appears in Mr. Froude's pages."—Friedmann's *Anne Boleyn*, ii. p. 352.

² In 1536 Easter fell on April 16th, and Ember Saturday on March 11th.

³ Wright, p. 36. Thomas Dorset, curate of St. Margaret's, Lothbury, to the mayor and others of Plymouth, March 13. The Greek traveller, Nicander Nucius, who was in England about the year 1545, gives what purports to be Henry's speech to this session of parliament, made for the purpose of securing the destruction of the religious houses. The speech is, of course, the Greek's own composition; but it is evidence of the story by which the king and his courtiers desired to account for the suppression of the monasteries and the seizure of their property. The bad lives of all, and in particular of the nuns, is much insisted on in this composition, as well as the great public advantages to be gained by the appropriation of the monastic revenues to almshouses, hospitals, schools, and the like. (*The Travels of Nicander Nucius*, Camden Soc., p. 57 *sqq.*).

⁴ Printed in Wright, p. 107.

should be made of the premises as well to the lords spiritual and temporal as to other his loving subjects the commons in this present parliament assembled. Whereupon the said lords and commons by a *great deliberation* finally be resolved, that it is and shall be much more to the pleasure of Almighty God" that the property of these religious "should be converted to better uses, and the unthrifty persons so spending the same be compelled to reform their lives."[1] And therefore they pray the king to take all the property of monasteries having an income under £200 a year.

From this preamble (which, it must be remembered, is practically all that is known about the measure) it would seem that parliament had no written documents placed before it, upon which to form any independent judgment as to the justice of the act they were asked to pass. The king, we are told, made a "full declaration" of what *he* knew to be true from the reports of the visitors and other sources. Upon this, after "a great deliberation," the members acted. Whether the report of the visitors in any shape was also submitted to their examination will probably never be ascertained with certainty. Sanders, it is true, speaks of the "publication of the enormities,"[2] but this might only refer to the king's "declaration." Bishop Latimer, who was possibly present in the house of lords, also says:—"When their enormities were first *read* in the parliament house, they were so great and abominable that there was nothing but down with them, but within a while after the same abbots were made bishops, for the saving of their pensions."[3] This is about the only authority for the statement that any such document as the famous "Black Book" was ever presented to parliament. The first mention of the name "Black book" occurs in a document called a declaration of the "mode of dissolving the abbeys." It is supposed to have been made for the information of Queen Elizabeth. "This appeared in writing," the author asserts, "with the names of the parties and their facts. This was showed in parliament and the villanies made

---

[1] H. VIII., cap. 28. The word used on the parliamentary roll, is "*compertes*," which were the visitors' reports.
[2] *Schism*, Lewis' translation, p. 129.
[3] *Two Sermons before Edward VI.* (Parker Society), vol. i. p. 123.

known and abhorred"[1] The villanies "made known and abhorred" (at least as to murders and forging of deeds and the number of those implicated) are certainly not borne out by any known letters or reports of the visitors, of which a great many are still in existence. It may be justly asked what reliance can be placed upon this account as a history of the event. It moreover professes to be no more than a recollection of what took place, and does not distinguish between the two acts of suppression by which the lesser and greater monasteries were destroyed.

"If this "Black book" was presented to parliament, as is so constantly asserted, nothing has since been seen of it." To explain the disappearance of this most important document, a theory started, as far as can be ascertained, by the ingenious Burnet explains that the catholics destroyed this dreadful indictment against the monks during the reign of queen Mary. Their object was to get rid of this damning evidence of the corruption of the monastic system. Burnet bases his assertion[2] on a commission issued in the fourth year of Mary's reign to Bonner bishop of London, Henry Cole dean of St. Paul's and others, to examine into the documents "*compertes, bokes, scroles, &c.,*" and also into "sundry and divers infamous scrutinies taken in abbeys and other religious houses tending rather to subvert and overthrow all good religion and religious houses than for any truth contained therein." The commissioners are ordered to get these documents together, "that the said writings and other the said premises be *brought to knowledge*,

[1] B. Mus. Cot. MSS. Titus, F. iii. fol. 266, printed by Wright, p. 114. The "vile lives and abominable facts in murders of their brethren," in unnatural sins, "in destroying of children, in forging of deeds and other infinite horrors of life, in so much that dividing all the religious persons in England into three parts two of these parts at least" were guilty of sins against nature. As this is the most important document on which is based the venerable tradition that the Black Book was laid before parliament it may be well to observe, in addition to what is said in the text: (1) that from an expression at the beginning it is clear the writer does not make his statement on inspection of records (he imagines that Wolsey's suppressions may have had the pope's approval, but is quite ignorant of the fact): (2) he clearly does not speak from personal knowledge of what passed in parliament: (3) as to the date of the document, all that Mr. Wright can say is that "it appears to have been written in the time of queen Elizabeth." This nameless, dateless production has not therefore even the value of sub-contemporary evidence; and in itself, apart from the use made of it, is not worth even the trouble of this note.

[2] *History of the Reformation* (ed. Pocock), ii. p. 547.

whereby they may be considered, read and ordered according to our will and pleasure." [1] They are further commanded to make their report to cardinal Pole. It is obvious that this commission is one of inquiry. There is not one word in the document to justify the assertion that it was one of destruction. Nevertheless, Burnet says he "soon knew which way so many writings had gone," when he saw the commission. The authority of the late Mr. Brewer may be given for the assertion that there is no trace among the records of this period of any such systematic destruction.[2]

If the book ever existed, its loss, whether destroyed on purpose or by accident, is greatly to be deplored. It is, however, obvious that the cause of the monasteries would be ill-served by the destruction. On the other hand, when uncorroborated charges had been made to serve their purpose against the monastic houses, when the spoils of sacred shrines and consecrated cloisters had been allowed to minister to the vices of the monarch or to replenish the empty purses of his corrupt courtiers, the sooner the evidence, upon which such destruction and spoliation had been wrought was destroyed, the better for the reputation of those who had profited by it. A modern Church of England authority writes:—"If I could visit the island of Glubbdubdrib, and wanted to know what became of this 'declaration' or 'black book,' I should call up the ghost of Crumwell to tell me: that is supposing such a document ever existed."[3]

For three centuries and a half the imaginations of writers hostile to the monastic institutions have supplied the details of the missing document. Even the most honest historians have neglected to distinguish between what is mere conjecture and what is certain. Dr. Lingard, for example, states "that from their (the visitors') reports a statement was compiled and laid before parliament, which, while it allotted the praise of regularity to the greater monasteries, described the less opulent as abandoned to

---

[1] Dec. 29, 1556, Rot. Pat., 3 and 4 Phil. and Mary. Pars. 12 m. (21), 30 d., printed in Burnet, *Records*, ii. No. 28.
[2] Dixon's *History of Church of England*, vol. i. p. 342. "Mr. Froude, with his usual disregard of facts, says 'The report itself is no longer extant. Bonner was directed by Queen Mary to destroy all discoverable copies of it, and his work was fatally well executed'"!!!
[3] *Ibid.*, note.

sloth and immorality."[1] It is, however, by no means certain that any "statement was compiled" from the reports of the visitors, still less that it was laid before parliament. On the other hand, it is expressly stated that the king's information was based on other "credible informations" besides the "accounts of his late visitation." And certainly from what we know of the royal agents and their methods, it is most unlikely that they would give the "praise of regularity" even to the greater monasteries.

From the records of this event it would seem therefore to be tolerably certain, that the visitors made their reports to Crumwell and in no sense to the houses of parliament. That Crumwell had an abstract of these reports prepared from time to time is more than probable,[2] and that they were gathered together into one book not unlikely. That they formed, however, a volume called the "Black book" and were in this way laid before the parliament cannot be proved, and on the evidence of the "preamble" of the act itself would appear unlikely. One thing seems to be certain: there was no attempt made to inquire into the truth of the charges suggested in the king's declaration. They were accepted on *his authority*, who had "knowledge that the premises were true."

The preamble[3] of the act of suppression commences by stating, that "manifest sin, vicious, carnal and abominable living is daily used and committed commonly" in religious houses of *less than twelve* in number, "*whereby* the governors of such religious houses and their convent spoil, destroy, consume, and utterly waste" their property "as well as the ornaments of their churches" and other goods. On the face of it, it is absurd to suppose that the serious charges here brought against the monasteries could be confined to

---

[1] *History*, vol. vi. (3rd ed.), p. 298.
[2] Ap Rice, one of the visitors, says he made this "Breve docket."
[3] Amos, *Statutes of H. VIII.*, p. 9 notes. "With regard to the *facts* detailed in *preambles*, their veracity will derive no support from a coincidence with State papers, such as confessions, depositions, verdicts, judgments, reports, provided both the preambles and such documents should appear to be the productions of the same laboratory, the handiwork of the same craftsmen. Such a coincidence might be anticipated if the king, by his subservient agents, stretched racks, examined prisoners, transcribed and read evidence, empannelled and reformed the pannels of juries, directed and terrified the *twelve*, pronounced criminal and ecclesiastical judgments, wove the tissue of vilifying reports, and afterwards, summed up the results in preambles."

those houses, which had less than twelve inmates. The limit was very probably suggested to the framers of the measure by the terms of the papal bull of 1528, authorizing cardinal Wolsey to suppress certain houses for the establishment of his colleges. This bull provided, that the religious in these monasteries be less in number than twelve and be transferred to the larger monasteries. Such a limit, however, is made ridiculous, when it is set as the line of demarcation between virtue and vice.[1]

The records of the visitation, which was the forerunner of this act, show who were the real "spoilers and destroyers" of the monastic treasuries. Those who, like Layton, "had packed up the stuff as the monks had," and the "crosses of silver and gold," intending to "bring you (Crumwell) the rest when I have received all," or the king who had taken a fancy to possess himself of the jewelled cross from the cathedral priory of Winchester, were best able to know that the religious houses were being spoiled of their "ornaments." The clause, as it stands in the preamble, seems to have no other object than to cover the fact of the disappearance from the monastic treasuries of valuables, which had already found their way into the king's possession through the hand of his visitors, or had been appropriated to their own private purposes.[2]

The professed desire of the king to reform the inmates of the smaller monasteries by sending[3] them to the greater

---

[1] *Vide* Amos, *ibid.*, p. 301. The number 12 was probably introduced *ad captandum*. It is never again referred to in the enacting clauses. It may have been thought that *numbers* could not be diminished so plausibly as *values*.

[2] *Ibid.*, p. 309, Amos says:—"It would appear that, with regard to their (the monastic) personal property, and such of their possessions as were capable of rapine or destruction, a great part of the damage they received was done them, under colour of the visitations, before any dissolution act had passed."

[3] This provision is also taken from the bull of 1528. How anxious Henry really was for the religious reformation of the monasteries may be judged from a letter written by Chapuys to the Emperor, on July 31, 1531. "At the request of the abbots of this country," he writes, "and by the advice and order of the General Chapter of the Order of Cisteau, there has come to this city an abbot of Chalon, (*sic*) a very learned and virtuous monk, for the purpose of visiting the monasteries of his order in this country, which are in great need of inspection. But notwithstanding the manifold juridical reasons and the right he had to undertake the said visit, as he himself told the nuncio and me when dining at my hotel, the king has never allowed him to make the said visitation, alleging that no one had a right to interfere in the affairs of his kingdom, saying that he was at once King, Emperor (and if I recollect right) Pope also in his dominions."—*Spanish State Papers*, iv. No. 775.

houses, "where they may be compelled to live religiously for the reformation of their lives," was not carried out in practice. Wholesale dispensations from the solemn obligations of the religious vows had already been granted. A priest's or layman's gown, with forty shillings out of the plunder of their own property, on being turned out into the world to live as best they might, was the usual form of "reformation" adopted to get rid of the monks from their homes and to get possession of their coveted property. Nevertheless, the same professed desire for perfect religious life and the spiritual welfare of the monastic establishments is repeated in another part of the preamble, where it is suggested that the ejected religious would go to raise the numbers in the "great, solemn monasteries wherein (thanks be to God) religion is right well kept and observed."

It is, moreover, well to note the only kind of reformation attempted by the king or his agents during the six months which preceded the passing of this act. It was the forcible suppression of several small monasteries, the seizure of their possessions, and the violent laying of hands on the treasures of others. In the enacting clauses of the bill, also, the number of the religious to be found in the monasteries is not laid down as the limit to mark them for dissolution or preservation, but a money value of under £200 a year. The monasteries were, moreover, given to the king and his heirs only in "as ample a manner" as they were possessed by the religious superiors. These were trustees for common purposes and never regarded their property in any other light than as held for the support of religion and the poor. Further, the purpose, for which the monastic property was diverted by this act from its possessors and given to the king, is stated to be "that his highness may lawfully give, grant, and dispose them, or any of them, at his will and pleasure *to the honour of God and the wealth of this realm.*"

However uncertain and vague the terms of this grant may appear, they can hardly be supposed to comprehend those purposes, private, secular and even vicious upon which Henry squandered the property thus obtained. It was ordered, also, that the king should provide occupation and pensions for the monks not transferred to other monasteries. It was further enacted, that on the site of every dissolved religious house the new possessor should be bound under heavy penalties to provide hospitality and service for the poor, such as had been given them previously by the religious foundations. By this provision not only is the patrimony of the poor recognised as being merged in the property of the monasteries, but a testimony is afforded as to the way the religious had hitherto discharged their obligations in this respect. The repudiation of these rights of the needy, by those who became possessed of the confiscated property, is one of the greatest blots on our national history. It has rightly caused the spoliation of monastery and convent to be regarded as the rising of the rich against the poor.

In the commons, there are some signs of opposition to the act of suppression, which made legal, but by no means just, this plunder of monastic property. The "preamble" of the act speaks of a "great deliberation" which preceded the final vote, and Sir Henry Spelman, who no doubt gave the traditional account of the matter, says:—"It is true the parliament gave them to him, but so unwillingly (as I have heard) that when the bill had stuck long in the lower house and could get no passage, he commanded the commons to attend him in the forenoon in his gallery, where he let them wait till late in the afternoon, and then coming out of his chamber, walking a turn or two among them, and looking angrily on them, first on the one side and then on the other at last, 'I hear' (saith he) 'that my bill will not pass, but I will have it pass, or I will have some of your heads,' and without other rhetoric or persuasion returned to his chamber. Enough was said, the bill passed, and all was given him as he desired."[1]

It has always been stated that the abbots of the greater monasteries, who sat in parliament, to save their own abbeys did not hesitate to vote for the suppression of the less powerful houses. Hall in his Chronicle says, that "in this time was given unto the king, by the consent of the great, fat abbots, all religious houses that were of the value of 300 marks and under, in hope that their great monasteries should have continued still. But even at the time one said in the parliament house that these were the thorns, but the great abbots were the putrified old oaks, and they must follow. And so will others do in Christendom, quoth Dr. Stokesley,

[1] *Hist. of Sacrilege* (ed. 1853), p. 206. Spelman was born in 1562, less than thirty years after the event.

bishop of London, or many years be passed."[1] There does not, however, appear to have ever been any actual voting in the upper house. Consequently all that the mitred abbots would have done, was to have been present during the passing of the bill. Probably those that were there had no choice in the matter. It is, moreover, certain that the king had grave fears that the opposition of these parliamentary abbots would defeat his intended spoliation, and that to prevent them "parrying the blow in store for them" and "complaining of the innovations introduced in their convents," he had prepared to exclude them from parliament altogether.[2]

Henry and his minister Crumwell appear to have been the first English rulers who realised the immense power of public opinion, and who endeavoured by definite and elaborate measures to educate it. Every effort was made to influence the people, by means of preachers selected for their known adherence to the policy of the king, and by stage plays and interludes, often acted in the very churches. These represented the "immoralities and disorders of the clergy" and "the pageantry of their worship," by which they "encouraged them all they could" to adopt their freedom of thought and contempt of religion.[3]

In the June of the previous year (1535) Chapuys had described the personal interest the king took in these plays. Henry, he says, had gone thirty miles, walking ten of the distance at two o'clock in the morning, in order to be present at a representation of a chapter of the Apocalypse. He had taken up his position in a house from which he could observe everything, "but was so pleased to see himself represented as cutting off the heads of the clergy, that in order to laugh at his ease, and encourage the people he discovered himself."[4]

The pulpit had been already used for the purpose of attacking the papal supremacy and instructing the people in the principles of revolt against authority.[5] Cranmer, whom

---

[1] *Union* (ed. 1548), fol. 227d.   [2] *Spanish State Papers*, vol. v. No. 221.
[3] See Blunt, *Reformation*, p. 273, note. "The horrible coarseness of such representations; the immorality and blasphemy of parodizing the H. Eucharist in the very house of God itself seem not to have struck these writers" (*i.e.*, Foxe and Burnet).
[4] *Calendar*, viii. No. 949.
[5] Privy Council Memoranda, anno 1533, *State Papers*, vol. i. 411.

Chapuys considered a kind of antipope[1] set up by Henry, used his short-lived supreme spiritual authority to revoke the licences of the preaching clergy. He granted his permission only to those whom he could trust to speak against the authority of the see of Rome.[2] For the purpose of more easily controlling the teaching of the people, all sermons and instructions in the ordinary parish churches were forbidden to be given after nine o'clock in the morning. At that time the services were to be finished, so "that then the curates, with the parishes, might come to Paul's cross and hear the preachers." These sermons were specially named as occasions when there was to be set forth the doctrine directed by the Privy Council. Moreover, a minute of the council strictly commands the mayor, aldermen and common council of London "liberally to speak at their boards" on this matter, and instruct their servants in the same, while provincial officers and the gentry are to see that their families "bruit the same in all places where they shall come."[3]

At a time when no individual was allowed to have an opinion of his own on the policy of the government, or, indeed, even on the faith of his forefathers, the influence of public preaching was necessarily most powerful in directing popular feeling and sympathy. No sooner, therefore, was the suppression of the monasteries determined upon, and the arrangements for effecting it complete, than the machinery of the public pulpits was set in motion to endeavour to forestall popular discontent. Coarse invective and unscrupulous insinuation, it was hoped, might alienate the affection of the people from the monks. In pursuance of this object Crumwell sent forth three kinds of preachers to attack the monastic institutions. "One sort must be railers against religious men, calling them hypocrites, sorcerers, crooked necks, slowbellies, idle drones, abbey lubbers, plants which the Heavenly Father never planted, mumblers of praises in the night, which God heard not, creatures of the pope's making."

"Another sort," like Cranmer, must needs tune their instruments on another string, "saying that they made the

---

[1] *Calendar*, vol. vii. No. 14.
[2] *Ibid.*, No. 463.
[3] Reminiscences of John Louthe, printed in *Narratives of the Days of the Reformation* (Camden Soc.), p. 23.

land unprofitable," whilst a third told the people that the king would never want their money again. "This part was well discharged by Cranmer at Paul's cross." So much so "that, although wise men saw there was no truth in it," still they allowed themselves to be influenced by the specious promises.[1]

The fact is, that the people were groaning under the weight of an almost insupportable taxation. They were only too ready therefore to listen to any voice promising them immunity in the future—more especially when this was to be purchased by sacrificing the property of others. "After his denial of papal obedience," writes Marillac, the French ambassador, in 1540, "Henry employed preachers and ministers who went about to preach and persuade the people that he could employ the ecclesiastical revenues in hospitals, colleges, and other foundations for the public good, which would be a much better use than that they should support lazy and useless monks."[2]

Cranmer, at Paul's cross, tried to stifle the natural feelings of dismay and opposition to the proposed suppression, by vague but captivating promises of future exemption from taxation. Nicholas Harpsfield, who was present, says[3]:— "This prelate (Cranmer) when the king went about to suppress the monasteries, was his chief instrument and worker, and, to bring the people asleep and cause them to have better contentation that (as it was doubted) would not patiently and quietly bear the suppression (as it proved afterwards by the rebellion of Lincolnshire and Yorkshire) came and preached at Paul's cross, and to sweet the people's ears with pleasant words told them, amongst other things, that they had no cause to be grieved with the evertion of the abbeys, but should rather be glad thereof, for the singular benefit 'that should redound to the whole realm thereby . . .' and that the king should, by the suppression of the abbeys, gather such an infinite treasure that from that time he should have no need, nor would not, put the people to any manner of payment or charge for his, or the realm's

---

[1] B. Mus. Sloane MS., 2495.
[2] *Inventaire Analytique*, No. 242. Marillac au Connétable, Aug. 6, 1540.
[3] Nicholas Harpsfield, *The Pretended Divorce*, ed. N. Pocock (Camd. Society), 1878, p. 292. The learned editor, in his preface, declares that he considers Harpsfield to be absolutely trustworthy.

affairs. This sermon, as no wise man did believe, so myself, that chanced to be there present," have known how false was the promise. "His said sermon was in effect nothing else but a plain invective against all monasteries as places and dens of all error and superstition." "The bishop of Canterbury," writes another of the audience, "saith that the king's grace is at a full point for friars and chauntry priests, that they shall away all that, saving those that can preach. Then one said to the bishop, that they had good trust that they should serve forth their life time, and he said they should serve it out at the cart then, for any other service they should have by that."[1]

Aided by much rough rhetoric, by the undisguised threats of the king's vengeance if "his bill" did not pass, and doubtless by the arrogance of Crumwell, who six months before had threatened an English jury unless they convicted the Carthusian fathers, the act was passed through the house of commons. Parliament acts for the commonweal. Just as it cannot without injustice take the property of the individual and bestow it without compensation at its caprice, so without sacrilege and robbery it cannot appropriate the wealth, which pious benefactors have bestowed on religion and the poor. More especially is this so, when the property thus taken is not made to serve any public purpose or to mitigate some of the miseries of poverty, but as a sop to the greedy appetite of a vicious and avaricious monarch and his needy favourites. Vice is a ground for reformation, not destruction. "Henry," it has been well said, "was ever prone to reformation when there was anything to gain by it." Here there was more to be gained by destruction. In charging the religious houses with being steeped in vice and immorality, the king did them, moreover, a greater wrong than in the mere robbery of their valuables. In asserting that the reports of his visitors bore him out in this accusation, Henry was but repeating a tale which they were sent by him to tell.

Sir James Mackintosh, in treating of this act of dissolution, thus summarises the uses for which the rights of property have been instituted. "Property," he remarks, "which is generally deemed to be the incentive to industry,

[1] Wright, p. 38.

the guardian of order, the preserver of internal quiet, the channel of friendly intercourse between men and nations, and, in a higher point of view, as affording leisure for the pursuit of knowledge, means for the exercise of generosity, occasions for the returns of gratitude, as being one of the ties that bind succeeding generations, strengthening domestic discipline, and keeping up the affections of kindred; above all, because it is the principle to which all men adapt their plans of life, and on the faith of whose permanency every human action is performed, is an institution of so high and transcendent a nature that every government which does not protect it, nay, that does not rigorously punish its infraction, must be guilty of a violation of the first duties of rulers. The common feelings of human nature have applied to it the epithets of sacred and inviolable." From this consideration the attention of the reader is invited to an examination of the charges which the king "knew to be true from the report of his visitors," and upon which royal knowledge parliament justified the suppression of the Lesser Monastic houses.

CHAPTER VII

The "Comperta Monastica" and other Charges against the Monks

PARLIAMENT suppressed the lesser monasteries on the faith of the king's "declaration" that vice was prevalent in them. This is certain from the terms of the preamble to the act. It is therein also declared that Henry himself knew "the premisses" to be true, by the "comperts of his late visitation as by sundry credible informations." It becomes therefore necessary to examine into the charges made against the monks by the royal inquisitors, so far as they can be learnt from their letters and reports.

It is hardly necessary to remark, how easy it is to make accusations of this nature and how difficult to disprove them. More especially must this be so, when these charges were made more than three centuries ago, and when many documents, which might have thrown much light on the matter, must have perished, and when the assertions, vituperations and insinuations of subsequent ages have been accepted as the testimony of contemporaries. These moreover have often been collected and embellished by the fertile imaginations of authors hostile to the monastic institute.

Putting aside whatever has been written against the English monks, by those who have endorsed the charges against them without weighing the grounds of the accusation, the reader's attention is invited to the original documentary evidence still remaining. In the first place, there are many letters from the visitors themselves, written whilst engaged on their task of inspection. A selection of these was published by the Camden Society from a volume in the Cotton manuscripts in the British museum.[1] Many others

[1] *The Suppression of the Monasteries*, edited by Mr. Wright. The volume is almost entirely taken from the Cotton MS. Cleop. E. iv., which evidently originally formed a part of the "Crumwell correspondence" in the Record

hitherto little known are to be found in the public Record Office. Besides these letters there is a document known as the "*Comperta.*"[1] This is merely an abstract of the letters or reports made to Crumwell by his agents. The greater part of the document is taken up with a report on the monasteries in the northern province of York and in the diocese of Coventry and Lichfield. The rest consists of two portions of a similar account of the diocese of Norwich, written by John Ap Rice. This visitor had joined with Dr. Legh in a request to Crumwell for the suspension of all episcopal powers during the progress of their visitation.[2] Ap Rice was occupied with Legh in this part of England, after the latter had finished his examination of the University of Cambridge, and before his meeting with Layton at Lichfield in December 1535, for their northern tour of inspection.

Besides the manuscript "*comperta,*" another document of the same nature has been preserved in the pages of "foul-mouthed Bale"[3] which refers to some fourteen of the southern monasteries. These "*comperta,*" "*comperts,*" or accounts were furnished to Crumwell by his visitors whilst on their rounds. For instance, in October 1535, Ap Rice

Office. The letters in both collections are endorsed in the same handwriting, which is probably that of Mr. R. Starkey, who lived in the beginning of the seventeenth century, when the Cotton collection was formed.

[1] The original in the Record Office is in the handwriting of one of the visitors, John Ap Rice. The two copies in the Museum are evidently taken from this document. There is, however, in the R. O. a fragment of a similar report not transcribed in the Cotton or Lansdowne MSS. It is in all probability a leaf from the abstract of the reports sent by the writer, John Ap Rice, as to the monasteries of Norfolk, Suffolk, Cambridge, &c. *Calendar*, vol. x. No. 364.

[2] A letter from Ap Rice (Wright, 85), written from Bury St. Edmund's, shows he was engaged in the diocese of Norwich. Also two joint letters, *Calendar*, ix. No. 808, from him and Legh as to West Derham show that they were engaged in this part of England in November 1535. The date of the "*comperta*" is important and is dealt with below. Canon Dixon (p. 352) thinks they are a report of a subsequent visitation. Mr. Gairdner (vol. x. No. 364) refers them to the visit of 1535-36.

[3] *Pageant of Popes.* A portion of this is to be found in the third ed. of Speed's "History," and probably not inserted by him, which was copied from Henri Estienne (called Henry Steven). This author in his *Apologie pour Hérodote* (ed. 1565) says his extract is "tiré d'un livre Anglois." As Bale's book was published in 1555 it is probably the work from which it was copied. The literary history of the extract in Speed (3rd ed.) is interesting, and accounts for some strange mistakes. For instance, Bale, probably not knowing the name of the prior of Bermondsey, calls him "*Blank*" (his real name being Richard Gill). Estienne gives the name as "Blanc," and the editor of Speed retranslates him into "*White.*"

writes from Cambridge to say that "herewith you have the abridgement of the *compertes* in such places as we have been at since we came from London." In the same communication he goes on to say of Walden abbey:—" Ye may see by the *comperta* of this house how they live, all the sort of them that professeth chastity." This house had a good name, and yet is "as some of the other where we have no comperte." "Here they declared the truth, because their superior always exhorted them so to do;[1] and in other houses they do not so because of considerations made between them to the contrary, as at St. Albans, where we found little, although there were much to be found."[2]

A month later the same visitor and Dr. Legh write from Westacre a joint letter, saying they had dispatched Crumwell another "abridgement of the 'comperts' from the last ye had unto Crabhouse."[3] At the same time they regret they cannot send more to him, for "at the greatest houses that we come to commonly they be so confederate, by reason of their heads being mere pharisees, that we can get little or no *comperte* there. And albeit that of the others, ye may soon guess what the rest be, yet if it shall please you hereafter to send a commission to certain houses, *ad melius inquirendum*, and give them that shall go somewhat *more leisure*, we doubt not but ye shall find them all naught."[4]

Again, on September 27th, 1535, Dr. Legh writes to Crumwell and encloses the "*compertes*" of Chertsey abbey, which is headed "*compendium compertorum apud Chertsey*."[5] This document is in precisely the same form and under the same heading as the other *comperta*, and leaves no doubt whatever that the documents are the actual reports forwarded to the visitor general by his instruments, during the progress of their work.

That the chief motive of the visitation and the special desire of the visitors was to discover evil, the letters them-

---

[1] Ap Rice had already said that this superior was "teaching in his daily lectures, that there was no virtue *in monachatu*," and was himself a fallen man.

[2] *Calendar*, ix. No. 661.

[3] "Evidently," writes Mr. Gairdner (*Calendar*, x. Pref. xlii.), "the third paper in No. 364 of the present volume."

[4] *Calendar*, ix. No. 808. Note the confession of the rapidity of their examination, and the expectation of finding all they wished against the religious.

[5] *Ibid.*, No. 472.

selves do not allow us to doubt. "We have no reason, indeed," writes Mr. Gairdner, "to think highly of the character of Crumwell's visitors; and the letters of Layton show that he really gloated over the obscenities that he unearthed."[1]

Individual members of the religious houses, who were tired of the restraints of monastic discipline or who were bad at heart, may perhaps have welcomed the chance of release afforded them in this visitation. From such, Layton, Ap Rice and Legh may have learned some of the stories, which they entered as charges against members of the various religious communities they visited. That there was even a shadow or semblance of investigation into a single one of the accusations, does not appear by any letter or paper in existence. The very rapidity with which the visitors executed their commission, and the eagerness with which, as their letters prove, they welcomed every indication of evil, would seem to render such an examination impossible and undesirable. From the monks, as a body, it is most unlikely that the inquisitors derived much knowledge or assistance. It is probable that most of their charges were the result of ill-natured gossip, magnified by their own ready imaginations. They found only what they hoped and expected, and in all probability those, whose reputations were at stake, were left in entire ignorance of the whole matter.

"It is not to be supposed," says Mr. Gairdner, "that abbots and convents generally submitted quietly to a new authority, intent on promoting offensive investigations as a pretext for their own destruction. Many of the principal houses, it is clear, would have nothing to say to the visitors; and it is quite possible that the monks in many cases refused even to exculpate themselves before men for whose character and commission they had very little respect. Considering the rapidity with which the work was done the investigations could hardly have been very judicially conducted."[2]

The date of the document, known as the *comperta*, is of considerable importance. Parliament passed the act of suppression on the faith of the king's "declaration" that the monks were immoral. This he knew to be the case by the *compertes* of his late visitations. Are the extant *compertes*

---

[1] *Calendar*, x. Pref. xliii.   [2] *Ibid.*, x. Pref. xlii.

The Charges against the Monks

those upon which Henry based his declaration? There is no reasonable doubt that these are the documents forwarded at this time to Crumwell, for Henry to use in pushing his measure of suppression through the parliament. They are, moreover, in the same form as they were originally despatched by the inquisitors as they progressed with their mission. This may be judged from the *comperte* of the great abbey of Chertsey, which document was written in 1535 during the royal visitation.[1] The larger *comperta* of Layton and Legh are the result of the northern tour of these two worthies, and agree with their letters written during this same visitation. The document commences with Lichfield, where it is certain they met on December 22nd, 1535.[2] It includes reports of the cathedral church of York, St. Mary's abbey and Fountains, where they were in 1536, on January 11th, the 13th, and before the 20th respectively.[3] The last letter, moreover, which describes their visitation of Fountains, corresponds with the *compertes* of this abbey.

The other manuscript *comperta* also, certainly relate to the same period, previous to the meeting of parliament in the spring of 1536,[4] and the portion of a similar document preserved by Bale undoubtedly refers to the inquisitions of Layton at the monasteries of Kent and Sussex made during the summer of 1535.[5] We may consequently conclude that all the documents of this nature were intended to serve, and did actually serve as the basis of the king's "declaration" to parliament in 1536. They are the *compertes* of his "late visitation."

The singular want of honesty in this assurance to parliament is apparent. Henry professed to go by the evidence of his visitors. Their *comperta* included the greater monas-

---

[1] *Calendar*, ix. No. 472. This document was sent with a letter to "The Right Hon. Mr. Thos. Crumwell, Chief Sect. to the King's Highness." It is, like the letter, in the handwriting of John Ap Rice, and is in form similar to the other *comperta* which Ap Rice copied from the originals.

[2] Wright, 91. Letter of Layton to Crumwell.

[3] Wright, pp. 95, 97, 100.

[4] The *compertes* for the abbey of Bury St. Edmund are founded entirely on Ap Rice's letter of November 11, 1535 (Wright, 85), and are almost certainly in his handwriting. Legh and Ap Rice can be also traced at work in the diocese of Norwich by other letters, *e.g.*, Wright, 82, 83; R. O. Crum. Corr., xxii., Nos. 14, 16, 17, 18, 22, &c.

[5] See letters, Wright, 58, 75. R. O. Crum. Corr., xx. Nos. 10, 13, 18, 19, 20, &c.

teries with the lesser in wholesale condemnation. The preamble of the act, passed on the strength of the royal assurance, however, declares that in the larger monasteries "thanks be to God religion is right well kept and observed." The fact that the greater monasteries are not spared in these reports, makes it impossible to believe that they were really submitted to the inspection of parliament. The *expressio falsi* in the preamble of the act, which (in the face of the *comperta* of Crumwell's agents) expressly declared that "in the great and solemn monasteries of the realm" religion was well conducted, demonstrates the dishonest purpose which actuated the framers of the measure. It is proof positive of the fraud by which parliament was induced to sanction the appropriation of the corporate property of the lesser monasteries.

It is well here to note in passing that, with very trifling exceptions, no accusations of the same nature are suggested after the bill had been forced through parliament. This fact, when duly considered, seems to show, that such charges of immorality and incontinence were brought against the religious for the distinct object of disarming opposition and securing the passing of the measure. In subsequent letters and reports there is hardly anything that can be construed into a charge of the gross nature, with which Layton, Legh, and Ap Rice delight to blacken the reputation of monastery and convent during their first tour of inspection.

There is no need to admit that both the letters and reports of the visitors at this period, if they are to be believed, are very damaging to the characters of the monastic houses. Still, even accepting their estimate, the proportion of the well conducted, or, at least, of those against whom no charge is suggested, is very much in excess of what is generally believed. "There were many monasteries named in these reports," writes Mr. Gairdner, "against which nothing is said; and there were more in the dioceses reported on which are not named at all. So that it may be presumed, in the opinion of the visitors themselves, not a few of the monastic houses were pure and well governed."[1] So far,

---

[1] *Calendar*, x. Pref. xlv. Of the 155 monasteries given in the *comperta* (No. 364), there are 43 against which nothing worse is alleged than the possession of certain relics, which is supposed to argue "superstition." "To judge," says Mr. Gairdner (note), "by the proportion in Yorkshire, the visitors examined only about *four out of ten houses.*"

therefore, from two-thirds of the religious being represented as hopelessly sunk in vice and immorality, even the visitors' *ex parte* reports really charge only a very small minority with vice of any kind.

In several instances, moreover, it is quite clear from the *comperta* itself, that mere idle rumour must have been the foundation of the charge. Malicious reports, also, fostered if not suggested by the visitors, ever anxious to further Crumwell's intentions, were evidently the sole basis of grave accusations. This is seen more clearly in the *comperta* of Legh and Ap Rice than in those of Layton and Legh. Ap Rice, for example, writes to Crumwell with regard to the visitation of Bury St. Edmund, which in conjunction with Legh he made in November 1535:—"Please it your mastership, forasmuch as I suppose you will have suit made unto you touching Bury, ere we return, I thought convenient to advertise you of our proceedings there and also of the *compertes* of the same."[1] He then proceeds to say, that they could find nothing against the abbot's character, except that he was much at his country house, was fond of dice and cards and did not preach. "Also he seemeth to be addict to the maintaining of such superstitious ceremonies, as hath been used heretofore." As "touching the convent, we could get little or no reports among them, although we did use much diligence in our examinations, with some other arguments gathered of their examinations." And they, therefore, conclude "that they had confederated and compacted before our coming that they should disclose nothing." "And yet it is confessed and proved that there was here, such frequence of women coming and resorting to this monastery as to no place more. . . . Here depart of them that be under age upon eight, and of them that be above age upon five would depart if they might, and they be of the best sort in the house and of best learning and judgment. The whole number of the convent before we came was 60 saving one and besides, three that were at Oxford."

The *compertes*, which these visitors sent their master after acknowledging that they could "get little or no *reports*, although using much diligence in their examinations," fortunately exist. They are in the handwriting of Ap Rice him-

[1] Wright, 85.

self. The abbot is charged with being fond of cards and dice and not doing his duty in preaching. It is added, that he delights in frequenting the houses of women, &c.[1] Ap Rice confessed in the very letter, with which these *compertes*, written in his own hand, were sent, that there was nothing but vague report against Abbot Melford's character. After this, it is not surprising that nine of his religious are bracketed together, as "defamed of incontinence from too great intercourse with women," and three others "are reported" (fatentur) guilty of other faults. Finally, the *comperta* adds: "There is a grave suspicion that the abbot and convent had agreed together not to tell anything against themselves, for though *report* says the monks here live licentiously, still there never was less confessed to."[2]

From this instance, and others that could be given, it must be allowed that the *compertes* are merely a collection of reports, tales or malicious informations. They cannot seriously be considered as any evidence of the moral state of the monastic houses. It is a curious revelation of the bias of Crumwell's agents that they suspect all monks against whom they could learn no ill of having agreed together to conceal everything.[3] This determination to see nothing but evil should surely throw discredit on the *ex parte* reports contained in the *comperta* documents. The same spirit is evinced in the letters the visitors addressed to Crumwell at various stages in their progress and which were doubtless sent with their reports or *comperta*, which we no longer possess. Layton, for instance, on his way to meet Legh at Lichfield, visits a Gilbertine convent at Chiksand, in Bedfordshire.[4] Here "they would not in any wise have admitted me as visitor," he writes, "but I would not be so answered, and visited them." From none of the sisters was he able to find out anything amiss, but on the report of "one old beldame" he accused two of the eighteen nuns of incontinence. In the same letter, Leicester abbey is declared to be "confederate and nothing will confess." "The abbot," Layton says, "is an honest man, and doeth very

---

[1] "Gaudet mulierum contubernio."   [2] *Calendar*, x. No. 364.
[3] *Ibid., e.g., Thetford*: "Etiam hic colligitur suspicio confederationis quum essent 17 numero." *Iklesworth*: "Et illic subolet etiam suspicio vehemens confederationis nam quum essset 18 numero, nihil tamen confessum."
[4] Wright, 91.

well, but he hath here the most obstinate and factious canons that ever I knew." "This morning," he continues, "I will object against divers of them the 'grossest of crime,' *et sic specialiter descendere*, which I have learned of others (but none of them). What I shall find I cannot tell." "If this method were put in practice generally," says Mr. Gairdner, "how much would have been taken for confession? Perhaps silence in some cases."[1] Certainly it would only have been reasonable to expect, that Doctor Layton would have taken some time to inquire into the particular charges of so grave a nature against the character of the Austin canons, who strenuously denied them. He expressly states, however, in the letter, that he was starting the same morning for Lichfield.[2]

A wide opinion has prevailed in the past, that confessions of conscience-stricken monks and nuns exist in abundance. Upon these, it has been thought, the chief part of the commissioners' reports are based. This notion is altogether false. As far as can be ascertained, no such confessions or self-accusations are in existence.[3] It is true that the king declared to the Lincolnshire rebels that "there be no houses suppressed where God was well served, but where vice, mischief, and abomination of living was used, and that doth well appear by their *own confession, subscribed with their own hands*, in the time of their visitations."[4] There is absolutely no record of any such self-accusations subscribed by the offenders. Moreover, the letters of the visitors and their *compertes* prove incontestably that they did not base their charges upon any such confessions.

There are, it is true, one or two so-called "confessions" existing. But these belong to a subsequent period, and were made when the religious were being compelled to

---

[1] *Calendar*, x. Pref. xliv.

[2] Wright, 93: "This morning we depart towards Lichfield church," &c., "and from thence," &c. For other examples of the rapidity of the visitors' progress, see Wright, 72, and Layton's letters as to Sussex, Somerset, &c., in R. O. Crum. Corr., vol. xx.

[3] Wright, in his preface to the Camden Society Volume, p. vi., says, "I think that even the various lists of the *confessions* of the monks and nuns of the several religious houses, entitled *comperta*, and preserved in manuscript, ought to be made public." To call the *comperta* by the name of *confessions* is to convey an entirely false and misleading idea to the readers of Mr. Wright's preface.

[4] Hall, "Union," &c. (written 1542), f. 229.

surrender their houses into the king's hands. Even these contain only general and vague self-accusations of "voluptuous living." They were evidently drawn up, not by the religious, but by the royal commissioners, who also appear not to have hesitated to sign the document with the names of the monks. Of these so-called confessions, the best known is that of the monks of St. Andrew's, Northampton.[1] On the face of it, this lengthy document was composed, not by the conscience-stricken monks, but by those who came to turn them out of their home and take possession of their property. When compared with another similar document from Westacre, it is seen to be merely one of a general type made use of by the commissioners.

It is well here to note, that in 1535 Layton had written from Northampton, where he was on his visitation:—"the prior now is a bachelor of divinity, a great husbond and a good clerk, and pity it is that ever he came there. If he were promoted to a better thing, and the king's grace would take it into his hands, so might he recover all the lands again which the prior shall never. In my return out of the North, I will attempt him so to do if it be your pleasure." Apparently the attempt was not made till later, when the so-called confession[2] was extracted from him and his community. What was thought of its real purport may be judged from the fact that pensions were arranged for all the religious. The prior, after having been pensioned,[3] was made first dean of the newly-created see of Peterborough. The history of this so-called "confession," in reality the concoction of Crumwell's agents, will speak for itself. It has often been quoted as one of the most damning pieces of evidence against the monastic institutions, and its reproduction has generally been accompanied with the insinuation that there are more of the same kind. As

---

[1] First printed by Weaver, pp. 106-110. It is a most verbose document, made in the presence of Legh and Layton. Fuller, "Church Hist.," ed. 1845, p. 398, gives the choice passages. It has been well dealt with by Canon Dixon.

[2] The "confession" (*Calendar*, xiii. (i.) No. 396) is dated March 1. We may note, however, that this is only a copy made apparently in the early part of the 17th century. The body and signatures are in the same handwriting. It may be added that the real surrender, as it appears enrolled on the Close Roll (Rot. Claus. 29 H. VIII., pars 2, m. 7), is a totally different document; being a surrender in the general form.

[3] R. O. Aug. Off. Misc. Bks., 232, f. 17.

far, however, as is known at present, this and its prototype of Westacre, composed and adapted to altered circumstances by the ingenuity of the same royal commissioners, are the only documents of the kind.

The *comperta* documents, therefore, cannot be considered as representing "confessions" of vicious life on the part of the monks. They are in reality only the biassed and, probably in many instances, baseless judgments of men who came to report evil. By far the larger number of charges contained in the "reports" are concerned with secret and personal vice, which could not have been easily matter of examination. The other accusations, in the *comperta* and letters of the king's visitors, refer some few to drunkenness, one or two to supposed theft, an insignificant number to unnatural crime, and the remainder to incontinence. Under this latter head, the total number of religious charged in all the known letters or reports bears a very small proportion to the entire body of religious at that time in England. In the *comperta* and letters, which report as to the monasteries of a considerable portion of England, scarcely 250 monks and nuns are named as guilty of incontinence.[1] In the same districts the religious must have numbered many thousands. Of these 250, more than a third part can be identified as having subsequently received pensions upon the dissolution of their houses, a fact which even Burnet would consider as disproving the charge in their regard.[2] Of the entire number of convents of women visited and reported upon by Layton and Legh in the North, they are able to relate very little amiss. Only some twenty-seven nuns in all are charged with vice, and of these, seventeen are known to have been afterwards pensioned. Further, in their whole visitation, extending over thirteen counties, they only report that some fifty men and two women are anxious to abandon the religious life, even under the restrictions imposed by Crumwell's injunctions. This latter fact would seem to show that in

---

[1] This number includes those named in the various MSS. *comperta*, Bale's printed portion, and the letters of the visitors.

[2] The difficulty of identifying the religious at this time is very considerable. They are variously described by their Christian, religious, or surnames, and often also by the name of their birthplace. Hence there is no doubt that a great number more really received pensions, but not under the same name as that by which they are entered in the *comperta*.

truth the monks and nuns were well content with their life and were not so desirous of freeing themselves from their obligations as is generally believed.

In the spring of 1536, or only a few months after the *comperta* were composed by Crumwell's agents, commissions were issued to re-examine the monasteries, with a view to the suppression of such as were under the annual value of £200. Besides this, the visitors were to report upon "the number of monks, and their lives and conversations." "Returns of the commissioners," writes Mr. Gairdner, "for a certain number of the monasteries in five several counties, are given in this volume, and it is remarkable that in these the characters given to the inmates are almost uniformly good. More remarkable still, in the return for Leicestershire, we find the inmates of Garendon and Gracedieu—two of the houses against which some of the worst *compertes* were found—reported to be of *good and virtuous* conversation. The country gentlemen who sat on the commission somehow came to a very different conclusion from that of Drs. Layton and Legh."[1] These country gentlemen, be it remarked, were "some of the leading men in each county." How the king appreciated this good report may be understood by the letter of one of the commissioners, George Gyffard, written on 19th June 1536, from the monastery of Garendon, whilst on this very tour of inspection. "And, sir," he says to Crumwell, "forasmuch as of late my fellows and I did write unto Mr. Chancellor of the Augmentations in favour of the abbey of St. James, and the nunnery of Catesby, in Northamptonshire, which letter he showed unto the king's highness in the favour of those houses, where the king's highness *was displeased*, as he said to my servant, Thomas Harper, saying that it was like that we *had received rewards which caused us to write as we did*, which might put me in fear to write. Notwithstanding, the sure knowledge that I have had always in your indifference, giveth me boldness to write to you in the favour of the house of

---

[1] *Calendar*, x. Pref. xlv. Since the publication of Mr. Gairdner's volume I was fortunate enough to discover several more reports of these commissioners in the Record Office. As they had been placed wrongly among the *Chantry Certificates* they had escaped the editor's notice altogether. It is sufficient here to say that they entirely bear out Mr. Gairdner's remarks upon the other documents he had before him as to the uniformly good character that is given to the religious in the houses visited.

Walstroppe. The governor thereof is a very good husbond for the house and well-beloved of all the inhabitants thereunto adjoining, a right honest man, having eight religious persons, being priests of right good conversation and living religiously, having such qualities of virtue, as we have not found the like in any place; for there is not one religious person there but that they can and do use either embroidering, writing books with very fair hand, making their own garments, carving, painting, or graving. The house without any scandal or evil fame, and stands in a waste ground, very solitary, keeping such hospitality that except by singular good provision it could not be maintained with half as much land more, as they may spend, such a number of the poor inhabitants nigh thereunto, daily relieved that we have not seen the like, having no more lands than they have. God be even my judge, that I write unto you the truth, and no otherwise to my knowledge, which very pity alone causes me to write."[1]

It has been pointed out that, besides the charges contained in the *comperta* of the visitors, the letters of Crumwell's agents also contain a variety of accusations against religious persons and houses. Some of these choice stories, reflecting on the character of the monastic establishments, have been told and retold by hostile writers, as typical illustrations of the natural tendency of the religious mode of life. One or two of the best known may now be examined. At the outset we may note that, like the rest of such charges, no evidence is offered in substantiation of their truth. No inquiry was apparently made, and no depositions of witnesses are forthcoming. As a rule, therefore, the stories have to be tested on their own merits, and usually they will be found to depend entirely on the ingenuity of the narrator.

An example very often given, which is supposed to be typical of the depravity prevailing among the monks, is that of the prior of the Crossed friars in London. This religious, "at the dissolution, the watchful emissaries of Crumwell caught *in flagranti delicto*, and down at once went the king's hammer upon the corrupt little brotherhood."[2]

[1] Wright, 136.
[2] Thornbury, *Old and New London*, vol. ii. p. 253. The story is also given in Burnet, ed. Pocock, i. p. 385.

This oft-told story is founded on a letter of one John Bartelot, to Thomas Crumwell.[1] The writer certainly says that he so caught the prior. In the first place, however, the circumstances are unlikely. The time, when the offence against good morals was said to have been committed, was eleven o'clock in the day on a Friday, in Lent. Then Bartelot himself admits that to keep him quiet the prior gave him £30, and promised him more "by his bill obligatory." This, as Mr. Wright concedes, "is not greatly" to the witness's credit.

Luckily however, the prior did not pay, and Bartelot summoned him before the Lord Chancellor. This judge, having heard the case, not only decided against the accuser, "making the premisses to be heinous robbery," but told him he deserved to be hanged. He further ordered him to refund the black-mail which he had already levied upon the unfortunate prior. This is absolutely all the evidence in existence, upon which so-called history has founded its accusation against the character of the prior of the London Crossed friars. As far as the facts speak for themselves, they are decidedly against the accuser. This judgment of the matter is somewhat sustained by the fact that the prior of this house "was reported by the visitors of the religious houses to lord Crumwell as a man of inoffensive life."[2]

Another story constantly repeated, and which has certainly not been allowed to suffer loss by repetition, affects the good name of the Premonstratensian abbey of Langdon in Kent.

This accusation is also connected in some measure with Crumwell's servant, John Bartelot, who was told by Chancellor Audley, that for his part in regard to the prior of the Crutched friars "he was worthy to be hanged." Layton, ever "so eloquent in accusations" according to his fellow-commissioner Legh, tells the story.[3] Froude declares, without the slightest grounds, that it was "the more ordinary experiences of the commissioners."[4] The letter describes how Layton skilfully caught that "dangerous,

---

[1] Wright, 59. The editor says: "His (Bartelot's) transaction with the prior is not greatly to his credit, and the chancellor appears to have formed no very unjust opinion of him."

[2] *Monasticon*, vi. p. 1586. Edmund Stretham was the name of the prior who, on April 17, 1534, subscribed to the royal supremacy.

[3] Wright, 75. Mr. Wright finds the story "singularly ludicrous."

[4] *History*, vol. ii. p. 425.

desperate, and hardy knave," the abbot of Langdon. The man Bartelot and other servants were left to watch the outer gates of the abbey house while Layton went to the door of the abbot's lodging. Not getting any answer to his knocking "saving the abbot's little dog that, within his door fast locked, bayed and barked," he broke it open with a pole-axe, found quite handy. He entered alone, but with his pole-axe, for fear of the abbot. Bartelot, guarding the outlets, caught a woman running away and took her to Layton, who, having examined her, sent her under her captor's charge to Dover. Layton does not say that the abbot was at his lodgings at all, but his letter adds: "I brought the holy father abbot to Canterbury, and here at Christchurch I will leave him in prison." A woman's dress was found, at least Layton says so, in the abbot's chest, which fact has been ingeniously rendered by Burnet, to serve his purpose, as: "in the abbot's coffer there was a habit for her, for she went for a young brother."[1]

Accepting the facts of the letter as they stand, what are they apart from insinuations, pleasantry and dressing up? That a woman was caught running away.[2] Also, if Layton is worthy of credit, that a female's dress was found in the "abbot's chest." The fact that some of Crumwell's own servants were actually in the house at the time, and yet "marvelled what fellow" it was who thus broke into it, looks suspicious. Moreover, both Dr. Layton and Crumwell had a motive in trying to defame the character of the religious, which appears at the close of this very letter. "*Now*," says the zealous visitor, "*it shall appear* to gentlemen of this country, and other the *commons* that ye shall not deprive or visit but upon substantial grounds. Surely I

---

[1] Burnet, i. p. 307. Layton in his letter only says:—"At last I found her apparel in the abbot's coffer." This gloss as to how the woman passed herself off is Burnet's own.

[2] "But for a conclusion his . . . gentlewoman bestirred her stumps towards her starting holes and there Bartlett, watching the pursuit, took the tender damoisel, and after I had examined her, to Dover there to the mayor to set her in some cage or prison for viij days." This is all the information vouchsafed. Layton is very circumstantial on accessories, very sober or reticent on the main point; he does not even say that the woman ran out of the "abbottes logeyng." Neither here nor hereafter does he so much as hint at what the examination elicited. The sequel of the story is told in the text; how far it agrees with the beginning as narrated in Layton's lightest, merriest vein, the reader can judge for himself.

suppose God himself put it in my mind thus suddenly to make a search at the beginning, because no canon appeared in my sight."

In a letter written the same night (October 23, 1535) from Canterbury, Layton, after describing the fire which took place at Christchurch on the night of his arrival, proceeds to speaks very ill of Dover, Folkestone, and Langdon. Although he gives the worst possible character to the abbot of the last-named monastery, nothing is said of the story of his capture, which he had reported shortly before. In place of this, another accusation is substituted against William Dare, the abbot who is called "the drunkenest knave living." The whole community are, in fact, included in one of Layton's sweeping charges of immorality. It is strange that there is not the least reference, even jocose, to the doctor's achievement the day previous, about which he had been so proud. Was it that, on reflection, he saw after all he had found out absolutely nothing upon which to found an accusation against the abbot? Did he hence desire to substitute another and a more hearsay charge against his character? At any rate his motive was the same, for he expressly warns his master to be "quick in taking the fruits" of the doomed abbey.[1]

A fortnight later, November 16, 1535, three commissioners attended at the chapter-house of Langdon to receive the surrender. These king's officers, although reporting badly of the abbot's administration, bring no graver charges against him. On the contrary, they recommend this man, whom Layton had described as most immoral and "the drunkenest knave living," for a pension.[2] This reward was granted him by the court of Augmentation for life, or until such time as he received a "fitting ecclesiastical benefice."[3] If Layton's accusations were true the abbot could have been got rid of without expense and without the scandal of proposing to place such a man in cure of souls. This fact, if fairly considered, should suffice to disprove Layton's insinuations and demolish the stock story founded on them.

Another charge against the character of a monk has been often repeated on the authority of the same Dr. Layton. This visitor, who could write the vilest accusations against

[1] *Calendar*, ix. No. 669.   [2] Wright, 89.
[3] R. O. Aug. Off. Misc. Bks., 232, f. 57.

a religious man and then add "it were too long to declare all things of him that I have heard, which I suppose are true,"[1] declares that the prior of Maiden Bradley, in Somerset, had six children. Further, that his sons were "tall men waiting on him," and that "the pope, considering his fragility, had given him license in writing *sub plumbo*," to discharge his conscience.[2] This story, so utterly improbable in itself, rests on no authority whatever, but the *ipse dixit* of the unblushing Layton. It is disposed of by the fact that the prior Richard Jennings was pensioned by the advice of the chancellor and court of Augmentation,[3] and subsequently became rector of Shipton Moyne, in Gloucestershire.

Something must be said in reference to accusations against the abbot of Wigmore, an abbey eight miles from Ludlow in Herefordshire. Of the long document in which the charges are made, Mr. Froude says:—"It is so singular that we print it as it is found—a genuine antique, fished up in perfect preservation out of the wreck of the old world."[4] The same author has made choice of this story as one of two specimens, which he believes completely justify Henry's measures against the monasteries. He goes into rhapsodies about this "flagrant case," which he declares to be "a choice specimen out of many" of an abbot "able to purchase with jewels stolen from his own convent a faculty to confer holy orders, though there is no evidence that he had been consecrated bishop," and to make £1000 by selling the exercise of his privilege. The charges are to be found in a letter to Crumwell from one of the canons of Wigmore, named John Lee. The articles are 29 in number, and give the worst possible character to the abbot. He had sold the jewels of the monastery to pay for the fees for his consecration. He took fees for ordination and acted as a bishop, on the strength of the papal bulls. He kept concubines and squandered money upon them. He was very malicious and wrathful, "not regarding what he saith or doth in his fury." He had murdered a man and his wife, who had purchased a corrody from the abbey, and had consented to another murder committed by his chaplain. This chaplain, it is added, is allowed to do what he likes, "to carry cross-bows,

[1] Wright, p. 48.   [2] *Ibid.*, p. 58.
[3] R. O. Aug. Office Mis. Bks., 244, No. 143. Original of grants.
[4] *Short Studies*, i. "Dissolution of Monasteries."

and to go fishing and hunting in the king's forests, parks and chases, but little or nothing serving the choir as other brethren do, neither corrected of the said abbot for any trespass he doth commit." Further, the abbot had not kept the injunctions given by Dr. Core from the king, and would have put the brother who denounced him into prison, had he not been prevented by the chapter. The writer of this strange document "will not name now" many acts of incontinence on the part of the abbot, "least it would offend your good lordship to read or hear the same." In a postscript he adds, "My good lord, there is in the said abbey, a cross of fine gold and precious stones, whereof one diamond was esteemed by Dr. Booth, of Hereford bishop, to be worth a hundred marks." In this is a piece of the true cross, which is used to be brought down to the church with lights and much reverence. "I fear least the abbot upon Sunday next, when he may come to the treasury will take away the said cross and break it and turn it to his use and many other precious jewels that be there." In conclusion John Lee declares that his articles are "true in substance," and that he is ready to prove them. He winds up by the suggestion, that Crumwell should appoint *him*, "or any man that will be indifferent and not corrupt, to sit at the said abbey" as his commissioner.

Much of this long document, and notably the accusation of murder, is absurd on the face of it and may be dismissed. For the rest, as no other evidence is forthcoming, it is necessary to fall back upon what is otherwise known of Wigmore and its abbot. The monastery had been regularly visited by the bishops of Hereford before its dissolution, and in the year 1518, the community placed the nomination of their superior in the hands of cardinal Wolsey. After due consideration, the cardinal made choice of a canon regular of Bristol for the post. This was John Smarte, against whom these grave charges were afterwards brought by his subject, John Lee. At this date, he was declared as publicly known to possess the qualities necessary for a worthy superior.[1] Smarte was a scholar of Oxford and a bachelor of divinity at that university.[2] After his election he was much esteemed

---

[1] Reg. Booth, Ep. Heref., f. 24.
[2] Boase, *Reg. Univ. Oxon.*, i. p. 53. "Smarte or Smerte, John, Reg. Can.," B.A. 1508, B.D. 1515.

by the bishop of Hereford, Charles Booth, who wrote to the pope asking that the abbot might be made his suffragan.¹ This request was granted. He became titular bishop of Pavada, and acted as coadjutor of Hereford from 1526 to 1535. During the first six years of this period, he also performed the same office for the diocese of Worcester.² In this capacity, as suffragan bishop, abbot John Smarte held the usual diocesan ordinations, some of which (notably that in the first year of his office, 1526) were very large. The fact that the bishop of the diocese had asked for this abbot's nomination as his suffragan, disposes of the insinuations which Mr. Froude makes, as to his having purchased a "faculty" to ordain, "though there is no evidence that he had been consecrated bishop."

The accusations brought against his character by the letter of John Lee are more difficult to meet. His appointment by Wolsey as abbot, and the good opinion certainly formed of him by bishop Booth, are considerable evidence that Lee's charge was malicious and false. Fortunately, however, a visitation of Wigmore was ordered by bishop Edward Fox in the autumn of 1536, and his injunctions were issued on 26th March of the following year.³ As these orders follow closely the lines of the charges in Lee's letter, it is difficult to resist the conclusion that this exceptional visitation was ordered, in consequence of the canon's complaints.⁴ Whether this be so or not, we have in the injunctions for Wigmore, entered in the register of bishop Fox, issued in the spring of 1537, an independent judgment about the state of the abbey and the character of its superior. As to the charges of incontinence against him, Dr. Hugh Coren or Curwen, the vicar general, who held the visitation, appears to have reported mere imprudence on his part. The bishop only enjoins him to avoid being too much with women. That no case had been proved against him, however, appears tolerably certain from the insertion of the clause "if there be any" (*si quæ sint*) into the body of this injunction. He is ordered to let the brethren know "whether he has redeemed the jewels which he has pledged," and to restore them to the monastery. The usual regulations are

---

[1] Reg. Booth, f. 9.   [2] Stubbs, *Registrum*, p. 147.
[3] Reg. Fox, Ep. Heref., f. 21.
[4] *Ibid.*, f. 8, says the king had directed these visitations by his letters.

made for the yearly accounts and for the custody of the monastic deeds. The abbot is warned to correct his subjects with mildness and not too roughly, and the subjects on their part are warned to be obedient in all things to their abbot, and to look upon the virtue of chastity as the gem of the religious life. Finally the abbot's chaplain, Richard Cubley, about whom Lee had complained in his letter, is ordered to attend the choir like the rest of the canons and to desist from hunting and other unmonastic occupations. Thus, after a careful examination, little appears against the character of Wigmore and its abbot, John Smarte. The visitation really discredits the charges and base insinuations of John Lee. If this examination followed upon his complaints to Crumwell, as we have every reason to suppose, then the injunctions must fairly be considered as a verdict in favour of the abbot. In any case, we have in this record a picture of the state of the monastery and a judgment on the character of its superior altogether at variance with that presented in the letter of the discontented canon.

In concluding this brief examination of the grave accusations made against the monasteries, it may be useful to point out how strong is the *negative* evidence, as it may be called, in favour of the general moral tone of these establishments, as against the biassed accounts of Henry's royal commissioners. The historian Strype says, that special injunctions were sent to the bishops by Crumwell to watch narrowly into the conduct of "the abbeys and religious houses that especially stuck to the pope and kept as much as they could to the old superstitions."[1] In spite, however, of these special instructions, although we have numerous letters[2] from the bishops of the time, there is hardly an expression that can be construed into a condemnation of the moral lives of the monks. This negative testimony is all the more important, as many of these ecclesiastics were known opponents of this method of life. The old and contemporary chroniclers—Hall, Stow, Grafton, Holinshed and Fabian—are also singularly silent as to the pretended vicious lives practised in the cloisters of England. And Wriothesley, although clearly in favour of the cause of the

---

[1] *Eccl. Mems.*, i. 1, p. 333 (ed. 1822).
[2] An immense number of letters are in existence from Cranmer, Stokesley, Latimer, Rowland Lee, and others.

reformers, makes no mention whatever of these charges in his chronicle. He says that in 1535 the lesser monasteries were granted to the king, "to the augmentation of the crown," and adds: "It was pity the great lamentation that the poor people made for them, for there was great hospitality kept amongst them, and, as it was reported, ten thousand persons had lost their living by the putting down of them, which was great pity."[1]

Lord Herbert declares that bishop Latimer was anxious to preserve some of the monasteries—at least two or three in each diocese. In bishop Latimer's arguments with king Henry VIII. against purgatory, he concludes thus:—"The founding of monasteries argueth purgatory to be, so the putting them down argueth it not to be. What uncharitableness and cruelty seemeth it to be to destroy monasteries if purgatory be? Now, it seemeth not convenient the act to preach one thing, and the pulpit another clear contrary."[2] This reference must have been to the act for the suppression of lesser monasteries (1535), because, at the date of the fall of the greater houses, Latimer was not in such circumstances as would allow him to controvert with Henry.

Cranmer also, who with others narrowly watched the monks of Christchurch, Canterbury, admitted that there was nothing whatever against their moral character. Many of these same monks became the first secular canons of the cathedral, although they were amongst those most seriously accused by the visitors. Moreover, Richard, the suffragan of Dover, who was much employed on the work of suppression and has left many letters, particularly as to the friars, makes no charge of so serious a nature as those brought by Layton, Legh and Ap Rice. This may be accounted for, possibly, because his mission was rather to suppress than to find motives for the work. As he was occupied in this, after parliament had given over the smaller

---

[1] *Wriothesley's Chronicle* (Camd. Soc.). This is a contemporary London chronicle, and its negative evidence is very valuable. Had there been much talk about the immoral lives of the monks, it is reasonable to suppose the author would have made some note of it. He had every means of knowing, as he had an official position among the heralds, having become Windsor herald on Christmas day, 1534. He was attached chiefly to the person of chancellor Audley. See editor's remarks, p. 274. It is also very remarkable that no mention of the great outcry against the monasteries is to be found in the letters of the well-informed Chapuys or of other writers at this time.

[2] Printed by Strype, *Eccl. Mems.*, i. p. 388.

houses to the king, there was no need for furnishing such evidence.

*In fact, there is very little evidence that the gross insinuations against the character of monks and nuns in general, and special charges such as were brought against a small proportion, by such men as Layton, Legh and Ap Rice, were either made or believed in by others. *There is, on the other hand, most positive evidence, to which subsequent reference will be made, of the esteem and respect in which many religious houses were held by those who had best reason to know their true character. If we add to this the singular silence as to such charges, maintained by contemporary chroniclers, we are led to the conclusion that these terrible accusations were not much insisted upon, even in the parliament which passed the bill of suppression. More than one authority clearly states that the chief motive, which actuated the servile parliament in passing the measure, was the hope that the property thus appropriated from the church and poor, would be a means of freeing them for some time from the constant and importunate exactions of the king. It was hoped that the people would thus be indirectly benefited. This conclusion is much strengthened by the fact that within a very short time after the first dissolutions it was proposed to present to the king a petition from the lords and commons, asking him to stay any further suppressions. The ground for this request was, that so far from the destruction of the religious houses doing good to the country, as had been promised, the measure had proved an unmitigated evil. "And albeit," this remarkable document runs, "most dread sovereign lord, at the making of the said act it was thought that we might full well thereby have advanced the revenues of your noble crown without prejudice or hurt of any your poor subjects, or of the commonwealth of this your realm; *yet nevertheless* they perceive those houses already suppressed showeth plainly unto us, that a great hurt and decay is thereby come and hereafter shall come to this your realm, and great impoverishing of many your poor obedient subjects for lack of hospitality and good householding, which was wont in them to be kept to the great relief of the poor people of all the country adjoining to the said monasteries, besides the maintenance of many servants, husbandmen and labourers that daily were kept, in the said religious houses." Then, after some suggested regulations for the property of monasteries already suppressed, the proposed petition asks that all monasteries, of whatever kind they were beyond the Trent, and which, although falling under the act, had not as yet been suppressed, "shall stand still and abide in their own strength and foundation, and the act aforesaid of suppression of religious houses that were not above the yearly value of £200 lands, to be frustrate as concerning them and of no effect."[1]

Such a petition would be impossible, if the chief cause of the suppression had been the hopeless state of immorality in which the monasteries were sunk. The truth is, that money was the object which Henry and his minister had in view. This is emphasized by the fact that many monasteries were allowed to purchase temporary continuance by heavy payments to the royal exchequer. As for the charges brought by Layton and his fellows, they are unsupported by any other evidence but their bare assertions. They are worth so much and no more.

[1] B. Mus. Cott. MS. Cleop., E. iv. f. 215 (182).

CHAPTER VIII

Thomas Crumwell, the King's Vicar General

FIRST and chief among the accusers of the monks must be reckoned Thomas Crumwell. His was the mind which first conceived the idea of attacking the papal power in its strongholds and procuring thereby the wealth to gratify the covetousness of the king. Perhaps no actor on the stage of history has ever possessed greater powers, personal and political. Certainly, no single minister in England ever exercised such extensive authority, none ever rose so rapidly, and no one has left behind him a name covered with greater infamy and disgrace.

Thomas Crumwell, so far as his early history is known, was born of parents in poor circumstances. His father is said to have been a blacksmith at Putney, and Thomas in his youth seems to have been apprenticed to a fuller named Wix.[1] He was not contented, however, to remain long in this humble state. As the gossip in the day of his power went, he had in youth been thrown into prison for some offence, and had been subsequently obliged to leave the country.[2] At an early period, we find him, or some one of his name, in the service of the Marchioness of Dorset, and all accounts agree in saying, that he passed a portion of his youth as a common soldier in Italy. He once told Cranmer that he had been at one time a "ruffian," and some authorities seem to think it not improbable that he was present

---

[1] B. Mus., Sloane MS., 2495, f. 8.

[2] *Calendar*, ix. No. 862. Chapuys to Granvelle, London, Nov. 21, 1535 (printed in Mr. Froude's ed. of "Thomas' Pilgrim," p. 106). "Sir Master Crumwell, of whose origin and antecedents your secretary, Antoine, tells me you desire to be informed, is the son of a poor blacksmith, who lived in a small village four miles from this place, and is buried in a common grave in the parish churchyard. His uncle whom he has enriched was cook to the late archbishop of Canterbury (Warham). The said Crumwell in his youth was an ill-conditioned scapegrace. For some offence he was thrown into prison, and was obliged afterwards to leave the country."

when Rome was assaulted and taken in May 1527, by the imperial army, under the Duke of Bourbon. Among those who took part in the sack of the city there is said to have been [1] "an Englishman of low, vicious habits and infidel principles, who afterwards became of terrific importance to the church of England." This is thought by some to have been Thomas Crumwell.[2]

From his own letters he appears to have been settled as a merchant at Middelborough in 1512, for in that year he employs a correspondent, in Antwerp, to buy an iron chest of considerable size, in which presumably to keep his money. Before 1520, Crumwell had added the occupation of scrivener to his other avocations, and was also engaged in accommodating members of the aristocracy with loans of considerable amount. This money-lending business appears to have always possessed special attractions for him, as he is found lending large sums of money, even when at the very height of his power.[3] In 1523, Crumwell entered parliament; and though, apparently, he did not take any very prominent part in the debates, it is possible that he was of service to Wolsey in obtaining the parliamentary grant of a very large subsidy voted in that year. In 1525 he was living near Austin Friars, in London, and engaged as a merchant, lawyer and money lender.[4] Amongst those who were obliged to have recourse to him in this latter capacity, was lord Henry Percy, then attached to the court of the cardinal of York—a court hardly less magnificent and costly than that of the king himself. By this client Crumwell may well have been introduced to the notice of Wolsey.

Whilst in the cardinal's service,[5] Crumwell was chiefly employed in the work of suppressing the monasteries, which had been doomed to extinction for the purpose of endowing the cardinal's colleges at Oxford and Ipswich. In this occupation he acquired a knowledge of the monastic houses, and of the methods useful to employ in seizing the property of

---

[1] Maitland, *The Reformation*, p. 228. The author thinks that if Crumwell was present it probably was in the service of Wolsey, and not at this time as a soldier.
[2] Lord Herbert, in Foss, *Judges of England*, vol. v. p. 147.
[3] R. O. Chapter House Books, B½.
[4] *Calendar*, iv. Nos. 1385, 1586, 1620, &c.
[5] Cardinal Pole says, that when Crumwell was in the service of Wolsey, he strongly recommended to him (Pole) the works and principles of Machiavelli, especially those contained in "Il Principe." Ellis, *Orig. Letters*, 3rd Series, iii. 278.

the monks.[1] This work may very possibly have suggested to his mind the subsequent wholesale confiscations. It certainly gave him opportunities, of which he was not slow to profit, to promote his own advancement and interests. Cardinal Pole declares that these violent suppressions, carried out under cover of authority from the pope, obtained by the masterful influence and diplomacy of Wolsey, proved a fortune to Crumwell. From this time his worldly prospects, as Pole says, were secured. "He (Crumwell) was certainly born," he adds, "with an aptitude for ruin and destruction."[2]

On Wolsey's disgrace, Crumwell's first thought was how to save himself from being involved in his master's ruin. He had reason to fear the consequences of acts which, although perpetrated in the cardinal's service and under cover of his authority, had placed him within reach of the law. Now that the strong arm which had shielded him was paralyzed, the popular resentment against him did not fear to make itself heard. In defending his patron in parliament it is possible that he may have been actuated by sincere motives of gratitude, but in defeating the bill of attainder, he was in reality only making the best possible defence for himself. To have allowed the bill to pass, would practically have been to acquiesce in his own ruin. The charges against the cardinal were founded, at least partially, on the grave injustice done in the work of suppressing certain monasteries. And it was on this very work that Crumwell had been specially employed and had earned for himself unenviable notoriety. His own, as well as his master's, safety consequently demanded the defeat of the attainder. "I have read," says dean Hook, "with attention the letters addressed to Crumwell by Wolsey, and I think that any one who does so will come to the conclusion that Wolsey had no confidence in Crumwell's sincerity; and that Crumwell did not treat his fallen master with consideration and kindness. He was obliged to defend him, for he had no other course to pursue."[3]

---

[1] R. O. Exchequer Q. R. Treasury of Receipt, $\frac{49}{29}$. The sales by T. Crumwell of Begham Priory, Kent, at this time. It might well be taken for an account of a suppression ten years later.

[2] "Apologia," *Epist. collectio*, vol. i. p. 127.

[3] *Lives of Archbishops*, vi. p. 128.

Moreover, the very fact of Crumwell's attitude towards the measure, at a time when no opposition to the king's wishes and intentions would be tolerated, shows that some secret understanding had been arrived at between the monarch and his future adviser.[1] The account given by Cavendish of the way Crumwell left the cardinal, proves that the former knew he was in great danger, and that he had the intention of trying to escape from the difficulties which beset him, by treating at once with the court. In no other way can the scene described by Cavendish be explained. Thomas Crumwell evidently thought it high time he should look to his own affairs. More especially was this necessary as there seems to have been a report current which affected him most seriously. When Wolsey's case was settled, the people said, then would come Crumwell's turn for punishment. In fact, the popular voice had already consigned him to the gallows. Cardinal Pole, who was in London at the time, asserts that he himself heard the expression of popular exultation over the expected punishment of one considered so well deserving of death. He declares also, that it was asserted Crumwell had already been arrested and cast into prison."[2]

It is not difficult to imagine what means Thomas Crumwell took to defeat the popular clamour for his punishment, and to change the king's views regarding him. Henry no doubt saw in him one who was likely to be a useful instrument in his hands. Something more, however, was needed to alter the king's known contempt and distrust into immediate reliance on his services, and to establish a secret understanding between them. It has appeared probable to some that Crumwell, at his interview with Henry, suggested a solution of the king's difficulties with the pope. It was nothing less than the entire withdrawal of England from spiritual allegiance to the Holy

---

[1] Dr. Pegge says, "The rejection of the bill may be justly ascribed to the relentment of the king, for Crumwell would not have dared to oppose it, nor the commons to reject it, had they not received an intimation that such was the royal will.—Singer, *Cavendish*, i. p. 209 note.

[2] "Apologia Reg. Poli. ad Carolum V. Cæsarem," *Epist. Collectio*, Brixiæ, 1744, vol. i. p. 126. "Ipse (Crumwell) omnium voce, qui aliquid de eo intellexerant ad supplicium posceretur. Hoc enim affirmare possum, qui Londini tum adfui et voces audivi, adeo etiam ut per civitatem universam rumor circumferretur, eum in carcerem fuisse detrusum, et propediem productum iri ad supplicium."

See, and the declaration that the king was henceforth to be considered the head of the Church in England. Others have imagined that he captivated the king by showing him how easily he might lay his hand on the riches of the Church and the broad lands of the monastic bodies. Whatever the motive or the inducement, it seems certain that at this interview Crumwell obtained the king's approval to the defeat of the "bill of attainder" and to the policy of proceeding against the cardinal under the statute of "præmunire." In this way the king would still possess himself of the fallen minister's property. Indeed, by this method Henry would be the gainer. For not only could the cardinal be brought under the law for acting as legate of the pope, but the entire body of clergy also. In fact, all who had admitted these legatine powers were involved in the meshes of the legal statute and were in danger of forfeiting goods and chattels to the king's majesty.

That Henry had granted his royal license for the cardinal to act as he had done, is unquestioned. The obvious way, therefore, of meeting the charge was by the production of the royal permission under the great seal. When the commissioners came to ask him what answer he could make to the indictment, Wolsey replied: "The King's highness knoweth right well whether I have offended his majesty and his laws or no, in using of my prerogative legatine for the which ye have indicted me. Notwithstanding, I have the king's license in my coffers, under his hand and broad seal, for exercising and using the authority thereof in the largest wise within his majesty's dominions, the which remaineth now in the hands of my enemies."[1] Not having the document, Wolsey threw himself on the king's mercy. By what means did this license under the great seal find its way "into the hands" of the cardinal's enemies? Was it the peace-offering of Crumwell to Henry? An early account of the transaction, which clearly took place between the king and the servant of the fallen cardinal, declares that the price paid by Crumwell to secure his own safety and the king's favour, was the theft of this document from the private papers of his master, to which he had access. "And so like an unfaithful and traitorous servant

---

[1] Singer, *Cavendish*, i. p. 209.

the said Crumwell stole from his master and delivered to the king."[1]

Crumwell's rise after this was rapid and unchecked as long as he served Henry's purpose. "It more resembled," writes Lord Campbell, "that of a slave at once constituted grand vizier in an Eastern despotism than of a minister of state promoted in a constitutional government where law, usage, and public opinion check the capricious humours of the sovereign."[2] He became successively master of the king's jewels, chancellor of the Exchequer for life, master of the Rolls, and secretary of state, the king's vicar general in matters ecclesiastical, lord privy seal, dean of Wells, and great chamberlain.[3] In 1533 he was knighted, and three years later became a peer of the realm under the title of Earl of Essex. By virtue of his commission as vicar general of the king, who had according to act of parliament taken on himself "all spiritual and temporal jurisdiction in the Church of England," he had power to "exercise all spiritual jurisdiction belonging to the king for the due administration of justice in all cases touching ecclesiastical jurisdiction, and godly reformation, and redress of errors, heresies, and abuses in the said church."

The position occupied by Thomas Crumwell during the years of his power is unique in English history. As vicegerent and vicar general he was placed above the archbishops and bishops, even in convocation and other strictly ecclesiastical assemblies.[4] Hardly was the venerable Fisher

[1] B. Mus. Arundel MS., 152, f. 426.
[2] *Lives of the English Chancellors*, i. p. 600; *Ibid.*, p. 230 *et seq.*
[3] Master of king's jewels, 1532; chancellor of Exchequer and knighted, 1533; master of Rolls, vicar general and secretary of state, 1534; lord privy seal and a peer of the realm, July, 1536; vicegerent in ecclesiastical causes, 1536; dean of Wells, 1537; great chamberlain, 1539.
[4] In a curious little volume by Alexander Alane, Scot., *Of the auctorite of the word of God agaynst the Bisshop of London* (1542), the author gives an account of one of the meetings which Crumwell held as vicar general. The following quotation will be of interest. The writer says: "I did mete bi chance in the streate the right excellent Lord Crumwell, going unto the parliament howse, in the yeare 1537. He when he sawe me, called me unto him and toke me with him to the parliament howse to Westmynster, where we fownd all the bisshops gathered together. Unto whom as he went and toke me with him, all the bisshops and prelates did rise up and did obeisance unto him as to their Vicar General, and after he had saluted them he sate him down in the highest place, and right against hym sate the archbishop of Cantorbery, after hym the archbisshop of Yorke and then London, Lincoln, &c.... Than the Lord Crumwell, being Vicar General of the realme, Lord of the Prevy Seale

executed, than he was elected his successor as chancellor of the University of Cambridge.[1] Though a layman, he did not scruple to hold the deanery of Wells and other ecclesiastical benefices.[2] In parliament, he took precedence of the nobility of every rank by virtue of his ecclesiastical title of king's vicar general.

Armed, as he was, with supreme and absolute power, both civil and spiritual, he succeeded in establishing and maintaining a complete reign of terror in England. How he used his authority for the appointment of other agents of destruction the foregoing pages have partly told. How they together accomplished their work, every ruined abbey and every desecrated shrine in England proclaims. Every pauper is made to feel, by the cold charity extended to him in the poorhouses of the country, how cruelly he was robbed of his inheritance, by the destruction and spoliation of the monastic houses of the land.

It is by no means easy to realise the completeness of the autocratic power which was placed by the king in Crumwell's hands at this time, and which he used unscrupulously to crush all opposition to his schemes, for the overthrow of the Church and the seizure of its revenues. His agents and spies were everywhere, and the most secret conversations were reported to him. The abbot in the midst of his community could not reckon upon his word being safe from the prying ears of the minister's agents. The sayings of a religious in the "shaving house" or the "frater" might be, and often were, repeated and distorted to his injury. The preacher had his sermons commented upon, and the conversations of noblemen at table were often carried to Crumwell. The mass of his correspondence that still remains, and the private notes for his "remembrances," prove conclusively that nothing was too trivial for him to inquire into. He was ever anxiously watching, in order to guard against any possible interference with his plans, and to entrap others whom he had reason to fear.

Dean Hook gives a picture of the times when he writes,

and chefe secret counceler unto the king, turned himself to the bisshops and sayd, 'Right Reverend fathers in Christ,'" &c. &c. (Ellis, *Orig. Letters*, 3rd Ser., iii. p. 196).

[1] *Calendar*, ix. No. 208 (Aug. 30, 1535).

[2] Record Off., Chapter H. Books, B. ⅜, *eg.*, April 2nd, 30 H. VIII. "Item. Mr. Gostwyke for the first fruits of my lord's divers benefices." *Ibid.* "29th. The tenths for deanery of Wells."

that "in every county and village, almost in every homestead, he had a secret force of informers and spies. They depended on the patronage of the vicegerent, who, generous and despotic, could give as well as take away. In the enthusiasm of their selfish loyalty they were on the watch for traitors, and in the well-paid piety of their hearts they had a terrible dread of superstition."[1] Every modern notion of justice, or of the certainty of fair and honest trials, must be altogether laid aside in regard to the charges and convictions of this period of our national history. Crumwell was on some occasions " prosecutor, judge and jury." For a word of disapproval about the king or his minister, for a jest or slighting remark at their expense, the offender might find himself summoned before the magistrates to answer for his offence. The accused and his accusers probably never met face to face. Cases of serious import, often of life and death, were decided on the depositions of men whose interest it was to obtain convictions. Words spoken against Crumwell, or in condemnation of a tyranny subversive of the first principles of freedom, were construed into treason against the king and the state. Even suspected persons, against whom no case could be made out, might be summoned to have the oath of supremacy tendered to them. Their houses could be ransacked for evidence of disaffection, and they themselves brought before the council in London, to be transferred untried or unconvicted, if thought to be obstinate or otherwise obnoxious, to the Marshalsea, the Tower, or Newgate.

Among the letters to Crumwell there is one from lord William Howard, who writes to his master, saying, "I hear it is your pleasure that I should go into the country to hearken if there be any ill-disposed people in those parts that would talk or be busy any way."[2] Another correspondent recommends for the service of Crumwell an informer against religious persons.[3]

The libraries of monasteries were ransacked for evidence of opposition to the new state of affairs, and even the cherished store of pious books belonging to the country priest—his service books and his very manuals of piety—were overhauled to search out proofs of his clinging to the faith and practice of his fathers. From Bath abbey, for

---

[1] *Lives of Archbishops*, vi. p. 98.   [2] *Calendar*, xi. No. 599.
[3] B. Mus. Cott. MS. Cleop., E. iv. 127 (106).

example, the zealous doctor Layton writes: "Ye shall herewith receive a book of Our Lady's miracles well able to match the Canterbury tales. Such a book of dreams as ye never saw, which I found in the library."[1] Another of Crumwell's agents, a certain "Ralph Lane, junior," reports that according to his master's commands he went after "the books of one Sir Thomas Cantwell, parson of Hardwick . . . which had been brought to a poor man's house in Whitchurch." Having examined them, he selected and forwarded to his employer five volumes "belonging to the said parson, whereof three are entitled *Homeliari Johis Echii*, being all three dated A.D. 1438; one book of the life of *St. Thomas Becket*, and a missal wherein is the word *papa* 'throughoutly uncorrected.'"[2]

Another informer of a different class, William Waldegrave, writes: "There is a chaplain of my lady Waldegrave, my grandam, which is a papist and causes (those) here to hold off from the truth, hath in his mass book daily this Thomas Beckett's name with all his pestiferious collects."[3] So also the curate of Wrington, Somerset, "will not abrogate the name of Thomas Becket." This was taken in all cases as a certain sign of wrong-headed obstinacy, and an intention to resist the king's changes. The monks of Christchurch, Canterbury, got into trouble for singing the old *domnum apostolicum* in their litanies, and the priest who sang high mass was reported for keeping the pope's name in the Canon.

All classes of society throughout the country were made to feel, that they were subjected to the omnipotent will of Thomas Crumwell and to the petty tyranny of those, who thought to win his favour by proving that his power was above all law and justice.[4] When the chapel of Our Lady of

---

[1] *Calendar*, ix. No. 42.

[2] R. O. Crum. Corr., xix, No. 20. See also 21, where the library of Dr. Lussh, the vicar of Aylesbury, is searched. Also xliv. 35, where the prior of Twynham is ordered to search for certain books.

[3] *Calendar*, xiii. No. 1179.

[4] Foxe, v. p. 896, ed. 1846, gives an instance of this. "Hereunto also pertaineth the example of friar Bartley, who wearing still his friar's cowl after the suppression of religious houses, Crumwell, coming into Paul's churchyard and espying him in Rheines shop, 'Yea,' said he, 'will not that cowl of yours be left off yet? And, if I hear by one o'clock that this apparel be not changed, thou shalt be hanged immediately for example of all others.'" Mr. Gairdner (*Calendar*, xiii. (ii) preface, p. viii.) points out that this "friar Bartley" was in

Walsingham had been despoiled by the king's commissioners and the image taken away, a report got noised abroad of some grace or favour granted at the old shrine. Sir Roger Townsend went there to find out the author of the report, which might remind the people of their old attachment to this place of pilgrimage, and so beget trouble. In a letter written to Crumwell on January 20th he thus describes the result of his visit :—

"There was a poor woman of Wells beside Walsingham that imagined a false tale. . . And upon the trial thereof by my examination from one person to another to the number of six persons, and at last came to her that she was the reporter thereof, and to be the very author of the same as far as my conscience and perceiving could lead me. I committed her, therefore, to the ward of the constables of Walsingham. The next day after, being market day there, I caused her to be set in the stocks in the morning,[1] and about nine of the clock, when the said market was fullest of people, with a paper set about her head, written with these words upon the same, '*a reporter of false tales*,' was set in a cart and so carried about the marketsted and other streets of the town, staying in divers places where most people assembled, young people and boys of the town casting snowballs at her. This done and executed, she was brought to the stocks again, and there set till the market was ended. This was her penance, for I *knew no law* otherwise to punish her but *my discretion*, trusting it shall be a warning to other light persons in such wise to order themselves. Howbeit I cannot but perceive that the said image is not yet out of some of their heads."[2]

A Worcester man named Thomas Emans, servant to Mr. Evans, got into difficulties for blaming the spoliation of the shrine of Our Lady of Worcester. He was tried by a mixed commission, headed by Latimer, the bishop of the city. It was proved against him that he had come to the church, and leaning on the shoulder of one Roger Cromps,

---

reality the celebrated Alexander Barclay, the poet and translator of Sebastian Brandt's *Ship of Fools*. It is probable that the incident here referred to took place in August or September 1538. Barclay was hostile to the royal theology, and is complained of as one who "doth much hurt in Cornwall and Devonshire both with open preaching and private communications."

[1] Note that it was in the depth of winter and snow on the ground, as will be seen.
[2] Ellis, *Orig. Lett.*, 3rd Ser. iii. p. 162.

had said:—"'Lady, art thou stript now; I have seen the day that as clean men hath been stript at a pair of gallows, as were they that stript thee.' Then he entered into the chapel" and "knelt down, saying his Pater and Ave, and kissed the image and turned to the people and said 'though Our Lady's coat and her jewells be taken away from her, the similitude is no worse to pray unto having sorrow, than it was before.'" The depositions carry on the story of this bold and turbulent fellow, who confessed to the charge made against him, no further than his committal to safe custody.[1]

It is impossible to peruse the records of these years of Crumwell's supremacy without feeling deeply, that even a pretence of justice and fair dealing was little thought of, that prisoners were left to languish untried in the gaols of the country, and to die in numbers from pestilence,[2] which was dignified on the public rolls into "a visitation of divine providence." The long lists of those who were each term called upon to find security for their good behaviour or convicted of assembling for riotous purposes, are sufficient proofs of the efforts made to extinguish the last remnants of a struggle for freedom from the masterful rule of Crumwell and his creatures.

We may judge, from an instance recorded by the historian Stow, that at the height of his fame the all-powerful minister was not less arbitrary as a man, than as the agent of a despotic king's will. In his "Survey of London" Stow says:—"On the south side and at the west end of this church" (Augustine friars in London) "many fair houses are builded, namely, in Throgmorton Street one very large and spacious, builded in the place of old and small tenements by Thomas Cromwell, master of the rolls, &c. . . This house being finished, and having some reasonable plot of ground left for a garden, he caused the pales of the garden adjoining to the north part thereof on a sudden to be taken down, twenty-two foot to be measured forth right into the north of every man's ground, a line there to be drawn, a trench to be cast, a foundation laid and a high brick wall to be builded. My father had a

---

[1] *Calendar*, xii. No. 587. The offence was committed on the eve of the feast of the Assumption, 1537. The examination took place on the 19th of August.
[2] See the lists, twelve and twenty at a time, on the "Controlment Rolls" for these years.

garden there, and a house standing close to his south pale, this house they loosed from the ground and bare upon rollers into my father's garden twenty-two foot, ere my father heard thereof, no warning was given him, nor other answer, when he spake to the surveyors of that work, but that their master Sir Thomas commanded them so to do; no man durst go to argue the matter, but each man lost his ground. My father paid his whole rent, which was six shillings and eight pence, for that half which was left. Thus much of mine own knowledge have I thought good to note, that the sudden rising of some men causeth them to forget themselves. The company of the drapers in London bought this house, and now the same is their common hall."[1]

It is impossible to read the numerous letters addressed to Thomas Crumwell and his instructions to his agents during the period of the suppression of the monasteries, and to credit him with even honesty in regard to his dealings with them. Although their destruction was a foregone conclusion, and the royal commissioners were fully instructed in their master's purpose, he bids them expressly repudiate any such intention on the part of the king. Doctor Layton writes from Norfolk to his master, that he has done his best to stop the rumour that the monasteries are all to go down; that he has told the monks and their neighbours that such a report is a slander on the king's majesty, and adds that he "now understands that your commandment therefore given me in your gallery was much more weighty, than I at the time judged or supposed or would have believed if I had not seen the very experience thereof."[2] The commandment was evidently intended to prevent the loss of plate or valuables got rid of by the monks, in view of the threatened seizure of their property, by falsely declaring that the king had no such designs of destruction.[3]

During the eight years that Crumwell ruled England the plunder he amassed by public and private spoliation was

[1] Stow, *Survey of London*, ed. 1602, p. 180. Foxe has recorded other instances of Crumwell's arbitrary mode of acting.
[2] *Calendar*, xiii. (i), No. 102.
[3] The same declaration that the king had no intention of suppressing the monasteries that remained, and that he " would not in any wise interrupt you in your state and kind of living," is made in the draft of a letter from the king to reassure the monasteries, probably in Crumwell's handwriting. B. Mus Cleop. E. iv. fol. 86.

immense. The only policy possible for the monastic bodies was one of attempted conciliation. By liberal donations, presents and bribes to their supreme governor, they hoped to buy off the evil day. Demands for leases, grants and pensions, were made on the monasteries by Crumwell, or in his name, without hesitation or consideration. Generally what was asked was at once granted. The monks had no option, except the prospect of involving their houses in greater difficulties by refusal. Sometimes they pleaded earnestly to be allowed to say no, when some farm or pension was asked, that was necessary to support their very existence or to maintain the poor who depended on them.

The account book[1] of Crumwell's steward, Thomas Avery, shows that large sums of money came to him by way of presents from all manner of persons, ecclesiastical and lay. Gifts of £10 and £20, for the new year, frequently appear in its pages. Archbishops, bishops, abbots, and priors, nobles and commoners, officials and unknown laymen, towns, colleges and cathedral chapters, all sent in their fees and new year donations, to propitiate the favour of the great man. Some of the amounts are startling. On the 1st January, 1539, for instance, the account book records money presents for the new year of £800 (more than £9000 of our present money). Fees of sums from £10 to £50, flow in for visitations of monasteries and dioceses and for installation to ecclesiastical and civil offices. In the year 1538, more than £300 was paid, by the prior of St. Swithin's, Winchester, into the private purse of Crumwell. At one time the prior of Rochester pays £100, at another the abbot of Evesham £266. The agents he has employed in the visitation of the monasteries, Layton, Legh, Ap Rice and Petre, pay large sums in discharge of debts, as their master's share in the visitation fees and as presents.

Cranmer, who certainly feared and distrusted his powerful ecclesiastical superior, thought it necessary to secure to him £40 a year "as a memorial of his friendship."[2] From Rowland Lee, the bishop of Coventry and Lichfield, Crumwell demands £100 in return for the grant of some priory secured to him, but this demand the bishop was bold enough

[1] R. O. Chapter House Books, B⅛.
[2] More than £400 a year of our money.

to refuse, saying that he had never promised it, and could not spare it.[1]

Bribes of all kinds, unmistakable in their purposes, were offered to him by those who had best reason to know the secret of gaining what they desired. Layton, the most unscrupulous of his tools, is frequently the channel by which money of this kind is offered. For the elections at Fountains, Gisborough, Whitby and many other places, large bribes are offered to Crumwell in return for a nomination. If he will make a certain monk abbot of Vale Royal "he will be contented," writes Sir Piers Dutton, "to give your mastership a £100 in hand, and further to do you as large pleasure as any man shall."[2] From a certain John Parkyns there are two offers of £100 for some coveted office "and faithful service during my natural life."[3]

Reports of the coming suppression produced many tempting bribes offered to the all-powerful minister to spare the doomed houses. The abbot of Pipwell will "do all that a poor man can to gratify your lordship . . . with £200."[4] If Peterborough[5] may be allowed to stand, Crumwell will find it worth his while; and to avert the fate of dissolution from Colchester he is offered as much as £2000 (£24,000 of our money). In fact, in the matter of bribes, the character of Crumwell had been rightly judged by the religious. For them, it was the last chance to purchase further existence by liberal donations. The prior of Durham, in a solemn letter, proposes to increase the annuity of £5 the monastery of S. Cuthbert had hitherto given him, to £10.[6] The prioress of Catesby will give him a hundred marks to buy a gelding, and the prayers of the convent for life, if he can persuade the king to accept the 2000 marks she has offered through the queen, as ransom for her house.[7] Richard, the abbot of Leicester, sends £40, as he understands "it should be your pleasure,"[8] and his successor, the abbot John, who had to pay a yearly tax of £240, and was deeply in debt, sends a present in kind, of "a brace of fat oxen and a score of fat wethers."

As for presents, they come pouring in upon him on all sides, fish from Croyland, apples from Kingslangley,

---

[1] R. O. Crum. Corr., xxv. No. 11.   [2] Ibid., ix. fol. 100.
[3] Ibid., xxxii. 15, 16.   [4] Ibid., xxxi. No. 51.   [5] Wright, 179.
[6] Ellis, Orig. Lett., 3rd Ser. iii. p. 44.   [7] Ibid., p. 50.   [8] Ibid., ii. p. 313.

partridges and pheasants from Harrow, Irish hawks from Bath, geldings from Tewkesbury—these are but samples of the endless variety and number of his presents, not the least curious of which is £40 from one John Hunter "towards furnishing of your cellar with wine, in recompense" for Crumwell's part in a law case relating to the property of the writer's wife. His accounts reveal that considerable sums were received in a way to leave little doubt that they were really "secret service" money. For example, "in a purse," "in a white leather purse," "in a crimson satteen purse," "in a handkerchief," "in a glove," "at Arundel in a glove," "in a pair of gloves under a cushion, in the middle window of the gallery." Some of the other items of receipt are hardly less suspicious; for example, "a chain which melted acquired for my lord £482" (more than £5000 of our money). "Trapes, the goldsmith, in full payment, £1348, 15s. 2d.," and "Bowes for 144 oz. of gold, £274, 11s. 0d."[1]

Crumwell's share of the monastic spoils has yet to be calculated. A great deal came into his hands by way of grant from the crown,[2] and much more by private arrangement with those to whom, perhaps through his instrumentality, it had been given. His accounts show, that during the years of suppression he was expending large sums in the purchasing of estates. In the last two years of his life he must have spent some £10,000 in this way, a very large sum in those days, and equal to about £120,000 of our money. Large amounts of money pass between him and his agents, which have a suspicious look. Sir Thomas Elliot[3] promises him the first year's fruits from any lands of suppressed monasteries granted to him by his intervention, and his "remembrances" are full of suggestive hints on this matter.[4] "Item," he notes, "to remember Warren for one

---

[1] R. O. Chapter H. Books, B. ⅛, fol. 25, &c.
[2] Amongst these must be enumerated Lewes priory, in Sussex, with its cell at Melton-Mowbray, in Leicestershire; the priories of Mickelham, in Sussex; Modenham, in Kent; St. Osithe's, in Essex; Alcester, in Warwick; Yarmouth, in Norfolk; and Laund, in Leicestershire. His nephew, Sir Richard, the great-grandfather of the Protector, had Ramsey abbey, Hinchinbrooke, Sawtry, St. Neot's, Neath abbey, St. Helen's, London, and other property of monasteries he helped to suppress as a royal commissioner.
[3] Strype, *Eccl. Mems.*, i. 1, 399, 407.
[4] B. Mus. Cott. MS. Titus, B. 1, fols. 446–459

monastery, Mr. Gostwyke[1] for a monastery, John Freeman for Spalding, Mr. Kingsmill for Wherwell, *myself* for Laund.[2] Item, to remember John Godsalve for something, for he hath need," and "Item, to remember to know the true value of the goods of Castleacre for my part thereof." Whether he got these goods does not appear, but those of the priory of Lewes came into his possession and were sold by him, as appears from his account book. "May 19th, Thomas Busshope, for the sale of divers goods and cattle at Lewes in part payment of a more sum, £467, 13s. 0½d." Other items of the sale produced nearly £1200, a large total from the spoils of one monastery for his private purse, representing some £17,000 of our money.[3] Crumwell also received a grant of the priory of Lewes, and having made some alterations and removed superfluous buildings, the record of which appears in his expenses, he allowed his son Gregory, then lately married, to go there with his wife to occupy the monastery from whence the monks had been expelled. Gregory writes to his father to say Mrs. Crumwell found the buildings "very commodious."[4]

In his expenditure Crumwell appears to have been lavish. His household cost him, for some time at least, more than £100 a month, and he indulged considerably his taste for building. In former days he had warned his master, Wolsey, to beware of this very attractive but dangerously fascinating and expensive taste, but when in the height of his power, he himself had buildings in progress at the "Rolls," Austin Friars, Hackney, Mortlake and at Ewhurst. He purchased estates [5] as he could get the oppor-

[1] There were large money transactions between Gostwyke and Crumwell at this period. The former, in one month, pays "on his bills obligatory" more than £3000, and, on the other hand, Crumwell pays by "way of *present*" at one time £1000, and eighteen months later £2000.

[2] Illustrating this "remembrance" of "Laund for himself" there is a letter from Thomas Frysby, a canon of the house, accompanying a present of cheese to Crumwell. In it he says that his good master need not thank the abbot for the gift, and concludes: "Pleaseth it your good mastership to call to your remembrance when ye lay here with us at Launde abbey some time, ye would take pains to talk with me or my brethren about our business." He made himself, so it seems, well acquainted with the property. See Blunt, i. p. 377.

[3] Chapter House Books, B. ⅛, fol. 70.

[4] R. O. Crum. Corr., vii. fol. 171.

[5] As examples, in his account book we find:—"Lord Latimer, the purchase of land, £280; the chancellor of augmentations, ditto, £800; Sir Gregory Somerset, purchase of his house at Kew, £200; Lord Clynton,

tunity, some the spoils of dissolved monasteries, some the hereditary lands of the old nobles, sold to meet their liabilities. No doubt, with Crumwell's eye for his own interests, many of them were as great bargains as the annuity of £84 a year seems to have been, which he purchased of Sir William Gascoyne for £333.

Crumwell also indulged considerably in a taste for goldsmith's and jeweller's work. Cups, ewers, and trenchers of gold; platters, dishes and saucers of silver by the dozen, are expenses incurred to "Mr. Trappes of London," John of Antwerp, and Bastian the jeweller; while we would gladly know something more of some of the items of account, such as "the cross of gold of Saint Albans," for which he paid £106 to "Aston the auditor," and "the diamond and ruby" sold by "Jenyns the jeweller" to him, for the enormous price of £2000.

On his amusements Crumwell spent his money freely. At bowls, cards and dice he appears to have lost sums varying from twenty shillings to £30. He was, moreover, liberal in treating the king and court to masks, shows and other spectacles, and minstrels, hobby-horses and players all come in for a share of the plunder of monastery and convent. More than the yearly pension of many a monk and nun went "for trimming of Divine Providence when she played before the king," and for " the collar of velvet for the strange beast my lord gave to the king."

It remains to speak of the ending to his career, which took place in well-merited infamy. By a nemesis of fate he passed to the scaffold suddenly, almost untried, and certainly unheard in his own defence, and this was possibly by virtue of an act he had devised and obtained, to get rid of inconvenient rivals and others bold enough to oppose his lawless policy or thwart his schemes. Rumours had not been wanting that the minister's influence over Henry had not been so paramount, for some time before his final disgrace. The king, to whom Wolsey had "kneeled the space sometimes of three hours to persuade from his will and appetite," but without success, did not become more easy to lead in

---

purchase of manors at Golston, Folkeston, and Walton, £2374; the prior of Folkeston, £263, 1s. 3d.; Sir John Dudley, manor of Holden, &c., £3490; Sir Thomas Pope, manor of Dunford by Wandsworth, £266, 13s. 4d.," &c., &c.

Crumwell's time. Report spoke of scenes in the audience chamber, when the royal wilfulness developed such an extreme of passion as to result in the boxing of Lord Crumwell's ears right soundly. Castillon, the French ambassador, had heard his majesty read a lesson to the lord privy seal, and tell him "he might be fit to look after household duties but not to manage the business of kings."[1]

On 11th June, 1540, Marillac, who had succeeded Castillon as ambassador of France, wrote that he had heard, an hour before sending his despatch, that Crumwell had been sent to the Tower. He added that it is impossible to foretell how this arrest might change the whole public policy of the king, "even as regards innovations in religious matters, in which Crumwell had been the prime mover."[2] Henry was anxious that Marillac should understand fully the reason of the minister's downfall, and at once sent, asking him to suspend his judgment till their next interview, when he would explain everything. In the meantime he was to believe that it was because Crumwell had been found to be a heretic at heart, and had supported false German teaching in spite of the king's wishes, boasting that he was powerful enough to do what he liked.[3]

On the 23d June, the ambassador received a full account of what had taken place, and wrote the substance of his information to the Constable of France. From this letter[4] it appears that Crumwell was altogether unprepared for his downfall. When the lieutenant of the Tower entered the council chamber at Westminster and informed him that he was ordered to take him prisoner, Crumwell, moved with indignation, threw his hat on the floor, and declared that he had never done anything but for the king and in his service. Some of the council called out that he was a traitor, and must be judged "by the laws he had himself made, and which," as Marillac explains, "were so sanguinary that a few words, often perhaps spoken inadvertently or in good faith, could be construed into the crime of high treason." The duke of Norfolk tore the order of St. George from his neck, and the Garter was also taken from him. Before the news spread, Crumwell had already been lodged in the

---

[1] *Inventaire Analytique des Archives, &c.*, ed. Kaulek, No. 62, May 14, 1538.
[2] *Ibid.*, No. 226.   [3] *Ibid.*, No. 189.   [4] *Ibid.*, No. 231.

Tower, and the people obtained their first knowledge of the arrest by seeing the king's officers, attended by a large retinue of archers, enter the fallen minister's house for the purpose of searching it.

Lord Crumwell had few friends and many enemies. The duke of Norfolk assured Marillac that he was to die "by the most ignoble punishment then in use,"[1] and, as the ambassador considered, his only staunch friend was Cranmer, "who dared not speak a word in his favour."[2] The day following the arrest, Henry began to distribute his fallen favourite's offices, and sent through the streets of London to proclaim "that henceforth no one should call him 'Lord Privy Seal' or by any other title or dignity, but simply 'Thomas Crumwell, cloth carder,' and that the king had taken from him every privilege and title of nobility which he had ever granted him."[3]

The record of his attainder[4] gives more information about the charges brought against him than can be learnt about many of his victims. After stating how much the king had done for him, the bill continues: "Yet nevertheless" it has been proved that he has been "a false and corrupt traitor," setting at liberty those he thought fit, and selling "for many-fold sums of money" various grants, even to foreigners and aliens.

Further, he hath of his own will granted passports, and being a "detestable heretic," has sent over England a great number of false and erroneous books, leading people to a disbelief "in the most holy and Blessed Sacrament of the altar and other articles of the christian religion." And after these books were translated, he declared the "material heresy so translated good," and also declared "that it was lawful for every christian man to be a minister of the said sacrament as well as a priest."

As vicegerent under the great seal, he "licensed divers persons detected and suspected of heresy, openly to preach and teach," saying "that he would fight even against the king to maintain these heresies. . . . And then and there most traitorously pulled out his dagger and held it up on high saying these words: Or else this dagger thrust me to the heart if I would not die in that quarrel against

---

[1] *Inventaire Analytique*, No. 197.   [2] *Ibid.*, No. 227.   [3] *Ibid.*, No. 231.
[4] Parliament Roll, 32 Henry VIII., m. 60.

them all, and I trust if I live a year or two, it shall not lie in the king's power to resist or let it if he would."

Furthermore the said Thomas Crumwell "hath acquired and obtained into his possession by oppression, bribery, extorted power and false promises" immense sums of money and treasure.

Posterity may be grateful that the avenging hand came upon him so suddenly. His arrest, unexpected by all, gave him no time to destroy the papers which had accumulated in the course of his administration, and which we may well believe he would have been unwilling for other eyes than his own to see. On the morning of the 10th of June, 1540, he was supreme in England,[1] the evening saw him a prisoner in the Tower, and his fate practically sealed. After begging in the most servile terms that his life might be spared, he was brought out to the scaffold on Tower hill, on the 28th of June. John Stow, the chronicler, records the following speech. "I am come hither to die, and not to purge myself, as some think peradventure, that I will. For if I should do so I were a very wretch and miser. I am by the law condemned to die, and thank my lord God that hath appointed me this death for mine offences. For since the time that I have had years of discretion I have lived a sinner, and offended my lord God, for which I ask him heartily forgiveness. And it is not unknown to many of you that I have been a great traveller in this world, and, being but of base degree, I was called to high estate, and since the time I came thereunto, I have offended my prince, for which I ask him heartily forgiveness; and I beseech you all to pray to God with me, that he will forgive me. And now I pray you

---

[1] In a letter to Bullinger from Rich. Hilles (*Zurich Letts.*, Parker Soc., 105) the following account is given:—"Not long before the death of Cromwell, the king advanced him, and granted him large houses and riches, and more public offices, together with very extensive and lucrative domains; and in the same way he also endowed queen Anne a short time before he beheaded her. But some persons now suspect that this was all an artifice, to make people conclude that he must have been a most wicked traitor... It was from a like artifice, as some think, that the king conferred upon Cromwell's son Gregory, who was almost a fool, his father's title and many of his domains, while he was yet living in prison, that he might more readily confess his offences against the king at the time of execution... There are, moreover, other parties who assert, with what truth God knows, that Cromwell was threatened to be burned at the stake and not to die by the axe, unless at the time of the execution he would acknowledge his crimes against the king, and that he then said, 'I am altogether a miserable sinner!'"

that be here to bear me record, I die in the catholic faith, not doubting in any article of my faith; no, nor doubting in any sacrament of the church. Many have slandered me and reported that I have been a hearer of such as have maintained evil opinions, which is untrue. But I confess, that like as God, by his holy spirit, doth instruct us in truth—so the devil is ready to seduce us—and I have been seduced."

Thus died unwept and unpitied the man for whose punishment the people had clamoured three years before, in their struggles for freedom from his tyranny. John Gostwyke, his trusted secretary, to whom he had lent considerable sums of money, and whom he had "remembered to a monastery," writes to the king:—"May it please your most excellent majesty to be advertised that I your most humble servant John Gostwyke have in my hands, which I treasured from time to time unknown to the earl of Essex, which if I had declared unto him he would have caused me to disburse by commandment *without warrant* as *hitherto I have done*, £10,000."[1]

A few days before the execution, the French ambassador wrote, that "Crumwell's effects appear, by inventory, to be less valuable than was expected, though enough and too much for a man of such base origin. He had in money £7000 sterling, which is equal to 28,000 crowns of our coinage. The silver vessels, including many crosses, chalices, mitres, vases, and other spoils of the Church, might amount to rather more than that sum.[2] All these were carried in the night to the royal treasury, a sign that the king has already no intention of restoring them. . . . The following day many letters were found."[3]

"Thomas Crumwell, the cloth carder" (to give him the style ordered by Henry VIII.), was regretted by very few in England. He had plundered defenceless men and women; he had endeavoured to rob the religious of their reputations as he had of their property; he had defrauded

---

[1] B. Mus. Cott. MS., Appendix xxviii. fol. 125.
[2] Considering the large sums that Crumwell had spent on the purchase of real property, building, &c., £7000 in money and about the same in Church spoils is a very great amount. To this must be added the £10,000 in Gostwyke's hands, making in all about £24,000, or more than a quarter of a million of our money!
[3] *Inventaire*, &c., *ut sup.*, No. 231.

the people of their rights, and had seized upon the patrimony of the poor; he had deprived the sick and aged of their hospitals and places of refuge; he had driven monks and nuns from their cloisters, to wander homeless in poverty and disgrace. But his day of reckoning came at last, and in merited ignominy his career closed.

CHAPTER IX

The Chief Accusers of the Monks, Layton, Legh, Ap Rice and London

THE instruments selected by Crumwell to carry out his designs in regard to the monasteries were from his point of view well fitted for the work. They were not troubled with scruples of conscience or unnerved by tenderness in effecting the end their master had in view. "The inquisitors," remarks Fuller, the historian, "were men who well understood the message they were sent on, and would not come back without a satisfactory answer to him who sent them, knowing themselves to be no losers thereby."[1] They were, and professed themselves to be, completely dependent on Crumwell. That they would not hesitate to serve him and their own interests, even at the expense of their honesty, is made clear from their own letters.

"Seldom in the world's history has a tyrant found baser instruments for his basest designs than Henry found for carrying out the visitation of the English monasteries. . . . That any monastery in England contained half-a-dozen such wretches as the more prominent of the visitors who came to despoil them is almost inconceivable. It is a sickening story. The reader . . . is in danger of disbelieving everything that these men report in his indignation at the audacious and manifest lying which characterises their reports."[2]

"Legh and Layton," writes Mr. Froude, "were accused subsequently of having borne themselves with overbearing insolence; they were said also to have taken bribes, and where bribes were not offered to have extorted them from the houses which they spared. That they went through their business roughly is exceedingly probable, whether needlessly so must not be concluded from the report of

[1] *History*, ii. p. 214. Dean Hook adopts Fuller's estimate of these tools of Crumwell.
[2] *Athenæum*, on Mr. Gairdner's *Letters and Papers*, ix. Nov. 27, 1886.

persons to whom their entire occupation was sacrilege. That they received money is evident from their own reports to the government, but it is evident also that they did not attempt to conceal that they received it."[1]

At various times between 1535 and 1538, a considerable number of commissioners appear to have been sent to visit the monasteries, to receive their surrender, or superintend their spoliation and destruction.[2] The chief of the inquisitors, however, were Doctor Richard Layton, Thomas Legh, Doctor John London, and John Ap Rice. Two others, Richard Yngworth, suffragan bishop of Dover, and William Petre were engaged principally in the subsequent work of dissolution. Upon the authority of the first four, and chiefly, if not entirely, on that of Layton, Legh and Ap Rice, rest the charges made against the monasteries. No inquiry was ever instituted (as far as can be ascertained) into the truth of their reports. They gathered them from the gossip of ill-disposed and malicious persons, and it becomes, therefore, of importance to understand who they were that made themselves responsible for these charges. "It is not impossible," writes a modern author, "that even such bad men *may* have told the truth in this matter: but the character of witnesses must always form an important element in estimating the value of their testimony, and the character of such obscene, profligate, and perjured witnesses as Layton and London could not well be worse. These men were not 'just Lots vexed with the filthy conversation of the wicked,' but 'filthy dreamers,' who defiled the flesh, despised ecclesiastical dominion, and spake evil of dignities in the very spirit of the evil one."[3]

The more the letters and reports of these royal agents are examined, the less worthy of credit does their testimony appear. The word of men of their stamp would be accepted in no matter of serious import. However hopeless, therefore, it may be, after this lapse of time, to disprove the charges made by them, the very fact that they rest only on such testimony should be enough to discredit them. For, as Mr. Gairdner says: "We have no reason, indeed, to think highly of the character of Crumwell's visitors."[4] It is

---

[1] *History*, iii. p. 97.
[2] The names of thirty-eight are given by Oldmixon. *History*, p. 107.
[3] Blunt, *Reformation*, i. p. 359.　　[4] *Calendar*, x. Pref. xliii.

absolutely upon the word of such men, unsupported by other evidence, that the monks have been condemned.

Dr. Richard Layton may be considered the most important of the four monastic inquisitors. He was without doubt the most active and zealous of the servants of Thomas Crumwell. His letters, which are the most numerous and most full of detail, abound in the most filthy accusations, general and particular. They manifest the prurient imagination of one who was familiar with vice in its worst forms. On the face of them, they are the outpourings of a thoroughly brutal and depraved nature; even still, they actually seem to soil the hand that touches them. He tells his stories in a way to allow of no doubt that evil has for him a zest, and that he believes his master will appreciate and approve his foul suggestions.

The origin of this unworthy priest was humble. In one of his letters to Crumwell he says that but for him, he would have been a basket-bearer;[1] yet he obtained considerable ecclesiastical preferments. He had the sinecure rectory of Stepney, the living of St. Faith's and that of Harrow on the Hill; was prebendary of Kentish Town, dean of the collegiate church of Chester le Street, archdeacon of Buckingham, and finally dean of York.

His letters to Crumwell show that a complete understanding existed between them as to the object of his mission. From the outset, when he petitioned for the employment, he professed to have a desire to serve his master's interests in every way. In return, he is constantly requesting some office or other reward, for himself or friends. In the late summer of 1535, he writes his excuses for having somewhat mistaken Crumwell's intentions, and then proceeds to make explanations as to the injunctions which he had given to houses already visited. On the representation of some of the other zealous visitors, Crumwell had blamed these orders "as very slender," and not pleasing to the king. Layton replied with all the confidence of conscious genius, "I dare say well that when you have known *my conceit* in the rules and injunctions premised, and what I have there done in every condition, the king shall have *no less expectation* of your affairs than his grace hath had heretofore. Praying

---

[1] Cooper, *Athenæ Cantab.*, i. p. 530.

God right effectuously that rather I may be buried quick than be the occasion why the king's highness should diminish any part of the confidence or expectation of your assured and proved mind towards his grace."[1] But confident as he was, Layton was made to see that his power and acceptability to his employers lay in one direction only.

In this same visitation Layton makes another mistake in praising the great abbey of Glastonbury. For this he was taken to task by Crumwell, who evidently told him he had not been sent on his round for the purpose of approving. He replies, "Whereas I understand by Mr. Pollard you much marvel why I would so greatly praise to the king's majesty at the time of visitation, the abbot of Glaston, who appeareth not, neither then nor now, to have known God, nor his prince, nor any part of a good Christian man's religion. So that my excessive and indiscrete praise that time unadvisedly made to my sovereign lord must needs now redound to my great folly and untruth, and cannot be well redubbed, but much diminish my credit towards his majesty, and even so to your lordship; whom I most humbly beseech to consider that I am a man and may err, and cannot be sure of my judgment to know the inward thoughts of a monk, being fair in words and outward appearance and inwardly cankered as now by your discreet inquisition appeareth. And although they be all false, feigned, flattering hypocritical knaves, as undoubtedly there is none other of that sort. I must therefore now at this my necessity, most humbly beseech your lordship to pardon me for that my folly then committed, as you have done many times heretofore; and of your goodness to mitigate the king's highness majesty in the premisses. And from henceforth I shall be more circumspect whom I shall commend either to his grace or to your lordship."[2]

Layton's letters show that he was on all occasions the mere subservient tool of Henry VIII. and his more immediate master, Crumwell. As Anthony Wood puts it, "He did much to please the unlimited desires of the king." Henry and his minister had determined to make out a case against the monasteries, and Layton was just the man to assist them. He did not hesitate to promise to be a very "*alter ego*" to Crumwell, who could "trust him even as well as your own-

---

[1] *Calendar*, ix. No. 7.   [2] R. O. Crum. Corr., xx. No. 14.

self." Both he and Dr. Legh, he says, have to depend entirely on Crumwell as their "*Mæcenatem et unicum patronum*," and their only desire, therefore, is to declare their "true hearts and faithful mind," and the "fast and unfeigned service" they bear him.[1]

If Layton's ingenuity, aided by promises or threats, failed (even from an "old beldame," upon whose gossipings two Gilbertine nuns are charged with grave crime) to extract any accusation against a house, the place is "confederated." In fact, the first principle with this visitor, in regard to monks and nuns, is, as he expresses it, that "they be all false, feigned, flattering hypocritical knaves."[2] If they are not, they must be made to appear so, and are treated as such. If they do not declare themselves to be vile, they must have agreed together to conceal their evil deeds. If, as in the case of the canons of the abbey of Leicester, for instance, he can bring no definite charges, still, "to divers of them" he intends "to object" the foulest accusations, which he "has learned of other (but not of any of them)."[3]

Dr. Layton's money transactions with Crumwell were considerable. There is abundant evidence to prove, that he knew when to tender a bribe and when to determine a special course of action by the suggestion of its pecuniary possibilities. He did what he promised to do, and kept his eyes open for his master's advantage. As Legh, his companion, writes: "Layton is now at Fountains to do your wishes."[4] In this instance these were, to get a large bribe for the appointment of a new abbot.

That he fully understood Crumwell's weakness for profitable transactions and accessibility to bribes cannot be questioned. In one of his letters, he points out that the injunctions to the bishops "shall be much profitable . . . to your mastership." Shortly after, he offers in behalf of Marmaduke Bradley, a large bribe for the office of abbot of Fountains.[5]

There is something about Doctor Layton's obsequious servility to his master which is particularly repulsive. Nothing could be more exaggerated in sentiment than one expression he used, when he invited Crumwell down to his rectory at Harrow and said:—"Surely Simeon was never

---

[1] Wright, 157. Layton to Crumwell.   [2] *Calendar*, ix. p. 157
[3] *Ibid.*, p. 93.   [4] *Ibid.*, xxii. 19.   [5] *Ibid.*, p. 101.

so glad to see Christ his master, as I shall be to see your lordship."¹ At one period of his career, Layton was anxious to get the office of chancellor to the diocese of Salisbury. For this, he did not hesitate to offer Crumwell a large bribe. "For your travail therein taken," he writes, "I will give you £100."² Subsequently he was made dean of York. To judge from his letter written to Crumwell in the January of 1536, he was on the look out for the office, even on his first tour of monastic inspection and three years before he got the coveted post. When at last he did obtain it through "the good mind" of Crumwell, he showed his old partiality for ecclesiastical plate by pawning what belonged to the Minster. After his death it had to be redeemed by the chapter.³

Layton does not, however, appear to have been contented with his deanery in the north, and probably desired more active employment. He wanted to come up to Convocation, but writes to his master, "I dare not without your leave." He concludes by reminding him that he had often said he would "get him placed beyond the seas."⁴ Crumwell aparently kept his promise and found him occupation abroad. This appears likely, as Layton's death occurred at Brussels in 1545.

Thomas Legh, a doctor of civil law, was the companion of Doctor Layton on more than one of his visitation tours. He had been a member of King's College, Cambridge, and visited that university as Crumwell's deputy in 1535. Shortly after, whilst engaged during the autumn with Ap Rice in visiting various monasteries, the latter gives Crumwell an account of the character of the man the king's vicar general had selected for this work. He describes him, as "a young man of intolerable elation," who went about with a retinue of twelve servants in livery. He dressed himself, John Ap Rice says, in a most costly fashion, and did not hesitate to browbeat and ill-treat the abbots and superiors

---

[1] Quoted in *Home and Foreign Review*, 1864, p. 181.
[2] R. O. Crum. Corr., vol. xx. 38.
[3] B. Mus. Harl. MS., 6971. Excerpts from York Registers. "Mem. March 27, 1544. Several jewells and plate appertaining to the Church of York, pawned by Richard Layton late dean, for a certain term of years, are now, by consent of the prebends, ordered to be redeemed with money extracted out of the chest of divident."
[4] R. O. Crum. Corr., xx. No. 27.

of the houses he came to visit, in an overbearing and insolent fashion. He had abused right roundly the abbots of Bruton and Stanley, the prior of Bradstock and others, for not being at the doors of their monasteries to meet him, although they had received no warning of his visit, and could not possibly have known what he expected from them.

Ap Rice, moreover, shows disinclination to be associated with him, "lest he with his bold excuses, wherein he is, I advise you, very ready, would have overcome me, being but of small *audacity* specially in *accusations*, for I am not *eloquent in accusations* as some men be." Even Ap Rice is thus unwilling to endorse the charges Legh was ever unscrupulously ready to prefer against the monasteries, the inmates of which he treated "in his insolent and pompatique" manner.

As to the fees and bribes Legh demanded from the monks, Ap Rice's letter, quoted above, tells us enough. "He asketh," he writes, "no less than £20 as of due for every election, which, in my opinion, is too much, and above any duty that was ever taken before." If the unfortunate victims of his tyranny did not tender him what he pleased to consider the value of his services, he refused their gift. They were then forced to send after him whatever sum he wished to get. "Surely," adds Ap Rice, "religious men were never so afraid of Dr. Allen as they be of him, he useth such rough fashion with them."[1]

These fees were, no doubt, shared by Crumwell, for considerable sums of money for elections and visitations certainly passed into the visitor general's private accounts. Sometimes, it is clear, that Dr. Legh did a good stroke of business for his master, as when he obtained from William Basing, on his election as prior of St. Swithin's, Winchester, a promise of £500 "under his writing obligatory."[2] The payments of this sum appear in Crumwell's account books. From the same prior of Winchester, Legh obtained for his master a patent for an annuity of £20, to be continued also to his master's son Gregory Crumwell.

It has already been pointed out that Ap Rice told Crumwell that he apprehended nothing less than murder,—

---

[1] *Calendar*, ix. No. 622.
[2] *Ibid.*, x. No. 485. A large sum in those days, and equal to nearly £6000 of our money.

"irrecoverable harm," as he puts it,—from Legh's familiar "rufflers and serving-men" did he, Legh, come to know that his conduct had been animadverted on to the minister by his fellow-visitor. Yet by the reports of such a man, as described by his own companion, has the character of the religious houses been judged. 'Nearly every unfavourable account given of the monasteries can be traced to the authorship of either Layton or Legh, or is a joint production of these two creatures of Crumwell.'

Legh, notwithstanding the complaints made against him, was not recalled, but, on the contrary, was employed more constantly than ever in the work of visitation. A letter of admonition, however, was sent. Legh returned a penitent reply, and promised to give up his velvet gown and to discharge some of his servants.[1] Very possibly Crumwell recognised by Ap Rice's description of Legh's excesses and unscrupulous violence, that he was a fit instrument for the special work of driving the religious in very despair to surrender their houses and themselves to the king's tender mercies. The explanation Legh gave of the necessity of strong coercive measures at first, in order that petitions for mitigation which would flow in might be a source [2] of gain to his master, would, no doubt, have great weight with Crumwell, and counterbalance the opinion of Ap Rice that it was not politic to press matters on the religious as hardly as Legh was doing.

The views Dr. Legh propounded as to the utility of united action on the part of the visitors, show that he clearly understood the object of the king and Crumwell in instituting the visitation. Dr. Layton did not, in his opinion, press matters forward in the way of enforcing impossible injunctions with proper vigour and determination. Although he admitted that the regulations were in reality unworkable in practice, still he thought that the religious should be compelled to observe them, in order that they might be brought all the sooner to abandon the useless struggle.[3]

It is with evident relish, that Legh also relates any story adverse to the reputation of monk or nun. It is impossible not to suspect that many of them spring from his own fertile imagination, without even the foundation of encouraged

[1] *Calendar*, ix. No. 651.   [2] *Ibid.*, No. 265.
[3] *Cf.* Mr. Gairdner's Preface, p. xx., to *Calendar*, vol. ix.

malicious suggestion. Of the prioress of Sopham he reports that she has bestowed a benefice on a certain friar, whom "they say she love well," and adds, "to *make you laugh*" I send you a letter which is supposed to have come to her from some lady, but "as is conjectured" was sent by the friar.[1] He well knows what Crumwell wants. Just as Layton thought his master would look upon the tale of the abbot of Langdon as a "comedy," so Legh thinks he will not fail to enjoy his scandalous "conjecture." On the same principle, when he "does not doubt" but that his master will find "many things worthy of reformation," he adds, "by the knowledge whereof I suppose the king's highness and you will be glad." And, not the less, for this reason, that "it shall be much profitable" to you.[2]

So notorious did the two visitors, Legh and Layton, become throughout the country, that against them and their master, Crumwell, the anger of the insurgents in Lincolnshire and the North was chiefly directed. "The chief commissioner, Dr. Legh," writes Chapuys to the queen regent, "who was specially obnoxious to the people, as the summoner of your aunt (queen Catherine) now in glory, before the archbishop of Canterbury, contrived to escape, but his cook was taken, and as a beginning the people hanged him. A gentleman belonging to the lord privy seal, who is called master Crumwell, tried to stop them, and he too was immediately laid hands on, wrapped in the hide of a newly killed calf and worried and devoured by dogs, the mob swearing they would do the same for his master."[3]

The Yorkshire "Pilgrims of Grace" also demanded "that Dr. Legh and Dr. Layton may have condign punishment for their extortions in time of visitation, in bribes of some religious houses £10 and £20 and other sums, besides horses, advowsons, leases under convent seals by them taken, and other abominable acts by them committed and done."[4] Mr. Froude even, admits "these two men bore themselves with overwhelming insolence, and to have taken bribes, and when bribes were not offered to have extorted them from the houses which he spared."[5]

Thomas Legh was given the mastership of Sherburn

---

[1] *Calendar*, ix. No. 708. [2] Wright, p. 96.
[3] Quoted by Froude, *Thomas Pilgrim*.
[4] Speed, p. 1022, "Ex originale MS." [5] *History*, iii. p. 97.

hospital, in the county of Durham, in September 1535. He took possession of his office and wrote his thanks to his master early in the following year.[1] By the statutes of this institution, the master was charged with the maintenance of thirteen poor brethren and two lepers, but Legh treated the goods of the poor as if they had been his own. "The delinquencies of former masters were but a type of his."[2] He leased the property of the hospital to his own relations, and granted away the patronage of many good livings. Moreover, he contracted with those who farmed the property, for the maintenance of only eight poor men and women. Although the leases he granted required the consent of the inmates, he sent the documents for their signatures already sealed with the common seal, and they set their names "for fear of master Legh's displeasure." During the whole of his office he never required the assent of the brethren to any of his improvident grants. Altogether in this office of trust he acted "to the utter disinheritance, decay and destruction of the ancient and godly foundation of the same house."[3]

The third of the names chiefly associated with the visitation and suppression of the monasteries is that of John Ap Rice. During the autumn of 1535 he was occupied as companion to Legh, and conjointly with him brought serious accusations against many of the religious houses they visited. He had been employed as scribe in the examination of prisoners and witnesses in the Tower, and had written out the blank forms of acknowledgment of the king's supremacy, which had been sent for signature to the various religious houses. For these services he asked Crumwell to obtain him some reward, and especially "as he made a breve

---

[1] *Calendar*, x. No. 288. [2] Surtees' *Durham*, i. 140.

[3] Depositions in 1557 before a Commission of Inquiry. Surtees' *Durham*, i. 130. That Henry himself distrusted Legh seems clear from an inquiry he ordered as to the sums of money he had received at the dissolution of various religious houses. Sir John Daunce, who made the inquisition, notes :— "Memorandum as touching the plate that was supposed to be sold by the late abbot of Merivale, to George Warren, goldsmith of London, to the value of £18, whereof information was given to Dr. Legh and William Cavendish after they had dissolved the said monastery, riding by the way, the same Dr. Legh and W. Cavendish sent unto the said late abbot for the said £18. This £18 they confess that the late abbot sent to them by one of their servants by the way (begging) to be good masters unto him and his brethren. And (this) the said Cavendish doth affirm by his answer. Also by the said Doctor Legh confessing the same. Daunce."—Exch. Q. R. Miscell. Suppress. Papers $\frac{334}{13}$.

docket" for the king "out of all his highness' late visitation, compendiously touching the name, the order, the state, the number and the dates of every religious house in the realm."[1]

We have seen how Ap Rice reported the conduct of his companion Legh, of whom he had a wholesome dread, and how he had besought Crumwell that it might never be known from whom the accusation came. He not unnaturally supposed that his master would set some one to spy upon him, as he had been made to do on Legh; consequently he says:—"For my own dealing and behaviour I trust you shall have no cause of complaint against me. One thing humbly desiring your mastership that you give no light credence till the matter be proved and my defence heard."[2] That he had been previously in serious trouble is evident from the fact that he feared to report about Legh, because Crumwell might then have thought he had done so in retaliation. "Supposing that you, considering how he was one of them that depraved me heretofore with your mastership, for no just cause, but for displeasure which he have towards me for certain causes, which I will declare unto you more at leisure."[3]

What the accusations were, which Legh had made against him, do not appear. They were, however, apparently of a nature discreditable enough, under ordinary circumstances, to have rendered his employment, as a visitor of monasteries, especially convents of ladies, most undesirable and unwarrantable. This may be gathered from his explaining that he could not at the time make any defence, because "I was *so abashed*, that I had not those things in my remembrance that were for my defence." Indeed, this would seem in some measure to bear out a statement made of him, that he was a priest who had been unfrocked for misconduct. He does not, moreover, appear to have received any spiritual promotions in reward for his services, like London and Layton. And it is obvious that he must have been in disgrace since he could write, "I had experience in myself not long ago how grievous yea and deadly it is for any man to have the displeasure of such a man as you are." His dependence on Crumwell was like that of the others, abject.

---

[1] R. O. Crum. Corr., xxxv. 39, 40.   [2] *Ibid.*, 38.   [3] *Ibid.*

The Chief Accusers of the Monks 169

In return for Ap Rice's services, Crumwell appears to have desired to appoint him to some office in the cathedral church of Salisbury. Against this the dean and chapter protested in several vigorous letters,[1] and the appointment was not made. In his reports of the monasteries Ap Rice proves how little reliance can be placed in the truth of the charges he brings in conjunction with Legh.

If he could discover nothing against the good name of a monastery, it was to him a sign that the religious had agreed together to conceal their iniquities, as at St. Albans, where he found nothing, "although there was much to be found."[2] It is characteristic of Ap Rice, with the other chief visitors, to speak commendably of persons, who are at the same time stated to be men of dubious or evil conduct, but compliant to the will of the ruling powers. In the same letter Ap Rice told his master that he had been visiting the abbey of Walden. The abbot Robert, "a man of good learning and right sincere judgment," he said, had confessed to him "an awful secret." This was, that he had privately married and would like to abandon the religious habit and give up his monastery "to your hands." Crumwell advised the unfortunate man to go on as he has done, to use caution and avoid scandal.[3] It hardly seems possible, that such a secret as the abbot's marriage could have been concealed very long. The whole story looks like an invention. One thing, however, is clear, Ap Rice knew quite well what Crumwell desired, since he added: "You may have the house soon de-relinquished if you like."

Doctor London, the last of the four principal visitors and destroyers of the monasteries, is no more reliable a witness against them than his fellows. He had considerable preferments in the Church, being canon of Windsor, dean of Osney, dean of the collegiate church of Wallingford, and, from 1526 to 1542, warden of New College, Oxford. His letters do not reveal any particular animosity against the monks. His zeal in Crumwell's service was principally displayed in collecting for him the plate and jewels of the monastic churches, and in defacing those sacred buildings.

[1] R. O. Crum. Corr., xxxvii.
[2] R. O. Crum. Corr., xxxvii. 36. Compare the letter of Legh and Petre to Crumwell in Wright, p. 250.
[3] *Ibid.*, xlv. 10.

In none of his many letters does he endorse distinctly any charge made by the other visitors, or suggest any but vague accusations on his own authority. He reports generally, that he finds many of the monks and canons "young lusty men, always fat fed," by no means "learned nor apt to the same," and he says he has advised them "to turn some of their ceremonies of idleness into some bodily exercise, and not sit all day lurking in the cloister idly."[1] But he does not appear to have gone beyond these general accusations, although evidently not biassed in favour of the religious.

In fact, there is some reason to believe, that Dr. London was induced to throw himself into the schemes of Crumwell and Henry, rather by motives of self-interest than conviction. He had most certainly been amongst those who considered the break with Rome a mere temporary phase of the quarrel about the king's divorce. He had even gone out of his way to prevent his nephew committing himself to any violent language or action against the pope. It is, moreover, quite possible that the doctor's interference upon this occasion, brought, as it certainly was, to the notice of Crumwell by the examination and confession of the nephew, may have been the means of placing him in the minister's power. It may have been this circumstance which afforded Crumwell a subservient tool to be used in the furtherance of his suppression schemes.[2]

In the work of devastation, Doctor London was certainly the most terrible of all the monastic spoilers. He writes, for instance, that he has pulled down the silver image of our lady of Caversham and will send it by the next barge from Reading. He has defaced the chapel, and thinks the lead had better be pulled off the roof. The lodgings of the priest from Noteley abbey, who served this place of pilgrimage, "with its large garden and orchard," he has kept, because, as he tells Crumwell, "it will do well for any friend of yours."[3] At the friar's houses in Reading[4] the people somewhat anticipated his work of destruction,

---

[1] Wright, p. 215.

[2] *Calendar*, viii. No. 146. The "confession" was made apparently about 1534, just after the final rupture with the pope, and we know that Bishop Gardiner, of Winchester, was in the April of this year in great danger of being sent to the Tower (*Calendar*, vii. No. 522). A like danger would probably have threatened London.

[3] Wright, p. 222.   [4] *Ibid.*

much to his disgust, helping themselves, "to the very clappers of the bells." However, he did not stay his hand on this account, but a few weeks later informs his master, "I did only deface the church (at Reading), all the windows being full of friars, and left the roof and walls whole for the king's use. I sold the ornaments and the cells in their dorter."[1] At the Grey Friars, in the same town, he did much the same barbarous work of destruction. "The inward part of the church," he writes, "thoroughly decked with Grey Friars, as well in the windows as otherwise, I have defaced."[2] In fact, the record of his work, as contained in his letters, tells everywhere the same tale of wholesale destruction. In this he had, as he informs Crumwell, the object of preventing the friars from again taking possession of their property. From Coventry he writes that he has partly destroyed the house of the Grey Friars "because the poor people lay so sore upon it." At Warwick he had defaced the windows of the friars' church, and as usual pulled down so much of the house as to prevent its being used again.[3]

Sometimes even this iconoclast appears to pause in his work of destruction, and to regret the havoc he is causing. "At Stamford," he says, "I have left as yet visibly at the Grey Friars a goodly image of copper gilt, and the said (image) laid upon marble made for dame Blanche of Lancaster. It is very beautiful, and I resolved to know of the king's grace concerning it."[4] The monument, which the aged countess of Salisbury, cardinal Pole's mother, had prepared for herself in the priory of Christchurch, Twynham, did not meet with the same sparing hand on his visit there. "In this church," he writes, "we found a chapel and monument curiously made of Caen stone, prepared by the late mother of Reginald Pole for her burial, which we have caused to be defaced and all the arms and badges clearly to be deleted."[5]

Dr. London's treatment of the abbess of Godstow is well known. He had been opposed to her appointment, and had "ever since," as she writes to Crumwell, "borne me great malice and grudge, like my mortal enemy." To him was

---

[1] *Calendar*, xiii. (ii) No. 719.   [2] *Ibid.*, No. 346.
[3] R. O. Crum. Corr., xxiii. No. 81.
[4] R. O. Chapter House Books, A. $\frac{4}{30}$, fol. 64.   [5] Wright, p. 232.

committed the task of suppression. As Katherine Bulkeley, the abbess, reports, he "suddenly came unto me with a great rout with him, and here doth threaten me and my sisters, saying he hath the king's commission to suppress the house spite of my teeth. And when he saw that I was content that he should do all things according to his commission, and showed him plain that I would never surrender to his hands, being my ancient enemy, now he begins to entreat me, and to inveigle my sisters one by one, otherwise than ever I heard tell of the king's subjects hath been handled, and here tarrieth and continueth to my great costs and charge. . . . And notwithstanding that Doctor London, like an untrue man, hath informed your lordship that I am a spoiler and a waster . . . the contrary is true, for I have not alienated one halporth of the goods of this monastery, moveable or unmoveable, but have rather encreased the same."[1]

"I have seen complaints of Dr. London's soliciting nuns," writes bishop Burnet, "yet I do not find Doctor Lee complained of." London's subsequent history makes it seem not unlikely that he would have availed himself of exceptional opportunities for entrapping the nuns in so diabolical a manner. Archdeacon South, writing about other matters than his connection with this visitation, gives him the following character: "But to what open shame Doctor London was afterward put, with open penance, with two smocks on his shoulders, for Mrs. Thykked and Mrs. Jennynges, the mother and the daughter, and how he was taken with one of them by Henry Plankney in his gallery, being his sister's son—as it was then known to a number in Oxford and elsewhere, so I think that some yet living hath it in remembrance, as well as the penner of this history."[2]

By this, Doctor London nearly lost the favour of Crumwell and his office as warden of New College, Oxford. Thomas Bedyll writes to Crumwell that "Master London, warden of the new college in Oxford is informed (I wot not by whom) that your lordship is sore amoved from him in the benevolence and favour which your lordship bore him, and you intend to put him forth of his college." I would beg you to remember, he adds, that he "hath done more good to the reformation of ignorance and superstition than all the other

[1] Wright, p. 230. [2] *Narratives of Reformation* (Camd. Soc.), p. 35.

visitors." He retained his office at this time, but only to be involved in deeper disgrace after Crumwell's execution.

Whilst London was warden of New College, the antiquary, Leland, applied to him for some information as to William of Wykeham. At his dictation were written some memoranda, giving a discreditable and wholly false account of that prelate. This was not only devoid of foundation, but must have been known to be so; an act of baseness and ingratitude on London's part, as he had not only been warden of Wykeham's college in Oxford, but, as bishop Lowth[1] remarks, "he owed his subsistence to Wykeham's bounty," having been educated at his school in Winchester.[2] "His history," the bishop considers, "is sufficient to show his want of credit"[3]

After Crumwell's fall, London paid his court to Gardiner, bishop of Winchester, and insinuated himself into his good graces as dexterously as he had before done, on Warham's death, into those of Crumwell. By this prelate he was used as an instrument to endeavour to ruin Cranmer, and to chastise the would-be reformers with the "whip of the six strings." Between Cranmer and Doctor London there was no love lost, and the archbishop calls him "a stout prebendary of Windsor."[4]

At this period of his life he is described rough and brutal in his determination to punish who rejected the six articles. At Oxford "he was of the three that prosecuted most rigorously the good students in the Cardinal's college, when by imprisonment and hard usage several of them died."[5] One of these students describes his demeanour when he learnt that the chief light among the opponents of the articles had escaped from Oxford. It was at Vespers in St. Friswide's that the news was brought to the dean and commissary, who, as the Magnificat was being sung, left the choir. And "about the middle of the church met them, doctor London, puffing blustering and blowing

[1] *Life of William of Wykeham*, 3rd ed., p. 288. The paper referred to is now in the Bodleian, and consists of 13 notes written on the cover of an old letter.
[2] London was admitted to New College 1505, took his LL.B. 1512, and LL.D. 1518. He was canon of York and Lincoln, and domestic chaplain to archbishop Warham.
[3] *Life of Wykeham*, p. 289.
[4] Extract from MS. Benet. Coll. Camb., "*accusatio Cranmeri.*" Mem. in the archbishop's own hand, quoted in Strype, *Memorials of Cranmer*, i. p. 158.
[5] Strype, *ibid.*, p. 156.

like a hungry and greedy lion seeking his prey." At a subsequent examination, the narrator says, "doctor London and the dean threatened me, that if I would not tell the truth . . I should surely be sent into the Tower of London and there be racked and put into *little-ease*."[1]

What Dr. London was at this time, he no doubt was a year or two before as visitor of monasteries and convents of nuns. One can well imagine the indignation of the abbess of Godstow at the unmannerly conduct of this strange kind of visitor, and one shudders to picture the lot of helpless ladies in the convents of England exposed to the rude questionings and intemperate threats of this immoral and unscrupulous man.

By means of informations and evidence collected by London and presented to the council by bishop Gardiner, several people suffered death under the "six articles." "He and one Symons a lawyer, and Ockham, that set traps for others," says Strype, "were catched at length themselves. They were men that busied themselves in framing indictments upon the six articles against great numbers of those that favoured or professed the Gospel, and in sending them to court to Winchester, who was to prefer the complaints to the council. The king being more and more informed of their base conspiracy, and disliking their bloody dispositions, commanded that the council should search into the matter, and so London, &c., being examined before the council, were in the end found to be perjured in denying upon their oaths what they had indeed done, and was proved manifestly to their faces. Hereupon they were adjudged perjured persons, and appointed to ride through Windsor, Reading and Newbury,"[2] their faces to the tails of their horses, and to stand in the pillory in each of these towns on a market day, with a paper on their heads proclaiming their offence. This done, they were committed to the Fleet prison, where London died miserably in 1543. Strangely enough it was Thomas Legh, another visitor, who was the chief instrument in proving London's guilt and obtaining his punishment.

"A dean," writes Mr. Blunt, "twice detected in immorality and put to open penance for it, and afterwards

---

[1] Anthony Delaber's account of Thomas Garret, printed in Foxe, *Acts*, v. p. 421.
[2] *Mems. of Cranmer*, i. p. 175.

convicted of perjury, is not the stuff of which credible witnesses are made."[1]

Probably, however, the fact that the avowed object of the visitors was plunder, and that the charges made against the religious were only means to attain that end, will be to most minds the most conclusive evidence of the untrustworthiness of their testimony. Whatever may be thought of monasteries and monks, it is unjust to convict them of shameless irregularities on the word of those who had a motive in endeavouring to blacken their good name. The words of Edmund Burke may here once more be recorded. "It is not with much credulity," he writes, "that I listen to any when they speak ill of those whom they are going to plunder. I rather suspect that vices are feigned or exaggerated when profit is looked for in the punishment. An enemy is a bad witness —a robber is a worse."[2]

The character of the men upon whose word the monasteries have been defamed would in these days be defended by no honest historian. No other evidence is forthcoming, and it may fairly be asked, in the name of common sense no less than of sacred justice, that the religious houses may not be condemned on the unsupported word of such miserable wretches as Layton, Legh, Ap Rice and London.

[1] *Reformation*, i. p. 358.
[2] *Reflections on the French Revolution*.

CHAPTER X

The Dissolution of the Lesser Monasteries

By the spring of the year 1536 Henry had partially succeeded in his designs against the monasteries. The parliament, acting according to his royal will and pleasure, had in March granted him power to deal with the possessions of every religious house, the income of which did not exceed £200 a year.¹ The time was marked by events of importance both to the church and the nation at large. Death had ended the troubles of the unfortunate queen Catherine in January. And the sudden fall and execution of Anne Boleyn four months later seemed to offer a favourable occasion for the reconciliation of Henry with the pope. The king of France had shown the English ambassadors, immediately upon the news of Anne's degradation, that there could not be "a better opportunity of wiping out the stains on Henry's character, and making himself the most glorious king in the world . . . that every one should do his duty, and that they would find in the pope that true piety and goodness which ought now to be known to all the world." The ambassador and the bishop of Winchester had with tears in their eyes assured the French monarch "that this was their only desire, and that they would do their part."¹ The English people, on their side, manifested a general joy at the disgrace and execution of the king's mistress, which was occasioned as well by the possibility of the breach with Rome being now healed, as by their belief that, as Cranmer had declared the marriage of Anne null and void, and the consequent illegitimacy of her daughter Elizabeth, the cruel injustice hitherto done to the princess Mary would be redressed.²

The entire freedom of the king at this moment from

---

¹ *Calendar*, vol. x. No. 956.   ² *Ibid.*, pp. 377-429.

matrimonial difficulties was looked upon abroad as a ground for hoping that he would now return to the communion of the church, from which he had only withdrawn by his determination to maintain at all costs his unlawful union with Anne.[1] Even the pope, if Sir Gregory Casale is to be believed, was only too anxious to smooth the way for Henry's return to obedience, and was merely waiting for some slight sign of the king's desire for reconciliation to welcome him back to the bosom of the church. He had spoken, so wrote Sir Gregory to the king himself, in the highest terms of his excellent natural qualities and ability, and of his former love for the faith. He was praying that at this favourable opportunity divine providence might effect this return, and reminded Casale how as cardinal he had used his influence with his predecessor, Clement VII., to further Henry's desires as far as possible.[2]

Unfortunately, however, for the accomplishment of this happy return of England to the unity of the faith, other matters besides the divorce of Katherine were now destined to keep the king and pope apart. Henry's title to royal supremacy might have been abandoned without much loss of dignity, for although all the terrors of the block and scaffold had enforced the royal pretension to spiritual jurisdiction over the consciences of his subjects, they were still at heart against it, and any alteration of the royal policy in this regard would have been welcomed by all but a small minority of very ardent innovators. A more real obstacle, however, was to be found in the fact, that the king had already seized upon a considerable amount of church property, and was at the moment occupied with schemes for further wholesale alienation of the goods of monk, priest, and poor. However much, therefore, the past might have been obliterated by a sincere though tardy return to duty, and former spoliation condoned by a profession of repentance, such a retrograde step in the royal policy must have infallibly stayed Henry's hand just in the hour when it was prepared to close upon the spoils of monastery and convent, which a subservient parliament had placed within his reach. Reconciliation would obliterate the visions of untold wealth conjured up in the royal imagination by pre-

---

[1] *Calendar*, x. Nos. 838, 956, &c.   [2] *Ibid.*, No. 977.

vious plunderings:—dreams which could only be realised by perseverance in the course of destruction upon which he had now embarked.

It is of course impossible now to say what finally determined Henry to maintain his attitude of hostility to the Holy See and to pursue his course of reckless spoliation. One event, however, at this time must have had its influence in checking the growth of the better feelings in Henry's heart. From the best of intentions, when not coupled with discretion and when zeal gives full play to angry feelings, the worst consequences often spring. Such must have been the result of the book " de Unitate Ecclesiastica," which Pole published at this time and addressed to the king.[1] Henry was the last man to be driven along the right path by whips, or coerced into doing his duty by denunciations or strong language. And Pole's book, however true its facts and cogent its arguments, was couched in language sufficiently vehement, for the time at least, to turn the king from his purpose. Too often, unfortunately, in the world's history has solid good been sacrificed to the vainglory of style and to the power of penning a caustic sentence and turning with a bitter remark an elegant or striking period, and the work " de Unitate Ecclesiastica " is overflowing with a rhetoric which would have stung many a milder man than Henry Tudor into rebellion, or turned him from purposes of amendment.

To be told that he, the English king, was worse than the Turk, and to be reminded that, whilst Charles V. was engaged in his glorious expedition to Africa, he, " bearing most untruly the name of defender of the faith, did not merely kill, but tore to pieces all the true defenders of the old religion in a more inhuman fashion than the Turk," was hardly the kind of argument to convince him of the errors of

[1] Gregorio Cortesi, writing to Cardinal Contarini, from Venice, 6 July, 1536, says that he was with Pole at Verona when the messenger, sent into England to convey the *de Unitate Ecclesiastica* to Henry VIII., returned. He had brought back a mild message and an invitation from the king to Pole to return to England. Cortesi, who suspected the truth, strongly urged Pole not to venture into Henry's power, and asks the cardinal to second his efforts to prevent his going, as he was more than half inclined to do. So far the book has been carefully suppressed in England, since the king " fears that were it published it would lead to a rising of the people, which he fears more than anything else." (*G. Cortesii, Monachi Casinatis . . . Omnia Scripta.* Patavii, 1774, p. 110.)

his ways. The unmistakable hints, moreover, which the author throws out as to a probable rebellion of his subjects, were quite sufficient to determine the imperious will of Henry to follow in its old course.[1] Nor was the language of the "instructions" forwarded by the author to England, explaining the purport of the work, calculated to soften the bitter feelings awakened in the king's heart by the attack. Indeed, in many ways, the letter must undoubtedly have added poison to the wound already inflicted.

Whatever the cause, the hopes reasonably entertained of reconciliation between England and Rome, or more truly between Henry and Paul, were disappointed. The king's good dispositions vanished, and he embarked seriously upon the work of realising the goods of the lesser monasteries, which parliament by its act had dissolved. Provision had already been made for carrying out the business arrangements necessitated by the transfer to the crown of so vast an amount of real property, from the corporations to which it had hitherto belonged. Almost the last measure passed through parliament at this time, previous to its dissolution, was the creation of a "Court of Augmentations." This body was established to deal with all lands and moveables coming into the king's possession through the suppression or surrender of the religious houses. It consisted of a chancellor, a treasurer, two legal officers — attorney and solicitor — ten auditors, seventeen particular receivers, a clerk of the court, with an usher and messenger.[2] The careful organisation of this office has been regarded by historians as an indication that, at the time of the dissolution of the lesser monasteries, the king contemplated further and more extensive measures in regard to ecclesiastical property than the first act of suppression intended. The officers of the "Court of Augmentations" were to receive and account to the king for all rents, tithes or proceeds of sales; to examine all leases, to take all surrenders and issue all grants, gifts or releases at their discretion. One singular reservation is made in the act, by which it is made clear that already Henry had in contemplation the refoundation or preservation of such monasteries as he willed to keep. "Except always are reserved," runs the act, "such and as

---

[1] *Calendar*, x. No. 975. [2] Rot. Parl. 27 Hen. VIII., 61.

many of the same monasteries, priories, and houses, with all their hereditaments and possessions, goods and cattles, which the king's majesty by his letters patent and under his great seal shall declare and limit to continue and be in their essential estate and to persevere in the body and corporation as they were before the making of the said act."[1]

The court forthwith commenced its functions. Its officers were appointed on the 24th of April, 1536, Sir Thomas Pope being made treasurer. From the rolls of his accounts and those of his successors in that office we are enabled to form a very fair estimate of the progress of the spoliation, to gather the totals of the sums of money received, and to understand in some measure the mysterious manner in which these vast sums appear to have melted away. The chancellor of the court, Richard Rich, received a salary of £750 a year, some £7500 or £8000 of our money, and the treasurer, for whose accounts posterity should be grateful, half that sum. If minute receipts are not recorded, almost scrupulous exactness is manifested in the disbursements. The first payments are for the necessary equipment of the office, such as "green cloth called counterboard cloths," scales and weights, large and small iron safes and bags to hold the looked-for money, jewels, and plate. The official character of the court is manifested by the purchase of "a book called a 'jury-book' with a silver crucifix fastened upon it," to be used in the court sessions, and of the seals of office, great and small, for which a long price is paid, and to which the sum of 12d. is added for wax bought to show the king the first impressions of these new seals.[2]

Preparations for extensive dissolutions having been made by the creation of this court, Henry proceeded to carry out his intentions with regard to the lesser monasteries. As the parliament had granted him only such houses as possessed an income of less than £200 a year, it became necessary to determine which monasteries were unfortunate enough to fall within this pecuniary limit. For this purpose the royal commission was issued to some of the leading men in each county to make a new survey of the houses

---

[1] R. O. Aug. Office Misc. Bk. 2.
[2] R. O. Exch. Augt. Office, Treas. Roll, 1 ; m. 10d. For a knowledge of the existence of these "Rolls," as well as for much other information, I am indebted to the late W. D. Selby, Esq., of the Record Office.

within certain appointed districts. As early as April 24th, the very day upon which the court of Augmentations was finally organised by the appointment of its officers, instructions were issued for the guidance of these surveyors. They were to form a body of six visitors; the auditor, the particular receiver appointed for the county, and a clerk were to be the royal officials, and they were to be accompanied by "three other discreet persons to be named by the king in every county." On their arrival at any monastery, they were ordered to summon the superior and show him the "act of dissolution" and their special commission. Next they were to make the officials of the house swear to answer truly the questions they put them. Having done this, they had to proceed with their examination into the state of the establishment and were to report the result of their inquiry. They were specially directed to state the number of the religious "and the conversation of their lives;" how many were priests and how many were willing to go to other houses, or would take "capacities," and what servants or other dependents were attached to the establishment. Having obtained this information, the royal commissioners were to call for the convent seal and all muniments of the house, and to make an inventory "by indenture" with the superior, of all plate, jewels and other goods and property, which belonged to the establishment on the 1st March of this year, 1536. They were then to issue their commands to the superior not to receive any rents nor to spend any money except for necessary expenses until the king's final pleasure was known. At the same time they were to enjoin him to continue his care over the lands, and to "sow and till" as before, till such time as the king's farmer should relieve him of this duty. As for the community, the officer was "to send those that will remain in the religion to other houses, with letters to the governors, and those that wish to go to the world to my lord of Canterbury and the lord chancellor for capacities." To the latter "some reasonable reward," according to the distance of the place appointed, was to be given. The superior alone was to have any pension assigned to him, and he was to go to the chancellor of the Augmentations for it.[1]

[1] *Calendar*, x. 721.

These instructions will afford the reader an idea of the methods employed by the king's officers to gather into the treasury of the court of Augmentations the revenues, proceeds of sales and precious plate and jewels from the houses and churches of the lesser monasteries. The system was the same in all cases, and the history of one dissolution is that of all. What the arrival of the six royal commissioners with their retinue of servants at monastery and convent must have been to the inmates can be well imagined. The act of dissolution, it is true, saved them from the necessity of surrender, to which many of their more powerful brethren were subsequently constrained. Still their position was pathetic. The homes, which pious benefactors had built generations before, and in which for centuries men and women of their order had served God and aided their neighbours, were passing away from them for ever, and the demand for and defacing of their convent seal was the outward sign of the ending of their corporate life. Henceforth they were to pass the remainder of their days as strangers in a larger house, or as wanderers in a world which many had left years before and to which they could never again belong. The desecration of their churches, in which they and their forefathers in religion before them had gathered by night and by day for the service of God; the seizure for the king's use of their altar plate, in itself perhaps often so poor, to them always so precious by association with the past; the rude appraising of their bells and the lead which covered the roofs over their heads; the hurried sales of the mean furniture of their cells, and of the contents of church, cloister and frater, were all so many heartrending evidences of the passing away of all that for which in this life most of the monks and nuns really cared.

The work was of course a process of time, but throughout England it was begun very shortly after the commissions were issued, and by Michaelmas of the year 1536, or in six months from the passing of the act of dissolution, large sums had been paid into the treasury of the court of Augmentations, and a considerable number of monasteries had been desolated. In many instances the actual process of suppression occupied many weeks. Thus, at Clementhorpe convent, in the city of York, the commissioners first arrived on June 13th, and it was not till August 31st that the final steps were taken, and the nuns turned out of their house. During that period Isabel Ward, the prioress, had been obliged to provide for her household, consisting of nine nuns, an equal number of servants and a lady, Alice Tocotts, who, with her servant, had a corrody in the house. Besides this, here, no doubt, as elsewhere, provision had to be found for the servants of the commissioners who were left to carry out the work. To meet these expenses the prioress was forced to sell a silver chalice and cup, together with some reliquaries.[1]

In the same way Isabel Savage, the prioress of St. Michael's convent, Stamford, was obliged to sell various pieces of plate to keep up the hospitality of the convent and to support the nuns from May 31, when the dissolution commenced, to July 18, when the work was completed.[2] And, from numerous examples which might be cited from the "Ministers' Accounts," it is probable that from six to ten weeks were usually occupied in the work of dissolving these religious houses. To many of the religious thus rendered homeless the hardship must have been more than would readily be believed. Many were of great age, or suffering from disease. Thus, to Elizabeth Johnson, a nun of Arden, a small pittance is allowed for her support, "because she is helpless and deaf and is said to be over eighty years of age."[3] In the same way to William Coventry, a religious of Wombridge Priory, the sum of £6, 8s. 4d. is given, upon his being turned out of his home, "because he is sick and decrepid,"[4] but such consideration was apparently only on rare occasions extended to the inmates of the dissolved houses. Of Esholt, a convent in Yorkshire marked out for dissolution at this time, it is said that two nuns, disabled by infirmities, were passed on to their friends. "Dame Elizabeth Pudsey prioress," the entry runs, "aged seventy years, infirm and unable to ride or walk—gone to her friends." Also, "Dame Johanna Hallynrakes, aged fifty-four years, decrepid; she is not able to be carried for she is lame; (to) continue in her habit and be with her friends."[5]

The returns made by the mixed royal commissions at this time are of great interest and importance. The different

[1] R. O. Exch. Augt. Off. Mins. Acct. 27-28 Henry VIII., No. 178, m. 14d.
[2] Ibid., No. 173, m. 5.   [3] Ibid., 178, m. 14d.
[4] Ibid., 165, m. 3.   [5] R. O. Exch. Q. R. Suppress. Papers, $\frac{882}{17}$.

estimate these gentlemen formed of the state of the religious houses in England, to that pictured in the *comperta* of Layton, Legh and their fellow-inquisitors, has already been pointed out, and it is unfortunate that comparatively few of these documents are known to exist.[1] As an example of the interesting particulars found in these returns, the first in the report of the commissioners for Warwickshire may be here given. The abbey of Pollesworth is stated to be a convent of "Black nuns of St. Benedict's Order." The valuation made at the last visitation of their clear annual income was £87, 16s. 3d., and the visitors now assess it at £110, 6s. 2d.[2] The nuns are stated to have been fourteen in number, "with an abbess and one 'ancress,' of a very religious sort, one close upon a hundred years old; all desire to 'keep out' their religion there or be transferred to other houses." The number of servants and others attached to the abbey was thirty-eight, namely, three priests, eight yeomen, seventeen hinds, nine women servants, and of "persons having living by promise one very old and impotent creature sometime cook of the house." The lead, bells and buildings were estimated to produce £52 when sold, and the house was declared to be "in good repair." The value of all moveable goods, stocks, stores, and debts owing to the house was calculated at £127, 13s. 8d., besides which there were 108 acres planted with trees, "whereof great woods about the age of 100 years" were priced at £114, 10s., and a great common with sixty acres of wood.[3]

In dealing with the lesser religious houses, those which claimed to be cells or dependencies of the greater monasteries, proved a difficulty. This had been foreseen, and the

---

[1] See *Calendar*, x. pp. 495–500. Reference has been made in a previous note to other reports not known to Mr. Gairdner when he published this volume of the *Calendar*. They may be found printed in an article entitled "Overlooked Testimonies to the Character of the English Monasteries," in *The Dublin Review*, April, 1894. They deal with the houses in Norfolk, Suffolk, Hampshire, Wilts, Gloucester, and in the city of Bristol. So far as concerns the moral state of these monasteries and convents, these reports of the country gentry are wholly different from those of Crumwell's visitors. Whilst the latter defame, the former are found to praise, and in the notes appended to the later reports there is evidence that this discrepancy was remarked upon by the official into whose hands the report came.

[2] It is curious to find that in almost every instance the new valuation was higher than that returned by the commissioners for the *Valor Ecclesiasticus* the year before. [3] *Calendar*, x. No. 1191 (2).

commissioners were instructed in the case of a cell "to deliver a privy seal to the governor, to appear before the chancellor and council of the Augmentations and not meddle with the same cell till the king's pleasure be known."[1] Accordingly, in Warwickshire, the royal visitors gave privy seals to the prior of Avecourte, Warwick, who alleged his house to be a cell of Great Malvern, and to Charles Bradewaye, prior of Alcester, who claimed exemption from the act of dissolution, as a dependent of the abbey of Evesham, ordering them to appear before the court in London within fifteen days. Into these cases strict inquiry was made. In the case of Malpas, for example, which claimed to be a cell of Montacute, in Somerset, a commission was ordered to sit at that priory on November 27, 1536, and to require all deeds and evidences of the claim, and to examine the prior and John Montague, prior of Malpas.[2] As might be expected, these claims for exemption from the operation of the act of dissolution appear to have failed. In the three cases given above, the priors of the cells seem to have returned to their monasteries, where two years later they are found in the list of those pensioned on the final dissolution of the mother houses.[3]

One curious fact about the dissolution of these smaller monasteries deserves special notice. No sooner had the king obtained possession of them than he commenced to refound some in perpetuity under a new charter. In this way no fewer than fifty-two[4] religious houses in various

[1] *Calendar*, x. No. 721.   [2] *Monasticon*, v. p. 173.
[3] R. O. Aug. Off. Misc. Bk. 245, ff. 72, 102, 187.
[4] Canon Dixon says (vol. i. p. 365): "Three hundred and seventy-six of the smaller monasteries came under the new act, and were dissolved. Out of which thirty-one were refounded for ever in August of this year, and continued a year or two longer." In this he follows Burnet so far as the number is concerned, who states that there were "in all thirty-one houses" thus restored. The names of the fifty-four are known. The treasurer of the court of Augmentations acknowledges sums of money received as "fines" from thirty-three houses, and twenty-one more, not including Bisham, are enrolled on the Patent Rolls. The dates of the grants will show that they were not all refounded in August. Stevens has, moreover (*Monasticon*, ii. Appendix 17–19), published an original document containing the names of the lesser monasteries which escaped immediate destruction, specifying the individuals to whom the king had previously granted, and distinguishing those houses which had been actually refounded when the paper was drawn up From this it appears that the whole number respited was 123. Forty-six had already been refounded, five were still doubtful; and of these fifty-one no less than thirty-three had been previously promised to different private persons.

parts of England gained a temporary respite from extinction. The cost, however, was considerable to themselves, and likewise to their friends, as they were finally suppressed before they were able to repay the sums borrowed to purchase this favour of their royal founder. In hard cash the treasurer of the court of Augmentations acknowledges having received "in part payment of the various sums of money due to the king for fines or compositions, for the toleration and continuance" of thirty-three of these monasteries some £5948, 6s. 8d., or about £60,000 of our money. The same Sir Thomas Pope ingenuously adds, that he has not counted the arrears due to the office under this head, "since all and each of the said monasteries before the close of the account have by surrender come into the king's hands, or by the authority of parliament have been added to the augmentation of the royal revenue. For this reason therefore the king has remitted all sums of money still due to him as the residue of their fines for his royal toleration."[1]

The sums paid by the re-established houses vary from £400, given by the two houses of Polleshoe, in Devon, and Albaland, in the diocese of St. David's, to the £20 furnished by the Carthusians of St. Anne's, Coventry, the two first paying nearly three times their annual revenue as a fine to the king for a grant under the great seal, enrolled on the Patent roll, of establishment "in perpetuity."[2] Besides these pecuniary payments, Henry had in some cases helped himself well to the monastic manors, and having lessened the income of houses already suffering from poverty, allowed them to be re-established for a perpetuity commensurate with his royal whims. Thus the convent of St. Mary's, Winchester, which according to the *Valor* possessed a clear income of £179, 7s. 2d., not only paid a fine of £333, 6s. 8d., but was re-established with the loss of some of its richest possessions.

It is well to note that several of the monasteries and convents thus re-established were among the number of those gravely defamed by Layton and Legh in their *comperta*, and in more than one case a superior incriminated by them was reappointed in the new foundation. Besides the sums paid to the king by the religious for the privilege of

[1] R. O. Augt. Off. Treasur. Rolls I., mm. 4d. 5.
[2] See "Rot. Pat.," 28 Henry VIII., pars i., ii., iv., v., and 29 Henry VIII., i., ii., iv., v.

continuance, there is hardly any doubt that in days when influence was to be purchased, other bribes were exacted from the houses so refounded, by Henry's hungry officials.[1] One example of the straits to which these exactions reduced many of the religious houses may be given. The convent of nuns at Stixwold, in Lincolnshire, wrote to Heneage, the king's visitor, to beg his good offices in their regard. "Right worshipful sir," they say, "as your poor and daily beads-women, we humbly commend us unto you, advertising you that by the goodness of my lord privy seal and by his only means and suit to the king's majesty, our house doth stand, paying to his highness nine hundred marks fine[2] besides our first-fruits, which is £150, and also a pension of £34 by the year for ever. Good Mr. Heneage, we most humbly pray and desire you, in the way of charity and for God's sake, to be mean to my lord privy seal that he will of his goodness be suitor to the king's majesty for to remit and forgive the said pension of £34 a year, or else we shall never be able to live and pay the king the aforesaid money.

"We be eighteen nuns and a sister in our house besides officers and servants to the number of fifty persons in all, and our stock and cattle being delivered up this year past; which was our chief hope and living. And if by my lord privy seal's goodness and yours we may obtain redemption of the said yearly pension we shall take pains to live poorly and serve God and pray daily for the king's majesty, my lord privy seal, and you during our lives. And if at your contemplation we cannot obtain grace of the said pension we shall upon necessity, for that we shall not be able to pay and perform all such payments as we be bound, give up the house into the king's highness' hand: which were great pity, if it pleased God and the king otherwise.

"From Stixwold the 8th day of January
"By your poor bedes-women
"The whole convent of Stixwold."[3]

---

[1] Burnet says, "It is not unlikely that some presents to the commissioners or to Crumwell, made these houses outlive this ruin: for I find great trading in bribes at this time, which is not to be wondered at, when there was so much to be shared."

[2] The treasurer of the augmentation office only acknowledged having received £21, 13s. 4d.

[3] Strype, *Eccl. Mems.* (ed. 1822), p. 395. The patent for the continuance of Stixwold is dated 9th July, a° 29 Hen. VIII. (1537). " Rot. Pat.," 29 Hen.

'It is difficult to estimate correctly the number of houses which passed into the king's power by the operation of this act of dissolution. Various numbers have been stated, but the authority of Stowe is usually relied upon, that "the number of the houses then suppressed was 376, the value of their lands then £32,000 and more by year." As these suppressions were not all carried out at the same time, but occupied the royal commissioners many months, the number can only refer to all the houses of religion with an income of £200 or under. This number is apparently fairly correct. In the contemporary "list of monasteries in England of a less yearly value than £200" the number stated is 362,[1] but in this are included "cells" belonging to the greater houses and several of the places are entered twice over in different counties.[2] Of the various counties affected, Yorkshire, including Richmond, had the most, numbering in all twenty convents of women, twenty-five houses of men and eight cells dependent on the greater abbeys. Lincolnshire contained within its borders thirty-seven houses which came within the operation of this act of dissolution.

In respect to the annual value of the property which passed to the king by these suppressions, the estimate given by Stowe and others is probably fairly correct. The total stated in the contemporary list above referred to is £28,858, 19s. 10¾d.,[3] and the difference is perhaps accounted for by the values of other monasteries which before the passing of the act, or subsequently by surrender or otherwise, had about this time passed into the king's possession. Indeed, lord Herbert puts the value at "about £30,000 or £32,000,"[4] the former figure not differing materially from the estimate given above. Of this sum, a very large proportion, no less

VIII., Part i. m. 29. The letter is evidence that much more was required by the royal founder than the sum acknowledged as received in the roll of the treasurer of the augmentation office.

[1] *Calendar*, x. No. 1238.

[2] The actual number of monasteries accounted for by the receivers from Michaelmas, 1535, to Michaelmas, 1537, is 243 (Exch. Augt. Office Mins. Accts., ann. 27–28 Hen. VIII., and ann. 28–29 Hen. VIII.). The first accounts of some are missing, but in this number are included others which had fallen into the king's hands by surrender, like Abingdon, or by attainder, like Whalley and Barlings. This number, 243, together with the 123 stated in the original document published by Stevens (*Monast.*, ii. Append. pp. 17–19) to have been respited, comes sufficiently near to the number above stated.

[3] It is added up in a later hand incorrectly £29,041, 0s. 3½d.

[4] Ed., 1683, p. 441.

than £3460, 11s. 1d., came from the lands of the Yorkshire monasteries, and the almost equal amount of £3062, 8s. 0½d. from those in Lincolnshire. It will be seen subsequently how the promises of large annual receipts from the confiscated estates proved illusory, and, in spite of the rack-renting of the crown farmers, the monastic acres furnished less money for the royal purse than they did under the thrifty management and personal supervision of their former owners.

As for the spoils of the religious houses, consisting of money, plate and jewels, which were sent in kind into the king's treasury, and the proceeds of the sales of lead, bells, stock, furniture, and even buildings, it is clear that lord Herbert, following Stowe's estimate of these "Robin Hood's pennyworth's," has placed the amount received at too high a figure. It is, of course, undeniable that these goods were worth much more than the £100,000 at which they were estimated; but, as will be seen later, nothing like that sum was received by the royal treasury, or at least acknowledged by Sir Thomas Pope as having been obtained from the sales of the moveables belonging to the lesser monasteries. Corruption, without doubt, existed everywhere, from the lowest attendant of the visiting commissioner to the highest official in the court of Augmentation, whose high salary might be supposed to have raised him above a suspicion of dishonesty; but allowing for the numberless ways in which the royal revenue could be robbed, it seems, judging by the paltry sums realised by the sales of monastic effects, that an average of £260 or £270 for each house would be altogether too high.

Previous to the passing of the act which authorised this wholesale suppression, some few houses had already come into the king's hands. Few though they were, it was yet clearly thought necessary to cover the illegality of these suppressions by a retrospective clause in the act. Three houses, those of Langdon, Folkstone and Dover, had been appropriated as early as the November of the previous year, 1535, and the cause of the surrenders as stated on the Close roll is, that they were burdened with debt,[1] and were thus unable to continue any longer, whilst on their northern

---

[1] "Rot. Claus.," 27 Hen. VIII., Pars i., 27, 28, 29.

visitation in February, Layton and Legh procured the surrender of two houses, Marton, a priory of Austin canons near York, and the priory of Hornby, in Lancashire. This last was a poor place, and had even to borrow a seal from a neighbouring abbey with which to seal its doom.[1] Two other monasteries in the south of England, Bilsington in Kent, and Tiltey in Essex, both much in debt, complete the list of houses which had fallen into Henry's hands before the dissolution was made legal by the parliament.

It is difficult to form any proper estimate of the number of persons affected by the dissolution of the lesser monasteries. Besides the monks and nuns that were turned out of their houses and lost their support, and the number of servants, farm labourers and others, to whom these houses gave employment and means of subsistence, there must have been a vast number of men and women whose means of livelihood were more or less dependent upon the religious houses. Putting the latter class altogether on one side, it is possible that the calculation given by Stowe, that " 10,000 people, masters and servants, had lost their livings by the putting down of these houses at that time," is not too high an estimate. From the particulars given in the returns of the royal commissioners it is known, that in the twenty-one religious houses for which their certificates exist, there was an average number of at least eight members in each monastery and convent, and that every house had besides some twenty-seven people directly dependent upon it. Taking the number of the lesser monasteries at only 350, and the average number of religious inmates at only six, it will be seen that over two thousand monks and nuns were at this time dispossessed. By the same method of calculation, it will appear that between nine and ten thousand people were direct dependents of the monasteries dissolved.

Of course the work was not accomplished without some earnest protests and some strenuous endeavours to deter the king from continuing his work of destruction and desolation. Thus no sooner was the passing of the act made known than Crumwell received letters from persons of all sorts begging his good offices with Henry for the preservation of houses in which the writers were specially interested. Sir Piers

---

[1] Rot. Claus.," 27 Hen. VIII., Pars i. 38.

Edgecombe, for example, writes that "here is much communication and bruits that all abbeys, priories, and nunneries under the clear value of £200 shall be suppressed, notwithstanding it is not as yet in these parts openly known the occasion of suppression, nor who shall take most benefit thereby, nor to what use it shall rest at length." He then goes on to say, that he is the founder of the priory of Totnes and the convent of Cornworthy, in Devonshire, both under £200 a year, and as the prior of Totnes is a man of "virtuous conversation and a good viander," he thinks it right to tell the king's secretary.[1] In the same way lord de la Ware begs for Boxgrave, and trusts it may be spared, as many of his ancestors and his wife's mother lie there. The parish church is under the roof of the church of the monastery, and there, he adds, I have made "a poor chapel to be buried in."[2]

Nor did the monasteries themselves quietly wait for the royal commissioners to dispossess them of their effects. There are many indications of goods and even plate being turned into money, often no doubt with a view of obtaining the means of subsistence. Thus as early as March 27th, shortly after the passing of the act, it is reported to Crumwell that the house of Marham nunnery, in Norfolk, had been stripped of all the lead and left uncovered and bare. Richard Southwell, the writer, says that the convents of "Blackborough, Shouldham and Crabhouse also make away with all they can, and make such pennyworths as they are not able to pay any part of their debts, so that all the goods will be dispersed." The writer concludes by a petition for Pentney: "We beseech your favour," he writes, "for the prior of Pentney,[3] assuring you that he relieves those quarters wondrously where he dwells, and it would be a pity not to spare a house that feeds so many indigent poor, which is in a good state, maintains good service, and does so many charitable deeds. We hear that great labour will be made unto the king for the same and large offers, the rather because the house is new made throughout and no house in the shire stands so commodiously. If you will prevent it, your labour will not be without remembrance."[4]

---

[1] Wright, p. 117. [2] *Ibid.*, 119.
[3] He was one of the monks defamed by Layton and Legh in the *comperta*.
[4] *Calendar*, x. No. 563.

One other document addressed to the king, giving reasons for the continuance of Carmarthen priory, may be here given as possessing considerable interest. It is urged that "at the first survey for the tenth" the yearly value was returned as £209, and it was by the fault of the commissioners that it was "presented as being under £200. 2. Beside the twelve canons, whereof four died but lately, there are daily and commonly found by the said priory about eighty persons. 3. The house is well built and in good repair. 4. As to the behaviour of the brethren, they refer to the report of the country and the commissioners. 5. The priory stands in Carmarthen, a notable market-town and common thoroughfare, and a great number of people have their meat and drink in the said house. 6. As there is but little good lodging for noblemen resorting to these parts on the king's or other business, the house is an open lodging for all such. 7. Hospitality is daily kept for poor and rich, which is a great relief to the country, being poor and bare. 8. Weekly alms are given to eighty poor people, which, if the house were suppressed, they would want. These charges are maintained more by good husbandry and provision of the house than by its revenues, which stand mostly in spiritualities. 9. When Henry VII. came to this country the prior made a new lodging for him, which is meet for the king or the prince if they happen to come to those parts. 10. Strangers and merchantmen resorting to those parts are honestly received and entertained, whereby they are the gladder to bring their commodities to that country. The king of Portugal thanked the house under his great seal for entertaining his merchants."[1]

In the middle of the year 1537 the king refounded one or two monasteries which had been suppressed. This was a different and more solemn act than the permission which had been accorded to some to continue undissolved, and to which reference has been made. On the 9th July, for example, he granted a charter of foundation to a convent of Premonstratensian nuns, to which he had given the site of the convent of Stixwold. It was ordered to be called "the new monastery of King Henry VIII.," and a grant in mortmain was made to Mary Missenden, who was appointed

[1] *Calendar,* x. No. 1246.

The Dissolution of the Lesser Monasteries

prioress "of the ground and site of the church, bell tower, church-yard, bells, ornaments, etc.," of the monastery of Stixwold, to be held at a rent to the crown of £15, 5s., "which is the true tenth."[1]

In the same way, on December 18th of this same year, Henry united several monasteries in one foundation at Bisham. William Barlow, bishop of St. David's and commendatory prior of Bisham, had surrendered that house to the king in July, 1536. A year later the abbey of Chertsey passed into the royal power by the act of the abbot and monks, and six months after, the abbot, "in consideration that the said John Cordrey, late abbot, and convent of Chertsey, had granted their possessions and monastery to the king," received a charter incorporating that house with a monastery the king desired to found at Bisham. It was to consist of an abbot and thirteen Benedictine monks, who were to pray for the king and queen Jane, and was to be called "King Henry VIII. new monastery of Holy Trinity, Bisham." The king also granted to Cordrey his royal permission "to wear a mitre like any other abbot of that order with large possessions in England."[2]

It is touching to see how some of the monks plead for permission to continue their religious life. To take but one example: on the 9th of June, 1536, the abbot of Waverley writes to Crumwell: "Pleaseth your mastership I received your letters of the 7th day of this present month, and have endeavoured myself to accomplish the contents of them, and have sent your mastership the true extent, value and account of our said monastery. Beseeching your good mastership, for the love of Christ's passion, to help me in the preservation of this poor monastery, that we your beadsmen may remain in the service of God with the meanest living that any poor men may live with in this world. So to continue in the service of Almighty Jesus, and to pray for the estate of our prince and your mastership. In no vain hope I write this to your mastership, forasmuch you put me in such boldness full gently, when I was in suit to you last year at Winchester, saying, 'Repair to me for such business as ye shall have from time to time.' Therefore, instantly praying you, and my poor brethren with weeping, yes!—desire you

[1] "Rot. Pat.," 29 Henry VIII., Pars. i. 29.
[2] *Ibid.*, Pars. iv. m. 12.

to help them; in this world no creatures in more trouble, and so we remain depending upon the comfort that shall come to us from you—serving God daily at Waverley."[1]

Meantime the progress of the dissolution went on apace. From the 12th May, 1536, when Calwich, in Staffordshire, a cell of the Augustinian monastery of Kenilworth, was taken by the commissioners as the first-fruits of the coming harvest, the work of destruction did not cease. On June 1st John Freeman wrote to Crumwell that he hoped to "bring a profitable inventory to the king worth £1000 in one shire, not reckoning Gilbertines nor cells which are ten houses. Of these," he continues, "I reckon a great part in lead and bells, not including woods. For other moveables they have left their houses meetly bare, nor can we make them bring all things to light."[2]

So quickly was the work accomplished that by July 8th Chapuys was able to write:—"It is a lamentable thing to see a legion of monks and nuns, who have been chased from their monasteries, wandering miserably hither and thither seeking means to live; and several honest men have told me that, what with monks, nuns and persons dependent on the monasteries suppressed, there were over 20,000 who knew not how to live."[3]

Everywhere throughout the country the same scenes were being enacted. The thoroughness of Henry's policy was brought home to the people by the same sickening story of destruction, wanton waste, pilfering, pillage and mock auctions worse than plain pilfering, going on up and down the land. As for the ejected monks and nuns themselves, to use Mr. Gairdner's words, "The full degree of hardship arising out of the king's proceedings was perhaps difficult even in that day to estimate—impossible in ours."[4]

Some of the religious, however, did not take the spoliation of their houses as quietly as the abbot of Waverley. Even before the general rising in Lincolnshire the canons of Hexham absolutely refused to be suppressed by the king's officers. They had apparently a good cause, for archbishop

---

[1] *Calendar*, x. No. 1097.   [2] *Ibid.*, No. 1026.
[3] *Ibid.*, xi. No. 42. Mr. Gairdner upon this (Preface xii.) says:—"The estimate may possibly have referred to the ultimate effects of the act, though the previous statement shows that the results were painful enough already. For as yet not half the work could have been done."
[4] *Ibid.*, Pref. xiv.

Lee had begged that their house might be spared, and it seems his request was granted, since, as will appear, they received a grant under the great seal to continue. Their bold Northumbrian spirit could not submit calmly to what they must have regarded as most unjust resolutions of a parliament composed of Henry's creatures. The story of their successful resistance is of great interest.[1] It is found in a report upon "the misdemeanours of the religious persons of Hexham in the county of Northumberland. First," runs this valuable record, "whereas Lionel Gray, Robert Collingwood, William Green, and James Rokeby, commissioners for the dissolution of the monasteries within the county aforesaid, the 28th day of the month of September, in the 28th year of the reign of our sovereign lord king Henry VIII. (1536), associated with their ordinary company, were riding towards the said monastery of Hexham, there to execute the king's most dread commandment of dissolution. Being in their journey at Delston, 3 miles from the same monastery (they) were credibly informed that the said religious persons had prepared them with guns and artillery meet for war, with people in the same house and to defend and keep the same with force." (Upon this report they) "assented that the said Lionel Gray and Robert Collingwood should with a few persons repair to the same monastery, as well to view and see the number of persons keeping the same house as to desire the subprior and convent of the same thankfully and obediently to receive the king's commissioners, coming near at hand to enter into their house, with due entertainment, there to execute and use the effect of their duties of dissolution, according to the king's most dread commandment. The said Lionel and Robert accordingly did enter into the said town of Hexham. Riding towards the said monastery (they) did see many persons assembled with bills, halberts, and other defenceable weapons, ready standing in the street, like men ready to defend a town of war. And in their passing by the street, the common bell of the town was rung, and straight after the sound of it the great bell in the monastery was likewise rung, whereby the people forceably assembled towards the monastery where

---

[1] *Calendar*, xi. No. 504. Printed in Raine, *Priory of Hexham* (Surtees' Society), Appendix, p. cxxvii., &c., from the MS. collections of the Rev. John Hodgson. The story is well told in the excellent preface to that volume.

the said Lionel and Robert found the gates and doors fast shut. And a canon, called the master of Ovingham, belonging to the same house, being in harness, with a bow bent with arrows, accompanied with divers other persons, all standing upon the leads and walls of the house and steeple. This master of Ovingham answered these words hereunder written: 'We be 20 brethren in this house and we shall die all, or that ye shall have the house.'

"The said Lionel and Robert answered with a request, and said: 'Advise you well and speak with your brethren, and show unto them this our request and declaration of the king's gracious writings, and then give us answer finally.' And so the master departed into the house. After his departure did come into the same place five or six of the canons of the house with divers other persons, like men of war in harness with swords girt about them, having bows and arrows and other weapons, and stood upon the steeple head and leads in the defence of their house, the said Lionel and Robert being without. About whom did come and congregate many people, both men with weapons and many women, and stood there a great space, assured by the said master of Ovingham that they should remain peaceably there until their answer were made and so to depart without bodily hurt.

"The said master of Ovingham being in harness with the subprior, being in his canon's apparel, not long after did repair again to the said Lionel and Robert, bringing with them a writing under the king's broad seal, and said these words hereafter written, by the mouth of the subprior: 'We do not doubt but ye bring with you the king's seal of authority for this house, albeit ye shall see here the king's confirmation of our house under the great seal of king Henry VIII. God save his grace! We think it not the king's honour to give forth one seal contrary to another, and before any either of our lands, goods or house be taken from us we shall all die; and that is our full answer.' And so the said Lionel and Robert returned and met the rest of the commissioners approaching near the town. And so all together recoiled back to Corbridge, where they lay all that night."

Next day they learnt "that immediately after the commissioners departed the town, the canons being all in harness, associated with a great company of tenants and servants belonging to the said monastery to the number of 60 persons and more, did issue forth of the monastery in defenceable array, by two together, all in harness, and so did walk from the monastery to a place called the green, towards where the commissioners did meet, and there stood in array with their weapons in their hands until the commissioners were past out of sight of the monastery. And so returned into the monastery again."

It would seem that from the 28th of September, when the royal commissioners were driven away, till the 15th of October, the canons held the monastery by force of arms. After that they wavered in their determination, and said "that the abbey should be delivered to the king's commissioners to be ordered at their pleasure, so that they might there serve God and remain, though they begged for their livings." Their message of submission, however, was not taken to the king, and Hexham remained untouched till, on the final suppression of the Pilgrimage of Grace, they could be dealt with. Probably many of the canons suffered for their temerity in resisting the royal will, for Hexham is mentioned by name in Henry's letter to the duke of Norfolk, as one of the places where the monks "are to be tied up without further delay or ceremony."[1] Prior Jay, who is not named in the account of the resistance offered to the suppression, was possibly, like so many superiors at this time, a crown nominee. He alone received the grant of a pension when Hexham finally fell into the hands of Henry in March, 1537.[2]

[1] Lemon, *State Papers*, i. 537.
[2] Exch. Augt. Off. Mins. Accts., 28–29 Hen. VIII., 200 m. 4d. The grant is dated 10 March, anno 28. Canon Raine says that tradition has it he was hanged at the gate of his monastery. This possibly was the subprior. It could not have been prior Jay.

CHAPTER XI

The Rising in Lincolnshire

THE resistance offered to the royal commissioners at Hexham was an indication of the popular disapproval of Henry's measures. Before punishment could be dealt out to the hardy northerners, and indeed even within a few days of the affair at Hexham, the smouldering flame of discontent had burst into the full blaze of open defiance in Lincolnshire. No part of England had a worse reputation for disorder, and the crown records for a long period previously afford ample proof of the bold and turbulent spirit of the inhabitants of the fen lands and the adjacent districts. They were the last people in England to see changes which they could not approve taking place in their midst without making an endeavour to stay the course of events by an appeal to arms.

Only one other county had been so greatly affected by the late act of parliament which had dissolved the lesser monasteries. By this measure some seven-and-thirty religious houses in Lincolnshire passed into the king's possession, and a rental of more than £3000 a year, which had hitherto been spent in the county and, in a great measure at least, for the good of the people, was transferred to the royal purse for the vague purpose of augmenting the crown revenues.

The full meaning of this change must have come home in a practical way to almost every class in the county. Not only were a large number of monks and nuns rendered homeless, and a still greater number of their dependents, deprived of their means of livelihood, become outcasts and beggars, but the clergy, who were vicars of livings appropriated to the dissolved monasteries, must have been uncertain whether they could continue to count upon their stipends, now that the greater tithes had passed into the hands of the royal officials and other laymen. The poor, also, long dependent in great measure on the charity and assistance of the religious, must have regarded the movement with feelings akin to despair, whilst even those who had been accustomed to relief left them by dead benefactors, and of which the monks had been the careful guardians, would have known that their trusts had likewise been swept away into the capacious purse of Henry.

In no part of England, moreover, was the ugly business of gathering in the spoils pushed on with greater vigour than in Lincolnshire. By the feast of St. Michael, 1536, or in six months from the passing of the act of dissolution, John Freeman, the royal receiver for the district, was able to account for a large sum to the treasurer of the court of augmentation. His receipts from the sales of the religious houses, including buildings, furniture, lead, bells, with stocks and moveables of all kinds, had reached the high total of £7484, 0s. 4¾d., or, in round figures, some £75,000 of our present money, to which a further sum of nearly £200 was to be added for "pictures, clocks," and other precious articles sold subsequently. Altogether, with rents and other items of receipts, John Freeman admitted having obtained for the king in the first six months no less a sum than £8756, 11s. 9¾d., of which about one fourth part had been paid away in the process of dissolution.[1]

It is, of course, impossible that the people could have witnessed the desecration of the monastic churches, the sales of the sacred vestments, the carrying away of the altar plate to the royal treasure-house, and the expulsion of the religious from monastery and convent without deep and angry feelings. They argued, rightly, as the event proved, that a power which could proceed to such extremities against ecclesiastical rights would not stop here, and that gradually the treasuries of parish churches would be searched and emptied to satisfy a greed which would only be whetted by the spoils already obtained from the monastic houses. Other causes of discontent were likewise at work on the popular mind. The religious changes, and in particular the renunciation of papal authority at the royal pleasure, were eminently distasteful to the nation at large. The ecclesiastical appointments made by Henry, especially those of bishops regarded by the Catholic instincts of the people as heretics

---

[1] Exch. Augt. Office Mins. Accts., 27-28 Hen. VIII., No. 166.

and false pastors, had stirred up feelings of resentment ready to burst out on the slightest provocation; and the late enactments of Henry's parliament about property appeared to attack a long-established right as to the free disposal of acquired estates and to destroy the possibility of making provision by will for the support of the younger members of a family.

Just at this time three commissions were issued by the crown which singly might have tried the temper of a nation, but which combined were irritating beyond the limits of popular self-control. In the autumn of 1534 a subsidy or tax of two and a half per cent. on all incomes of more than £20 a year had been voted by the parliament. The first part had been paid, and the second now being due, the royal officials were endeavouring to enforce the payment and to push their inquisitorial demands for the correct returns of income.

At the same time other commissioners were busy conducting the work of suppressing the lesser monasteries. With bands of retainers and workmen imported from distant places, they were carrying on the forced sales, dismantling the conventual churches and other buildings, and dispatching convoys with plate and muniments to London, or with the lead of church roofs and gutters melted into fodders and pigs, and the metal of broken bells to some place where they were to be stored for use or sale.

Simultaneously a third set of royal agents were busy carrying round certain injunctions, which Crumwell, as vicar-general in spirituals, had made for the clergy at large. Their powers were extensive, and were intensely disliked by those whom they most concerned. They were directed to call before them every individual parish priest, to inquire into his character, habits and reputation, to examine into his qualifications and learning, and to dismiss from their cures those they considered unfit.

As might be expected, rumours were busily circulated which served to inflame the popular mind. According to the declaration of the abbot of Barlings, for about a month or six weeks before Michaelmas day, 1536, reports were going about the country "that two or three parish churches should be put in one." Also "that about the same time, it was likewise bruited that all chalices, crosses and other jewels of the church should be taken away from the same churches, and chalices of tin should be given to the said churches in lieu of them;" also "that all manner of gold, coined and uncoined, should be brought to the Tower of London to be touched."[1] According to another witness, it was commonly said at this time that the churches were to be destroyed, "that all the abbeys of England should be suppressed save only the monastery of Westminster. And further. . . that all the jewels of the church, that is to say crosses, chalices, censers, should be taken away from the churches, and chalices, crosses and censers of tin put in their places."[2]

The first outbreak of the storm took place at Louth.[3] By the close of September the monastery of Louth-park had been dissolved, and the people had witnessed the sales of the ornaments and vestments of the church, which, together with the other effects of the place, realised close upon the large sum of a thousand pounds.[4] At the feast of St. Michael the process of dissolution was going on at the convent of Legbourne, just outside the town, and two of Crumwell's servants, Millicent and John Bellow, had been left by the commissioners to complete the work.

On Saturday, the last day of September, Dr. Raynes, chancellor of the bishop of Lincoln, held a court of examination at Bolingbroke, and the priests of the district had been much exercised by his inquiries. According to the declaration of a former monk of Louth-park, it was the chancellor's scribe, Peter, who fanned the spark into flame by "recommending the priests to study up their books, for they should have straight examination taken of them shortly."[5] One was heard to say: "They will deprive us of our benefices because they would have the first-fruits."[6] Another declared that "they would not be ordered nor yet examined of their ability in learning or otherwise in keeping of cure of souls."[7]

---

[1] Chapter House Bk., A. $\frac{2}{19}$, p. 12.
[2] *Ibid.*, p. 25. In this declaration, as to the popular belief that Henry coveted the treasures of the parish churches, all the numerous witnesses examined as to the rising agree.
[3] Only a slight sketch of both the Lincolnshire rising and the Pilgrimage of Grace is here attempted, in so far as they bear upon the question of the dissolution of monasteries.
[4] Exch. Augt. Off. Mins. Accts., 27-28 Hen. VIII., 81, m. 43.
[5] Chapter House Bk., A. $\frac{2}{19}$, p. 143.   [6] *Ibid.*   [7] *Ibid.*, A. $\frac{2}{28}$, p. 8.

And the parson of Farforthe, Simon Maltby, "returned home to his parish and reported amongst his neighbours that the church goods should be taken from them." He also said that "there were divers chalices made of tin which should be delivered to them in exchange for their silver chalices, and the said silver chalices to be had to the king's use. And further the said Sir Simon said, that he with other priests were determined that if the said chancellor did sit any more they would strike him down, trusting that their neighbours would take their parts in that behalf."[1]

The report that the king was going to take possession of all church plate was fully believed on all sides. "One William Man that singeth bass in the choir at Louth and parson Sotbye going to board with Thomas Manby at Louth," just before the rising, said, that "the common fame was that the inhabitants of the town of Hull had sold the church stuff to prevent the king's commissioners."[2] And whilst dining at Grimsby, a sailor, "a very tall man having a tall woman for his wife," was heard to say: "We hear at Hull that ye should have a visitation here shortly, and therefore we have taken all our church plate and jewels and sold them and paved our town withal. And so, if ye be wise, will ye do too and mend your town, which is foul withal."[3]

There were, however, other matters which moved the people more deeply than any question about their church plate. Kendal, the vicar of Louth, declared that there was much grumbling about the supremacy question, although he could not give the names of those who "murmured that the king's highness should be head of the church." And also that "all men with whom he had any communication did grudge and murmur at the new opinions touching our Lady and Purgatory, and himself also did grudge at the same. Item," runs the record of the vicar's examination in the Tower, "he saith it was reported that the sacrament was irreverently taken down at Hagneby by the king's officers at the time of the suppression and dissolution of the same house."[4]

It is impossible to inspect the depositions of witnesses and examinations of prisoners on this matter, without a conviction that the men of Lincolnshire rose in arms in

---

[1] Chapter House Bk., A. $\frac{2}{28}$, p. 7. [2] *Ibid.*, A. $\frac{2}{29}$, p. 3. [3] *Ibid.*, p. 144.
[4] *Ibid.*, p. 3.

defence of what they held to be matters of both Christian faith and practice. The vicar of Louth advised them most strongly "in no wise to meddle with the king's highness, but only for the repression of heresies and maintenance of the faith of Christ."[1] They regarded Crumwell and some of the bishops as banded together to destroy the Catholic faith, and they were loud in their demands for their punishment. "Item," said one witness, "they intended if they might have prospered in their journey to have slain the lord Crumwell, four or five of the bishops, the master of the Rolls, and the chancellor of the Augmentations." Also—and to this part of the examination an ominous hand with a finger pointing is placed in the margin with the remark, "Note this specially"—the gentlemen "demanded of the commons whether they would have the lord Crumwell and others before named, saying to them: "The lord Crumwell was a false traitor, and that he and the same bishops and master of the Rolls and the chancellor of Augmentations—calling them two false pen-clerks—were the very imaginers and devisers of all the false laws.'"[2]

Against Crumwell in particular, the feeling of the priests and people was extremely bitter. One priest is accused of saying that "the king's most noble counsel were false harlots in devising of false laws for spoiling of the goods of the spirituality, and named the procurement thereof to be the lord Crumwell,"[3] and many threats of personal violence are recorded as being uttered against him. Altogether there can be no doubt that the people, as one witness has it, "called my lord privy seal most vilipendiously at their pleasure."[4]

Besides the religious questions there were also social matters which irritated the people at this time. Parliament, in the last session but one, had passed the celebrated "Statute of Uses."[5] Up to this time, land had not been subject to disposition by will, but this bar to the free disposal of real property had been practically removed by a system of "uses" or "trusts," under cover of which it had been the practice to make provision for younger children, for the payment of debts and for other charges, which were often tantamount to a transfer of such property. The king's

---

[1] Chapter House Bk., A. $\frac{2}{25}$, p. 6.   [2] *Ibid* p. 28.   [3] *Ibid.*, A. $\frac{2}{25}$, p. 5.
[4] *Ibid.*, A. $\frac{2}{25}$, p. 169.   [5] 27 Hen. VIII., Cap. 10.

anxiety in the passing of the "Statute of Uses" was to prevent the failure of his feudal dues. Some three years before the measure passed into law, he had endeavoured to effect what he wanted by a measure relating to "wardships."

The populace were thus at this time thoroughly roused by the temporal and spiritual innovations which they were compelled to witness. In Lincolnshire also the extensive suppressions of religious houses coming at this time, in conjunction with the constant reports of yet further destruction and desecration of churches, and of the greater seizure of ecclesiastical property meditated by Henry, determined the people to have recourse to arms for the preservation of the rights of church and nation.

The story of the rising may be best told in the words of those who were present, and which are preserved in the depositions of witnesses and the examination of prisoners after the close of the rebellion. "Sir William Moreland, priest, late monk of Louth-park," deposed[1] that he was a monk in the abbey up to the 8th of September, 1536, and that on "Holy Rood day (14th September) next following" he had received his capacity, "and ever since then hath gone in secular habit, saving at such time as he was at Pomfret with Sir Robert Constable, when he did wear their white jacket and a scapulary." After leaving his monastery, he had lodged at the house "of one Thomas Wrightson of Kedington," a little village about a quarter of a mile from his old religious home, and had only been away twice, when he went to a house in Louth "to meet two or three of his late brethren."

"About three weeks before Michaelmas," this exiled monk declares, "a great rumour was busily spoken (specially after the commissary's visitation kept at Louth church, in Saint Peter's choir, by one Master Peter, then scribe to the commissary of Lincoln) that the chalices of parish churches should be taken away, and that there should be but one parish church within six or seven miles compass. Also, that every parson and vicar should be examined and tried by their learning whether they were able and sufficient of their learning to have and take upon themselves the cure

---

[1] Chapter House Bk., A. $\frac{2}{15}$, pp. 91 to 129.

of souls or not. Wherewith this deponent was right glad, and thought to himself that it might perchance be his fortune to succeed some of such unlettered parsons or vicars in some of their rooms.

"And the Monday (2nd October) next after Michaelmas day, as this deponent remembereth, the said inquiry and visitation should have been kept at Louth aforesaid. And the same Sunday (1st October) when the insurrection first began at Louth, he rode forth by four o'clock in the morning on a bay gelding, which he borrowed of one Dane Thomas Lilborne, late subprior of Louth-park, and so rode on to Markby and Hagneby to deliver there certain 'capacities' to the number of ten, into divers of the brethren of the monasteries there also late suppressed. And the same afternoon about three o'clock he came home again to Kedington. And then he heard say that the vicar of Louth, called Kendall, had made a certain collation[1] that same Sunday unto his parishioners, in which, amongst other things, he advised them to go together and to look well on such things as should be inquired of on the next morrow at the visitation. And the same Sunday at evensong (as this deponent heard say, for he was not thereat), the parishioners 'commoning' amongst themselves of the premises, the head men of the parish and the poor men all together, or the most part of them, at last fell at such diversity of sundry opinions amongst themselves that in conclusion, the poor men took the keys of the church from the rich men and churchwardens there, and said they would keep the keys themselves. And that night, he heard say, that the parishioners did put into the church to keep the same ten or twelve of their neighbours."

On the Monday morning, Moreland, after having "said matins," hearing of the disturbance of the night before, went into Louth to make inquiries. "And then," he continues, "this deponent would have gone into the church to hear mass, but such of the parishioners as kept the church would not suffer him nor none other to enter into the same, but only such as they liked." Not being able to hear his mass, he retired "from the church unto the house of one William Hert, a butcher," where, amongst others, he met one of his old brethren of Louth-park, "Robert Hert." They, of

---

[1] *i.e.*, sermon or address.

course, discussed the events of the previous evening, "and as they sat together there at breakfast with puddings, suddenly the common bell was rung by such as were within the said church."

At the sound of the alarm the people rushed towards the church, where its meaning was soon discovered, by the appearance of John Heneage, "the proctor," who riding into the town had been seized by the excited populace, who would have killed him. Some of the better disposed, however, hurried him to the church, where they managed to get him into the choir, "and to lock the door between him and the commons." He was, however, forced to take the oath to be true to God and the people. Nicholas Melton, "whom afterwards they named captain Cobler," was the chief leader of the people at this time.

This excitement had somewhat subsided when, as the people were turning home, "suddenly, at the coming into the town of one master John Franke, the registrar of the bishop of Lincoln, the common bell was rung again, and then all the commons in like manner with weapons, as they did before, ran again unto the house of one William Goldsmith, where the said registrar was alighted, and there they took all his books from him. And one John Taylor, of Louth, 'webstar,' brought out of the said house a great brand of fire, and by the commoners the said books were conveyed to the market-place."

The witness declares that he did his best to prevent this destruction of the registers, but could not. "And then they by force carried this deponent under the high cross there, and said that he, with others to the number of six, being there of the same opinion should look in the books to know what was in them." He commenced to read the king's commission in order to declare its meaning to the people, when the others, frightened by the noises of the mob, "'flang' all the books down unto them beneath the cross, and then every man that was beneath got a piece of them and hurled them into the fire."

Whilst this scene was being enacted at the market-cross, some of the crowd went and brought the registrar to the square, "and caused him, by a ladder, to climb up to the altitude of a half-part of the cross. And when he came up, he said unto this deponent, 'For the passion of Christ, priest, if canst, save my life. And as for the books that be already burnt, I pass not of them;' so as a little book of his reckoning of such money as he had laid out might be saved, and also the king's commission, which to be saved this deponent promised as much as in him was." Meantime the mob clamoured for the registrar to come down from the cross and burn his own books, which he was forced to do. The monk of Louth-park tried to save the small book of accounts, but as he was carrying it off "they all drew about him, and demanded of him what book was that which he had in his hands." He told them that it was a book of reckonings. But they would not believe him, "and carried him with strength the breadth of the market-stead, unto a shop window of one Thomas Grantham, tailor, and then he read unto them some parts of the contents of the book." At length they permitted him to keep the volume, but as he was carrying it to the registrar he was surrounded again by three or four hundred people, who "took it out of his sleeve." He informed the king's officer of the loss, who, however, for his good service "paid for his dinner," and promised him "his letters of orders." In the afternoon the registrar was conveyed out of danger.

"Whilst this deponent," he continues, "was thus at dinner with the said registrar, the commons of the said town went unto the monastery of Legbourn, a mile and a half from Louth, and from thence they fetched and brought to Louth with them one Millicent and John Bellow, servants unto my lord privy seal, and put them in great fear and jeopardy of their lives." In the evening they put these two men and another, George Parker, into prison.

Thus passed the first day of the rising. Early on the morning of the following day, Tuesday, the common bell at Louth was again set ringing. The king's commissioners were reported to be at Caistor; and Melton, otherwise Captain Cobbler, harangued the mob and gave order, that at the "next ringing of the bell" all should set out for that neighbouring town. Four priests and four laymen were appointed to speak with the commissioners, and of these "Dane William Borowby *alias* Moreland," the chief informant, was one. They set out on foot till they came to Irford, a convent of Premonstratensian nuns, where they "borrowed for this deponent, of the prioress there, a white trotting gelding, ready bridled and saddled." On their way they were met by contingents from the neighbouring villages, and at Caistor hill they found about a thousand men, unarmed, waiting for them. Seeing the commissioners, Borowby, with some eighteen or twenty others, rode on to speak with them, "and with his cap in his hand desired them, in the name of the said company of commoners, to return and speak with them." This, most of them consented to do, and they were forced to take the oath to aid the commons. Lord Borough, however, who was with the gentry when they were overtaken by the people, set spurs to his horse and escaped. The rioters thought that his servant Nicholas had aided him in his flight, and angry at not having secured the master, they turned upon the servant. "And," continues the witness, " so great a number of them striking at him, as I never saw man escape such danger as he was in, having so many strokes and wounds as he had. And at last when he had fled evermore backward from them almost a quarter of a mile, saving himself always amongst the horsemen, he was stricken down by the footmen of Louth and Louth-Esk. And then, when he was stricken down they cried for a priest for him. And at last with much pain this deponent came unto him, and so at length he caused him to be conveyed unto the town and then confessed him, and sent two surgeons unto him from Louth."[1]

On the same day, Tuesday, October 3rd, the country round about Horncastle rose with even greater unanimity than at Louth. Some of the townsmen discovered that Dr. Raynes, the chancellor of the bishop of Lincoln, was still at Killingbroke, and unable to move from sickness. Upon this information they came thither "with a great company to take the chancellor, and did ring the common bell. And then the commons did cry, 'Kill him!' and would have drawn him out of his bed" had they not been dissuaded by others from violence.[2] The people of Killingbroke promised, however, to come to a great muster on Ancaster heath near to Horncastle, and thither they brought with them Dr. Raynes, the chancellor of Lincoln, "being very sick." The following day the gentry of the county were

---

[1] The whole of the above narrative is taken from the depositions of Moreland, *alias* Borowby, the Louth-park monk. A. $\frac{2}{29}$, pp. 91-129.
[2] *Ibid.*, A. $\frac{2}{28}$, p. 3.

present, with the sheriff, Mr. Dymmoke, at their head, who "gave divers of the rebels, being poor men, money for their costs."

As the chancellor rode into the field with his captors the passions of the mob were stirred, and there occurred one of the two acts of violence, which alone in this or the subsequent Yorkshire rising, disgraced the movement.[1] "At his coming into the field," declares one witness named Brian Staines, "the rebels, whereof were many parsons and vicars, cried out with a loud voice, 'Kill him, kill him.' And upon that one William Hutchinson, of Horncastle, and William Balderstone, by the procurement of the said parsons and vicars, pulled him violently off his horse, kneeling upon his knees, and with their staves they slew him. And being dead, this deponent saith the priests continually crying 'Kill him, kill him,' he also struck the said chancellor upon the arm with a staff."[2]

As the body of the murdered chancellor lay upon the ground in the midst of the mob, "his apparel was divided amongst them, and his purse brought to the sheriff, who afterwards distributed the money that was in the same to the poor men that were amongst the rebels." And the

---

[1] Canon Dixon (vol. i. p. 457, *note*) rightly says: "It (the 'Great Insurrection') was throughout more of a demonstration than a civil war, and with the exception of the murder of the chancellor and of a serving-man, the behaviour of the so-called rebels was wonderfully temperate and orderly. On the other hand, the bloody perfidy of the strangely chosen hero of Mr. Froude comes out more conspicuously in his excited narrative than in any of the histories."

[2] Chapter House Bk., A. $\frac{2}{20}$, pp. 24-25. The deposition of this witness, Brian Staines, is the authority for supposing that the priests were the chief instigators of this crime. Mr. Froude accepts the statement without question, and exclaims: "These, we presume, were Pole's seven thousand children of light who had not bowed the knee to Baal—the noble army of saints who were to flock to Charles' banners." Canon Dixon (vol. i. p. 457) has followed his guidance, and stated that the chancellor "was killed at the instigation of the clergy." The authority of the witness is, however, not altogether beyond suspicion. To judge from the depositions in this matter, those implicated were generally ready to excuse themselves by casting the blame on others. In fact, Staines himself was accused of perpetrating the deed; and this seems to have been considered the true version. For in the notes which were intended to sum up the evidence, the following is entered: "Brian Staines was he which killed the chancellor" (*Ibid.*, A. $\frac{2}{28}$, p. 3). There is no reason to suppose, as would be natural from Mr. Froude's and Canon Dixon's narratives, that Dr. Mackarel, the abbot of Barlings, and "all his fraternity" were present at the murder of the chancellor; in fact, it appears that the abbot was not with them till some days afterwards (*Ibid.*, A. $\frac{2}{20}$ p. 13), and knew nothing of the insurrection till the day after the murder.

priests and vicars then advised them strongly to proceed on their journey, saying "they should lack neither gold nor silver." Banners were made and carried at the head of the detachments. A tenant of the abbot of Barlings "tied a white towel on the top of a banner and pinned a picture of the Trinity painted in parchment on the same towel, and caused his son to bear it."[1] And another, called Dymmoke's banner, was thus described by the man who carried it. "Item, the said Trotter saith the meaning of the plough borne in the banner was to encourage the husbandmen. The meaning of the chalice and the host was borne in remembrance that chalices, cross and jewels of the church would be taken away. The meaning of the five wounds was to 'couraging' of the people to fight in Christ's cause. The meaning of the horn was borne in taking of horn cattle."[2]

Before, however, the assembly broke up at Horncastle they devised certain articles of grievance which were to be forwarded to the king. They were drawn up by the gentry, including the sheriff Dymmoke and his brother, who held their discussion a mile or so from the body of the people, and were written out by one of their number "on the field upon his saddle-bow." When they were finished, Dymmoke and the rest rode up to the mob, and in a loud voice proclaimed the articles, saying: "Masters, ye see that in all the time we have been absent from you we have not been idle. How like you these articles? If they please you, say yea. If not, ye shall have them mended." And then the commons held up their hands, with a loud voice, saying: "We like them very well."[3]

The demands thus made to the king were six in number. They complained, (1) of the dissolution of the religious houses and of the consequent destitution of "the poorealty of the realm;" (2) of the restraints imposed on the distribution of property by "the statute of uses;" (3) of the grant to the king of the tenths and first-fruits of spiritual benefices; (4) of the payment of the subsidy demanded of them; (5) of the introduction into the king's

---

[1] Chapter House Bk., A. $\frac{2}{10}$, p. 7.
[2] *Ibid.*, p. 37. It was reported that the king was going to levy a tax on all cattle.
[3] *Ibid.*, A. $\frac{2}{10}$, p. 31.

council of Crumwell, Rich, and other "such personages as be of low birth and small reputation;" and (6) of the promotion of the archbishops of Canterbury and Dublin, and the bishops of Rochester, St. David's, and others, who, in their opinion, had clearly "subverted the faith of Christ."[1] These articles were dispatched at once to the king at Windsor, and Heneage, the royal commissioner, was allowed to accompany[2] the messenger.

At Lincoln itself there had been a rising of the people also. The town was occupied by armed insurgents, and bishop Longland's palace had been broken into and sacked, the people doing there "as much hurt as they could."

For the first week the course of the insurgents was unchecked. They armed themselves as best they might, and did not hesitate to seize upon weapons and armour wherever they could be found.[3] They set beacons blazing and alarm-bells ringing throughout the county, but the movement lacked a leader of ability, and it collapsed almost as suddenly as it had come into existence.

The messengers from the meeting at Horncastle were detained by the king for a short time, while preparations were hurried on to collect forces and forward munitions of war to the north. In a week from the first commencement of the movement Sir John Russell, with the advance guard, was at Stamford, and the duke of Suffolk, to whom the supreme command had been given, was coming up in his rear.

On Wednesday, October 11th, just ten days after the outbreak, the king's herald arrived in Lincoln with the royal answer to the articles. It was couched in angry and vigorous language. "Concerning choosing of counsellors," the king wrote, "I never have read, heard nor known, that

---

[1] Canon Dixon, vol. i. p. 457, on the authority of Speed's account of the Lincolnshire articles, says that the insurgents acknowledged the king "to be by inheritance the supreme head of the Church of England." There is no indication of this as far as can be known. In the original depositions rather the opposite would appear, both in their case and that of the "Pilgrims of Grace," who subsequently adopted the same articles.

[2] "Perhaps to save him from being murdered by the priests!!" is Mr. Froude's remark on this permission accorded to Heneage.

[3] An interesting example of this may be given. "Philip Trotter, of Horncastle, is accused by Edward Dymmoke, saying he took the coat armour of Sir Lyon Dymmoke out of Horncastle church, where he was buried, and wore it upon his back."—*Ibid.*, A. $\frac{2}{18}$, p. 13.

princes' counsellors and prelates should be appointed by rude and ignorant common people; nor that they were persons meet or of ability to discern and choose meet and sufficient counsellors for a prince. How presumptuous then are ye, the rude commons of one shire, and that one of the most brute and beastly of the whole realm, and of least experience, to find fault with your prince for the electing of his counsellors and prelates, and to take upon you, contrary to God's law and man's law, to rule your prince whom ye are bound to obey and serve with both your lives, lands, and goods, and for no worldly cause to withstand.

"As to the suppression of houses and monasteries," they were granted to us by the parliament, "and not set forth by any counsellor or counsellors upon their mere will and fantasy, as you, full falsely, would persuade our realm to believe. And where ye alledge that the service of God is much thereby diminished, the truth thereof is contrary; for there are no houses suppressed where God was well served, but where most vice, mischief, and abomination of living was used: and that doth well appear by their own confessions, subscribed with their own hands, in the time of our visitations. And yet were suffered a great many of them, more than we by the act needed, to stand; wherein if they amend not their living, we fear we have more to answer for than for the suppression of all the rest. And as for their hospitality, for the relief of poor people, we wonder ye be not ashamed to affirm that they have been a great relief to our people, when a great many, or the most part, hath not past four or five religious persons in them and divers but one, which spent the substance of the goods of their house in nourishing vice and abominable living. Now, what unkindness and unnaturality may we impute to you and all our subjects that be of that mind that had rather such an unthrifty sort of vicious persons should enjoy such possessions, profits and emoluments as grow of the said houses to the maintenance of their unthrifty life, than we, your natural prince, sovereign lord and king, who doth and hath spent more in your defences of his own than six times they be worth."

The king's proclamation dismisses the "act of uses" as a subject which they cannot comprehend, and coming to speak of their demand to be relieved of the subsidy imposed upon them, he upbraids them for "so unkindly and untruly" dealing with him, who has done so much for them "without any cause or occasion."

Lastly, as to the "*first-fruits*," Henry declared that the people ought to be glad for him to have them, to enable him to bear "the great and excessive charges for the maintenance" of the commonwealth. "Wherefore," he concludes, "we charge you, eftsoon, upon the aforesaid bonds and pains, that ye withdraw yourselves to your own houses, every man; and no more to assemble, contrary to the laws and your allegiances; and to cause the provokers of you to this mischief to be delivered to our lieutenant's hands or ours, and you yourselves to submit to such condign punishment as we and our nobles shall think you worthy."[1]

On Thursday, October 12, the people were ordered to be at the Castle-garth, in Lincoln, to hear the king's answer to their petition. Difficulties had by this time arisen between the gentlemen and the common people. They mutually distrusted each other, and at the reading of the royal letter the dissensions became apparent. "We the gentlemen," says one of them, when the letters came, "thought to read them secretly among ourselves, but as we were reading them the commons present cried that they would hear them read or else pull them from us. And, therefore, I read the letters openly; and because there was a little clause there, which we feared would stir the commons, I did leave that clause unread, which was perceived by a canon there, and he said openly the letter was falsely read, by reason whereof I was like to be slain."[2]

From that hour agreement was impossible, and on the following morning, Friday, October 13, the Lincolnshire resistance to Henry's measures was at an end. The gentry went forward to Stamford to meet the duke of Suffolk, and in their company he, with Russell and Richard Crumwell, rode through Lincoln, the streets of which were crowded with a sullen and disheartened populace. On that same day, Friday, October 13, the royal proclamation was read at the cross in the market-place at Louth, and by Sunday, Henry had received at Windsor the news of the complete collapse of what threatened to be a formidable popular protest against his policy and government.

[1] *State Papers*, i. p. 463.
[2] "Confession of Thomas Mayne," quoted by Froude, iii. p. 117.

The king saw at once how prejudicial to his position abroad was this overt expression of popular dissatisfaction with his domestic policy. He did not even wait for the news of the suppression of the rising, but on October 13th, even before Suffolk had entered Lincoln, he had written to his ambassadors at the court of France, bishop Gardiner and Sir John Wallop, to counteract any evil which might arise from the news of the rebellion. "You shall understand," he says, "that, by the blowing abroad of certain false tales—that is to say, that we should intend to take all the ornaments, plate, and jewels of all the parish churches within our realm into our hands and convert the same totally to our own use; and that we should also therewith intend to tax all our commons, as the like thereof was never heard of in any Christian religion, when we assure you there was never word spoken, or thing thought, by us or any of our council touching such matters; which certain traitors (whereof two be already executed, and we have more of the authors ready to suffer like punishment) devised and invented, being they otherwise in the danger of our laws, and thinking, in this tombeling to fly and escape— certain of our subjects, with a number of boys and beggars, assembled themselves together in our county of Lincoln. And for as much as the matter of this insurrection may be there noted a greater thing than it is and so spoken to our dishonour, we thought meet to advertise you, as of the cause and the state of the thing we have done already." He concludes by saying that Suffolk, "who is now there, with a great force," will, without doubt, "give the traitors the reward of their traitorous attempt very shortly." And he adds that in six days he has "levied and conveyed" to Ampthill "an army of" 80,000 tried men, which he hopes his ambassadors "may declare it" to the king of France, "and to all others whatsoever shall be bruited of the same, and that we can at all times return every man home again to his house or dwelling-place, in as short space, without tumult or any manner of inconvenience."[1]

[1] Tierney, *Dodd's Church Hist. of England*, vol. i. App. xlii., "from the original, in my possession." No such army as the king speaks of was in existence. Eleven days later the privy council ask the duke of Norfolk's advice whether it was "expedient that his grace should levy an army." (*Hardwicke State Papers*, i. p. 26.)

Upon the submission of the men of Lincolnshire, Henry issued another proclamation giving them his pardon and extolling his own generosity in so doing. They were ordered to "leave all their harness and all other weapons in the market-place of our city of Lincoln," and to depart peacefully to their homes. "And if," the document concludes, "you will not take this most gracious and merciful clemency at this present time, but continue one whole day longer after the receipt hereof, we shall execute all extremity against you, your wives and children without mercy; to the most terrible and fearful example of all others, whilst the world shall endure hereafter."[1]

It is well to enter more in detail into the part taken by the monks in the insurrection. They must doubtless have given their best wishes to a movement which was initiated in their defence, but beyond this and the fact that they had given food, and perhaps money, to the mob, and that some few were violently compelled to go with it, there is nothing that can be construed into a proof of complicity. The first with whose name the Lincolnshire rising is especially associated is Dr. Mackarel, abbot of Barlings.[2] He and his brethren, who were of the Premonstratensian order, are accused not only of taking an active part in fomenting the disturbance, but the abbot is made by Mr. Froude and those who follow him the head of the rising.

In his own examination, taken in the Tower of London on January 12th, 1537, abbot Mackarel declares that: "By command of Mr. Dymmocke, the sheriff, he brought a cartload of victuals to the rebels. And at his coming amongst them, for fear of his life and for safeguard of his house, and to the intent they should not spoil his said household, he said to the sheriff these words, or like in effect following: 'Mr. Sheriff, I beseech you to be good master unto me and save my house from spoiling, and I will help you with such victual and goods as I have.'" Further, after declaring that he knew nothing about the insurrection till the Wednesday (October 4th), and ex-

---

[1] *State Papers*, i. p. 468.
[2] He was titular bishop of Chalcedon and suffragan of Lincoln. As chosen agent of so prudent and experienced a prelate as Longland in the administration of his diocese, it is to be presumed he was not naturally of the temper of a brawler, or disposed to rush to the head of a rabble.

plaining what he considered to be the causes which led to the rising, he asserts that the sheriff Willoughby, "with great bragging and menacing words commanded him to bring victuals," and denies utterly that "he did at any time persuade the people by sermon or oration or any kind of persuasion."

"Item," the record runs, "he saith that upon Friday after the commencement of the insurrection (October 6th), when he had sure knowledge that the rebels would come into his monastery—and at that time there were in his house a hundred of the same rebels—he then weeping declared to his brethren and some of his servants these words, or like in effect following: 'Brethren and servants, I perceive that these rebels will have both you and me with them, and what shall become of us God knoweth; but this ye shall understand, that their cause is nought, and surely God and man must of justice take vengeance on them.'

"Item he saith, that he would have fled at the beginning of the insurrection, saving he feared the burning of his house and the utter destruction of the same and spoiling of all his goods."

"Be it remembered," continues the document, "that a canon of the abbot of Barlings, now prisoner in the Tower of London, being examined what words the said abbot had to his canons, servants and the rebels, at their being in his house as is aforesaid, declared that the abbot, being by them required to send his canons to the rest of their company, answered, it was against the laws of God and man that any religious person should go to battle and specially against their prince. And said further, that the said abbot was so sorrowful that he could not, in a great while after their departure from his house, say any part of his divine service for weeping."[1]

In a subsequent examination on March 23rd, 1537, before Legh, Layton and Ap Rice, abbot Mackarel made certain admissions about the way in which he viewed the work of suppression. He says that when they were prisoners in Lincoln gaol the cellarer was admitted to bail by Sir William Parr in order that he might collect the rents due to the abbey, and of these Sir William got £20.

---

[1] Chapter House Bk., A. $\frac{2}{15}$, pp. 11-13.

He also confessed that "he was in much fear of deprivation (at the) time of the king's late visitation. And the visitor Mr. Bedyll came so suddenly on him that he had no leisure or deliberation to tell the money which he delivered in a purse to 'one Thomas Osegarby.' Also he says," continues the record, "that when Freeman and Wiseman, the king's surveyors, were suppressing the lesser abbeys in Lincolnshire, the report was common, that they should return to resolve the greater, and he then gathered his brethren together and said to them thus: 'Brethren, ye hear how other religious men be treated and how they have but forty shillings given to each of them and so let go; but they that have played the wise men among them have provided beforehand for themselves and sold away divers things, wherewith they may help themselves hereafter. And ye hear also this rumour that goeth abroad as well as I, namely, how that the greater abbeys should go down also. Wherefore by your advice, this shall be my counsel, that we do take such plate as we have and certain of the best vestments and set them aside and sell them if need be, and divide the money coming thereof among us, when the house is first suppressed. And I promise you, on my faith and conscience, ye shall have your part thereof and of every penny that I have during my life. And thereupon the said brethren agreed thereto.'" Upon this, concludes the abbot, "I sent plate worth £100 and some of the best vestments to one 'Thomas Bruer.'"[1]

The only real witness against the abbot of Barlings was one Bernard Fletcher. He deposed "that the rebels being within a flight shot of the said abbot's pastures, the same abbot brought them 80 wethers, 6 oxen, and a wain laden with bread and drink." Further on in his examination he declared that when the abbot "brought his said victual to the rebels, he there openly declared unto them these words, or like in effect following: 'Masters, I have brought you here certain victuals. Go forward and stick to this matter. I have a lordship at Sweton, and I will prepare for you as much more victual and bring the same to you to Ancaster heath.'"

But "be it remembered," runs the record, "that after

[1] Brit. Mus. Cleop., E. iv. f. 245.

the examination of this deponent named Bernard Fletcher, the same deponent and the abbot of Barlings were brought face to face. And there the abbot denied utterly that he brought any sheep to the rebels, and further said that there came no sheep in his company. Whereupon this deponent being asked the question whether he did or no, saith that he cannot perfectly tell whether the 80 sheep expressed in his examination were the same abbot's or no, or to whom they did belong or appertain."

"The same abbot also denieth that he said to the said rebels at his repair to them: 'Go forward and stick to this matter, etc.' . . . But saith that, being amazed and fearing lest they would have killed him, forasmuch as a great many of them were his mortal enemies, said unto them: 'Masters I have according to your commandment brought you victuals, beseeching you to be good unto me and preserve my house from spoil. And if ye will let me have a passport, I will go to a lordship of mine called Sweton, where against your coming to Ancaster heath I will prepare for you as much more victual.' And the same abbot being asked why he spake these words, said he intended if he might have had his passport to have stolen from them clean and gone his way, for without he should use such policy it was not possible."[1]

The depositions of Thomas Bradley, subprior of Barlings, and other canons of the house agree with their abbot's in the main facts. Compelled by the insurgents, six of the brethren appear to have borne arms for some days and gone along with the host. From the evidence, it certainly does not appear that the abbot and all his canons "rode at the head of the host in full armour," or that he and one of his brethren were justly executed for having "been concerned in the murder of the chancellor."[2]

As to Bardney and Kirksted, the evidence of complicity is even more meagre. Seven monks of the first monastery were examined in November, and confessed that four or five of their number went for a short time with the rebels, "by command of William Wright."[3] Some other witnesses confessed having seen them in the ranks, and one "heard say that the said traitors" had help from the abbey.[4]

---

[1] Chapter House Bk., A. $\frac{2}{18}$, pp. 19–22.   [2] Froude, iii. p. 212.
[3] *Calendar*, xi. No. 828.   [4] Chapter House Bk., A. $\frac{2}{18}$, p. 116.

The Kirksted monks acknowledged their part in the rising when questioned. Under threats that, "if they came not forth to the host, (they) should be (burnt in) their own house" . . . about four o'clock in the evening, the abbot, cellarer, bursar and all the monks able to go, 17 in all, went to the outer gate, where they met a servant of the abbey, who told them they could wait till the next day. At eleven o'clock the following morning all except the abbot departed, "the cellarer and bursar horsed and with battle-axes, the rest unhorsed." Two days before, a band of sixty of the insurgents had carried away all the servants of the abbey to the muster. The abbot, "as being sick," was excused, but he gave the bursar 20s. and a horse laden with victual. The day upon which the monks arrived at the head-quarters of the insurgents two of them returned home sick, four went the following day (Friday), and four more on Saturday; the rest remained "till Tuesday morning." As for the abbot, he "was glad of their return, and thanked God there was no business."[1]

The punishment meted out to the insurgents was terrible. About a hundred are said to have been carried away to London, and lodged in the Tower. The following year they were tried by Sir William Parr and a special commission sitting at Lincoln on Tuesday in the third week of Lent, March 6th. The jury was apparently in their favour. Thomas Moigne, a gentleman of the county and one of the accused, spoke skilfully for a long time in their behalf, and "but for the diligence of the king's serjeant" they would have been acquitted. As it was, they were condemned, although sixty-three were immediately respited. The other three-and-thirty, including the abbot of Kirksted and three of his monks, six monks of Bardney, four canons of Barlings, and seven secular priests, were ordered for immediate execution. Towards the end of March the abbot of Barlings, William Moreland, monk of Louth-park, Thomas Kendal, vicar of Louth, with two other priests and twelve laymen, were tried in London before chancellor Audeley, found guilty, and condemned to death.

[1] *Calendar*, xi. No. 828.

CHAPTER XII

The Pilgrimage of Grace

THE sudden termination of the Lincolnshire rising did not by any means relieve Henry from his domestic difficulties. Popular protests against his policy and active interference with his agents in carrying out his orders were not confined to the fen district and its immediate neighbourhood. "Alarming reports came in of the temper of the north-midland and eastern counties. The disposition of the people between Lincoln and London was said to be as bad as possible." A servant of Sir William Hussey reported, that "in every place by the way as his master and he came, he hath heard as well old people as young pray God speed the rebellious persons in Lincolnshire, and wish themselves with them, saying that if they came that way that they shall lack nothing that they can help them unto. And the said Hugh (the servant) being asked what persons they were which so reported," replied "*all.*"[1] Another witness declared that "he heard some say in the south parts (as he rode towards London, between Stamford and London) that the commons of those parts were in one mind with 'the northerners,' and wished they had come forward an end, for then they should have had more to take their parts." And also when in London, a shopman said to him: "Because you are a northern man you shall pay but sixpence for your shoes, for ye have done very well of late, and would to God you had come an end, for we were in the same mind that you were."[2] But the inquisitorial severity of the king and his advisers visited with the extremity of punishment even the slightest approval of the popular movement. The English terror had now fully set in. "The ninth of October," writes Stowe, "a priest and a butcher were hanged at Windsor, by martial

---

[1] Sir W. Fitzwilliam to Crumwell, quoted by Froude, iii. p. 112.
[2] Chapter House Bk., A. $\frac{2}{16}$, p. 66

law, for words spoken in the behalf of the Lincolnshire men. The butcher wished the good fellows (as he termed them) in Lincolnshire to have the flesh on his stall rather than to sell it at such a price as he was offered. The priest standing by likewise wished them to have it, for he said they had need of it. Also James Mallet, doctor of law, late chaplain to Queen Catherine, for like words was executed at Chelmsford."[1]

Simultaneously with the movement in Lincolnshire the king experienced opposition to his schemes of suppression in Cheshire, which but for the prompt action of Sir Piers Dutton, the sheriff, might have proved serious. The abbey of Norton, in that county, did not come strictly within the act for suppressing monasteries under £200 a year, its income having been returned at £258, 11s. 8d. Still, as early as August, 1536, it had by some means or other fallen into the king's power. On the third of that month Sir Piers informed Crumwell that he had "taken the bodies of the abbot of Norton, Robert Jamyns and the stranger, a cunning smith, two of the said abbot's servants, also Randal Brereton,[2] baron of the king's exchequer of Chester, and John Hall, of Chester, merchant, and have them in my custody and keeping."[3] Shortly after Anne Boleyn's disgrace, the bishop of Salisbury had interceded with Crumwell for "the poor abbot of Norton" and the religious of "that house, for the poor people" of that neighbourhood were much "refreshed there."[4] But by October the abbey was in the hands of the king's receiver, John Byrkhed, who in his Michaelmas account acknowledges that he has received nearly £350 from the rents and sales of the abbey moveables, and has already remitted about £100 to the king. The greater part of the rest had been given to Thomas Byrkhed, the then called abbot, to keep up the house till the final dissolution.[5]

[1] Stowe, ed. 1615, p. 572. Hall places this circumstance in the Yorkshire rising. Wriothesley, however, gives the date "9th October." The nephew of the imperial ambassador (*Calendar*, xi. No. 714) refers to the fact, but calls the man "a shoemaker."
[2] Brereton is supposed to have been uncle to Sir William Brereton, who had been beheaded in May preceding for his alleged connection with Anne Boleyn. (Ormerod, *Cheshire*, i. p. 502, *note*.)
[3] Wright, p. 52.   [4] *Calendar*, x. No. 942.
[5] Exch. Aug. Off. Mins. Accts., 27-28 Hen. VIII., 80, M. 3. It would hence appear that a relation of the receiver Byrkhed had been appointed to the office of abbot. Robert Hall was the last regular abbot (*Monasticon*,

By this time Robert Hall, the true abbot, had been released or had escaped from prison, and apparently arrived at his monastery as the royal commissioners were packing up the valuables previous to removing them. "Pleaseth your good lordship," writes Dutton to Crumwell on October 12th, "to be advertised that Mr. Combes and Mr. Balles, the king's commissioners within the county of Chester, were lately at Norton, within the county of Chester, for the suppressing of the abbey there. And when they had packed up such jewels and stuff as they had there, and thought upon the morrow after to depart thence, the abbot gathered a great company together, to the number of two or three hundred persons, so that the said commissioners were in fear of their lives, and were fain to take (to) a tower there, and thereupon send a letter to me ascertaining me what danger they were in, and desired me to come and assist them or else they were never like to come thence.

"Which letter came to me about 9 o'clock in the night upon Sunday last (October 8th), and about two o'clock in the same night I came thither with such of my lovers and tenants as I had near about me, and found divers fires made as well within the gates as without. And the said abbot had caused an ox and other victuals to be killed and prepared for such of his company as he had then there. And it was thought on the morrow after he had comfort to have had a great number more.

"Notwithstanding, I used some policy, and came suddenly upon them, so that the company that were there fled. And some of them took to poles and the waters, and it was so dark that I could not find them. And it was thought if the matter had not been quickly handled it would have grown to further inconvenience, to what danger God knoweth.

"Howbeit, I took the abbot and three of his canons, and brought them to the king's castle of Halton, and there committed them to ward to the constable, to be kept as the king's rebels upon pain of £1000, and afterwards saw the same commissioners and their stuff conveyed thence, and William Parker, the king's servant, who is appointed to be the king's farmer there, restored to his possession."[1]

vi. p. 313). Thomas Byrkhed received a pension of £24 (Aug. Off. Mins. Bk., 249, f. 22), while the real abbot was condemned to death, as will be seen.

[1] Ellis, *Orig. Letters*, 3rd Series, iii. p. 42.

On receipt of this letter Henry sent to thank Sir Piers Dutton for his great service. In reply to the sheriff's implied question as to the punishment of the abbot and his three canons, the king wrote: "For answer whereunto ye shall understand that for as much as it appeareth that the said late abbot and canons have most traitorously used themselves against us and our realm, our pleasure and commandment is, that if this shall fully appear to you to be true, that then you shall immediately upon the sight hereof without any manner further delay cause them to be hanged as most arrant traitors in such sundry places as you shall think requisite, for the terrible example of all others hereafter. And herein fail ye not . . . Travail with such dexterity as this matter may be finished with all possible diligence."[1]

The execution was not carried out immediately, because, as Dutton explains a month later (30th November), before there was time he learnt from the earl of Derby that the Pilgrimage of Grace was at an end, and concluded to wait till the king's "further pleasure were made known." He tells Crumwell that he writes for instructions, as his fellow commissioner, Sir William Brereton, refuses to follow this course, and he adds that he has "the said evildoers and offenders in straight endurance of imprisonment within his castle of Chester, there surely to be kept to abide his grace's pleasure."[2] The final fate of the abbot and his companions, like that of so many others at this time, remains uncertain, but no record appears of their pardon.

The most formidable opposition which Henry experienced at this time was without doubt the popular movement known as the "Pilgrimage of Grace." In the numbers who joined the agitation, in the high position of their leaders, and in the extent of the disaffection, the king and his counsellors had reason for the utmost alarm, especially as they felt the southern population could not be relied upon to support a policy which they detested; and from over the seas were floating rumours of foreign combinations to aid the English people in their struggle for the rights of the church, their ancient faith, and their own temporal good. In five counties, from the borders of Scotland to the Lune and the Humber, the agitation remained for a short time unchecked.

---

[1] Ormerod, *Cheshire*, i. p. 502.   [2] *Ibid.*

As in Lincolnshire, so in the more northerly parts the effect of the late act of suppression had been patent to all. In Yorkshire, with the archdeaconry of Richmond and the bishopric of Durham, including the cells of larger monasteries, some forty-seven houses of men and twenty-three convents of women came within the pecuniary limit for dissolution, and a yearly income of £4384, 8s. 8d. had been transferred from the district to the king's purse.[1] By the feast of St. Michael of this year, 1536, Hugh Fuller, the royal receiver for the county of Yorkshire, reported that he had gathered in for the king's use from the half-yearly rents, the sales of goods and the estimated value of plate, bells and lead, above £4500. Five hundred and three ounces of gilt plate, 657 ounces of parcel gilt, and 321 ounces of silver—in all 1481 ounces of plate, valued at £224, 7s. 6d.—had besides this sum been already forwarded to Henry's treasure-house, and 133 fodders of lead, worth £440, with thirty-seven bells, valued at an average of £3 each, the spoils from the church roofs and belfries of the district, were stored up for subsequent sale.[2]

That the people were stirred most deeply by these auctions of monastic effects and by the fear of even more extensive desecration of consecrated churches and seizure of ecclesiastical property in the near future does not admit of doubt. The causes which led to the armed protest were fully and boldly declared by the leader of the movement, Robert Aske, when he wrote to the lords holding Pomfret Castle urging them to deliver up their charge and join the popular movement. "And in the same letter the said Aske rehearsed

---

[1] *Vide* list, *Calendar*, x. No. 1233
[2] Exch. Aug. Off. Mins. Accts., 27-28 Hen. VIII., No. 178, mm. 5d. 18d. One or two instances of hardships in particular monasteries and convents of this district have been already referred to. We may here add a few more. One monastery, *Warter*, which supported a prior and twelve canons, with fifty dependents and boys, was sold with all its goods to the earl of Rutland for £800 (*Ibid.*, 178, m. 5). At *Nunburnholme*, a small convent, there were twelve dependents and "many poor living there" (*Ibid.*, m. 15). At *Molseby*, a convent of eight nuns, a certain Elizabeth Ward had received a corrody, and on August 4th, when the nuns were dismissed, in consideration of £3, 6s. 8d. paid by the commissioners, she renounced all further right. She was "*impotens et surda*," and in consideration of her debility and poverty the commissioners gave the sum to a man of trust, who promised to keep the poor lady during her life (*Ibid.*, m. 15). At *Drax* there were thirty-nine "dependents and boys," besides other poor people (*Ibid.*, 14d.). At *Ferriby* thirty-four servants with boys and poor supported in the house (*Ibid.*, m. 15).

how the said commons were gnawn in the conscience with spreading of heretics, suppression of houses of religion and other matters touching the commonwealth." In his subsequent interview he "declared to the said lords, as well spiritual as temporal, the griefs of the commons. And how first, that the lords spiritual had not done their duties in that they had not been plain with the king's highness for the speedy remedy and quenching of the said heretics and the preachers thereof and for the suffering of the same; and for the ornaments of the churches and abbeys suppressed and the violating of relics by the suppressors, with the irreverent demeanour of the doers thereof, with abuse of the visitors and their impositions taken extraordinary. . . . And to the lords temporal the said Aske declared they had misused themselves in that they likewise had . . . not declared to his said highness the poverty of his realm and that part specially; in so much as in the north parts much of the relief of the commons was by succour of the abbeys, and . . . now the profits of abbeys suppressed, tenths and first-fruits went out of those parts." By reason of this "within short space of years there should be no money nor treasure in those parts; neither the tenant to have (money) to pay his rents to his lord, nor the lord to have money to do the king's service withal."[1]

At the close of his narrative to the king, Aske again insists upon the same points. "In all parts of the realm," he says, "men's hearts much grudged with the suppression of abbeys, and the first-fruits, by reason the same would be the destruction of the whole religion in England.' And their especial great grudge is against the lord Crumwell, being reputed the destroyer of the commonwealth, as well amongst most part of the lords as all other the worshipful commons. And surely, if he continue in favour and presence with your grace it will danger the occasion of new commotions which will be very dangerous to your grace's person; for as far as the said Aske can perceive, there is no earthly man so evil believed as the said lord Crumwell is with the commoners. . . . And also the said Aske saith that the most part of all the realm greatly impugneth against certain bishops of the new learning, reputing them and their folks as heretics and the

[1] Chapter House Bk., A. $\frac{2}{18}$, p. 53. Aske's narrative to the king.

great causes of this late commotion: and also against the lord chancellor for so general granting of injunctions and for playing of '*ambi-dexter*' in granting and dissolving of injunctions."[1]

But if the popular leader was bold in his declaration to the king, he is more explicit still as to the nature of the popular desires when examined in the Tower. Asked as to whether he considered that false reports "were not one of the greatest causes of the" insurrection,[2] he replies "that he thinks those bruits were one of the greatest causes, but the suppression of abbeys was the greatest cause of the said insurrection which the hearts of the commons most grudged at." And further he adds "that he thinks that only the suppression of the abbeys and 'dimission' of preachers had caused an insurrection though the said bruits had not been spoken of at all."[3]

Another fragment of his examination goes more particularly into the reasons which actuated the people in this movement. "To the 23rd article," runs this record, "the said Aske saith: First, to the statute of suppressions, he did grudge against the same, and so did all the whole country, because the abbeys in the north parts gave great alms to poor men and laudably served God. In which parts of late days they had but small comfort by ghostly teaching; and by occasion of the said suppression the divine service of Almighty God is much diminished, great number of masses unsaid, and the blessed consecration of the Sacrament now not used and showed in those places, to the distress of the faith and spiritual comfort to man's soul. The temple of God (is now) razed and pulled down, the ornaments and relics of the church of God unreverently used; the tombs and sepulchres of honourable and noble men pulled down and sold. No hospitality (is) now, in those places, kept, but the farmers for the most part let and tavern[4] out the farms of the same houses to other farmers for lucre and advantage to themselves. And the profits of these abbeys yearly go out of the country to the king's highness, so that in short space little money, by occasion of the said yearly

[1] Chapter House Bk., A. $\frac{2}{28}$, p. 64.
[2] *Ibid.*, p. 87. "Interrogatories" signed by "T. Crumwell."
[3] *Ibid.*, A. $\frac{2}{15}$, pp. 198-199. [4] "Underlet."

rents, tenths and first-fruits, should be left in the said country, in consideration of the absence of the king's highness in those parts, want of his laws and the frequentation of merchandise.

"Also divers and many of the said abbeys were in the mountains and desert places where the people are rude of condition and not well taught of the law of God. And when the said abbeys stood, the said people not only had worldly refreshing in their beds, but also spiritual refuge both by the ghostly living of them, and also by spiritual information and preaching. And many their tenants, whether feod[1] servants to them or serving-men, (were) well succoured by abbeys. And now not only these tenants and servants want refreshing there both of meat, cloth, and wages, and know not now where to have any living, but also strangers and baggers of corn (who) betwixt Yorkshire, Lancashire, Kendal, and Westmoreland, and the bishoprick (were) greatly helped both horse and men by the said abbeys; for never was in these parts denied either horsemeat or man's meat, so that the people were greatly refreshed by the said abbeys, where now they have no such succour. Wherefore the said statute of suppression was greatly to the decay of the commonwealth of that country; and all its parts of all degrees greatly grudged against the same, and yet doth, their duty of allegiance always saved.

"Also the abbeys were one of the beauties of this realm to all men and strangers passing through the same. Also all gentlemen (were) much succoured in their needs, with many their young sons there assisted, and in nunneries their daughters brought up in virtue, and also their evidences (*i.e.*, title-deeds) and money left to the use of infants in abbeys' hands—always sure there.[2] And such abbeys as were near the danger of sea-banks, were great maintainers of sea-walls

---

[1] *i.e.*, holding leases.
[2] As examples see the wills in *Testamenta Eboracensia* (Surtees Soc.), vol. iii. pp. 203-205; vol. v. pp. 189-191, 222; in *Archæological Journal*, vol. xxv. p. 72, see the provision of Sir John Stanley on his becoming a monk of Westminster, whereby his young son and heir is to be brought up until twelve years old by the abbess of Barking, and from that age until manhood under the care and guardianship of the abbot of Westminster. When in 1503 Margaret of Richmond, with the advice of Bishop Fisher, finally settled her Divinity lectureship at Cambridge, the abbey of Westminster was made trustee of the estates with which it was endowed, and charged with the payment of the salaries.

and dykes, maintainers and builders of bridges and highways (and) such other things for the commonwealth."[1]

Aske then goes on to state his reasons for objecting to the statute by which the princess Mary was declared illegitimate. "Also it was thought," he concludes, "that the divorce made by the bishop of Canterbury, hearing that appeal, was not lawful. Yea! and then men doubted the authority of his consecration, having not his pall as his predecessor had."

Passing on to speak of the statute of "first-fruits," Aske calls attention to the way in which houses still standing were hampered by the new legislation; "it was thought good that the statute should be annulled because it would be the destruction of the state of religion, which was and is profitable for the commonwealth both in soul and body, as before rehearsed. For it may chance so that in some year by death, deprivation or resignation the king's highness may be entitled thereunto two or three times, or more. And for the pain of the same, worshipful men and friends must be bound, and so they to be in danger and the house not able to pay the same. For now, in manner, what with the king's money granted by them and the tenths yearly by them paid, all or most part of their plate is gone and cattle also and their houses in debt. So that, either they must minish their household and hospitality and, enforced, keep fewer monks than their foundation; or else surrender their abbeys into the king's hands as forced (to do) for need, and the money thereof always coming out of that country to the great detriment of the commonwealth there. Whereby all the riches and treasures of religion was and is esteemed the king's treasure, as ready at his commandment. Also because they had plenty of riches they adorned the temple of God and always succoured their neighbour in their need with part of the same—their money for the most part current amongst their people.[2]

When questioned about the statutes of the "royal supremacy" Aske replied, "that then all men much murmured at the same and said it could not stand with God's law. And divers reasons thereof (were) made, whereof he delivered one to the archbishop of York in Latin, containing

---

[1] Chapter House Bk., A. $\frac{2}{19}$, pp. 209-210.   [2] *Ibid.*, p. 211.

a whole sheet of paper or more. . . . But the great bruit in all men's mouths then was, that never king of England since the faith came within the same realm claimed any such authority. And it would be found to be an increase of a division from the unity of the Catholic Church, if men might without fear, and by the king's favour declare their learning without his grace's displeasure."

With regard to the "statute of words that be treason," he declared that except in relation to the supremacy question "he heard few men grudge thereat." But on that matter "every man is fearful to show his learning or to labour for the same intent to show their learning, because there is a temporal law whereby they should incur the danger, or else the displeasure of their prince. And if the cause touch the health of man's soul, then it were a gracious deed that the king's highness would annul that statute and that learned men in divinity might show their learning either in convocation or preaching."[1]

Examined as to the popular opinion about the bishops and the griefs of the commons on that score, Aske said that they declared them to be heretics, "because they were so noted in the petitions of Lincolnshire and because they were reputed to be of the new learning and (holding) many tenets of Luther and Tyndal. And to the bishop of Worcester (Latimer), because it was said, either he was before abjured or else should have borne a faggot for his preaching. And that the archbishop of Canterbury was the first that ever was archbishop of that see that had not his pall from a spiritual man or from the see of Rome. And because he took upon him to make the divorce betwixt the king's highness and the lady Catherine dowager, where it was appealed to the Church, and for other his opinions, which the said Aske much noted, not because they were so openly bruited with all men. And as to the other two bishops,[2] surely they be marvellously evil spoken of, to be maintainers of the new learning and preachers of the same; and that because of their information religion was not favoured and the statute of suppression taken place, for they preached as it was said against the benefit of habits in religion and such like, and against the common orders and rules before used in the

---

[1] Chapter House Bk., A. $\frac{2}{29}$, p. 215.
[2] Hilsey of Rochester and Allen of Dublin.

universal Church. This was the common voice of all men." . . . And also "because they varied from the old usages and sermons of the Church, and because they preached contrary to the same, therefore they were bruited so to be schismatics."[1]

As Aske the leader thought, so thought the rest who followed him. Lord Darcy, speaking to him of the supremacy question, assured him "he had in the parliament chamber declared before the lords his whole mind touching any matter there to be argued touching their faith."[2] At another time the same lord in regard to the preaching of the new bishops said "that he would be no heretic."[3] Others deposed that they demanded the deprivation of the bishops "because they were supposed to be occasion of the breach of the unity of the Church."

Thus in the "Pilgrimage of Grace" the causes of the armed resistance to the royal policy appear to have been chiefly ecclesiastical. The suppression of the abbeys was felt to be a blow to religion in those parts no less than a hardship to the poor, and a detriment to the country at large. The royal supremacy was looked upon as founded only on Henry's whim and as a pretension without precedent in history, while the renunciation of papal authority was held to be subversive of the principle of unity in the Christian Church, and the first step towards diversity of doctrine and practice.

The story of the actual rising is well known. The sketch that it is needful to give here may be best taken

---

[1] Chapter House Bk., A. $\frac{2}{15}$, pp. 227–228.

[2] *Ibid.*, p. 233. Lord Darcy's account of the method followed in parliament is of interest. "Before this last parliament," he said, "it was accustomed amongst the lords, the first matter they always discussed after the mass of the Holy Ghost . . . to affirm and allow the first clause of *Magna Charta* touching the rights and liberties of the Church, and it was not now so." Also, "that in any matter which touched the prerogative of the king's crown or any matter that touched the prejudice of the same, the custom of the lords' house was they should have upon their request a copy of the bill of the same," to examine it and get counsel about it. But "that they could now have no such copy upon their suit, or at the least so readily as they were wont to have in parliament before. And to his remembrance he thought default in those of the chancery, in their use of their office amongst the lords, and in the hasty reading of the bills and request of the speed of the same." The statute which gave the king generally all monasteries under £200 both Aske and lord Darcy considered "little better than void," as the particular houses were not stated.

[3] *Ibid.*, 241.

chiefly from the account given of it by Robert Aske himself. At the beginning of October in the year 1536, Robert with his two brothers, John and Christopher, met at the house of their brother-in-law, William Ellerkar, for a hunting party. On the father's side the Askes were Yorkshire gentry of good descent. Their mother was a Clifford, daughter of John lord Clifford, the stout Lancastrian who was killed on Towton field; and aunt of the first Clifford, earl of Cumberland. John, the eldest of the three brothers, had the family estate of Aughton; Christopher possessed a property at Marshland, and Robert himself, with a manor in Yorkshire, was a barrister in good practice at Westminster. The latter was on his way back to London, when, crossing over the Humber in the Barton ferry, he learnt from the boatman for the first time "that the commons on the Lincolnshire side were up."

On landing at Barton, on the Lincolnshire side of the river, he proceeded to the house of a brother-in-law at Sawcliffe. When two miles on his road he was met by a band of mounted insurgents, who forced him to take the oath to be true to the commons, and then conducted him to his destination. A few nights after, he and his three nephews were taken out of their beds by the people, but the three youths were allowed to go over to Yorkshire, "because two of them were heirs apparent." Robert Aske himself was forced to become the leader of the insurgents in this part, who were in number some 4000. He appears to have accepted the position thus forced upon him and for some days endeavoured to organise the movement.

Leaving the southern side of the Humber after a short time, he crossed back into Yorkshire, where the rumour that he had been a leader in Lincolnshire had already preceded him. Almost immediately he prepared to return, but before he could do so he learnt the complete failure of the popular movement, and was obliged to fly. That night (October 13th), as he crossed the Trent, he saw the beacons blaze out over the waters and heard the clash of the alarm-bells calling upon the northern counties to rise in defence of their rights. The people of the north country had adopted the demands of the commons of Lincolnshire, and as the spark was stamped out in the fen districts, the flame burst forth again in all the country from the Humber to the Scotch marches and from the Irish sea to the German ocean.

Aske turned back, and passing once more over the Ouse into Howdenshire, found all the country far and wide astir. In places the "cross of the church" was with the villagers as their standard, and everywhere they "enforced gentlemen and heirs apparent to come unto them."[1]

To most the "Pilgrimage of Grace" was undoubtedly a rising in defence of religion and Catholic practice, and the actors bound themselves by an oath to fight "for the preservation of Christ's church, of the realm, and of the king." Aske at once fell into his place as leader, and with 9000 men or more he marched on York. In a letter to the mayor he urged him to give free access to the host, and as the city was fortified "neither with artillery nor gunpowder," this was conceded. The chiefs published an address in which the causes of the "assembly or pilgrimage" are stated, and an invitation is given to all to join in the work.[2] In the two days that the insurgents then remained at York, Aske "took order for religious houses suppressed, because the commons would need put them in again. Which order was set on the minster door at York, to the intent all the houses suppressed should resort there and know how they should use themselves."

Acting on this, many of the monks and nuns who had been ejected from their houses returned. "Work is done rapidly by willing hands in the midst of a willing people. In the week which followed, by a common impulse, the king's tenants were universally expelled. The vacant dormitories were again peopled; the refectories were again filled with exulting faces."[3] "Though it were never so late when they returned," the monks "sang matins the same night."[4] The Abbey of Sawley, which had been vacant since the 14th of May, and which had been, with all its moveables, sold to lord Darcy for close upon £400, was again occupied by the abbot and his twenty-one brethren,[5] and "being the charitable relief of those parts, and standing in a mountain

---

[1] Chapter House Bk., A. $\frac{7}{28}$, pp. 47–51.
[2] *State Papers*, i. p. 466.
[3] Earl of Oxford to Crumwell, quoted by Froude, iii. 133.
[4] *Calendar*, xi. No. 1319.
[5] Exch. Aug. Off. Mins. Accts., 27–28 Hen. VIII., No. 178, m. 5.

country and among three forests," the men of Craven, Kendal, Furness, and the districts, bound themselves together to resist any attempt to take it from the monks a second time.[1]

It was on Sunday, October 15, that Aske and his followers entered York. The people of Richmondshire and Durham had by this time also risen in arms, had seized the persons of lord Lumley, the earl of Westmoreland, and lord Latimer, and by Tuesday, the 17th, Aske had information that they were coming to join him. Pomfret castle, held by lord Darcy, was surrounded by the insurgents, and the garrison was known to incline to the popular movement. On Thursday Aske summoned lord Darcy to surrender, and the following morning, October 20th, after a long parley, Aske was allowed to take possession of the stronghold, and Darcy, Sir Robert Constable, the archbishop of York and the others who had sheltered within its walls, took the oath of the "Pilgrimage of Grace."

Of all the Yorkshire strongholds, Skipton and Scarborough alone held out for the king. The people daily flocked to the banner, and the host increased to an alarming size. "Lords Nevill, Latimer, and Lumley and 10,000 men, with the banner and arms of St. Cuthbert," and the men of Pickering and Blackmore, "with knights and gentlemen about 5000," came to the support of Aske. So great grew the multitude that when he moved forward on Doncaster he was followed by between thirty and forty thousand men "well tried on horseback." They marched under the banner of the pilgrims, which was practically that which the Lincoln men had adopted, and each wore on his arm a badge either with the "five wounds" worked upon it, or with a cross and I.H.S., which was used especially by those who marched under "Saint Cuthbert's banner."

The earl of Shrewsbury was now at Doncaster with his armed tenantry, together with the duke of Norfolk and some 5000 men. The river Don separated the opposing forces, and had battle been given, there is little doubt that victory would have been on the side of the people. The duke of Norfolk, on his side, had received the king's special commandment, "above all things, never to give stroke . . . unless you shall think yourself to have great and notable

[1] Chapter House Bk., A. $\frac{2}{28}$, p. 57.

advantage for the same." [1] And particularly if he found the rebels too strong for him, or if he thought "any of the company" with the earl of Shrewsbury "evil willing," he was to retire, and not hazard a fight. How he was to do this he left to the judgment of Norfolk himself, only recommending him his own "politic device," and warning him as to his "promises, to be made to the rebels for the stay of them, till your forces shall be come and joined with the others. Albeit we certainly know," the royal letter concludes, "that you will pretermit no occasion wherein, by policy or otherwise, you may damage our enemies; yet we doubt not again, but in all your proceedings you will have such temperance, as our honour, specially shall remain untouched and yours rather increased than, by the certain promise of that which you cannot certainly promise, appear anything defaced." [1]

On their side the insurgents appear to have been by no means anxious to shed the blood of their countrymen. Some, indeed, of the younger lords and gentry were eager to proceed to extremities at once; but their leader, Aske, reminded them that "it was no dishonour," and that "their whole duty was to declare their griefs to their sovereign lord, to the intent that evil counsellors about his grace might be known and have punished." [2]

Actuated by such motives—the one side by what Henry called a "politic device ... wherein you may damage our enemies," and the other apparently by a sincere desire to obtain their demands without bloodshed—the leaders of the two forces agreed to a conference. The desires of the "pilgrims" were, at the request of the duke, drawn up in a set of articles, and at a second meeting on Doncaster bridge it was agreed that Norfolk should accompany two of the northern leaders to the king to present their demands; that the king's forces should retire from Doncaster, and the "pilgrim" army return to Pomfret.

A fortnight passed in suspense. Many of Aske's followers returned to their homes, weary of waiting, and he himself was fully occupied in his endeavours to keep the remainder from active aggression pending the royal reply. From Craven came the news one morning that the earl of Derby

[1] *State Papers*, i. p. 494.
[2] Chapter House Bk., A. $\frac{2}{28}$, p. 55. (Note Lord Darcy "*playing the fool*.")

was marching with a force to expel the reinstated monks of Sawley Abbey, and that the people of the district were gathering to resist. Through the earl of Shrewsbury, Aske managed to stop the movement of lord Derby, and sent messages to the commons, "who had already attained Whalley Abbey," to "withdraw them to the mountains" again.

The next day the leader had to be in York to quiet the people there; and then again the following morning he was off fourteen miles away, at Watton Priory of the order of Sempringham, on the same errand—"to stay the commons there who would have chosen a new prior because the said prior was fled to the lord Crumwell, being one of his promotion, and had left behind him brethren and sisters of the same house, nigh sixty or eighty and not forty shillings to succour them." Aske managed to pacify the people, and "deputed the sub-prior for the time to order the same house," as the prior was yet absent.

Again, the day following, Aske was at Hull, to see Sir Robert Constable, who held the town for the commons, and to examine the fortifications made against the duke of Suffolk, who was "directly against the town." That town had fallen into the possession of William Stapleton, one of the insurgent leaders, about the middle of October.

Meantime, whilst Aske was fully occupied in his endeavour to keep the people quiet in the hopes that their petitions to Henry would be accepted, the royal agents were busy over two futile plots to secure the leader's removal by assassination or betrayal. "Alas, my lord!" wrote lord Darcy to Norfolk, "that you, being a man of so great honour, should advise or choose me to betray any living man, Frenchman, Scot, yea, or even Turk. To win for me or for mine heirs the best duke's lands that be in France, I would not do it to no living person."[1]

In the middle of November the two insurgent envoys, Ellerkar and Bowes, were sent back to the north "with general instructions of comfort," and with the information that the duke of Norfolk, with other commissioners, would follow after them with the royal reply. Henry had essayed several answers to the Yorkshire articles, but in each draft,

[1] Quoted by Froude, iii. p. 169.

annexed to the general pardon, was a reservation of certain persons to be excluded from it, and it was only finally, in deference to the advice of the duke of Norfolk, that he could be induced even to undertake to forego his royal vengeance entirely.

On November the 21st the insurgent leaders met at York to consider their future action. They had been invited to meet the king's commissioners at Doncaster, but they "debated long whether they should do so or not, because of a letter sent by Lord Crumwell to Sir Ralph Evers. Wherein were these threats or such like: 'Except the commons of those parts soon would be pacified, there should be such vengeance taken upon them that the whole world should speak thereof and take example by them."[1]

It was agreed finally, however, to meet the duke at Doncaster with 300 persons, and "letters were sent to the clergy to stand for the articles profitable for the faith of the Church and liberties of the same." "But," writes Aske to Henry, "by reason of the same letters, and also for the extreme punishment of the great jury of Yorkshire, for Wickliff's cause and for the extreme assessment of their fines, the lord Crumwell was and yet (at the close of the first rising) is in such horror and hatred with the people in those parts that in a manner they would eat him, and esteem their griefs only to arise by him and his counsel, as the said commons there declared their minds to the herald Lancaster nigh Hampall in Yorkshire, who can recount their words to your highness."[2]

Before the meeting at York broke up it was settled that two days before the meeting at Doncaster the lords should assemble at Pomfret. As the royal commissioners approached the borders of Yorkshire, towards the close of the month of November, the beacons were lighted, and "bells rung backward," again recalling the scattered forces of the insurgents to the banner of their "pilgrimage." Norfolk sent letters back to the king "in such extreme and desperate sort, as though the world should be in a manner turned upside down, unless we," as Henry writes, "would in certain points condescend to the petition of the rebels."[3] The forces which

---

[1] *Chapter House Bk.*, A. $\frac{2}{28}$, p. 59.   [2] *Ibid.*, p. 60.
[3] *State Papers*, i. p. 512.

the king had been able to get together during the delay were considered by his lieutenant altogether inadequate to face the 20,000 insurgents ready to meet them and hear the king's answer to their complaints. Henry again enjoined Norfolk "not indeed to meet with them but in such sort as shall be for your perfect surety." Still, he was to try and get them peacefully to accept the pardon he was instructed to offer. If, however, they refused to entertain such an offer, unless the pardon was "*general* and without exception," or demanded a parliament or proposed any other article, Norfolk was to say that his commission did not contemplate "the granting of any of those things," but that such was his love for them, and his fear lest they should act against the king foolishly, that he would himself go to the king, and, writes Henry, "join with them as humble suitors and petitioners unto us."

Further, if the duke found that the people only demanded a free and general pardon and a parliament, then the king instructed him to pretend to go away for six or seven days as if for the purpose of going to him, "and when that time shall be expired, at the day to be prefixed, declare unto them that, with great dint, you had obtained their petitions, and so present unto them the general pardon." In fact, so far did this diplomacy of Henry go that Sir John Russell already had in his possession the general pardon, with instructions not to let any one know of its existence.[1] It is obvious that for the purpose of obtaining delay, Henry, as he himself puts it, "therein waded, as far as possible, with our honour." As for Norfolk himself, he wrote to the king "all desperately," but, as the latter reminds him, "in the end you said you would esteem no promise that you should make to the rebels, nor think your honour touched in the breach and violation of the same."[2]

On Monday, November 27, the leaders of the insurgents met at Pomfret. The assembly comprised five peers, more than thirty knights, and, as Aske afterwards declared, "all or most part of the esquires of the said shire and gentlemen also."[3] They agreed to certain articles and conditions upon which they would lay down their arms. Simultaneously the clergy who were in the town, with archbishop Lee at their

---

[1] *State Papers*, p. 511. [2] *Ibid.*, p. 51. [3] Chapter House Bk., A $\frac{2}{78}$, p. 60.

head, met in the church to consider their answer to a set of ten articles proposed to them, or, as one witness described it, the archbishop took "certain clerks to discuss their griefs." And "as it was amongst them that were in his company, the archbishop of York held the same opinion" (that the movement was "good and gracious") "at the beginning, but now at the last meeting he preached to the contrary."[1] Still, as Aske afterwards declares, the people "would have the clergy's opinions touching the articles concerning our faith, to the intent they should make their articles to the lords at Doncaster certain." And, he added, "if the clergy did declare their minds contrary to the laws of God it was a double iniquity."[2]

The assembly of clergy, in spite of the sermon of archbishop Lee, drew up a brief set of articles which rejected as unlawful all that Henry had done in his ecclesiastical legislation. Convocation, they declared, should condemn preaching against purgatory, pilgrimages, saints, and images, and also all books against the same teaching should be condemned; the pains and punishment of heretics decreed by Henry IV. ought to be executed. Holidays, bidding of bedes, and preaching should be observed according to the ancient custom of the Church. "No temporal man might be supreme head of the Church, or exercise any jurisdiction or power spiritual therein; no temporal man had authority by the laws of God to claim the tenths or first-fruits of any spiritual promotion." Lands given to God, to the Church, or religion might not be taken away and put to profane uses. The pope of Rome ought to be taken for the head of the Church. Clerks now in prison or fled the country for withstanding the king's superiority in the Church should be set at liberty and restored; apostates from religion, not dispensed by the pope, should be obliged to return to their houses.[3] The articles, of which the above are the most important, were presented to the leaders of the movement, who sent forward to Doncaster for a safe conduct from the duke. And on Wednesday Aske and 300 followers crossed the bridge over the Don into the town. They were lodged at the Grey Friars, and on Thursday, the last day of November, they made choice of "twenty knights, squires

---

[1] Chapter House Bk., A. $\frac{2}{28}$, p. 232.   [2] *Ibid.*, A. $\frac{2}{29}$, pp. 91-93.
[3] Dixon, *History*, i. p. 473.

and commons," with Aske as their spokesman, to proceed to "the White Friars to the duke and earls." Entering into Norfolk's presence, "and all making their low obeisance and kneeling on their knees," they asked for the king's pardon, and Norfolk appears to have satisfied the leader of the king's intention in respect to their demands, and chiefly as regards the general pardon and the parliament to be held within the year in some place appointed by the king.

Aske retired first to the Grey Friars, where he told his followers what had happened, and then to Pomfret to the main body of the host. Early the following morning he sent the "bellman" round the town ordering the commons to come to the "market-cross" to receive the king's pardon, telling them they were to receive it under the great seal. The people "gave a great shout of joy" at the news, and the whole body of the insurgents moved onward with their leader. "And incontinent," continues Aske's narrative, "came there a letter from the lord Lumley how the said commons would not be satisfied except they saw the king's most merciful pardon under seal, and that the abbots new put in of houses suppressed should not void their possessions to the parliament time," adding that "the parliament should be at York or else they would burn beacons and raise the whole country."

But Aske himself was satisfied with the assurances of Norfolk and trusted to the honour of Henry, and so returned at once to Pomfret, where he persuaded the people who were assembled there, to the number of some 3000, to accept the pardon. His reasoning prevailed, and the royal herald arriving the same night with the document, early the following morning they all assembled on "St. Thomas' Hill," outside Pomfret, and receiving the pardon, at once departed to their homes.

Once more Aske returned to Doncaster, and, in the presence of the duke of Norfolk and the earls, he and his followers tore off the "badges and crosses with five wounds" as a token that their "pilgrimage" was at an end, exclaiming: "We will wear no badge nor figure but the badge of our sovereign lord."[1]

[1] Chapter House Bk., A. $\frac{2}{28}$, p. 63.

Thus ended the first act of the "Pilgrimage of Grace." The sequel of the story, the part borne in the movement by the monks and the punishment meted out to the vanquished, will be briefly related in the next chapter.[1]

[1] As to the position of affairs at the close of the year 1536 Mr. Gairdner writes:—"It was a new experience to Henry VIII. that he had been, even for a time, completely checkmated by his own subjects. But this was the state of matters at the end of the year 1536. He had not been able to bring the North of England back into subjection without entrusting Norfolk with a large authority to make concessions, and Norfolk had been obliged . . . (to dispense) the pardons without even the reservation of a few notable offenders to satisfy the king's vengeance. With what feelings Henry endured such a rebuff, the events of the next six months enable us to judge without misgiving. But at present he could not afford to give ready vent to his anger." (*Calendar*, xii. (i.) preface, p. i.)

CHAPTER XIII

The Second Northern Rising

INFLUENCED by Aske's advice, the northern bands quickly dispersed to their homes. The leader himself trusted implicitly to the royal promises made through the duke of Norfolk, and unhesitatingly performed his part in the compact. That the king's government had been in the greatest danger of overthrow cannot be questioned, and the persistency and earnestness with which the fidelity of the few troops Henry had collected to oppose the forward movement of the insurgents is asserted, leads to a suspicion of even their loyalty to his cause. As early as the beginning of November, the king had been anxious to discount the effect of the news of this fresh rising at the foreign courts. For this reason, as he had done in the case of the Lincolnshire disturbances, Henry wrote to his ambassadors in France the account he wished circulated abroad. So that, as he tells them, "you may boldly affirm the same to be true to all men and in all presences where you shall have any occasion, cause or opportunity to speak thereof." Judged by the documents, the king's account of the movement is far from being correct in any particular. The whole insurrection, he declares, was planned by those who wished to obtain plunder during the tumult, an intention which is conspicuously absent during the entire affair. He says further that when the people learnt they had been deceived by their leaders, they "much lamented their offences therein committed," and humbly "desired pardon for the same." "And as concerning the Yorkshire men," he continues, "they do already, being thus retired, lament their traitorous attempt and make great suit and labour for their pardon; so that we have no doubt but we shall in time dispose of them as we will and bring them to like submission, as is already made by them of Lincolnshire. . . . And yet do both shires remain wholly at our commandment, neither having our pardon, nor any certain promise of the same. And therefore you may be bold not only to declare the premises, as they be before specified, but also to affirm that, against every of the insurrections of those shires (being one attempted after another, and yet chiefly by one principal actor) we had in readiness, and that within six days for every of them, such two armies as we think would first have devoured the said rebels and yet have remained right able, every of them, after to have given battle to the greatest prince christened. And surely we be as much bound to God as ever was prince, both for that we found our subjects so forward, so willing, and so ready to have fought against the rebels, that we were rather enforced to keep them back and to cause great numbers to retire home to their countries, than, by any manner of allurements, to prick them forward. . . . We have them again in so good quiet, without effusion of blood or the striking of any stroke by either party, which is somewhat strange, and, peradventure, hath not been often seen—they (the insurgents), being, as is said, such a multitude, as, doubt you not, had been able, well furnished with artillery, ordnance, and good captains, to have overthrown the better of either the emperor's or French king's army."[1] The manifest contradictions and falsehoods contained in this royal letter need not be pointed out; but the document is of interest as showing the worth of the king's word, upon the faith of which the insurgents had laid down their arms.

But notwithstanding the king's round assertions the truth had been understood. On the 24th of December Crumwell wrote to the same ambassadors, Gardiner, bishop of Winchester, and Sir John Wallop, with respect to rumours which had been circulated as to the methods employed in staying the insurrection, and the need in which the king stood which compelled him to come to terms. It was altogether false, he says, that the "commons assembled for the king's part, were so faint and unwilling that they would not have done their duties if it had come to extremity." Still he admits that it was so reported in the country, but states "that the most part of the king's retinue in manner wept when they were commanded to return, considering the

[1] Tierney, *Dodd's Church Hist. of England*, i. p. 430. Quoted from "the original in my possession."

rebels were not more extremely punished."[1] However this may be, it is certain that the duke of Norfolk had no confidence in the forces at his disposal. Both he and Henry were unwilling to "adventure the king's honour in battle," and the king left the matter to his discretion, although the council told the duke of their "regret to receive so many desperate letters, and, in the same, to hear no mention of the remedies."[2]

With regard to the promises made to the rebels, the conclusion of Crumwell's letter, written a few weeks after the duke of Norfolk had made them in the king's name, shows how little Henry regarded them as obligatory on his part. "It is reported," the letter runs, "that the matter should be taken up with conditions and articles. It is true that, at the beginning, the rebels made petition to have obtained certain articles; but in the end they went from all, and remitted all to the king's highness pleasure, only in most humble and reverent sort desiring their pardon, with the greatest repentance that could be devised; insomuch as in their chief article, which, next their pardon, was for a parliament, for that they might have their pardon therein confirmed, they remitted the appointment of the same wholly to the king's majesty, without the naming of time, place, or any other thing touching that matter: and this discourse may you declare to all men for truth; for no man with truth can impugn the same."[3]

If the people were deceived, they had at the time no notion of any such deception, neither did they in any way abandon their demands, as Crumwell in the foregoing letter implies. Aske, in his narrative to the king, speaks of "the articles now concluded at Doncaster, which were drawn, read, argued and agreed among the lords and esquires" at Pomfret, and whether Norfolk exceeded his power or not in treating with Aske and his followers, a distinct agreement was made and signed.

From the meeting at Doncaster Aske had gone to the abbeys of Haltemprice and Ferriby, into which the expelled religious had been again brought by the "pilgrims," and pending the decision of the expected northern parliament he arranged that the king's farmers should be reinstated in

[1] Tierney, *ut sup.*, i. p. 432. [2] *Hardwicke State Papers*, i. 28.
[3] Tierney, i. p. 433.

their charges.[1] The resumption by the religious of their old houses and lands during the few weeks of the insurrection and the consequent expulsion of the royal officials had been a bold step. It is probable that, however willing the monks had been to regain possession of their monasteries, they had no part in the actual work of dispossessing the king's receivers. From Aske's narrative it is clear that the people had determined not only to put a stop to future suppressions, but to demand the restoration of those houses which had already passed into the hands of Henry.

After the meeting at Doncaster and the dispersal of the people to their homes, the king's heralds were sent round about the northern counties to proclaim the royal pardon. In so doing the envoy was directed to note well the demeanour of the people and to find out whether they had settled down to their occupations or were still disturbed. If he thought well, he should declare the king's sorrow that, after twenty-eight years, during which he had "ever tendered them in all things rather like his natural children than like his subjects," they should listen to false tales about him. What the king had done had the approval of the parliament and the clergy. Then "with gentle words" the envoy should declare "how the king having a main army of 50,000 men besides that force which was addressed against them," still on account of his affection for them, directly he heard they had retired, determined not to advance and punish them as they deserved. Having said this much, the herald was to read the proclamation, and have it fixed to the Market Cross or other public place, which shall be strictly watched to see whether anyone tear it down. "And finally," the officer "shall in all his journey, diligently, secretly and substantially ensearch what monks, canons, nuns or other religious persons, of any religious houses, within the limitation of the act of suppression, having been discharged by his grace's commissioners, be again restored by any of the rebels to the possessions of their said houses; how they use themselves in the same; and of what inclination the people is for their continuance."[2]

An instance of the way in which the directions issued by the king for the proclamation of his pardon were observed, is given in the examination of William Colyns, the bailiff of

---

[1] Chapter House Bk., A. $\frac{2}{23}$, p. 63. [2] *State Papers*, i. 473.

the town of Kendal. "And on the morrow after our Lady's day before Christmas," runs the record, "they received the king's gracious pardon at Pomfret, which they have to show in Kendal town under the king's broad seal at this examinat's house, brought by Clarencieux the herald about fourteen days before our said Lady's day. Which herald made proclamation in Kendal town the said fourteenth day of the king's said pardon. And because certain farmers of priories about sent to him showing him how divers brethren took away their corn from them, and therefore like to have been murder between them about the same, therefore the said herald gave commandment openly in the king's name, upon pain of high treason, that no man should disturb any man about the possession of lands and tithes; but they should be in like manner as they were at the last meeting at Doncaster, and so continue till the duke of Norfolk came again to the country, which should be about the twentieth day after Christmas. Which done, as the herald was departing away, came two of the brethren of the late priory of Cartmell, and desired the herald to write unto them the same order that they might show it to their neighbours. And he said he could not tarry so to do, but desired this examinat to write them a word or two of the effect of the said order. And thereupon this examinat at his request and to the intent to have the said brethren to keep them out of danger of the king's statutes, wrote unto them the said order of this effect: 'Neighbours of Cartmell, so it is that the king's herald has made proclamation here that every man (under) pain of high treason should suffer everything, as farms, tithes and such other to be in like stay and order concerning possession, as they were in the time of the last meeting at Doncaster, except you will of your charity help the brethren there somewhat towards their board.'"[1]

As he "showed me," says a witness, "that all the canons of Cartmell had entered the house except the foolish prior, who would not go to them," I wrote to him. As far as I remember "it was to this effect: Forasmuch as all religious persons in the north parts had entered their houses by putting in of commons, and I am informed that you, meaning the prior of Cartmell, being required so to enter, do withdraw

[1] Chapter House Bk., A. $\frac{2}{29}$, p. 250.

yourself, I think you may safely enter and do as others do, keeping yourself quiet for the season and praying for the king. And at the next parliament then to do as shall be determined, and I have no doubt but so doing you may continue in the same with the grace of God who keep you." The letter was written from York on the ninth of December, and the writer declared that he sent it, because it was openly said at the time both at Pomfret and York that the abbey should continue "in such manner as they were put in, unto the next parliament." For this same reason, and because he "understood that such was the promise made at Doncaster," he spoke in the same way to prior Coke of St. Agatha's.[1]

The letter to Cartmell probably confirmed the brethren there in their determination to hold to their old home. Their trust in thus relying on the herald's word was terribly expiated, for as Colyns, the bailiff of Kendal, declared in his examination: "After this, four of the brethren of the said house of Cartmell and eight yeomen were put to execution for withstanding the king's farmer Mr. Holcrofte and stirring up a new commotion about eight weeks after (the letters) without the knowledge of this examinat or any other man of Kendal to his witting."[2]

It does not seem open to doubt that Aske endeavoured to restrain the people and prevent any further attempt at insurrection, in the expectation that Henry would redeem his promises made at Doncaster. A fortnight after the people had dispersed to their homes the king wrote to him pressing him to come and see him. "We have conceived," he says, "a great desire to speak with you and to hear of your mouth the whole circumstance and beginning of that matter," and he promises that he will "accomplish towards you and all others our general and free pardon, already granted unto you."[3]

In obedience to this summons Aske travelled to the south and remained some time with the king. At his wish he wrote out a full and complete history of his connection with the rising and a straightforward and honest declaration of the various causes which led to the disturbance. It is from this invaluable document that many of the details of

[1] Chapter House Bk., A. $\frac{2}{18}$, p. 345.
[2] *Ibid.*, A. $\frac{2}{16}$, p. 250.   [3] *State Papers*, i. p. 523.

the rising are known, and that it is known how keenly the people of the North felt the destruction of the religious houses and the various ecclesiastical innovations introduced by Henry.[1]

Aske was then sent back to the North with fresh assurances of the king's intention of abiding by the pledges given by Norfolk. But meantime the people were becoming disheartened by the long delay and doubtful of the royal intention. The fact that Crumwell remained apparently as secure as ever in Henry's favour in spite of all the objections they had urged against him; that rumour had spoken of the massing of royal troops round about the disaffected counties, and of the strengthening of the defences of Hull and elsewhere, seemed to suggest that Henry had no real intention of keeping faith with them. On his return to Yorkshire Aske saw the danger and immediately wrote to inform the king of the agitation. "I do perceive," he said, "a marvellous conjecture in the hearts of the people, which is, they do think they shall not have the parliament in convenient time; secondly, that your grace hath by your letters written for the most part of the honourable and worshipful of the shires to come to you, whereby they fear not only danger to them, but also to their ownselves; thirdly, they be in doubt of your grace's pardon by reason of a late book answering their first articles, now in print, which is a great rumour amongst them; fourthly, they fear the danger of fortifying holds, and especially because it is said that the duke of Suffolk would be at Hull and to remain there; fifthly, they think your grace intendeth not to accomplish their reasonable petitions by reason now the tenths is in demand; sixthly, they say the report is my lord privy seal (Crumwell) is in as great favour with your grace as ever he was, against whom they most specially do complain; finally, I could not [but] perceive in all the shires, as I came from your grace homewards, that your grace's subjects be wildly minded in their hearts towards commotions or assistance thereof, by whose abetment yet I know not; wherefore,

---

[1] It is significant that whilst the filthy scribbles of Layton and his compeers have been printed and reprinted and their reports dinned into people's ears for the last two centuries, such a weighty document as Aske's "expostulatory narrative to the king," drawn up at Henry's express request, has never yet seen the light.

sir, I beseech your grace to pardon me in this my rude letter and plainness of the same, for I do utter my poor heart to your grace to the intent your highness may perceive the danger that may ensue; for on my faith I do greatly fear the end to be only by battle."[1]

It would appear that Aske was loyal to the king in his implicit belief that the promises made at Doncaster would be adhered to. The letter given above, together with his narrative of the events, hardly admit of a doubt that he was honest in his endeavour to restrain the people from any further aggressive measures. John Hallom, one of those most deeply compromised by the second rising, declared at his examination that Aske had done what he could to prevent it,[2] and in this opinion he was borne out by most of the witnesses. Lord Darcy also joined Aske in this attempt to preserve the peace. He, like the leader, had been invited to journey to Windsor to see the king, but although he had excused himself on the plea of such ill-health that "he was more like to die than to recover thereof,"[3] he wrote several letters advising the people to trust to the king's promises and to his looking to their grievances.[4] He also declared to the lord admiral, in a letter written on the 20th of January, 1537, that Aske, Babthorp, Ellerker, Constable and he himself were doing their best to quiet the restless humour of the people. "And Sir Richard Tempest." he adds, "is sent home . . . with good comfortable words of the parliament for spiritual and temporal men, and of the king's free and mere pardon of his own benign grace granted, and that true justice shall have place against all that was in the bill of article." And if the duke of Norfolk only come to promise this, he concludes, "he will accomplish more than 40,000 men could."[5]

On the eve of Sir Francis Bigod's rising, letters were sent to him and the commons with him urging them to pause. With these Sir Robert Constable, on January 18th, sent a paper saying that "the king's highness hath declared by his own mouth unto Robert Aske that we shall have our parliament at York frankly and freely for the ordering and reforming of all causes for the commonwealth of this realm;

---

[1] Froude, iii. p. 182.   [2] Chapter House Bk., A. $\frac{2}{19}$, p. 48.
[3] Ibid., B. $\frac{2}{11}$, p. 40.   [4] Ibid., pp. 1, 3, 7.
[5] Ibid., p. 21.

The Second Northern Rising

and also his frank and free convocation for the good stay and ordering of the faith and other spiritual causes."[1]

Bigod, however, had no belief in the honesty of the royal promises. "You are deceived," he said in a speech to his followers, "by a colour of a pardon, which is but a proclamation. It is as if I should say the king will give you a pardon, and I bade you go to the Chancery for it. You are there (in the pardon) called rebels, and if you accept it you will acknowledge yourselves to have acted against the king. A parliament, too, is promised, but neither place nor time appointed; and the king claims to have cure both of your bodies and souls, which is against the Gospel."[2]

But Aske and others had no suspicion of double dealing; and in fact it was this very confidence in the royal honesty which was afterwards construed into high treason, and for which lord Darcy, Aske and many others were executed. In the notes upon the evidence against them it is stated that a letter from Darcy to Aske, written on January 21st, declared that the duke of Norfolk was to come into the North "to proclaim a free parliament to be kept there, and also free liberty to the spirituality to utter their learning;" also that in this parliament all grievances were to be considered. This shows, the author of the "note" rightly infers, that lord Darcy still looked for reform, "which," he continues, "is high treason." Moreover, in a letter to the duke of Suffolk, he asked that "the appointments made at Doncaster on the king's part should be observed," and this again, says the annotator, proves that he is a "traitor" still. The same deductions are made from the letters and actions of Robert Aske subsequent to the pardon, whereby the very reliance he placed upon the plighted word of Henry is counted as proof of a traitorous disposition.[3]

In March Norfolk wrote to Crumwell that he had successfully lured Robert Aske into his toils. Whilst affecting to treat him with perfect confidence the Duke was in reality setting traps to catch him for the king. He wrote to Crumwell that he had induced the late popular leader to go to London, giving him letters of recommendation, to which, however, the all-powerful minister was to attach no importance, as they were "only intended to lull the bearer

[1] Chapter House Bk., B. $\frac{2}{21}$, p. 131.   [2] *Calendar*, xii. (i), No. 369.
[3] Chapter House Bk., A. $\frac{2}{28}$, pp. 241-247.

into false security." At the same time "he recommended the king to pursue the same policy, affecting to repose great trust in him till he had wormed out all his secrets"[1] and had him in his power. "It was rather superfluous work," writes Mr. Gairdner, "to teach Henry double-dealing. From the time of his previous conference with Aske he had been constantly studying how to get both him and all the other leaders entirely within his power, and have them judicially convicted of offences committed since the pardon, or such as the pardon did not cover."[2]

It is unnecessary to follow the history of the several sporadic risings, by which the people endeavoured to force attention to their disappointed hopes. Sir Francis Bigod and others endeavoured to seize Hull and Beverley in the beginning of January, and were captured in the attempt. The leaders of the first rising lost no time in repudiating the new movement, and Aske received a letter from the king, thanking him for his services in endeavouring to put an end to it.[3] Various commotions followed in the northern parts, which culminated in an attack upon Carlisle by some eight thousand men of Westmoreland. They failed in their attempt, and only afforded the duke of Norfolk a pretext for advancing into the disturbed districts with an army upon which he could rely. Martial law was proclaimed and remorseless executions finally broke the resistance of the people.

These ill-judged and hopeless disturbances afforded the king an excuse for breaking off the convention of Doncaster. Even those who, in reliance upon the royal promises, had done their best to restrain the impatience of the people, found themselves involved in the consequences of their former acts although they had sued and obtained pardon for them. Aske, whose good offices in keeping the people quiet had been acknowledged by Henry, and lord Darcy, who had certainly taken no part in such risings, found themselves prisoners in the royal power.

Before speaking of the final act in the drama of the Pilgrimage of Grace—the trials and executions of those implicated in the movement—the special attention of the reader must be directed to the part taken in it by the

---

[1] *Calendar*, xii. (i), Nos. 710, 712. [2] *Ibid.*, preface, p. xxix.
[3] *State Papers*, i. 529.

religious. The king, in his letter just quoted, declared that "all these troubles have ensued by the solicitation and traitorous conspiracies of the monks and canons of those parts." It will be of interest to see how far such an assertion, borne out apparently by the numerous executions of abbots and monks, is confirmed by the depositions and examinations of witnesses and prisoners, on which alone, if justice had had its course, their condemnation or acquittal should have rested.

Speaking of the beginning of the insurrection, one witness, William Stapleton, accuses an Observant friar of being implicated in the movement. He was staying, he says, at the Grey Friars, Beverley, with his elder brother Christopher, "a very weak, crazed and impotent man," who had been ill for some sixteen years and was at that time at the Friars "for change of air," as he "had been the summer before from May till after midsummer." William, who was on his way to London, did not leave as he intended on October 4th, because he heard that the "commons of Lincolnshire" had risen, and so he remained on from day to day, till Sunday, the 8th, when the people about Beverley joined in the movement. William Stapleton tried to keep his people indoors, but his brother's wife would not be controlled, and went to the hedge, crying out, "God's blessing have ye and speed ye well in your good purpose." The people asked where her people were, "and she replied, 'They be in the Friars. Go pull them out by the heads.'" For this she was blamed by both brothers, but she replied "that it was certainly God's quarrel." At this time, as Stapleton declared, there was with the people "one Sir Thomas Johnson, otherwise called Bonaventure, an Observant friar, who was sworn, and had been much with the said Christopher both at his house at Wighill and at Beverley, and before that time was assigned to the said house of Beverley by Doctor Vavasour, warden of the Grey Friars at York. And the said Bonaventure supervised much the rising, and was very busy going betwixt the wife of Sir Christopher and the said wild people, oft laying scriptures to maintain their purpose."[1]

It was apparently at the suggestion of the same friar that William Stapleton was forced to become the leader of

[1] Chapter House Bk., A. $\frac{2}{8}$, p. 150.

the people, and subsequently, as he says, "the Observant offered himself to go into the quarrel in harness to the field, and so did to the first stay." The same witness accuses "Sir Robert, a friar of St. Robert's of Knaresborough,"[1] of working hard to stir up the people to join the movement, and these two are about the only individual names mentioned as connected with the rising and not belonging to abbeys well known in history as attainted for their supposed part in the Pilgrimage of Grace.

In the second rising, the Gilbertine priory of Watton, on which a new prior had been imposed against the wish of the community by Crumwell, was said to be mixed up with the movement. The story is best told in the words of one William Horsekey when examined as to his knowledge of the matter. "Upon Monday was a fortnight," he says, "which was plough-day after that (Christmas day) the said Hallam, Hugh Langdale and this examinat had a drinking together at one John Bell's in Watton with many other of the parishioners, being there together in great number as the manner is there of plough-days, and every man departed homeward. The said Hallam, Hugh Langdale and this examinat, with the vicar of Watton, as they passed by the church of Watton turned in the same to say a *pater noster*, and there being, the said Hallam called this examinat and the said Langdale to an altar, called our Lady's altar, and said unto them: 'Sirs, I fear me lest Hull do deceive us the commons, for there is ordnance daily received there by ships.'" He then went on to declare that the king was not going to keep his promises and that they must look to themselves. Aske, as the witness declared, did all he could to prevent the second rising, which was "for the pulling down abbeys" and the payment "of tenths."

"Also he saith," continues the document, "that the subprior, the confessor of the nuns, and the vicar of Watton . . .

---

[1] The king personally examined all the evidence against those accused, and in regard to this "friar of Knaresborough" Mr. Gairdner thus characterises Henry's action. He acted generally "in the spirit of a detective policeman, and writing marginal comments (on the evidence) for the instruction of Norfolk. As a specimen of these it may be worth while to note the observation made upon the first information about the friar of Knaresborough:—'This Knave is to be taken, and, well examined, to suffer;' the fate of the victim, it will be observed, being quite decided by the king himself before any judicial investigation. How to satisfy his thirst for blood and save appearances as regards the law might sometimes be a problem." (*Calendar*, xii. (i), preface, p. xxix.)

are great favourers and setters forth of this matter of sedition, for he heard them and every of them since Christmas last, at sundry times say that it would never be well as long as the king's grace should be the supreme head of the Church, and that the same would not be reformed without the people did set forward again with a new insurrection. And upon his conscience he thinketh that there is never a good one of all the canons of the said house of Watton, but that every one of them is glad to set forward this business. And he saith that they all great(ly) grudge their prior and would fain have a new one."[1]

In the examinations of the religious of Watton themselves much the same evidence was elicited. The subprior, "D. Harry Gill," says they were asked by the insurgents for money and horses. They gave only £10 and a gelding, and "also Master Aske had one spice plate of silver, which was a pledge of the earl of Northumberland," and if it had not been given the house would have been "spoiled." He declared that the archbishop of York sent a letter "to all curates and religious that they should go a procession every day and send their minds out of Holy Scripture and the four doctors touching the commons' petition." From their house two replies were sent, one from a "Dr. Swinburne" and another "from a young man of our habit called Thomas Asheton" . . . "and they were both one as touching the Supreme Head."

With regard to the election of a prior in place of the one appointed over them by Crumwell, who had fled on the first sign of the rising, the subprior deposed that at the time of the first insurrection Hallam came "with a great number of his soldiers after him into the infirmary of Watton where the brethren were bound to dinner, and there in the presence of the prior of Ellerton and the prior of St. Andrew's, York, charged the brethren to elect them a new prior. And they said it was against their order and statutes of their religion, their prior being alive, and not lawfully removed. Then he said if they did not, he would spoil their house, and would nominate one himself. And he said: 'Methinks this man' —pointing to the prior of Ellerton—'is meet to be your prior.' Then for fear of spoiling of their goods, as they

[1] Chapter House Bk., A. $\frac{2}{15}$, pp. 41–45.

say, they met together and did nominate the said prior of Ellerton to be their prior." He, however, would not take the office, "nor they receive him for such indeed, but to have him to bear the name only through fear of the commons."[1]

Lastly, examined as to the crucial question of the "Supreme Headship" of the king, the subprior declared that for himself "he had no learning to discuss the matter; but as he saith it was in every man's mouth that if that were not laid down[2] it should not be well."

The answers of two other religious of Watton[3] do not add anything material to the declaration of the subprior, although they confirm its accuracy in every particular. It may, therefore, be supposed that in these various informations and examinations the various ways in which alone the priory of Watton was implicated in the rising are stated. None of the canons took any active part in the movement, their contributions were small, and even these were extorted by force. As for the matter of the election, however much they disliked the superior appointed by Crumwell, and whatever cause they had to endeavour to get rid of him, they appear to have acted loyally to him, except in so far as they were compelled to give way to force.

Beyond the foregoing isolated instances, none of the numerous depositions and relations furnish any accusation against monastery or monk of active co-operation with the insurgents, with the exception of the abbeys of Jervaulx and Whalley, the priory of Bridlington and the individual connection of the quondam abbot of Fountains with the movement. These cases must now be considered.

With respect to Jervaulx, the chief witness against the monks is one Ninian Staveley, himself one of the leaders of the movement and a representative of the swashbuckler element among the insurgents. He engaged in the movement as an adventurer rather than as a "pilgrim," and having compromised himself, endeavoured to save his own

---

[1] Chapter House Bk., A. $\frac{2}{25}$, pp. 77–80. It will be remembered that Aske declared he had gone at this time to Watton to prevent this new election from taking effect.

[2] *i.e.*, if the king did not put aside the title of Supreme Head which he had assumed.

[3] That of "J. D. Thomas Lather, cellarer and granator," is prefaced by the expressions, "*Jesus sit in adjutorio*," "*Jesu adjuva me*," and "*Deus in adjutorium.*"

The Second Northern Rising

neck by incriminating others. By his deposition it would appear that the abbot during the second rising had promised to join the insurgents "with all his brethren;" and had sent a messenger to Sir Thomas Percy "to have him come forward," and also a servant into Lincolnshire to find out the state of the country, and to let them know whether the duke of Norfolk was advancing "with arms or no."[1] These form the chief points of the abbot's offending, and they may be considered best in the light of his own examination in the Tower on 27th of April, 1537. "Adam Sedbar, abbot of the monastery of Jervaulx, 'sworn and examined,' said that during the first rising, about Michaelmas day, there 'came to the garth or court of the abbey of Jervaulx,' some two or three hundred men. He knew nothing about it at that time, but hearing that their captains, Middleton and Staveley, were asking for him, 'he conveyed himself by a back door' to a place 'called Wilton Fell.' He only had a boy with him, and 'bade his other servants get them every man to his house and save their cattle and goods.' He remained thus concealed for four days, only coming home at night," and during all those days the said commons wandered about the said house in the country about. "At the last, hearing say that this examinat had said that there should no servant of his ever after do him service, nor tenant dwell on no land of his that should go with them, they therefore turned back to Jervaulx and inquired for this examinat, and they were answered that this examinat was not at home. And then said they: 'We charge you brethren to go and choose you a new abbot.' Whereupon the brethren rang the chapter bell and went towards making of a new election. And certain among them would in no wise agree to make any new abbot. Then the commons gave them half an hour's respite to choose one; and if they did choose none in that space they would burn their house over their heads. Then the brethren sent several ways about to seek this examinat, and at last one William Nelson came where this examinat was upon Wilton Fell in a great crag, and showed him that the commons would burn the house except he should come home, and all the brethren cried 'Woe be (us).'

[1] Chapter House Bk., A. $\frac{2}{28}$, pp. 117-118.

"Then for saving of the house this examinat came home (and) about the outer gate he was torn (from his horse) and almost killed, they crying 'Down with that traitor.' At last by means of some of his friends he was carried in from them, and when he came to the hall entry Leonard Burgh, one of the ringleaders, drew his dagger and would have killed him, but for them that stood by. Then he came further where one William Asleby, chief captain of these parts, was, and he said to this examinat: 'Horeson traitor, where has thou been?' and said: 'Get me a block to strike off his head upon,' and there this examinat was commanded to take the oath, which he took, the said Burgh ministering the same to him. And so took this examinat with them forthwith and gave him no respite, but caused him to ride with them upon a brown horse, which he rode upon his coming into them."

He was forced to remain with them for some days, but at last, through the intercession of one of the leaders, was allowed to return home. During this time, letters were sent to Jervaulx from the "commons" of the district, to receive which and forward to their destination, certain of the insurgents were quartered on the monks. This continued till the settlement at Doncaster, when the strangers left.

In answer to an inquiry as to what aid he had given the insurgents, the abbot replied "that the commons took all his servants with them . . . but (that) he never gave one of them one penny of wages." Further, "he saith," continues the record, "he never sent victuals unto them, and that the commons took with them two of this examinat's brethren[1] among them, against this examinat's mind and will, who returned again with this examinat."

Further examined, the abbot said that "there came to this examinat's chamber immediately after breakfast" one day in the winter Staveley and Middleton, "and his son and heir, and many more were in the hall." Staveley told the abbot that formerly he had deceived the people, "and therefore bade him come with them and half a dozen of his brethren forthwith. And this examinat desired them to forbear and said they were his neighbours and should be his friends and were his enemies. . . . And

---

[1] From the notes on this examination (Chapter House Bk., B. $\frac{2}{11}$, p. 140) it appears that the names of these two were Roger Hartlepool and John Stanton.

partly by his importunity and refusal and partly by the entreaty of one Beckwith that came with them, they let this examinat and his brethren alone. But they took against this examinat's will certain of his friends with them."

The following day the abbot fled to Bolton Castle to Lord Scrope, where he remained until the insurgents were "broken at Richmond," when he returned home. "Since that time," he says, "he heard nothing of the matter. And other comfort, aid or assistance he gave not them by word deed or writing, by the virtue of his oath and upon his allegiance."

Lastly, as to the special points upon which Staveley accused him, he denied "utterly that ever he sent or caused to be sent, nor that he was privy that any messenger should be sent to Sir Thomas Percy, or that he put his servants and tenants with Staveley or gave them any aid or comfort, or that he sent any man to lie in Lincolnshire to consider the state of the country there, but saith that the cellarer of the house sent one Jackson to Lincolnshire at the latter end of the Christmas holidays to gather their rents, and for no other purpose to this examinat's knowledge as he saith."[1]

The quondam abbot of Fountains, William Thirsk, was implicated in the movement,[2] together with the abbot of Jervaulx. Thirsk had been deprived of his office at Fountains by Crumwell's visitors in the beginning of the year 1536. Layton and Legh had written to Crumwell about his having made away with the plate and jewels of the abbey, and of their success in getting him to "resign privately into their hands."[3] On the appointment of his successor, Marmaduke Bradley, who had offered Crumwell six hundred marks, and the king £1000 as "first-fruits" if he could

---

[1] Chapter House Bk., A. $\frac{2}{19}$, pp. 259 to 263.
[2] *Ibid.*, B. $\frac{3}{11}$, p. 101.
[3] Layton and Legh, the king's commissaries, accepted the resignation of William Thirsk in "The Church Chamber," at the monastery of St. Mary's Fountains, 19 January, 1536. They granted him a pension of 100 marks a year (*Calend*. x. No. 131). In a letter written by his successor on March 6th, it appears that there were considerable difficulties about the money arrangements. The pension of £40 was objected to as excessive, and Thirsk is said to want to keep all the house goods above the value of £1000 (No. 424), and according to archbishop Lee he had not resigned by the end of March, as he wished to be made secure as to his proper and promised pension (No. 521).

R

obtain the office, abbot Thirsk retired first to London and afterwards to Jervaulx. How far he had any part in the insurrection for which he was executed must be judged from his examination, as there is little else known about him. On April the 24th doctors Layton and Legh, his old enemies, had him before them in the Tower, and, being sworn, he said: "About the beginning of the last Lent (1537), as this examinat was in his chamber at Jervaulx abbey, came to him one of the servants of the house, called James Thwaites, desiring this examinat in the abbot of Jervaulx's name to deliver to Middleton that came with him forty pence: one Staveley being there also. And he said he would, and with that took out an angel noble and bade them change it. And Staveley took the same in his hands and said it was cracked. Then this examinat took out another angel and bade them change that. And the said Staveley took both and put them up, saying, 'Ye churle monks ye have too much and we have nothing. Neither of these thou gettest again.' Then this examinat said again, 'Ye shall not have my money so. If ye be true men ye will not take my money away. Ye should have but forty pence of me.' Middleton, however, promised to repay the money if Staveley did not, 'and so they departed without any more words.'"

About a week after this "the said Middleton and Staveley in harness came to the said abbot of Jervaulx as he and this examinat were in his chamber, and bade the said abbot and this examinat upon pain of death, and all their brethren and servants go with them forthwith. And many other of the commons were in the hall and about the house. And he desired them instantly to suffer him and his brethren to be still, seeing it was not meet that religious men should go about any such business. And so this examinat desired them also to let him likewise alone, for he was old and feeble and nothing meet for such business. Nevertheless, as this examinat heard say, they took with them the servants of the house, but whether it were by the abbot's command or not he cannot tell."

Further he denied absolutely that he had ever desired Staveley or any other "if there should be any new insurrection . . . 'to help to put him in his room again.'" And he declared he knew nothing of the first rising, "being in

London all the time," and never heard of any message being sent to Sir Thomas Percy.¹

If the abbots of Jervaulx and Fountains do not appear to have afforded active assistance to the insurgents, the part played by the abbot of Whalley was of a still less compromising nature. William Rede, a baker of Oxford, said that he had carried letters from the abbot "to his scholars being in Oxford," and also "another to the abbot of Hayles." The abbot had told him to recommend him specially "to the abbot of Hayles, and tell him that I am sore stopped and acrazed. And pray him to send me word when he purposeth to come over to this country, for I would be glad to see him once ere I depart out of this world, seeing I brought him up here from a child." The baker on his way received a packet of letters from a schoolmaster to give to "Philip, his son, at Oriel college." And when he came to Wotton, having told the constable there what he was carrying, he found himself taken prisoner and conveyed to Kenilworth castle. The letters were examined, and, as far as can be judged from the document, only implicated the schoolmaster and not the abbot.²

One witness, indeed, declared that the abbot of Whalley had lent a horse to Nicholas Tempest, of Brashall. But Tempest's account of the matter is very different. He says that he went to the abbey "with three or four hundred men," and after "being kept out about two hours, were at last let in for fear of burning their barns and houses. And there this examinat swore the abbot and about eight of his religion according to Aske's oath."³ So that according to Nicholas Tempest even the oath of the pilgrims was extorted from the monks by threats of violence. The only other matter which appears to tell against the abbey of Whalley is that lord Darcy had some communication with the abbey. "Memorandum," it is noted, "also that lord Darcy this Lent last past sent a copy of a letter which my lord of Norfolk wrote to him unto the prior of Whalley who is now attainted of high treason, whereby appeareth that the lord Darcy favoured the said prior, being a traitor."⁴

¹ Chapter House Bk., A. $\frac{2}{19}$, pp. 257–258.
² *Ibid.*, p. 134.
³ *Calendar*, xii. (i), No. 1014.
⁴ Chapter House Bk., A. $\frac{2}{18}$, p. 247, *i.e.* the lord Darcy being the traitor.

Lastly, as to Bridlington the only item of information is obtained in a note possibly in Crumwell's hand. "Item," it runs, "the prior of Bridlington and Dr. Pickering, the friar, had been great setters forth of both the first and last insurrections. And the said Dr. Pickering, a great writer of letters, to move and stir as well the first as the last. And also the prior of Bridlington had in readiness as well all his household servants as also divers his tenants in harness, for to have given assistance to Bigod and Lumley in the last insurrection."[1] In a list of those implicated, the names of "Nicholas Tempest, Hammerton and Pickering, friar," are associated with that of "the abbot of Bridlington." These four names have been subsequently erased. Against the names of Hammerton and Tempest is the note: "The petition made to Thomas Percy by the abbot of Sawley, wherein is no apparent matter against them but before the pardon.[2] And even as to this, Nicholas Tempest denied upon oath that he knew anything about that "supplication," and declared that his connection with Sawley abbey was confined to advising the abbot's chaplain to lay their cause before the meeting at Pomfret, and "when the commons had put in the abbots and monks," to giving "them a fat ox, one mutton, and two or three geese."[3] In like manner Sir Stephen Hammerton denied having had anything to do in the matter. His declaration is of interest, as it shows that it was for the crime of taking possession of their old home that the abbot of Sawley, and doubtless some of his brethren, perished on the scaffold. "And he saith," runs the record of Hammerton's examination, "that the abbot of Sawley, as he was condemned to die, sent divers persons to this examinat to desire his forgiveness for that he had named this examinat in the said letters . . . and he took it upon his death that neither this examinat nor no other gent or other person of the county was counsel to the making or devising of the said supplication but only he himself and the said Estgate (his chaplain), and two of his said brethren called Bradford and Parish."[4]

---

[1] Chapter House Bk., B. $\frac{2}{21}$, p. 143.   [2] *Ibid.*, p. 101.
[3] *Calendar*, xii. (i), No. 1014.
[4] Chapter House Bk., A. $\frac{2}{28}$, p. 30. The *Monasticon*, v. p. 511, says that William Trafford, last abbot of Salley, was hanged at Lancaster for opposition to the crown in 1538. The declaration of Hammerton, made in 1537, states that he was condemned to death, and it would seem to imply that he had

The punishment meted out to the insurgents now that the last resistance was at an end was, as might be expected, not wanting in severity.

"Norfolk," writes Mr. Gairdner, "had really little to do except to arrange for some further butcheries and terrify all the other malcontents into the most abject submission. The wretched country people—'poor caitiffs'—as he himself said they might well be called, having lost their horses, harness and everything in their flight—flocked into Carlisle to submit to the King's mercy. The Duke's answer was to select seventy-four of the chief insurgents and lock them up in prison till they should be sentenced by martial law and hanged, letting the rest go home without any promise of pardon. 'Dreadful execution' was the one great object with Norfolk. It had been insinuated that some old feeling of regard for those monastic establishments now being remorselessly overturned would make him less zealous in the execution of the King's orders; and he was anxious to clear himself of any such imputation. His only regret was that he could not find iron chains enough in the country to hang the prisoners in; ropes must serve for some. He flattered himself, however, that so great a number put to death at a time had never been heard of."[1]

The chief prisoners were first tried by a commission in York.[2] In forcing friends and even relations of the prisoners to take part as jurors in this trial, Norfolk perpetrated a

---

already been executed. Walcott says his execution was at Lancaster on March 10th, 1537, and this is the year assigned by Stowe (ed. 1615, p. 573), who says that "one Astlebe, a monk of Jervaulx," was executed with him.

[1] *Calendar*, xii. (i), preface, p. xxvi.

[2] It is well to understand the kind of pressure which was exerted upon the northern juries to find verdicts of guilty. On March 23rd and 24th, 1537, one William Levenyng was tried at York for complicity in Bigod's rebellion. The majority of the jury were for an acquittal, believing that the only witness was actuated by malice, "having had a promise of his lands from the king." The jury were locked up from nine on Friday morning until Saturday night, and as "a more effectual way of promoting unanimity, they were deprived of all warmth." In the end they acquitted the prisoner. Norfolk was dissatisfied, and further examined Levenyng, and even proposed sending him up to Crumwell. "A few days later," writes Mr. Gairdner, "we find the Duke promising to ascertain for Crumwell the names of the grand juries who found indictments in Yorkshire, and who apparently had disappointed expectations by finding so few, but he cannot help suggesting that if they were sent for to appear before the Council, it would lead to rumour 'that men should be compelled to pass otherwise than their consciences should lead them.'" (*Calendar*, xii. (i), preface, p. xxxi.)

cruelty which could hardly have been believed as intentional were it not for the testimony of his own letter to Crumwell. After telling him that the king's commission had arrived "with two books of indictments and two schedules; the one of such as should be indicted and the other of gentlemen to be impanelled," he goes on to say: "I doubt not to have the greatest appearance that was seen at York of many years, on Tuesday night and Wednesday morning (May 9th, 1537). I will sit upon those that be named in the schedule on Wednesday by nine o'clock, and also upon two monks of the Charterhouse for not knowing of the king to be supreme head of the Church, unless they do openly recant from their false opinion, which I think they will not do."[1]

The duke then goes on to say that, as he presumes Crumwell intends, he thinks it well to have "two divers inquests; for they being so kept that one of them shall not know what another doth shall make them the more quick to find the matter. And I have so provided that we shall lack no number if I would have four inquests. And I am at this time of such acquaintance with the gentlemen that I dare well adventure to put divers on the quests (of whom) some hath married with the lord Darcy's daughters and some with Sir Robert Constable's.[2] And I will put John Aske thereupon, who is eldest brother to Robert Aske. Doubt ye not, my lord, but the matter shall be found according to the king's pleasure."

Continuing, he says he hopes to have the evidence before Thursday, which "is no day to sit, considering as it shall be Ascension day," and if so, "Crumwell shall have the result and be able to proceed with the London arraignments on Monday or Tuesday. My good lord," he goes on, "I will not spare to put the best friends these men have upon one of the inquests, to prove their affection whether they

---

[1] The names of these two were "John Rochester and James Walwercke," two of the heroic members of the London Charterhouse. They were hanged in chains at York. *Vide* p. 74, *ante*.

[2] Raine, *Hexham Priory* (Surtees Soc.), i. App. clxii., *note*, says: "These were Brian Stapleton, of Carlton; Henry Babington, of Dethick; Sir William Fairfax, of Gilling; Sir Thomas Dawney, of Cowick; and Sir Thomas Metham. Sir Thomas Metham was a grand juror.

Sir Robert Constable's daughters married into the houses of St. Quintin, Gower, Pudsey, Cholmeley, and Husee: Sir Roger Cholmeley and Sir Edward Gower were on the York grand jury.

will rather serve his majesty truly and frankly in this matter, or else to favour their friends, and if they will not find, then they may have thanks according to their cankered hearts. And, as for the other inquest, I will appoint such that I shall no more doubt of than of myself."[1]

The commission was held at York Castle on "Wednesday, the vigil of the Ascension, May 9th," before the Duke of Norfolk, Sir Thomas Tempest and others. The jury, amongst whom was John Aske, the brother of Robert, found the prisoners guilty of conspiring with lord Darcy on the 10th of October "to deprive the king of his dignity, title, name, and royal state, namely, of being on earth the supreme head of the English Church." Also they found them guilty of endeavouring to compel the king "to summon and hold a parliament and convocation, and other divers high treasons." Further, that having been pardoned, they repeated these treasons in January.

A week later they were brought up before chancellor Audeley at Westminster, and pleading not guilty, May 24th was appointed for the trial. On that day all the prisoners except Ralph Bulmer[2] were condemned to death.[3]

There can be no doubt that the abbots and monks now tried and put to death fell victims to Henry's cupidity and sanguinary vengeance, and that they did not suffer for their own misdeeds, or for any real connection with the insurrections. Among the rest the following religious were ordered to be executed: Adam Sedbar, abbot of Jervaulx; William Thirsk, quondam abbot of Fountains; William Wood, prior of Bridlington; James Cockerel, prior of Gisborough and rector of Lythe; and John Pickering, late of Bridlington, and a friar of the Dominican Order. Lord Darcy was executed on Tower Hill. The abbots, with Percy, Bigod, John Bulmer, Hammerton, Lumley, and Tempest, were hanged and quartered at Tyburn, while Constable and Aske were hanged in chains at Hull and York. The fate of those who had withstood the royal will and appealed even to arms to save the ancient abbeys of England from spoliation and

---

[1] Raine, *ut sup.*, i. App. clxi.
[2] Coram Rege. Roll, 33 Hen. VIII., Easter, M. 9. Ralph, son of Sir John Bulmer, by a letter dated 29 Jan., A° 32 Hen. VIII., was pardoned and discharged.
[3] *Ibid.*, and *Baga de Secretis*, in iii. Rept. Dept. Keeper, App. ii.

to protest against the changes in religious faith and practice imposed upon an unwilling nation, struck terror into the hearts of the English people. The collapse of the rising removed every restraint upon the autocratic power of the crown and opened the way for further seizures of monastic and church property.

CHAPTER XIV

Dissolution by Attainder

THE Northern disturbances, in the autumn of 1536 and the spring of the following year, acted as a check upon the suppression schemes of Henry. From Michaelmas of the former year to the same feast in the latter, according to the accounts of his ministers, very few religious houses passed into his possession. In Yorkshire and the adjoining counties during the spring months of 1537 the royal officers were occupied in once more ejecting the monks and nuns who had been reinstated by the insurgents in their old homes. The king's instructions to the duke of Norfolk on this point were precise. He was immediately after the execution of Constable and Aske to restore the keeping of the monasteries formerly suppressed to the royal farmers, "and aid such commissioners as his majesty shall appoint to dissolve the other monasteries within the limit of the said act not yet dissolved." Further, the instructions run, "the said duke shall cause all the religious persons that were or be in any of the said houses either to take their livings in such other monasteries of their religion as they shall be assigned to, or else if they shall refuse so to do, he shall punish them as vagabonds and enemies of the commonwealth, so as no one of that sort remain at large in that country."

Norfolk and the earl of Sussex had, indeed, in behalf of the king, made large promises at the meeting of Doncaster that the restored religious should be left undisturbed until the Northern parliament had finally settled the question of the dissolution. But the king evidently did not consider himself bound by the acts of his plenipotentiaries. "And forasmuch," his instructions continue, "as the said duke of Norfolk and the lord admiral at their late being at Doncaster promised to be suitors to the king's majesty that the monks, canons, and nuns of such religious houses suppressed should have *victum* and *vestitum* of the goods of the monasteries they were of, till further determination should be taken touching that matter, by reason whereof some ringleaders may perchance make some argument for the continuance of the said monks, nuns and canons with such sustentation at their liberties, the said duke in such case shall make a discourse to all men appearing so much affectionate towards them, of their essential wilful poverty, chastity and obedience, and dilate how far they vary from good religious men, from them that will be wilfully poor: yea, from true subjects that would direct their prince and sovereign lord; that will not live but as they list themselves, and therewith declare how the king's majesty is by his laws rightfully entitled to those monasteries, and that those that will so direct his majesty therein be not esteemed for his great true subjects, but to be punished as his traitors and rebels."[1]

In a previous letter, written by Henry at the time when the duke had proclaimed martial law, the commander had been praised for the way he had "discreetly, plainly and truly," painted and set forth to the people in their true colours "those persons that call themselves religious." "And we doubt not," continues the king, "but the further you shall wade in the investigation of their behaviours, the more ye shall detect the great number of them and the less esteem the punishment of such, as you shall find, in will or deed, culpable in things that may touch us or the common quiet of our realm. . . ."

"Thirdly," the letter continues, "we do right well approve and allow your proceedings in the displaying of our banner. And forasmuch as the same is now spread and displayed, by reason whereof, till the same shall be closed again, the course of our laws must give place to the ordinances and estates martial, our pleasure is, that, before you shall close up our said banner again, you shall in any wise cause such dreadful execution to be done upon a good number of the inhabitants of every town, village and hamlet, that have offended in this rebellion, as well by the hanging of them up in trees, as by the quartering of them and the setting of their heads and quarters in every town, great and

---

[1] Chapter House Bk., A. $\frac{2}{18}$, pp. 367 *et seq.*

Dissolution by Attainder

small, and in all such other places, as they may be a fearful spectacle to all other hereafter that would practice any like matter: which we require you to do, without pity or respect, according to our former letters; remembering that it shall be much better, that these traitors should perish in their wilful, unkind and traitorous follies, than that so slender punishment should be done upon them, as the dread thereof should not be a warning to others." Further, Henry expressed his desire that after "such execution" had been done by the summary processes of martial law, the ordinary legal forms of "ordinary justice" should, at the duke's discretion, complete the work of punishment.

"Finally," the letter concludes, "forasmuch as all these troubles have ensued by the solicitation and traitorous conspiracies of the monks and canons of those parts; we desire and pray you, at your repair to Sawley,[1] Hexham,[2] Newminster,[3] Lanercost,[4] Saint Agatha's,[5] and all such other places as have made any manner of resistance, or in any wise conspired or kept their houses with any force since the appointment at Doncaster, you shall without pity or circumstance, now that our banner is displayed, cause all the monks and canons that be in any wise faulty to be tied up without further delay or ceremony to the terrible example of others."[6]

The rigours of martial law are only by chance recorded, and it is now impossible to calculate the numbers of religious, and of the people who rose to defend them, that perished during the months when legal trial was suspended in the North, and Sussex and Norfolk acted upon the royal command "to cause all the monks and canons that be in any wise faulty to be tied up without further delay or ceremony." And even when Sussex stayed his hand in compassion, Henry would hear of no pleading for those who had offended against his majesty. "Concerning the old man," he writes, "whom you wrote you had respited, upon the lamentation he made at the bar and the allegation of his service thrice heretofore against the Scots and otherwise done unto us; albeit we cannot but take your stay of him in good part, yet, considering he hath so often received our wages and would

---

[1] In Craven, West Riding.
[2] In Northumberland.
[3] In the same county.
[4] In Cumberland.
[5] At Richmond, Yorks.
[6] *State Papers*, i. 537.

nevertheless at the last be thus corrupted against us, we think him for an example more worthy to suffer than the rest that before had not experience of our princely puissance, nor had received any benefit of us; and so remit him unto you to be executed according to his judgment." [1]

Under the terror of the royal vengeance and with the example of these remorseless punishments inflicted on all who came within reach of the royal arm, the commissioners do not appear to have experienced much difficulty in regaining possession of the confiscated monasteries. At the beginning of February, Norfolk had anticipated a very different result, and declared that, although the nobles and gentry had promised "to put the king's farmers in possession of the religious houses," no one would dare to do so.[2] But a couple of months later, what with the paralyzing effect of the executions actually carried out, and the dread each one had of being involved in the same fate, resistance was at an end.[3] A correspondent writing to reassure Dr. Legh, the royal visitor whose punishment had been demanded by the Pilgrims of Grace, says on April 24th: "Loving to God, the country is quiet enough, saving that every malefactor dreads himself. . . . And as concerning any complaint against you or other for the visitation, there is nothing spoken of that matter. I dare well say there is no religious man that will avow any grief for that matter."[4]

According to the directions given by the king to his generals, the monasteries of Sawley, Hexham, Newminster, Lanercost and St. Agatha's were quickly retaken from the monks.

Newminster was finally suppressed on August 20th, after the commissioners had been there from July 1st. The value of the moveables was counted at close upon a thousand pounds; more than one-half of which was represented by the lead and the worth of 660 ounces of plate. Pensions were promised to the community, consisting of seventeen

---

[1] *State Papers*, i. p. 541. [2] *Ibid.*, i. 534.
[3] At heart, there can be no doubt, the people remained as opposed as before to the king's ecclesiastical policy generally, and in particular to his assumption of the supreme headship of the Church of England. Two years later, in the opinion of Mr. James Gairdner (*Calendar*, xiii. (i), preface ii), "We have ample evidences at this time of ill-concealed disaffection" towards the king in these matters.
[4] *Calendar*, xii. (i), No. 1025.

priests, three junior monks, as well as to four choir boys;[1] but the following year only the abbot, Edward Tirry, and a former abbot, Edward Dunfield, received anything.[2] The suppression of St. Agatha's, Richmond, followed about the same time; one only, Robert Brampton, receiving any pension. The goods and plate were valued at close upon £1000, and some rich vestments from St. Agatha's and Calder were handed to Sir Thomas Pope for the king's use. Much of the property was, however, seized by the insurgents during the northern rising, as it still remained in the possession of the receiver, and some was not recovered[3] for the royal purse. Sawley, Hexham and Lanercost had already been dealt with in the same fashion.

Several of the larger monasteries, moreover, fell into the royal power at this time by the attainder of their abbots. In the statute for the settlement of the royal succession (25 Hen. VIII., c. 22), under the ambiguous terms "estate of inheritance" and "successors," were introduced two great changes into English law. By the first, estates tail were made liable to forfeit for treason, and by the second—"other than such persons as shall have been so convict, their heirs and *successors*"—may have been intended, as is suggested by Sir Matthew Hale, to fasten upon lands held in the right of a corporation, as by a bishop or abbot. The king had a personal concern in all property so confiscated, and it was to his interest to make the meaning of the act as wide as possible. Hitherto the attainder of a bishop or abbot would not affect the property of the diocese or abbey over which the attainted superior ruled. It was left to Henry to include the forfeiture of possessions of a corporation in the punishment awarded to its head for supposed or real treasonable practices. Even Burnet argues that such a proceeding was unjustifiable. "How justly soever these abbots were attainted," he writes, "the seizing on their abbey lands, pursuant to those attainders, was thought a great stretch of law, since the offence of an ecclesiastical incumbent is a personal thing, and cannot prejudice the church; no more than a secular man, being in office, does by being attainted

[1] Exch. Aug. Off. Mins. Accts., 27-28 Hen. VIII., 200, m. 4d.
[2] *Ibid.*, 29-30 Hen. VIII., No. 204, m. 1d.
[3] *Ibid.*, No. 169, m. 5.

bring any diminution of the rights of the office on his successors."[1]

Upon this novel interpretation of the law of treason, however, Henry now determined to act, and the supposed complicity of some of the abbots in the Pilgrimage of Grace gave him the opportunity of laying hands upon the possessions of their houses. The part taken by John Paslew, abbot of Whalley, has already been remarked upon. According to the evidence, there was very little, if indeed anything, which could be construed into active co-operation with the insurgents. Still he was tried, probably by martial law, at Lancaster, together with two of his monks, John Eastgate and William Haydock, and the abbot of Sawley. William Trafford, the abbot of Sawley, was hanged at Lancaster on March 10th, and the abbot of Whalley, with Eastgate, two days later at Whalley. Haydock, the other monk of Whalley, suffered the same punishment the following day, March 13th, in a field a few miles from his monastery, where his body was left hanging for some time.[2]

Writing to the earl of Sussex about this time, Henry conveys his thanks for the punishment inflicted upon those who had offended him. "And whereas," he continues, "upon the execution of the abbot of Whalley, you have taken order for the good direction of the house, and the safe keeping of the goods without embezzlement, till further knowledge of our pleasure; approving much your good foresight thereof, we have thought convenient to signify unto you, that forasmuch as it appeareth that the house of Whalley hath been so sore corrupt amongst others, that it should seem there remaineth very few therein that were meet to remain and continue in such a corporation, we think it shall be meet that some order be taken for the remotion of the monks now being in the same. And that (it is proper) we should take the whole house into our own hands; as, by our laws, we be justly, by the attainder of the said late abbot entitled unto it; and so devise for such a new establishment thereof, as shall be thought meet for the honour of God, our

---

[1] *Hist. of Reformation* (ed. 1679), Bk. iii. p. 240.
[2] Whittaker, *Hist. of Whalley*, p. 123. The actual date seems uncertain. From the king's letter to Sussex it would seem that the abbot of Whalley was dead before Sussex wrote letters which Henry speaks of receiving on March 11th. (*State Papers*, i. p. 540.)

surety and the benefit of the country. Wherefore our pleasure is, that you shall, with good dexterity, lay unto the charges of all the monks there their grievous offences towards us and our commonwealth, and therewith assay their minds, whether they will conform themselves gladly." They may either go to other houses or "receive secular habit," but Sussex is enjoined to endeavour to get them to go to some other monastery, as, says the king, "it cannot be wholesome for our commonwealth to permit them to wander abroad."[1]

The directions of Henry were acted upon, and by Michaelmas, 1537, John Kechin, the receiver, had sold goods and got in rents to the value of £957, 11s. 7d. from the abbey of Whalley, and had sent up to Brian Tuke, the king's treasurer, some £500.[2] Thus in a few months the king had apparently given up all idea of "devising the new establishment" which was to be more "meet for the honour of God and the benefit of the country" than the old monastery of Whalley. Perhaps, however, he considered that by filling the royal purse he was but carrying out his original idea of "honouring God" and benefiting the country.

In the same way the abbeys of Barlings, Jervaulx and Kirksted, and the priory of Bridlington, came at this time under the law of attainder. Bishop Mackarel, the abbot of Barlings, was executed in March. His supposed offences have already been spoken of, and his monastery shared the fate of Whalley. The minster church, 300 feet in length, was defaced, the lead on the buildings, both here and at Kirksted, being torn from the roofs and melted down at the special direction of Crumwell.[3]

Bridlington, an important priory of Austin canons in Yorkshire, possessing an income of £547 a year, likewise came to Henry by the attainder and execution of the prior. The previous year Crumwell had pressed the house to recognize the king as founder, a request which the community refused.[4] By Michaelmas, 1537, public sales of the monastic property had been conducted by Tristram Teshe, the royal receiver for the district, and had realized more than £800. The canons had been ejected some months

[1] *State Papers*, i. p. 540.
[2] Exch. A. O. Rec. Gen. Accts., 28-29 Hen. VIII., No. 211.
[3] *Calendar*, xii. (i), No. 676. [4] Wright, 80.

before, and in May, Crumwell had written to the duke of Norfolk of the king's intention to look after the interests of the poor people round about Jervaulx and Bridlington. He thought of trying to get "some substantial person meet and necessary to stay the country and keep hospitality, to dwell in the principal part of the monastery," and thus in some measure to keep up the traditions of the place.[1] The Bridlington people had petitioned that the church, "which is the parish church for 1500 houseling people," and the shrine of St. John of Bridlington, might be kept and not defaced.[2] The early English choir of five bays had an east end like those of Whitby and Rievaulx. The altar possessed a magnificent reredos, and between it and a chapel aisle with five altars stood the shrine of the saint[3] from appropriating which the people begged the king would restrain his hand. But Henry had a scruple. "As for the shrine," Crumwell says in the letter to Norfolk already quoted, "the king's highness, to the intent that his people should not be seduced in the offering of their money, his grace would have taken down, which and all other jewels and plate appertaining to his highness, except such as you desire to have for your money," are to be sent to him. The vestments, he adds, and other goods not fit for the royal use are to be sold.[4] The actual demolition, however, did not take place till a few months later. Richard Bellasis, who had been engaged in this work for the king, wrote in November that he would delay the destruction till March "because the days now are so short." But, he added, "from such time as I begin I trust shortly to dispatch it, after such fashion, that when all is finished, I trust your lordship shall think that I have been no evil husband in all such things as your lordship hath appointed me to do."[5] The nave of ten bays with its aisles, which alone remain to this day, indicates the faithful way in which this agent of destruction kept his promise to Crumwell.

The people of the neighbourhood might well petition for the safety of the priory, for the poor of the district annually received in alms from the benefactions left in trust to the religious more than £250 of our money. The four vicars

---

[1] *Calendar*, xii. (i), No. 1257.   [2] *Calendar*, xii. (i), No. 1307.
[3] Walcott, *Eng. Minsters*, ii. p. 77.   [4] *Calendar*, xii. (i), No. 1257.
[5] Wright, p. 165.

and four deacons who served the parish church of Scarborough received a yearly stipend from the funds of the monastery,[1] while more than one aged priest found an asylum within its walls.

The neighbouring abbey of Jervaulx, situated in the vale of the Ure, fell likewise a prey to the royal rapacity in consequence of the insurrection. Adam Sedbar, the abbot, was hanged, and his brethren soon found themselves turned out of their monastery. "The house of Jervaulx," wrote the king with keen prevision, to the earl of Sussex, shortly after the death of the abbot, "is in some danger of suppression by like offence as hath been committed at Whalley,"[2] and the danger was not long delayed. At the beginning of June, Sir Arthur Darcy informed Crumwell that he had been "at the suppression. . . . The houses within the gate," he says, "are covered wholly with lead, and there is one of the fairest churches that I have seen." In fact, he was so delighted with the place, that he suggested it would make a good stable for the royal "stud of mares," which were so costly to the king, "at Thornbury and other places."[3]

By the middle of November, what Darcy declared to be "one of the fairest churches" he had ever seen had been desecrated and demolished through the energetic action of Richard Bellasis. Crumwell had ordered the lead to be taken from the roof, and this zealous officer soon wrote to say that "all the lead of Jervaulx" was melted down into pieces of half fodders, amounting to the number of eighteen score and five fodders, with thirty-four fodders and a half that were there before. "The said lead," he continues, "cannot be conveyed nor carried until the next summer, for the ways in that country are so foul and deep that no carriage can pass in winter. And as concerning the razing and taking down the house, if it be your lordship's pleasure, I am minded to let it stand to the spring of the year, because the days are now so short, it would be double charges to do it now." As to the bells, "I can," he says, "get only fifteen shillings a hundredweight" for them, and would gladly know whether I shall take the price "or send them up to London."[4]

[1] *Valor Eccl.*, p. 120.
[2] *State Papers*, i. 542.
[3] Wright, 158.
[4] *Ibid.*, 164.

By Michaelmas, 1537, the king's officer was able to account for receipts from the attainted monastery of Jervaulx exceeding £600, or more than £6000 of our money. The following year the same property brought to the exchequer £764, 13s. 8d.

The great abbey of Furness, in Lancashire, was also now induced to surrender to Henry. Roger Pyle, the abbot, and some of his monks, were thought to be incriminated with the northern insurgents. The members of the community, "with the tenants and servants, were successfully examined in private."[1] The result was summed up in a bill of accusations against some members of the abbey. The abbot had been guilty of "falsehood at the time of the visitation in causing his monks to be forsworn." The monks of Sawley, on the suppression of that monastery, had been sent to Furness, and the abbot had induced them to go back to their monastery during the rebellion. "The abbot concealed the treason of Henry Sawley, monk, who said no secular knave should be head of the Church; which abbot also made suit to his brethren to hold with him in all things that should be laid to his charge, promising to be for the same good unto them." These were the accusations of a friar named Robert Legat. A priest named Roger Pele, vicar of Dalton, said that the abbot did not keep the king's injunctions; and one of his monks, John Broughton, added that he knew of the prophecies of the Holy Maid of Kent and others. One of the abbey bailiffs said that the abbot had told the brethren to be of good heart, "for he was sure on both sides both for the king and the commons." And a tenant said that he had ordered the monks to do the best for the commons; but this, runs the document, "the abbot in his confession doth flat deny."

As regards the monks, the prior, Brian Garner, and one of the seniors, John Groyn, were reported as assembling their tenants on "All Hallows" Eve, when the latter said that "the king should make no more abbots there, but they would choose them themselves." Another monk had spoken against the king as rightful possessor of the crown of England, while others had said that "the bishop of Rome was unjustly put down."[2]

[1] Lingard, *History*, vi. 339. [2] West, *Antiq. of Furness*, 165.

The result of the examinations at Furness was communicated to Henry by the earl of Sussex. Sufficient matter had been reported against the abbot to have secured his sharing the fate of the abbots of Whalley and Sawley, and the passing of the monastery to the king by his attainder. Sussex, however, hit upon another plan. "By such examinations as you have sent us," wrote the king to him, "it appeareth that the abbot of Furness and divers of his monks have not been of that truth towards us that to their duties appertained. We desire and pray you (therefore) with all the dexterity you can, to devise and excogitate to use all the means to you possible, to ensearch and try out the very truth of their proceedings, and with whom they, or any of them, have had any intelligence. We think verily, that you shall find thereby such matter as shall show the light of many things yet unknown. And our pleasure is, that you shall, upon a further examination, commit the said abbot and such of his monks as you shall suspect to have been offenders to ward; there to remain till you shall, upon the signification unto us of such other things as by your wisdom you shall try out, know further our pleasure."[1]

In reply to this communication Sussex wrote on the 6th of April that he had in his previous examination at Furness used "the said abbot and his brethren in such wise as . . . it was impossible to get any more than was had before" out of them. He told the king that he "had committed to ward and sure custody in the castle of Lancaster two of the same monks,[2] which was all we could find faulty." Seeing, therefore, it was not likely that any "material thing" done "after the pardon" would be discovered by further examination against the abbot and his monks "that would serve for the purpose," the earl now exposed his plan for obtaining the rich possessions of the abbey for the king. "I, the said earl," he says, "devising with myself, if one way would not serve, how and by what other means, the said monks might be rid from the said abbey, and consequently how the same might be at your gracious pleasure, caused the said abbot to be sent for to Whalley, and thereupon, after we had examined him, and indeed could not perceive that it was possible for

[1] *State Papers*, i. 541.
[2] Henry Sawley was apparently one of these, as his name does not appear on the deed of surrender.

us to have any other matter, I, the same earl, as before by the advice of other of your council, determined to essay him as of myself, whether he would be contented to surrender, give and grant, unto your heirs and assigns the said monastery."[1]

With the fate of his brother abbots brought so clearly before his mind, and with the bodies of abbot Paslew and his companion still perhaps swinging before the gate of Whalley, where this examination was conducted, it is scarcely a matter of surprise that Sussex carried his point. It was a choice between death or surrender.[2] In either case the royal hand would seize the coveted possessions, and, as Sussex so clearly said, "the monks would be rid from the abbey, and the same be at" the king's gracious pleasure. The abbot chose the course most in accord with the weakness of human nature. He saved his life, but at the cost of his honour and his house. On the 5th of April, 1537, in the presence of Sussex and others, he signed a paper surrendering the monastery to the king on account of the "misorder and evil lives, both unto God and our prince, of the brethren of the said monastery."[3] He did not doubt, the earl continues, "but that we and he together shall easily obtain the ratification of the same gift of the convent, under their convent seal, as shall be requested."

---

[1] West, *Antiquities of Furness*, p. 166.

[2] Mr. Gairdner (*Calendar*, xiii. (i), preface xxviii.) says: "How easy it was to entangle heads of houses in such charges may be seen by the case of an abbot who, under rather trying circumstances, contrived not to commit himself very seriously. At Pershore, a groom of the King's Privy Chamber took advantage of that free hospitality which all monasteries offered to the wayfarer to listen to the conversation at the abbot's table and report it to the king." A neighbour, one Ralph Sheldon, having commended the King for throwing off the "usurpation of the Church of Rome," the abbot blamed him for what he said, and declared that for his part he hoped to die a child of Rome, and added that any one was accursed who resisted "a power" ordained by God. Harrison, the groom, wished to continue the conversation, but the abbot only "scornfully smiled and made no answer." He purposely turned the conversation; but it was no use. A remark about the great mortality about Pershore at the time made by a man from the North, led the abbot to say, "You died fast enough in the North last year" (alluding of course to the savage executions on the suppression of the rebellion); "and as for us in this country, we be smitten with the plagues of David for David's offences." Harrison understood the allusion, and the words were taken to the King. "If this conversation was truly reported," says Mr. Gairdner, "it is strange that the abbot, notwithstanding his discreet reticence on some points, escaped examination and indictment."

[3] Wright, 153.

Immediately this document had been obtained from the abbot of Furness three knights were dispatched from Whalley "to take into their hands the rule and governance of the said house to the use of your highness, and to see that the monks and servants of the same be kept in due order and nothing to be embezzled." Sussex was evidently pleased with what he had done, and, as he informed the king, Fitzherbert, to whom he unfolded his plan, "liked the same very well, saying, that he thought it was the most convenient way that could be to conduct that monastery to your grace's hands, and that now they may be ousted." It was Fitzherbert who drew up the deed of surrender ready for the monks' signatures, which the earl proposed to demand a few days later.[1]

On the following Monday, therefore, April 9th, when the commissioners arrived with the abbot, and the deed prepared by Anthony Fitzherbert had been read to the community in their chapter-house, they took the only possible course left for them and ratified the act of their superior. Thirty monks, out of the thirty-three named as the community by Sussex, signed away their rights; two were in prison; only one apparently did not affix his name to the instrument.[2]

None of the monks, it seems, received any pension in return for the surrender of their monastery, which was worth, free of all charge, more than £800 a year. All they received on being turned out into the world was forty shillings each; three of the thirty-one, "being sick and impotent," were given three pounds.[3] Abbot Roger, a year later, was provided for by the grant for life of the profits of the rectory of Dalton, which were then valued at £33, 6s. 8d. a year.[4] Apparently he lived in the parsonage, for he was subsequently directed by Crumwell to give it up to "John Bothe, one of the king's servants." In his reply, which he dates from Furness, he pleads that he has "nothing else to live upon," and adds, "but for your displeasure I should be there now." To propitiate the all-powerful minister he sends him forty shillings in gold, and promises to send as much more at Easter.[5]

[1] West, *ut sup.*   [2] Eighth Rep. Dep. Keep. App., ii. 21.
[3] Exch. Augt. Off. Mins. Accts., 29–30 Hen. VIII., No. 187, mm. 13–14.
[4] West, p. 190.   [5] R. O. Crum. Corr., viii. f. 18.

"The vast and magnificent edifice of Furness was forsaken," writes Canon Dixon, "the lamp of the altar of St. Mary went out for ever, and in the deserted cloisters no sound was heard but the axe and hammer of those who came to cut away the lead, dash down the bells, hew away the rafters, and break in pieces the arches and pillars. Thus dismantled, the ruin was left as a common quarry for the convenience of every countryman who could cart away the sculptured stones for building a pigsty or a byre."[1]

Here as elsewhere the suppression was felt most keenly by the poor. From "time immemorial" on Maunday Thursday alms had been liberally bestowed on the poor at the abbey gate, while a hundred poor boys in the cloister each received a sum equal to more than a shilling of our money. Yearly on the feast of St. Crispin, according to the will of the founder, five oxen were given to the poor of the neighbourhood with a request for prayers for his soul. "Each week eight widows" had their bread and beer at the monastic kitchen, while from the foundation of the abbey to the day of dissolution thirteen poor people had been entirely maintained within its walls. Thus the regular charities alone, for which the monks of Furness were the trustees, amounted to a yearly sum of nearly £500 of our money.[2] This loss to the poor of the neighbourhood, even if no account is taken of the numerous other services done to them under no strict obligation of justice, may be well imagined. The money to furnish bread and alms, which pious benefactors had left to the needy of the district, passed away from them for ever into the king's purse or the pockets of his courtiers. The thirteen "poor almsmen who had their living" within the old monastic walls, were, through the generosity of the royal commissioners, enriched by the gift of one mark each on being turned out into the world to beg for their living.[3] What the commonwealth at large lost by the destruction may be gathered from the fact that four hundred horsemen and twice that number of foot are said to have formed the monastic contingent at Flodden field.[4]

Another great Cistercian house, at no great distance from Furness, passed into Henry's hands by surrender. The

---

[1] Dixon's *Hist. of Ch. of Engl.*, vol. i. 496. [2] *Valor Eccl.*, v. 270.
[3] Exch. Augt. Off., *ut sup.* [4] Walcott, *English Minsters*, ii. p. 124.

abbey of Holm Cultram was situated on the coast, and looked over the waters of the Solway Firth towards Scotland. At the time of the dissolution it possessed an income of £535, 3s. 7d. It was a royal foundation, and among its annual expenses were pensions for priests who at the "Jesu altar" in the church offered the daily mass for the soul of Henry II. and the good estate of Henry VIII. Every year on Maunday Thursday alms were distributed equal in value to more than £30 of our money to the "boys brought up in the cloister" and "to the poor at the abbey gate," that they might remember to pray for the king, while five poor people received their support in the house for the same purpose. At the expense of the monks likewise were maintained the sea-dykes and walls by which alone the waters of the Solway Firth were prevented from devastating the adjacent country.[1] At the time when Layton and Legh visited the northern monasteries, in the beginning of 1536, Thomas Carter held the office of abbot, and his community consisted of five-and-twenty religious. He and several of his monks received a bad character from the royal commissioners, which may or may not have been deserved.[2]

But whatever desire the king might have had for the reformation of monks, nothing was apparently done until, the northern insurrection breaking out, Thomas Carter was involved in the suspicion of treason in aiding the rebels. Before the outbreak of the Lincolnshire rising he had been summoned to London, "to answer before the king and council such things as" should be objected against him, and on October 1st he replied to the order asking to be allowed to appear by "a friend."[3] The insurrection had already broken out, and Crumwell was obliged to delay his dealing with the refractory abbot until the rising had been quelled in the spring of 1537. A commission was then appointed to consider the matter, and it sat in the abbey church. "The articles against the abbot of Holm Cultram for high treason" were presented and signed by a religious, Thomas Graham; and two other monks gave evidence. The gist of the accusation is, that at the first rising abbot Carter forced his tenants, "upon pain of hanging," to join the commons: that he had contributed forty shillings to the

[1] *Valor Eccl.*, v. p. 282.   [2] *Calendar*, x. No. 364.
[3] R. O. Crum. Corr., xvii.

expenses of the insurgents: that he was one of the commissioners from the people to Carlisle, and rode near to demand that the city should be delivered up to them: and finally, that at the last rising when the people laid siege to Carlisle he had said "almighty God prosper them, for if they speed not this abbey is lost," and upon the saying, "he sent for his subprior and commanded him to cause the brethren to go daily with procession to speed the commons' journey."

Beyond the above, the abbot was accused of violating the injunctions of the king's visitors. It was said that he had admitted women to dine and sup within the precincts of the abbey: that he had sold the monastic plate to the value of £100 or more: that he had given out leases and "convent seals:" and that he had given the abbot of Byland "for helping him to his promotion, a salt of gold and silver worth twenty shillings."[1] The commission was, however, never concluded.

The abbot appears to have died on the 10th of August, and thus to have anticipated his fate.[2] Writing from Carlisle on August 17th (1537), Sir Thomas Wharton, one of the commissioners, states that he has attended the assizes at Carlisle and desires to plead the cause of the abbot's chief accuser, the monk Graham, who had given his late superior grave cause for anxiety by the irregularity of his life. "It may further please your lordship," he writes to Crumwell, "to know that, since the death of the late abbot of Holm, there were labours made unto me to sue for one Graham, monk of that monastery, who would besides his first fruits to be paid to the king's highness bestow for his preferment to be abbot there 400 marks."[3]

Graham was unsuccessful, for Crumwell had another worthy candidate for the appointment. Gawin Borodale about five years before had been for some months in prison at Furness Abbey on the charge of having caused the death of his abbot, Thomas Carter's predecessor, "in poisonning him." In a letter to Crumwell he had declared his innocence, and had asked to be tried "according to the statutes of the holy" Cistercian religion.[4] Dr. Legh, at the request of the abbots of Furness and Byland, "the visitors and reformators

[1] Raine, *Hexham Priory*, i. App. cliv. [2] *Calendar*, xi. No. 276.
[3] *Ibid.*, 319. [4] R. O. Crum. Corr., iv. f. 118.

of the Cistercians," had begged Crumwell's favour for him, as "he had well served the king in his house," and was "kept out of his monastery through the sinister information of some evil-disposed persons."[1] It was this Gawin Borodale who received the office of abbot of Holm Cultram in the autumn of 1537, and who, in the March following, resigned the abbey into the king's hands. As in the cases of Jervaulx, Whalley, Kirksted and other monasteries, the superiors of which had been executed for treason, so Holm Cultram would no doubt have come into the royal power by attainder if other arrangements had not been made.

On February 18th, 1538, the king issued a special commission to Thomas Legh, William Blithman, and James Rokeby to repair to the abbey. The commission states that "whereas the abbot and convent of our monastery of Holm Cultram . . . freely and willingly be determined and concluded to surrender all the title and interest of the monastery and of the goods and possessions thereunto belonging into our hands and disposition," the king appoints the above to obtain from the abbot and convent "such sufficient writing under their convent seal as shall be expedient." Further, that at the dissolution they shall promise the abbot and monks "such things as shall be necessary for them and his living according to their discretion; shall make an inventory and survey of the goods and lands, and conduct the sales of the monastic effects."[2]

Acting upon these instructions, the commissioners attended at the monastery upon March 6th, 1538, and at once dispatched James Rokeby to London "to declare the surrender." In their account at the following Michaelmas they acknowledge having sold 802 ounces of plate for £147, 11s. 4d., and 146 fodders of lead worth £486, while they have left the covering on the church roof for the further "pleasure of the king, because it was the parish church." The monks on being dispatched had various sums given to them, varying from £6 to Robert Langton, the prior, to £2 to each of the three novices.[3] Gawin Borodale secured for himself a pension of £100 a year, a house and stables, and all the tithes as rector of Holm Cultram.[4] Most of the

---

[1] R. O. Crum. Corr., xxii. No. 9 (Aug. 16, 25 Hen. VIII.).
[2] Exch. Aug. Off. Mins. Accts., 28-29 Hen. VIII., No. 165.
[3] Ibid.   [4] Aug. Off. Misc. Bk., 232, f. 43.

community were pensioned at the same time.¹ To Thomas Graham, the chief accuser of abbot Carter, Dr. Legh, as royal commissioner, made the special grant of "a chapel called Saint Thomas chapel to make him a chamber of there."²

The dissolution of two other houses may be here noted, not that their fate had any apparent connection with the northern rising, but that they were brought by some means or other under the law of attainder. These were the Cluniac priory of Lenton, in Nottinghamshire, and the Cistercian abbey of Woburn, in Bedfordshire. The former house, like so many others, had been much disturbed by the action of Crumwell's visitors. One of the monks, Dan Hamlet Pencriche, had brought an accusation against the prior before the council, and finally fled from his monastery, as he had twice before done, carrying away goods belonging to the house.³ He was, however, subsequently lodged in the Fleet prison by order of the Chancellor,⁴ and although Nicholas Hethe, the prior, had originally been promoted to his post by the good-will of Crumwell himself, he soon discovered that his duty to his house forced him to break with his patron. As early as April, 1536, apparently not long after coming to his office, Hethe wrote to say that his predecessor had left the house much in debt, and that although he had promised Crumwell, through his nephew Richard, £100, he was then only able to pay £60; he hoped that the rest might stand over to Martinmas, or otherwise he would have to borrow money "in London of some merchant" to "keep up hospitality." He concludes by asking that the rule banishing all young men from the cloistered life may be relaxed for Lenton. "I beseech," he says, "I may have your favour concerning two young men in our religion at Lenton. All my brethren, except four or five, are very impotent and of great age, and request your favour that they may continue in their religion."⁵

On the 29th of June the same year, 1536, the prior is said to have committed some act of treason against the king.⁶ What the treason was does not appear, unless it be

---

¹ Aug. Off. Misc., Bk. 233, ff. 2, 170.   ² Exch. Q. R. ⁷⁄₅, No. 5.
³ *Calendar*, x. No. 655.   ⁴ R. O. Crum. Corr., xxxii. No. 38.
⁵ *Calendar*, x. No. 1234.
⁶ R. O. Exch. Augt. Off. Misc. Bk., 3136, f. 8, a curious list of the dates of the treasons of those attainted.

the sale of some of the plate of the monastery, disposed of doubtless to relieve the needs of his community, and for which Godbery, a London goldsmith, who had purchased it, was subsequently forced by Crumwell to refund nearly £20 to his private purse.[1] Whatever his act may have been, the prior was seized and thrown into prison in February, 1538, where he remained till the middle of the following month,[2] when he, together with eight of his monks and four labourers of Lenton, were indicted for treason at Nottingham.[3] In the Crumwell's "Remembrances" at this time is entered the following note :—" The suppression of Lenton and the execution of the prior,"[4] and on the "Controlment Roll" is found the record of the conviction of "Nicholas Hethe, prior of Lenton, William Gylham, monk of Lenton," four labourers and a priest for high treason, after whose names are entered the ominous "T et S," "to be drawn and hanged," as the sentence passed upon them. What became of the rest of the monks is not known. None of them obtained any pension from the king, nor apparently did the five poor men kept by the monastery alms[5] receive any compensation upon being deprived of their inheritance. A clear revenue of upwards of £329 a year passed into Henry's hands by the attainder of the monastery, and more than £252 were obtained by the sales of the monastic goods.[6]

The story of the destruction of Woburn and the fate of the abbot is rendered even more pathetic by the touching details which have been preserved. By it the veil is lifted and a glimpse is afforded of the fears, hopes and despair which filled the souls of the religious in the short time during which the sword of destruction hung over their heads. Their hearts appear chilled by the uncertain fate which awaited them, their actions paralyzed by the masterful policy of Crumwell, and the very fountain of religious life dried up by injunctions conceived with the deliberate purpose

---

[1] R. O. Chapter House Bk., B. ⅛, f. 40.
[2] R. O. Exch. Aug. Off. Mins. Accts., 29-30 Hen. VIII., 181.
[3] R. O. Control. Roll, 30 Hen. VIII., m. 39. The names of the monks were: Ralph Swenson, Richard Bower, Richard Atkinson, Christopher Browne, John Trewnam, John Adelenton, William Bery, William Gylham.
[4] Brit. Mus. Cott. MS., Titus B. i. f. 468d.
[5] *Valor Eccl.*, v. 149.
[6] R. O. Exch. Aug. Off. Mins. Acct., 29-30 Hen. VIII., 181.

of making the cloister unbearable and compelling rebellion or surrender.

Richard Hobbes had been abbot of Woburn for many years, and, together with his monks, had given in to the royal demands and sworn to the king's "headship." It was clearly against his better judgment and that of many at least of his monks, that the oath was taken, and they were troubled in conscience at their weakness in not standing out for what they believed to be the only truth. Dan Ralph, the subprior, subsequently acknowledged his scruples and begged Henry's pardon for his "erroneous estimation of Mr. More and the bishop of Rochester, whose death he a great while thought meritorious, wishing he had died with them." In fact, he asserted that it was the abbot himself who, "by counsel and menaces," persuaded him to take the required oath of supremacy. Another of the community, Dan Laurence, the sexton, declared that when he was first sworn he could not touch the book on account of the numbers, and so he considered his conscience was free, although he had signed "the carte of profession."[1]

Even at the beginning of the year 1536 rumours were circulated about the probable fate of the abbey, and it was said that "it and other more should go down ere Twelfth-tide."[2] But it was really not until the spring of the year 1538 that any steps were taken against it. The final catastrophe was hastened through the malicious informations of discontented monks, who, here as in many monasteries of England at this time, served Crumwell as spies upon the acts and words of their superiors and brethren.

On the 12th of May, 1538, abbot Hobbes and certain of his monks were examined in the Tower. The subprior and some others deposed that at the time when the Carthusians were put to death the abbot had called them together and said these words:—"Brethren, this is a perilous time; such a scourge was never heard since Christ's passion. Ye hear how good men do suffer death. Brethren, this is undoubtedly for our offences. Ye read, so long as the children of Israel kept the commandments of God, so long their enemies had no power over them, but God took vengeance on their enemies; but when they broke God's commandments, then

---

[1] *Calendar*, x. No. 1239.   [2] *Ibid.*, No. 5.

they were subdued by their enemies, and so be we. Therefore, let us be sorry for our offences and undoubtedly he will take vengeance on our enemies; I mean these heretics that cause so many good men to suffer thus. Alas! it is a piteous case that so much Christian blood should be shed. Therefore, good Christian brethren, for the reverence of God, every one of you devoutly pray and say this psalm—*Deus venerunt gentes* through, and say this versicle—*Exurgat Deus et dissipentur inimici.* This foresaid psalm to be said every Friday, immediately after the litany, prostrate, when ye lie before the high altar, and undoubtedly God will cease this extreme storm."

This injunction the monks faithfully carried out, although some murmured at the command, and when at the beginning of 1536 parliament passed the act by which the lesser monasteries were suppressed, the abbot again spoke to his monks. "The abbot," says the deposition of four of the monks, "with such like exhortation in the said chapter-house, with lamentable mournings for the dissolving of them, enjoined us to sing, '*Salvator mundi salva nos omnes*' every day after Lauds. And we murmured at it, and were not content to sing it for such cause. And so we did omit it divers times, for which the abbot came unto the chapter and did in manner rebuke us, and said we were bound to obey his commands by our profession. And so he did command us to sing it again with versicles: '*Exurgat Deus,*' etc., and enjoined us to say at every mass that every priest did sing, a collect: '*Deus qui contritorum,*' etc. And he said if we did thus with good and pure devotion, God would handle the matter so that it should be to the comfort of all England, and so show us mercy as he showed unto the children of Israel. And surely brethren, he said, there will come over us a good man that will re-edify these monasteries again that are now suppressed, 'quia potens est Deus de lapidibus istis suscitare filios Abrahæ.'"[1]

Meantime during the period of waiting for the final doom there arose excitement and contentions among the monks, and cross-accusations of one party against the other. In the "shaving house" Dan John Croxton was openly accused by a brother, Laurence Blonham, of being one of the "new

[1] *Calendar,* xiii. (i), No. 981.

world." Dan John replied with bitter words, saying that such ideas would get them into trouble, but Blonham answered: "Neither thou nor yet any of us all shall do well as long as we forsake our head of the Church, the pope." Croxton retorted that if Blonham really thought this, he was "a false, perjured knave to his prince," and upon his saying that "he never was sworn to forsake the pope as head, and never would be," said, "Thou shalt be sworn spite of thy heart one day, or I will know why nay."[1] Another monk, called Crowe, complained that, having spoken against the bread supplied to them, the abbot told him "to go further and fare worse."

These and such like tales, duly carried to the ears of Crumwell, brought the abbot under suspicion. He was arrested and conveyed together with other of his monks to the Tower. He with his monks had tried, it seems, to anticipate the event by a joint letter handing over themselves and their monastery to the king's mercy. They indeed acknowledged Henry "to be supreme head" and their "comfort and joy," and declared that they were innocent of the charges brought against them, including "high treason."[2] But the submission, ample and humble as it was, either came too late, or the king had determined to discourage disobedience in other monasteries by another example of an abbot ending an honoured life on the scaffold.

In his examination Richard Hobbes practically allowed all that had been advanced against him. With regard to the pope, he does not hesitate to admit that in "much preaching" he has not declared the king "supreme head;" not out of malice, as he says, "but only for a scrupulous conscience he then had touching the continuance of the bishop of Rome." He had got Dan William Hampton, his secretary, to transcribe a book written by John Mylward, priest of Todington, called "De potestate Petri." He will not allow that he spoke of England as an heretical country, for not joining in the general council; nor that he neglected to give up all the "papistical bulls" he could find to "Mr. doctor Petre" at the visitation; nor that he neglected to have the pope's name erased out of the "calendars and other books, as mass books, grayles and other usual books of the choir." He commanded

---

[1] *Calendar*, xiii. (i), No. 981.   [2] Wright, 145.

the cantor, Dan Robert Neve, and others to obey the king's order in this matter, and himself put the name out of "such books as he had to say his service."

On the other hand, he confesses that, when the papal bulls were sent up to doctor Petre, he got Dan Robert Salford "to write the principal bulls in a fair hand," and the junior monks not priests to transcribe the others in a running hand, so that when the quarrel between the king and pope was settled he might have evidence of his old privileges and exemptions. These copies, he said, "remained yet in my chamber at my coming away."

He fully admitted his sermons to his brethren, and even himself says he likened Henry to Nebuchodonosor taking away the sacred vessels of the Temple. Also on several occasions he had spoken to young men, "commensals" of the house, as "Mr. Morice, Mr. Carye and Mr. Hervy," whose schoolmaster was very earnest against the "new learning," in the same strain. "And I the said abbot," he says, "confess that in all audiences from time to time I have stood stiffly in my opinions of the old trade unto this present day, maintaining the part of the bishop of Rome, so far as I durst, thinking that it was the true way, and the contrary of the king's part but usurpation desiderated by flattery and adulation."[1]

As abbot Hobbes had spoken to his brethren and those living in his house, so he had declared for the old faith to his friends outside. To lord Grey of Wilton he had been explicit as to his opinions, and also to Dan Augustin, "the quondam" of Wardon, who was staying at Woburn. Most plainly of all had he opened his mind to Sir Francis Brian, and throughout his examinations he manifests a fear lest his friendship with Sir Francis should be considered detrimental to that gentleman's interests. He had often been at Ampthill with him, and always took care to extol the teaching of the "old fathers Catholic," and specially condemned the preaching of Latimer "as touching our Lady and the saints." On one occasion in particular, after the Lent of 1538, he was with a large company at Sir Francis's house at Ampthill. He went, "after loving cheer and disports," with Brian to his bedroom, where he saw a "goodly book," which proved

---

[1] Brit. Mus. Cott. MS., Cleop. E. iv. f. 108.

to be the new English translation of the Bible. He took advantage of the chance to speak about it. "It is a fair book," he said, "but in my opinion not well interpreted in many places, which hereafter may be the cause of much error." Sir Francis opened the volume and turned to the place in St. Luke which speaks of the "consecration of the blessed Body and Blood." Having read it, he asked the abbot what he thought about it. He confessed that it was good, but took occasion to say again that there were many false translations in the volume.[1]

The abbot admitted that he had wished he had died with the Carthusians, More and Fisher. He was ill at the time, a few weeks before his imprisonment, and, as the accuser says, "Dan Ralph Woburn, subprior, reported in his own chamber to one Dan William Hampton, in the presence of this examinat, that the abbot from whom he came a little before said to him (after he had asked him how he did) that he wished himself to have died with the good men that died for holding with the pope, and said that his conscience doth grudge him daily for it. Whereunto this examinat," says the accuser, "answered, 'If he be disposed to die for that matter, he may die as soon as he will.'"[2]

"And finally," says abbot Hobbes in his confession, "as touching acts of the archbishop of Canterbury in ordaining and consecration of bishops, dispensations of matrimony, capacities given to religious men, I have thought he had no authority so to do without power of the bishop of Rome, and in likewise all such things done by him, not lawfully exercised by those that have received such dignities and dispensations from him."

This ample confession, which was evidently made by the advice of Crumwell, pitifully reveals mind and soul and heart in all their perplexities. But the abbot had also vividly before him the horrors of imprisonment and the thought of a terrible death. Under stress of this fear, before his examination is concluded, he, in accents more pitiful still, admits that he may have been mistaken after all, and prays for pardon.

This is but a picture of the anguish of conscience and the sinking of heart in dread of an uncertain end which must

---

[1] Brit. Mus. Cott. MS., Cleop. E. iv. f. 109.
[2] *State Papers*, Dom. 1538, *ut sup.*

have been the experience of thousands in that terrible time. The storm burst first and most heavily, as usual, not on the practised theologian and skilled dialectician, but on men who mostly lived by authority and tradition. By instinct they knew what was right. Their conscience "was scrupulous touching the continuance of the bishop of Rome." They maintained his part "as far as they durst, thinking it was the true way," and regarding with equal distrust and fear the ecclesiastical policy of Henry and the acts of Cranmer, believing that the archbishop "had no authority to do as he did without power of the bishop of Rome." The expectation was general that the "quarrel," as it was esteemed, between the king and the pope would be made up again, and that at no very distant time. To men wise after the event, such an expectation may seem to betoken a simplicity bordering on foolishness, but to men in those days it was a sheet-anchor of hope.

To those in the position of the abbot of Woburn the immediate interests were pressing, involving both the welfare of brethren, servants, dependents, friends, and the fate of a home they loved. Such considerations must have added a moral weight to suggestions prompted by personal fears, and perchance may have helped them even to deceive themselves. Like prior Houghton of the Carthusians, they might come to believe that they were making themselves anathema for the sake of their brethren, and even "the daily grudge of conscience" would appear to men of this stamp but part of the sore burden to be borne in their Master's service, so subtle is the mind in finding the highest motives to avert an evil before which the flesh quails and the heart sinks. All that could be done for the moment was to hold out and gain time.

But such a surrender of convictions as that to which abbot Hobbes had brought himself was all in vain. His prayer for pardon was denied; he was not allowed to live. Henry had passed beyond the stage of compassion for any human weakness, of pity for any living soul. The abbot was apparently tried at Lincoln, together with Laurence Blonham or Peck, and Richard Woburn or Barnes, two monks of the abbey, and all three being found guilty, were ordered to be drawn, hanged and quartered.[1] Of the two

---

[1] R. O. Control. Roll, 30 Hen. VIII., m. 6d.

T

monks thus condemned, one, Laurence Blonham, was he who in the "shaving house" had declared he never would "be sworn to forsake the pope." The other, Richard, or as he is otherwise called, "Ralph," Woburn or Barnes, was the subprior of whom abbot Hobbes has left it on record, that he "always held the strongest views and expressed them" on the matter of the pope's authority.[1]

The abbot, together with the vicar of Puddington and others, was hanged before the gate of Woburn abbey, and tradition as late as the beginning of this century pointed to an old oak tree in front of the monastery as the gallows upon which the monks were executed.[2]

The possessions of the abbey, producing a clear income of nearly £400 a year,[3] thus passed into the royal hands by the new interpretation of the law of attainder on the 20th of June, 1538. By the 29th of September the royal receiver for attainted lands acknowledged from sales of the monastic goods the sum of £266, 12s.[4] A few years later this property was granted, together with many other broad acres belonging to the Church and the poor, to Sir John Russell.

[1] Cleop. E. iv. f. 106d.
[2] Brit. Mus. Add. MS. 27,402, p. 47, gives only *one* monk—"the prior" executed with the abbot. The parson of Puddington's name was *John Henmersh*. Cont. Roll., 31 Hen. VIII.; Dodd's *Woburn*, 1818, p. 38.
[3] *Valor Eccl.*, iv. p. 213.
[4] R. O. Exch. Augt. Off. Mins. Accts., 29-30 Hen. VIII., 181, m. 3.

CHAPTER XV

The Suppression of Convents

SEVERAL circumstances relating to the destruction of English nunneries render some particular account of them advisable. Many things combined to render the dissolution of conventual establishments of women and the disbanding the inmates more terrible to nuns than to monks. A woman compelled to exchange the secluded life of a cloister, with all its aids to piety, for an existence in the world, to which she could never rightly belong, would be obviously in a more dangerous and unbearable position than a man. To the monk, who was also a priest, there was always a possible future in the exercise of his sacred calling, and however remote his chance of obtaining a cure of souls or other sacerdotal employment, when the tendency of Henry's policy was on every hand to destroy the influence and diminish the occupation of the clergy, still the bare possibility must have rendered expulsion from home less hopeless in its outlook. The nun's lot, however, had no such ray of consolation. Even had the circumstances attending her dismissal from conventual life been more fortunate, or had it been the result of her own act and choice, her future must have been dark and uncertain, since the vows which bound her heart and conscience must keep her always apart from the secular surroundings in which she was compelled to exist. The cleric, even although his monk's garb were torn from him, and he was forced to trudge the world in poverty, could not be deprived of the sacred character of the clerical state; but the nun, driven from the dismantled walls of her convent, and the veil of her profession denied to her, could not but suffer the pains of daily martyrdom in the rough surroundings of an uncongenial world.

At the time of the dissolution there were in England some hundred and forty convents of women. Of these, rather more than half belonged to the Benedictine order. They were scattered over the face of the country; Yorkshire containing a greater proportion than any other county. The majority were not possessed of a yearly income sufficient to exempt them from the operation of the act by which the lesser houses passed into the king's hands. In Yorkshire alone, more than half the convents were suppressed under cover of this act of dissolution.

With regard to the regularity and order which prevailed in the English nunneries at the time of their destruction, it will be sufficient here to indicate that even Layton and Legh in their celebrated "*comperta*" are able to bring comparatively few charges against their good name. It will be remembered that the reports of these worthy emissaries of Crumwell embraced some thirteen counties, and only twenty-seven nuns in all the convents they visited are charged with vice of any kind. Even of these seven-and-twenty all but ten can be identified as subsequently receiving the grant of a pension. It is, moreover, most remarkable that even Layton and his fellow-visitor can only name two nuns, out of all the convents visited, who are anxious to cast off the restraints of religious life; and this even after the imposition of vexatious injunctions, the very acknowledged purpose of which was to render the practice of religious life unendurable.

In the subsequent reports of the mixed commissions of gentry and officials, the character given to the convents is uniformly most excellent. Thus the White nuns of Grace Dieu in Leicestershire, the only convent of the order in England, are declared to be "of good and virtuous conversation and living, and all desirous to continue their religion there, and none willing to have capacities" to return to a life in the world. They were fifteen in number, and their convent, situated in the wilds of Charnwood forest, was a blessing to the neighbourhood. Although their whole available income was under £100 a year, they yet gave employment to thirty-six dependents, and twelve people, nine of whom were absolute paupers, were supported in the convent.[1] Besides this, out of their scanty income they had to distribute on the anniversary of the death of their

[1] *Calendar*, x. p. 497.

foundress a sum equal to £20 of our money, to obtain the prayers of the poor for the repose of her soul.[1]

A few months before this report the previous royal visitors had accused two of the nuns of the worst offences,[2] who are now declared to be "of good and virtuous conversation." The house came, of course, within the pecuniary limit appointed by the act dissolving the lesser houses of religion, but on August 17th the prioress, Agnes Litherland, received the king's licence to continue. For "divers causes and considerations," the convent was allowed to be re-established "in perpetuity," and the prioress was continued in her office.[3] On October 21st, 1538, however, the house was suppressed by Dr. Legh, who promised Cecily Bagnald, then apparently the prioress, a pension of £40 a year.[4] On the 20th of the following December, fifteen other nuns, amongst whom were the two so grievously incriminated by doctors Layton and Legh, were also granted pensions.

In the same way the poor priory of Black Benedictine nuns at Langley, in the same county, received an equally good character from the mixed commissioners. There were six nuns besides the prioress, "who is," says the report, "of great age and impotent; all are of good and virtuous living and conversation; one is sister to the late Sir Richard Saccheverell, almost 80 years old; 'one other is in regard a fool.' All are desirous to continue in religion."[5] They had a chaplain, fourteen dependents, and two people living in the house to whom they had granted a perpetual corrody. Of a thirtieth part of their small revenue they were only the trustees, being bound by their founder to distribute corn and money, worth in these days some £10, every year, on the Wednesday in Holy Week, to twelve widows, that they might pray for the repose of his soul.[6] On the 24th of June, 1536, the royal commissioners descended upon the priory, and the process of dissolution took them exactly three months. The plate and jewels belonging to the church and house, including a silver vessel weighing 108 ounces, and a "pix" for the blessed Sacrament of 16 ounces, were estimated to be worth nearly £60, and were forthwith

---

[1] *Valor Eccl.*, iv. 175.   [2] *Calendar*, x. p. 183.
[3] Rot. Pat., 28 Hen. VIII., Pars ii. m. ($\frac{10}{8}$).
[4] R. O. Augt. Off. Misc. Bk., 245, f. 225.
[5] *Calendar*, x. p. 247.   [6] *Valor Eccl.*, iv. 176.

dispatched to the royal treasury. The prioress, Dulcosa Bothe, was obliged during these months of weary waiting to sell a silver salver and eleven spoons in order to keep up the hospitality and almsgiving of the house.[1] The vestments and moveables of the convent were sold for more than £81; while the lead on the roofs and gutters, together with two small bells, were appraised at £34 more. When all arrangements had been made, on September 24th, the nuns were expelled, and thirty-six shillings and eightpence was distributed amongst them.[2] There were no pensions, apparently, granted to any of the nuns. Very probably the prioress, to whom, according to the rule followed in most of the early dissolutions, some small allowance would have been made, did not long survive her expulsion, since she was "of great age and impotent" at the time. In Mary's reign, one nun only, Isabel Seton, appears on the pension list of the survivors of the dissolved monasteries.[3]

Among the religious houses, which ought to have been suppressed under the act for the dissolution of the lesser monasteries, but which purchased from the king a royal grant to continue, were twenty-one convents of women. The nuns who thus obtained a temporary respite were some 273, and their dependents may be considered to have equalled four or five times that number. The price they paid to the king's treasury as purchase-money for their own convents and for leave to continue in the cloister was, in almost every case where payment had been made before the final catastrophe, greatly in excess of their annual revenue. About half the number, however, chiefly those situated in the northern counties, had apparently paid nothing when their property was again seized by Henry. The others, although the treasurer of the Augmentation Office is careful to note that the sums entered were only "part payment," and that the arrears due had been forgiven them as they had come into the king's hand before the settlement of the debt, paid dearly for their continuance. Thus Lacock, a convent of eighteen nuns in Wiltshire, actually paid £300,

---

[1] Besides this, she accounted for £47, 4s. 2½d., received from rents, as spent on the support of the house. Exch. A. O. Mins. Accts., 27–28 Hen. VIII., 90, m. 28.
[2] R. O. Exch. Augt. Off. Mins. Accts., 27–28 Hen. VIII., 168, m. 4.
[3] Brit. Mus. Add. MS., 8102, Co. Leicester.

its annual income being only £168; and St. Mary's, Chester, which maintained its thirteen nuns upon the slender income of £66 a year, was compelled to purchase exemption by a payment of £160.[1]

If these sums are large, there can be little doubt that many other payments were also made, either as bribes to induce the king's officials to interest themselves in the preservation of various houses, or to obtain the royal favour by money offered personally to him. Thus the prioress of Catesby wrote to Crumwell that "the queen had moved the king for me, and offered him 2000 marks for the house of Catesby, but has not yet a perfect answer." She begs the all-powerful minister in her "great sorrow" to get the king to allow the house to stand, "and," she adds, "get me years of payment for the 2000 marks. You shall have 100 marks of me to buy a gelding, and my prayers during my life, and all my sisters during their lives." She concludes by reminding Crumwell of the good report the commissioners had sent of her house, and although, as she hears, a grant has already been made of the convent to some royal favourite, still she trusts to the queen's efforts and his that its destruction may be averted.[2]

On May 12th the commissioners themselves anticipated their report of the visitation in Northamptonshire to try and save the convent. The "house of Catesby," they say, "we found in very perfect order, the prioress a pure, wise, discreet and very religious woman with nine nuns under her obedience, as religious and devout, and with as good obedience as we have in time past seen or belike shall see. The said house standeth in such a quarter much to the relief of the king's people, and his grace's poor subjects there likewise much relieved, as by the report of divers worshipful (men) near thereunto adjoining, as of all other that is to us openly declared. Wherefore if it should please the king's highness to have any remorse that any such religious house shall stand, we think his grace cannot appoint any house more meet to show his most gracious charity and pity to than to the said house of Catesby." They praise the "discreet entertainment" the prioress showed to the commissioners, and write thus, "lest peradventure there may be

[1] R. O. Exch. Aug. Off. Treasurer's Roll, i. m. 4d.
[2] *Calendar*, x. No. 383.

labour made to her detriment and utter undoing, before knowledge should come to his highness and to you from us," and that the king "may stay the grant" of the house.[1]

This petition on behalf of the nuns of Catesby, from the very commissioners who had been sent to conduct the dissolution of their convent, perhaps did harm to the cause they wished to serve. The chancellor of the Augmentation Office showed Henry the letter, and subsequently declared that "the king's highness was displeased, as he said to my servant Thomas Harper, saying that it was like that we had received rewards, which caused us to write as we did."[2] George Gyffard, the writer of the above letters, informed Crumwell on the 27th of June that by order of "Mr. Chancellor and Mr. Attorney of the Augmentation," the commissioners had returned to Catesby "to begin our suppression." Even then, however, they were loath to execute the decree of expulsion, and asked whether the order from the Augmentation Office was "a sufficient warrant."[3]

Crumwell's reply was, no doubt, an order to proceed with the unwelcome work, for the suppression was immediately commenced. The establishment consisted of nine nuns besides the prioress, twenty-six dependents, the vicar of Catesby, two assistant chaplains and one parish clerk paid by the convent. The royal officers seized plate to the value of £29, 4s., sold the furniture of the house, with the vestments and other ornaments of the church, for more than £400, and estimated that the lead, which had been torn from the roof and melted, would bring in £110 more, besides £3 for the broken metal of two handbells.[4]

The work of dissolution took some time, and it was not till after September 27th that the nuns were finally turned adrift. John Tregonwell, one of Crumwell's emissaries, gave them a good character to the last. "The prioress there," he says, "is a right sad matron; the sisters also there now being by the space of twenty years hath been (by as much as I can learn) without suspicion of incontinent living."[5]

Joyce Bykeley, the prioress, was granted by letters patent a pension of £20 a year from July 2nd, 1536.[6] The payment

[1] Wright, 129.   [2] *Ibid.*, 136.   [3] *Calendar*, x. No. 1215.
[4] R. O. Exch. Aug. Off. Mins. Accts., 27–28 Hen. VIII., 173, m. 2.
[5] R. O. Crum. Corr. xliii. No. 59.
[6] Exch. Augt. Off. Misc. Bk., 244, f. 32, "Orig. of Grants."

for this sum was made to her, as appears in the "Minister's Accounts," until Michaelmas, 1541, when no charge is entered on her behalf and the pension apparently ceased.

The fines paid to the king for the continuance of the convents reduced some of them, as already pointed out in the case of Stixwold, to a state of absolute beggary. It was made a plea by the commissioners for an increase of pension in some instances when the final doom came upon them. Thus Dr. London, writing to the chancellor Rich on the final dissolution of the convent of Pollesworth, says :— "The convent to the great charge of the friends lately purchased again of the king, in your high court, the house to continue." And, as "the abbess hath always been reputed a virtuous woman and a good housewife," he strongly advocates giving her a pension of £26 13s. 4d. a year.[1] In the same way Alice Baldwin, the abbess of Burnham, is recommended for a small annual allowance " in consideration that she redeemed her house ;"[2] and, to give but one more example, the same royal commissioner writes that he and Dr. Baskerfield had dissolved the Cistercian house of Delapray, although the nuns had purchased "the same of the king that it should continue." They have consequently promised, he says, £40 a year to the abbess, for "she is very sickly and an aged woman, and hath been abbess there about thirty years, and hath lived always like a virtuous woman, and her house in like manner was well ordered."[3]

The convents of England were mostly small as regards numbers and poor in their resources. In fact, had not the king been persuaded to hold his hand for a time, the act dissolving monasteries and convents under £200 a year would have swept away all but eighteen of the houses of religious women. Only twelve out of the eighty-four convents of the Benedictine order were possessed of revenues greater than the pecuniary limit assigned by the act. Of the twenty-six Cistercian houses, one only, that of Tarrant, in Dorsetshire, was exempted from the operation of the act; whilst of

---

[1] R. O. Exch. Augt. Off. Misc. Bk., 245, f. 15. The reason here assigned for granting the prioress a good pension is also urged in other cases.
[2] *Ibid.*, f. 29. The grant for this convent to continue is enrolled on Rot. Pat., 29 Hen. VIII., Pars. v. m. 17. The account of the treasurer does not mention any money.
[3] *Ibid.*, f. 38.

the rest, only one Augustinian, the Bridgettines of Sion, the ladies of St. John of Jerusalem at Buckland, and two houses of nuns of the order of St. Gilbert, were rich enough to escape suppression in the year 1536. Special legislation was apparently made for the latter order, and one-and-twenty of the smaller convents purchased a temporary existence from the king; but, with all the exceptions, there could not have been fifty convents throughout England spared when once the process of destruction commenced in 1536.

The method of life in one convent must have been much what it was in every other throughout the land. The nuns in many cases came from the highest families, and mixed with their neighbours in kindly intercourse, and were by them well known and loved. Rigid enclosure was then almost unknown. The sisters, as has been well said, " were indeed not of the world, but they were in it, actively and intelligently to do a good work to it—to elevate, to console, to purify and to bless."[1]

It is unnecessary to speak of the many blessings which must have accrued to a neighbourhood by the presence of a convent of cultivated English ladies. Their gentle teaching was the first experience of the youthful poor; from them they derived their early knowledge of the elements of religion and of Catholic practice; to them they went in the troubles and cares of life as to a source of good advice; theirs was the most potent civilising influence in the rough days of the Middle Ages; and theirs was the task of tending the sick and smoothing the passage of the Christian soul to eternity.

To the bounty of these religious ladies, as the " titles " to ordination in the episcopal registers show, a large number of the secular clergy of England owed their ecclesiastical position, while there is abundant evidence that the ranks of the regular orders received many recruits through their generosity and self-sacrifice. In the convents the female portion of the population found their only teachers,

---

[1] The portrait of the prioress given in Chaucer, who

" Was so charitable and so pitous,
And al was conscience and tender herte,"

will recur to many when considering the pre-reformation conventual life of England.

the rich as well as the poor,[1] and the destruction of these religious houses by Henry was the absolute extinction of any systematic education for women during a long period. Thus at Winchester convent, the list of the ladies being educated within the walls at the time of the suppression shows that these Benedictine nuns were training the children of the first families in the county.[2] Carrow, in Norfolk, for centuries gave instruction to the daughters of the neighbouring gentry, and as early as A.D. 1273 a papal prohibition was obtained from pope Gregory X. restraining the nobility from crowding this monastery with more sisters than its income could support.[3] And according to the evidence of Robert Aske, the people of Yorkshire objected strongly to the suppression scheme, because "in nunneries their daughters (were) brought up in virtue."

The declaration made by the royal commissioners as to the good done by the convent of Pollesworth in Warwickshire is worthy of being here given in its entirety. It may be premised that these Benedictine nuns possessed an income of only £87 a year, and previous to this letter had paid some £50 for the king's permission to remain in religion, which money, as before noted, they had borrowed from their friends.

"After our duties of humble recommendation unto your good lordship made," Crumwell's agents write to him, "it may please the same to be advertised that we have surveyed the monastery or nunnery of Pollesworth in the county of Warwick. Therein is an abbess named dame Alice Fitzherbert, of the age of 60 years, a very sad, discreet and religious woman, and hath been head and governor there twenty-seven years. And in the same house, under her rule are twelve virtuous and religious nuns and of good conversation, as far as we can hear or perceive, as well by our examinations as by the open fame and report of all the

---

[1] In the "Canterbury Tales" the miller of Trompington is described as both well to do and well married:—

"A wyf he hadde, come of noble kyn;
Sche was i-fostryd in a nonnerye...
Ther durste no wight clepe hir but *Madame*
What for hir kindred and hir nortelrye
That sche had lerned in the nonnerye."
Reeve's Tale, ll. 3940, &c.

[2] *Monasticon*, ii. p. 452.   [3] Taylor, *Index Monasticus*, viii.

country. And never one of the nuns there will leave nor forsake their habit and religion. Wherefore in our opinions, if it might so stand with your lordship's pleasure, ye might do a right good and meritorious deed to be a mediator to the king's highness for the said house to stand and remain unsuppressed; for as we think ye shall not speak in the preferment of a better nunnery nor of better women.

"And in the town of Pollesworth are 44 tenements, and never a plough but one, the residue be artificers, labourers and victualers, and live in effect by the said house. And the repair and resort there is made to the gentlemen's children and sojourners that there do live to the number sometimes of thirty and sometimes of forty and more, that there be right virtuously brought up. And the town and nunnery standeth in a hard soil and barren ground, and to our estimation if the nunnery be suppressed the town will shortly after fall to ruin and decay, and the people therein, to the number of six or seven score persons, are not unlike to wander and to seek their living as our Lord God best knoweth."[1]

The general occupations of the nuns in their cloisters were the same as those described by an eye-witness at a Wiltshire convent. There, says John Aubrey, "the young maids were brought up (not at Hakney Sarum Schools, &c., to learn pride and wantonness, but) at the nunneries, where they had examples of piety, and humility, and modesty, and obedience to imitate and to practise. Here they learned needlework, the art of confectionery, surgery (for anciently there were no apothecaries or surgeons—the gentlewomen did cure their poor neighbours: their hands are now too fine), physic, writing, drawing, &c. Old Jacques could see from his house the nuns of the priory (St. Mary's near Kington St. Michael) come forth into the nymph-hay[2] with their rocks[3] and wheels to spin: and with their sewing work. He would say that he had told threescore and ten: but of nuns there were not so many, but in all, with lay-sisters, as widows, old maids and young girls there might be such a number. This," concludes the author, "was a

---

[1] Wright, 139.
[2] A meadow "on the east side of the house, with a delightful prospect on the south-east."
[3] *i.e.* distaff.

fine way of breeding up young women, who are led more by example than precept; and a good retirement for widows and grave single women to a civil, virtuous and holy life."[1]

It is impossible to reflect on the trials and difficulties to which the nuns were exposed during the few years which elapsed before their final dispersion without a sense of horror. To be subjected to the questionings of such men as Layton, Legh and London in their visitation must have been an experience for ladies happily unique in the annals of England. Dr. Ortez, writing at the time, charges one of the commissioners with speaking "immodestly to the nuns," while Sander has mentioned Legh as "tempting the religious to sin," and as "more ready to inquire into and speak about uncleanness of living than anything else."[2]

When the final doom of all monastic houses was decided on, only some fifty convents of women were left to seize. It was important that the surrender of the greater houses, by which means alone the king could legally become possessed of their property, should appear to be voluntary, and every pressure was brought to bear upon the monks and nuns to induce them to resign their charges into Henry's hands. The methods pursued in this matter can best be understood by the precise instructions issued for the guidance of those engaged in the work. These agents are ordered to take "the consent of the head and convent by way of their fair surrender under their convent seal to the same. If they shall willingly consent and agree, the said commissioners shall appoint unto the said head and every of their convent pensions for term of their lives, and also give unto them by way of reward such sums of money for the change of their apparel, and likewise such portions of the household stuff," as they think proper.

"And if they shall find any of the said heads and con-

---

[1] *Aubrey's Collections* (Wilts Archæological Society), p. 12. The last prioress of the convent of Kington was Mary Dennys. She "lived," says the same authority, "a great while after the Reformation, and died within the memory of man in Somersetshire. (*From my grandfather Lyte*)." The editor notes that "she died 1593 at Bristol, and was buried in the church of the Gaunts on the green."

[2] *Anglican Schism*, Lewis' transl., p. 129. Those who wish to see this most repulsive side of a sad record may turn to the pages of Fuller, where it is drawn out in sufficient detail. It is evident that the blood of the old Puritan was stirred within him, and he must have felt that the disgraceful relations made to him were only too true. *Church Hist.* (ed. 1837), ii. 216.

vents, so appointed to be dissolved, so wilful and obstinate that they will in no wise submit themselves to the king's majesty in manner and form aforesaid; in that case the said commissioners shall take possession of the house and lands, the jewels, plate, cattle, stuff and all other things belonging to them, to the king's majesty's use by force of the last act made for the alteration of all spiritual tenures at his majesty's pleasure.

"And in that case," if they will not resign at the king's wish, the commissioners "shall cause the brethren or sisters" to change their religious dress and give them money for the purpose, but they shall neither give pensions nor any part of their household goods to "such obstinate and wilful persons, till they shall know further of the king's pleasure."

"And if they shall find any of them so indurate that they will not yield thereunto according to their bounden duties, they shall commit such persons to such place or keeping for their punishment as for the time and opportunity their wisdom shall think convenient."

Further, as regards the property, the royal officers are ordered to retain all plate, jewels and ornaments "meet for the king's use," and compare what they find with previous inventories, that they may see that the property has been "well administered." Also they are to examine well what plate or other valuables are missing, "to the great damage of the king's majesty."[1]

It would be natural to suppose that when pressure of a nature disclosed in these secret instructions to the royal agents was brought to bear upon convents, the ladies would readily acquiesce in Henry's designs. The two methods adopted to secure a voluntary surrender—the one a promise of a pension and other substantial advantages, the other the threatened deprivation of even a scanty means of subsistence, and perhaps further punishment—were calculated to allure or alarm the helpless inmates of monastic houses, and in particular the nuns, to compliance. But the design was only very partially successful as regards the convents, and even this success was marked by some extraordinary drawbacks. It is true, that of the fifty convents which survived

---

[1] R. O. Chapt. House Bk., A. $\frac{24}{30}$ f. i. *seqq.*

the first dissolution the surrenders of some three-and-thirty are enrolled on the Close Rolls. But the original documents preserved in the Record Office prove that, for some reason or other, in the majority of cases, numbering no less than twenty-eight, the papers drawn up in blank form by the commissioners never received the signatures of the nuns at all. Of the remaining five, one, the surrender of the great abbey of Shaftesbury, a convent of fifty-six nuns, and at the dissolution of which Crumwell himself assisted, is signed only by Elizabeth Zouche, the abbess.

A second document, that of Tarrant, although having twenty signatures, is worthless, as all are written in the same hand.[1] Of the whole number of convents, therefore, only three signed surrenders exist. In the case of Nuneaton convent the document is dated the 12th of December, 1539, and has no names, but twenty-seven crosses appended to it.[2] Nesham, the surrender of which, without signatures, is dated December 9th, was suppressed by four commissioners on the 21st of the same month.[3] And the Benedictine nuns of Newcastle, the surrender of which to Dr. Layton, also unsigned, is said to have been made on January 3rd, 1540, was already suppressed by Dr. Legh and three others on December 31st, 1539.[4] Other evidence exists besides the absence of surrender deeds to show that the nuns of England resisted, in a heroic manner, the tempting offers to resign their trusts and abandon the religious life itself at the bidding of the king. At the end of March, 1539, three royal commissioners, Tregonwell, Petre and Smyth, came to the Benedictine convent of Ambresbury, in Wiltshire. They had received the surrenders of both Shaftesbury and Wilton, and no doubt expected to work their will at Ambresbury without difficulty. But they were soon undeceived. "We yesterday came," they say, "and communed with the abbess[5] for the accomplishment of the king's highness' commission in like sort. And albeit we have used as many ways with her as our poor wits could attain, yet in the end we could not by any persuasions bring her to any conformity. At all times she rested and so remaineth in these terms : 'If the king's highness command

---

[1] Eighth Rep. of Dep. Keeper, App. ii. p. 43.   [2] *Ibid.*, p. 35.
[3] R. O. Exch. Augt. Off. Misc. Bk., 246, f. 9.   [4] *Ibid.*, f. 7.
[5] A mistake for "prioress." Ambresbury was not an abbey.

me to go from this house I will gladly go, though I beg my bread; and as for pension, I care for none.' In these terms she was in all her conversation, praying us many times to trouble her no further herein, for she had declared her full mind, in the which we might plainly gather of her words she was fully fixed before our coming."[1]

Some months went by, during which it is more than probable that pressure of every kind was brought to bear upon Florence Bonnewe, the staunch and fearless prioress. At the end of that time she announced to Crumwell her resignation "at the king's bidding."[2] In December, 1539, Dr. London, John Ap Rice and others arrived at the convent and suppressed it.[3] The successor of the intrepid Florence Bonnewe received a pension of £100 a year, one of the largest granted to any nun, and 33 of her sisters were also promised a pittance.[4] The name of the former prioress does not appear. No doubt she kept her word to go forth, "though I beg my bread." "As for pension," she had said, "I care for none," and none she received.[5]

One other example of the same pressure put upon a convent to secure its compliance with the king's wishes is furnished by the abbey of Godstow. This convent, in Oxfordshire, is well known as the place where fair Rosamond Clifford, the mistress of Henry II., passed her last years in penitence. The royal visitors had given it an excellent character; "where there was great strictness of life, and to which were most of the young gentlewomen of the county sent to be bred; so that the gentry of the country desired the king would spare the house."[6]

---

[1] *Calendar*, xiv. (i), No. 629.   [2] *Ibid.*, ii. No. 27.

[3] Speaking of Dr. London's employment in the task of suppressing the religious houses of women, Mr. Gairdner (*Calendar*, xiv. (ii.) preface xxviii.) writes: "When we think of the shame in which Dr. London ended his days, a few years later, committed to the Fleet for perjury, not to mention other stories against him; and when we consider that Crumwell himself, the year before this, had been obliged to pay some regard to the abbess of Godstow's remonstrance against his conduct towards her and her companions, it might seem strange that the task of suppressing nunneries should have been more specially committed to him than to any other. But perhaps indelicacy was rather a recommendation for the kind of work that was to be done."

[4] R. O. Exch. Aug. Off. Misc. Bk., 245, f. 98.

[5] It may be of interest to note about Ambresbury that upon its surrender "rewards" were given to 33 nuns, 4 priests, and 33 servants. Pensions were granted to 35 nuns. *Ibid.*, Bk. 494, f. 31.

[6] Burnet (1st ed.), i. p. 238.

On Tuesday, November 4th, 1539, that valiant visitor, Dr. London, appeared at the abbey to dismiss the nuns and take possession for the king. The following day Katherine Bulkeley, the abbess, wrote to Crumwell begging his protection. She had, as she says, "been appointed to her office through his influence, and up to that time had never been moved nor desired by any creature . . . to surrender and give up the house." She will do as the king commands, but she says, "I trust to God that I have never offended God's laws nor the king's, whereby this poor monastery ought to be suppressed. This notwithstanding, my lord, so it is that doctor London, which, as your lordship doth well know, was against my promotion, and hath ever since borne against me great malice and grudge, like my mortal enemy, is suddenly come unto me with a great rout with him, and here doth threaten me and my sisters, saying that he hath the king's commission to suppress the house, spite of my teeth. And when he saw that I was content that he should do all things according to his commission, and showed him plainly that I would never surrender to his hand, being my ancient enemy, now he begins to entreat me, and to inveigle my sisters one by one otherwise than ever I heard tell that any of the king's subjects hath been handled. And he here tarrieth and continueth to my great cost and charge, and will not take my answer, that I will not surrender till I know the king's gracious commandment or your good lordship's." She adds that she will do what the king wants, but that it is not true that she has wasted the property of her house, as Dr. London told Crumwell.[1]

London's letter, written the following day, after saying that the abbess takes his coming "something pensively," adds that, while waiting for an answer, he intends to "something ripe" himself "in knowledge of the state of the house." And if the king insist on dissolving the house "notwithstanding her desire (to have a statement of) such considerations as moveth his grace, for the reformation of such abuses, to take the house by surrender," he begs that the nuns may be allowed suitable pensions. The abbess has had to borrow the money for payment of her "first-

[1] Wright, 229.

fruits," many of the nuns are old, and "few of the others have any friends."[1]

Crumwell sent his orders to let the house alone for a while. Then on November 26th, 1538, the abbess wrote her thanks "for the stay of doctor London, who was here ready to suppress this poor house against my will and all my sisters, and had done it indeed if you had not sent so speedily contrary commandments." She adds that according to further orders she has handed over the "domains and stock" to "master doctor Owen," and that she is ready to go any lengths if the house may be spared. In fact, she assures her master that "there is neither pope nor purgatory, image nor pilgrimage, nor praying to dead saints used or regarded amongst" them, and that they do not too much cling to "this garment and fashion of life."[2]

A year after Katherine Bulkeley had penned this miserable surrender of her faith and principles, on November 17th, 1539, she surrendered her trust.[3] Sir John Williams and others were sent down to effect the transfer of the convent property to the king, in place of her "old enemy" London, and they forwarded to Henry the deed of surrender, which, however, was signed by none of the nuns. The abbess and fifteen nuns were promised pensions; three of them for the somewhat strange reason "because they cannot marry."[4]

Besides the trials incidental to the uncertainty of the fate which awaited them, the nuns, at this time deprived of the aid and direction of their spiritual superiors in the episcopate, must have suffered extremely. This the prioress of Wilton, Joan Gybbart, writes in so many words to Crumwell. "We stand and have done long," she says, "for lack of a head in great unquietness and danger, as God knoweth not only in the decay, lack and disturbance of the service of God according to our religion, but also of the destruction and desolation of our monastery. We are so threatened by our ordinary, master doctor Hylley, that we know not what to do. He cometh to us many times, and among us as he says he does but order us after the law; but as God knoweth we are unlearned, and not wont to such law as he doth exercise

---

[1] Wright, 227.   [2] Ellis, *Historical Letters*, 3d Series, iii. 233.
[3] *Calendar*, xiv. (ii), No. 539. There are no signatures to the deed of surrender.
[4] R. O. Exch. Augt. Office Misc. Bk., 245, f. 157.

amongst us. And because that we differ such matters as he would that we should consent to, the which as we suppose and think are not lawful, nor yet profitable to us or our house, he does sore and grievously threaten us. And he hath heretofore put us to great vexation and trouble, and yet mindeth so to do and continue. He hath admitted to bear rule with us, in this our vacation,[1] one Christopher Willoughby and another. This Christopher, for his subtle, crafty and false demeanour has been expelled first by dame Cecily Willoughby, the abbess, and then after, his service was utterly refused by Isabel Jordan, our last abbess."[2]

Over the community at Stratford a superioress, or, as they preferred to call her, a "supposed prioress," named Sibilla Kirke, had been appointed, who was the cause of great trouble in the community. "As soon as we speak to have anything remedied," they say, "she bids us go to Crumwell and let him help us. And the old lady, who is prioress in right, is like to die for lack of sustenance and good keeping, for she can get neither meat, drink, nor money to help herself." The chancellor of the bishop of London, they complain, told them that the intruder should continue "in spite of our deaths and of their deaths that say nay to it. He commanded her to look to us and to punish us, that all others may beware by us." . . . "Sir," they continue in their appeal to Crumwell, "it is not possible for us to continue in the manner that we be in now. Sir, the chancellor rebuked us, and said that we had got a temporal man over us for our ordinary and that he spake by you. But our learned counsel, who we had before we put our matter to the king's grace, told us it was not lawful for him to be a chancellor, for he is not a priest, and hath no power to hear confession, nor yet to give absolution as he doth."[3]

Very few of the convents were rich enough to bring any great amount of spoil to the king. The spoil, however, from Barking, the home of so many saints, the most ancient and venerable, and almost the richest nunnery in England, which came into the royal hands in November, 1539, proved

---

[1] Vacancy of the office of abbess.
[2] *Calendar*, vi. No. 285. Dame Cecily Willoughby, the abbess, died in 1528, and was succeeded by Dame Isabel Jordan, who died in 1533. Her successor was Cecilia Bodenham, who surrendered the abbey to the king.
[3] *Ibid.*, vol. xli. Nos. 2, 4.

a valuable prize. The plate consisted of over 3000 ounces, the greater part being parcel gilt, besides what was found to be only copper gilt when broken. There was discovered here "a monstrance" weighing 65 ounces, enriched with a beryll; and numbers of copes and other vestments of cloth of gold and tissue were reserved for the king's use. Besides this, the goods of the abbey sold for nearly £200;[1] so small a sum in so wealthy a house shows the poverty actually observed by the religious.

One circumstance with regard to the suppression of the Bridgettine house of Syon is worth recording. In one of Crumwell's interesting remembrances is the following item: "Touching the monastery of Syon, the king may dissolve it by *premunire* as he will."[2] This power possessed by Henry over the convent arose from a singular circumstance. On May 29th, 1538, the attorney-general, in behalf of the king, had presented a bill of complaint against John Stokesley, bishop of London, who was brought up from the Marshalsea, where he had been in prison. The charge was, that on February 5th, 1537, he had, in the ceremony of professing Thomas Knotton, a brother of Syon, and Godfrey, a lay brother, under the obedience of John Copinger, the father confessor, made use of the form of profession approved of by pope Paul II. In acting thus, he publicly proclaimed the jurisdiction of the bishop of Rome, and made use of "papistical rites, cultus and ceremonies;" and by any one upholding the authority of the bishop of Rome after 31st July, 1536, as well as all aiders and abettors, the penalties of *premunire* had been incurred. Moreover, he had acted in the same way on two later occasions, and it was contended that both the bishop, Agnes Jordan, the abbess of Syon, and others had thus forfeited their property to the king. Stokesley confessed the bill, and was bound over to appear under a bail of 10,000 marks and the surety of several London merchants.[3] And although Henry subsequently pardoned all concerned, his hand already fingered the thread by which the sword of destruction hung suspended over the community. In December, 1539, the convent passed, apparently without surrender, into his possession.

[1] R. O. Exch. Aug. Off. Mins. Accts., 31–32 Hen. VIII., 257, m. 5.
[2] *Calendar*, xiv. (ii), No. 424.
[3] Coram Rege, 30 Hen. VIII. Easter, Rex. Roll, m. 20.

One word must be said as to the number of nuns who were turned adrift into the world on the destruction of their homes. Hooper, in a letter written in 1546 to Bullinger from Strasburg, says:—" He (the king) has caused all their (the monastic) possessions to be transferred into his exchequer; and yet they are bound, even the frail female sex, by the king's command to perpetual chastity. England has at this time at least 10,000 nuns, not one of whom is allowed to marry."[1] Such an estimate is obviously much exaggerated. The fact is, that allowing for the four or five convents about which some uncertainty exists, there do not appear to have been more than some 1560 religious women in England at the time of the dissolution. Of these, more than one-half, or some 850, belonged to the Benedictine Order.

[1] Original Letters, Parker Society, No. 21.

CHAPTER XVI

Fall of the Friars

THE autumn of 1538 witnessed the destruction of the English friaries. From the thirteenth century the mendicant orders had taken an important part in the religious life of the country. They were actuated by a different fundamental principle from that which was the mainspring of the monastic state. In the latter, whatever may have been the work the members of the great religious orders were at times called upon to undertake, the basis upon which they rested was conventual life and seclusion from the cares of even parochial matters, in order that their lives might be given up to the calmer service of the cloister. The principle that inspired the friars, on the other hand, was devotion to the external needs of the Church. In its primary conception, the ideal of a friar's life was to be found in the performance of active religious duties among the people. Untrammelled, on the one hand, by the stricter traditions of the old monastic observance, and on the other by the petty exigencies of parochial management, they could devote their energies to the duties of preaching and teaching. Their houses were built in or near great towns; but to the friar the convent was a very different place to what it was to the monk. To the latter, from the day of his profession the monastery became his home, and the brethren gathered within its walls his family; to the former, the convent cell afforded but a temporary shelter in which to recruit his powers, physical and mental, for new labours in the cause of religion. He had no home, properly so called, as the monk had in his monastery, and no special place could claim his services. His profession bound him to the general body of his brethren, not to any particular family. The friars were itinerant preachers, living to a great extent among the people, and endeavouring to influence their religious views and practices by every means at their command, and in the early days of their mission they achieved great and striking successes. The whole history of the Church does not present a parallel to the enthusiastic reception given by the people to the reforms they preached, and their popularity in England, almost down to the day of their suppression, is evinced by numerous gifts and testamentary dispositions in their favour.

In the sixteenth century the friaries throughout the country numbered some two hundred. Of these, the followers of St. Francis had sixty, the Dominicans about fifty-three, the Austin friars forty-two, and the Carmelites six-and-thirty. The rest were held by the Trinitarians and other less important bodies of men. Of the four great orders of mendicant friars, looking at them so far as England is concerned, the Dominicans or 'Black Friars,' small though some of their churches may have been in country towns, ever preserved a certain dignity, and, so to speak, an aristocratic character. It would appear as though, whilst retaining the canon's dress first worn by St. Dominic in the cathedral of Osma, they bore with it something of the pre-eminence which naturally attaches to the clergy. The Franciscans or 'Grey Friars' were the most popular, in the widest sense of the word, with high and low. The Carmelites or 'White Friars' were simple, homely, and spread through the country as if an order of native origin.

The two or three greatest houses of Franciscans, as London or York, might vie whether in buildings or quantity of plate and richness of vestments with a Benedictine abbey of all but the first rank. The Carmelite houses and churches form a striking contrast. The church of so important a convent as Cambridge, for example, was furnished with a poverty which among these friars was not incongruous with their profession, but of which the smallest parish church would have been ashamed. It is remarkable how prolific the English Carmelites were in writers, although it is not impossible that their number was not really greater than those of the Franciscans or Dominicans. These latter orders, however, lacked a Bale;—for even Bale has a redeeming point in his literary character. Whilst it was yet possible, he gathered up with scrupulous care the memorials of his order in England, and thus showed, in spite of violence and virulence of speech and pen, that there was somewhere in his heart a tenderness for the men of his old habit.[1]

The total number of friars is somewhat difficult to estimate, and can only be stated in general terms. From the list of names given in the "surrenders" and other documents, it would appear that the average number of inmates in each Dominican friary was about nine, in each Franciscan about eleven, in each Augustinian about eight, and in each Carmelite about nine. Taking these averages as approximately correct, it would appear that the total number of friars in England at the time of their dispersion was about eighteen hundred. Richard Ingworth, the suffragan bishop of Dover, writing to Crumwell on April 1st, 1539, says that in the North of England he has received for the king twenty-six houses. In these there were "nine score friars;" but he adds that these were "the poorest houses that ever" he went to, and that the best houses had been undertaken by other visitors.[2] The average of seven, therefore, for the smaller houses given up to the bishop would seem to show that the estimate of eighteen hundred is not excessive.

For some reason or other, the various orders of friars had not been included in the dissolutions which had been carried out under the act for suppressing houses of less than £200 a year.[3] It is probable that as, in accordance with their several constitutions, they were possessed of very little real property, it did not suit the king's purpose to risk the unpopularity of attacking them when so little was to be gained by so doing. When, however, the royal policy of plunder had been firmly established, and the complete overthrow of the northern rising had rendered resistance almost impossible, Henry could contemplate the seizure of the friaries and the absorption of their trifling possessions into the regal revenues without fear of the consequences. Small as their belongings really were, still some few manors, farms and houses were to be got out of their wholesale destruction. Each convent, however poor, had the site upon which it

---

[1] It is to be regretted that Bale's Carmelite collections in the Harleian MSS. at the British Museum (Nos. 3838, 7031, &c.) have not been printed.

[2] *Calendar*, xiv. (i), No. 661.

[3] It is curious to note the mistakes into which some authors have fallen upon this point. More than one writer could be cited who state that these "lesser monasteries" were chiefly the houses of friars.

stood; and even if the plate in the sacrist's keeping was generally worth but a trifling sum, the lead on the roof and gutters of the church would add a few pounds to the grand total of these ecclesiastical spoils.

In the work of suppressing the friaries Crumwell found an energetic lieutenant in Richard Ingworth, formerly prior of the Dominican house of King's Langley, the richest possessed by the Black Friars, having an income of £125 a year. On December 9th, 1537, Ingworth was consecrated suffragan bishop of Dover,[1] and much about the same time he received two commissions "to visit and vex" his brother friars. In the first, power was bestowed upon him to depose or suspend incriminated superiors, and to appoint others in their places. In the second, he is directed to visit their convents, to take possession of their keys, to sequestrate goods, and make indentures and inventories.[2] No mention is made of suppression, and such a work was apparently entirely beyond the powers granted either to him or other visitors,[3] although their instructions quoted in the last chapter leave on the mind no doubt as to the royal intention.

In the time that elapsed from 1534, when the troubles began, to the autumn of 1538, when the active suppression of the friars commenced, a considerable number of these religious evidently succeeded in leaving the country. Thus, rather than take the oath to hold Henry as head of the Church, the Franciscan Observants and others in the island of Guernsey had given up their convent in September, 1537. "I have called unto me," writes a correspondent to Crumwell, "all the Friars Observant strangers which were left in the convent of the Friars Observant of Saint Francis within the Isle of Guernsey," and ordered them immediately to take the required oath. They refused, and asked to be allowed to cross over "to Normandy, their natural country," saying "they would rather forsake their convent and country

---

[1] Stubbs, *Episcopal Succession*, p. 78.
[2] Wilkins, *Concilia*, iii. 829, 835.
[3] Dixon, *History of Church of England*, ii. p. 37, says: "This was well contrived. If the visitors suppressed a house quietly, they were not complained of, though they exceeded their commission: the king pocketed the money. But if (which never happened) there had been a disturbance, the king and Crumwell were safe: they would have said that the visitors had exceeded their commission, and would have punished them exemplarily if public feeling had required a victim."

than make" such an oath. The writer adds that he sent them over in a boat and took possession of their goods, an inventory of which he encloses.[1]

The way in which the number of friars was diminished before the final suppression of their convents may be illustrated by the house of Dominicans at Derby. Previous to 1534 the community consisted of about thirty religious. When Dr. London visited it in the January of 1539 he only obtained the signatures of some half-a-dozen. It is said on the highest authority that "a great part of the friar preachers of England in 1534-35 withdrew from the country into Ireland, Scotland and Flanders,"[2] rather than conform, and in consequence of the poverty to which they were reduced.

At this time numerous charges were preferred against priests and others for their hostility to the royal supremacy and the general policy of Henry in ecclesiastical matters. In April, 1537, the popular discontent manifested itself in a serious way in Norfolk. Men met in the streets of Walsingham and "condemned the suppression of so many religious houses in which God was well served and many good deeds of charity done." One man said, "See how these abbeys go down and our living goeth away with them. For within a while Burnham shall be put down and also Walsingham, and all other abbeys in this country. And further he said that the gentlemen there had all the farms and all the cattle in the country in their hands, so that poor men could have no living by them. And therefore, quoth (he), when these men shall come to put down the abbeys some men must step to and resist them." "I hear say," said another, "that all the abbeys in the country shall go down." "More pity if it pleased God," cried a third.[3]

The late experience of the northern rebellion had taught the king the necessity of prompt action. Some thirty or forty men of the district were seized and tried. They were charged with saying "that if they could get any company they would make an insurrection as well for the staying of

---

[1] Ellis, *Orig. Letts.*, 2nd Series, ii. p. 91.
[2] Rev. C. R. F. Palmer, O.P., in the *Reliquary*, vol. xviii. p. 71. The volumes of this valuable periodical contain many communications from Father Palmer's pen on the English Dominican Convents.
[3] *Calendar*, xii. (i), No. 1056.

the abbeys putting down as for reformation of gentlemen for taking of farms." Their object was to take Lynn and to seize and fortify Thetford and Brandon bridges. A special commission sitting at Norwich Castle on May 22, 1537, tried and found them guilty.[1] Amongst them were John Grigby, rector of the church of Langham, two Augustinian canons of Walsingham, Nicolas Myleham and Richard Vowell, a cleric of Walsingham, William Younger, and two Carmelite friars of Burnham Norton, William Gybson and John Pecock. Friar Gybson was condemned to perpetual imprisonment,[2] together with another cleric, John Punte, rector of the parish church of Waterlow. This latter was specially charged with having approved the action of the others by saying, "Peradventure what they did was for the commonwealth."[3].

Of the rest, twelve were executed at different towns in Norfolk. Amongst these were George Gysborough, Ralph Rogerson and William Gysborough, whose avowed condemnation of the destruction of the religious houses has been quoted above, and two religious: the Augustinian canon Mileham, executed at Walsingham on Wednesday, May 30th, and the Carmelite friar Pecock, who suffered at Lynn on Friday, June 1st, 1537.[4] The terror inspired by the constant accusations, trials, convictions and cruel executions of those guilty only of verbal treason, or of expressing disapproval of the king and his actions, bore down all opposition. None was safe. As one man who was accused and examined expressed it, "If two or three good fellows be walking together, the constables come to them and will know what communication they have or else they shall be stocked."[5]

The case of another friar, Anthony Brown, who was condemned to death in the summer of 1538 for his belief in the old doctrine of papal supremacy, may be here briefly referred to, before passing on to relate the circumstances of the general dissolution of the friaries. The duke of Norfolk, writing to Crumwell on August 4th, 1538, told

---

[1] *Coram Rege*, 29 Hen. VIII., Hilary, m. 2.
[2] *Controlment Roll*, 29 Hen. VIII., m. 33d.
[3] *Coram Rege, ut sup.* These two were afterwards pardoned (Rot. Pat., 29 Hen. VIII. Pars. i. m. 9).
[4] *Calendar*, xii. (i), No. 1300.
[5] *Ibid.*, No. 1212. Confession of Richard Bishop, of Bungay.

him that the justices of assize lately sitting at Norwich had before them "one called Anthony Brown, some time a Friar Observant of Greenwich, and of late taking upon him as a hermit." He wrote out "his own confession with his hand, which," says the duke, "you shall receive with this." The friar was found guilty, "giving respite to the sheriff for his execution ten days following, which they showed me the said duke, they did for this consideration, which was they thought it convenient that a sermon should be made by the bishop of Norwich, as was by the bishop of Worcester at the execution of Forest."

The views of the bishop of Norwich were apparently considered doubtful, and it was thought well that the duke of Norfolk should thus make trial of both the friar and him. "And because," continues the duke, " Mr. Townsend is the only one of the king's council in these parts, I sent in likewise for him to be present at all the examinations. And this afternoon we so handled the said friar that we brought him to this point, that he would not stick upon the authority of the bishop of Rome to be supreme head of the Church, but in no wise could we bring him from the opinion that the king ought not to be supreme head of the Church, saying that no temporal prince was *capax* of that name and authority." Neither "Dr. Call, a Grey friar," who was present and took the king's part, nor the bishop of Norwich, who argued well on the point, could move the friar. And so "we have delivered him," continues Norfolk, "to the sheriff to be carried to the gaol and there to suffer according to his foolish doings upon Friday next. Before his death the said bishop shall make such a sermon as we trust shall be to the king's highness contentation and apparent to the people (who, we think, will be there in great number) that this unhappy foolish friar is well worthy to suffer and that his opinions be false and untrue. My lord, the cause of the sending of this man in so great haste unto you is because that if the king's majesty and you shall think it convenient to have him to be brought to the Tower, there to be more straightly examined and to be put to torture, you may despatch this bearer or some other with command to the sheriff accordingly, so that the same may be with him at Norwich by Friday at ten o'clock."

"After writing" this much, the bishop of Norwich tried

Fall of the Friars

once more to induce the friar to change his opinions, but without success. As the duke expresses it, "yet finally he persisted in his errors,"[1] and though an actual record of the execution has not been found, there can be little doubt that the sentence of death was carried out on Friday, August 9th, 1538.

The various dissolutions of religious houses and desecration of churches, which had been witnessed in all parts of England from the spring of 1536, had a disastrous but natural effect on the friaries. These religious were almost entirely dependent upon the alms of the faithful for their support, and one immediate result of the royal seizure of ecclesiastical property was to dry up the spring of charity given for religious purposes. It could hardly be supposed that donations would be given for objects marked out for destruction, and which would only go to swell the total amount of the royal plunder.

There were exceptions, of course, to the general rule, and there are instances of donations being given to the friars on the very eve of their dispersion.[2] Thus, on October 9th, 1537, just fifteen months before the surrender, Robert Davell, archdeacon of Northumberland, made an interesting covenant with friar Roland Harding, the successor of Richard Marshall at the Black Friars, Newcastle. The Dominican brethren promised that "between six and nine o'clock in the morning daily, before the picture of our Lord, called the crucifix, which was between the cloisters and the outer door of the choir within the church, the friars kneeling, would sing devoutly the anthem of the cross, beginning '*O crux*,' with the versicle *Adoramus te Christe Jesu Fili Dei vivi*, etc., and the collect of the same, *Domine Jesu*, etc. And after then (they were) devoutly to say, for the souls of William Davell and John Brigham, late of Newcastle, merchant, their wives and children, with their benefactors and all Christian souls, the *De profundis* with the *preces* belonging, ending with the oratio *Absolve*. In return of all which Robert Davell gave the friars £6, 8s. in their

---

[1] Ellis, *Orig. Letts.*, 1st Series, ii. p. 86.
[2] Mr. Gairdner (*Calendar*, xiii. (i) preface xxiv.) says that at this time the friars clung "no doubt to the fond hope entertained by so many, that the royal supremacy would not last very long, and that much of the old order would be restored, when the Pope was able to bring the King to reason."

great need. And the friars agree that if the anthem and prayers were not sung for two days, they would sing a solemn dirge with mass of requiem by note, sending the bellman round the town to notify the same in order that the people might come to the friars and make an offering for the souls. And if none of the premises were observed, truly and without delay the £6, 8s. should be refunded."[1]

The very terms of this contract would show, were there not ample evidence of the fact, that by this time the friars had been reduced to a state of extreme poverty. In fact, it is impossible to read the letters of bishop Ingworth and doctor London to Crumwell whilst they were engaged in the work of suppressing the friaries without seeing that their poverty left them no alternative but surrender. "Since that I last was with you," writes the former, "I have received to the king's use twelve houses of friars: that is, one in Huntingdon, four in Boston, four in Lincoln, one in Grantham, one in Newark and now one in Grimsby. They all were in poverty, and little left, scarce to pay the debts and in some places not so much as £3 or (so). In these houses the king's grace shall have but the lead, which I think in all twelve houses shall be, as I can judge it, about twelve score fodders or more and twenty-four bells, such as they be; and of every house a chalice of six to ten ounces apiece, in some places more. These chalices I bear with me, and other silver if I find it."[2] So, too, according to the same authority the three houses of friars at Canterbury were all in debt. The Austin friars, for example, owed £40, while all their belongings, exclusive of plate, which the bishop estimated at eighty-five ounces, would not fetch £6.[3] In the twenty-six houses of friars in the north which he dissolved in the first months of 1539, he obtained little except the worth of the sacred vessels.[4] It is the same story wherever this episcopal commissioner goes. At Dunstable, Ware, Walsingham and innumerable other houses the goods are reported as "some sold, some stolen and some pledged," so that little was left either in plate, lead or other valuables,[5] while at Scarborough the three houses

---

[1] Brand, *History of Newcastle*, quoted by Fr. Palmer. *Reliquary*, vol. xviii. p. 164.
[2] R. O. Crum. Corr., viii. f. 112.
[3] *Ibid.*, 114.   [4] *Ibid.*, 115.   [5] *Ibid.*, 117.

were so impoverished as to be obliged to sell the very stalls and the screenwork from their church, "so that nothing is left but stone and glass," and all that the king can expect to get is the lead off the roof and "very poor chalices."[1]

The testimony of the redoubtable Dr. London, to whom much of the work of dispatching the friars was committed, is to the same effect. At Northampton the Carmelites were so much in debt that all they had would not pay it off. The friars of Aylesbury were in the same plight. Dr. London thought their ornaments "very coarse," and sold them all with "the glass windows and their utensils."[2] Thus, with few exceptions, if any, the friars throughout England had fallen into a state of poverty which rendered their continuance almost an impossibility.

The chief object of bishop Ingworth, Dr. London and other royal agents was to force the alternative of submission upon the unwilling friars. "Good my lord," writes the bishop to his master, "I beseech you think not that I am any feigner to you, for I assure you I am not, but am and will be as true and as secret to you as any servant that you have. . . . I would do all things with so much quiet and without any clamour so near as I know; if I knew your pleasure, there shall be no part left undone so near as I may. My commission giveth me no authority to put any out, without they give up their houses, but if I knew your pleasure, I may find causes sufficient to put them out of many places for their misliving and for disobeying the instructions and the king's acts."[3] "Divers of the friars," he writes again, "are very loath to forsake their houses, and yet they are not able to live," as their debts are so great all they have will not pay them.[4]

At Gloucester, as the memorandum of the mayor records, Ingworth gave the friars their choice either to "continue in their houses and keep their religion and injunctions according to the same," which, be it remembered, were framed for the purpose of making religious life impossible, "or else to give their houses unto the king's hands." The mayor considered the injunctions "reasonable," and even the friars

---

[1] R. O. Crum. Corr., viii. f. 120. The letters of the bishop, printed by Wright, pp. 191-200, tell the same tale as to the poverty of the friars at this time.
[2] *Ibid.*, xxiii. 81. See also London's letters, printed by Wright.
[3] Wright, 200. [4] R. O. Crum. Corr., viii. f. 127.

confessed "that they were according to their rules, yet as the world is now they were not able to keep them and live in their houses, wherefore voluntarily they gave their houses into the visitor's hands to the king's use." The visitor said to them, continues the declaration, "Think not, nor hereafter report not, that you are suppressed, for I have no such authority to suppress you, but only to reform you, wherefore if ye will be reformed according to good order ye may continue," as far as I am concerned. They, however, confessed that they could not remain on the terms offered them, and so "the visitor took their houses and charitably delivered them, and gave them letters to visit their friends and so to go to other houses with which they were content."[1]

The fact is that the methods adopted were admirably conceived to force compliance to the royal will. When the chief source of their revenue, the charity of the faithful, had been cut off, the only means left to the friars to secure sufficient to live upon were sales of their effects or leases of the little property they possessed. For both, the free use of their corporate seal was required, and the first design of the visitor was to secure possession of this, and thus cut them off from any possibility of raising money. "In every place," says the bishop of Dover, "is jewels selling and other shift by leases. But in all these places I have set stay by making indentures and sequestering the common seals, so that now they have no shift to make." By this means "I think before the year is out there shall be very few houses able to live, but (they) will be glad to give up their houses and provide for themselves otherwise, for there they shall have no living." He then goes on to speak of the same two houses in Gloucester, from which he wrote, and the surrender of which has been recorded above. Of these he says, "I think there be two houses that will give up, for they have no living."[2]

In some of the houses, however, bishop Ingworth did not have it all his own way. He thus relates his experience at the house of Austin friars at Canterbury: "Being there

[1] Wright, 202.
[2] Wright, 193. In another communication he says that in "all places" he has been to he has "sealed up the common seals, so that they shall sell or alienate no more of their jewels nor other stuff, wherefore I am sure that within a year the more part shall be fain to give up their houses for poverty."
—*Ibid.*, p. 202.

the 14th day of December (1538), one friar there very rudely and traitorously used him before all the company, as by a bill here enclosed ye shall perceive. I seeing his demeanour, straight sequestered him so that none spake with him. I sent for the mayor, and before he came I examined him before master Spylman and also afterwards before the mayor and master Spylman, and at all times he still held and still desired to die for it, that the king may not be head of the Church of England, but that it must be a spiritual father appointed by God. Wherefore I required of master mayor to have horses and men to send him to you, charging both the men that no man should speak with him."[1]

At the Austin friars at Droitwich, bishop Ingworth found in the prior's coffer "eleven bulls of the bishops of Rome and above a hundred letters of pardons, and in all the books in the choir the bishop of Rome still standing as he did twenty years past." The prior had been only a year in the office when the bishop arrived, but he had already "felled and sold seven score good elms, a chalice of gilt of 90 ounces, a censer of twenty-six ounces, two great brass pots each able to seeth a whole ox, as men say, spits, pans and other things, so that in the house is not left a bed, a sheet, a platter or dish." For all this, the writer adds, "I have charged the bailiffs that he shall be forthcoming."[2]

---

[1] Ellis, 3rd Ser. iii. 181. This was probably friar Stone, who was executed at Canterbury about this time. The following account of the expenses incurred by the city in carrying out the sentence may be here quoted from the city records:—

"A.D. 1538-9.—Paid for half a ton of timber to make a pair of gallaces (gallows) to hang Friar Stone. For a carpenter for making the same gallows and the dray. For a labourer who digged the holes. To four men that helped set up the gallows. For drink to them. For carriage of the timber from stable gate (Staplegate) to the dungeon (now Dane John). For a hurdle. For a load of wood, and for a horse to draw him to the dungeon. For two men who set the kettle and parboiled him. To two men who carried his quarters to the gate and set them up. For a halter to hang him. For two halfpenny halters. For sandwich cord. For straw. To the woman that scoured the kettle. To him that did execution, 4s. 4d."—(Hist. MSS. Comm., 9th Rept., Append., p. 153, "City of Canterbury Records.") It has been thought by some that the 'Friar Stone' of this account was really Dom John Stone, a monk of Christchurch, Canterbury. It is however clear from A. Cope, *Dialogi Sex*, p. 373, that the John Stone put to death was an Austin friar. The Christchurch monk, although in trouble at this time, appears subsequently on the pension lists.

[2] Wright, 195. Other friars at this time got into difficulties. Sir Peter Egerton, for example, wrote to Crumwell that he had sent to Launceston gaol a "priest secular and two late friars priests." The secular, "Andrew Furlong,

But with all his activity, bishop Ingworth was hardly the kind of man that the king's work required. Although he evidently from the first appreciated that the purpose of his commission was to drive the friars to surrender or abandon their houses, still he seems to have thought that some of them might be spared. He hesitated to desecrate the church of the friars at Droitwich, and appointed one of the religious to continue to say mass there, even although Sir John Russell wanted the place, and two other magnates of the county were making suit to the king and Crumwell for it.[1] The latter wrote him a sharp rebuke, and in his humble reply Ingworth says he shall act now that he knows his master's mind. "And where it hath pleased your lordship," he says, "to write to me, as ye judge, that though I have changed my habit I have not changed my friar's heart, good my lord, judge me not so. For God shall be my judge, my friar's heart was gone two years before my habit, saving only my living. But the favour I have shown has not been for my friar's heart, but to bring all things with the most quiet to pass. And also till now that your letter came to me I never could perceive anything of your pleasure, but ever feared that if I were too quick, that I should offend your lordship." He then goes on to edify Crumwell with some general accusations, which he thinks "would not a little have moved" his lordship,[2] and which are well-nigh the only suggestion of evil living the bishop makes against the friars in the whole of his many letters.

He quickly amended his method of dealing with the religious, and although he had previously given leave to his brother of St. Dominic's order, the prior of the Black friars, Winchester, "to say mass" in his old church till further notice, on the receipt of Crumwell's letter he wrote "to avoid him thence." At the end of his career as a royal

priest and schoolmaster at Saltash, Co. Cornwall, was sent by me to gaol," he says . . . "for this cause, there was a Bible of his found in his chamber. In the beginning thereof were three or four leaves cancelled and blotted out in such a manner that no man could read the same." Also "John Hunt and Robert Ellis, late Grey friars of Plymouth, by the confession and handwriting of the said Hunt, said to one that questioned them when they were put out of the Grey friars whether they would buy them new habits or not, and they both said that they would not for a year or two, and by that time perchance there would be another change." For this they were sent to gaol (R. O. Crum. Corr., x. f. 26).

[1] Wright, 195.   [2] *Ibid.*, 199.

visitor, in August, 1539, he wrote, however, to beg that a house of his own order in Shrewsbury might be allowed to continue. But on August 27th, he again sent to beg Crumwell not to grant his former request, for although he "could find no great cause in them to cause them to give up,"[1] still he thought their "standing" would perhaps give him greater "business in divers places than (he) should have." He was specially thinking of the Franciscans and the Austin friars of Bristol, who "are stiff and bear themselves sore by (the) great favour" in which they are.[2] The following day he returned to the subject. "I have left," he says, "but one convent standing, and that is (the) Black friars of Shrewsbury. For this there will be great suit made to you to have it stand still, and that specially by one of the bailiffs, master Adam a Mytton, who, as he saith, is much bound to your lordship. For your sake he made me great cheer. Yet for all that, I would that he had some pleasure, but not that pleasure."[3] Before Michaelmas the friars, who had been left in their house by the bishop, were dispossessed.

The suppression was, of course, not carried to a conclusion without some severe handling of the friars. Instances of such measures have been noticed. No record, doubtless, was kept of much of the suffering endured by the religious before they were finally dispersed, but the glimpse that is afforded in the papers of this period is sufficient to show that the most extreme measures were often resorted to. Robert Buckenham, a member of the Dominican Order, was attainted of high treason and condemned to death for promulgating the "venomous serpent, the bishop of Rome, to be supreme head of the Church."[4] He, however, escaped out of Henry's power. Another friar, William Storme, was kept in the Fleet prison for "honouring images and maintaining the use of pilgrimages,"[5] and Robert Southwell, writing to Crumwell, informs him of the condemnation of a Franciscan for maintaining, or remaining staunch to, the old Catholic doctrine of papal supremacy. "Pleaseth it your

---

[1] Wright, 204. [2] *Ibid.*, 211. [3] *Ibid.*, 210.
[4] R. O. Rot. Parl., Hen. VIII., 147, No. 15.
[5] R. O. Crum. Corr., xl. 67. Dr. London writes about a "Black friar" who had been put in prison at Northampton at "All-Hallowes," and was there still on January 27. His offence was "certain words."

good lordship to understand that William Dickinson, clerk and priested in Rome, with William Petty, sometime a friar minor in Jersey, were yesterday attainted of high treason upon their several denying the king's supremacy. In this they stuck as arrogantly as any traitors that I have much seen in my life, and more would have done if they might have been permitted thereto. Surely, sir," he continues, "they were and yet be two weeds not meet to grow in our garden, nor none of their seed that they have sown, whereof we can as yet learn nothing by their confession. Dickinson was apprehended by the seaside in Sussex in journey towards Rome if he had not been stayed. Petty is subtly witted as he is ingenious, and hath as pleasant an instrument for the utterance of his cankered heart as I have heard." The writer concludes by desiring to know "the king's pleasure concerning the time of the execution of these two traitors that be attainted."[1]

The character of doctor London was more fitted than that of his fellow, bishop Ingworth, for the rough work they were called upon to do in the suppression of the friars' houses. His letters give ample evidence that he did not scruple to perform any act of vandalism necessary to complete the wrecking of friaries built up by generations of pious benefactors, or for the desecration of churches which had for centuries been dedicated to the service of God. At Reading he says, "I did only deface the church, all the windows being full of friars, and left the roof and walls whole for the king's use. I sold the ornaments and the cells in their dormitory." ... At Aylesbury "I only did deface the church;" and so too at Bedford and Stamford. At Coventry he partly razed the Franciscan house, "because the poor people lay so sore upon it." At Warwick he only smashed in the windows of "the friars' church," and added in his account to Crumwell, "I never pulled down any house entirely, but so defaced them that they could not be used again."

Of the friars themselves we hear but little from this valiant destroyer. That little, as may be expected, is not complimentary in its character. The prior of the Austin friars at [2] Northampton is untruthful, "like a very friar;"

[1] Ellis, *Orig. Letters*, 3rd Ser. iii. 95. [2] *Calendar*, xiii. (ii), No. 719.

but when all is over he has to confess that the town of this same Northampton and the villages round about are falling into decay, a good deal of which is popularly attributed to the destruction of the friaries. The warden of the Grey friars at Reading, London says, is "a friend of mine," which probably will not now be accounted much to his credit. This friar "also desired me," the doctor writes, "to be a humble suitor for him and his brethren that they may, with your lordship's favour, also change their garments with their papistical manner of living. The most part of them are very aged men, and not of strength to go much abroad for their livings, wherefore their desire is that it may please your lordship to be a mediator unto the king's grace for them that they might during their lives enjoy their chambers and orchard."[1] A fortnight later, however, (September 14th, 1538) the doctor says that he has got the surrender, "and this day they all shall change their grey coats. Of friars," he adds, "they be noted here honest men." And after a description of the house and grounds he says, "the inward part of the church, thoroughly decked with Grey friars, as well in the windows as otherwise, I have defaced."[2]

Of the friars' houses at Oxford London gives some special information. The commission to visit them consisted of the mayor, "master aldermen," and the doctor himself. They first went to the Carmelites. Here he found that the friars, in anticipation of their dissolution, had sold an annuity of £3 their house had from the abbot of Evesham, for £40 and divided the money. They were on the point of disposing of a similar annuity paid from the abbey of Westminster.[3] Moreover, the land, small as it was which this friary possessed, was all let on a thirty years' lease. Their ornaments, "as copes and vestments," Dr. London considered "pretty," and these he took. The rest of their belongings he thought not worth £5 the lot. At the Augustinian friary all the trees had been felled. The Franciscans had good lands, woods and a "pretty garden." The house, however, was large and ruinous, and the religious had been obliged to pawn most of their plate. Even the lead pipes of their conduit had been lately dug up "and cast into 68 sows," twelve of which had

---

[1] Wright, 217.   [2] *Calendar*, xiii. (ii), No. 346.
[3] These instances are interesting as showing how the great abbeys helped the poorer friaries.

been sold to pay the expenses of taking up," but the indefatigable doctor secured the rest and "put into safe custody." He adds that the wind had lately blown down many of the trees, and, worse than all, the "house is roofed with slate and not with lead." In the case of the Dominicans they were more fortunate. "They have behind their house," he reports, "divers islands well-wooded," and although their convent was only covered with slate, the choir, "which was lately built, was covered with lead." The plate also was valuable, especially a great "chalice of gold set with jewels, worth more than a hundred marks."[1]

After what has been so far said about the state to which the friaries had been reduced by the middle of 1538 there is little need to dwell upon the surrenders which were extracted from them. The chief object of a formal document was to secure to the crown the legal possession of the property belonging to the religious corporation, and for this purpose the deed was, as a rule, carefully entered on the "Close Roll." As the friars possessed real property so slight in amount, the "surrender" was of comparatively minor importance, and out of the two hundred convents of friars only some forty-five official deeds are known to exist. Of these, more than a fourth are not found enrolled, several have not been dated, and some not legalised by the convent seal. In the case of one, that of the Franciscans of Aylesbury, although the convent apparently consisted of fifteen members, the signatures of only seven are attached to the document. Besides these forty-five, a book of surrenders made to bishop Ingworth seems to contain the signed resignations of some five-and-twenty more, none of which are sealed documents or have been enrolled.

The form of surrender employed in many cases is curious. After stating that the act was altogether voluntary, the document proceeds to say that the house is resigned into the king's hands under the conviction that the religious who sign it have been guilty of crimes and vices. The same form is made use of in a great many instances,[2] and chiefly where doctor London was engaged in the work. And although the document has often been pointed to as

---

[1] *Calendar*, xiii. (i), No. 1335, 1342.
[2] *e.g.*, Stamford, Franciscans and Carmelites; Bedford and Aylesbury, Coventry, &c.

proof that the religious themselves confessed the iniquity of their lives, no reasonable man can doubt that, like other so-called "confessions," this was a ready-made document.

Were there any doubts left on the mind as to the authorship of such documents, after examining their terms, they can be removed by the knowledge that there exists a draft of a surrender couched in a similar form, written in the hand of doctor London, and intended for the Carmelite friars of Oxford.[1]

How far this was to be a voluntary act may be understood from a letter written by the doctor on July 7th, 1538: "We find," he says, "the White friars (these Carmelites) and the Augustins to be most out of order and brought into such poverty, that if they do not forsake their houses, their houses will forsake them, wherefore we are well onward in such order with them as they shall put themselves and their houses in the king's hands." At the end of this communication he says: "If Mr. Fryer, now newly come from London, had not said in the Blackfriars that he heard say in London that the four orders in Oxford and Cambridge should stand, the Black had made their submission yesterday. The Grey and Augustins have done it already under their writings and seals."[2] It was thus, according to London's own admission, only when the friars were given plainly to understand that they must go, that their voluntary submission was executed. Even a rumour that they might be allowed to remain caused them to hesitate and draw back.

The spoils obtained for the royal treasury by the suppression of the friars were in the first instance very small. Beyond the plate seized for the king, which was seldom more than the sacred vessels, often only one chalice, a few shillings, or at most a few pounds, represented the amount credited to the king after the expenses of the commissioners had been paid. Thus at Pontefract the goods sold amounted, in the Dominican friary, to only 110s. 4d., all the furniture of "the cells" fetching but eight shillings. Prior Day was given thirteen shillings and fourpence and each priest five shillings. Sixty-two shillings was the balance obtained by the king, besides a small amount of lead, two bells, "a

---

[1] *Calendar*, xiii. (i), No. 1335 (2). [2] *Ibid.*

conduit and a brass 'hallywalter fatt'" left in the keeping of the mayor.¹

At Newcastle, to take but one instance more, bishop Ingworth sold the vestments and other moveables in the Black friars' house and church for less than £5; the mayor bought the tiles of the roof and everything in the dormitory for ten shillings; two chalices, weighing 38 ounces, were sent to the royal treasure-house; the lead was melted into 18 fodders, and the episcopal visitor went away with thirty shillings as the price obtained by all the desecration and ruthless destruction. As for the community, six shillings and eightpence was given to the prior, five shillings to two other priests, to two lay brothers three and fourpence each, and to another, Robert Burrall, who did not sign the surrender, as much as ten shillings. The bishop "gave them a few hours' grace to quit their convent," and turned them out in the depth of winter without any other provision.²

As to the sites and buildings, the crown, no doubt, made some profits by the sales of these. Situated in the heart of great towns, the space, and even the actual buildings, were much sought after. Thus, "in Lincoln," writes the bishop of Dover, "in the Grey friars is a goodly conduit, for which the mayor and the aldermen were with me to make suit to have the conduit into the city."³ So, too, the mayor and aldermen of Grimsby wanted to beg half the friars' church "to make of it a common house for ordnance and other necessaries for the defence of the king's enemies if need be." It "stands very well for the purpose," writes John Freeman, who had conducted the dissolution, "near the water and open on the sea." And the thing asked he believes is "very necessary for the common wealth."⁴ In Reading also the town wished for the church of the Grey friars to make a town-hall, and in several places the buildings were purchased by the cities in which they were situated. Thus in December, 1539, the king sold to the inhabitants of Worcester the sites, lands, churches, belfries and bells, churchyards and other belongings of the convents of the Black and Grey friars there for £541, 10s.,⁵ and this was

---

¹ Fr. Palmer in *The Reliquary*, xx. p. 73.   ² *Ibid.*, xviii. 165.
³ Wright, 192.   ⁴ *Calendar*, xiii. (ii), No. 567.
⁵ Rot. Pat., 31 Hen. VIII., p. 1, m. 28.

after the superfluous buildings had been sold to private wreckers by men who took four days over the job at a cost of seventy-eight shillings and eightpence.

It is necessary to say a few words about the lot of the disbanded friars. Only one or two individuals were granted any pension for their support. As a rule, a few shillings (on an average apparently about five shillings) was delivered to each one on being turned out into the world to find his own living as best he might. Even when they secured what is known as a "capacity"—that is, permission to act as one of the secular clergy—employment was by no means easy to be obtained. The bishops were no lovers of the wandering friars, and the great destruction of churches diminished the possibility of obtaining any cure of souls, even had the ordinaries been willing to employ them. This is evident in many letters of the period. "I beg your lordship," wrote Ingworth to Crumwell, "to be good lord for the poor friars' capacities. They are very poor and can have little service without their capacities. The bishops and curates are very hard to them without they have their capacities."[1] In another letter he says, "I pray you be good lord to me, that the warrants for their habits may be had according to my promise, for they (the friars) may not be suffered to say mass abroad in churches till they have their exemptions. I have written to divers of the bishops, and with divers I have spoken to license them till after Michaelmas, and at that time I have promised to send their license to certain places where they shall have them free, for the most part of them have no penny to pay for the charge of them."[2]

Lastly, to give but one more instance of the hardship to which the expelled friars were exposed, another letter of the same bishop Ingworth, who was the chief instrument in producing such misery, may be quoted. "Further my good lord," he writes, "in these parts within the diocese of York the poor men (the disbanded friars) that surrender their houses are hardly ordered by the bishop's officers at the bishop's commandment. They cannot be suffered to sing nor say in any parish church without they show the letters of their orders, my letters or their capacities notwithstanding.

[1] Wright, 193.   [2] *Ibid.*, 210.

And, the charge for these letters of their orders be so great, that the poor men be not able to bear it. Some must go a hundred miles to seek them. And when they come there the charge of searching the register is so great that they are not able to pay it, and so they come home again confounded. I have been with my lord of York and showed him your lordship's letter, that your commandment is that they who have surrendered their houses should be suffered without interruption to sing and say in any church. The bishop made many objections and said that it must be known whether they were priests or not. And I certified him that we who received the houses made due search which were priests and which were not, and so made certificate to your lordship and your lordship to the king's grace. So that by that means (only) their capacities were granted. Wherefore I desired him to accept their capacities from the king's grace with as much favour as the bishop of Rome's capacities had been before received, for which there never was any search made." Still, Ingworth does not think archbishop Lee was satisfied, and he begs that Crumwell will write his directions that these men may "sing and say" mass without having to show "any proof of orders."[1]

[1] R. O. Crum. Corr., viii. 120.

CHAPTER XVII

Progress of the General Suppression

THE story of one dissolution, at least as to the general circumstances attending the work, is practically the history of all. The steps of the royal commissioners engaged in disbanding monks, in destroying what were accounted superfluous buildings, and in sweeping the spoils into the king's treasure-house, have been so closely followed by Canon Dixon,[1] that little need be said here as to the mere sequence of events which culminated in the total extinction of the monastic body in England.

For a year after the "Pilgrimage of Grace" few dissolutions, except of some of the lesser monasteries previously doomed by act of parliament, are recorded. The only exceptions were those houses seized by Henry on account of the attainder of their superiors for their supposed connection with the northern rising. From Michaelmas, 1537, to the same date in the following year, the work of destruction was pushed on very vigorously. Besides the houses of friars, and the monasteries of Woburn and Lenton, which in this year fell under the law of attainder, many other of the larger monasteries either surrendered or in some other way came into the king's hands before the feast of St. Michael, 1538. The circumstances attending the destruction of one or two of these may be taken as a sample of the methods employed in the work.

The need of voluntary surrenders for the legal possession of the monasteries not included by parliament in the pecuniary limit assigned for suppression has already been pointed out. The instructions given to the royal agents were, by all methods known to them to get the religious "willingly to consent and agree" to their own extinction.

[1] In the second volume of his *History of the Church of England*.

And it was only when they found "any of the said heads and convents so appointed to be dissolved so wilful and obstinate that they would in no wise" agree to sign and seal their own death warrant that the commissioners were authorised to "take the possession of the house" and property by force.[1] For many months, in fact, since the first wholesale dissolution of the lesser monasteries commenced, popular rumour had spoken of the total destruction of the abbeys of England, and the seizure of their lands and wealth, as the ultimate goal to which the royal intentions aimed. The religious themselves, whilst hoping against hope that some change of regal whim might bring again union with Rome and the dismissal of the then all-powerful, and, as they regarded them, evil counsellors, could have had little expectation that, under existing circumstances, their lot would ultimately prove more fortunate than that of their poorer brethren. Against such a notion it was to the king's interest to protest. A belief that within a brief period, to be measured, probably, by weeks or months, their property would pass into the royal power would naturally tend to make the monks not alone careless in the supervision of buildings and lands, but anxious to save something for themselves, if possible, from the general spoliation. Hence the visitors frequently in their letters urge rapidity of action when once the resolution is taken to deal with a particular abbey or convent. Hence, also, the care with which Henry and his agents endeavoured to dissemble the royal intention of suppressing the monastic body throughout the country.[2]

Thus the unscrupulous doctor Layton, in a letter written in the middle of January, 1538, describes his efforts to prevent the spread of reports detrimental to the king's interests. "On my coming to Barnwell priory on the 12th day in the evening," he says, "it was immediately bruited in Cambridge that the priory should be even then suppressed,[3] and that I would go from thence to Ely and to Bury and suppress wheresoever I came: and that the king's

---

[1] R. O. Chapter House Bk., A. $\frac{4}{80}$, f. 1, *et seq.*

[2] Mr. Gairdner (*Calendar*, xiii. (i), preface vi) says: "In spite of Dr. Layton's denial—in spite even of the king's own denial conveyed to some monasteries by Cromwell—it is impossible not to suspect that the complete suppression of monastic houses had already been resolved on."

[3] The house was surrendered on the 8th November following, to Dr. Legh (App. ii. to 8th Rept. Dep. Keeper, p. 9).

highness was fully determined to suppress all monasteries: and that Mr. Southwell and I were sent into Norfolk only for that purpose. Which bruit to stop, and to satisfy the people, I went with expedition to the abbeys and priories, calling unto me all such gentlemen and honest men as were nigh inhabitants there. I (then) openly in the chapter house commanded and charged the abbots and priors with their convents in the king's behalf that they should not in any wise, for fear of any such bruit or vain babbling of the people, waste, destroy or spoil their woods, nor sell their plate or jewels of their church, nor mortgage or pledge any part or parcels of the same for any such intent: nor let out their granges, pastures or glebe, ever retained in their hands for the maintenance of their house and hospitality, nor to make excessive fines for renewing any manor's lease for a hundred years . . . nor to sell or alienate their lands and revenues nor diminish their rents; nor sell any manor, portion, pension, quit-rent or any such like appertaining to their monastery. And finally (I ordered them) to keep everything in the same state as they have done always heretofore, and as they of right are bound, and not to give any credit to the vain babbling of the people. And whatsoever they were that persuaded them to make any such alienation or sale, alleging that the king would suppress them and all other religious houses, and that it would be better for them to make their hands betimes than too late, no matter of what condition the people who said this were," the doctor continues, "in this they utterly slandered the king their natural sovereign lord." He told them not to believe such reports, and "commanded the abbots and priors to set" those who related such things "in the stocks," unless they were gentlemen, when they were to acquaint Crumwell.

"This digression," Layton concludes, "hath somewhat hindered us for Westacre, which if I should not have sped before the dissolution of the same, the rumour would have so greatly increased in the heads of the common people, that surely all abbots and priors would have made foul shifts before we could have made full expedition and all finished at Westacre. Your (*i.e.* Crumwell's) commandment therefore given me in your gallery in that behalf was much more weighty than I at that time judged or supposed or would have believed if I had not seen the very experience thereof."[1]

That the far-seeing minister had been fully alive to the danger is evident from the draft of a letter sent to various monasteries to assure them that no intention of suppressing them existed. "Albeit," this letter of Crumwell's runs, "I doubt not but, having not long since received the king's highness's letters wherein his majesty signified to you that, using yourselves like his good and faithful subjects, his grace would not in any wise interrupt you in your state and kind of living; and that his pleasure therefore was that in case any man should declare anything to the contrary, you should cause him to be apprehended and kept in sure custody till further knowledge of his grace's pleasure,—you would so firmly repose yourself in the tenour of the said letters as no man's words nor any voluntary surrender made by any governor or company of any religious house since that time, shall put you in any doubt or fear of suppression or change of your kind of life and policy." The king, however, feels that there are people who "upon any voluntary and frank surrender would persuade and blow abroad a general and violent suppression." And because some houses have lately been surrendered, the king commands me to say "that unless there had been overtures made by the said houses that have resigned, his grace would never have received the same. And his majesty intendeth not in any wise to trouble you or to devise for the suppression of any house that standeth, except they shall either desire of themselves with one whole consent to resign and forsake the same or else misuse themselves contrary to their allegiance." In this last case, the document concludes, they shall lose "more than their houses and possessions, that is, the loss also of their lives." Wherefore take care of your houses and beware of spoiling them like some have done "who imagined they were going to be dissolved."[2]

The royal fears that the work of spoliation might be anticipated by the monks themselves if they were allowed to suspect his designs were not altogether groundless. Numerous examinations held some years later as to sales and leases of lands, gifts of annuities and pledging of plate

---

[1] *Calendar*, xiii. (i), No. 102.　　[2] Brit. Mus. Cott. MS. Cleop., E. iv. f. 86.

and jewels, prove that even a suspicion of the coming destruction was enough to make the monks anticipate it. Thus, to take an example of the many that might be cited.

The priory of Launde (of which Crumwell notes: "Item, to remember Launde for my part thereof,") affords an interesting instance of the way in which some of the coveted plate and other valuables disappeared on the eve of the catastrophe. A gentleman of the county of Leicester, some years after the dissolution of this priory, informed the chancellor of the court of Augmentation that, shortly before the suppression, when he was "riding from Sowerby to Sir John Villiers, he met with a cart laden at Old Thorpe. With this cart there rode a canon and three servants of the prior of Launde." He asked them what was in the cart, "because the cart-horse swetted very fast." One of the servants replied, "'It is some of the shortest stuff of Launde priory,' and so went his way smiling." Also the same informer had been told that a basket of plate had been carried from the priory to a house at Sowerby, and remained there for six weeks after the dissolution, when it was taken to the late prior at "Frisby parsonage."

Other witnesses deposed that "three geldings and a mare" belonging to the priory were brought to a neighbour's stable shortly before the suppression, whence they were taken to the parsonage of Frisby; that "three suits of vestments," formerly belonging to the monastery, were saved from the sale of the effects by the same means, and that in the same place were hidden in a chest several pieces of plate—goblets, spoons and other silver articles—for a year or more after the dissolution.[1]

In the same way a curious story is told about some plate that belonged to the abbey of Croyland. The person examined had been one of the monks, and, when the exiled abbot, John Briggs, was dying shortly after, "was his confessor and one of his executors." He had heard that the late abbot had some plate given him by the king's commissioners. And "the said deponent," continues the record of the examination, "saith that he required of the said abbot on his death-bed to know where his plate was, and he said that after his death it should be found in his chamber . . .

[1] R. O. Aug. Off. Misc., Bk. 133, ff. 32–33.

in a spruce coffer by his bedside." Besides this box there was another chest "bound with iron," which contained several pieces of plate. And "this deponent saith that about eight weeks before the surrender he went by the command of the abbot to one John Mereshouse at Croyland and there opened a long chest," in which there was some of the silver plate found on the abbot's death, "and a standing piece which was after given to the earl of Essex that then was."[1]

Instances such as these could be multiplied, but the above are sufficient to show that the monasteries were often not inclined to wait calmly for the coming of the spoiler. Examples of leases made conditionally upon the suppression are very frequently met with, and more than one in which, for a similar purpose, a lease made on the eve of the dissolution was antedated. Frequently the monks were no doubt moved by the desire or need to meet the liabilities of their convent, which were in all cases great, in some positively overwhelming. In most instances, however, their intention in thus anticipating the royal seizure was probably the outcome of a natural desire to save something from the general ruin.

As to the "surrenders" themselves, little need be said. About 150 monasteries of men appear to have signed away their property, and by the formal deed to have handed over all rights to the king. Their act, however, can hardly with justice be called free and voluntary. With Henry's hand upon their throats it was a question between life and possessions. Even staunch resistance to the royal will would not save the property of which they were the guardians, from the covetous designs of king and minister. Refusal to resign at their bidding meant certain loss of the pittance generally allotted to those who acquiesced in the spoliation, and possible death for such temerity. It is not given to all to offer life for honour when no real advantage is purchased by the sacrifice. However much, therefore, the compliance of the monks is to be regretted, it must be confessed that the heroism of refusal could hardly be looked for in many. Moreover, Henry had carefully prepared the way for his design by the removal of refractory abbots, the substitution

---

[1] R. O. Aug. Off. Misc. Bk., f. 42.

of others more pliable, and by other methods calculated to ensure success, to which reference will be made hereafter. It is well, also, to bear in mind that the idea of any general attack on monasticism was not only kept in the background, but actually repudiated by both king and agents. The monasteries stood alone. Singly they were attempted, and singly they fell.

It was in the years 1538 and 1539 that most of the "surrenders" were made. Some three or four houses only had come into the king's possession in this way during the latter half of 1537. The convent of the London Carthusians is the earliest recorded instance; but the document has no signatures appended to it, and the surrender of the Benedictine abbey of Chertsey may be regarded as the first legal document of this kind. It was signed by John Cordrey, the abbot, and fourteen of his monks, who, however, were not disbanded, but transferred to Bisham, which had been "dissolved and granted to the king by William Barlow bishop of St. David's and late commendatory prior," on the 5th of July, 1536. Here, on December 18th, 1537, the old community of Chertsey were established by royal charter, as "King Henry's new monastery of the Holy Trinity," "in consideration that the said John Cordrey, the late abbot, and convent granted their monastery and possessions to the king."[1] This royal foundation, however, although endowed with lands to the value of nearly £700 a year, was very short lived, for on the 17th of June, 1538, or just six months after its establishment, it was resigned, or surrendered, into the king's hands.[2]

Doctor Layton, who was engaged in this work of suppression, wrote on June 22nd to Crumwell:—"We have taken the assurance for the king. The abbot a very simple man, the monks of small learning and much less discretion. Plate very little, household stuff none but the abbot's bed and one mattress for two of his servants. I caused a bed to be borrowed in the town and brought into the abbey for Dr. Carne and myself. In lieu of hangings bare walls throughout the house; cattle none, but bought this day and to-morrow to the larder, saving a few milch kine not twelve in number. In the garners not one bushel of wheat,

---

[1] Rot. Pat., 29 Hen. VIII., Pars. iv. m. 12.
[2] Eighth Rept. Dep. Keeper, App. ii. p. 13.

malt or other grains. Vestments small store and not one good, for the abbot hath made money of all the best and sold them in London and even so the church plate." He then goes on to attribute this to the abbot's fondness for "white wine, sugar and burage," and says he has been obliged to raise money out "of the rotten copes and bells" to "dispatch" the monks. On the other hand, this visitor gives a good account of the state of the crops growing on the land, and concludes thus:—"This day we dispatched the monks, for they be much desirous to be gone, for yesterday when we were making sale of the old vestments within the chapter-house, then the monks made a new mart in the cloister, every man bringing his cowl cast upon his neck to be sold, and sold them indeed."[1]

On the 16th November, 1537, William Petre visited and received the surrender of Lewes priory,[2] together with its rights over the cell of Castleacre, which resignation was confirmed at Castleacre before the same royal commissioner six days later.[3] The prior of the latter place had tried to propitiate Crumwell with "four marks as a token of my love" and a patent for the same amount each year, but he had been finally forced to send up the deeds of "foundation" and other things demanded of him, together with a fruitless prayer for "pity on me and mine."[4] By March 24, 1538, with the lengthening days, the work of destruction had commenced at Lewes. "I advertised your lordship," writes Crumwell's agent to him, "of the length and greatness of this church, and how we had to pull the whole down to the ground and what manner and fashion they used in pulling it down. I told your lordship of a vault on the right side

---

[1] Ellis, *Orig. Letters*, 3rd Ser. iii. p. 265. The house was endowed with lands of the late dissolved abbey of Chertsey, and with the possessions of the priories of Cardigan, Bethkelert, Ankerwyke, Little Marlow, &c. On the present letter Ellis notes:—" From its contents we must conclude that the re-endowment by Henry VIII. could only have been promised ... the poverty of the house is little reconcileable with the increased endowment." As the foundation only lasted from December 18, 1537, to July 19, 1538, it is more than probable no revenues were received. The goods of Bisham had already been sold on the first dissolution.

[2] Rot. Claus., 29 Hen. VIII., Pars. i. m. 9.

[3] *Ibid.*, m. 10. The original surrender, without any seal, but signed in the margin by Prior Thomas and ten monks, is in the Brit. Museum (Add. Charter, 15,495).

[4] R. O. Crum. Corr., iv. 178. No pension was apparently granted to any monks of either place.

of the high altar, that was borne up by four great pillars having about five chapels which are compassed in with walls" 210 feet in length. "All this is down on Thursday and Friday last. Now we are plucking down a higher vault borne up by four thick pillars 14 feet from side to side (and) 45 feet in circumference. These shall down for our second work. As it goeth forward I will advise your lordship from time to time and that your lordship may know with how many men we have done this, we brought from London 17 persons, three carpenters, two smiths, two plumbers, and one that keepeth the furnace. Every one of these attendeth to his own office. Ten of them hewed the walls about, among which there were three carpenters; these made props to underset where the others cut away, the others broke and cut the walls. These are men exercised much better than the men we find here in the country." He then requests more men and concludes: "On Tuesday they began to cast the lead, and it shall be done with such diligence and saving as may be." At the close of the letter, the dimensions of the church which they were calmly engaged in destroying are given. It was a hundred and fifty feet long and sixty-three high.[1] Its walls were five feet thick and the walls of the steeple, which was ninety feet high, were ten thick. There were two-and-thirty pillars which carried the groined roof, which over the high altar rose to the height of eighty-three feet from the ground.[2] Such was one of those magnificent creations of English architectural skill which at this time in almost every part of the country the government were occupied in wrecking.

The first monastery to surrender in the year 1538 was the abbey of Westacre. The history of this transaction has already been referred to. The actual resignation of the monastery could hardly have been freely made, since a month before, on December 16 (1537), Sir Roger Townsend wrote to say that, "as directed" by Crumwell's letters, he and others had repaired to the priory, "sequestered all the property" and taken inventories[3] of their possessions. As to the surrender itself, two documents exist, one dated on

---

[1] The church, from other dimensions given in the letter and from recent excavations, must have been 400 feet long. The 150 feet refers to the eastern limb only. The letter says the circumference of the church was 1558 feet.

[2] Wright, 180. [3] *Calendar*, xii. (ii), No. 1219.

the 14th January, 1538, and the other the following day. The first is a confession of maladministration and other general self-accusations in much the same form as the Northampton document. The second is the surrender proper, and apparently neither have been enrolled upon the Close Roll. Even had all been regular, the surrender could hardly have meant much more than the "confession," as the property of the priory was already in the hands of Crumwell's commissioners. What makes it somewhat more strange is, that Layton, on the 18th of January, wrote, in a letter already quoted, implying that the suppression was not an accomplished fact at that date. The work of putting a stop to the rumours of the coming suppressions had "hindered" him, he says, at "Westacre," and he adds:—"What untruth and dissimulation we find in the prior! What falsehood in false knaves amongst the convent! What bribery, spoil and ruin with crafty colours of bargains contrived by the inhabitants it were too long to write; but for a conclusion all their wrenches, wiles and guiles shall nothing prevail them, and so God willing we shall serve the king truly."[1]

The surrender of Abingdon on the 9th of February of this same year, 1538, presents one or two remarkable features worth recording. Like many of the monasteries, the financial state of this great abbey does not appear to have been very flourishing. There had been difficulties with tenants, implying costly lawsuits and compromises detrimental to the interests of the house. Internally the discipline of the cloister had suffered by the interference of the king and his vicar-general. Shaxton, the bishop of Salisbury, had safe in prison a monk of the house, who, when by the royal orders two of his brethren "were scraping out the bishop of Rome's name," came and told them that they

[1] *Calendar*, xiii. (i), No. 102. When the commissioners reached Westacre on January 18th, 1538, they found that they had been anticipated in their intention of securing the property before the rumours of the intended suppression had got about. Not only had much of the land been let on long leases, but as early as the beginning of the previous December, the convent had been visited by one Charles Wyngfield, who had declared to the members that it was the royal pleasure they should sell their house to him and his heirs. This they had accordingly done, granting him a deed "to hold good only if the king's pleasure were such as he declared" (*Calendar*, xiii. (i), No. 101). This transaction gave Layton and his companion some anxiety and considerable trouble.

"who set knife and pen to the book were cursed."[1] More than this: the exactions and demands of Crumwell hampered the abbot in the administration of his house. "Your letters," writes the abbot to him, demand that I give the office of "chamberer" to one Richard Birrall, "a monk of this my monastery, by convent seal for the rest of his life. It hath not been seen in time past that any monk hath ever had a convent seal of any office. For if he had it, I think it were my duty to take it from him. Also it is against his religion and standeth not with his profession. Wherefore seeing that it standeth neither with the good custom of the house nor doth agree with the good order of religion, I therefore beseech your good mastership with all my heart to be good master unto me that I may order a monk as he ought to be ordered according to the good rule of religion, and that no such precedent may be had."[2]

The good order of the abbey, however, mattered little to Crumwell, who in the year 1537 enters among his notes, together with other similar matters to be held in memory: "Item, the suppression of Abingdon."[3] How this was accomplished may be judged from one circumstance. On the 7th of February, 1538, a sum of £600, more than £6000 of our money, was paid by royal warrant to doctors Tregonwell and Petre, "to be spent by them on bringing about the dissolution of the monastery of Abingdon."[4] The monastery surrendered two days later. Thomas Pentecost, *alias* Rowland, the abbot, obtained the grant of a pension of £200 a year and a house to live in, and each of the monks a suitable sum for their lives. On February the 22nd, Sir Richard Ryche wrote his report of the royal prize. The buildings he found in a great state of decay. The abbot's house was unfit for habitation, and would require a large amount of money to make it fit for the king. The ground was not fit to make a park, for if the fields on the south side of the Thames were taken for the purpose, the writer believes that the town of Abingdon, which was very populous, "will decay." He concluded by asking "what part of the church,

---

[1] R. O. Crum. Corr., xxxviii. 52.
[2] *Ibid.*, i. 9. It is curious to note the peculiar form in which Richard Birrall signs the deed of surrender, "concedo et ego Richardus Birrall."
[3] Brit. Mus. Cott. MS. Titus, B. i. f. 468d.
[4] R. O. Exch. Aug. Off. Mins. Accts., 28 Hen. VIII., 1 Edw. VI. 155. This sum is also entered as paid on Treasurer's Roll, I. m. 12d.

cloister, dorter, chapter-house and frater shall be defaced. I think," he adds, "a great part thereof may be defaced and sufficient left to the king's contentation."[1]

The spoils were gathered into the royal treasure-house. Two mitres were purchased by Sir Thomas Pope, the treasurer of the Court of Augmentations, and three pontifical rings with precious stones with a silver gilt cross were saved from the common melting-pot for the royal use. In the latter, set in a piece of gold, was a portion of the holy cross called "an esse."[2]

The dissolution of the abbey of Vale Royal affords an interesting insight into the methods employed to force compliance, and a criterion by which to estimate the value of the surrenders. Here, as elsewhere, the demands upon the resources of the abbey had been met until it became impossible with further exactions to keep up the house. "My lord," writes the abbot to Crumwell in answer to a repeated demand, "I most humbly beseech your good lordship, for the love of God and our Blessed Lady and for the maintenance of good service and poor hospitality to be kept in the house, to pardon our refusal."

On the 22nd of August, 1538, one of the most energetic of the king's commissioners, Thomas Legh, was at the abbey, and on the 7th of September a surrender is said to have been made by the abbot and convent. It was entered in due course on the Close Roll as a valid document, but was repudiated by the abbot. At Lichfield, on his way to London, he wrote his protest against the surrender which Holcroft, the subsequent grantee,[3] was evidently the chief agent in extorting, if not in forging. The commissioners, so said John Harwood, the abbot, had brought the royal demand that we should "clearly of our own consents surrender . . . our monastery." "My good lord," he writes to Crumwell, "the truth is, I nor my said brethren have never consented to surrender our monastery, nor yet do, nor never will do by our good wills, unless it shall please the king's grace to give us commandment so to do, which I cannot perceive in the commission of master Holcroft. And if any information be given unto his majesty or your lordship,

[1] *Calendar*, xiii. (i), No. 332.   [2] Aug. Off. Treas. Roll, I. m. 3.
[3] He paid £450, 10s. 6d., with an annual fee of £3, 5s. 8d., for the property.

that we should consent to surrender as is above said, I assure your good lordship upon my fidelity and truth, there was never any such consent made by me or my brethren, and no person or persons had authority so to do in our names." He adds a prayer that the king may spare the monastery, and forwards "a bill indented made by me and my brethren" which the commissioner had refused.[1]

Abbot Harwood's journey failed in its purpose. Still the king could neither force the unwilling monks to surrender nor, at this date, was he apparently desirous of seizing the property without some pretence of justice. Mr. Ormerod remarks that the difficulty was overcome in this instance by bringing a capital indictment against the abbot. "The jurisdiction of the abbey courts," he writes, "afforded an easy opportunity of gratifying the royal wishes, and lord Crumwell, the seneschal of the abbey, presided in person at a court held at Vale Royal on the Monday after the feast of the Annunciation, 1539, in which fourteen jurors found a bill against the late abbot and others for the following offences:—

"That John Harwood, late abbot of the monastery of O. B. Lady of Vale Royal, consented to the slaying of Hugh Chaliner, his monk; and that the day before the said monk's throat was cut, the said monk said unto a child, being his brother's son of twelve years of age or thereabouts, that he the said monk would be with his brother at Chester before the Assumption, or else he should suffer death if he tarried any longer in the said monastery."

The jury further found that the abbot threatened a tenant of his that he would have nothing more to do with him if he fought against the northern men in the general rising. Also that the abbot's brother approved of the northern men, and one of his vicars refused to marry a couple upon a license obtained from the king as supreme head.[2]

A true bill being found against the abbot on these charges his life was in grievous peril. In fact, the Cheshire tradition

---

[1] Wright, 244.
[2] Ormerod, *Cheshire*, i. 503. See also *Monasticon*, vi. 701, *note*. The document is said to be a transcript of the Original Inquisition, and addressed "to Thomas Holcroft be these directed with speed." For the Inquisition, see *Calendar*, xiv. (i), No. 639.

is said to be that he was executed.[1] This, however, was not the case, as in the year 1542 "John Harwood, late abbot of Vale Royal, was in receipt of a pension,[2] which he continued to receive till the first year of Edward VI.[3] The effect of the condemnation was, however, sufficient doubtless to place the abbot in the royal power, and thus to overcome his opposition to surrender his charge, of which John Harwood had given such unmistakable proofs.

Of course by the middle of the year 1538 it became obvious to all that the king intended nothing less than the total destruction of the monastic orders. Rumours sprang up that not only the friars but monks generally would soon be expected to abandon their religious habits, and Prior Goldstone of Christchurch, Canterbury, wrote to Crumwell earnestly begging that such a measure might not be applied to himself and his brethren. Crumwell, he says, had sent him word that they should never be constrained to do this against their wills, and he assures him that they will never voluntarily break the profession they have made to serve God in their monastic dress, or give up a mode of life which had been led by the sons of St. Benedict at Canterbury for more than nine hundred years.[4] His entreaty was naturally of no avail. Crumwell, who happened to be at Canterbury with the king early in September, 1538, "intimated to the monks in the chapter-house that the change was actually resolved on, and Dr. Richard Thornden, warden of the cathedral manors, who was accustomed to provide new apparel for them yearly at All Hallows' day, wrote to ask when it was to take place."[5]

The pressure put upon the monks to resign their property may be further illustrated by two letters relating to houses in the county of Somerset—the one from the prior of the Charterhouse of Hinton, the other from a priest employed to bring about the surrender of Athelney Abbey. "In the Lord Jesus shall be your salutation," writes prior Horde to his brother Alan, a barrister of the Middle Temple. "And where ye marvel that I and my brethren do not freely and voluntarily give and surrender up our house at the motion of the king's commissioners, but stand stiffly, and as you

---

[1] *Ibid.* [2] R. O. Aug. Off. Misc. Bk., 248, 41.
[3] R. O. Aug. Off. Treasurer's Roll, III. m. 106.
[4] *Calendar*, xiii. (ii), No. 139. [5] *Ibid.*, preface, viii.

think obstinately, in our opinion; truly, brother, I marvel greatly that you think so, but rather that you would have thought us light and hasty in giving up that thing which is not ours to give, but dedicate to Almighty God for service to be done to His honour continually, with other many good deeds of charity which daily be done in this house to our Christian neighbours. And considering that there is no cause given by us why the house shall be put down, but that the service of God, religious conversation of the brethren, hospitality, alms-deeds, with all other our duties, be as well observed in this poor house as in any religious house in this realm or in France; which we have trusted that the king's grace would consider. But because that ye write of the king's high displeasure and my lord privy seal's, who ever hath been my especial good lord, and I trust yet will be, I will endeavour myself, as much as I may, to persuade my brethren to a conformity in this matter; so that the king's highness nor my said good lord shall have any cause to be displeased with us, trusting that my poor brethren who know not where to have their living, shall be charitably looked upon." [1]

After dissolving the abbey of Keynsham, John Tregonwell and William Petre, the two royal commissioners, arrived at Hinton on January 25th, 1539, for the same purpose. "Immediately after our coming," they write to Crumwell, "we entered conversation with the prior there about the cause of our coming, and used such means and persuasions unto him for the purpose as we thought most meet and might best take place in him. His answer in effect was, that if the king's majesty would take his house, so (that) it proceeded not of his voluntary surrender, he was contented to obey; but otherwise he said his conscience would not suffer him willingly to give over the same. In the end, after long conversation, he desired delay to make us answer until this morning. At this time, we often using like diligence in persuading him as we did before, he declared himself to be of the same mind he was 'yester-

---

[1] Ellis, *Orig. Letters*, 2nd Ser. ii. p. 130. "Of pressure being applied we have express evidence—as at the Carthusian priory of Hinton. . . . The abbot of Winchcombe also wrote in August to Cromwell, saying he hoped that he had not done anything against the laws of God or the King to merit the suppression of the Monastery" (*Calendar*, xiv. (ii), preface, xxix).

night,' or rather more stiff in the same. In conversation with the convent we perceived them to be of the same mind the prior was, and had much like answer of them as we had from the prior (three only excepted who were conformable). And amongst the rest one Nicholas Balland, monk there, being incidentally examined of the king's highness' title of supremacy, expressly denied the same, affirming the bishop of Rome to be the vicar of Christ, and that he is and ought to be taken for supreme head of the Church."[1]

Crumwell had long had his eye upon this house. Lord Stourton had written to him about a vision the prior was said to have had, which appeared to forecast the execution of one of Henry's queens,[2] and he had entered on his "remembrances" "of the Charterhouse at Hinton."[3] And so, by March 31st, 1539, the opposition to the king's demands was broken down, and the surrender signed by prior Horde and fourteen monks. Two others, one of whom was Nicholas Balland, apparently did not sign the document.[4] The house was sold by Tregonwell to Sir Walter Hungerford, but although he paid his money, he complains three months later that Sir Thomas Arundel had on a royal grant sold and "despoiled and quite carried away a great part of the church and other superfluous buildings next."[5]

In much the same way evidently the surrender of the abbey of Athelney was procured by pressure. On November 2nd, 1538, the parson of Holford writes an account of his visit to the abbot at the instigation of Crumwell and chancellor Audley. "I found," he says, "the said abbot in the church coming from mass at the hour of ten o'clock before noon. And, as reverently as I could, I delivered the said my lord and master's letters, and showed him that my lord Audeley recommended him to him. And the said abbot answered: 'I am glad to hear of my lord's welfare.' And

---

[1] *Calendar*, xiv. (i), No. 145. In a letter written on the 24th June, Sir W. Hungerford says he "kept in his house till I know your pleasure" this Nicholas Balland, who publicly declared he would die for the belief that the pope was the only head of the Church" (*Ibid.*, No. 1154).

[2] R. O. Crum. Corr., xl. 71.

[3] *Calendar*, ix. No. 498.

[4] Eighth Rept. Dep. Keeper, App. ii. p. 23.

[5] R. O. Crum. Corr., xviii. 11. On April 4th, 1540, grants of pensions were made to the prior and 22 monks, including Nicholas Balland (R. O. Augt. Off. Misc. Bk., 233, f. 242). For payment see A. O. Mins. Acct., 30-31 Hen. VIII., 224, m. 8d.

so he read his letter and said: 'Go with me to my chamber and you shall know my mind.' And I followed the said abbot, and suddenly he stopped and said: 'What, is my lord Audeley a man of the new set or after the old sort?' 'My lord,' said I, 'he is after the best sort, and like a kind-hearted subject to the king's grace and a good Englishman that loveth all the realm.' 'Well,' said the abbot, 'do you think he doth not judge there will be another world shortly?' 'My lord,' said I, 'there will be another world when we be out of this world, but in this I think there was never so gracious a prince as the king's grace is, for he loveth virtue and will punish vice.' Wherewith the said abbot shook his head and said: 'Hear you no new tidings of this great council beyond the sea?' 'No, my lord,' said I, 'there is no matter to be passed upon in their council, for the king will provide surely for all such matters.' And therewith I was in a study, for I wist not what that matter meant. And the abbot said again: 'Well, if I wist what would come of these matters I would soon be at a point with my lord.' With that the abbot went forth and said: 'I will write a letter to my lord and ye shall learn my mind.' And then he went to his chamber, where he called me in secret to him and said: 'Is it not my lord's mind to have me resign my house to him?' 'No, my lord,' said I, 'but it may fortune upon good considerations and causes that he would have you resign your house into the king's hands.' And then said he: 'Our house would be destroyed and all the country undone by that means, as it is about Muchelney.' 'No, my lord,' said I; 'my lord master will come and dwell here, and I think he will be a petitioner to the king's highness to have some part of the order here, as it is at Saint Mary's Altar' (?). This I said, somewhat to satisfy the abbot's mind. 'Why,' said he, 'then what should I have?' 'My lord,' said I, 'I dare undertake, if you will be advised by my lord, he will get you a hundred marks, and he will get you some prebend of the bishop of Sarum, whereby ye shall wear a grey almuce, and all your brothers shall be provided for and shall have services and promotions as shall be meet for them.' 'Well,' said the abbot and shook up his hand, 'if I would have taken a hundred marks I could have been stayed ere this time, but I will fast three days on bread and water than take so little.' 'My lord,' said I, 'I speak of the least. You will find my lord much better when you speak with him.' 'Well,' said he again, 'if I wist what should come of it, I would soon be at a point.' And therewith he sat himself down and eat bread and butter and made me eat with him." The writer then tells how the abbot wrote his letter to the chancellor, and how going to see the steward, he spoke with the community, and found them willing to take Audley's advice, and resign their house at the king's bidding.[1]

The abbey was surrendered to the king on February 8th, 1539, by the abbot and six brethren, who all received pensions for their compliance with the royal will.[2] The effects of the monastery were sold for £80, of which sum Audley, who showed such anxiety to obtain the abbot's resignation, paid £20 for the whole of the buildings.[3]

The action of Audley was not confined to Athelney. He says himself that he sent for the abbot of Osyth's "before the dissolution, and induced him to yield the house to the king's majesty's good will, and that he should exhort his convent to conform themselves to the same, who by my advice and exhortation conformed themselves as humble subjects without murmur or grudge, wherein I trust that I have not for my part served the king's highness amiss." He then goes on to ask Crumwell to obtain him some return, for "I have no fee nor office of his highness," he says, "but the chancellorship, and although it be high and honourable, yet it is cumberous and chargeable."[4]

In the same way, even Burnet allows that the king prepared the way for the suppression by skilfully selecting men who were likely to resign their houses when called upon. Thus John Capon or Salcot, abbot of Hyde, although made bishop of Bangor in 1534, was allowed to remain commendatory of his monastery, and upon surrendering it in 1539 into the king's hands was rewarded with the See of Salisbury. So, too, Robert Pursglove, the prior of Gisburne, who was bishop of Hull, as a suffragan of York, not only surrendered himself, but was active in persuading others to act in the same way. He obtained a pension of £200 a

---

[1] Brit. Mus. Cott. MS. Cleop., E. iv. f. 135.
[2] R. O. Aug. Off. Misc. Bk., 223, f. 105.
[3] R. O. Aug. Off. Mins. Accts., 30-31 Hen. VIII., 224, m. 6d.
[4] Wright, 239.

year.¹ Stephen Sagar, abbot of Hayles, having been sent for to London, made a "privy surrender,"² and was dispatched to his convent to obtain the general consent. This he managed so well that he obtained high praise from the commissioners, who said he "did surrender his house with such discreet and frank manner, as we have seen no other do better in all our journey."³

"What could not be effected by arguments and fair promises," writes the learned Dugdale, "was by *terror* and severe dealing brought to pass. For under pretence of dilapidation in the buildings or negligent administration of their offices, as also for breaking the king's injunctions, they deprived some abbots and then put others that were more pliant in their room." Thus Richard Boreman *alias* Stevenage, the abbot of St. Alban's, was placed in the room of abbot Catton in April, 1538.⁴ On the 10th of December of the previous year, two royal commissioners, Legh and Petre, had written about Saint Alban's that "by confession of the abbot himself," there appears to be "just cause of deprivation, not only for breaking the king's injunctions, but also for manifest dilapidation, making of shifts, negligent administration and sundry other causes, yet, by what means we know not, in all communications or motions made concerning any surrender he showeth himself so stiff, that, as he saith, he will choose to beg his bread all the

---

¹ The royal visitors had compelled the predecessor of Pursglove to resign his office in February, 1537, and had appointed "a friend" of Crumwell. Pursglove was sent to Whitby in October, 1538, to be present at an election of the abbot. He tried to force the community to let him "nominate" the one desired by Crumwell. This they refused. He then endeavoured to get them to allow his master to have the election; they again refused, and claimed the right of free election. This the royal agents would not allow. The prior started for London to lodge a complaint (Wright, 249). The whole letter shows clearly how the elections were managed, in the last years of the existence of the monasteries, and many other instances could be given of the strenuous efforts made by the crown to secure superiors pliant to the royal will. Whitby was dissolved on December 14th, 1539; no legal surrender was apparently made, but the monks were pensioned, Henry Darell, the abbot, receiving 100 marks (R. O. Aug. Off. Misc. Bk., 246, f. 14). For some time efforts had been made to force the late abbot of Whitby, John Hexham, to resign. He had refused, and although reports had been spread that he was willing, he wrote denying them. In the end he gave up his office to W. Petre in August, 1538 (*Calendar*, xiii. (ii), No. 108).

² R. O. Crum. Corr., xx. 15.

³ Wright, 237.

⁴ The *congé* on the "deprivation" of Catton is dated 23rd January, 1538. Rot. Pat., 29 Hen. VIII., Pars. iii. m. 9.

days of his life than consent to surrender." The visitors tried every means to change him, but, as they say, "he waxeth hourly more obstinate and less conformable." They asked for instructions. If they deposed him, the house was in such debt "that no man will take the office of abbot here upon him, except any do it for that purpose to surrender the same to the king's hands; and by this means" they think "this may most easily and with least speech be brought to the king's highness' purpose." Another method they suggest is to leave the unfortunate abbot for a time in suspense "in utter despair of any favour," and perhaps he will then, expecting "to be deprived," "sue to have his surrender taken, because he would be assured of some living."[1]

But abbot Catton kept his word. Neither pressure from without nor the burden of difficulties could move him to do the king's will by surrender or resignation. Deprivation soon followed this letter. The last free abbot of St. Alban's had no pension.

Richard Boreman, who was appointed by Crumwell to succeed, had his difficulties as abbot. He failed to pay his "first-fruits" to the king, and got locked up. "Mr. Gostwick," he writes to Crumwell, "hath detained me from my liberty and keepeth me within his gates, so that I can have no friendly means of him for my liberty. Notwithstanding I have offered him to pay out of hand £300, which is as much as I have and can make friends for in this short time, he demandeth of me besides other great sums the first payment of the first-fruits, which is above all my power to do. . . . Now this evening I am like to be imprisoned in the compter to my bitter shame and undoing."[2]

On December 5th, 1539, abbot Boreman, who, as the commissioners suggested, had doubtless taken the office for the purpose, surrendered the abbey into the king's hands. Not more than half a century before, abbot William of Wallingford had built the rich and sumptous high altar at a cost of above £733, and had beautified the church with gifts worth, as Weaver calculated, more than £8000. This noble minster was only redeemed from destruction and sacrilege by the townspeople, who purchased it from the

---

[1] Wright, 250.   [2] *Calendar*, xiii. (i), Nos. 180, 181.

king for £400. On the 17th December the sacred vessels and the treasures of St. Alban's shrine were brought into the royal jewel-house, and formed a rich prize of no less than 122 ounces of gold, 2990 ounces of gilt plate, and 1144 ounces of parcel gilt and silver. Golden buckles, in which were set "great agates, cameos and coarse pearles," three pontifical mitres, and 400 ounces of copper, formed but part of the plunder.[1]

In the same way Clement Litchfield was compelled to resign the abbey of Evesham to one who would surrender it to the king. The royal inquisitors had reported this abbot to be "chaste in his living and to right well overlook the reparations of his house." He it was who built the noble gateway which still remains a memorial of him, and, although he had been obliged to pay £160 for his temporalities, with large sums as loan to the king and Wolsey, as well as for a whole year to keep four-and-twenty royal lacqueys and their horses, he still managed to adorn the choir and to add two chantries to the churches of St. Lawrence and All Saints.[2] To Latimer, the bishop of Worcester, he was, in the vigorous language employed by that ecclesiastic, a "bloody abbot," which probably means that he did not agree with him in his reforming tendencies.

On the 17th of March, 1538, William Petre, the royal commissioner, wrote to Crumwell:—"According to your commandment I have been at Evesham and there received the resignation of the abbot, which he was contented to make immediately upon the sight of your lordship's letters, saying that he desired me very instantly that I would not open the same during the time of my being here, because (as he said) it would be noted that he was compelled to resign for fear of deprivation."[3] On the 4th of April Philip Harford succeeded.[4] Latimer had assured Crumwell that he

[1] *Monastic Treasures* (Abbotsford Club), p. 29. Among these jewels was doubtless the "lapide preciosum qui constat ex sardonice, calcedonio et onic," presented to the church by king Ethelred II. Matthew Paris (*Additamenta*, ed. Luard, vi. p. 387) describes how the king "coming one day to Saint Albans, entered the chapter-house, brought with him the said stone, and kindly and lovingly offered it to the church, praising it and pointing out its merits. He asked," says the historian, "that the abbot and convent should lay a sentence of excommunication against all who should at any time take away this his gift." (See too the facsimiles in that volume.)
[2] May, *History of Evesham*, p. 72.
[3] Wright, 177.   [4] Rot. Pat., 29 Hen. VIII., m. 14.

would find him a true friend,"[1] and so on January 27, 1540, the monastery was surrendered, the young abbot getting a pension of £240 a year as his reward.[2]

Another example of the personal pressure exerted by the king's agents to induce the religious to surrender may be here given. The important convent of Romsey, in Hampshire, on the eve of its dissolution maintained a community of twenty-five nuns, ruled over by an abbess, Elizabeth Ryprose. They appear to have been unwilling to fall in with the royal views or to abandon the religious life in order that their property might pass into Henry's possession. Eight nuns, nearly a third of the entire community, had made their religious profession on July 28th, 1534, only a few years before their troubles commenced.[3] One of these was Catherine, youngest daughter of Sir Nicholas Wadham, governor of the Isle of Wight, whose sister Jane had been for some years a professed nun in the same abbey of Romsey. At this time the convent steward was a certain John Foster, who lived at Baddesley, near Romsey, and rented the greater tithes of that place from the Hospitallers of St. John of Jerusalem.[4] Foster's position would have given him accurate information as to the extent and value of the property, and his intercourse would have afforded him the means of bringing influence to bear upon the nuns. It was this man who was apparently selected by the king's agents for the delicate service of sounding the nuns as to their disposition to satisfy Henry's desire for their property. In the report he forwarded to Sir Thomas Seymour,[5] "of the king's Privy Chamber," he says:— "According to your request, I herein signify and subscribe unto you the state of the house of Romsey. . . . First you shall understand that the house is out of debt; also the plate and jewels are worth £300 and more; six bells are worth £100 at least; also the church is a great sumptuous thing, all of free stone and covered with lead, which, as I

---

[1] R. O. Crum. Corr., xlix. 42.
[2] R. O. Augt. Off. Misc. Bk., 245, f. 105. There is no deed of surrender and no enrolment on the Close Roll.
[3] For this and much other valuable information I am indebted to F. J. Baigent, Esq., of Winchester. His cordial co-operation and encouragement in my work I desire here gratefully to acknowledge.
[4] Mr. Baigent's MSS. Collections.
[5] Brother of Jane Seymour, one of Henry's wives.

esteem it, is worth £300 or £400 or rather much better."¹ He then goes on to give particulars of the revenue coming from the abbey lands, on some at least of which Seymour had set his heart.² He then concludes:—"And where you wrote unto me by Mr. Fleming, that I should ascertain you whether I thought the abbess with the rest of the nuns would be content to surrender up their house: the truth is I do perceive throughout the motion that your kinswomen and other (of) your friends made for you, (that) they will be content at all times to do you any pleasure they may. But I perceive they would be loath to trust to the commissioners' gentleness, for they hear say that other houses have been straightly handled."³

Attached to this letter is a list of the nuns in the abbey. From this it appears that Catherine Wadham, who had only been four or five years in the convent, had mounted up to the office of subprioress, while her sister held the next rank. These, and another nun, Elizabeth Hill, were the kinswomen of Sir Thomas Seymour, through whose influence John Foster hoped to accomplish the voluntary destruction of the convent.⁴ Apparently his design was unsuccessful. There is no surrender deed of the abbey; neither are the names of the abbess and her nuns found in the pension lists.

If there were some who showed themselves ready to urge the monks to do all that Henry wished and surrender their houses and goods into his hands, there were not wanting others who exhorted them to remain staunch to their religious vocation. Above others, Dr. Richard Hill-

¹ This building was afterwards purchased of the king by the inhabitants for some £100.
² Tenth Report Deputy Keeper, p. 268. "Particulars for Grants."
³ Brit. Mus. Royal MS., 7, C. xvi. f. 147.
⁴ Sir Nicholas Wadham, the father of the two nuns of that name, married twice. His first wife was daughter of Robert Hill, of Antony; and his second Margaret, daughter of Sir John Seymour, of Wolfhall, Wilts, and sister to queen Jane Seymour and Sir Thomas Seymour. The high connection of the Wadhams seems to suggest a reason for the early promotion of Catherine to a high office in her convent. Of John Foster, of Baddesley, the writer of the above letter, one who lived at the end of the sixteenth century records a rhyme popular in the neighbourhood when he went to school as a boy:—

"Mr. Foster of Baddesley was a good man
Before the marriage of priests began,
For he was the first that married a nun,
For which he begat a very rude son."

—(Mr. Baigent's MSS. Collections.)

yard, the late secretary to bishop Tunstal, of Durham, endeavoured to instil the spirit of heroic resistance into the souls of the religious. Fortunately for himself, he escaped from Henry's hands into Scotland, or he would certainly have paid for his boldness with his life. As it was, he was attainted and condemned to death in his absence.[1] The doctor, writes an informer, "says in Edinburgh that he fled away because he had given counsel to sundry religious houses, yet unsuppressed, not to render their houses into the king's hands until they were violently put therefrom." Another writer informed Sir William Eure "that the said Hillyard saith himself that he being in company with certain gentlemen would lament the suppression of the house of Mountgrace and spake large words in favour of the same house. Unto which, as the same Hillyard affirmeth, a gentleman answered: 'that for as small offences as the said Hillyard did commit by speaking these words at that time he had seen men taken as traitors to the king's majesty.' And so the same Hillyard fearing to have been accused for the said words, did so suddenly convey himself out of the realm."[2]

The only religious mentioned by name as connected with Hillyard was the prior of Mountgrace. He was supposed to have helped him to escape, and Eure gave information to Crumwell, in order that "further search, as well touching the prior as his 'conversants and familiars,' might be made."[3] John Wilson, the prior of Mountgrace, was examined, and confessed having talked to Dr. Hillyard about the suppressions. He acknowledged that he did not wish to surrender his house "if it might have stood with the king's pleasure that he might have kept it." And "finally, there never was any one that gave unto them con-

---

[1] Rot. Parl., Hen. VIII., 147.

[2] Brit. Mus. Cott. MS. Calig., B. vii. f. 249. The story of the escape of Hillyard through the help of the prioress of Coldstream is full of interest, but foreign to the present subject. Henry demanded that Hillyard should be given up to him by the Scotch king as one who "had laboured to sow in the realm much sedition." The envoy was to bring him back at once if possible, "having special watch for the sure conveyance of him, and specially noting in his return who shall be desirous to talk with him" (*Sadler Papers*, i. p. 12). The later editions of Sander, *Schism* (*e.g.* 1590, p. 167) give a quotation from his account of the destruction of the monasteries.

[3] *Ibid.*, f. 255.

trary counsel but doctor Hillyard, who said it was in a manner selling the house to surrender up their house for money or pensions."[1]

Another witness, Nicholas Wilson, a "prisoner in the Tower," being examined as to his relations with the escaped doctor Hillyard, wrote: "First I had a conversation with him touching the putting down of monasteries, which, as I remember now, began by my asking him to give the prior of Mountgrace, to the north, one of my friends, advice to be obedient and conform himself to the king's highness in giving up his monastery when he should be required. . . . Upon this motion the said doctor began to doubt, touching the suppression of monasteries, how it might be done. Whereunto I answered him, that their deed, who were then in the houses and had government of them, by their common consent and seal, must needs be of value in the law. And that all such things must be under the disposition and government of the king's highness and his realm as should be thought most meet for the commonwealth. Which words of mine and such other, as far as I perceived, did not fully then satisfy him." In this matter, continues the declaration, "I have certainly tried to satisfy my own conscience and also to take away other men's scruples in obeying the act of suppression. I have told them that the king and his council did this for the common good, although I and other mean men did not perceive the whole considerations for it, and that it was matter for subjects to be under lowly obedience and think the best of their rulers in all things. And further, that as monasteries were founded and endowed" by the licence of princes, so they ought to be able to put them to other uses if they thought it good for the state.[2]

[1] *Calendar*, xv. No. 125.
[2] *Ibid.*, No. 747. Mountgrace fell into the king's hands on December 18, 1539. John Wilson was the prior who surrendered it (Rot. Claus., 31 Hen. VIII., Pars. iv. m. 3). He obtained a pension of £60 and the house and chapel called "le Mounte." Sixteen priests, four novices and six lay brethren were also pensioned (R. O. Aug. Off. Misc. Bk., 246, f. 13). In a list of those executed in this reign (Brit. Mus. Add. MS., 27,402, f. 47) occurs the name of "— Wilson, monk of the Charterhouse, Mountgrace." This could not have been the prior, and it hardly appears likely that it could have been his namesake, Nicholas Wilson, who, although "a prisoner in the Tower," was not a monk of Mountgrace. Dr. Nicholas Wilson was a Yorkshire man, and educated at Cambridge. He refused to take the oath of succession, and was sent to the Tower with Sir Thomas More. He finally took the oath, however, and died June 8, 1548. Hall (838) says that he and

It has been possible in this chapter to take notice of only some few points to illustrate the general dissolution of the monasteries in the years 1538-1539. The methods employed by the agents of the king in suppressing these houses of religion may be best understood by the account given of the destruction of Roche abbey by one who was a boy living in the neighbourhood at the time. "In the plucking down of these houses," he writes, "for the most part, this order was taken: that the visitors should come suddenly upon every house unawares . . . to the end to take them 'napping,' as the proverb is, lest if they should have had so much as an inkling of their coming, they would have made conveyance of some portion of their own goods to help themselves withal, when they were turned forth of their houses. And both reason and nature might well have moved them so to have done, although it may be said all was given to the king before by act of parliament, and so they had neither goods nor houses nor possessions.[1] And thus they had to give the king great thanks—yea, pray for him upon their black beads—that was so gracious a prince to them, to suffer them to stay so long after all was given from them. And therefore, if the visitors, being the king's officers and commissioners in that behalf, took their dinner with them and then turned them forth to seek their lodging where they could get it (at night or at the furthest the next day in the morning), as was done indeed, they did no wrong nor truly no great right.

"For so soon as the visitors were entered within the gates they called the abbot and other officers of the house, and caused them to deliver all the keys and took an inventory of all their goods, both within doors and without. For all such beasts, horses, sheep and such cattle as were abroad in pasture or grange places, the visitors caused to be brought into their presence. And when they had done so, (they)

bishop Sampson, with Richard Farmer, a London grocer, were implicated "in relieving of certain traitorous persons which denied the king's supremacy." Richard Hilles (*Ep. Tigurinæ*, p. 140; *Orig. Letters*, Parker Soc., No. 105) says: "The treason they had committed, as I hear, was sending alms to that papist Abel, then brought down to the lowest misery through his long detention in a most filthy prison, and, as the papists say, almost eaten up by worms, vermibus fere necatus."

[1] It is not, of course, accurate to say that parliament had given all houses and goods to the king. It can hardly be expected, however, that the writer should know the niceties of the changing law.

turned the abbot and all his convent and household forth of the doors.

"This thing was not a little grief to the convent and all the servants of the house, departing one from another, and especially such as with their conscience could not break their profession. It would have made a heart of flint melt and weep to have seen the breaking up of the house, the sorrowful departing (of the brethren), and the sudden spoil that fell the same day of their departure from their home. And, every one had everything good, cheap, except the poor monks, friars and nuns who had no money to bestow on anything. This appeared at the suppression of an abbey hard by me, called Roche abbey [1]—a house of White monks, a very fair built house, all of freestone, and every house vaulted with freestone and covered with lead as the (abbeys were in England, as the churches are (now)). At the breaking up of this an uncle of mine was present, being well acquainted with certain of the monks there. And when they were put out of the house, one of the monks, his friend, told him that every one of the convent had given to him his cell in which he lived, wherein was not anything of price, but his bed and apparel, which was but simple and of small price. This monk wished my uncle to buy something of him, who said, 'I see nothing which is worth money for my use.' 'No,' said he, 'give me two shillings for my cell door, which was never made with five shillings.' 'No,' said my uncle, 'I know not what to do with it' (for he was a young man unmarried, and then neither stood in need of houses or doors). But such persons as afterwards bought their corn or hay or such like, finding all the doors either open or the locks and 'shackles' plucked down, or the door itself taken away, went in and took what they found and filched it away.

"Some took the service books that lay in the church and put them upon their wain 'coppes' to piece them; some took windows of the hay-loft and hid them in their hay, and likewise they did of many other things. Some pulled forth

[1] The Cistercian abbey of Roche was surrendered on June 23rd, 1538, by the abbot and seventeen monks (Eighth Rept. Dep. Keeper, App. ii. p. 39). The deed has not been entered on the Close Roll. Henry Crundall, the abbot, was granted a pension of 50 marks, and most of the monks £5 a year (Augt. Off. Misc. Bk., 232, f. 59). A short inventory of the goods found on the dissolution of this priory is given in the *Monasticon*, v. p. 506.

the iron hooks out of the walls that bought none, when the yeomen or gentlemen of the county had bought the timber of the church. The church was the first thing that was put to spoil and then the abbot's lodging, dorter and frater, with the cloister and all the buildings thereabout within the abbey walls. Nothing was spared but the ox-houses and swine-cots and such other houses of office that stood without the walls, which had more favour shown them than the very church itself, which was done by the advice of Crumwell, as Fox reporteth in his book of Acts. It would have pitied any heart to see what tearing up of the lead there was, what plucking up of boards and throwing down of spires. And when the lead was torn off and cast down into the church and the tombs in the church all broken (for in most abbeys were divers noble men and women—yea, in some abbeys kings whose tombs were regarded no more than the tombs of inferior persons—for to what end should they stand when the church over them was not spared for their sakes), all things of price either spoiled, carried away, or defaced to the uttermost.

"The persons who cast the lead into fodders plucked up all the seats in the choir, wherein the monks sat when they said service, which were like to the seats in minsters, and burned them and melted the lead therewith, although there was wood plenty within a flight shot of them, for the abbey stood among woods and rocks of stone. In these rocks were found pewter vessels that were conveyed away and there hidden, so that it seemeth that every person bent himself to filch and spoil what he could. Yea, even such persons were content to spoil them that seemed not two days before to allow their religion and do great worship and reverence at their matins, masses and other services and all other of their doings. This is a strange thing to consider that they who could this day think it to be the house of God, the next (did hold it as) the house of the devil; or else they would not have been so ready to have spoiled it. . . . I demanded, thirty years after the suppression, of my father, who had bought part of the timber of the church, and all the timber of the steeple with the bell frame, with others partners therein—(in the steeple hung eight—yea nine—bells, whereof the least but one could not be bought at this day for £20, and which bells

I myself did see hang there more than a year after the suppression)—whether he thought well of the religious persons and of the religion then used. And he told me 'Yea, for,' said he, 'I saw no cause to the contrary.' 'Well,' said I, 'then how came it to pass you were so ready to destroy and spoil what you thought so well of?' 'Might I not as well as others have some profit from the spoil of the abbey?' said he. 'For I saw all would away, and therefore I did as others did.' . . .

"No doubt there have been millions and millions that have repented the thing since, but all too late. And thus much, upon my knowledge, touching the fall of Roche abbey, which had stood about 300 years, for the church was dedicated by one Ada, bishop of Coventry (A.D. 1244). By the fall of this it may be well known how all the rest were used."[1]

It is, of course, somewhat difficult to estimate the number of monasteries and of religious that were affected by the final suppression. Judged by the lists of surrenders, the grants of pensions and other sources of information, the abbeys and priories, exclusive of convents of women and friaries, which have already been spoken of in previous chapters, as being swept away between the years 1538 and 1540, numbered some two hundred and two. From the same source of information, it would appear that there were living in these houses at the date of suppression about 3221 monks and regular canons. If to these be added 1560 the estimated number of the nuns, 1800 that of the friars, and excluding the nuns, 1500, religious who were turned out of their homes under the act dissolving the lesser houses, it will be seen that as a rough estimate there were in the monasteries some 6521 monks, regular canons and friars, and some 1560 nuns of various orders at the date of the suppression. In round numbers eight thousand religious persons were expelled from their homes at this time, besides probably more than ten times that number of people

[1] Brit. Mus. Add. MS., 5813 (Cole xii.). It is said by Cole to be a copy of an old MS. written about the year 1591, which he had from Thomas Porter, of Nottinghamshire and Cambridge. Ellis, *Orig. Letters*, iii., Series iii., pp. 31-36, has printed the more interesting portions. The editor remarks that the "extracts probably exhibit what was at that time the genuine as well as general feeling of the English public." This document will be again referred to in the concluding chapter.

who were their dependents or otherwise obtained a living in their service.[1]

It would be easy to multiply the incidents, often so significant and touching, which occur in the correspondence of the time in regard to the suppression of this or that great house, the name of which is still held in honour by Englishmen; to relate how prior Goldstone of Christchurch, Canterbury, pleaded to be left to die in his old rooms; how the ruin of St. Edmundsbury broke the heart of abbot Melford; how abbot Malvern, of St. Peter's, Gloucester, unable to avert the doom of his house, could never be brought to sign the fatal surrender. Who shall tell the sorrow that filled the hearts of thousands and thousands of lay people, when they saw the shrines they honoured, the houses of God which had been to them a rest and a delight, profaned, despoiled and brought to destruction?

This chapter in the tale of ruin may be fitly closed in the words of one who deeply felt its sadness and its meaning. What he says of the abbey of St. Peter's, Gloucester, holds good of many another home of piety and religion swept away by the tyrant who, if any, deserves the name "the Ruthless." "Having existed for more than eight centuries under different forms, in poverty and in wealth, in meanness and in magnificence, in misfortune and in success, it finally succumbed to the royal will; the day came, and that a drear winter day, when its last mass was sung, its last censer waved, its last congregation bent in rapt and lowly adoration before the altar there, and doubtless as the

---

[1] The number of monasteries suppressed or surrendered between 1538 and 1540 is thus obtained:—

Benedictine	54 houses and	1,300 monks.
Cluniac	8 houses and	108 monks.
Cistercian	40 (including attainted houses) and	596 monks.
Carthusian	9 houses and	134 monks.
Austin Canons	59 houses and	773 canons.
Premonstratensian	12 houses and	159 canons.
Gilbertine	20 houses and	151 religious.

Houses . 202 Monks and Canons	3,221
Friars according to estimate	1,800
Monks and canons in lesser monasteries	1,500
Nuns according to estimate	1,560
Total	8,081

last tones of that day's evensong died away in the vaulted roof, there were not wanting those who lingered in the solemn stillness of the old massive pile, and who, as the lights disappeared one by one, felt that for them there was now a void which could never be filled, because their old abbey, with its beautiful services, its frequent means of grace, its hospitality to strangers and its loving care for God's poor, had passed away like an early morning dream, and was gone for ever."[1]

[1] *Hist. et Cart. Mon. S. Petri Gloucestriæ* (Chronicles and Mem.), edited by the late W. H. Hart, iii., Introduction, xlix.

CHAPTER XVIII
The Three Benedictine Abbots

THE circumstances attending the fall of Glastonbury, Reading and Colchester are deserving of special record. By the autumn of 1539 Henry's designs upon the monastic property had so far succeeded that comparatively few houses still remained in the possession of their religious owners. County after county was laid desolate by the royal commissioners, and the monks and nuns turned from their homes. Every expedient was resorted to in order to obtain the so-called voluntary surrenders[1] of houses and property into the king's hand, and few, indeed, were found bold enough to withstand the royal methods of persuasion. Where resistance was offered, the ready process of attainder, with its accompanying confiscation of the common goods of a monastic corporation, which, "against every principle of received law,"[2] was held to follow upon the treason, supposed or real, of the superior came to effect what the threats or promises of the royal officials had been unable to accomplish. Some examples of the working of the mysterious law of attainder in bringing about the desired end have been already given. The execution of the three mitred abbots of Glastonbury, Reading and Colchester, and the seizure of the great possessions of these abbeys by virtue of their attainder for treason, are instances of the working of Henry's laws which cannot be passed over.

Few spots in England were counted more sacred than Glastonbury. To the people of pre-reformation days it was a "Roma secunda." The scene, according to mediæval legend, of the burial of St. Joseph of Arimathea and the home of the earliest followers of Christ in this land of

---

[1] "A step of very questionable legality."—Hallam, *Constitutional Hist.* (10th ed.), i. p. 72.
[2] *Ibid.*

Britain, Avalon or Glastonbury had become recognised as the principal sanctuary of the island. Almost alone among the churches of Britain it was spared by the destroying hands of the invaders, and when St. Augustine came from pope St. Gregory to plant the faith, it was already associated with the names of St. Patrick and St. David. For a period St. Paulinus is said to have been at this renowned sanctuary before setting out for the scene of his apostolate in northern England. Rendered more renowned in later times by the fame and virtues of St. Dunstan, the abbey of Glastonbury was the centre of the monastic revival which marked the reign of Edgar the Pacific. With varying fortune but with unbroken life the monastery continued to flourish till, at the close of the year 1539, the venerable Richard Whiting, the last of a long line of abbots, was hanged as a traitor to Henry VIII., and its possessions thus passed into the royal power.

It is, perhaps, difficult to understand fully why abbot Whiting was singled out as an example of the royal severity. It was "probably," writes an historian, "to show forcibly the overpowering character of the royal will by destroying an ecclesiastic of immense moral weight and territorial influence. To adopt the language used ten years before respecting his friend Wolsey, the abbot of Glastonbury was probably considered to be the 'bell-wether' of the mitred abbots, and when he had fallen the others would be without hope and an easy prey."[1]

The position of an abbot of Glastonbury was one of great dignity. The house was one of the largest and richest monasteries in the kingdom, and the church in length was exceeded in England only by that of old St. Paul's. The abbot was a great local magnate, a peer of parliament, and the master of vast estates. Four parks teeming with game, domains and manors of great extent and number, bringing to the monastery an income of more than £3000 a year, or ten times that amount in our money, gave him an influence of the highest importance in the west, and even throughout all England.

What the monastic buildings themselves were can be well imagined. "The house is great, goodly and so princely

---

[1] J. H. Blunt, *History of the Reformation*, p. 345.

as we have not seen the like,"¹ write those sent to seize the possessions for Henry. The library filled Leland with amazement. It was second to none in the land, and he had scarcely passed the threshold when the very sight of so many treasures of antiquity struck him with such awe that for a moment he hesitated to enter. He spent days making a list of the most valuable manuscripts.²

The rule of abbot Whiting over the vast establishment at Glastonbury had to be exercised in very difficult times. Within a few months of his election Sir Thomas Boleyn was created by Henry viscount Rochfort, and this marked the first step in the king's illicit affection for the new peer's daughter, Anne, and the beginning of the troubles of Church and State. Four years of wavering counsels on the great matter of the desired divorce led in 1529 to the humiliation and fall of the hitherto all-powerful cardinal of York.

The sequel is well known. The clergy, caught in the cunningly-contrived snare of premunire, were at the king's mercy. With his hands upon their throats Henry demanded, what in the quarrel with Rome was at the time a retaliation upon the pope for his refusal to accede to the royal wishes, the acknowledgment of the king as supreme head of the Church in England. Few among the English churchmen were found bold enough to resist this direct demand, or who even, perhaps, recognised how they were rejecting papal supremacy in matters spiritual. As a rule, the required oath of royal supremacy was apparently taken wherever it was tendered, and the abbots and monks of Colchester, of Glastonbury, and probably also of Reading, were no exception, and on September 19, 1534, abbot Whiting and his community attached their names to the required declaration.

It is easy, after this lapse of time, and in the light of subsequent events, to be loud in reprobation of such com-

---

¹ *State Papers*, i. p. 620.
² *Cf.* Walcott's *Engl. Minsters*, ii. 129. The antiquary spoke of abbot Whiting as "homo sane candidissimus et amicus meus singularis," "and though," says Warner (*Hist. of Glastonbury*, p. 219) "the too cautious antiquary in after times passed his pen through this language of praise and kindness, lest it should be offensive to his contemporaries, yet happily for the abbot's fame the tribute is still legible and will remain for ages a sufficient evidence of the sacrifice of a guileless victim to the tyranny of a second Ahab."

pliance; to wonder how throughout England bishop Fisher, Sir Thomas More, and the Observants, almost alone, should have been found from the beginning neither to hesitate nor waver. It is easy to make light of the shrinking of flesh and blood, easy to extol the palm of martyrdom. But neither is it difficult to see how to abbot Whiting, no less than to blessed John Houghton and his other holy companions of the Charter House, reasons suggested themselves for temporising. To most men at that date the possibility of the final separation of England from Rome must have seemed incredible. They remembered Henry in his earlier days, when he was never so immersed in business or in pleasure that he did not hear his daily mass; they did not know him as Wolsey and Crumwell, or as More and Fisher knew him; the project must have seemed but a momentary aberration, under the influence of evil passions or of evil counsellors. The king had at bottom a zeal for the faith, and would return by-and-by to a better mind, a truer self, and would then come to terms with the pope. Meantime the oath was susceptible of lenient interpretation. The idea of the headship was not absolutely new: it had in a measure been conceded some years before, without, so far as appears, exciting remonstrance from Rome. Beyond this, to many the oath of royal supremacy of the Church of England was never understood as derogatory to the see of Rome; while even those who had taken this oath were in many instances surprised that it should be construed into any such hostility.[1]

---

[1] *Calendar*, viii. Nos. 277, 387, &c., are instances of the temper of mind described above. No. 387 especially is very significant as showing the *gloss* men put on their supremacy oath, distinguishing tacitly between Church of England and Catholic Church, and "in temporalibus" and "in spiritualibus." It is usually stated that, however unwillingly, Convocation of 1531, in acknowledging the king as *Supreme Head*, allowed him "absolute spiritual jurisdiction and legislative power." A comparison of what Henry demanded from the clergy, and what after a long deliberation in two-and-thirty sessions Convocation granted, makes it absolutely clear that any direct acknowledgment of "spiritual jurisdiction" was avoided by the final vote of the Convocation. Warham in his protest (Wilkins, *Concilia*, iii. p. 746) makes the attitude of the clergy certain, as he maintains that the title *Supremum Caput* had reference to temporal matters only, and must not be twisted in "derogation of the Roman Pontiff or the Apostolic See." Moreover, the very last act of Warham's life was to draft an elaborate exposition to be delivered in the House of Lords of the impossibility of the king having spiritual jurisdiction, from the very constitution of the Church of Christ. The supreme *spiritual* jurisdiction, he

However strained this temper of mind may appear to us at this time, it undoubtedly existed. One example may be here cited. Among the State Papers in the Record Office for the year 1539 is a long harangue on the execution of the three Benedictine abbots in which the writer refers to such a view:—

"I cannot think the contrary [he writes], but the old bishop of London [Stokesley], when he was on live, used the pretty medicine that his fellow, friar Forest, was wont to use, and to work with an inward man and an outward man; that is to say, to speak one thing with their mouth and then another thing with their heart. Surely a very pretty medicine for popish hearts. But it worked madly for some of their parts. Gentle Hugh Cook by his own confession used not the self-same medicine that friar Forest used, but another much like unto it, which was this: what time as the spiritualty were sworn to take the king's grace for the supreme head, immediately next under God of this Church of England, Hugh Cook receiving the same oath added prettily in his own conscience these words following: 'of the temporal church,' saith he, 'but not of the spiritual church.'[1]"

Nor from another point of view is this want of appreciation as to the true foundation of the papal primacy a subject for unmixed astonishment. During the last half-century the popes had reigned in a court of unexampled splendour, but a splendour essentially mundane. It was a dazzling sight, but all this outward show made it difficult to recognize the divinely ordered spiritual prerogatives which are the enduring heritage of the successors of St. Peter. The dignified titles expressing those prerogatives might pass unquestioned in the schools and in common speech in the world, but from this there is a wide step to the apprehension of the living truths they express, and a yet further step to that intense personal realization which makes those truths dearer to a man than life.[2]

---

argues, must of necessity rest with the Pope (see Mrs. Hope's *First Divorce of Henry VIII.*, Introduction, pp. viii–xiv. (where this point is treated fully). Even the later renunciations of the Pope's "usurped jurisdiction" were certainly understood by many to have reference to questions of temporals only.

[1] *Calendar*, xiv. (ii), No. 613.

[2] The words of Cardinal Manning on this point may be here quoted:—
"It must not be forgotten that at this time the minds of men had been so

To some that realization came sooner, to some later; some men there are who seize at once the point at issue and its full import. They are ready with their answer without seeking or faltering. Others answer to the call at the third, maybe the eleventh hour; the cause is the same, and so is the reward, though to the late comer the respite may perhaps have been only a prolongation of the agony.

The royal visitation of Glastonbury was conducted by Layton. He came to the abbey on Saturday, August 21st, 1535; and from St. Augustine's, Bristol, whither he departed on the following Monday, he wrote to Crumwell a letter showing that even he, chief among a crew who "could ask unmoved such questions as no other human being could have imagined or known how to put, who could extract guilt from a stammer, a tremble or a blush, or even from indignant silence as surely as from open confession"[1]— even Layton retired baffled from Glastonbury under the venerable abbot Whiting's rule, though he covered his defeat with impudence unabashed. "At Bruton and Glastonbury," he explains, "there is nothing notable, the brethren be so straight kept that they cannot offend: but fain they would if they might, as they confess, and so the fault is not with them."[2]

---

distracted by the great western schism, by the frequent subtraction of obedience, by the doubtful election of popes, and the simultaneous existence of two or even three claimants to the holy see, that the supreme pontifical authority had become a matter of academical discussion *hinc inde*. Nothing but such preludes could have instigated even Gerson to write on the thesis *de Auferibilitate Papæ*. This throws much light on the singular fact attested by Sir Thomas More in speaking to the jury and the judge by whom he was condemned, when the verdict of death was brought in against him: 'I have, by the grace of God, been always a Catholic, never out of communion with the Roman Pontiff; but I have heard it said at times that the authority of the Roman Pontiff was certainly lawful and to be respected, but still an authority derived from human law, and not standing upon a divine prescription. Then, when I observed that public affairs were so ordered that the sources of the power of the Roman Pontiff would necessarily be examined, I gave myself up to a most diligent examination of that question for the space of seven years, and found that the authority of the Roman Pontiff, which you rashly—I will not use stronger language—have set aside, is not only lawful, to be respected, and necessary, but also grounded on the divine law and prescription. That is my opinion; that is the belief in which, by the grace of God, I shall die.'"— *Dublin Rev.*, Jan. 1888, p. 245.

[1] Dixon, *History*, i. p. 357.
[2] Wright, p. 59. Godwin, the Protestant bishop of Hereford, says that the monks, "following the example of the ancient fathers, lived apart from the world religiously and in peace, eschewing worldly employments, and

At this period it would seem that Richard Layton even spoke to the king in praise of abbot Whiting. For this error of judgment, when some time later Crumwell had assured himself of the abbot's temper, he was forced to sue for pardon from both king and minister. "I must therefore," he writes, "now in this my necessity most humbly beseech your lordship to pardon me for that my folly then committed, as ye have done many times before, and of your goodness to instigate the king's highness majesty in the premises."[1]

The letters of abbot Whiting which still exist, for the most part, answers to applications for benefices or offices in his gift, are marked by a courteous readiness to comply in everything up to the limits of the possible. It is evident, moreover, that he had an intimate concern in all the details of the complex administration of a monastery of such extent and importance, no less than a determining personal influence on the religious character of his community; and that public calls were never allowed to come between him and the primary and immediate duties of the abbot. He is most at home in his own country, among his Somersetshire neighbours, and in the "straight" charge of his spiritual children. Confident too in the affection with which he was regarded by the population, he had no scruples, whatever may have been his mind in subscribing to the Supremacy declaration of 1534, in securing for his monks and his townsfolk in his own abbey church the preaching of a doctrine wholly opposed to the royal theories and wishes on the subject. Thus on a Sunday in the middle of February, 1536, a friar called John Brynstan, preaching in the abbatial church at Glastonbury to the people of the neighbourhood, did not hesitate to declare that "he would be one of them that should convert the new fangles and new men, otherwise he would die in the quarrel."[2]

Knowing doubtless what would be the nature of its wholly given to study and contemplation;" and Sander, writing when the memory of the life led at Glastonbury was still fresh in men's minds, says that the religious were noted for their maintenance of common life, choral observance and enclosure.

[1] *Calendar*, xiv. (ii), No. 185.
[2] *Calendar*, x. No. 318. That the royal supremacy was unpopular does not admit of doubt. Even in 1540 Mr. Gairdner says "it was evidently a trying question for the conscience—a thing opposed by many in principle and disliked by others in its operation, even when the principle was conceded." (*Calendar*, xv., preface, p. xiv.)

business, abbot Whiting, excusing himself on the plea of age and ill-health, did not attend the parliament of 1539, which so far as it could do, sealed the fate of the monasteries as yet unsuppressed. He awaited the end on his own ground and in the midst of his own people. He was still as solicitous about the smallest details of his care as if the glorious abbey were to last *in ævum*. Thus an interesting account of abbot Whiting at Glastonbury is given in an examination about a debt, held some years after the abbot's execution. John Watts, "late monk and chaplain to the abbot," said that John Lyte, the supposed debtor, had paid the money "in manner and form following. That is to say, he paid £10 of the said £40 to the said abbot in the little parlour upon the right hand within the great hall, the Friday after New Year's Day before the said abbot was attainted. The said payment was made in gold " in presence of the witness and only one other: "for it was immediately after the said abbot had dined, so that the abbot's gentlemen and other servants were in the hall at dinner." . . . Also, "upon St. Peter's day at midsummer, being a Sunday, in the garden of the said abbot at Glastonbury, whilst high mass was singing," the debtor "made payment" of the rest. "And at that time the abbot asked of the said master Lyte whether he would set up the said abbot's arms in his new buildings that he had made. And the said master Lyte answered the said abbot that he would; and so at that time the said abbot gave unto the said Mr. Lyte eight angels nobles. . . .

"And at the payment of the £30 there was in the garden at that time the lord Stourton. . . . I suppose," continues the witness, "that the said lord Stourton saw not the payment made to the abbot, for the abbot got him into an arbour of bay in the said garden and there received his money. And very glad he was at that time that it was paid in gold for the short telling, as also he would not, by his will, have it seen at that time."[1] Thus too almost the last glimpse afforded of the last abbot of Glastonbury in his

---

[1] R. O. Exch. Augt. Off. Misc. Bk., xxii., Nos. 13-18. In view of the circumstance of the time, it seems likely that the witness was anxious to ward off any possibility of lord Stourton being mixed up in the affair. This anxiety to save friends from embarrassing examinations is a very common feature in documents of this date.

time-honoured home shows him in friendly converse with his near neighbour, lord Stourton, the head of an ancient race which popular tradition had justly linked for centuries with the Benedictine order, and which even in the darkest days of modern English Catholicity proved itself a firm and hereditary friend.[1]

To understand the closing acts of the venerable abbot's life it is necessary to premise a few words on suppression in its legal aspect. Many writers have assumed that the monasteries were really dissolved by parliament, and that accordingly an unwillingness to surrender, however morally justifiable as a refusal to betray a trust, and even heroic when resistance entailed the last penalty, was an act in defiance of the law of the land. And in this particular case of Glastonbury, it has been suggested that in insisting on its surrender the king was only requiring that to be given up into his hands which parliament had already conferred on him. However common the impression, it is not accurate. What the act (27 Hen. VIII., cap. 28) of February, 1536, did, was to give to the king and his heirs only such monasteries as were under the yearly value of £200, or such as should within a "year next after the making of" the act "be given or granted to his majesty by any abbot," &c. So far, therefore, from giving to the king the goods of all the monasteries, the act distinctly recognises, at least in the case of all save the lesser ones, the rights of their present owners, and contemplates their passing to the king's hands only by the voluntary cession of the actual possessors. How these surrenders were to be brought about was left to the king and Crumwell, and the minions on whose devices there is no further need to dwell. Before a recalcitrant superior, who would yield neither to blandishment bribery nor threats, the king, so far as the act would help him, was powerless.

For this case, however, provision was made, though but indirectly, in the act of April, 1539 (31 Hen. VIII., cap. 13). This measure, which included a retrospective clause covering the illegal suppression of the greater monasteries, grants to him all monasteries, &c., &c., which shall hereafter happen to be dissolved, suppressed, renounced, relinquished, for-

---

[1] For the first may be seen Hoare's *Modern Wiltshire*. The evidence of the second is written in the domestic annals of my own house of St. Gregory's.

feited, given up or come into the king's highness. These terms seem wide enough, but there is an ominous parenthesis referring to such others as "shall happen to come to the king's highness by attainder or attainders of treason." The clause did not find its way into the act unawares. We shall see it was Crumwell's care how and in whose case it was to become operative. And with just so much of countenance as is thus given by parliament with the monasteries of Glastonbury, Reading and Colchester, from which no surrender could be obtained, " were, against every principle of received law, held to fall by the attainder of their abbots for high treason."[1]

The very existence of the clause is, moreover, evidence that by this time Crumwell knew that among the superiors of the few monasteries yet standing there were men with whom, if the king was not to be baulked of his intent, the last conclusions would have to be tried. To him the necessity would have been paramount, by every means in his power, to sweep away what he rightly regarded as the strongholds of the papal power in the country, and to get rid of these "spies of the pope."[2] Such unnatural enemies of their prince and gracious lord would fittingly be singled out first, that their fate might serve as a warning to other intending evil-doers. Perhaps, too, Whiting's repute for blamelessness of life, the discipline which he was known to maintain in his monastery and his great territorial influence may all have gone to point him out as an eminently proper subject to proceed against, as showing that where the crime of resistance to the king's will was concerned there could be no such thing as an extenuating circumstance, no consideration which could mitigate the penalty.

In the story of what follows we are continually hampered by the singularly defective nature of the various records relating to the closing years of Crumwell's administration. This holds good in particular with regard to the three Benedictine abbots who suffered in 1539. We are, therefore, frequently left to supply links by conjectures, but conjectures in which, from the broad facts of the case, and such documentary evidence as remains, there is sufficient assurance of being in the main correct.

[1] Hallam, *Constit. Hist.*, i. 72.   [2] R. O. Crum. Corr., xv. No. 7.

It was in the autumn that final steps began to be taken in regard to the monastery of Glastonbury and its venerable abbot. Among Crumwell's "remembrances" of things to do, or to speak to the king about, still extant in his own handwriting, occurs the following about the beginning of September this year: "Item. For proceeding against the abbots of Reading, Glaston and the other in their countries."[1] From this it is clear that some time between the passing of the act in April, and September, these abbots must have been sounded, and it had been found that compliance was not to be expected.[2] By the sixteenth of this latter month Crumwell's design had been communicated to his familiar Layton, and had elicited from him a reply in which he abjectly asks pardon for having praised the abbot at the time of the visitation. "The abbot of Glastonbury," he adds, "appeareth neither then nor now to have known God, nor his prince nor any part of a good Christian man's religion."[3] Three days later, on Friday, September 19, the royal commissioners, Layton, Pollard and Moyle, suddenly arrived at Glastonbury about ten o'clock in the morning. The abbot had not been warned of their intended visit, and was then at his grange of Sharpham, about a mile from the monastery. Thither they hurried "without delay," and after telling him their purpose, at once examined him "upon certain articles, and for that his answer was not then to our purpose, we advised him to call to his remembrance that which he had forgotten, and so declare the truth."[4] They at once took him back to the abbey, and when night came

---

[1] Brit. Mus. Cott. MS. Titus, B. i. f. 446a.

[2] At this time Glastonbury, in common with other churches in England, was relieved of what it pleased the king to consider "superfluous plate." Pollard, Tregonwell and Petre on May 2nd, 1539, handed to Sir John Williams, the keeper of the royal treasure-house, 493 ounces of gold, 16,000 ounces of gilt plate, and 28,700 ounces of parcel gilt and silver plate taken from the monasteries in the west of England. In this amount was included the superfluous plate of Glastonbury. Besides this weight of gold and silver there was placed in the treasury "two collets of gold wherein standeth two coarse emeralds; a cross of silver gilt, garnished with a great coarse emerald two 'balaces' and two sapphires lacking a knob at one of the ends of the same cross; a superaltar garnished with silver gilt and part gold called the great sapphire of Glastonbury; a great piece of unicorn's horn, a piece of mother of pearl like a shell, eight branches of coral" (*Monastic Treasures*, Abbotsford Club, p. 24).

[3] The whole of this account is from the letter of the commissioners to Crumwell, in Wright, p. 255.

[4] Wright, p. 255.

on proceeded to search his papers, and ransack his apartments "for letters and books, and found in his study, secretly laid, as well a written book of arguments against the divorce of the king's majesty and the lady dowager, which we take to be a great matter, as also divers pardons, copies of bulls, and the counterfeit life of Thomas Becket in print; but we could not find any letter that was material."

Furnished with these pieces of evidence as to the tendency of Whiting's opinions, the inquisitors proceeded further to examine him concerning the "articles we received from your lordship" (Crumwell). In his answers appeared, as they considered, "his cankered and traitorous mind against the king's majesty and his succession." To these replies he signed his name, "and so with as fair words as" they could, "being but a very weak man and sickly," they forthwith sent him up to London to the Tower, that Crumwell might examine him again.

A week later, on September 28,[1] they again write to Crumwell that they "have daily found and tried out both money and plate," hidden in secret places in the abbey, and conveyed for safety to the country. They could not tell him how much they had so far discovered, but it was sufficient, they thought, to have "begun a new abbey," and they conclude by asking what the king will have done in respect to the two monks who were the treasurers of the church, and the two lay clerks of the sacristy, who were chiefly to be held responsible for the hidden plate.

Again on the 2nd of October the inquisitors write to their master to say that they have come to the knowledge of "divers and sundry treasons" committed by abbot Whiting, "the certainty whereof shall appear unto your lordship in a book herein enclosed, with the accusers' names put to the same, which we think to be very high and rank treasons." The original letter, preserved in the Record Office, clearly shows by the creases in the soiled yellow paper that some small book or folded papers have been enclosed. Whatever it was, it is no longer forthcoming, and, as far as can be ascertained, is lost or destroyed. Just at the critical moment we are deprived, therefore, of the most interesting source of information. In view, how-

[1] Wright, p. 257.

ever, of the common sufferings of these abbots, who were dealt with together, their common cause, the common fate which befell them, and the common reason assigned by contemporary writers for their death—viz., their attainder "of high treason for denying the king to be supreme head of the Church," as Hall, the contemporary London lawyer, phrases it, there can be little doubt that these depositions were much of the same nature as those made against Thomas Marshall, abbot of Colchester, to which subsequent reference will be made. It is quite certain that with abbot Whiting in the Tower and with Crumwell's commissioners engaged in "dispatching" the monks "with as much celerity" as possible, Glastonbury was already regarded as part of the royal possessions. Even before any condemnation whatsoever the matter is taken as settled, and on October 24th, 1539, Pollard handed over to the royal treasurer the riches still left at the abbey as among the possessions of "attainted persons and places."[1]

Whilst Layton and his fellows were rummaging at Glastonbury, abbot Whiting was safely lodged in the Tower of London. There he was subjected to searching examinations. A note in Crumwell's own hand, entered in his "remembrances," says: "Item. Certain persons to be sent to the Tower for the further examination of the abbot of Glaston."[2]

It is more than strange that the ordinary procedure was in this case never carried out. According to all law, Whiting and the abbots of Reading and Colchester should have been arraigned for treason before parliament, as they were members of the House of Peers, but no such "bill of attainder" was ever presented, and in fact the execution had taken place before the parliament came together.[3]

---

[1] *Monastic Treasures*, (Abbotsford Club), p. 38. These consisted of 71 ozs. of gold with stones, 7214 ozs. of gilt plate, and 6387 ozs. of silver.
[2] Brit. Mus. Cott. MS. Titus, B. i. f. 441 *a*.
[3] According to Wriothesley's *Chronicle*, they were arraigned in the "Counter." "Also in this month [November] the abbates of Glastonburie, Reding and Colchester were arrayned in the Counter." Mr. Gairdner (*Calendar*, xiv. (ii), preface, p. xxxii) says :—The "account or 'book' of his treasons unfortunately seems to be lost, and the nature of the charges on which Abbot Whiting was condemned can only be a matter of speculation. The book found in his study against the king's divorce and the printed life of Becket had been, of course, the justification of his committal to the Tower. But at first it was supposed that he was to be tried in Parliament, which had been

The truth is, that Whiting and the other abbots were condemned to death as the result of the secret inquisitions in the Tower. Crumwell, acting as "prosecutor, judge and jury,"[1] had arranged for their execution before they left their prison. What happened in the case of Whiting at Wells, and of Cook at Reading, was a ghastly mockery of justice, enacted merely to cover the illegal and iniquitous proceedings which had practically condemned them untried. This Crumwell has written down with his own hand. He notes in his "remembrances:"—

"Item. Councillors to give evidence against the abbot of Glaston, Richard Pollard, Lewis Forstell and Thomas Moyle. Item. To see that the evidence be *well sorted* and the indictments *well drawn* against the said abbots and their accomplices. Item. How the king's learned counsel shall be with me all this day,[2] for the full conclusion of the indictments."

prorogued in June to 3rd November. It was known, however, to the French ambassador, on the 25th October, that there would be a further prorogation till after the arrival of Anne of Cleves—in fact, till the 14th January—and the trial of the abbot, as he very naturally presumed, would not take place till then. The King and Cromwell, however, had more summary proceedings in view."

[1] Froude, *Hist.*, iii. p. 432.

[2] In curious agreement with the care of Crumwell in devoting the whole of one of his precious days to the final settlement of the indictment against the abbots, is the solicitude of his panegyrist Burnet (from whom, be it said, in fact though unwittingly, even Catholics have derived their ideas of so many men and events of the Reformation period) to "discover the impudence of Sanders" in his relation in the matter of the abbots' suffering for denying the king's supremacy, and to prove that they did not. It would take up too much space here to expose the mingled "impudence" and fraud of his own account of the matter. It may suffice to quote Collier on this point : " What the particulars were (of the abbots' attainder) our learned Church historian (Burnet) confesses 'he can't tell; for the record of their attainders is lost.' But, as he goes on, ' some of our own writers (Hall, Grafton) deserve a severe censure, who write it was for denying, &c., the king's supremacy. Whereas if they had not undertaken to write the history without any information at all, they must have seen that the whole clergy, and especially the abbots, had over and over again acknowledged the king's supremacy.' But how does it appear our historians are mistaken ? Has this gentleman seen the abbot of Colchester's indictment or perused his record of attainder ? He confesses no. How then is his censure made good? He offers no argument beyond conjecture. He concludes the abbot of Colchester had formerly acknowledged the king's supremacy, and from thence infers he could not suffer now for denying it. But do not people's opinions alter sometimes, and conscience and courage improve? Did not bishop Fisher and cardinal Pool, at least as this author represents them, acknowledge the king's supremacy at first? and yet 'tis certain they afterwards showed themselves of another mind to a very remarkable degree. . . . Farther, does not himself tell us that many of the Carthusians were executed for their open denying the king's supremacy [which it may be added they had previously admitted], and why then might not some of the abbots have the same

And then, to sum up all:—

"Item. The abbot of Glaston to be *tried* at Glaston, and *also executed* there."[1]

But amidst these cares Crumwell never forgot the king's business, the "great matter," the end which this iniquity was to compass. With the prize now fairly within his grasp, he notes:—

"The plate of Glastonbury, 11,000 ounces and over, besides golden. The furniture of the house of Glaston. In ready money from Glaston, £1100 and over. The rich copes from Glaston. The whole year's revenue of Glaston. The debts of Glaston, £2000 and above."[2]

The circumstances of Whiting's last journey homeward must now be told. In face of documentary evidence of unquestionable authenticity it is impossible to credit many of the oft-repeated statements in the second and subsequent editions of Sander's *Schism*.[3] They seem to be of a traditionary character, to embody the gossip of the countryside current half a century later; in some points running near enough to the truth, in others partaking of legend; such as the sensational scene, wanting alike in sense and probability, in the hall of the palace on the abbot's arrival at Wells; the assembly prepared to receive him, his proceeding to take the place of honour among the first, the unexpected summons to stand down and answer to the charge of treason, the old man's wondering inquiry what this meant, the whispered assurance that it was all a matter of form to

---

belief and fortitude with others of their fraternity?"—*Eccl. Hist.*, ii. 173. Hence, counter to Burnet's method of making abbot Whiting suffer for "burglary" and imaginary treasonable connection with the Pilgrimage of Grace, Collier asserts " neither bribery nor terror nor any other dishonourable motives could prevail " with the abbots of Colchester, Reading and Glastonbury. "To reach them, therefore, another way, the oath of supremacy was offered them, and upon their refusal they were condemned for high treason" (p. 164). A letter written to Bullinger early in 1540 says: "The two abbots of Glastonbury and Reading have been condemned for treason and quartered, and each of them is now rotting on a gibbet near his abbey gate" (*Orig. Letters*, Parker Soc., 627). A second letter from Oxford at this same time (*Ibid.*, 614) says the three abbots were executed because they "had secreted property and conspired to restore popery."

[1] Brit. Mus. Cott. MS. Titus B. i. f. 441.   [2] *Ibid.*, f. 446 a.
[3] The original edition of Sander simply says that the three abbots and the two priests, Rugg and Onion, "ob negatam Henrici pontificiam potestatem martyrii coronam adepti sunt." In the second and later editions this is cut out, another reason is assigned for their death, and an obviously legendary narrative about Whiting is inserted in the text.

strike terror—into whom or wherefore the story does not tell.

If it is hard to believe that Henry and Crumwell could amuse themselves by ordering the enactment of such a farce, it is more difficult still to conceive of Whiting as the unsuspecting victim of it. As we have seen under Crumwell's hand, his fate was already settled before he left the Tower. In the interrogatories, preliminary but decisive, he had there undergone, the abbot had come face to face with the bare duty imposed on him by conscience at last. He must himself have known to what end the way through the Tower had, from the time of More and Fisher to his own hour, led those who had no other satisfaction to give the king than that which he could offer. It is not impossible, however, that hopes may have been held out to him that in his extreme old age and weakness of body he might be spared extremities; this supposition seems to be countenanced by the account given below. Is the suggestion too horrible that Henry may have remembered Wolsey's [1] end, and have reflected that the death of the abbot in similar circumstances, before the last penalty was paid to his law, would render useless the pains taken to make a terrible example?

Some two months after the venerable abbot had been conveyed to London, he was brought back on his homeward journey. He reached Wells on November 14, where there awaited him (Russell is warranty for the fact) "as worshipful a jury as was charged here these many years. And there was never seen in these parts so great an appearance as were here at this present time, and never better willing to serve the king." [2] Besides the care taken over the indictments, every caution had been evidently adopted to make all secure on the spot. The duty of the jury at Wells was marked out in their charge; they might refuse to take the part assigned to them at their peril. No words are wasted over the sentence. Russell, in his report to Crumwell, does not so much as even mention it: "The abbot of Glastonbury was arraigned, and the next day put to execution, with

[1] Wolsey died in the end of fright. Dr. Brewer writes: "His despondency and waning health anticipated the sword of the executioner, and disappointed the malice of his enemies" (Introd. *Cal. Letters and Papers*, vol. iv. p. 613).

[2] Russell to Crumwell, Wright, p. 260. The similarity of the language here used by Russell and that of Norfolk about the northern jury should be noted.

two other of his monks, for the robbing of Glastonbury church."¹

On this "next day" (November 15, 1539) the aged abbot was taken in his horse-litter to Glastonbury.² In his case there was no mercy, no pity. The venerable man, who in a long life had passed through obedience and through honours alike blameless, now bowed under the weight of eighty years, was tied on a hurdle like a common felon and dragged to the top of Tor hill, where, with John Thorn and Roger James, two of his monks, he was handed over to the executioner.

Even here he was not allowed to die in peace. With the ghastly apparatus around—the gallows, the boiling cauldron, the butcher's knife—Pollard pestered him yet once more with "divers articles and interrogatories;" but "he could accuse no man but himself of any offence against the king's highness, nor he would confess no more gold nor silver, nor any other thing more than he did before your lordship in the Tower." Then "he asked God mercy and the king for his great offences towards his highness. And thereupon took his death very patiently and his head and body (are) bestowed in like manner as I certified your lordship in my last letter."³

"One quarter standeth at Wells," writes Russell on the following day, November 16, 1539, "another at Bath, and at Ilchester and Bridgewater the rest; and his head upon the abbey gate at Glaston"—an example, as a scribbler in Henry's service has put it, "of the rewards and ends of traitors, whereby subjects and servants might learn to know their faithful obedience unto their most dread sovereign lord the king's highness."⁴

The history of the fall of Reading abbey and the execu-

---

¹ Hearne, the antiquary, stated of Whiting that "to reach him the oath was offered to him at Wells," and that refusing it, he had the "courage to maintain his conscience and run the last extremity" (*Hist. of Glast.*, p. 50). These are the words of Collier, ii. p. 164. The "offering" the oath at Wells is probably a misunderstanding on the part of Hearne.

² The editor of Sander, consistent throughout, writes: "Glasconiam dimissus est, nihil minus tamen cogitans quam tam celerem sibi vitæ exitum." A priest approaches to hear his confession; he prays to be spared for a day or two to prepare for death, and to be allowed to say good-bye to his monks; he sheds tears, &c. The authentic report of Pollard is here followed in preference to his narrative.

³ Wright, p. 261.   ⁴ *Ibid.*, p. 260.

tion of Hugh Cook or Faringdon, the abbot, is in its main features but a repetition of the story of Glastonbury and abbot Whiting. If we may credit the account of his origin given by a contemporary, abbot Cook appears to have been born in humble circumstances. He thus apostrophises the abbot after his fall: "Ah Hugh Cook, Hugh Cook! nay Hugh Scullion rather I may him call that would be so unthankful to so merciful a prince, so unkind to so loving a king and so traitorous to so true an emperor. The king's highness of his charity took Hugh Cook out of his cankerous cloister and made him, being at that time the most vilest, the most untowardest and the most miserablest monk that was in the monastery of Reading, born to nought else but to an old pair of beggarly boots, and made him, I say ruler and governor of three thousand marks by the year."[1] But the testimony of the writer on a point of fact such as this cannot be rated high.

It is probable that abbot Cook belonged to that class from which the English monastic houses were so largely recruited, "the devouter and younger children of our nobility and gentry, who here had their education and livelihood."[2] His election to the office of abbot took place in 1520, and although Grafton and Hall in their chronicles, and some other writers of the Reformation, give him the character of an illiterate person, "the contrary will appear to such as will consult his *Epistles to the University of Oxford* remaining in the register of that university, or shall have an opportunity of perusing a book entitled *The art or craft of Rhetorick*, written by Leonard Cox, schoolmaster of Reading. 'Twas printed in the year 1524, and is dedicated by the

---

[1] *Calendar*, xiv. (ii), No. 613. This long harangue seems to have been prepared for delivery or publication soon after the execution of the three abbots. Its purport is first to justify their condemnation on the ground that by their loyalty to the Holy See they had been guilty of treason, and secondly to bring them and their fellow-sufferers by all means into contempt. As it is the chief document about the abbots, and in particular about the abbot of Reading, which is known to exist, considerable use is here made of it. It is clearly the composition of some tool of Crumwell, probably of some antipapal preacher.

[2] Bodleian MS. Wood, B. vi. Woodhope's "Book of Obits." It has been considered doubtful whether the name of the last abbot of Reading was Cook or Faringdon. He is sometimes called by one, sometimes by the other name. In the entry of his conviction for treason upon the Controlment Roll, usually very exact, he is called only by the name of "Cooke."

author to this abbot. . . . He speaks very worthily and honourably of Faringdon on account of his learning."¹

According to the writer of the contemporary document before quoted, abbot Cook "could not abide" the preachers of the new-fangled doctrines then in vogue, and "called them heretics and knaves of the new learning." He was also "ever a great student and setter forth of St. Benet's, St. Francis', St. Dominic's and St. Augustine's rules, and said they were rules right holy and of great perfectness." In fact, "these doughty deacons," as the writer calls the abbots and their companions, "thought it both heresy and treason to God to leave matins unsaid, to speak loud in the cloisters and to eat eggs on the Friday."²

On the question of the royal supremacy abbot Cook was equally clear. "He thought to shoot at the king's supremacy," as the contemporary witness has put it, and he was apparently charged with saying "that he would pray for the pope's holiness as long as he lived and would once a week say mass for him, trusting that by such good prayers the pope should rise again and have the king's highness with all the whole realm in subjection as he hath had in time past. And upon a *bon voyage* would call him pope as long as he lived."³

It would appear, however, probable that abbot Cook did not refuse to take the oath of royal supremacy,⁴ although

---

¹ Browne Willis, *Mitred Abbeys*, i. 161. For Leonard Cox consult *Dict. of National Biography*, xii. 136. Among the abbots, priests, monks and nuns whose names appear on the roll of the Palmers' Guild of Ludlow is that of " Hugh Farington, monk, now abbot of Reading."—*Shrewsbury Archæological Soc.*, vii. p. 97. ² *Calendar*, xiv. (ii), No. 613.

³ *Ibid.* After a page of abuse, the writer continues: "I cannot tell how this prayer will be allowed among St. Benet's rules, but this I am certain and sure of, that it standeth flatly against our Master, Christ's, rule. . . . What other thing should the abbat pray for here (as methinketh), but even first and foremost for the high dishonouring of Almighty God, for the confusion of our most dread sovereign lord, king Henry VIII., with his royal successors, and also for the utter destruction of this most noble realm of England. Well, I say no more, but I pray God heartily that the mass be not abused in the like sort of a great many more in England which bear as fair faces under their black cowls and bald crowns as ever did the abbat of Reading, or any of the other traitors. I wiss neither the abbat of Reading, the abbat of Glassenbury, nor the prior [*sic*] of Colchester, Dr. Holyman, nor Roger London, John Rugg, nor Bachelor Giles, blind Moore, nor Master Manchester, the warden of the friars; no, nor yet John Oynyon, the abbat's chief councillor, was able to prove with all their sophistical arguments that the mass was ordained for any such intent or purpose as the abbat of Reading used it."

⁴ No actual record exists of this oath, as in the case of Glastonbury, Colchester, &c.

there can be little doubt that in so doing he did not intend to separate himself from the traditional teaching of the Catholic Church on the question of papal authority. "I fear me," writes the authority so often quoted, "Hugh Cook was master Cook to a great many of that blackguard (I mean black monks), and taught them to dress such gross dishes as he was always wont to dress, that is to say, treason; but let them all take heed."[1]

At the time of the great northern rising, the abbey of Reading, together with those of Glastonbury and Colchester, is found on the list of contributors to the king's expenses in defeating the rebel forces. Reading itself appears to have had some communication with Robert Aske, for copies of a letter written by him, and apparently also his proclamation, were circulated in the town. Amongst others who were supposed to be privy to the intentions of the insurgent chief was John Eynon, a priest of the church of St. Giles', Reading, and a special friend of abbot Cook. Three years later this priest was executed with the abbot, but at the time it is clear that there was no suggestion of any complicity on the part of Cook, as he presided at the examinations held in December, 1536, as to this matter.[2]

The first sign of any serious trouble appears about the close of 1537. The king's proceedings, which were distasteful to the nation at large, naturally gave rise to much criticism and murmuring. Every overt expression of disapprobation was eagerly watched for and diligently inquired into by the royal officials. The numerous records of examinations as to words spoken in conversation or in sermons are evidence of the extreme care taken by the government to crush out the first sparks of popular dis-

---

[1] *Calendar*, xiv. (ii), No. 613. The following bears on the same point: "But like as of late by God's purveyance a great part of their religious hoods be already meetly well ripped from their crafty coats, even so I hope the residue of the like religion shall in like sort not long remain unripped, for truly so long as they be let run at riot thus still in religion they think verily that they may play the traitors by authority. . . . But now his grace seeth well enough that all was not gold that glistered, neither all his true subjects that called him lord and master, namely, of Balaam's asses, with the bald crowns. But I would now heartily wish that as many as be of that traitorous religion [*i.e.*, order] that those abbats were of, at the next [assizes?] have their bald crowns as well shaven as theirs were." This testimony to the steadfastness of the Benedictines to the Holy See fully corroborates Collier's statement given above.

[2] *Calendar*, xi. 1231.

content. Rumours as to the king's bad health, or, still more, reports as to his death, were construed into indications of a treasonable disposition. In December, 1537, a report that Henry was dead reached Reading, and abbot Cook wrote to some of his neighbours to tell them what was said. This act, so natural in itself, was laid to his charge, and Henry acquired a cheap reputation for magnanimity and clemency by pardoning "his own abbot" for what, at the very worst, at all times save during this reign of terror, would have been but a trifling act of indiscretion.[1]

Circumstances had brought abbot Cook into communication with both the abbots whose fate was subsequently linked with his own. In the triennial general chapters of the Benedictines, in parliament, in convocation, they had frequently met; and when the more active measures of persecution devised by Crumwell made personal intercourse impossible, a trusty agent was found in the person of a blind harper named Moore, whose affliction and musical skill had even brought him under the kindly notice of the king. This staunch friend of the papal party, whose blindness rendered his mission unsuspected, apparently travelled about from one abbey to another, encouraging the imprisoned monks, bearing letters from house to house, and, doubtless, finding a safe way of sending off to Rome the letters which they had written to the pope and cardinals.

"But now amongst them all let us talk a word or two of William Moor, the blind harper. Who would have thought that he would have consented or concealed any treason against the king's majesty? or who could have thought that he had had any power thereto? Who can muse or marvel enough to see a blind man for lack of sight to grope after treason? Oh! Moor, Moor, hadst thou so great a delight and desire to play the traitor? Is this the mark that blind men trust to hit perchance? Hast thou not

[1] *Calendar*, xiv. (ii), No. 613. This paper thus treats the incident:—
"For think ye that the abbat of Reading deserved any less than to be hanged, what time as he wrote letters of the king's death unto divers gentlemen in Berkshire, considering in what a queasy case the realm stood in at that same season? For the insurrection that was in the north country was scarcely yet thoroughly quieted; thus began he to stir the coals *à novo* and to make a fresh roasting fire, and did enough, if God had not stretched forth his helping hand, to set the realm in as great an uproar as ever it was, and yet the king's majesty, of his royal clemency, forgave him. This had been enough to have made this traitor a true man if there had been any grace in him."

heard how the blind eateth many a fly? Couldst not thou beware and have kept thy mouth close together for fear of gnats? Hath God endued thee with the excellency of harping and with other good qualities to put unto such a vile use? Couldst thou have passed the time with none other song but with the harping upon the string of treason? Couldst thou not have considered that the king's grace called thee from the wallet and the staff to the state of a gentleman? Wast thou also learned, and couldst thou not consider that the end of treason is eternal damnation? Couldst thou not be contented truly to serve thy sovereign lord king Henry VIII., whom thou before a great many oughtest and wast most bound truly to serve? Couldst not thou at least for all the benefits received at his grace's hand, bear towards him thy good will? Hadst thou nought else to do but to become a traitorous messenger between abbat and abbat? Had not the traitorous abbats picked out a pretty mad messenger of such a blind buzzard as thou art? Could I blazon thine arms sufficiently although I would say more than I have said? Could a man paint thee out in thy colours any otherwise than traitors ought to be painted? Shall I call thee William Moor, the blind harper? Nay, verily, thou shalt be called William Moor, the blind traitor. Now, surely, in my judgment, God did a gracious deed what time He put out both thine eyes, for what a traitor by all likelihood wouldst thou have been if God had lent thee thy sight, seeing thou wast so willing to grope blindfolded after treason! When thou becamest a traitorous messenger between the traitorous abbats, and when thou tookest in hand to lead traitors in the trade of treason, then was verified the sentence of our Master, Christ, which sayeth, When the blind lead the blind both shall fall into the ditch. Thou wast blind in thine eyes, and they were blind in their consciences. Wherefore ye be all fallen into the ditch, that is to say, into the high displeasure of God and the king. I wiss, Moor, thou wrestest thine harpstrings clean out of tune and settest thine harp a note too high when thou thoughtest to set the bawdy bishop of Rome above the king's majesty."[1]

[1] *Calendar*, p. 25. "William Moore" appears in a list of prisoners in the Tower, 20th November, 1539 (Brit. Mus. Cott. MS. Titus, B. i. f. 133). The list, as far as Reading names are concerned, runs :—" Roger London, monk

Abbot Cook, like Whiting of Glastonbury, underwent examination and practical condemnation in the Tower before being sent down to his "country to be tried and executed." What was the head and chief of his offence we may take from the testimony of the same hostile witness so freely invoked in this chapter.

"It will make many beware to put their fingers in the fire any more," he says, "either for the honour of Peter and Paul or for the right of the Roman Church. No, not for the pardon of the . . . pope himself, though he would grant more pardon than all the popes that ever were have granted. I think, verily, our mother, holy Church of Rome, hath not so great a jewel of her own darling Reynold Poole as she should have had of these abbats if they could have conveyed all things cleanly. Could not our English abbats be contented with English forked caps but must look after Romish cardinal hats also? Could they not be contented with the plain fashion of England but must counterfeit the crafty cardinality of Reynold Poole? Surely they should have worn their cardinal hats with as much shame as that papistical traitor, Reynold Poole. . . . Could not our popish abbats beware of Reynold Poole, of that bottomless whirlpool, I say, which is never satiate of treason?"

From such scanty evidence as may be gathered from these passages, one or two things are made clear. First, that the abbots of Glastonbury, Reading and Colchester were singled out for execution because of their loyalty to the Holy See and their influence with their brethren; secondly, that the venerable Hugh Cook was conspicuous for his devotion to the vicar of Christ, and, spite of Henry's favour and spite of his threats, would never in his heart accept the king's supremacy, but week by week would offer the holy sacrifice on behalf of the bishop of Rome, and call him pope till his dying day.

of Reading; Peter Lawrence, who was warden of (the) Grey friars, Reading; Gyles Coventry, who was a friar of the same house; George Constantine; Richard Manchester; William Moor, the blind harper." In one of Crumwell's "remembrances" at this time we have "Item to proceed against the abbots of Reading, Glaston, Rugg, Bachyler, London, the Grey friars and Heron" (R. O. State Papers, Dom., 1539, $\frac{7}{551}$). Perhaps Moor is the same person mentioned by Stowe (ed. 1614, p. 582): "The 1 of July (1540) a Welchman, a minstrel, was hanged and quartered for singing of songs which were interpreted to be prophecying against the king."

When carried down to Reading for the mockery of justice called a trial, the abbot did not waver in his determination. "When these traitors were arraigned at the bar, although they had confessed before and written it with their own hands that they had committed high treason against the king's majesty, yet they found all the means they could to go about to try themselves true men, which was impossible to bring to pass."

On November 15th, the same day upon which abbot Whiting suffered at Glastonbury,[1] the abbot of Reading and two priests were brought out to suffer the death of traitors. Abbot Cook, standing in the space before the gateway of his abbey, spoke to the people, who, in great numbers, had gathered to witness the strange spectacle of the execution of a lord abbot of the great and powerful monastery of Reading. He told them of the cause for which he and his companions were to die, not fearing openly to profess that which Henry's laws made it treason to hold—fidelity to the see of Rome, which he declared was but the common faith of those who had the best right to know what was the true teaching of the English Church. "The abbot of Reading," says the old authority, "at the day of his death, lamenting the miserable end that he was come unto, confessed before a great sight of people, and said that he might thank these four privy traitors before named of his sore fall, as who should say that those three bishops and the vicar of Croydon had committed no less treason than he had done. Now, good Lord for his Passion, who would have thought that these four holy men would have wrought in their lifetime such detestable treason?" And later on, speaking of the three abbots: "God caused, I say, not only their treason to be disclosed and come abroad in such a wonderful sort as never was heard of, which were too long to recite at this time, but also dead men's treason that long lay hidden under the ground; that is to say, the treason of the old bishop of Canterbury [Warham], the treason of the old bishop of St. Asaph

---

[1] Some give November 14th as the date of the execution. Browne-Willis says: "Hugh Faringdon, opposing the surrender of this abbey at the dissolution, *an.* 1539, and also refusing to attest the king's supremacy, became attainted of high treason," and was executed "at Reading, November 14, 1539, at which time two of his monks, Rugg and Onion, suffered with him." *Vide* also *Monasticon*, vol. iv.; Holinshed (ed. 1586), iii. p. 948. Some authorities make abbot Whiting's execution the 14th (Brit. Mus. Add. MS., 27,402, f. 47).

[Standish], the treason of the old vicar of Croydon, and the treason of the old bishop of London [Stokesley], which four traitors had concealed as much treason by their live's time as any of these traitors that were put to death. There was never a barrel better herring to choose [among] them all, as it right well appeared by the abbat of Reading's confession made at the day of [execution], who I daresay accused none of them for malice nor hatred. For the abbot as heartily loved those holy fathers as ever he loved any men in his life."

The abbot's "chief counsellor," John Eynon or Oynyon,[1] who had been particularly vehement in his protestations of innocence, also spoke, admitting his so-called treason, begging the prayers of the bystanders for his soul, and craving the king's forgiveness if in aught he had offended.[2] This over, the sentence of hanging with its barbarous accessories was carried out upon abbot Cook and the two priests, John Eynon and John Rugg.[3]

[1] The usual spelling of this name has been Onyon or Oynyon, but it really was Eynon. It is so spelt in the document already referred to (*Calendar*, xi. No. 1231), and also in the accurate entry of the conviction to be found on the Controlment Roll, 31 Hen. VIII., m. 28 d.: "Recordum attinctionis, &c., Hugonis abbatis monasterii de Redyng in dict. com. Berks. alias dicti Hugonis Cooke, nuper de Redyng in eodem com. Berks. clerici; Johannis Eynon nuper de Redyng in com. pred. clerici; Johannis Rugge nuper de Redyng in com. Berks. clerici alias dict. Johannis Rugge nuper de Redyng capellani pro quibusdam altis proditionibus unde eorum quilibet p. se. indict. fuit. T. et S."

[2] Of John Eynon the hostile witness writes that he not only denied the charge of treason, "but also stoutly and stubbornly withstood it even to the utmost, evermore finding great fault with justice, and oftentimes casting his arms abroad, said: 'Alas, is this justice to destroy a man guiltless? I take it between God and my soul that I am as clear in this matter as the child that was this night born.' Thus he prated and made a work as though he had not known what the matter had meant, thinking to have faced it out with a card of ten. And in this sort he held on even from the time of the arraignment till he came to the gallows. Marry then, when he saw none other way but one, his heart began somewhat to relent. Then both he and his companions, with their ropes about their necks, confessed before all the people that were present that they had committed high treason against the king's most noble person, but namely Oynyon, for he said that he had offended the king's grace in such sort of treason that it was not expedient to tell thereof. Wherefore he besought the people not only to pray unto God for him, but also desired them, or some of them at the least, to desire the king's grace of his merciful goodness to forgive his soul, for else he was sure, as he said, to be damned. And yet not an hour before a man that had heard him speak would have thought verily that he had been guiltless of treason."

[3] Eynon was, as before stated, a priest attached to the church of St. Giles, Reading. John Rugg had formerly held a prebend at Chichester, but had apparently retired to Reading. In December, 1531 (*Calendar*, v.), Rugg

The attainder of the abbot, according to the royal interpretation of the law, placed the abbey of Reading and its lands and possessions at Henry's disposal. In fact, as in the case of Glastonbury, on the removal of the abbot to the Tower in September, 1539, before either trial or condemnation, the pillage of the abbey had been commenced. As early as September 8th, Thomas Moyle wrote from Reading that he, "master Vachell and Mr. Dean of York" (Layton), had "been through the inventory of the plate, &c., at the residence" there. "In the house," he said, "there is a chamber hanged with three pieces of metely good tapestry. It will serve well for hanging a mean little chamber in the king's majesty's house." This is all they think worth keeping for the royal use. "There is also," the writer adds, "a chamber hung with six pieces of verdure with fountains, but it is old, and at the ends of some of them very foul and greasy." He notes several beds with silk hangings, and in the church eight pieces of tapestry, "very goodly" but small, and concludes by saying that he and his fellows think that the sum of £200 a year "will serve for pensions for the monks."[1]

On September 15th another commissioner, Richard Pollard, wrote from Reading that he had dispatched certain goods according to Crumwell's direction, "and part of the stuff reserved for the king's majesty's use." "The whole house and church" are, he says, still "undefaced," and "as for the plate,[2] vestments, copes and hangings, which we

writes for his books to be sent to Reading from Chichester. Another letter, dated Feb. 3, 1532, from "your abbey-lover Jo. Rugg" shows that the writer had obtained dispensation for non-residence at Chichester. Coates (*History of Reading*, p. 261), on the authority of Croke, says that John Rugg was indicted for saying "the king's highness cannot be Supreme Head of the Church of England." On being asked, "what did you for saving your conscience when you were sworn to take the king for Supreme Head?" Rugg replied, "I added this condition in my mind, to take him for Supreme Head in temporal things, but not in spiritual things."

[1] *Calendar*, xiv. (ii), No. 136. In the "Corporation diary," quoted in Coates' *Reading*, p. 261, is the entry "before which said nineteenth of September (1539), the monastery is suppressed and the abbot is deprived, and after this suppression all things remain in the king's hands." Mr. Gairdner (*Calendar*, xiv. (ii), preface, p. xxx) says :—"The abbot, in all probability declined to give up his monastery. Just a year before . . . Dr. London . . . gave it distinctly as his opinion that while both the abbot and monks professed to be entirely at the King's command, they would be very loth to surrender."

[2] In Pollard's account of the plate of "attainted persons and places" (*Monastic Treasures*, Abbotsford Club, p. 38) Reading is credited with 19½

have reserved also to the use of the king's majesty," they are left in good custody and are to be conveyed to London. "Thanks be to God," he adds, "everything is well finished, and every man well contented and giveth humble thanks to the king's grace."[1]

The abbot of St. John's, Colchester, Thomas Marshall,[2] writes Browne Willis, "was one of the three mitred parliamentary abbots ... that had courage enough to maintain his conscience and run the last extremity, being neither to be prevailed upon by bribery, terror or any dishonourable motives to come into a surrender, or subscribe to the king's supremacy; on which account, being attainted of high treason, he suffered death."

Thomas Marshall succeeded abbot Barton in June, 1533, and entered upon the cares of office at a time when religious life was becoming almost impossible. At the outset he had apparently considerable difficulty in obtaining possession of the temporalities of his abbey. "I, with the whole consent of my brethren," he writes to Crumwell, "have sealed four several obligations for the payment of £200 to the king's

---

ozs. of gold, 377 ozs. of gilt plate and 2660 of silver. It is also stated that the abbot put "to gage to Sir W. Luke three gilt bowls of 152 ozs. and six silver bowls of 246 ozs."

[1] Wright, 220. Mr. Wright thinks this letter "must refer to the priory and not to the abbey." A letter from William Penison, to whom Pollard says he committed the charge "by indenture," says that on September 11th he "received possession of Mr. Pollard and other commissioners here (Reading, September 21) of the abbey of Reading and all the domains which the late abbot had in his hands at his late going away" (*Calendar*, xiv. (ii), No. 202). This leaves no doubt that the letter printed by Wright refers to the *abbey*, and that the property was seized early in September. According to Penison's information, abbot Cook was "*late*" abbot—in other words, had ceased to hold the office when he was taken to the Tower for the so-called examination. Penison, it may be added, made Crumwell a rich present to obtain the office of receiver, and had informed him that abbot Cook was getting rid of the monastic property.

[2] It has already been pointed out that Thomas Marshall was also called Beche. It may be worth while, as some confusion has existed as to the last abbot of Colchester, to give here the evidence of the Controlment Roll, 31 Hen. VIII., m. 36d., which leaves no room to doubt that Beche and Marshall are *aliases* for the same individual. "Recordum attinctionis Thomæ Beche nuper de West Donylands, in com. Essex, clerici, alias dicti Thomæ Marshall nuper de eisdem villa et comit., clerici, alias Thomæ Beche nuper abbatis nuper monasterii S. Johannis Bapt. juxta Colcestr., in com. pred. jam dissolut, alias dicti Thomæ Marshall nuper abb. nuper mon. S. Johis. Colcestr. in com. pred. pro quibusdam altis proditionibus." West Donylands was a manor belonging to the abbot, and the name occurs in exchanges made by the abbot with chancellor Audley in 1536 (see *Calendar*, xi. Nos. 385, 519).

use ... trusting now by your especial favour to have restitution of my temporalities with all other things pertaining to the same. ... Unless I have your especial favour and aid in recovering such rents and dues as are withdrawn from the monastery of late, and I not able to recover them by the law, I cannot tell how I shall live in the world, saving my truth and promises."[1]

Of the earlier career of Thomas Marshall little is known except that he, like the majority of his order in England, who were selected by their superiors for a university course, was sent to Oxford, where he resided for several years, and passed through the schools with credit to himself and his order. During this period he was probably an inmate of St. Benedict's or Gloucester Hall, the largest of the three establishments which the Benedictines possessed in Oxford, and to which the younger religious of most of the English abbeys were sent to pursue their higher studies.[2]

Very shortly after abbot Marshall's election his troubles commenced. At Colchester, as elsewhere in the country at this period, there were to be found some only too anxious to win favour to themselves by carrying reports of the doings and sayings of their brethren to Crumwell or the king. In April, 1534, a monk of St. John's complained of the "slanderous and presumptious" sayings of the subprior, "D. John Francis." This latter monk, according to Crumwell's informer, had "declared our sovereign lord the king and his most honourable council, on the occasion of a new book of articles, to be all heretics, whereas before he said

---

[1] R. O. Crum. Corr., vi. f. 145. The temporalities were restored on Jan. 23, 1534, and on March 30th of this same year the new abbot took his seat in the House of Lords. It has been thought that Marshall is the same Thomas Marshall who ruled the abbey of Chester until 1530, and is counted as the 26th abbot of that house (*Monasticon*, iv., Browne Willis, &c.). Whether, on his retirement from Chester in favour of the reinstated abbot, John Birchenshaw, he went to Colchester, is uncertain. If he had been long at this latter monastery it is somewhat strange that the witnesses against him in 1539 should have professed to be unacquainted with him until his election.

[2] St. Benedict's is now represented by Worcester College; Canterbury Hall, destined for the monks of the metropolitan church, is now merged in Christ Church; and Trinity College has succeeded to St. Cuthbert's Hall, the learned home of the monks of Durham. D. Thomas Marshall, O.S.B., supplicated for B.D. January 24, 150$\frac{8}{9}$; disputed 3rd June, 1511; admitted to oppose 19th Oct.; received the degree of S.T.B. 10th Dec.; sued for D.D. and disputed 20th April, 1515. (Boase, *Register of the University of Oxford*, p. 63.)

they were but schismatics." These and other remarks were quite sufficient to have brought both the bold monk himself and his abbot into trouble at a time when the gossip of the frater or shaving-house was picked up by eavesdroppers and carried to court to regale the ears of the lord Privy Seal. In this case, however, the report came on the eve of the administration to the monks of Colchester of what was to be henceforth considered the touchstone of loyalty, the oath of supremacy. On the 7th of July, 1534, the oath was offered to the monks in the chapter-house of St. John's, and taken by abbot Marshall and sixteen monks, including this John Francis, the subprior complained of to Crumwell.

Very little indeed is known about Colchester or the doings of the abbot from this time till his arrest in 1539. At the time of the northern rising, whilst the commissioners for gaol delivery sat at Colchester, they were invited to dine at the abbey with the abbot of St. John's. When they were at dinner, as Crumwell's informant writes to him, one Marmaduke Nevell and others came into the hall. I asked him, says the writer, "How do the traitors in the north?" "No traitors, for if ye call us traitors we will call you heretics." Nevell then went on to say that the king had pardoned them, or they had not been at Colchester. They were, he declared, 30,000 well-horsed, and "I am sure," he said, "my lord abbot will make me good cheer;" and asked why, said, "Marry, for all the abbeys in England be beholden to us, for we have set up all the abbeys again in our country, and though it were never so late they sang mattins the same night." He added that in the north they were "plain fellows," and southern men, though they "thought as much, durst not utter it."[1]

About the time of the arrest of the abbots of Reading and Glastonbury, in September, 1539, reports were spread as to the approaching dissolution of St. John's, Colchester. Sir Thomas Audley, the chancellor, endeavoured to avert what he thought would be an evil thing for the county. He had heard the rumours about the destruction of the two abbeys of St. John's, Colchester, and St. Osyth's, and, writing to Crumwell, he begs they may continue, "not, as they be, religious; but that the king's majesty of his good-

[1] *Calendar*, xi. No. 1319.

ness to translate them into colleges. . . . For the which, as I said to you before, his grace may have of either of them £1000, that is for both £2000, and the gift of the deans and prebendaries at his own pleasure. The cause I move this is, first, I consider that St. John's standeth in his grace's own town at Colchester, wherein dwell many poor people, who have daily relief of the house. Another cause, both these houses be in the end of the shire of Essex, where little hospitality will be kept if these be dissolved. For as for St. John's, it lacketh water, and St. Osith's standeth in the marshes, not very wholesome, so that few of reputation, as I think, will keep continual houses in any of them unless it be a congregation as there is now. There are also twenty houses, great and small, dissolved in the shire of Essex already." Audley then goes on to protest that he only asks for the common good, and can get no advantage himself by the houses being allowed to continue, and concludes by offering Crumwell £200 for himself if he can persuade the king to grant his request.[1]

The circumstances attending abbot Marshall's arrest are unknown, but by the beginning of November, 1539, he was certainly in the Tower. On the 1st of that month Edmund Trowman, who had been his servant ever since he had been abbot, was under examination. All that was apparently extracted from this witness was that, a year before, the abbot had given him certain plate to take care of and "£40 in a coser."[2]

The abbot's chaplain was also interrogated as to any words he had heard the abbot speak against the king at any time, but little information was elicited from him. The most important piece of evidence is a document which, as it contains declarations as to abbot Marshall's opinions upon several important matters, and as it is almost the only record of the examinations of witnesses against any of the three abbots, may here be given as nearly as possible in the original form.

[1] Wright, p. 246.
[2] *Calendar*, xiv. (ii), No. 439. In a curious list, giving apparently the dates of the supposed acts of treason committed by various people, is the entry: "Thos. Marshall abbas de Colchester. 17 die Septembris anno. 30°" (1538). The date of abbot Whiting's treason is given as "4th August a° 27°" (1535), and abbot Cook's as "1 March anno. 27°" (1536). See R. O. Exch. Augt. Off. Misc. Bk., 313 *b*, f. 8.

"Interrogatories ministered unto Robert Rowse, mercer, of Colchester, 4^(to) Novembris anno regni Henrici octavi tricesimo primo (1539). Ad primam, the said Rowse sworne upon the Evangel, and sayeth that he hath known the abbat of Colchester the space of six years at midsummer last past or thereabout, about which time the said —— was elected abbat.[1] And within a sennight after or thereabout this examinant sent unto the said abbat a dish of bass (baces) and a pottle of wine to the welcome. Upon the which present the said abbat did send for the examinant to dine with him upon a Friday, at which time they were first acquainted, and since was divers times in his company and familiar with him unto a fortnight before the feast of All Hallows was two years past.—ROBERT ROWSE.

"2. Ad secundam, he sayeth that the principal cause why that he did leave the company of the said abbat was because *Supremacy.* that abbat was divers times communing and respuing against the king's majesty's supremacy and such ordinances as were passed by the act of parliament concerning the extinguishment of the bishop of Rome's usurped *The whole authority committed to Peter.* authority, saying that the whole authority was given by Christ unto Peter and to his successors, bishops of Rome, to bind and to loose, and to grant pardons for sin, and to be chief and supreme head of the Church throughout all Christian realms immediate and next unto Christ, and that it was against God's commandment *Against the supremacy.* and His laws that any temporal prince should be head of the Church. And also he said that the king's highness had evil counsel that moved him to take on hand to be chief head of the Church of England, and to pull down these houses of religion which were founded by his grace's progenitors and many noble men for the service and honour of God, the commonwealth, and relief of poor folk, *Against man's law and God's law.* and that the same was both against God's law and man's law; and, furthermore, he said that by means of the premises (?) the king and his council were drawn into such an inordinate covetousness that *Covetous.* *A vengeance.* if all the water in the Thames were flowing gold and silver it were not able to slake their covetousness, and said a vengeance of all such councillors.—ROBERT ROWSE.

[1] D. Thomas Marshall or Beche was elected June 10, 1533.

"3. Ad tertiam, he sayeth that he is not well remembered of the year nor of the days that the said abbat had the foresaid communications, because he spoke at divers times, and specially at such times as he heard that any such matters were had in use; and furthermore of this he is well remembered of that at such time as the monks of Sion, the bishop of Rochester, and Sir Thomas More were put to execution, the said abbat would say that he marvelled greatly of such tyranny as was used by the king and his council to put such holy men to death, and further the abbat said that in his opinion they died holy martyrs and in the right of Christ's Church.— ROBERT ROWSE. Tyranny.
Died martyrs.

"4. Ad quartam, he sayeth that the last time that ever he heard the said abbat have any communication of such matters was immediately after that he heard of the insurrection in the north parts, he sent for this examinant to come to sup with him, and in the mean time that supper was making ready the abbat and the examinant were walking between the hall and the garden in a little gallery off the ground, and then and there the abbat axed of this examinant what news he heard of the coast? and this examinant said that he heard none. Then the abbat said: 'Dost you not hear of the insurrection in the North?' and this examinant said 'no.' 'The northern lads be up and they begin to take pip in the webe (*sic*) and say plainly that they will have no more abbeys suppressed in their country;' and he said to this examinant that the northern men were as true subjects unto the king as anywhere within his realm, and that they desired nothing of the king but that they might have delivered unto their hands the archbishop of Canterbury, the lord chancellor, and the lord privy seal; and the abbat said 'would to God that the northern men had them, for then (he said) we should have a merry world, for they were three arch-heretics,' which term this examinant never heard before; and so then they went to supper, and since this time, which was as this examinant doth remember a fortnight or three weeks before the feast of All Saints was two years.—ROBERT ROWSE."[1] Northern men.
That these lords might be delivered to the northern men.
Arch-heretics.

---

[1] *Calendar*, xiv. (ii), No. 458. The marginal notes, copied from the original document, indicate the chief points on which the examination turned.

The evidence of Thomas Nuthake, a "physition," of Colchester, is to the like effect. He had not, he said, to his knowledge seen or known abbot Thomas before his election, although he had divers times repaired to the abbey before that time. In reply to the third question, this doctor "sayeth that concerning the marriage of queen Anne this examinant remembers he hath heard the said abbat say that the reason why the king's highness did forsake the bishop of Rome was to the intent that his majesty might be divorced from the lady dowager and wed queen Anne, and therefore his grace refused to take the bishop of Rome for the supreme head of the Church, and made himself the supreme head."[1]

Another of the witnesses against the abbot of Colchester was a cleric, John Seyn, who deposed that when he had informed him of the abbot of St. Osyth's surrender of his monastery to the king, answered "I will not say the king shall never have *my* house, but it will be against my will and against my heart, for I know by my learning that he cannot take it by right and law, wherefore in my conscience I cannot be content, nor he shall never have it with my heart and will." Whereunto John Seyn, clerk, answered in this wise: "Beware of such learning as ye learned at Oxenford when ye were young. Ye would be hanged and ye are worthy. I will advise you to conform yourself as a true subject, or else you shall hinder your brethren and also yourself."[2]

Little more is known of abbot Marshall's last days but the fact of his execution on December 1st, 1539. The story of his sudden arrest and instant execution, as told by the Colchester historian, looks improbable.[3] Even if true, the abbot's journey to London, his examinations, his imprisonment in the Tower,[4] and the various measures taken with his servants[5] must have quite prepared him for the

---

[1] *Calendar*, xiv.(ii), No. 454.   [2] R. O. Crum. Corr., xxxviii. No. 41.
[3] *Monasticon*, iv. 605. "Morant says there was a tradition in his time in the town of Colchester that the magistrates invited abbot Beche to a feast and then showed him the warrant, and went and hanged him without further warrant or ceremony."
[4] His name appears in the list of prisoners, Brit. Mus. Cott. MS. Tit., B. i. f. 133.
[5] *Calendar*, xiv. (ii), No. 416, is "an account of money paid by Dr. Belassis unto the late servants of the abbat of St. John's besides Colchester, as well for their charges and horsemeat since they came to London, as for the arrearages of their wages and the king's majesty's reward bestowed upon them."

fate awaiting those who resisted the will of Henry. Under the stress of imprisonment in the Tower, and the examinations to which he was there subjected, abbot Marshall's courage appears somewhat to have failed him for a time. His replies to interrogatories addressed to him were mainly directed to explain away the accusations which, as we have seen, had been made against him and to turn away if possible the royal wrath.[1] His excuses, however, as we know, were made in vain, and in the end he, like the abbots of Glastonbury and Reading, laid down his life for conscience sake.

As in the case of Glastonbury and Reading, the abbot's imprisonment was the signal for commencing the pillage of church and monastery. By November 19th, 1539, the plate, consisting of 15 ounces of gold, 672 of silver gilt, and 1557 ounces of parcel gilt or silver had been sent by the king's receivers into the royal treasury, together with a couple of mitres and "a crozier staff" of gilt plate and iron.[2] Within six weeks of the execution of the abbot, the monastic buildings of St. John's with the abbey church, which had been consecrated nearly 450 years before, were dismantled. It took four men under the charge of one who designates himself " Francis Jobson, gentleman," eight days to strip the lead from the roof and melt it into pigs. The account of the expenses incurred in the process proves that they lived on the fat of the land whilst engaged on this work of desolation. At the end of the week the broken bell metal was packed in barrels and carted away to be sold.[3]

The landed property of the abbey was granted to Thomas, lord Darcy, whose family became extinct in the fourth generation. In the first two centuries no fewer than nine families and fifteen individuals had become the possessors of the abbey spoils by inheritance or purchase. History does not relate what became of the " many poor people " who dwelt " at Colchester," of whom chancellor Audley wrote that they " had daily relief of the house."

It is necessary to revert once more to the singular mystery which surrounds the fate of these abbots. Suddenly the *Baga de secretis*, which affords information as to earlier " treasons," fails. In vain has search been made through

[1] *Calendar*, xiv. (ii), No. 459.
[2] *Monastic Treasures* (Abbotsford Club), p. 27.
[3] R. O. Exch. Q. R. Suppression Papers, $\frac{832}{22}$.

books, rolls of legal proceedings and detached papers of the date of their execution and subsequent years. The records in the country do not begin at such an early date, and saving the possibility of further revelations from the archives at Woburn, this chapter contains all that can be found on the subject. From these gleanings the reader may form his own conclusion.

The execution of these three powerful abbots was well-nigh the last act in the drama of the Suppression. "Each of them now rotting on a gibbet near his abbey gate," as a contemporary wrote to a friend abroad, no doubt echoed the terror inspired by the fate of those who had dared to stand out against the royal will. So, as Mr. Gairdner writes:—"Of course, these examples did not encourage resistance, and surrenders of monasteries now came with a rush."[1] And before the year 1539 came to a close, with the exception of Westminster and one or two houses in the country, not a single monastery had been left "undefaced."

---

[1] *Calendar*, xiv. (ii), preface, p. xxxvii.

CHAPTER XIX

The Monastic Spoils

IT is by no means easy to determine with anything like accuracy the value of the property which passed into the royal possession by Henry's ecclesiastical depredations. The annual revenue of the various houses, including lands and the proceeds from the spiritual benefices held by them, is reckoned by Speed at £171,312, 4s. 3¼d. Other valuations place it at a somewhat higher figure, so that a modern calculation of £200,000, in round numbers, as the annual receipts of the confiscated property does not appear to be excessive.[1] Hence the fall of the monasteries transferred an income of more than two million pounds sterling a year of the present money value from the Church and poor to the royal purse.

It is well, however, to state at once that Henry did not derive by any means so large a benefit as this from his policy of spoliation. Gratuitous grants, sales of lands at nominal prices, and other ways whereby the capital value of the prize was diminished, prevented the income actually received by the royal treasury from reaching at any time the sum at which the revenue of the monastic houses was computed. In fact, the entire amount paid by the royal receivers into the Court of Augmentation as representing the revenue derived from the confiscated estates was only £415,005, 6s. 10½d. for the eleven years between Michaelmas, 1536, and the same date in 1547. That is to say, merely an average yearly income of £37,000 was secured to the king by the seizure of Church property which had formerly produced at least five times that sum. Further, in no single year did the income exceed £45,000, although for five years, from 1539 to 1544, the average approached that figure. In

---

[1] Blunt, *History*, p. 369.

other words, the king actually obtained by his confiscations an average yearly revenue only slightly exceeding the estimated income of the smaller houses.[1]

During this period, however, the crown obtained a large sum by the sale of the monastic lands, ecclesiastical benefices and other property from which the religious houses derived their income. The papers of the period contain ample evidence of the eagerness with which the hungry courtiers sought to profit by the destruction of the time-honoured monastic corporations. Much of the property, no doubt, the crown officials parted with unwillingly. But it was necessary to make the strong ones of the nation sharers of the plunder, that thus committed to the policy, they might resist any future cry for restitution. Other lands were quickly exchanged with noble landowners and even churchmen for the same reason, and much was sold to lords, merchant venturers and speculators at good prices. "Thus," says an old writer, "was the Church pared and pruned and made a prey, every bird being desirous to beautify herself with her fair feathers."

A veritable scramble followed the dissolution, and very rapidly a vast amount of land changed hands. Many obtained grants or purchased the Church property only to exchange or sell it again at an enhanced price. Some special supporters of Henry's policy secured large shares for themselves and their families through their own or Crumwell's influence. Thus, to take but one or two examples, lord Audley obtained as his part of the plunder the possessions of more than nine religious foundations;

---

[1] The figures are taken from the accounts of the treasurer of the Court of Augmentation (R. O. Aug. Off. Treas. Rolls, i. to iv.). As the yearly receipts from the confiscated lands may be of interest they are here given:—

	£	s.	d.
From April 24th, 1536, to September 29th, 1538, including certain receipts for goods sold which cannot be ascertained and deducted . . .	27,732	2	9¾
From 1538 to 1539	24,223	7	2¾
From 1539 to 1543	177,806	7	3¾
From 1543 to 1544	44,945	2	11½
From 1544 to 1547	140,298	6	6¾
Total for 11 years	£415,005	6	10¼

Edward, lord Clinton, secured twelve, including the rich lands of the Benedictine abbey of Barking; the duke of Northumberland became master of eighteen, while Suffolk was the successful spoiler of no less than thirty monastic properties. The net result to the royal exchequer of Henry's traffic in these Church lands was after all only £855,751, 18s. 5d.[1] This sum, equivalent to more than eight and a half millions sterling of the present money, although large in itself, can by no means represent the real value of the property disposed of by the king. There are certain indications that for some of the lands fair prices, equal to twenty years' purchase of the rents, were given to the king. Thus Sir Richard Gresham, father of the more celebrated Sir Thomas, wrote to Crumwell, "to be advertised" that he had "moved the king's majesty to purchase of his grace certain lands belonging to the house of Fountains, to the value of £350 by year, after the rate of twenty years' purchase. The sum of money," he adds, "amounteth to £7000."[2] This amount apparently he subsequently paid, as at one time he is credited with £11,137, 11s. 8d. in discharge of what was owing for the lands of Fountains, together with those of the two Benedictine nunneries of Swine and Nunkeling.[3]

Other purchasers, however, must certainly have obtained their share of the plunder at very much lower rates. Thus Crumwell's nephew, Richard Williams, apparently paid under £5000 for Ramsey abbey and its entire property, which was sold to him on March 4th, 1540, while the income of the monastery was returned at more than £1700 a year. Lord Crumwell himself, to take but one more instance, paid but £1446, 10s. for Launde priory with its revenue of £400 a

---

[1] The largest sales of lands took place in the year from Michaelmas, 1544, to Michaelmas, 1545, when the sum of £164,495, 1s. 5d. was realized. The sales include certain lands of attainted persons, such as the countess of Salisbury, Sir Stephen Hammerton, &c. In this year John Ap Rice bought the priory of St. Guthlac's, Hereford, for £1570, 1s. 9d. (R. O. Exch. Augt. Off. Treas. Rolls, ii., mm. 8d. to 28d.).

[2] Ellis, *Orig. Letters*, 3rd Ser. iii. 270. On this basis Blunt (p. 371) calculates the capital value of the income which came into the king's hands at £48,000,000. For a very considerable proportion, however, as the actual figures prove, Henry really only obtained about a sixth part of that sum.

[3] R. O. Exch. Aug. Off. Treas. Roll., ii. m. 100d. Whether the sum was actually paid in cash seems somewhat doubtful. The king had large transactions with Gresham. At one time he owed him for silks nearly £800, and a note in the accounts makes it appear probable that this and other debts were set off against Fountains Abbey.

year.[1] But notwithstanding the easy terms upon which much of monastic land was granted, the royal agents experienced considerable difficulty in obtaining the promised payments. No less a sum than £76,141, 8s. 3d. was due to the crown on this account when Henry died.

It would be impossible within the limits of an ordinary book to follow in detail the dispersion of the Church lands among the band of royal retainers, who all hungered and clamoured for a share in the booty. Little by little the broad acres and ecclesiastical benefices, upon the revenues of which not only had the religious themselves subsisted, but which had served to assist the poor, the aged and the sick of the country, and to further other public and national purposes, passed into private hands. Without the confiscation having contributed in any substantial way to the advantage of the country or crown, the property passed from the control of the State unburdened by any condition of service to the commonwealth or the particular district, which had hitherto characterised its tenure. Compared with the revenue derived by the religious establishments from their endowments and with the capital value of their property as estimated from that income, the net result of the suppression of the monasteries to the nation at large was from a financial point of view cruelly disappointing. For a brief period the royal revenue was augmented; but the income derived by the king from the confiscated lands at no time approached what the same estates produced under the thrifty management of their monastic owners. The sale of the acres obtained a large sum of money for the royal purse, but even this was small when compared with their intrinsic worth, or with what their real value was to the nation at large.

Those who reaped advantage from the work of desolation, from the overthrow of so many architectural monuments and destruction of almost countless works of art, from the seizure of lands bestowed upon the monks for purposes ecclesiastical and patriotic, were the "new men." To them good came from the hardships and misery inflicted upon hundreds of religious men and women and their retainers. They mounted into power and place upon the ruins of the old monastic houses, and laid the foundation of their family

[1] R. O. Exch. Aug. Off. Treas. Roll, ii. m. 11.

fortunes upon wealth filched in the name of the law from the patrimony of the poor.

From the consideration of the value of the monastic lands, which thus came into the royal possession, it is necessary to turn to the work of the royal agents in effecting the transfer of the estates and other property from the religious to the king. The story of the dismantling and destruction of so many sanctuaries and houses of religion in every part of the kingdom presents many points of pathetic interest. Some of these have been touched upon in previous chapters, and the present pages must be occupied principally with cold calculations about pecuniary results.

The method adopted by Henry to realize the moveables and other saleable effects of the monasteries was apparently much the same in every case. In each of eleven monasteries included in one commission, for example, a district jury was impanelled to witness the valuation, and a retinue of "strangers" from London travelled with the chief commissioner.[1] The costs of these men engaged upon the work of gathering in the spoils were considerable, and include such items as "minstrels 4d." and evening "wine and sugar 2s." It is pleasing to find in the accounts indications that the people of a neighbourhood were not too ready to assist in the work of demolition. In the above account twenty pence had to be paid for "a guide from Repton to Gracediew," while the demand for help in the case of the destruction of the church at Lewes, previously noticed, would seem to show that it was at any rate sometimes necessary to bring hardened ruffians from London to accomplish such work.[2]

As was almost inevitable in a work of this nature, the king by no means received the value of things sold or seized. From Crumwell downwards the officials appear to have looked well after their own interest[3] at this time. To

[1] R. O. Exch. Augt. Off. Misc. Bk., 172. Printed by Mackenzie E. Walcott, *Archæologia*, vol. xliii. pp. 201-249.

[2] Stow relates (*Survey of London*, p. 58) that "the church and steeple" of the priory of Holy Trinity, in the ward of Aldgate, "were proffered to whomsoever would take it down and carry it from the ground, but no man would undertake the offer." Stukeley, speaking of Glastonbury (*Itinerarium Curiosum*, ed. 1776, Iter. vi.), says, "I observed frequent instances of the townsmen being generally afraid to make such purchases (of stone from the ruins), as thinking an unlucky fate attends the family where these materials are used, and they told me many stories and particular instances of it."

[3] For an indication of Crumwell's share in this general scramble, see *ante*.

2 C

adopt the expression used by Dr. London whilst engaged in the work of taking over plate and jewels and expelling monks and nuns, it was indeed "a pretty bank,"[1] not only to the king, but to all lucky enough to be employed in such a service. Even such a man as Rich, chancellor of the Court of Augmentation, was not free from suspicion. An early writer states that had Henry lived a day or two longer he would certainly have brought this minister to justice;[2] and there is documentary evidence to prove that the king charged this official with allowing him to be cheated out of £570 a year in the exchanges of land made with the duke of Suffolk, as well as with having received money for the sales of lands and lead without accounting for it.[3]

Sir Ralph Sadler, to give but another instance, was gravely compromised in the same way. "At his first coming from Scotland of the insurrection of Yorkshire," runs the record of a subsequent examination, one Oswald Sisson, "perceiving then that many abbeys in Yorkshire would be surrendered, willed and procured the said Sir Ralph to ask of the king's majesty the preferment of the monastery of Selby . . . before the surrender thereof and promised to give to the said Sir Ralph Sadler for a fine for a lease of 21 years £100 in money and a horse, which he afterwards did." Sadler took the money and horse and granted the lease before the surrender of the monastery and before obtaining the grant from the king. Subsequently, when he had got the monastery from Henry, he offered it to Sisson at a profit of £110 more than he had agreed to pay. Sisson paid the money, and in his turn went into Yorkshire, where he "marked certain woods," intending to pay Sadler with the proceeds and to make more by the granting of other leases. Falling ill, he sold the lands of Selby to the royal receiver of the district, Leonard Beckwith, for £1240.[4]

[1] Wright, p. 235.
[2] Brit. Mus. Arund. MS. 152, in the contemporary collections for the lives of Fisher and More.
[3] R. O. Exch. Q. R. Ancient Misc., $\frac{7 \cdot 2}{4 \cdot 3}$.
[4] R. O. Exch. Augt. Off. Misc. Bk., 113, No. 31. In two other documents (Nos. 86 and 99) of the same volume a series of charges are laid against this Leonard Beckwith. He had sold lead and other things to his relations at less than their value. He had returned a false survey of the woods at Selby, making them less than half their real extent. Before the dissolution of monasteries he had endeavoured to get annuities from them, promising "if the houses did stand that he would not take so much as they did grant." In

The Monastic Spoils

"By the frauds of the officials of the Court of Augmentation, to whom was committed the gathering in of the great spoils," writes a contemporary, "the king was robbed. This much is certain, that a great number of men who when appointed to the office were possessed only of inkhorn and pen, were after two years able to rank in wealth and estates with 'the highest in the land.'"[1]

What was done in the case of lands and false surveys was more easily accomplished with regard to the plate and other precious moveables of the dissolved monasteries. An interesting example of the private purses made by the commissioners is afforded in the case of Thomas Bedyll.[2] He died apparently early in September, 1537, and thus before he had such opportunities of obtaining plunder as others had. Still he had apparently not neglected his chances; and Crumwell's nephew, Richard, who had been sent to seize what he could find, wrote: "Before my coming to Mr. Bedyll's house in Aldersgate Street, London, his woman had sent thither two of his servants . . . who had ransacked and conveyed this night, so that nothing but bedding, books and such other there remain." Having heard, however, that he was acquainted with Raynes,[3] "I came to the said John Raynes and declared to him that my coming was to see such money, plate and jewels as Mr. Bedyll had left in his custody. He forthwith confessed that he had a 'gardiviance' (ambry) of his, and brought out the same to me, wherein is such plate and gold as your lordship by a bill of particulars herein enclosed may perceive." It is now, the writer adds, in the custody of "Williamson at your place by friar Augustines."[4]

this way he procured no less than 23 patents from the religious, all dated in 1538 or 1539. These and other charges were examined into, and many were acknowledged by Beckwith himself.

[1] Brit. Mus. Arund. MS., 151, f. 386 (written about 1557).

[2] An account of Bedyll is to be found in Wood's *Athenæ*, vol. ii. He was one of those appointed to examine the "Holy Maid of Kent," and employed to get the Charterhouse monks to conform. As clerk of the council, he and Richard Layton examined blessed John Fisher. He was one of the commissioners for visiting religious houses previous to their dissolution. "This appointment," says Ellis, "probably made lord Crumwell anxious to get possession of his papers and effects."

[3] John Raynes was a well-known bookseller of the day in St. Paul's Churchyard.

[4] Ellis, *Orig. Letters*, 3rd Ser. iii. p. 104. Speaking of Sir Thomas Pope, his biographer writes: "His prodigious property was accumulated in conse-

The plate of the doomed houses, principally, indeed, the chalices and other sacred vessels of the altar, were the first solicitude of the royal spoilers. It is impossible even to guess at the worth of this portion of the king's booty. During centuries of undisturbed possession the monasteries of England must have been enriched by what would to-day be accounted priceless works of art in silver and gold. To the agents of Henry they represented merely so many ounces of metal, and as such only is there any record whatever of the precious contents of the monastic treasure-houses.

Only in very few instances do the spoilers add to the record of weight any detail of the precious work, frequently enriched with jewels, or enamelled bosses, or richly chased and beaten into artistic form by the hammer of the cunning smith, before it is swept into the bag of plunder to be "dispoiled" at the mint, and ultimately to find its way into the royal melting-pot, from which it issued forth as the debased money by which Henry cheated his subjects in his later years. Thus, to take one or two examples, from Westminster the record notes specially "a cup called the 'maser belle, or saint Edward's maser,'" a "cross of beryl" and "a dish or basin of precious stone called agate, ornamented with gold, precious stones and pearls."[1] From Canterbury, too, there was taken "a crozier of silver ornamented, called Thomas Beckett's staff," besides the mass of gold and silver and precious stones. And in rare instances particular inventories have been preserved of the precious church ornaments and plate found at some monastery and carried off to the royal treasury.

A very large amount of spoil was obtained through the royal crusade against relics, and, without weighing Henry's motives, it would have been more easy to believe in his good intentions had he not enriched himself so considerably by his attack upon the honour shown to the tombs and remains of holy men. As the noble author of his life remarks, "Henry promoted no other reformation but only that which

quence of the destruction of the religious houses, and the lucky opportunity of raising an estate from this grand harvest of riches which now lay open before him seems to have diverted his thoughts from making a fortune by law." Wharton, *Life of Pope* (ed. 1780), p. 23.

[1] R. O. Exch. Augt. Off. Treas. Roll, ii. m. 109d.

would turn the penny and increase the exchequer." And, whatever view may be taken as to the good or evil resulting to the Church by this action, the actual dishonour shown to the remains of the saints by the royal agents must on all hands be condemned. Even if it be allowed that some of the venerated relics had in fact little title to be what they claimed, still by far the greater number had a history which alone should have shielded them from positive disrespect, whilst many of them were undoubtedly the mortal remains of men and women whose names were written in no less honour on the pages of English history than on the diptychs of the Church. They were, to adopt Mr. Froude's language, "the peculiar treasures of the great abbeys and cathedrals —the mortal remains of the holy men in whose memories they had been founded, who by martyr's deaths, or lives of superhuman loftiness, had earned the veneration of later ages. The bodies of the saints had been gathered into costly shrines which a beautiful piety had decorated with choicest offerings. In an age which believed, without doubt or pretence, that the body of a holy man was incorporated into the body of Christ, that the seeming dust . . . would form again the living home of the spirit which had gone away but for a while, such dust, was looked upon with awe and pious fear."

Although no general seizure of the shrines of the saints was attempted by Henry till the year 1538, as early as May, 1537, the duke of Norfolk was directed to remove that of St. John at Bridlington. "As for the shrine," the letter runs, "the king's highness, to the intent that his people should not be seduced in the offering of their money, would have it taken down. This and all other jewels and plate appertaining to his highness, except such as you desire to have for your money," are to be dispatched to London.[1]

About the middle of the year 1538 general orders were apparently dispatched to the officers of various counties, directing them to repair to the several churches within the limits of their jurisdiction and effect the demolition of every noted shrine. Under cover of a pretended zeal against superstition, they were directed to take away the "shrine and bones with all the ornaments of the said shrine

[1] *Calendar*, xii. (ii), No. 34.

belonging, and all other relics, silver, gold and all jewels belonging to the said shrine, and . . . see them safely and surely conveyed unto our Tower of London." Further, they were ordered "to see that both the shrine and the place where it was kept be destroyed even to the ground."[1]

The circumstances attending the destruction of one or two of these precious monuments may be here recorded as examples. Pollard, one of the royal agents, in a letter to Crumwell describes the desecration of St. Swithin's at Winchester. It was "about three o'clock in the morning," he writes, that "we made an end of the shrine here." The prior and convent "were very conformable," he says, and he was assisted in his work, which lasted on through the night, by "the mayor with eight or nine of his brethren, the bishop's chancellor, Mr. doctor Crawford, with a good appearance of honest personages besides." The scene presented by that varied crowd who through the darkness of an autumn night watched from among the shadows of the venerable cathedral, whilst Pollard and his barbarous crew hacked and tore down the shrine which for centuries had been the glory of Winchester, may be easily pictured to the imagination. By the dim light of a candle the commissioner, who knew so well what he came for, must have eagerly scanned the metal as it was torn from the stones of the structure, and noted that "there was in it no piece of gold, nor one ring or true stone, but all great counterfeits," but that "the silver alone" would "amount near to two thousand marks." On that same night, too, he says, he "took possession of the cross of emeralds, the cross called 'Hierusalem,' another cross of gold, two chalices of gold with some

[1] The order for the destruction of the shrine of St. Richard of Chichester is given in Wilkins, iii. 840. This commission to take down and convey to the Tower of London the bones, shrine, &c., now in Chichester Cathedral of "a certain bishop of the same which they call Saint Richard," dated 14th December, is in the Record Office (*Calendar*, xiii. (ii), No. 1049). On the 20th December Sir William Goring, the commissioner, returned an account of 118 ounces of gold, "with stones, enamel and agate," 5255 ounces of silver gilt, 162 ounces of parcel gilt, one mitre, four copes and one vestment, as the result of this crusade against St. Richard (*Monastic Treasures*), p. 43. The details are given in *Calendar*, xiii. (ii), No. 1103. In a ship coffer 55 images of silver and gilt. In a long coffin, wherein bishop Richard's bones were, 57 pieces of silver and gilt. Three other coffers full of broken silver. "A cover with three locks . . . with relics and other jewels, parcel of the said shrine." In a little box 31 rings with stones and three other jewels. In a casket 51 jewels set with stones and pearls.

silver plate."[1] And on the Sunday morning, when the shrine had been disposed of, "going to bed-ward," they went round into the choir and stood with their lights before the magnificent reredos. There, he writes, "we viewed the altar, which we purpose to bring with us. It will be worth the taking down and nothing thereof seen; but such a piece of work it is, that we think we shall not rid it, doing our best before Monday night or Tuesday morning. This done," he adds, "we intend both at Hyde and Saint Mary's to sweep away all the rotten bones that be called relics; which we may not omit lest it should be thought we care more for the treasure than for avoiding of the abomination of idolatry."[2] The result of the work, so far as the main point was concerned, was $1035\frac{1}{2}$ ounces of gold, 13,886 ounces of silver gilt, 300 ounces of silver and parcel gilt, and one mitre received by the treasurer of the royal jewel-house.[3] No mention whatever is made of the reception of the magnificent jewels spoken of by Pollard in his letter.

Probably no shrine in the world could compare with the riches of that St. Thomas at Canterbury. For three centuries treasures of every kind had been bestowed upon the tomb of the martyred archbishop from every part of the Christian world. Even at the beginning of the fourteenth century the inventory of jewels belonging to the shrine presents a goodly list of precious and artistic treasures.[4] According to Erasmus, "the least valuable portion was gold; every part glistened, shone and sparkled with rare and very large jewels, some of them exceeding the size of a goose's egg. . . . The principal of them were offerings sent by sovereign princes."[5] So, too, Madame de Montreuil, who saw it just prior to its destruction when on her return from Scotland to France, "marvelled at the great riches thereof, saying it to be innumerable, and that if she had not seen it,

---

[1] These precious objects were probably gifts of Bishop Henry de Blois. The "cross of emeralds" is doubtless the "*alia crux aurea cum xxxiiii smaragdis*," No. 6 of the inventory printed in *Downside Review*, vol. iii. p. 41. "Hierusalem" is probably No. 1 of the inventory, and the two golden chalices Nos. 9 and 10.
[2] Wright, p. 218.
[3] *Monastic Treasures* (Abbotsford Club), p. 40.
[4] See *Erasmus' Pilgrimages*, by J. Gough Nichols (2nd ed.), p. 191.
[5] *Ibid.*, p. 49.

all the men in the world could never have made her believe it."¹

In the autumn of 1538 St. Thomas was declared a traitor, and it was enjoined that henceforth "his images and pictures through the whole realm shall be put down and avoided out of all churches, chapels and other places; and that from henceforth the days used to be festival in his name shall not be observed, nor the service office, antiphons, collects and prayers in his name read, but rased and put out of all the books . . . upon pain of his majesty's indignation and imprisonment at his grace's pleasure."²

As a necessary consequence of this condemnation of the saint came the spoliation of his tomb. Sander suggests that "the offence for which the most holy martyr was thus severely punished was nothing else but the wealth lavished upon his tomb and the necessity of finding some excuse for the pillage."³ Even if this was not the case, the result was the same; and the process of casting down the shrine, col-

---

¹ *State Papers* (ed. 1830), Part ii. p. 583. Polydore Vergil, *Relation* (Camden Society, 30), contains the account of a Venetian who visited the shrine about the year 1500. "The tomb of St. Thomas the martyr, archbishop of Canterbury," he says, "exceeds all belief. Notwithstanding its great size, it is wholly covered with plates of pure gold; yet the gold is scarcely seen because it is covered with various precious stones, as sapphires, balasses, diamonds, rubies and emeralds; and wherever the eye turns something more beautiful than the rest is observed. Nor, in addition to these natural beauties, is the skill of art wanting, for in the midst of the gold are the most beautiful sculptured gems both small and large, as well such as are in relief as agates, onyxes, cornelians and cameos; and some cameos are of such size that I am afraid to name it; but everything is far surpassed by a ruby, not larger than a thumbnail, which is fixed at the right of the altar. The church is somewhat dark, and particularly in the spot where the shrine is placed, and when we went to see it the sun was near setting and the weather was cloudy; nevertheless I saw the ruby as if I had it in my hand. They say it was given by a king of France." This jewel was no doubt the "Regal of France," of which subsequent mention will be made. It seems, however, to have been a diamond.

² Burnet, *Records* (ed. Pocock), vi. 220. It is difficult to conceive that the so-called citation, trial and condemnation of the saint by a court sitting at Westminster can have taken place. The story passed current on the Continent, and is given by Pollini. Lingard thinks that the Bull "Cum Redemptor" of Paul III., dated Dec. 17, 1538, confirms the story. Canon Dixon (ii. p. 72 *note*) has shown that it does not necessarily do so.

³ Lewis' transl., p. 142. In this Marillac, the French ambassador, agrees. After declaring that Henry was so avaricious and covetous "that all the wealth of the world would not be enough to satisfy and content his ambition . . . from which has come the ruin of the abbeys and the spoiling of every church in which there was anything to take," he then adds: "St. Thomas is declared a traitor because his relics and bones were adorned with gold and stones" (*Inventaire Analytique*, ed. Kaulek, p. 211).

lecting the plate and jewels as already described in the case of Winchester, was repeated at Canterbury. Here, however, the relics, which had been venerated for many generations, were apparently treated with special indignity, and torn from the sheltered tomb were committed to the flames.[1]

The plate was carried away to London. From the descriptions quoted above it is evident that the prize was worth having. "All above the stone work was first of wood, jewels of gold set with stone . . . wrought upon with gold wire," says the account from which Stowe derived his information. "Then again with jewels of gold, as broch[es images of angels and rings] ten or twelve together, cramped with gold into the ground of gold. The [spoils of which filled two] chests, such as six or eight men could but convey out of the church. At [one side was a stone with] an angel of gold pointing thereunto, offered by the king of France: [which king Henry put] into a ring and wore it on his thumb."[2]

In the Treasurer's Roll the weight of the plate obtained is thus recorded: The gold (including $2\frac{3}{4}$ ounces fine gold of coins) was no less than $4994\frac{3}{4}$ ounces; the gilt plate weighed 4425; the parcel gilt 840; and the plain silver 5286.[3] At a subsequent date twenty-six ounces of gold

---

[1] *The Relics of St. Thomas*, by Rev. J. Morris, S.J. Fr. Morris shows that it is almost certain that the relics were burnt. In *The Travels of Nicander Nucius* (Camden Soc.), p. 75, the Greek gives the account of this burning current in England when he was there about 1545. The bones of the saint, he says, after being "treated with every indignity, were committed to the fire in the middle of the city, and reduced to ashes; and having put the ashes into a cannon, they discharged them into the air."

[2] Nichols, *ut sup.*, p. 190, from Cott. MS. Tib., e. viii. f. 269. The history of this great jewel is interesting. In 1179 Louis VII. of France came to visit the shrine in company with king Henry. He offered at the tomb his golden cup and a rent of a hundred measures of wine yearly. Having passed the night in prayer before the saint's relics, he in the morning asked and received the "fraternity" in the chapter-house. Amongst his offerings is supposed to have been the great glory of the shrine, "that renowned precious stone that is called the Regal of France." From the thumb-ring, for which Henry VIII. used the jewel, it was apparently transferred to a collar. In the inventory of precious stones delivered to queen Mary the 10th of March, 1553-4, was "a collar of golde set with sixteen faire diamountes, whereof the Regal of Fraunce is one, and fourtene knottes or perles, in every knotte four perles" (Brit. Mus. Harl. MS., 611, 22). See Nichols, Introd., lxxxvi.

[3] *Monastic Treasures*, p. 40. Sander says (Lewis' trans., p. 143): "The king's receiver confessed that the gold and silver and precious stones and sacred vestments taken away from the shrine filled six-and-twenty carts. We may judge from this," he adds, "how great must have been the wealth of which the king robbed the other shrines, churches and monasteries."

with 4090 of silver gilt or plain were added to the spoils from Christ Church, Canterbury. Besides this wealth of precious metal, and the jewels of which there is no record, there were carried away to London four precious mitres, "two of silver gilt over-worked with pearls and precious stones;" a wooden throne covered at the parts called pommels with crimson velvet, and the handles of silver gilt; and a crozier ornamented with silver, called "Thomas Becket's staff."[1] Further, besides a number of fastenings for copes of gold and precious stones, nine pontifical rings and "a golden shell adorned with divers precious stones," there were taken for the king "eleven copes of gold cloth called 'gold Bawdekin.' Of these ten were white, with the arms of . . . Morton, formerly archbishop, and the eleventh was ornamented with red roses." Also, "one covering for the upper part of an altar of white and red velvet splendidly worked."[2] These, with other things, formed the plunder which Henry gathered into his treasure-house "from the goods of the late monastery of Christ Church, Canterbury."

In a similar way to that in which the shrine of St. Thomas was demolished other sanctuaries were invaded and pillaged. Throughout the length and breadth of England the same hands which were levelling the monasteries and the same spirit which was at work on them were engaged in the war against the departed saints and in appropriating the gifts with which generations of pious Englishmen had honoured their tombs. It was the same story everywhere, with the place and actors alone changed.

[1] In the inventory made in 1315, the pastoral staff of St. Thomas is thus described:—"Item. Baculus Sancti Thomæ de pyro, cum capite de nigro cornu." It was thus made of pear-wood with a crook of black horn. Erasmus says: "There (in the sacristy) we saw the pastoral staff of Saint Thomas. It appeared to be a cane covered with silver plate; it was of very little weight and no workmanship, nor stood higher than to the waist" (Nichols, p. 44, and *note*, p. 175).

[2] R. O. Exch. Augt. Off. Treas. Roll, i. m. 110. Speaking of the treasures of Canterbury, Erasmus says: "Good God! what a display was there of silken vestments, what an array of golden candlesticks." The inventory (1315) before referred to, which may be seen printed in the Appendix to Dart's *History of the Church*, pp. iv.–xviii., must be consulted fully to understand the amazing treasures which have perished. There were 65 "copes of profession" given by suffragan bishops and abbots, besides many more. The list of crosses, chalices and church furniture is very lengthy. Among the chasubles belonging to the shrine was one given by Sir John Plukenet, knight, of purple cloth with golden pine-apples, and a large orfrey before and behind. (See Nichols, p. 192.)

It is not to be supposed that this rough treatment of the relics of saints hitherto so much venerated was approved of by the people. Indications are not wanting that they saw with sorrow what they were powerless to prevent, for, as Marillac, the French ambassador, informed his master about this time, "the people were much more attached to the old religion than to the new opinions."[1] One of Crumwell's numerous spies reported the opinions of the servant of bishop Tunstal, of Durham, on this matter. The document is of considerable length, but portions of it are of very great interest. "I would gladly," he writes, "have found an occasion that the servant should declare his mind in the evidence of others, and so at supper and in the presence of the goodman of the Taberd, at Royston . . . as we talked of the suppression of houses of religion, by his own occasion, (he) show(ed) us, that before he came to Huntingdon he overtook certain men that came from the commissions, and brought with them in their males (trunks) behind them copes and other abbey gear. He showed us that the prior of Mountgrace was fully minded not to give up his house, and that he answered the servant of a friend of his, who had sent to him for very friendliness that he should meet Mr. Henley, coming towards his house to suppress it, three or four miles from the house and present him with a gelding of the price of five marks, and desire him to be a good master to him, which would serve his purpose well. Unto which messenger he said, he thanked his master for his good will, but he had no gelding of such a price, and in case he had, he neither intended to meet him, nor give him a hair of the tail to be good to him. . . . 'Lord,' quoth I, 'what manner of man is that prior? Is he a man of any discretion?' 'Yea, marry he is,' quoth he, 'and a great learned man, and so be all his brethren, and they be like-minded all to him.' 'How doth the country favour him?' quoth I. 'Marry,' quoth he, 'wondrously well, and they lament and bewail his cause very sore in their hearts.'

"And after that he told us another tale; how he was with the visitors one time when they handled relics very irreverently and spoiled them of the gold and silver that was about them, and cast them away when they had done, and

---

[1] *Inventaire Analytique des Archives*, ed. Kaulek, No. 119.

gave unto him certain bones garnished with silver, and bade him pluck off the silver and garnish his dagger withal. (These) he took at their hands and keepeth them yet and other bones likewise, which the visitors had cast away and he gathered up afterwards. And, he added, he had rather go a begging than he would take the silver from them."[1]

From the spoiling of shrines and relics, and from the pillage of cathedral and monastic treasuries, Henry amassed a booty of immense value. Putting on one side the actual jewels, which were undoubtedly worth considerable sums of money, and the amount of plate appropriated by the royal commissioners and other agents engaged on the work of gathering the harvest, the mass of ecclesiastical plate which reached the treasure-house was very considerable. Besides the adornments torn from the tombs of saints and the reliquaries from out of which their bones had been cast, the plunder comprised miscellaneous church ornaments of all sorts: sacred chalices and patens, monstrances for exposing the Blessed Sacrament and vessels for reserving it, crosses and candlesticks for the altar, processional and pastoral staves, pontifical mitres, rings and gloves, cruets, censers and silver dishes of every kind, and even jewelled clasps torn from missals and other service books were conveyed to London to the king.[2] The sacred character of the greater number of the articles was no protection against

---

[1] *Calendar*, xiv. (ii), No. 750.

[2] Besides the weight of plate, a miscellaneous variety of ecclesiastical ornaments were brought to the treasure-house. For example: "A monstrance having a great beryl in the midst and set with divers counterfeit stones," from Ramsey; a silver crown, mitres without number, "a pair of beryl candlesticks garnished with silver gilt," "great agates, cameos, coarse pearls" set in gold, from St. Albans; a monstrance from Gloucester; a mitre "garnished with flowers of silver and silver bells with counterfeit stones" from Canterbury; "a table of silver gilt with two leaves, the inside set with sapphires and other stones" from Ely; "a gospel book plated upon with a crucifix, Mary and John, of silver, and a text of a gospel book plated," &c., &c. (*Monastic Treasures*).

Curious deductions are made from the accounts, thus: The king took the use of a "Gospeller," ornamented with silver and precious stones, and 60s. is allowed for its price; £15, 12s. 1d. was deducted for lead, wax and paper in a parcel of plate which had been priced as silver, and 40s. 5d. because a silver gilt image of St. John from Abingdon proved lighter than was estimated" (Exch. Augt. Off. Treas. Roll, i. m. 13d.).

In the accounts of the keeper of the jewel-house, $7101\frac{1}{2}$ ounces of plate are said to be lost in the melting by wax, lead, &c. (*Monastic Treasures*, pp. 54–63).

profanation, just as artistic value and costly workmanship did not save them from the royal melting-pot. The worth of the plunder was calculated by its weight, and this, as entered upon the roll of the treasurer, may be stated as follows:—Pure gold, 14,531¾ ounces; silver gilt, 129,520 ounces; parcel gilt, 73,774¾; and silver, 67,600¼.[1] This vast collection was estimated by Sir John Williams, at the melting price, to be worth in money of that date £63,531, 15s. 1d. To this, however, certain additions must be made. The keeper received in money for plate and other ornaments sold at the dissolution £15,550, 1s. 3½d.[2] and nearly £7000 worth of plate was forwarded to the Augmentation Office in the earlier years of the dissolutions.[3] Hence the money value of the gold and silver spoils actually received by the king, and estimated only at the weighing price, was more than £85,000, or very nearly a million sterling of the present money.[4]

From the ecclesiastical plate thus appropriated by Henry to the sacred vestments the transition is natural. Ancient inventories show that there were in the monastic sacristies copes, chasubles, and much other altar furniture, of gold and silver cloth, of silver richly and artfully embroidered with the needle, of brocades and stuffs of Eastern origin, which would have been esteemed priceless works of art in this age. Much must have perished in the wanton destruc-

---

[1] *Monastic Treasures* (Abbotsford Club), p. 53, *et seq.*
[2] *Ibid.*, pp. 68–69.
[3] R. O. Exch. Augt. Off. Treas. Roll, i. m. 4d.
[4] For the full account of the amount of plate and what became of it see the Appendix. A good deal was expended for "new trimming images of gold," *e.g.*, an image of Our Lady. Plate and money to the value of no less than £46,636, 1s. 1¼d. was given "to the proper hand of the king" (*Monastic Treasures*, p. 92), and £810 was spent in the expenses of offices and collecting, nearly £70 being for the carriage of plate "as well by boats as carts to Westminster and Greenwich" (p. 93). As an example of the way the plate was relegated to the melting-pot may be given a few items from an account of "plate molten by order of the king's council," 1 July, 1557 (Ed. VI.). In this there are "gold coming from defacing 3 books, a mitre, two gloves;" "glass garnished with gold from three books;" "two candlesticks, 2 cruetts, 2 chalices;" "a ship of mother of pearl and silver;" "silver from a 'glass of berryl';" "three mitres, 2 gold crosses and an 'ark';" "a ring of gold called a pontifical having an eagle and in her breast a small ruby;" "a plate of gold being of a monstrance;" "3 cross stars all gilt;" "4 rings of silver called pontificals, 2 having stones therein and the third a pearl." It is noted that the stones coming from the mitres, rings, &c., defaced are still in hand (R. O. Audit Office, Bundle 1533, Roll. 1).

tion that characterised the work of the royal commissioners at the time of the suppressions. The skilfully-wrought metal work of shrine and reliquary, more precious for the art of the workman than for the worth of the material, when torn from its place by the tools of despoilers became but a mass of broken metal fit only for the melting. So, in like manner, the triumphs of loom and crewel, amid the desolation of places where they had been prized and cared for, were too often regarded as pieces of useless lumber.

Vestments, altar frontals, and the like, which had been looked on "as objects of joy and beauty" by generations of religious, who knew the history of each, and who would recall with gratitude the memory of the various donors, were looked upon merely as things upon which a little money was to be raised to pay the expenses of the commissioners or the wages of their servants. "Money to dispatch the household and monks," writes the indefatigable Dr. Layton, of Bisham abbey, "we must make of the rotten copes and bells;" and he further says that they had already "made sale of the old vestments within the chapter-house."[1] The accounts of such auctions show that a few shillings, or in many instances only a few pence, represented the sums which the sacred vestments fetched.[2]

Scores of copes and chasubles, chiefly of cloth of gold and silver, of tissue, or worked in pearls, were preserved for the king's use. Thus, a set of "cloth of gold with ornaments of blue velvet" and three altar frontals from Beaulieu, another of "cloth of silver worked with fleur-de-lys and angels" from Canons Ashby,[3] were saved from the general sales[4] and sent up to London. So, from St. Swithin's, Winchester, "six copes of blue tissue and one

---

[1] R. O. Crum. Corr., xx. No. 11.
[2] See Scudamore's account. Wright, p. 266, &c.
[3] These vestments have a history of their own. Richard Colles, the prior, ordered them from "Thomas Typlady, citizen and broderer of London," and a "cope and two tunicles," for which the convent promised to pay £39; they were brought to Stourbridge fair and delivered to the servants of the abbey only a short time before the dissolution (Exch. Augt. Off. Misc. Bk., 120, f. 215). £29 was still due to Typlady when the vestments were taken for the king and handed to Sir Thomas Pope, the treasurer of the Court of Augmentations. This sum Typlady claimed from the king (*Ibid.*, Bk. 404, f. 220), and he was ultimately paid in full (*Ibid.*, Treas. Roll, i. m. 12d).
[4] R. O. Exch. Aug. Off. Treasurer's Roll, i. These are merely haphazard examples of many such entries.

piece of arras, with the image of the Passion;" from St. Augustine's, Bristol, "certain garnishing of vestments of silver gilt, enamelled, and fret with small pearls;" from Cirencester, "a cope embroidered with the story of Jesse, with cloth of gold upon crimson velvet and two copes of cloth of gold;" from St. Peter's, Gloucester, "three copes of silver tissue, two of gold and one of blue"[1] were reserved for royal service.[2]

The vestments purchased at the various sales, which took place in every part of England, were dispersed throughout the country, and large numbers even were shipped to foreign lands. In many instances the auctions were attended by merchants who followed the footsteps of the royal commissioners and purchased largely for speculative purposes. Thus, one Hugh Payne appears to have purchased the vestments of St. Martin's-le-Grand; John Blackewall, a cleric, "divers capes of Worcester;"[3] Joan Mynne, three copes of silk and four of bawdekin of Westminster, and Edward Elrington obtained other copes and ornaments of the same place for £102.[4] A market was found in places beyond the seas for the ecclesiastical ornaments and vestments thus discarded, and not only were the sentiments of the nation at large outraged by the pillage of churches, and at the sight of the royal visitors riding along the roads with "copes and other abbey gear" as their chief luggage, but the seaport towns of the Continent were astonished at the desecration. "The lord of Barrow," wrote an English priest from Holland in 1540, "showed me that there were brought to his town

---

[1] R. O. Exch. Aug. Off. Misc. Bk., 494.
[2] The portion of ecclesiastical spoils so reserved from Westminster is rich. Of altar furniture there is specially noted : " A basin or dish of a precious stone named agate, ornamented with gold, precious stones and pearls, and weighing 38 ounces. Two altar hangings, called frontals, of cloth of gold worked with lions, fleur-de-lys and the arms of the late — Islip, formerly abbot of the monastery." "Five copes of needlework (one called St. Peter's cope, one the cope with angels of pearl and three others called Jesses) with two tunicles, one chasuble and seven silver gilt buttons, together with albs, stoles and maniples of the same work." "Sixteen copes of cloth of gold of various colours: one of blue with a chasuble, two tunicles, an alb, stole and maniple belonging to the same; another cope of cloth of gold with the orpheries splendidly worked with 'Islips' and adorned with golden images : 14 other copes of cloth of gold of velvet and golden portcullises worked on them." These and other altar furniture were taken for the king's use (Treasurer's Roll, i. m. 109d).
[3] *Ibid.*, Roll, ii. m. 9d.   [4] *Ibid.*, m. 106d.

and Antwerp so many rich and goodly copes out of England to sell these years past that it caused them all no less to marvel than in a manner to mourn to see them come to a sale that were prepared to the service of God. Whereupon rose rumours that we had no masses in the realm (of England)."[1]

A large proportion also of the Church spoils were without doubt scattered over England, and possibly used by many for secular purposes. "Nothing more is said about the abbeys," wrote the Venetian ambassador at the time; "they are all suppressed and their revenues annexed to the crown, some being given and usurped by the nobility, who convert them into palaces, furnishing them with the church ornaments (when there are any) and rendering them heirlooms in their families."[2] A learned historian, speaking of what followed upon the pillage of churches under Edward VI., draws a picture which must equally have represented the results of ecclesiastical spoliation under his father. "Although," he says, "some profit was hereby raised to the king's exchequer, yet the far greatest part of the prey came to other hands: Insomuch that many private men's parlours were hung with altar-cloths, their tables and beds covered with copes, instead of carpets and coverlids; and many made carousing cups of the sacred chalices, as once Balshazzar celebrated his drunken feast in the sanctified vessels of the Temple. It was a sorry house, and not worth the naming, which had not somewhat of this furniture in it, though it were only a fair large cushion made of a cope or altar-cloth, to adorn their windows, or make their chairs appear to have somewhat in them of a chair of state. Yet how contemptible were these trappings in comparison of those vast sums of money which were made of jewels, plate and cloth of tissue, either conveyed beyond the seas or sold at home."[3]

It is unnecessary to dwell further upon the sales which preceded and accompanied the destruction of the religious houses, and at which the furniture of the churches and effects of the convents were disposed of to the highest bidder, often at ridiculously small sums. Altars and images, the

---

[1] R. O. State Papers, Dom., 1540, $\frac{w}{205}$.
[2] *Venetian State Papers*, v. p. 347.
[3] Heylin, *Eccl. Restaurata*, ed. 1670, p. 134.

wood of choir stalls and chapel screens, candlesticks and lamps, tables and forms, tombs, gravestones, pavement, timber, iron and glass—in fact, everything which would add a penny to the total of the plunder came to the hammer. In some cases the grant of an entire building with all its effects, in others the purchase of the goods as a whole, did away with the necessity of a public auction; but these were comparatively few in number, and, as a general rule, a sale, conducted in the chapter-house, church or cloister, was the method by which a monastery was cleared out as a preparatory step to dealing with the building itself.

Wanton waste was, of course, inseparable from such wholesale destruction, but it is impossible to suppress the word of grief at what the world has in this way lost beyond recovery. No other instance is needed to rouse in all feelings stronger than regret than the loss of the precious manuscripts and other contents of the monastic libraries which disappeared in the general havoc. How little such things were cared for may be gathered by the contemptuous references which occur in the account of the sales which took place. "Old books in the choir, 6d.;" "old books in the vestry sold to Robert Dorington, 8d.;" "old books and a cofer in the library, 2s.;"[1] "a flat chest with five books in it, 8d.;" "a mass book with its desk, 8d.;" "fourteen great books in the choir, 14s.,"[2] are samples of the sales of manuscripts which would now be of immense value.

"The English monks," says Fuller, "were bookish themselves, and much inclined to hoard up monuments of learning." John Bale has left on record his experience as to the way in which the treasures described by Leland disappeared upon the destruction of the monasteries. The purchasers of the houses used the manuscripts for every vile and common necessity. "Grocers and soap-sellers" bought them for their business purposes, and "whole ships full" were sent "over the sea to the bookbinders." While one merchant bought "the contents of two noble libraries for forty shillings' price," and "this stuff hath he occupied instead of grey paper," adds the author, "by the space of more than these ten years: and yet he hath store enough for as many years to come."

Nothing illustrates this wholesale and wanton destruction

[1] Scudamore accounts. Wright, p. 269, &c.
[2] R. O. Augt. Off. Misc. Bk., 408, f. 74, &c.

better than the dearth of English Church service and music books, so much lamented in these days. That the choral schools of the country produced good results in the way of music, and that they were in full swing at the time of the destruction of the monastic houses, cannot be doubted. And yet practically nothing is known of the compositions of later English musicians or their works, so complete has been the destruction of this manuscript music.[1] In the same way how very few copies of the various service books, such as Antiphonals, Graduals, Ordinals, Missals, &c., does the present age possess. And yet many thousands—in fact, not fewer than a quarter of a million, according to the highest authority upon the matter—must have been in actual use at the various churches at this period.[2]

[1] Erasmus speaks of the English love of choral song. "It is," he says, "so agreeable to the monks, especially in England, that youths, boys, &c., every morning sing to the organ the mass of the Virgin Mary, with the most harmonious modulations of voice" (Owen and Blakeway, *Shrewsbury*, ii. 50, *note*). As a sample of the music which must have existed in every monastery, a portion of a much-mutilated inventory of Worcester may be given. It will be found printed in Green, *Worcester*, App. vii. A glance at the original (Brit. Mus. Harl., 604) will show what a small fragment it is. "The maister of the chapell." "Item, a surples for the maister of the children and 6 surpliesses for the children: A masse bocke of—with prycksonge wheryn is 5 parts and 4 parts. Four prycksonge mass books of paper. Two other books—one with anthems and *salves* in him. Four little prycksong books of masses. Five mass books of 5 parts. Five books—with *Salve Festa Dies* and scrolls belonging to the 2 paper books. In them be the 5 parts of other songs—a singing note book 'burdyde'—a parchment book of *Salves* 'burdyde,' 2 masses of 5 parts in parchment scrolls—a paper book of 4 parts—a paper book with the '*invitatories*,' *Benedictus, Te Deum* in prickynge. There be 3 or 4 anthems in *scroll*."

[2] Speaking of the destruction of service books, Mr. Maskell (*Monumenta Ritualia*, 3rd ed., i. p. cxcvii.) says: "Of each (*i.e.* the eight or nine books previously named) not only must there have been almost countless copies in manuscript in the year 1530, but there had been many large editions of several of them printed. Yet now, in about three hundred years, we may say of them that as a class they have all but totally disappeared. Examples of any one, missal or breviary or manual, it matters not, are of extraordinary rarity. Of some none are extant, and by far the greater part of those we do possess are mutilated and imperfect." The learned author calculates that when the old ritual ceased at least two-thirds of the copies must have been good, since the greatest care was taken of them. "Every church and chantry and chapel was supplied." At St. John the Baptist's, Glastonbury, in 1421, there were "3 missals, 3 graduals, 1 psalter, 3 antiphonals, 1 legend, 2 collects and 1 processional" (Warner, App. xcix.). "Monasteries had hundreds." At Ramsey there were "70 breviaries, 100 psalters, 4 hymnals, 32 graduals, 39 processionals" (Brit. Mus. Cott. Roll, xi. 16). And altogether, Mr. Maskell calculates (p. ccii.) that there could have been "not less that 250,000 volumes in actual use, besides those which might have been laid up and treasured in the Archives." He further adds that they must have been purposely destroyed to prevent men "worshipping any longer after the manner of their forefathers."

After a monastery had been dismantled, and the churches, to use Dr. London's expression, "defaced," then came the process of realizing the value of the materials of the building itself. The chief source of profit was the lead with which the monasteries were mostly covered. It was stripped from the roof of the finest church without hesitation, and melted at a fire made probably with the wood of the stalls, screen-work or rood. Orders were sent, in what appears at this date the most cold-blooded manner, to wreck the roof and "pull" the lead off some of the most glorious architectural monuments which England then contained. Bands of workmen went about from place to place throughout the country, lit their fires in the naves or chancels of abbey churches, and occupied themselves for days, and even in some cases weeks, in melting the coverings of roofs, and the gutters, spouts and pipes from the building into pigs and fodders, the sale of which might add a few pounds to the royal plunder. The same story was repeated in every place. Like a swarm of locusts the royal wreckers went forth over the land, and what they found fair and comely they blackened with their smelting fires and left useless ruins. For eleven weeks, as an example, the commissioners wandered about Somerset, " defacing, destroying and prostrating the churches, cloisters, belfreys, and other buildings of the late monasteries." At Keynsham £12 was paid to one Richard Walker for melting the lead on church, cloister and steeple. At Hinton Charterhouse, Witham, Montacute, Bruton, Athelney and Buckland the work was repeated, and at Bath half-a-crown was paid for the casting of each of 156 fodders, the result of the process at the priory church, when the metal from the roofs of the church and other monastic buildings passed into the melting-pot.[1] At Wigmore abbey, to quote but one more example, it took James Reynolds, the royal metal melter in those parts, more than eight days to tear down the lead and cast it into pigs. Day and night the process was watched, "for fear some" of the royal spoil "should be stolen by the people."[2]

The casting completed, other workmen arrived to convey the fodders to a place of safety, where they might remain till purchased or used. Along the roads teams of horses

[1] R. O. Exch. Augt. Off. Mins. Accts., 30-31 Hen. VIII., 224, m. 17.
[2] *Ibid.*, 230, m. 26d.

dragged waggons weighted with the lead, and down the navigable rivers barges carried it to the sea-coast. The metal from Wigmore, for example, was carried into the castle, and thither also was brought in waggons the stuffs from Bordesley and Lylleshull; while from the latter house a caravan of ninety-three carts took a portion of it to a royal manor some twenty miles distant.[1] The lead from off the great cathedral church of Coventry, estimated to be worth £647, was stacked, together with that from other churches in the town, within the desecrated building,[2] while that from the church and monastery of Bury St. Edmunds, "now pulled off," as the account has it, and worth, according to the estimate, £3302, remained on the site. Many of the royal castles, as, for instance, those of Worcester and Tutbury, were turned into storehouses. Round the cathedral of Lincoln the metal melted from the roofs of the monastic churches of the district was piled for use, and thousands of tons were floated down the Severn to Bristol to be sold for export.[3]

What has been said of the lead is equally true of the bells found in the monasteries. They were a source of great profit to the king, as the metal was valuable for the making of guns, and was readily purchased by the London merchants, if they were not saved from destruction by the immediate payment of their estimated value by the people of the neighbourhood for their parish church. Thus £832 worth of metal, from the broken bells of Lincolnshire, was given, in 1542, to Sir Charles Morris, under royal warrant, to make guns and other engines of war. At the same time it was noted that 68 bells still remained unsold[4] in that district. Of purchases by private adventurers there were many examples. Thus Henry Over, a grocer of Coventry, purchased many of the bells in that town; William Gerard, a London haberdasher, and Thomas Walker, a vintner, speculated jointly in 80,000 lbs. weight of broken metal, for which they paid £800; Sir Richard Gresham paid £31 for the bells of Blakeney and Burnham, in Norfolk, and

---

[1] R. O. Exch. Augt. Off. Mins. Accts., m.m. 27–27d. [2] *Ibid.*, 226, m. 11d.
[3] R. O. Exch. Augt. Off. Misc. Bk., 472. Grant "to one John Smith of Bristol for his ship ready to sail, in consideration of £200, two hundred fodders of lead out of such our store as there remaineth, good weight." The Scudamore papers show what vast quantities went down the Severn. Brit. Mus. Add. MS., 11,041, ff. 93, *et seq.*
[4] *Ibid.*, Mins. Accts., 34–35 Hen. VIII., 220.

John Core, a grocer, of London, who bought very largely at one time, took 144,500 lbs. of the metal for £1345.[1]

The accounts for the delivery of part of this large order are extant. They include the expenses for dismantling belfreys and pulling down bells; for carriage of the metal to London to the "king's weighouse," where they were to be delivered to Core the grocer; for the wages of labourers engaged in breaking up; and "14d. paid to each man riding to Gracedieu and Leicester to look at the bells." Also charges were made for "hammers, iron wedges, crowes of iron, chisels and other instruments bought and used at different times for breaking" them up, as well as for sundry barrels bought at different times and places in which to pack the broken metal. In this work of destruction the labourers were employed for seventy-five days.[2]

Some, however, of the bells were sold unbroken to merchants, who carried them abroad. Thus, in a letter written in the year 1539 to one of Thomas Crumwell's gentlemen, an Englishman complains of the treatment he had received from the Spanish Inquisition. "The causes of the persecution," he says, "were refusal to acknowledge Henry VIII. a heretic and alleged approval of the destruction of monasteries and selling church bells." The whole matter arose from Thomas Edwards, a London merchant, bringing in a ship "a brazen bell, which might weigh two kintals." A priest, who passed and saw it, said, in the hearing of the writer of the complaint, "What a good Christian is your king of England to put down the monasteries and to take away the bells!" The Englishman defended his sovereign, and thus involved himself in difficulties with the authorities of the Inquisition.[3]

In some few instances the monastery bells were saved from destruction by being purchased by the inhabitants of neighbouring parishes. Thus those of Buckfastleigh, in Devon, paid £33, 15s. to Sir Thomas Arundel for the five bells of the old abbey;[4] at the dissolution of Ford the people bought five bells for their parish, and those of Churchstoke

---

[1] R. O. Exch. Augt. Off. Treas. Roll, ii. m. 9.
[2] *Ibid.*, Mins. Accts., 31–32 Hen. VIII., 236, m. 37. This portion of the 144,500 lbs. bought by Core came from Leicestershire. The bells broken up numbered 56, and weighed 48,000 lbs. (m. 7d).
[3] Ellis, *Orig. Letters*, 2nd Ser. ii. p. 139.
[4] R. O. Exch. Aug. Off. Mins. Accts., 30–31 Hen. VIII., 223, m. 12.

collected £26, 13s. 4d. to save the bells of Newnham[1] from destruction. Out of the two hundred bells collected by Sir John Scudamore from the monasteries of Hereford, Shropshire, Staffordshire and Worcester, the inhabitants of Roucester claimed three as belonging to their parish church, since they had been rung for their services as well as for the choral offices of the canons.[2] In the same way the people of Abergavenny laid claim to three bells of the dissolved priory upon the ground that their ancestors had collected money for them, and they had been always regarded as the property of the people.[3]

Something must now be said about the destruction of the buildings themselves. In some instances the entire structure was disposed of by the king. Thus, for example, the city of Worcester paid £541 for the two convents of the Black and Grey friars,[4] and chancellor Audeley purchased the buildings of Athelney abbey for £20.[5] As a rule, however, the buildings were sold piecemeal. Thus, to take one or two examples, at Bath one Anthony Payne bought "all the iron and glass of the monastery for £30. Another, Robert Cocks, purchased the entire 'dorter' for £10, a third, Walter Dennys, obtained the 'fratry' for £6, and Henry Bewchyn 'the cloisters' for £8."[6] At Walsingham the "windows, doors, stone called freestone, glass, iron, slate and tiles" were disposed of in lots for a total of £55, 15s. 11d.[7] At the destruction of Dover priory one "Adrian the brewer" paid £7 for the tiles and timber; another, Thomas Portway,

---

[1] R. O. Exch. Off. Mins. Accts., m. 26. [2] *Ibid.*, 230, m. 6.

[3] *Ibid.*, Misc. Bk., 117, f. 18. The reasons assigned are curious. 1. Thomas Ap Letham, aged 66 years, deposed at the inquiry "That one called Jenkyn Ap Letham, of Abergavenny, his father, being a smith, did work of his own proper costs and charges to the setting up of the said bells in the late priory, and also besides paid his part to the being of the said bells, how much he cannot tell." 2. John Ap Poll Ap John, aged 80 years, deposed that "One John Ap Vaughan, of Abergavenny, his father-in-law, did pay 20s. for his part, and his father-in-law's brother 13s. 4d. to the being of the said bells. Furthermore he saith that the parish of Abergavenny should ring and did ring the same bells if any of their servants died without license or restraint of the prior or convent, and so did use to do till the suppression of the said late priory. And also the said parish did find all manner of costs and charges belonging to the said bells. Also further, he saith that he was one of them with Jenkyn Ap Letham" and others "that went into the country with games and plays to gather money to pay for the aforesaid bells."

[4] *Ibid.*, Mins. Accts., 30-31 Hen. VIII. 230, m. 5.

[5] *Ibid.*, 224, m. 6d.

[6] *Ibid.*, m. 5d. [7] *Ibid.*, 31-32 Hen. VIII., 255, m. 10d.

obtained "the roof of the Lady chapel" for thirteen shillings and fourpence, and the "grave stones and altar stones" for twelve shillings, and the commissioner admits having taken twenty tons of "rotten timber" for his own use.[1]

That there was, throughout the whole process of destruction, great waste, that in comparison with the original cost of the buildings the paltry sums received were altogether inadequate, and that the crown actually only obtained a tithe of the real value of the confiscated property, does not admit of doubt. As an example of this, the dissolution of the abbey of Pipwell may be cited. At the first coming of the commissioners, Sir William Parr obtained as a gift the paving of the dormitory, and carried some of it away at once. Then followed apparently a general scramble of the people in the neighbourhood, and a great deal of glass, iron and lead was stolen. One man carried off the two doors of the brewhouse, and another, a tinker, caught in the act of appropriating some lead, was hanged at Northampton. Sir William Parr helped himself to the fish out of the east and west ponds and "stored" them. Each monk carried away the contents of his chamber. Shortly after the suppression "a strong press in the dormitory," which contained the title deeds, was broken open, and it was impossible to determine what had been abstracted. The floor of the steeple was pulled down when the commissioners dismounted the bells, "and at the same time the desks in the choir and all the windows in the infirmary were broken up and sold by the servants" of the royal officials.[2]

In the work of wrecking the finest monuments and most costly buildings, which took place all over the country, there does not appear to have been any hesitation on the part of Henry or his servants. There was never any question of sparing anything which could not be used for farm or other purposes, or by the demolition of which a few pounds might be added to the sum total of the plunder.

[1] R. O. Exch. Augt. Off. Misc. Bk., 109, Nos. 22, 26.
[2] *Ibid.*, No. 29. Numerous examples of the destruction of buildings for the sake of the lead might be given. The roofing of the magnificent minster of Sherborne, with that of the bell tower and dormitory, was purchased for £230. The stone, iron, &c., of the Friars in Fleet Street, London, for £125. The lead on the church of St. Elphege, Cripplegate, fetched £60; that on St. Mary's Abbey, York, £800; that on Evesham, £260, &c., &c. (*Ibid.*, Treas. Roll, iii. m. 17d.)

Thus in every case, as at St. Mary's, Winchester, the superfluous buildings were declared to be church, chapter-house, dormitory, frater; and those allowed to stand were the superior's "lodging with offices."[1] The "superfluous buildings" were demolished without any scruple. Thus John Freeman, one of those engaged in the work, wrote that he was to pull down all monastic buildings except what might be of use for farm purposes. In Lincolnshire, where he was then occupied, there were more great houses than in any other part of England. The walls were thick and there were few to buy. "To pull them down," he says, "will cost the king a good deal," and so it is best to get the bells and lead, "which will rise well." And "this done, to pull down the roofs, battlements and stairs, and let the walls stand, and charge some with them as a quarry of stone to make sales of as they that have need will fetch."[2]

All this destruction, however, was not accomplished without an attempt being made to stay the king's hand in some cases. Thus Roland Lee, the bishop of Coventry and Lichfield, and the mayor and aldermen of Coventry vainly tried to induce Henry to spare the cathedral church of that city. The bishop begged Crumwell most earnestly for this favour. "My good lord," he says, "help me and the city both in this, that the church may stand, whereby I may keep my name and the city have commodity and ease to their desire."[3] The mayor also declared that "the lack and decay of it will be not only a great defacing of the said city, but also a great hurt and inconvenience to all the inhabitants there in time of plagues; the friars' churches there being already suppressed and no place for the infected people and

---

[1] R. O. Exch. Augt. Off. Misc. Bk., 494, f. 11.

[2] R. O. Crum. Corr., xii. 64. In the same way Crumwell is informed from Boston that as there was very little stone in those parts the building would be most useful (*Ibid.*, xxxii. 27). The mayor and aldermen of Worcester also asked for the friars' houses there, which they afterwards purchased, to repair the walls, roads and bridges (*Ibid.*, l. 13). The buildings of St. Augustine's, Canterbury, were used in the same way. On portions of the old monastery considerable sums were spent to adapt it to the requirements of a royal residence, the rest became the city quarry. Thus in 1542-3 "St. Michael's gate (Burgate) was extensively repaired. Nine loads of stone were obtained from the recently dissolved monastery of St. Augustine's. Nothing was paid for the material, but a man received 13½d. for carriage and two labourers were paid for the destructive work, which lasted four days" (Hist. MSS. Comm. 9th Rept., App. p. 153; City of Canterbury Records).

[3] Wright, p. 238.

others, who are no small number in plague time, to resort to, but only to the parish churches having but two in all the city." Wherefore the city begs that letters may be sent to Dr. London "to stay and give sparing to the defacement of the said church."[1] These appeals, however, were unheeded. The cathedral church was dismantled, unroofed, and, although a magnificent example of English architecture with three spires, was pulled to pieces for the sake of its materials. Its fate is only a sample of what befell hundreds of monastic churches at this period. Some churches, or in several instances portions of the entire buildings, were saved by the prompt action of the people, who by an offer of ready money redeemed them from destruction. Thus the parishioners of Crowland paid £26 "for the south aisle of their church" and £30 for two of the old abbey bells.[2] Those of Romsey saved the fine convent church from destruction with £100.[3] Richard Berdes and the inhabitants of Malvern purchased the church, bell-tower, dormitory, refectory and great barn of the monastery for £20,[4] and the people of Atherstone bought the priory church and two bells for £35.[5] In the same way the church of Southwark was obtained from the king by the inhabitants of the borough, "Dr. Gardiner, bishop of Winchester, putting to his helping hand."[6] The townspeople of St. Alban's gave £400 for the great abbatial church, and those of Crediton £200 for the collegiate building in that place.[7]

[1] *Calendar*, xiv. (i), No. 34.
[2] R. O. Exch. Augt. Off. Mins. Accts., 30–31 Hen. VIII., 217, m. 5. As a matter of fact the north aisle was the one saved.
[3] Mr. Baigent's MSS. collections. The deed, dated 20 Feb., 35 Hen. VIII. (1545), shows that only £100 was expended by the inhabitants. This is much below John Foster's valuation (*ante*), and very possibly the building had been despoiled and neglected during the interval. A portion also of the church belonged to the inhabitants, and served as their parish church.
[4] *Ibid.*, 210, m. 6.
[5] *Ibid.*, 226, m. 12d. These are only given as samples, and could be multiplied to almost any extent.
[6] Stow, ed. 1615, p. 579.
[7] Blomefield (*Hist. of Norfolk*, i. pp. 733–4) relates that the inhabitants of Wymondham claimed part of the church there and petitioned Henry for certain other parts, paying him for the bells, lead, &c., according to their value. They wanted to save the steeple with its bells, the vestry with all the "right up aisle" to the transept, with "the monks' lodgings builded on the south aisle," the chapel of St. Margaret, "the choir and our lady's chapel, with all the whole work as it standeth." Also "the whole chapel of Becket, standing in the midst of the town, with two little bells there hanging to give

In concluding this brief account of the spoils which Henry gathered into the royal purse by the overthrow of the monastic system and the destruction and sacking of the abbeys and convents of England, it is well to state, as far as it is possible to do so, the total amount of ecclesiastical plunder actually received by him. It is necessary, however, to bear in mind that many sums of money were disbursed, as well as royal grants of lands and possessions made, which do not enter into the ordinary accounts,[1] and that the figures as stated here represent only the actual receipts of the treasurer of the Court of Augmentation and those of the keeper of the royal jewels. The amount received from rents coming from the confiscated lands and from the sale of them has already been stated, as well as the value of the gold and silver plate taken by the royal commissioners during Henry's reign. The only other regular item of receipt which calls for notice here is that which represents the proceeds of the various sales of vestments, lead, bells, furniture, glass and building material of every kind, and from all of these only £26,502, 1s. 0¼d. is acknowledged by the Court of Augmentation. It is possible that the proceeds of some of the sales are entered under the heading of revenue by the particular receiver of a county; but even were the sum double, it would be but a paltry amount to represent the result of such wholesale pillage and destruction and as a set-off against all the misery inflicted upon the religious and the poor.

In round figures, the money received by Henry from the entire work, from 1536 till his death, was £1,338,500. To

---

warning to the people of every chance of fire or other sudden business happening." Although the people had paid the king, their good intention was frustrated. The lead was torn off and the stone carried away from the south aisle and lady chapel. "The choir being demolished, the inhabitants were obliged to pull the whole down and new built the present south aisle."

[1] One or two instances of this may be given here. From the priory of Bridlington the duke of Norfolk took everything, plate, vestments, cattle, &c., and none of these are in the accounts (R. O. Crum. Corr., xxxiii. 39). In one year the receiver of Yorkshire, Leonard Beckwith, paid £8200 coming from the dissolved monasteries for the fortifications of Berwick. This large sum does not come into the Augmentation Office accounts (R. O. Exch. Augt. Off. Treas. Roll, ii. m. 7). Other sums paid for the same purpose at another time are £666, 13s. 4d. (*Ibid.*, Mins. Accts., 32-33 Hen. VIII., 211, m. 8) and £570 (*Ibid.*, 239). From the receipts of the Somerset dissolved monasteries in the same year £1200 was "paid to the master of the works at Portland and Weymouth for the mole, fortifications and other new works" (*Ibid.*, 219, m. 16d).

this must be added £85,000, the melting value of the plate, as before stated, so that £1,423,500, or between fourteen and fifteen millions sterling of the present money, was the actual cash value of the work of dissolution to the king. Besides this, of course, there was the worth of the vestments and other ecclesiastical furniture reserved for the king's use, and what Crumwell seemed to take more account of than even of the plate itself, the countless precious stones and jewels from all the churches in England." [1] What the money value of these was it is of course impossible to guess. What became of the sums Henry actually obtained will be briefly told in the next chapter.

[1] It is much to be desired that the magnificent inventories of the plate, jewels and household stuff in the royal palaces and treasure-house at the date of Henry's death should appear in print. It is true the MSS. (now among the Harleian collection and at the Society of Antiquaries) are voluminous; but a French society has been found to print sumptuously the not less extensive " Mobilier de la Couronne sous Louis XIV.," and a zealous editor has not been wanting. Our English documents are of vastly greater interest, historical, artistic, antiquarian, social; and in view of the character of more than one series of thick volumes of mediocre and restricted interest issued of late by our publishing societies, the regret is all the more keen that some one of them has not summoned up courage to print a piece of such capital importance, the value of which is now generally acknowledged.

CHAPTER XX

The Spending of the Spoils

THE wealth amassed by the plunder of churches, monasteries, colleges and hospitals was quickly dissipated. It would serve no purpose to inquire too minutely into the history of its disappearance, or to explore with any very scrupulous care the various channels by which the riches, which for some years came pouring into the royal exchequer, were as quickly disposed of, leaving the king as needy and as great a burden upon his subjects as before.[1] Much of the spoil, indeed, melted away so quickly that it would be impossible to account for its disappearance. One thing is, however, quite clear from the accounts of the Augmentation Office, that although large sums were spent upon coast-defences and in preparation for possible foreign wars, the greater portion passed out of the royal possession without serving any public purpose whatever. Lord Coke, in his fourth Institute, lays stress upon the fact that "ad faciendum populum," the lesser monasteries were granted to Henry to use according "to the pleasure of Almighty God and the honour and profit of the realm," and noticing the two statutes legalising monastic suppressions, he observes that, amongst other promises, "the members of both Houses had been informed in parliament" that the "monasteries should never in time to come be converted to private use, and the subject never again be charged with subsidies, fifteenths, loans or other common aids." How utterly this was ignored it is needless to point out, for, says the same high autho-

---

[1] It has been pointed out as singular that Henry's attacks upon ecclesiastical property occurred in regular intervals of about five years. In 1530 he imposed an enormous fine on the clergy; in 1535 he commenced to dissolve the lesser monasteries; in 1540 he completed the dissolution of the larger houses; and in 1545 he attacked the universities and chantry chapels. (See Blunt, *Hist. of Reformation*, p. 293, *note*.)

rity, "since the dissolution of the monasteries" the king "has exacted divers loans and received the same against law."

Before stating briefly the chief ways in which the monastic property disappeared, one word must be said as to the second act of parliament dealing with it. It has been before pointed out that the action of the royal agents in regard to the greater monasteries was not strictly legal, and that when all opposition to Henry's policy had been defeated, a measure was introduced by which all the devastation, desecration and plundering of the previous years was legalised.[1] The object of the act, passed in the parliament which commenced on April 28th, 1539, was not to dissolve monasteries, but to secure to the king the property of those which "by any means had come into his hands by supersession, dissolution or surrender since the 4th of February," 1536. The bill was introduced by the chancellor on the 13th May. On Friday, the 16th, the house having adjourned over the feast of the Ascension, the bill was read the second time, in the presence of twenty abbots, and the following Monday, May 19th, it passed into law.[2] Unlike the act of 1536, this one does not allege any reasons for its action, but simply states that "sundry abbots, priors, abbesses, prioresses and other ecclesiastical governors and governesses of divers monasteries . . . of their own free and voluntary minds, good wills and assents, without constraint, co-action or compulsion of any manner of person or persons," having resigned their houses into Henry's hands, the king and his heirs are to hold them for ever. And furthermore this permission was to extend to all houses afterwards to be surrendered or dissolved.

Although in the words of the act itself there do not appear any considerations urged upon the parliament to induce them to grant what the king desired, it would seem quite clear that many inducements were really placed before them. "And now," writes Dugdale in his "History of

[1] 31 Hen. VIII., c. 13.
[2] Lords' Journals (Brit. Mus. Cott. MS., Tib. D. i. f. 58). In the parliament which assembled for its second session on April 12th, 1540, a note says, "No abbots present."

Warwickshire," "when all this (*i.e.* the dissolution) was effected, to the end it might not be thought that these things were done with a high hand, the king having protested that he would suppress none without the consent of his parliament (it being called April 28, 1539, to confirm the surrenders so made), there wanted not plausible insinuations to both houses for drawing on their consent with all smoothness thereunto: the nobility being promised large shares in the spoil, either by free gift from the king, easy purchases, or most advantageous exchanges; and many of the active gentry advancement to honours, with increase of their estates: all which we see happened to them accordingly. And the better to satisfy the vulgar, it was represented to them that by this deluge of wealth the kingdom would be strengthened with an army of forty thousand men, and that for the future they should never be charged with subsidies, fifteenths, loans or common aids. By which means the parliament ratifying the above surrenders, the work became completed."[1]

That some promises of this nature were actually made is more than probable. A document exists which is apparently the preamble of a projected act drawn up at this time, and having direct reference to the dissolution of the great monasteries. It is written and corrected by Henry himself, and proposes to take the revenues of the monasteries to establish schools, almshouses and new bishops' sees. It was withdrawn, as Tanner believed, "when the bill for the suppression was actually passed."[2]

---

[1] Within a year a loan was again asked and granted. "In a parliament which began the 18th of April (1540) was granted to the king a subsidy of 2s. the pound lands and 12d. goods and four fifteens towards the king's great charges in building of block-houses" (Stow, *Flores Historiarum*, 974).

[2] The projected act in Henry's writing is in the Cotton MSS. Cleop. E. iv. f. 305. The following portion is printed in Wright, p. 262:—"Forasmuch as it is not unknown the slothful and ungodly life which hath been used amongst all sort which have borne the name of religious folk, and to the intent that henceforth many of them might be turned to better use (as hereafter shall follow), whereby God's word might the better be set forth, children brought up in learning, clerics nourished in the universities, old servants decayed have livings, almshouses for poor folk to be sustained in, readers of Greek, Hebrew and Latin to have good stipends, daily alms to be ministered, mending of highways, exhibitions for ministers of the Church, it is thought therefore unto the king's highness most expedient and necessary that more bishopricks, collegiate and cathedral churches should be established instead

Some portion of the confiscated property, although only a very small portion, found its way back to the Church. Six new bishoprics were created out of the ruins of the monastic houses at Westminster, Oxford, Chester, Gloucester, Bristol, and Peterborough, and the endowments made for the bishops and chapters amounted to about £100,000 of modern money.[1] Besides this, some small sums were allotted to educational purposes at Oxford and Cambridge, but beyond these comparatively insignificant amounts the whole sum realized by

of these aforesaid religious houses, within the foundation whereof other titles before rehearsed shall be established."

On a second sheet of paper is another document written by the king, but apparently incomplete:—

"Bishopricks to be new made."

Essex	Waltham.
Hertford	St. Albans.
Bedfordshire and Bucks	Dunstable, Newenham, Elnestowe.
Oxford and Berks	Osney and Thame.
Northampton and Huntingdon	Peterbro'.
Middlesex	Westminster.
Leicester and Rutland	Leicester.
Gloucestershire	St. Peter's (Gloucester).
Lancashire	Fountains and Archdeaconry of Richmond.
Suffolk	Bury.
Stafford and Salop	Shrewsbury.
Notts and Derby	Welbeck, Worksop and Thurgarton.
Cornwall	Launceston, Bodmin with another.

"Places to be altered according to our device which have sees in them."

Christ Church in Canterbury.
St. Swithin's (Winchester).
Ely, Durham, Rochester.
Worcester and all others having the same.

"Places to be altered into colleges and schools only."

Burton super Trent.

[1] In 1541, John Chambers, last abbot of Peterborough, was made first bishop. About the same time Thomas Thirlby became first and only bishop of Westminster, and Robert King, late abbot of Osney, was made bishop of Oxfordshire, with Osney abbey church as his cathedral. Shortly after the see was moved to Christchurch, Oxford. Paul Bush became first bishop of Bristol, John Wakeman of Gloucester and Richard Sampson of Chester, all about the same time. Seven other cathedrals hitherto served by Benedictines were occupied by secular canons, many of the monks, however, obtaining stalls in the new foundation. These were Canterbury, Durham, Winchester, Ely, Carlisle, Norwich and Worcester.

the dissolutions was spent upon secular and private purposes, and even the tithes of parishes, which had been appropriated to the religious houses, passed away by grant or purchase from the royal appropriator to lay owners, to be henceforth used by them as part of their general revenue."[1]

The way in which a great deal of the monastic property was got rid of by the king is notorious. Fuller describes how "not only cooks, but the meanest turn-broach in the king's kitchen did lick his fingers," and he gives on good authority instances of Henry's prodigality with the abbey lands. Estates of considerable value were parted with readily as gifts to those who won his favour. "I could add," says the historian, "how he gave a religious house of some value to mistress —— for presenting him with a dish of puddings which pleased his palate."[2]

In the same way Fuller states that Henry lost a great deal by play. "Once, being at dice," he writes, "he played Sir Miles Partridge (staking a hundred pounds against them) for Jesus' bells, hanging in a steeple not far from St. Paul's in London, and as great and tunable as any in the city, and lost them at a cast."[3]

---

[1] With regard to Henry's gifts to Oxford and Cambridge the following is of interest:—

Money appointed to be paid towards the dotation and erection of colleges at Oxford and Cambridge from 25 March anno 36° to Michaelmas anno 38°

The revenues of Osney to Oxford	£702 9 4¾	Oxford	£3102 9 4¾
By warrant to Treasurer	2400 0 0		
To Cambridge revenues of King's Hall and Michaelhouse	329 15 8	Cambridge	£2329 15 8
By warrant	£2000 0 0		

After paying the ordinary "wages and stipend" there remained for building purposes at Oxford £1617, 18s. 1¾d., and at Cambridge £971, 7s. (R. O. Exch. Aug. Off. Misc. Bk., 415, f. 108).

The last year of Henry's reign, however, the revenues were not paid, and the college of Christchurch, Oxford, was in debt. Edward VI., to meet this, paid Dr. Coxe, the dean, £2400 (*Ibid.*, Treas. Roll, iii. m. 201).

[2] Much the same story is told by a writer of about the year 1557 (Brit. Mus. Arund. MS., 151, f. 387). In this version a cook who pleased the king with a well-cooked sucking pig had as his reward "the college of St. Edmund, Salisbury, with certain rectories," and thus, says the old writer, was given to a layman to whom it could not belong "the cure of souls."

[3] This story is also given (*Ibid.*), but with a slight change. Miles Partridge is represented as a gambler who had lost everything, and Henry gave him the belfry bells and lead to retrieve his fortune with. The writer adds that Partridge was afterwards hanged.

The Spending of the Spoils

The manner in which the king was robbed by all connected with the work of spoliation has frequently been illustrated in these pages. The inquiry made by queen Elizabeth, and the information presented to her, evidently by an authority on the matter, leaves no doubt that the king was cheated out of a very large portion of the plunder by the officials he employed.

How the rest went is shown on the rolls of the Treasurer of the Augmentation or the accounts of the keeper of the royal jewels.[1] It is only fair, however, to point out that some proportion of the plunder went for national purposes. To fortify the coasts, to establish a fleet, to support Henry's foreign policy, and to collect and maintain his armies, the ecclesiastical spoils were freely used. Thus, of the £1,338,500 actually acknowledged as received by the Augmentation Office from the beginning of the work of suppression till Henry's death, about £64,500 went to coast fortifications, £28,000 for naval matters, £137,000 for purposes of foreign war, including the defence of Calais and other towns on the Continent. Very nearly half-a-million of money was also spent upon the general military affairs of the nation, about one-half that sum being expended on the purchase and manufacture of guns, to which also the metal of a large number of the monastery bells was devoted. It may therefore be allowed that more than half the money received by the Augmentation Office from the plunder was disbursed for public purposes.

Of the rest, a large sum was expended upon the royal palaces at Westminster, Hampton Court, Chelsea, Hackney, St. James' and elsewhere, as well as upon enclosing the king's parks and adapting some of the old abbey buildings to the royal requirements. Nearly £52,000 was spent upon the purchase of lands, £23,000 on the household expenses of the young prince Edward, and £274,086, 19s. 8¾d. was either paid to the king in cash or went to support his household. Such are the chief channels which quickly carried off the wealth obtained from the destruction of the monastic houses.

The accounts of the keeper of the royal jewels show that

---

[1] It would be impossible to give full details without copious notes. The general sources of expenditure found in the Appendix are taken from the Treasurer's Rolls.

about £10,000 was spent on coast fortifications, and nearly the same sum was sent, for the king's purposes, to Ireland. Of the plate itself, a great deal was either handed to Henry for his use, or other gold and silver articles were purchased for him with the proceeds. In this account and on the Treasurer's Rolls no less than £30,860 was entered under this heading, as well as more than half the entire value of the plate obtained by the spoilers, that is, £46,636, 1s. 1¼d., was given over "to the proper hand" of the king.[1]

[1] *Monastic Treasures* (Abbotsford Club), p. 93. For further particulars see Appendix.

CHAPTER XXI

The Ejected Monks and their Pensions

SOMETHING must now be said about the pensions which were paid to the disbanded monks and nuns out of the funds coming into the king's possession on the dissolution of their houses. At the outset it is well to state that there is every reason to suppose that the promised annuities were fairly well and punctually paid, at least during the reign of Henry VIII. Still, it is necessary to bear in mind that by no means all the religious who were deprived of their homes and turned out into the world to begin life afresh were provided with any pittance whatever to secure them against poverty, or even, in many cases, it is to be feared, absolute starvation. In the first place, upon the dissolution of the monasteries which possessed an income of under £200 a year, the superiors only were granted a pension. By the terms of the act of parliament passed in February, 1536, the king's "majesty is pleased and contented, of his most excellent charity, to provide to every chief head and governor of every such religious house" a yearly pension for life. As for the community, "his majesty will ordain and provide that the convents of every such religious house shall have their capacities, if they will, to live honestly and virtuously abroad, and some convenient charity disposed to them toward their living, or else shall be committed to such honourable great monasteries of this realm wherein good religion is observed, as shall be limited by his highness there to live religiously during their lives."[1]

But although many of the monks and nuns thus disbanded found homes for a time in other houses of their order, it is probable that the majority were forced to take the alternative offered them and accept Henry's dispensation to seek

---

[1] 27 Hen. VIII., cap. 28.

their living in the world. Thus, as an example, William Morland, a monk of Louth Park, whose name is connected with the Lincolnshire rising, declares that when he went to Bourne abbey to obtain his "capacities," "a late canon of Bourne, then also suppressed," gave him six-and-twenty other dispensations to distribute [1] to his fellow-monks.

To those who thus went out into the world it may be taken as certain that the king never extended the promised "convenient charity disposed to them toward their living." In most instances only the abbot or superior received anything. In a small number of cases the religious obtained a few pounds, or generally shillings, on quitting their cloisters. Thus at Louth Park the abbot, George Walker, was granted a pension of £20 a year, but apparently none of his ten monks received anything whatever.[2] At Bourne in the same way John Small, the abbot, was allowed £24 a year, but none of his ten canons received anything on the dissolution of their house.[3] Other communities were somewhat more fortunate. Thus the five nuns of Cannington convent, in Somerset, received twenty shillings each on their dismissal, and Cecilia Verney, their prioress, was pensioned.[4] The seven Cistercians of Buildwas, in Shropshire, had fifty-five shillings divided between them.[5] And, to take but one more example, at Cleeve abbey, in Somerset, the abbot was pensioned, the prior had a present of £4, 3s. 10d., and each of the thirteen other monks went out of their cloister with twenty-six and eightpence in their purses.[6]

⸨In no known instance among the early dissolutions was any entire community pensioned, and, with only one or two exceptions, no provision was made for any one but the superior.⸩ In fact, the list of grants during the period of these suppressions shows that not above 204 monks, canons and nuns, out of the entire number of those dismissed, had any pension assigned to them.[7] As this number amounted to at least 2000, it is obvious that a very small fraction only

---

[1] R. O. Chapt. H. Bk., A. $\frac{2}{19}$, p. 96.
[2] R. O. Exch. Augt. Off. Mins. Accts., 27–28 Hen. VIII., 81.
[3] *Ibid.*, 166.   [4] *Ibid.*, 169, m. 2.   [5] *Ibid.*, 165, m. 2.
[6] *Ibid.*, 169, m. 2d.
[7] R. O. Augt. Off. Misc. Bk., 244, "Original of Grants;" also *Ibid.*, Bk. 232, "Enrolment of Grants." The pension was only paid to those who had a "patent" from the king, and many instances can be given of payment being refused when the letters patent were not forthcoming.

of those whose property was confiscated continued to be chargeable upon it or to interfere with Henry's full enjoyment or free disposal of the Church lands so obtained.

Even the case of those religious who elected, under the provisions of the act of dissolution, to be transferred to other monasteries, was scarcely more fortunate. For a year or two they were, perhaps, spared the hard fate of their brethren who had passed at once into the world, but in the end the same lot befell them. The conditions upon which general pensions were subsequently granted to the members of a community would seem to exclude these new-comers from participation in the benefit. Each individual grant provided that the recipient of the royal favour must have been for a considerable time (*diu antea*) before the dissolution an inmate of the monastery. While a comparison of the pension list of a monastery with any previous records of the names of the community[1] will certainly bear out the view that, as a general rule, only professed members of a house were made chargeable upon its revenues.[2]

[1] *e.g.*, the lists of monks contained in the Augmentation Office Book, 245, with the acknowledgments of royal supremacy printed in Dep. Keeper's Rept., vii.

[2] Under the act dissolving the lesser monasteries more than two-thirds of the Cistercian houses were suppressed. The inmates were, as a rule, transferred to other greater houses of the Order (Mr. Baigent's "Abbey of Waverley," p. 46). On the dissolution of Netley in February, 1537, all the monks went back to their mother house at Beaulieu. In the early part of March, 1536, John Browning, the abbot of Beaulieu, died, and Thomas Stephens, then abbot of Netley, was elected his successor. This was no sooner done than Netley was suppressed and all the Netley monks accompanied their abbot to Beaulieu. On April 2, 1538, this abbot and 20 monks signed the surrender of Beaulieu. In February, 1540, abbot Stephens was instituted to the rectory of Bentworth, near Alton, vacant at that time by reason of the deprivation of John Palmes. This latter was most unwilling to submit, and on March 1st (1540) wrote a letter of complaint to Crumwell saying that "his cousin Cooke, with gentlemen and farmers of Sir John Wallop's tenants, assembled upon St. Mathias' even (February 23) last past and inducted as parson of Bentworth the abbot quondam of Beaulieu, and with great violence and blows given entered into the parsonage and sealed up the barn doors, and hired men, with money, to gangle and ring the bells above all measure and custom of a charitable induction, whereof great clamour and wonder is of men in the whole shire, so that my name and estimation is clean gone and destroyed in all this disturbance at Bentworth." In 1548 Thomas Stephens was collated to the treasurership of Salisbury Cathedral and died in 1550 holding both these preferments (Mr. Baigent's MSS. Collections). It may be here noted that indications of disbanded religious obtaining livings are only by chance lighted upon. In the registers abbot Stephens, for example, is called "T. Stephens, *capellanus*," and in 1548 he is "Mr. Thomas Stephyns, *infirmus*." This is an instance of the difficulty experienced in tracing the expelled religious.

Even in the later suppressions, by no means all the disbanded religious were provided with pensions. The friars, as a class, received no yearly allowance. Only in the case of one or two individuals does there appear any exception. Thus the superiors of some of the London friaries obtained small grants, as £10 to John Gibbs, prior of the Carmelites; £13, 6s. 8d. to Thomas Chapman, prior of the Franciscans; £60 to John Hilsey, bishop of Rochester and commendatory superior of the Dominicans, and five marks to Ralph Turnor, of Crutched friars.[1] These, with the superiors of the Franciscan and Dominican convents in York, were very nearly the only members of the four orders of friars who were granted any pensions whatever. The rest were dismissed from their houses with some small gratuity, generally only a few shillings, and left to provide for themselves. Thus, when the Carmelites of North Allerton were disbanded, two days before the feast of Christmas, 1538, William Humfrey, the prior, was given six shillings and eightpence, four of his brethren five shillings, and six of the younger members three and fourpence apiece, and this, as the record has it, was paid by the special "consideration of the commissioner."[2]

In the same way, when, on November 21st, 1538, the Franciscans of Doncaster were dismissed, sixty shillings was distributed amongst them "out of the abundant benevolence of the lord king," who, at the same time, relieved them of their house, the vestments and other ornaments of their church, as well as three chalices and two cruets of silver. It was calculated also by his agent that there were 44 fodders of lead upon the roofs of the monastic buildings and four bells which would be worth some £200 to sell.[3] Even these were more fortunate than some others, who, like the Trinitarians of Newcastle, were ejected without any "reward," and the prior left to pay the convent's debts with what he could collect out of money due to the house.[4]

As a rule, therefore, it may be taken for granted that no pension whatever was allotted to any of the friars. The whole number, at the lowest estimate some eighteen hundred, were cast adrift in the world and left to find a living

---

[1] R. O. Exch. Aug. Off. Misc. Bk., 233, "Enrolments of Grants, annis 30°–31°," ff. 161, 163, 146.
[2] *Ibid.*, Mins. Accts., 29–30 Hen. VIII., 197, m. 12d.
[3] *Ibid.*, mm. 2d. 3. [4] *Ibid.*, m. 15.

as best they might. Even those who were priests experienced great difficulties in obtaining clerical employment, as has been before stated. The lot of those not in sacred orders must have been harder still.

With respect to the rest of the great body of monks and nuns who were pensioned, their grants were no doubt chiefly obtained by compliance with the king's wishes. Those that resigned their houses at the royal invitation were promised annuities. Those that resisted every suggestion of "voluntary surrender" not only got nothing, but acquired for themselves the deadly animosity of a king who would take no contradiction. "If they," runs the instructions to the royal commissioners, shall willingly consent and agree "to the proposed suppression," the said commissioners shall appoint unto the said head and every of their convent pensions for (the) term of their lives. But "if they shall find any of the said heads and convents so appointed to be dissolved so wilful and obstinate that they will in no wise submit themselves to the king's majesty," then they shall take possession of everything by force. "But they shall in no wise assign any pensions . . . to any such obstinate and wilful persons till they shall know further of the king's pleasure."[1]

To many of the monks, no doubt, the alternative here expressed in the royal instructions was clear, and they elected to go out with a pension rather than be turned out with nothing to secure them against absolute starvation. Others, however, preferred even death to the dishonour of betraying a trust which they had for the Church and the poor; and, to use Dr. Hillyard's words to the prior of Mountgrace, they held "that it was a manner of selling the house to surrender up their house for money or pensions."[2] The resistance of the prioress of Ambresbury to the suggestions of the king's agents has already been related. She preferred to go out and beg her bread rather than take a pension for a surrender. Her successor, Joan Darrell, put into the office for the purpose of giving up the convent, obtained £100 a year for her compliance. The name of the brave Florence Bonnewe does not appear upon the pension roll of the house, and she was, no doubt, left to

[1] R. O. Chapter House Bk., A. $\frac{4}{30}$. This document has been quoted more at length in a previous chapter.
[2] *Calendar*, xiv. (ii), No. 750.

carry out her design of begging for her support. It would be difficult to suppose that there were not many others in the English houses at the time possessed of a similar spirit, whilst the recorded pensions prove that of the entire number of religious at that time in England not one half were given any annuity whatever.[1]

A large number of those not pensioned have already been accounted for, and to these must be added the members of all houses which were made to fall into the king's hands by the attainder of the superior. Thus no monk at monasteries such as Kirksted, Jervaulx or Whalley in the northern parts, and Glastonbury, Reading, Colchester or Woburn in the south, obtained anything. Moreover, even a surrender does not appear to have furnished an absolute title to such a reward. Thus, to give one example, Furness abbey, the surrender of which has been related, was dissolved apparently without the monks having any promise of pension, and no grant is found enrolled in the Augmentation Court. On dismissal, each of them received only forty shillings except three, "who were sick and impotent," to whom an extra twenty shillings was granted. The following year, however, the abbot was provided with the profits of the rectory of Dalton, valued at £33, 6s. 8d. per annum, which may have been given him in lieu of pension, but, as far as is known, none of the thirty monks who composed his community obtained anything for their compliance with the royal demands.

The amount of the pensions varied considerably. Some of the abbots appear to have had large payments for those days. Thus John Lawrence de Wardeboys, the last abbot of Ramsey, had a grant of £266, 13s. 4d. a year with a house, woods and swans for life.[2] Abbot Wardeboys, however, who had been appointed to the office in 1507, was a very old man at the time of the surrender and was not likely

---

[1] The total number of patents for religious pensions enrolled in the Augmentation Office books is under 4000. Without this patent no pension was paid, and it may, therefore, be presumed that this number is fairly correct. According to a previous estimate there were some 8081 religious of all orders at the time of the suppression in England. The enrolled grants found in the Record Office Exch. Augt. Off. Misc. Bk., No. 232, Part I., contains those granted anno 28°; Part II., those in 29° and 30°; No. 233, those in 30°-31°; and Nos. 234-5, those in 31°-32°.

[2] R. O. Exch. Augt. Off. Misc. Bk., 245, f. 64.

to draw the pension very long, and he had not only readily resigned his trust when called upon, but had been, it is said, busy in persuading other abbots to follow his example. Even larger was the pension given to the late abbot of Bermondsey, Robert Wharton, who since 1536 had been bishop of St. Asaph's, a sum of £333, 6s. 8d. being assigned him out of the revenues of the monastery. Some other bishops, who were commendatory abbots, also received large sums, as the bishop of Down in Ireland, by royal letters patent abbot of Thorney; John Draper, a suffragan and prior of Twynham, Christchurch, and several others.

The ordinary pension, however, for the superior of one of the large monasteries appears to have been about £100 a year, and the average grant to each religious between £5 and £6. In the case of smaller houses the pension was proportionally less, and in some cases the superior did not receive more than £15 or even £10. Of the convents, Syon was the most highly paid. Agnes Jordan, the abbess, received no less a sum than £200 a year, while none of her sisters had less than £6, and several more than that sum. Very few of the nuns, however, had anything like that amount; £40 being the ordinary pension for an abbess and £3 or £4, and very often less, for a nun. In some places lay sisters and novices were not allowed to be entered on the pension list, possibly because they could have had no part in resigning the house.

Sometimes, as in the case of the abbot of Ramsey just quoted, besides the actual grant of money the pensioner was allowed certain houses, lands or privileges. Thus the abbot of Ford had the use of a house and grounds, the prior of Bath had "appointed to him for his dwelling-house one tenement set and lying in Stall street within the Southgate of Bath,"[1] and the abbot of Winchcombe was allowed to cut yearly forty loads of firewood out of "Deepwood" thicket. To others, members of old monastic churches or cathedrals, an office in the new establishment, over and above a small pension, was often given. Thus, at Rochester, Thomas Grey had forty shillings a year "besides the office of Gospeller" and Thomas Cope the same amount and "the office of Epistoler."[2] At Ely, in the same way, three monks,

---

[1] R. O. Exch. Augt. Off. Misc. Bk., 245, f. 109. "Wherein one Jeffry Stainer lately dwelled, being of the yearly rent of 20/." [2] *Ibid.*, f. 76.

noted to be "good choir men," received an office as well as a pension of £8 a year.[1] In certain other cases a living or cure of souls was granted in lieu of a pension. Thus, to give one or two examples, at Missenden, in Buckinghamshire, Thomas Barnard obtained the vicarage of the abbey, and another, John Slythurst, became curate of Lee with a pension of £8; at Pulton, in Wiltshire, John Hogge was appointed by Petre, the royal commissioner, "to serve the cure there, and for his wages" to have 106s. 8d., "and if he were unable to serve, then forty shillings."[2] One other example from the neighbouring county of Dorset is worth recording: at Bindon, one of the monks obtained "the cure" of the place, and for his services he was to get yearly £6, 13s. 4d., "and the king to have all manner of tithes and oblations."[3]

If some of the promised pensions appear somewhat high, there was a reason for this, especially in the beginning of the work of suppression. From Coventry, Dr. London in writing about the Benedictine cathedral priory there gives the reason clearly. "The prior," he says, "is a sad honest priest, as his neighbours do report him, and (he) is a bachelor of divinity. He gave his house unto the king's grace willingly and so in like manner did all his brethren." After declaring what pensions he had promised, the commissioner concludes: "Beseeching your good mastership to confirm and authorize the same by your high authority, and thereby others perceiving that these men be liberally handled will with better will, not only surrender their houses, but also leave the same in the better state to the king's use."[4]

---

[1] R. O. Exch. Augt. Off. Misc. Bk., 245, f. 61.   [2] *Ibid.*, f. 122.

[3] *Ibid.*, f. 145. Instances of cures being served by religious prior to the dissolution are sometimes met with. Thus the abbot of Quare, William Repon, was instituted to the vicarage of Carisbrooke, Isle of Wight, in 1533. On 24th February, 1536, on the dissolution of the abbey, he was called *capellanus*, and instituted to the vicarage of Newchurch on the presentation of Sir Richard Lyster, Kt. He resigned this the following year, and was succeeded by John Austen, canon of Tichfield, then dissolved, on the presentation of the abbot of Beaulieu (Mr. Baigent's MSS. Collections). This instance would seem to show that the larger monasteries gave livings to the disbanded inmates of the smaller houses. One or two more examples may be added. In 1520 Thomas London, abbot of Quare, was vicar of Carisbrooke, and one of his monks was serving curate at Binsted. In 1532 Lainston, near Winchester, was served by a Carmelite friar. Littleton was always served by a monk of St. Swithin's priory, and the proceeds of the cure went to purchase books for the choir of this monastic church (*Ibid.*).

[4] R. O. Exch. Q. R. Miscellanea, $\frac{14}{5}$, No. 15. Thomas Camswell, the prior, was granted £133, 6s. 8d. a year (Augt. Off. Misc. Bk., 233, f. 118).

The same reason prompted Dr. London in the case of Combe abbey. Robert Bate had been made abbot only "the same day twelve months" before he was invited to resign. He had, it appeared, already "paid part of his first-fruits and tenths." Dr. London assigned him £80 and hoped that Crumwell would ratify the grant, "as your mastership so doing," he writes, "will give occasion to others the more rather to make like surrender."[1] The same visitor also thought large pensions were deserved by those who so short a time previously had redeemed their houses by large money payments to the king, who had under his great seal granted that they should continue for ever. Thus he urges that the Carthusians of Coventry, the nuns of Delapre, the Austin canons of Ulvescroft and others who had "lately obtained the king's grace's charter for the continuance of the same to their and their friends great charge,"[2] might reasonably hope for good pensions.

Not every royal commissioner, however, cared to plead for generous pensions. It was naturally to the interest of the king's officials to reduce obligations on the received estates as much as possible, and much bargaining, no doubt, was resorted to to make the conditions upon which surrender would be made as easy as possible. Thus Robert Southwell, one of these officials, writing to Crumwell of St. James's abbey, Northampton, says: "We have practised with the poor men for their pensions as easily to the king's charge and as much to his grace's honour as we could devise."[3]

It has already been stated that the promised pensions were, as far as can be ascertained, fairly well paid. The disbanded religious received their annuities either directly from the Court of Augmentation in London, or from the royal receiver, appointed to administer the estates coming from the religious houses in any particular county. It is difficult to understand the reason of the distinction, especially when some members of a house were paid by the office in London and others by the particular receiver of the county. Some religious, especially in the earlier dissolutions, were especially directed to receive their annuities in London,[4]

---

[1] R. O. Exch. Augt. Off. Misc. Bk., 245, f. 42.
[2] Ibid., ff. 36, 38, 39.   [3] Wright, p. 173.
[4] Thus at Fosse, in Lincolnshire, Dr. London promised the nuns a pension, and added, "All are to come to London for them" (R. O. Exch. Augt. Off.

and as in process of time the various lands diminished by royal grants or sales, and receipts from them dwindled in proportion, the number of monks and nuns paid by the general treasurer in London increased.

Thus, in the first two years after the creation of the Augmentation Office only seventeen individuals drew their annuities directly from the treasurer in London, and in the last years of Henry's reign more than 200 monks and nuns were paid by him.[1] The great bulk of the pensioners, however, continued to draw their allowances from the king's officers in the different counties in which their monasteries had been situated.[2]

In the process of paying the money considerable abuses crept in. Many of the pensioned monks and nuns, either from age, infirmities or other causes, were unable to attend and receive their annuities personally, and were consequently forced to employ agents. Thus at one time a certain Anthony Emery, servant to Richard Pollard, was sent to obtain the pensions of some fifty or sixty monks and nuns of the west country. Another agent journeyed to London to fetch the money due to the abbess of Canonleigh and seventeen of her nuns, and a third acted in a like capacity for the prior of Plympton and his canons.[3] The necessity of sending long distances, with the "reasonable costs" of the requisite agents, considerably reduced the pittances, already small enough; but the various charges made by the officials concerned in the disbursement of the royal bounty still further diminished the sums awarded. For each quarterly payment the official was entitled to a fee of fourpence, but in practice there is little doubt that much more was demanded.[4]

Misc. Bk., 245, f. 23). They were, however, paid subsequently by the Lincolnshire receiver.

[1] Payments made by the office are entered on the Rolls of the Treasurer of the Court of Augmentation. The Miscellaneous Books of that Office (Nos. 246, 249, 250, 256) are the ledger books of these payments during Henry VIII.'s reign.

[2] These payments appear in the Ministers' Accounts, and are shown as deducted from the receipts accounted for to the Treasurer in London.

[3] R. O. Exch. Augt. Off. Treas. Roll, ii. m. 20d.

[4] As an example, the case of the nuns of Limbroke, in Herefordshire, may be given. They had fallen under the act for the suppression of the lesser monasteries, having an income of only £22 a year, but had purchased from Henry the perpetual continuance of their convent by a payment of £53, 6s. 8d., more than double their annual income (Aug. Off. Treas. Roll, i. m. 4d.). At the close of 1539, however, they were called upon to surrender to the king,

Further reductions were made in the pensions promised by the amounts being subjected to deduction on account of every subsidy granted by parliament to the king. Thus in the first year after the general dissolution a tenth part of the payment was withheld as "the first subsidy due to our sovereign lord the king."[1] Two years afterwards "one-fourth part of the pensions of all the late religious persons . . . having £20 and upward" was deducted "by way of loan" to Henry, and when the half year was due, on March 25th, 1543, the religious only received one quarter of the annual payment.[2] By these two methods Henry retained from the promised pensions a sum of £9443, 15s. 6d. for himself.[3] Beyond this, he received in 1544 from the clergy, and amongst them from many of the pensioned religious, the sum of £12,870, 16s. 8d. as a war contribution, but a portion of this sum was subsequently repaid.[4]

Necessity compelled some at least of the disbanded religious to part with their patents, and speculators were ready enough to purchase the annuity "for little or no money, or other thing given to the said pensioners, supplanting them to their utter undoing." It was, therefore, found necessary in the third year of the reign of Edward VI. for parliament

and the five nuns were promised pensions; the prioress £6, and each of the others 53s. 4d. In all they were to have £16, 13s. 4d. a year. The following are the charges made for obtaining that sum for them :—

William Thomas to John Scudamore, enclosing a bill for getting the pensions for the "poor nuns of Limbroke."

	£	s.	d.
"First to write Mr. Chancellor's clerk for making the warrant and getting it signed	0	6	8
"Item to Mr. Duke's clerk for writing out the pensions	0	6	8
"Item paid to Glascocke to dispatch them from the seal	0	5	0
"Item my lord Privy Seal's fee for the head of the house	1	0	0
"Item Mr. Chancellor's and Mr. Duke's fees of every 'pentionary' at 11s.	2	15	0
"Item for mine owne labour	1	0	0
Summa	5	13	4"

—(Brit. Mus. Add. MS., 11,041, f. 60.)

[1] Bib. Bod. Tanner MS., 343, f. 1, *et seq.*, contains the Scudamore accounts for four counties showing this deduction.
[2] Brit. Mus. Harl. MS., 604, f. 108.
[3] R. O. Exch. Augt. Off. Treas. Roll, ii. mm. 45-48.
[4] *Ibid.*, Roll, ii. m. 32. Amongst the names of those contributing are: The late abbot of York, £100; ditto of Evesham, £66, 13s. 4d.; ditto of Hayles, £66, 13s. 4d., and others.

to apply some remedy to this state of things. An act was consequently passed ordering all persons who had obtained pension patents in any fraudulent manner to restore them within six months. They were to receive back whatever they had originally paid, and if they failed to deliver the grant it was to be forfeited and all future payment made to the original owner. At the same time the officers and receivers were commanded to pay all pensions upon reasonable request under a penalty of £5, and if they demanded more then their legal fee they were to forfeit ten times the amount taken.[1]

A subsequent examination was made by a commission appointed to inquire into the pensions paid in each county. From the report of the officials, which still exists for some counties, many interesting particulars are learnt about the monks' pensions.[2] Many of the religious did not appear to claim their annuity. Many were proved to have died, and others had not been paid for the past year or so. Of a great many, who ought to have been in receipt of a pension, no tidings could be learnt, and in a good number of instances the original owner had long before parted with the grant. Thus, to give one or two examples of these sales, Laurence Sterkbone, a religious of Worksop, took £10, 13s. 4d. for his annuity of £5, 6s. 8d. from the bailiff of the town, who nine months later sold it again to one William Bolles for £16. The original pensioner, Laurence Sterkbone, had only received his annuity for a couple of years when he sold it at little more than two years' purchase. Another canon of the same monastery had got rid of his grant of £4 on somewhat better terms—for £12.[3]

Of Bury St. Edmunds the commissioners mention that one "Thomas Cole, about eight or nine years ago, did give and assign over his annuity to Ambrose Jermyn, Esq., upon condition that the said Ambrose did procure and obtain for him the benefice of Flempton, in Suffolk, of the gift of one Thomas Lucas, Esq." Another former monk, "Thomas Rowte, upon his oath saith and thereupon showeth an indenture bearing date the 1st day of March, in the thirty-sixth year of Henry VIII., declaring that he then sold and

---

[1] 2 and 3 Ed. VI., cap. 7.
[2] R. O. Chapter House Box, 154, Nos. 2, 15, 25, 54, 61, 63, 64.
[3] *Ibid.*, No. 25.

assigned over his letters patent to one Ralph Cockerell for the sum of £26, 13s. 4d., whereof he saith he never received but only £19."[1]

These instances of the sales of pensions are only examples of others to be found in the same report, and they would almost certainly have been found to be much more numerous had it not been for the act of parliament passed a year or two before, which made the possession of purchased grants illegal. As it was, the receivers had been ordered to refuse payment to all but the original owners.

A brief answer must now be given to a question so often asked: "What became of the ejected religious?" At the outset it must be confessed that the information available on this point is so meagre that no satisfactory reply can be given. Turned out of their houses, the monks and nuns, especially those to whom no pensions were assigned, must have endured great suffering and undergone many privations in their endeavours to gain a livelihood. This much can be certainly said without in any way exaggerating the hardship of their lot. But hardly any detail of the subsequent lives of those ejected from the dismantled cloisters of England is known to exist. The muse of history has perhaps mercifully spared the world what would have been a picture of deep distress and misery.

Some of those who were priests (and most of the monks, canons and friars appear to have been in sacred orders) would no doubt have been provided with livings. It was obviously to the advantage of the crown that a pensioned priest should be presented to a living as quickly as might be, since every annuity was granted only until some ecclesiastical benefice of suitable money value should be found for the holder. Still, the pension lists do not show that this was carried out to any very great extent, and the fact that the royal policy in religious matters tended considerably to diminish the call for priests, would render it more difficult to obtain any preferment of this kind for the disbanded monks. The great falling off in candidates for sacred orders at this time would have been more than counterbalanced by the diminution of possible cures. Some small proportion, however, of

---

[1] R. O. Chap. H. Box, 154, No. 15.

the monks and friars clearly found occupation and a livelihood in congenial clerical occupations.[1]

Even to obtain a living, however, formalities had to be gone through which must often have been impossible, and frequently have debarred an exiled religious from undertaking the task. The peculiar hardship of a friar's position in this respect has been remarked upon in a previous chapter. And although it is impossible to blame a bishop's care in preventing the chance of profanation from pretended orders, it is no less difficult to contemplate without shame the miserable spectacle of educated Englishmen, by episcopal consecration ordained for the service of the sanctuary, driven by want to beg that they might be put "into one of the priest's offices for a piece of bread."

The eagerness with which a "capacity," or permission to take a living or other cure, was sought after is illustrated in a curious way. In the ordinary course it was necessary first to prove the reception of orders, next to obtain a dispensation from the archbishop of Canterbury to leave the cloister, to put off the religious habit, and to undertake the care of souls, and thirdly, to obtain the king's confirmation of this dispensation.[2] Whether this was always required is

---

[1] A few of the most compliant abbots were provided with bishoprics during the schism. Thus Salcot, of Hyde, became bishop of Bangor and subsequently of Salisbury. Thomas Spark, a monk of Durham, was given the see of Berwick; Wharton, of Bermondsey, had St. Asaph's; Rugg, of Hulme, Norwich; Holbeach, prior of Worcester, the new see of Bristol; abbot Chambers, the new see of Peterborough; Kitchen, that of Llandaff; Wakeman, of Tewkesbury, became first bishop of Gloucester, and John Salisbury, prior of St. Faith's, was made the new suffragan of Thetford.

[2] The archbishop's dispensation and king Henry's confirmation in the case of the abbot of Feversham are printed by Southouse, *Monasticon Favershamiense*, pp. 136–7. The *Archæologia Cantiana* (viii. pp. 50–58) prints several documents of great interest on this matter. A monk of Battle, one Thomas Bede Twysden, received a dispensation from Cranmer and a confirmation from Henry. He was only in deacon's orders and on being turned out of his monastery lived in the world, and, amongst other things, acted as executor to the will and guardian to the children of his brother. In 1556 he obtained a dispensation and absolution for thus acting from Cardinal Pole. The following year Thomas Bede Twysden petitioned for pardon for having put on a secular dress without permission of the pope, for living out of his monastery, and for dealing with property by permission only of the parliament. His petition was granted by David Pole, the cardinal's vicar-general in 1557. He was allowed to receive ordination and to live in a secular priest's dress out of a monastery, "donec regularia loca restaurata fuerint," on condition that whatever money came into his hands more than sufficient for his necessities should be devoted to pious uses or the poor, and that "bona præfata post

not certain, and probably the comedy was not kept up in the
final suppressions. But at the time of the expulsion of the
friars from their houses it appears to have been the rule. In
the ordinary course, therefore, a Franciscan friar named John
Young obtained from archbishop Cranmer his capacity and
the "letters of dispensation" from the king to enable him
to get a living when chance offered. Another friar minor,
Richard Sharpe, who apparently had some difficulty in
obtaining similar documents for himself, borrowed the parchments from Young, and forged a like "capacity" and "dispensation" in his own name. The forgery was discovered.
Sharpe was tried at Norwich in April, 1539, and condemned
to be hanged, drawn and quartered. The sentence, however,
was not carried out, and he was subsequently pardoned.[1]

In the case of monks belonging to the old monastic
cathedrals or to those of foundations such as Gloucester and
Peterborough, which were upon the dissolution created into
new sees, several obtained positions in the reconstituted
establishments. The abbot or prior in several cases became
the dean, and some of the monks continued to occupy their
old stalls as secular canons. A conservative spirit which
prompted them to cling to the old spot, sacred with every
association of their lives, and a reluctance to turn out in old
age into an unknown world, is really the key to this strange
want of principle which must be deplored in so many of the
monks of the old foundations. An instance of this is afforded
by Thomas Goldwell, cathedral prior of the great Metropolitan
church of Canterbury. When first the coming changes were
reported at the monastery, prior Goldwell wrote to Crumwell:
"There is a common speaking here about us that religious
men shall leave or forsake their habits and go as secular
priests do. Whether they mind of some certain religious
or of all I know not. As concerning this matter your lordship has been so good unto me that you have sent me word
before this time that I and my brethren should not be constrained so to do. And as for my part I will never desire
to forsake my habit as long as I live, for divers considerations
that move me to the same. One is because religious men

mortem tuam præfato monasterio de Battell, vel religioni, etc., arbitrio ordinarii tui pro tempore existentis applicentur." Thomas Twysden died at Wye,
near Battle, in 1584.

[1] R. O. Coram Rege, 33 Hen. VIII., Trinity Rex Roll, 5.

2 F

have been and continued in this our church these 900 years and more also. I made my profession to serve God in a religious habit as much as lay in me so to do. Also if we that be religious men do forsake our habits and go about the world, we shall have many more occasions to offend God and to commit sin than we have now. For this and other considerations which your lordship knoweth better than I, I beseech your lordship to continue good lord to us, me and my brethren, that we may keep our habits of religion still. And if any motion be made to the contrary that it may please you to be our helper and defender therein."[1]

It is impossible not to admire the honourable sentiments expressed in this letter, and the love Thomas Goldwell declares both he and his brethren had for their religious habit. But when it came to the point his resolve gave way. He was, as six years before he had told Crumwell, "somewhat in age and weak and much disposed to a palsy," and he could not contemplate the idea of having to surrender his old rooms in Christchurch monastery. He wrote an earnest letter to the all-powerful minister begging him to remain his friend, "specially now in the change of the religion of this cathedral church of Canterbury from prior and convent into dean and canons. For I am informed," he continues, "that such as be or shall be assigned and appointed by the king's majesty to be commissioners and visitors for the said change of the said church of Canterbury shall be at the same church within a little time. And of the which commission my lord of Canterbury, as I hear, shall be the chief (who is not so good lord unto me, as I would he were). Wherefore without your especial lordship I suppose my lord of Canterbury will put me to as much hindrance as he can, and also I have heard of late that my brother the warden of the manors, Dr. Thornden, is called in my lord of Canterbury's house, 'Dean of Christchurch in Canterbury.' This office of dean by the favour of your good lordship I trusted to have had, and as yet trust to have. I have been prior of the said church above 22 years, wherefore it would be much displeasure to me in my age to be put from my chamber and lodging which I have had all these 22 years.

"It hath also been shown unto me that my lord of Canter-

[1] *Calendar*, xiii. (ii), No. 139.

bury at his coming to the said church will take from me the keys of my chamber, and if he do, I doubt whether I shall have the same keys or chamber again or not. I have or can have none other comfort or help in this matter but only by your lordship. And where it pleased your good mind towards me to write unto me of late, by your letters, that I should have my said chamber with all commodities of the same as I have had in times past, the which your said writing to me was and is much to my comfort. And with the favour of your lordship I trust so to have for the term of my life, which term of my life by course of nature cannot be long, for I am above the age of 62 years."[1]

Prior Goldwell, however, was doomed to disappointment. Dr. Thornden became first dean of Christchurch, and the old superior of twenty-two years' standing had to content himself with a pension of £80 a year and one of the prebendal stalls in the new foundation.

Many of the exiled monks probably found their way abroad and into Scotland, both on the suppression and after queen Mary's premature death had destroyed every hope of a monastic revival. An old monk of Westminster, named Henry Stils, who had been born blind, after wandering on the Continent, came to the abbey of Saint Ghislain,[2] in the Low Countries. On May 18th, 1579, he had visited the new seminary at Doway, in company with Dr. Allen, its president and founder,[3] and on October 17th, 1588, he died at Saint Ghislain, "where," as the annals relate, "he had a long time before taken refuge from the religious troubles in England and the persecutions of Catholics, and above all of the religious, a great number of whom came to seek an asylum in the Low Countries." He had been brought over from London by a youth who remained with him till his death.[4]

The Syon nuns are said to have always kept together. Many of them upon the suppression of their house retired to the Continent, where they continued to lead a conventual life. They were residing in a convent of their order at Dermond, in Flanders, when Cardinal Pole brought them

---

[1] R. O. Crum. Corr., v. f. 82.
[2] A celebrated Benedictine abbey in Hainaut, near Mons.
[3] Records of Eng. Caths., *Douay Diaries*, p. 153.
[4] Annales de l'Abbaye de Saint Ghislain, in Reiffenberg's *Monuments pour servir à l'Histoire des Provinces de Hainaut, Namur, &c.* (Bruxelles, 1848), t. viii. p. 800.

back to England in Mary's reign.[1] On their expulsion from England by Elizabeth, these nuns did not cease to keep up regular conventual life, which has been continued until the present day. The house of Syon is now settled near Chudleigh in Devonshire, and is (perhaps with one exception) the most ancient existing of the order of St. Bridget of Sweden.

In the same way there is little doubt that some of the disbanded religious managed to reunite and for a long time live a kind of conventual existence. Thus Dame Isabel Sackville, the last prioress of Clerkenwell, is reported to have kept one or two of her nuns near her for a long time. Dame Elizabeth Shelley, last abbess of St. Mary's, Winchester, also lived for some years, with a few of the nuns, in the neighbourhood of her dismantled convent. Her last will and those of several of her nuns are yet preserved, and afford some interesting particulars of the way in which these devout women clung to their religious profession. Thus in 1556, Agnes Badgecroft, who was subprioress of St. Mary's Abbey at the dissolution, died. She was living close to her old home and desired to be buried in the neighbouring church of St. Peter, Colebrook. "Also I bequeath," she says in her will, "my professed ring to the Blessed Sacrament, to be sold and to buy therewith a canopy for the Sacrament."[2]

In the same way the will of Jane Wayte, "lately a religious woman within the walls of Winchester," makes bequests to four of her "sisters" in religion; it is witnessed by Richard Woodlock, formerly a monk of Hyde, and Thomas Cooke, also a Benedictine.[3] The abbess herself, Dame Elizabeth Shelley, died in March, 1547. She left

---

[1] Aungier, *History of Syon*, p. 97.

[2] Mr. Baigent's MS. Collections. In the inventory of her goods taken on Oct. 5, 1556, are mentioned her monastic veils, her psalter, pair of beads and four altar cloths. "Item received for her pension 31s. 6d."

[3] *Ibid.* Another nun of the abbey, Edburga Stratford, whose will is dated March 18, 1552, leaves a legacy to "John Erle, rector of Empton, formerly monk of Winchester." In 1555 James Clayton, curate of the parish of St. Peter, Colebrook, leaves a legacy to one of the disbanded nuns, "Agnes Badgecroft," and to Sir Thomas Cooke, named above, "all my books to distribute as he shall think fit." The will of Morpheta Kyngsmill, last abbess of Wherwell, made 31st March, 1569, leaves bequests to seven of her old community, who were apparently living with her at her death (Mr. Baigent's MS. Collections).

The Ejected Monks and their Pensions 453

twenty shillings to each of seven nuns named, and "to every sister of the sistern house, near to St. Mary's (abbey) 12d." John White, the warden of Winchester college, was her executor, and she was buried by him in the college chapel. The reverence in which this abbess was held is evinced by a direction found in the will of Thomas Bassett, priest, and fellow of Winchester college, who died in June 1554. His last wish is, that he be buried "in the college chapel, by the side of the grave of Mrs. Shelley."[1]

Besides what the last abbess of Winchester bequeathed in her will, she disposed of several things by indenture. "Dame Shelley," writes Bishop Milner, "continued to reside in this city (of Winchester), and it appears she had not lost all hopes of seeing her convent once more established, as she made the present of a silver chalice, which she had probably saved from the sacrilegious wreck, to the college of this city, on the express condition that it should be given to St. Mary's abbey in case it was ever restored."[2]

On the other hand, some of the monks and nuns cast out into the world appear to have accommodated themselves to the circumstances of the times and fallen away from their religious obligations. Still, from such returns as exist it does not appear that this was, at least in the case of the nuns, an ordinary matter. A certain proportion, no doubt, in the process of time would have married, but in the returns made by the commissioners sent by Edward VI. to inquire into the state of the religious pensioners, although there are a considerable number reported on, only two nuns are named as married. These two are "Elizabeth Grimston, of the age of 26," married to "one Pyckerd of Welbeck," and "Elizabeth Tyas, who lives at Tykhill, and now married to

[1] Mr. Baigent's MS. Collections.
[2] Milner, *Winchester*, ii. 193. Some few scattered memorials of the disbanded nuns are to be found. Thus at Isleworth in Middlesex was a small brass commemorative of Margaret Dely, "a sister professed in Sion," formerly treasurer of the house, who died in 1561 (Haines, *Manual of Brasses*, p. xxxix. In the second edition this brass is said to be "now on a pew door"). At Denham, Bucks, is the well-known brass of Agnes Jordan, last abbess of Sion, who died apparently in 1545 (Waller, *Brasses*, plate xiii.). An entry in a 17th century description of Yorkshire speaks of a nun of Esholt. "Mr. Baildon, 1619, saith," it runs, "that Dame Margaret Martiall, sometime a nun of Esholt, lived at Fawether, adjoining (her old convent), and had a pension of £4 or £5 a year during her life, and died some 12 years since and was a good churchwoman" (Brit. Mus. Harl. MS., 804, f. 14).

one John Swyno, gentleman."[1] Both were young nuns of Swine convent, in the East Riding of Yorkshire, and very possibly were never professed at all.

It is certain that out of the large number of disbanded monks many must have conformed to the religious opinions and practices of the times. One interesting anecdote of an old monk, who lived till the beginning of the seventeenth century, may be allowed to find a place here. His name was William Littleton, and on the dissolution of Evesham abbey he was "subsexton," and appears as such on the pension list.[2] The story of the end of his life may be told in the words of an old writer.[3] Speaking of Father Augustine Bradshaw (prior of the house of St. Gregory's, Doway), it is related that "at his coming to Henlip in 1603 he was met by chance there by one Lyttleton, who had formerly been a monk of Evesham, and was now best known by the nic-name of 'parson tinker.' This man was observed to cast his eyes much upon Father Augustine, and being not able to hold, he asked Mr. Thomas Habington what this gentleman was, who confidently told him that it was a brother of his. 'A brother of mine!' said Mr. Lyttleton, 'I have not had any living these forty years.' 'I mean,' replied the gentleman, 'a monk of St. Benedict's Order.' At these words he seemed to alter countenance and be much moved, and at length besought Mr. Habington, for the passion of Christ, that he might speak to him. All being related to father Austin, a way was made to bring them together. As soon as Lyttleton came into the room he fell upon his knees and with floods of tears told what he was beseeching Fr. Austin to reconcile him, which he, remaining there a day or two, did. This old man being thus reclaimed went home and presently fell blind, and so remained almost two years deprived of his benefice, and had he not been bed-ridden he had been imprisoned for his conscience, and so died with great repentance, being near 100 years old."[4]

[1] R. O. Chapter H. Box, 154, No. 61.
[2] Exch. Augt. Off. Misc. Bk., 245, f. 105.
[3] Fr. Thomas White *alias* Woodhope.
[4] Bib. Bod. Wood. MS. B. 6, f. 16. "Benedictine Obits." Fr. White mentions that he "had the story from the mouth of the worthy gentleman who brought them together" (evidently Mr. Habington, of Henlip), and that "Mr. Hall of the Society assisted this old man at his death."

The Ejected Monks and their Pensions 455

When first expelled from their monasteries, Wood relates that the monks flocked in great numbers to Oxford. Canterbury college, Gloucester college, Durham, St. Bernard's, St. Mary's, and other halls were full of them,[1] but it is curious to remark how quickly every trace of many of the monks and nuns appears to have been lost. Considerable numbers died off in the first few years after their expulsion. Many were old and sickly, and the hardships to which they were inevitably exposed, and even the change of life itself, would probably have soon carried off the aged and infirm. In the "Ministers' Accounts" are to be found numerous entries of the passing away of these religious. Thus, in the receiver's account for the counties of Norfolk and Suffolk, during the twelve months from Michaelmas, 1540, to the same feast 1541, which was practically the first year after the general dissolution, the following are recorded as having died since the last account: The prioress of Marham, the prior of Bromholme, the prior of Holy Trinity, Ipswich, the abbot of Wendling, the prior of Westacre, and his predecessor, three canons and one nun of the Gilbertine priory of Shuldham, one canon of Walsingham, and three others who had not applied for their pensions, one canon of West Derham, and the abbot of Bury with three of his monks.[2]

By 1552, or twelve years after the suppressions, very many no longer appear. The reports of the commission appointed by Edward VI. to inquire, and to which frequent reference has been made, show that a great change had taken place in the lists of pensioners. Out of twenty-two, for example, who were named on the last list as receiving annuities as monks of Durham, seven are reported as dead, two did not appear, but were supposed to be living, the one at Lytham, the other at Stamford, former cells of Durham. Only four, apparently, had received their payments.[3]

Throughout the reports great numbers are noted as "absent" or "not heard of." Thus at St. Leonard's, York, more than a third of the religious had disappeared in this way. At St. Andrew's, York, of the three names mentioned, two had died recently and one had "not been heard of" by the commissioners. In the same way, to take one more

[1] *Fasti*, i. p. 61.
[2] R. O. Exch. Mins. Accts., 32–33 Hen. VIII., 235.
[3] R. O. Chapter H. Box, 154, No. 63.

example, of the fifteen canons of Welbeck who had been pensioned, only nine are named in the report of 1552. Three of these nine, including the abbot, Richard Bentley, who had been granted a pension of £50, are "unheard of," and one had sold his pension directly after it had been granted. In other places it is the same story: at Mathersey, in Nottinghamshire, out of five two are "unheard of;" at Wallingwells out of four nuns two are "unheard of," and the rest "unpaid."[1]

In the brief re-establishment of some of the monasteries during Mary's reign a few of the old religious found their way back to the cloisters. Thus the Bridgettine nuns were brought back to their old home at Syon, the Dominicans to Smithfield, the Observants to Greenwich, the Carthusians to Sheen, and the Benedictines to Westminster.[2] At the latter abbey Dr. Feckenham, previously a monk of Evesham, was appointed abbot, and he gathered round him a community composed of former members of the Benedictine order, comprising, amongst others, four of the old Glastonbury monks.

The restoration of that renowned sanctuary of the west was also contemplated, and, in fact, the work of repairing the ruined buildings was begun. So sure were these monks of the affection of the people of Somerset that they asked only for the ruins, feeling confident that their old neighbours would gladly help to build up the dismantled walls.[3] It was intended also to restore St. Albans under its old superior, Abbot Boreman.

[1] R. O. Chapter H. Box, 154, No. 2.
[2] Mr. Baigent points out that amongst other houses which were restored in Mary's reign was that of the Franciscan Observants at Southampton. This is evident from several entries in wills at this time. Thus John Tanner, of South Stoneham, on 9 Dec., 1558, bequeaths 10s. to the Friars of Hampton. So, too, in the will of Charles Harrison, physician, of the parish of Holy Rood, Southampton, dated 5 Oct., 1558, are the following items:—"My body to be buried in the church of St. Francis in Southampton aforesaid;" "I give and bequeath to the brethren of St. Francis' Rule, within the town of Southampton, 40s.;" "also I give and bequeath all my books of philosophy, divinity and stories (history) to the friars observant in Southampton, to the intent that they shall be and always remain in the library of the said friars;" "I will that all my books of physic be given to a student of physic at Oxford, who hath not money to buy books, and that such a one be inquired after by such as cometh and goeth to Oxford." It may be added that Charles Harrison must have been a man of substance as he leaves his wife 256 ounces of plate and £60 in ready money.
[3] *Monasticon*, i. 9.

Mary's death put an end to these projects, and Westminster once more passed away from the keeping of the monks of St. Benedict. The closing scene may be given in the words of the historian Fuller:—"Queen Elizabeth coming to the crown, sent for abbot Feckenham to come to her, whom the messenger found setting of elms in the orchard (the college green) of Westminster abbey. But he would not follow the messenger till first he had finished his plantation, which his friends impute to his being employed in mystical meditations—that as the trees he then set should spring and sprout many years after his death, so his new plantation of Benedictine monks in Westminster should take root and flourish, in defiance of all opposition." "But how his trees thrive," he continues, "at this day is to me unknown. Coming afterwards to the queen, what discourse passed between them they themselves know alone. Some have confidently guessed she proffered him the archbishopric of Canterbury on condition he would conform to her laws, which he utterly refused."[1] "Sure I am," adds Fuller, "that these monks long since are extirpated;" but in this assurance he was wrong; the line is continued through Feckenham to this day.

The Carthusians who were gathered together at Sheen under Prior Maurice Chauncy, when Mary came to the throne, were the scattered members of the Charterhouses of England. Many died during the few years of their sojourn in England and the rest followed their superior into the Low Countries on the accession of Elizabeth. When they came to Bruges in 1568, many members of their community had received the habit in their English houses. Prior Chauncy died in Paris, July 12th, 1581, and the last of the old monks to pass away was Father Roger Thomson, the vicar, who had been a novice at Mountgrace on the dissolution, and who died on October 20th, 1582.[2]

After Mary's death little is known of the fate of the

[1] Fuller, *Church Hist.*, quoted in Stanley's *Memorials of Westminster* (5th ed.), p. 405. The Dean notes that "the elms, or their successors, still remain. There was, till 1779, a row of trees in the middle of the garden which was then cut down."

[2] As so little is known about the dispersed monks the following may be of interest. The dates of the deaths are taken from a valuable MS., "History of the English Carthusians," in the library of J. Blount, Esq., of Mapledurham. The last death recorded is in 1663, and the MS. was compiled about that time. Among the old English Carthusians who were at Sheen and died in Mary's reign are: Fr. Fletcher (either of Mountgrace or Hinton), Robert

surviving monks. Only very trifling items of information have been preserved to posterity. Thus, in 1576, it appears that amongst those indicted for being at mass in "the house of John Pinchin," of Westminster, "sometime of the Middle Temple, and an attorney at the common law," was "Hugh Phillips, late monk of Westminster, the priest who said mass,"[1] and who had before the suppression been a member of the Ramsey community.[2]

Three years later there were two septuagenarian monks in the Marshalsea prison—Thomas Cook and Thomas Rede,[3] the latter probably a monk of Hayles, in Gloucestershire, the former a canon of Christchurch, Twyneham. In 1585 John Almond, a Cistercian of about 76 years of age, died in the castle of Hull, having been a prisoner there in 1579.[4] Two years previously, Thomas Madde, a monk of Jervaulx, died in the prison of York. Of him it is said that in the reign of Henry VIII. he "did take away and hide the head of one of his brethren of the same house, who had suffered death, for that he would not yield and consent 'to the royal supremacy.' Afterwards he fled, lest he should offend God and trouble his conscience by the doing of any unlawful acts, unto St. Andrew's in Scotland, where he did remain unto the end of king Edward's reign. He, returning in queen Mary's reign, did spend his time about Knaresbro' in serving God according to his vocation, and teaching of gentlemen's children and others."[5]

One other instance of a like nature and recording the end of a nun may be added here. Dame Isabel Whitehead

Abel (Mountgrace), Robert Marshall (Mountgrace), Robert Thurlby (Sheen). Those who followed Prior Chauncy abroad: Maurice Chauncy (London), *ob.* 1581, July 12; Roger Thomson (*novice* Mountgrace), *ob.* 1582, 20 Oct. ; Tristan Holimans or Hyckmans (Witham), *ob.* 1575, Dec. 6; Nicholas Dugmer (Beauvale), *ob.* 1575, Sept. 10; Leonard Hall or Stofs (Mountgrace), *ob.* 1575, Oct. 10; Nicholas Bolsand (Hinton), *ob.* Dec. 5, 1578; William Holmes (Hinton).

Besides these there were one or two others, probably belonging to ancient houses, but whom it is difficult to identify on the pension lists. To the above must be added Br. Hugh Taylor, a lay-brother. Additional MSS. 17,085 (f. 106), and 17,092 (ff. 78, 114, 152, 196), contain obits (*year* only) of this community from 1662 to 1757. The lists include the good old Catholic names of Gerard, Constable, Dolman, Brigham, Towneley, Yates. Earlier obits are scattered in various places through the latter volume.

[1] Brit. Mus. Lansd. MS. 19, f. 59.
[2] R. O. Exch. Augt. Off. Misc. Bk., 245, f. 64.
[3] Brit. Mus. Lansd. MS., 28, f. 96. [4] *Ibid.*
[5] *Records of Eng. Prov. S. J.*, vol. iii. p. 239.

was professed at the convent of Arthington, in Yorkshire, "until it was suppressed. Yet," says the account of her, "she continued her state as she could, so far as I know." She lived with "lady Midelton, at Stuborn, or Stokell (Stockeld), until she died and then wandering up and down, doing charitable works . . . till she stayed" with a Mrs. Ardington. There she became ill, and whilst in that state the house was searched at Michaelmas, 1587, for Catholics. The officers took Mrs. Ardington and her daughter, and "also entered the place wherein dame Isabel Whitehead, a nun, lay sick in her bed. They stood over her with their naked swords and rapiers, and did threaten to kill her unless she would tell where David Ingleby and Mr. Winsour were." She was carried away to York castle, where she died in the following March, "and was buried under the castle wall."[1]

[1] *Records of Eng. Prov. S. J.*, vol. iii. p. 731.

CHAPTER XXII

Some Results of the Suppression

IN entire consistency with the infamy heaped upon the monasteries has been the current estimate of the social consequences of their suppression. Grave writers no less than partisans have treated the matter as though their spoliation had resulted in great advantage to society at large, inasmuch as by it the honey was taken from the drones of the hive and handed over to the working bees. It is difficult to say which branch of this comparison is the more absolutely false as to fact. Even supposing that the thousands then living under vows had led the aimless and dissipated existences attributed to them by their despoilers, it might be asked, not without reason, whether any signal amount of private or public virtue was displayed by the courtiers and creatures of Henry VIII. If the buildings wherein the monks were housed and the churches they had raised to the glory of God were vast in extent and magnificent in design, so that, to use the words of a contemporary witness, they constituted "one of the beauties of this realm to all men and strangers passing through the same,"[1] what particular advantage accrued to the state from their desecration and wholesale destruction? If the hospitality dispensed to all comers by the monastic owners was generous and profuse, was the public interest greatly advanced by the private consumption of the very sources of that charity amongst a few royal or noble appropriators?

Such a line of argument, however, though serving fairly enough to expose the facility with which some writers, of cool judgment in other matters, accept transparent fallacies when dealing with monasticism, so far from covering the whole case, leaves room for the retort always tacitly implied,

---

[1] R. O. Chapter H. Bk., A. $\frac{2}{25}$, p. 210, Aske's examination.

if not openly expressed, that no matter what evils may come from the suppression of the religious houses, they could not equal those which would have resulted from their continuance. Certainly had those institutions been the abodes of wickedness and strongholds of oppression depicted by the false witnesses whom our English Ahab commissioned to slander the Naboth whose fair vineyard he coveted; had the sole business of the monks consisted in extorting by spiritual intimidation, and by chicanery and fraudulent deceits, the means for living in feasting and drunkenness; had their occupation been that of wallowing in unmentionable vice, for that in plain English is the picture drawn by their spoliators—then unquestionably, whatever scars may have been inflicted by the cautery, they would have been incomparably more tolerable than the canker.

Nor, it may be here observed, is excuse altogether wanting for those who at a later day gave credence to the statements of Henry's commission without examining into the credibility of the wretched men whom modern research is denouncing to the world as perjured robbers. If such a denunciation may appear at first sight strong, even to violence, it will upon reflection be seen rather to fall short of the truth. For although, in describing the actual events, the pen may, not without difficulty, be confined to a simple narration, yet when the mind contemplates the innumerable miseries entailed upon successive generations by that wholesale appropriation of the property of the Church and the poor, it is almost incompatible with any instinct of justice to refrain from characterising in language only too abundantly justified those infamous instruments of a ruler who alone was their rival in infamy. For when we look into the case in detail and reflect, it is impossible not to see in the spoliation and destruction of the monasteries the fount and origin of many of those appalling sores in the body of the nation from which at times the veil is torn away. Not in figure merely, but in grim, literal, earnest truth, the sacred heritage of the English poor was eaten up by the house of Tudor; and to such an extent did extravagance of food, of dress, and of every kind of living ensue, that not a few of the spoilers paid in their own ruin the penalty of their transgression.

To trace in detail the consequences which this act of wholesale waste entailed upon society at large would be a task beyond the present scope; partly because such a discussion would evidently be of a magnitude exceeding the original subject, and partly because the design of the present work is to deal with direct testimony, whereas any deductions as to the effects of this lawless act, however clearly they may be supported by evidence, must of necessity be in a measure inferential. Still, any description of the events which led up to and accompanied the suppression of these institutions, which should take no account of the important social effects which followed from it, would be imperfect.

Though the service of God was beyond all question the prime object of monastic life, yet the more closely that life is examined the more clearly does it exhibit the element of associated labour. In the popular estimate current at the present day, and derived in great measure from those kindly misdescribers, Sir Walter Scott and the author of the "Ingoldsby Legends," it is not unusual to imagine that a monk, although possibly a pious, was at all events a very indolent personage, and that the utmost he accomplished was to mumble—he was always supposed to mumble—a good many more prayers than other people, and to live on the fat of the land in return.

In strong contrast with the caricature drawn from the imagination of novelists, who at best clothe the cloistered life with a poetic unreality, the description given of it by a deeply-read writer of modern times may be here quoted. "The monks," says Mr. Thorold Rogers, "were the men of letters in the middle ages, the historians, the jurists, the philosophers, the physicians, the students of nature, the founders of schools, authors of chronicles, teachers of agriculture, fairly indulgent landlords and advocates of genuine dealing towards the peasantry."

It was the possessions of the monastic houses in particular that, to use the words of an old writer, were popularly regarded as "oblations to the Lord" and "the patrimony of the poor, 'to be bestowed accordingly.'"[1] The monks whereof "taught and preached the faith and good works, and practised the same both in word and deed; not only within the monasteries, but also all abroad with-

[1] Brit. Mus. Cole MS., xii. Written about the year 1591. A portion of this document has already been quoted, giving a description of the dissolution of Roche abbey.

out." . . . "They made such provision daily for the people that stood in need thereof, as sick, sore, lame or otherwise impotent that none or very few lacked relief in one place or another. Yea, many of them, whose revenues were sufficient thereto, made hospitals and lodgings within their own houses, wherein they kept a number of impotent persons with all necessaries for them, with persons to attend upon them: besides the great alms they gave daily at their gates to every one that came for it. Yea, no wayfaring person could depart without a night's lodging, meat, drink and money; (it not) being demanded, from whence he or she came and whither he would go.[1]

"They taught the unlearned that was put to them to be taught; yea, the poor as well as the rich, without demanding anything for their labour, other than what the rich parents were willing to give to them of mere devotion.[2]

"There was no person that came to them heavy or sad for any cause that went away comfortless. They never revenged them of any injury, but were contented to forgive it freely upon submission. And if the price of corn had begun to start up in the markets, they made thereunto with wainloads of corn and sold it under the market price to poor people, to the end to bring down the price thereof. If the highways, bridges, or causeways were tedious to the passengers that sought their living by their travel, their great help lacked not towards the repair and amending thereof: yea, oftentimes they amended them on their own proper charges.

"If any poor householder had lacked seed to sow his land or bread or corn or malt, before the harvest and come to the monastery, either of men or women, he should have had it until harvest, that he might easily have paid it again. Yea, if he had made his moan for an ox, horse or cow, he might have had it upon his credit. And, such was the good conscience of the borrowers in those days, that the thing borrowed needed not to have been asked at the day of payment.

"They never raised any rent, or took any incomes or garsomes of their tenants; nor ever took in or improved any commons: although the most part and the greatest was ground belonging to their professions." . . . "All sorts of

[1] P. 5.   [2] P. 6.

people were helped and succoured by abbeys. Yea, happy was that person that was tenant to an abbey, for it was a rare thing to hear that any tenant was removed by taking his farm over his head. He was not afraid of any re-entry for non-payment of his rent, if necessity drove him thereunto. And thus they fulfilled all the works of charity in all the country round about them to the good example of all lay persons that now have taken forth other lessons, that is *nunc tempus alios postulat mores.*"

It might be objected that this is a fancy picture drawn after date; but not merely is it the work of one who well remembered the ancient days, but it agrees entirely with the declaration of Robert Aske, written half-a-century before, to say nothing of so many other contemporary testimonies and well-ascertained facts. Even if it were granted that in this or that detail the picture be heightened by an old man's fancy playing upon early memories, as a whole and in substance it is unquestionably true, and it shows the "common fame" which the monasteries left after them, a fame wholly incompatible with the infamies of later repute; for the works of Christian charity can flow from but a single source, the love of God, and the love of man in Him.

The same writer points out how by the property obtained from the dissolutions the rich mounted up to place and power, whilst the poor, deprived of their protectors and inheritance, sank deeper into the slough of poverty. For the suppressions "made of yeomen and artificers, gentlemen, and of gentlemen, knights, and so forth upward, and of the poorest sort, stark beggars."[1]

And the commons, he says, were robbed not only in the actual taking away, but in the consequences. For the owners, who succeeded the monks, always try "to make the most of everything," which "abbots, abbesses and such like never did." . . . "Inferior persons made gentlemen," always desiring to make a show, are not "content, as other ancient gentlemen in times past did," and hence are constantly compelled to raise their rents.

Moreover, the new owners of the soil everywhere took

---

[1] P. 18. It is worth while to note how singularly the description of this anonymous writer, speaking with the facts before his eyes, agrees in regard to the degradation of the English labourer with the results obtained from purely documentary evidence by Professor Thorold Rogers.

hold of waste ground and common land. By this practice, he continues, "the poor cottagers that always before might have kept a cow for sustaining himself, his wife and children, and twenty sheep towards their clothing, now is not able to keep so much as a goose or a hen." Yea, the common arable fields that were common to all persons dwelling within the townships (as well the poor as the rich) are taken in and enclosed. By reason thereof the ground is worth so much that the poor cottagers, now innumerable (for in most *towns* for every cottage [at the time of the suppression] there are five now, and far more poor persons in them),[1] and other poor husbandmen, can neither have their common therein as they had before the inclosure, nor are able to pay for as much as a 'beastgate' within it, the rent is so great. Hence only wealthy farmers with money to buy cattle" can use the land; the poorer class "are brought to such poverty" that they cannot maintain their families "and pay their landlords their rents."[2]

By the enclosure of the commons the artificer in the town was no longer able to keep a cow for his household or a horse to carry his wares to market, for the people's pasturage was gone. Since the fall of the abbeys "great woods" had been cut down and sold, every one thinking of himself and "the present gain," so that the poor had great difficulty in getting wood for firing and for their various industries. By the dearth of cattle both leather and wool had become dearer. The poor, moreover, had less acknowledged right to a share of Church revenues. For, on the one hand, the married clergy supported their families out of their dues, and little would be left for those in want; and, on the other hand, the tithes "which belonged to vicarages now in temporal men's hands" were very considerable, but the owners "did not think they were more bound to contribute on this account to the poor than others."[3]

It is impossible to read any account of the work done by the monastic institutions for the poor without perceiving in how many directions this present generation has been com-

---

[1] In this he is calling attention to the migration of the country population to the towns, forced on by the increasing difficulty of remaining on the soil. As there was no corresponding increase in manufacturing industry, it is patent what an aggravation of poverty must have resulted.

[2] P. 35. [3] Pp. 36-38.

pelled by very necessity to devise some substitute for the consideration thus exercised. Our modern workhouses, our burial-clubs, our hospitals and charities, ever crying out for funds, much of which is swallowed up by paid organization and management, what are they but awkward and imperfect agencies for executing a portion of those duties to society which flowed naturally and unobtrusively from the religious communities in their ordinary practice of Christian charity?

That the wholesale uprooting of institutions so organic and so beneficent must have occasioned incalculable misery is rarely denied, though its extent is little understood. Amongst the writers who have treated this subject from the economic point of view a tolerably general consensus prevails that the condition of pauperism, as distinguished from that of poverty, may be traced distinctly to this event. Many, however, seem to consider such a condition as a kind of self-curable, if not self-engendered, disease. Even so just and usually well-informed a writer as Professor Thorold Rogers expresses a doubt whether the monks did not create much of the poverty which they alleviated. Of course, to those who consider almsgiving universally and essentially objectionable, no general answer can here be given beyond observing that they who would maintain this must at least be prepared to throw over the commands of the gospel, the example of the apostles, the teaching of the Christian Church, the instincts of humanity, and the universal practice of every civilized state. And, as a matter of fact, pauperism, which immediately after became a rampant evil, was kept within bounds so long as the monasteries remained untouched.

But many causes were even then at work, which in all probability would in process of time have rendered the old monastic methods of dealing with the evil inadequate. Still, the overthrow of the existing sources of charity, and their appropriation to quite other uses, was a fertile source of misery at the time, and up to the present. Nor is it easy to see how it could be good policy to disband corporations to whom the disposal of alms, in the spirit of Christian charity, was not merely a duty, but had become a familiar habit, and who, open as they were to the great waves of public feeling, and by tradition not unmindful of the public welfare, would not in the future have been less thrifty stewards had the need of strenuous effort and modified methods to meet a growing public evil been brought before them.[1] This would have been easy in view of the influence which the so-called "founder" could bring to bear in every case. Not only were the channels through which all relief flowed to the people destroyed, but the very fountain-head of the accumulated charity of previous generations was dried up at its source when the property of the religious houses was, without inquiry or discrimination, swept into the capacious purse of Henry. Even had the wealth acquired by the spoils of monasteries, churches, schools and hospitals been entirely applied to useful and national purposes, it would still be true that these objects were achieved in great measure at the expense of the poorer members of the nation. As it was, a considerable part went to minister to the private wants of the king, and to enrich his noble and ignoble courtiers. They grew great, whilst the poor became "stark beggars."

Nor must it be forgotten that the process, which consumed the very sources of charity, cast many thousands upon the world without sufficient means of livelihood. Not only numbers of monks and nuns, for whom clearly no provision was made in the way of pension, were turned adrift to swell the ranks of the poor, but far the greater number of those dependent on the monastic houses were dismissed to find occupation or living as best they could! At the same time, the new proprietors of the abbey lands treated the old tenants, with whom they had no sympathy, most harshly, and reduced many to a state of destitution. The monks had the character of being easy landlords, and one of the first objects of the royal agents was to rackrent the holders of the monastic farms. Thus, in his first account, John Freeman boasts that of the houses he has received in Lincolnshire, and the rental of which had been returned as £8100 a year, "there hath been more increased by my survey than was presented . . . yearly by £800."[2] To give another illustration. On the granges belonging to Fountains abbey, rented

---

[1] It has been pointed out that the incomes of a few modern millionaires would cover the revenues of all the religious houses. To make the monastic revenues suffice for all calls on them, it is clear that whatever may have been the case at this or that date, with this or that particular monastery, their administration as a whole must have been marked by thrift.

[2] R. O. Chapter H. Bk., A. $\frac{4}{30}$, f. 155.

at £156, 13s. 4d. by the monks, the king's valuers, in 1540, put a price of £30 a year more; and thirty-five years afterwards, in 1575, Gresham's rental, without including five of the granges, was £45, 7s. more than the whole were rented at in the royal valuation of 1540.[1]

But beyond this consumption by the "classes" of the heritage of their poorer brethren at the time of the suppression, an additional and heavy wrong was done them by branding poverty with the mark of crime. To be poor was not before regarded as a reproach in itself, but rather upon every Christian principle poverty was held in honour. To Henry belongs the singular distinction, which few will be inclined to dispute with him, of having invented literally no less than figuratively "the Badge of Poverty," and of being the first to dress a "pauper" in a "pauper dress." It may fairly be doubted whether any single act of monarch or statesman ever did so much to vulgarize the character of an entire nation as Henry's when he bestowed ninepence a week on each of the thirteen poor men, hitherto supported by the monks of Gloucester, on condition that their caps and cloaks should bear a badge emblazoned with a token of the royal munificence.[2]

How soon the effect of the transfer of land from the old to the new owners and the desolation it brought in its train was visible in the country may be learnt from a description of the state of the land addressed to Henry VIII. himself by a travelling artisan.[3] Speaking of the great increase in the number of poor people, the writer proceeds to explain what

---

[1] J. R. Walbran, *Memorials of Fountains* (Surtees Soc.). The editor in a note, p. 254, noticing the above facts, states that it "will show that the monks were just and merciful landlords; and that the lament on the fall of the abbeys in these parts, which old Henry Jenkins lived to report to the Cavaliers and Roundheads, might have partially arisen from more material reasons than a change of religion."

[2] R. O. Exch. Mins. Accts., 31–32 Hen. VIII., 263 m. 9d. A curious instance may be cited of the way the poor and sick simply disappeared when deprived of the care of the religious who attended them, and left to the mercy of the royal officials. The hospital for poor and sick at Bishopsgate, in London, was taken by the king on December 1st, 1539. There were at the time 34 poor in the establishment attended by six canons and two sisters. The first week each of these poor people received eightpence. For the next four weeks there were only 32 paid, then 30, and by March 19th there were only 20. At the end of the month they had been reduced to 16, and by September to only 8 (R. O. Exch. Mins. Accts., 31–32 Hen. VIII., 253, m. 12).

[3] A native of Wiltshire, John Bayker. *Calendar*, xiii. (ii), No. 1229.

he takes to be the causes. "For where," he says, "that your grace and your grace's predecessors have given and put in fee-farm lordships to your rulers and gentlemen of your realm, whom your grace puts in trust to the intent that they should aid and defend your poor subjects and commons in all right and justice. But alas! I think your poor subjects had never more need to complain unto your grace in any matter than they have in this, which if it please your grace to pardon me your subject I shall shortly show. . . .

"Your grace shall understand that I am a poor artificer or craftsman who has travelled and gone through the most part of your realm to get and earn my living. I have been in the most part of the cities and great towns of England. I have also gone through many little towns and villages, but, alas! it did pity my heart to see in every place so many monuments where houses and habitations had been, and now nothing but bare walls standing. . . . Now if it please your grace to hear what is the cause of such decay and ruin within your realm, your grace shall understand that in every place where your grace's majesty hath given in fee-farm any lordship to any gentleman, or such as be your grace's fee-farmers, (they) should let them again unto your poor subjects to inhabit and till, that they, paying their rent truly to their lords, might have a sufficient and complete living by their labour.

"But alas! how far are these fee-farmers or rulers wide in either point. For if so be that any of these fee-farmers have any tenement or farm in their hands, if a poor man come unto any of them desiring him to be good unto him in this tenement or farm that he might have it to inhabit, paying the rent for it as it hath been before time: he answers and saith, 'If thou wilt have this tenement of me, thou must pay me so much money at your coming in for a fine;' so that he raiseth what never was at any fine before to a great sum of money, and the rent to be paid yearly besides. The poor (man) then seeing there is no remedy but either to have it or be destitute of an habitation, sells all he hath from wife and children to pay the fine. Then the landlord perceiving the house in decay will not repair it, although the tenant paid ever so much for his fine, and the tenant comes to a decayed thing. Then the landlord perceiving that the house is ready to fall down, calls the tenant into court and there commands him to build up his house before a certain day under pain of forfeiting a certain sum of money. Then the poor man, because he paid so great a sum of money for the fine, is not able to build up his house so quickly. Then a second time is he called up again to the court and there commanded under pain of forfeiting his tenement to build it, so that the poor man being not able to repair it, forfeits it again unto the lord."

In later times still the evils here recorded were intensified, and the poverty of the nation at large could not be disguised. Everywhere we read of a host of mendicants, of thieves, of vagabonds, so that for one beggar in the reign of Henry there were a hundred in the days of Elizabeth.[1] Then those who had seized the inheritance proclaimed the poverty of those they had robbed a crime. Merciless and monstrous statutes enacted by the spoliators was the remedy by which it was sought to reduce the disease, and the rulers of the state did not shrink from introducing slavery, and inflicting even death for the crime of poverty, of which they had been the patent origin.

Hundreds of men and women, whose birthright had been divided amongst the rich and powerful, were cast into prison, scourged, and reduced to the condition of slaves, or hanged for the crime of going about the country to seek a livelihood, or for asking an alms when failing to find employment in the midst of the general distress and the disorders of national bankruptcy.[2]

---

[1] Brit. Mus. Cole MS., xii. p. 41.

[2] It is right to state that as early as 22 and 27 Hen. VIII. two statutes assigned punishments to promiscuous begging, and to "men and women, being whole and mighty in body," who were found vagrant. These latter were "to be had to the next market-town, and there to be tied to the end of a cart, naked, and to be beaten with whips throughout the same town till his body be bloody by reason of such whipping." These and other severe measures were found necessary, even before the dissolution of the monasteries. After that event the evil was augmented. By a statute (1 Edw. VI., c. 3) the vagrant is styled a "slave." If he was 18 years old, it was ordained that on a second conviction he should suffer death unless some one would take him into service for two years. On the third conviction, the *sturdy* rogue had no escape from the gallows.

The 14 Elizabeth, c. 5, made it criminal to be a vagrant. Every such one over 14, male or female, should, on the conviction of so odious an offence, be grievously whipped and burned through the gristle of the right ear with a hot iron of the compass of an inch, unless some one would take him into service. The branding was sent clean through the gristle of the ear. The condition of the convicted in service was that of a slave.

In one year (14–15 Elizabeth) 20 vagrants were so convicted at the Middlesex

The effect of Henry's policy in dividing the monastic estates among his courtiers was in reality to create a monopoly in land. So long as they remained in the hands of their rightful owners, those corporations, not being subject to demise, dealt with the tenants according to immemorial custom, and never aimed at extorting the last penny of profit from the cultivator. But the new grantees were not actuated by a like consideration and rents were everywhere increased.

This was tantamount to nothing less than a revolution effected by the powerful against the weak. "The further we look back into history," says Mr. J. S. Mill, speaking especially in regard to rent, "the more we see all transactions and engagements under the influence of fixed customs. The reason is evident. Custom is the most powerful protector of the weak against the strong; their sole protector where there are no laws or government adequate to the purpose. Custom is a barrier which even in the most oppressed condition of mankind tyranny is forced in some degree to respect." But in the revolutionary proceedings of Henry's reign no degree of respect was paid to custom, and, that protecting barrier thrown down, the weak were left to the mercy of the powerful.[1]

If the effects of the dissolution were felt to operate prejudicially to the material comfort of the people, the blow inflicted on higher interests was still more fatal. Of course, as regards religion itself, the Protestant must be bound to consider that, however grievously spiritual interests may have suffered, yet the substitution of Protestantism for Catholicity outweighs all other considerations. But learning, sacred and secular, is a more neutral ground, on which both

---

Sessions. On one occasion, in 1591 (the year referred to in the last note), 71 persons, male and female, aged 14 and upwards, were sentenced to be whipped and branded, an average of seven a week during that period.—*Vide Middlesex County Records*, i., Introd. i.

[1] See in Blunt, *Reformation*, p. 385, the plain words of Latimer on this subject. The absolute change of tenure, and rejection of "*custom*," is well illustrated in the *Durham Halmote Rolls*, published by the Surtees Society. Mr. Booth, the editor, in his preface speaks in the highest terms of the relations which existed between the tenants and the old monastic officials. "Notwithstanding the rents, duties and services, and the fine paid on entering," he writes, "the inferior tenants of the priors had a beneficial interest in their holdings, which gave rise to a recognised system of tenant-right, which we may see growing into a customary right." With the dissolution of the monastery all this came to an end; the dean and chapter who succeeded the monks flatly refused to recognise a customary estate in their tenants.

Catholic and Protestant may meet. Deterioration was felt in all grades of education, from the university downwards. The rise in rents, says Latimer, prevented the yeoman sending his son to school. Most of the schools at this time were closed, without any provision being made for a substitute. Moreover, the monasteries and convents had supported scholars at the universities, or provided for young clerics until their ordination, when they supplied them with a title. This change was felt immediately. At Cambridge the scholars in 1545 petitioned King Henry for privileges, as they feared the destruction of monasteries would altogether annihilate learning.[1] At Oxford, as is well known, the result was no less fatal, and for a time these great homes of learning were threatened with nothing less than ruin. At the very moment of the suppression the danger was foreseen, and to meet the case it was enjoined that every clergyman beneficed to the amount of £100 a year or more should find "an exhibition to maintain one scholar or more, either at grammar schools or at one of the universities." It is, however, clear that this injunction had no more effect than that laid on the new owners of monastic lands to keep up the hospitality always maintained by their predecessors.

Looking back from the days of Edward VI. to the times before the suppression, Bishop Latimer exclaimed: "In those days what did they when they helped the scholars? Marry! they maintained and gave them livings that were very papists and professed the pope's doctrine; and now that the knowledge of God's word is brought to light, and many earnestly study and labour to set it forth, now almost no man helpeth to maintain them."

"Truly," he said, in another sermon, "it is a pitiful thing to see schools so neglected: every true Christian ought to lament the same . . . to consider what hath been plucked from abbeys, colleges and chantries, it is marvel no more to be bestowed upon this holy office of salvation. It may well be said by us that the Lord complaineth by His prophet . . . 'My house ye have deserted, and ye run every one to his own house.' . . . Schools are not maintained; scholars have not exhibitions. . . . Very few there be that help poor scholars. . . . It would pity a man's heart to hear that,

---

[1] Fuller, *Hist. of the University of Cambridge.*

that I hear of the state of Cambridge; what it is in Oxford I cannot tell. . . . I think there be at this day (A.D. 1550) ten thousand students less than were within these twenty years and fewer preachers."[1]

So far as Oxford is concerned, "most of the halls and hostels," writes Anthony Wood, "were left empty. Arts declined and ignorance began to take place again."[2]

It is vain to speculate on what might have been, but it is certain that the progress of sound learning represented by such men as Warham, More, Colet and their friends was arrested. In view of the monasteries as they actually were, and the tendencies clearly perceptible among some of the most important in the last decades of their existence, what might not have been hoped from them for the promotion of letters had events been allowed to take their natural course? It might be objected, although there is no ground in the facts to countenance such an objection,[3] that the monasteries could have had no part in this new movement. But objectors such as these fail to take into account the capacity of the monastic order to adapt itself to new circumstances, and that wonderful recuperative power which is one of the most prominent as it is one of the most interesting features of monastic history.

One other serious result of the monastic suppression cannot be passed over without some notice. A large proportion of the conventual revenues were derived from parochial tithes impropriated to monasteries and convents. However great an abuse it may be considered to transfer such dues from one object to another, these tithes were granted in the first instance for charitable and other strictly ecclesiastical purposes. On the suppression of the religious houses no distinction was made between monastic revenues derived from this source and from the ordinary estates. Tithes were thus granted away and sold like the fee-simple of the land to laymen, and converted altogether to secular purposes. "These impropriations were in no one instance, I believe," writes Hallam, "restored to the parochial clergy,

---

[1] Quoted by Blunt, p. 387. For the state of affairs in Elizabeth's reign see W. Harrison's *Description of England*, written in 1577 (ed. New Shakespeare Society), p. 77, &c.).

[2] *Hist. and Antiquities of University of Oxford* (ed. Gutch), ii. p. 67.

[3] Compare the remarks of Dr. Jessop, *Visitations of the Diocese of Norwich* (Camden Society), p. xxviii.

and have passed either into the hands of laymen, or of bishops and other ecclesiastical persons who were frequently compelled by the Tudor princes to take them in exchange for lands."[1]

Vast sums of money—amounting to millions of pounds in these days [2]—originally belonging as tithes to the parish priest and the parish poor, found their way into lay hands in the course of what has been well called "The Great Pillage" initiated by Henry VIII. in the suppression of the monasteries. These revenues have been used ever since for secular purposes wholly alien to those for which they were intended. In view of the evidence available, it is impossible to deny that the monastic houses had acted as responsible almoners of the portion of the tithe which law or custom had assigned to the support of the needy. "There is no deduction in our value made for alms," write the royal commissioners for the survey of the monasteries of Norfolk, "which ought to be remembered in case the king's highness depart with the whole possessions of any house." And here, be it remembered, they are writing specially about the "parsonages that are parcel of our value within written." It is hardly necessary to say that this plea for some consideration of the claims of the poor found no response in the heart of the king or his officials. In the social and religious changes of this period the needy came unquestionably to have a less acknowledged right to any share in the Church revenues generally, just as *Individualism*, which became the dominant philosophy of "the new men," denied their claims as members of the one Christian family.

In this respect it seems quite clear that not only were the results of the destruction of the religious houses at once

[1] *Constitutional Hist.*, 10th ed., i. p. 77. In the diocese of Norwich, according to Taylor (*Index Monasticus*, p. xxvi.), there passed into the royal hands 221 endowments. Of these, only 13 were again invested in the Church, and 11 of them had been previously annexed to the see in exchange for half its revenues. Out of 96 endowments belonging to colleges, &c. (exclusive of 10 alien priories) 80 were granted to lay proprietors. Out of a total of 256 endowments confiscated by Henry in the diocese, four-fifths, or 184, were sold or granted to laity. It has been calculated that Henry VIII. "sold or gave away the tithes of 5000 parishes, together with those belonging to 2374 free chapels and chantries, 110 hospitals and 90 colleges," and that at the present time, while the Church is possessed of tithes to the amount of £3,413,697, as much as £2,404,233 is held, either directly or indirectly, by impropriators.

[2] For details the reader is referred to Mr. H. Grove's work *Alienated Tithes*.

manifest, but that the people at the time attributed the effect to its obvious and natural cause. A paper certainly penned before the close of the reign of Henry VIII., and, what is more important, by one who was no *laudator temporis acti*, but a firm believer in the new religious movement, makes it quite clear that at least in the popular opinion the increasing poverty of the time was ascribed to the suppression of the old monasteries. "The priests," writes the author, "mark such universal extremity and increase of misery, poverty, dearth, beggars, thieves and vagabonds, that it is hardly now possible to longer bear it." When asked the cause for all this distress, they reply: "What marvel is it, though we have no money, how many thousand pounds a year go to London for the rents of abbey lands, for first-fruits, for tenths, &c., besides the innumerable treasures that hath come to the king's highness by the purchase of plate and implements of the same houses, all of which heretofore was wont to be spent here in the country for victuals amongst us. Surely, surely, good neighbours, we have never had a merry nor wealthy world since abbeys were put down and this new learning brought in place."[1]

To this account of the matter may be added the description of the state of London immediately after the dissolution of the religious houses which Dr. Sharpe's studies of the city records have enabled him to give. "The sudden closing of these institutions," he writes, "caused the streets to be thronged with the sick and poor, and the small parish churches to be so crowded with those who had been accustomed to frequent the larger and more commodious churches of the friars, that there was scarce room left for the parishioners themselves. The city authorities saw at once that something would have to be done, if they wished to keep their streets clear of beggars and of invalids and to invite the spread of sickness by allowing infected persons to wander at large. As a means of affording temporary relief, collections for the poor were made every Sunday at Paul's Cross after the sermon, and the proceeds were distributed weekly among the most necessitous." After petitioning the king in vain to grant the city some of the dissolved houses and their revenues, in order that provision might be made

[1] Brit. Mus. Royal MS., 17 B. xxxv. f. 9a.

for the sick and needy, the authorities resolved in 1540 to make an offer to purchase some of them for 1000 marks, "yf thei can be gotten no better chepe." Henry only upbraided them for being "pynch pence" or stingy in their offer, and so nothing was done in the matter for four years.[1]

Another, although, as it may be thought, indirect effect of the dissolution of the monastic houses, was the subsequent seizure of ecclesiastical property of all kinds. The old abbot who was reported to Crumwell as having said that "all the water of the Thames would not slake the royal thirst once the king had tasted the fruits of the monastic spoliation," was in the event justified in his forecast. Even had Henry been able to draw back and once more bridle his spirit of avarice and lust for plunder, there were plenty of hungry courtiers on the look out for their share, who were only too ready to urge him forward in the career of spoliation upon which he had embarked. So the seizure of all the hospitals, chantries, schools and parish guilds was next determined upon. Henry's death alone put a temporary stop to a measure which was the most direct, deliberate and heartless robbery of the English poor. It was left to the ministers of Edward VI. to accomplish this infamy, and to add to it the seizure of the plate and other rich ornaments with which generations of Englishmen had adorned their parish churches, and to cover up the robbery by a general wrecking of the sacred fabrics themselves. There is evidence to show that had not the premature death of the boy-king brought the confiscations to a sudden close, the Church revenues would have entirely disappeared in the vain attempt to satisfy the craving of the men in power after the goods of the Church under the guise of a desire for the purity and simplicity of the gospel. Before the accession of Mary the temporalities of the see of Exeter, which on Edward's accession had been £1566, 14s. 6d., had been reduced to £421; and those of Winchester from £3885, 3s. 3¾d. to £1333, 6s. 8d.; whilst, as a whole, the richer bishoprics of England were stripped of two-thirds of their income, the poorer of about a half.

Such are some of the momentous social results of sweeping away the monastic houses. They may be summed up in a few words. The creation of a large class of poor to

---

[1] *London and the Kingdom,* i. p. 404.

whose poverty was attached the stigma of crime; the division of class from class, the rich mounting up to place and power, the poor sinking to lower depths; destruction of custom as a check upon the exactions of landlords; the loss by the poor of those foundations at schools and universities intended for their children, and the passing away of ecclesiastical tithes into the hands of lay owners.[1]

It has become habitual with many persons to regard the greatness of the Elizabethan era as in some way rendered possible only by the dissolution of the monasteries. By this the national energies are vaguely supposed to have now first obtained a fair field and fair play. That society should have re-settled itself, and a new and great day should have dawned is nothing wonderful. The constitution of human society appears to be such as never to lose the power of re-creating itself on a new basis, however desperate the condition to which it may be for a time reduced. Out of revolution order once more will surely be evolved, however much may have been irretrievably lost in the cataclysm which suddenly arrested a natural and normal development. It is in no spirit of concession to a sentimental and sterile feeling of regret for a dead past that it is desired to bring home the fact that the dissolution of the monasteries did inflict a terrible blow on the social state and made life harder for the nation at large. It is always an advantage to know the truth and to learn how to face it. Besides, the past has ever its lesson for the present, and to know how grievous was the deception in the bright promises of national happiness and individual prosperity which the distribution of so noble a prize was to secure, may have its lessons even in our own day.

[1] Regrets are sometimes expressed that at least a distinction was not made between colleges of secular clergy, the hospitals, chantries and other eleemosynary foundations, and the religious houses properly so called. The distinction between these two classes of institutions seems to be clear to the minds of many persons in these days, but only because the real state of the case is misapprehended. In fact, all alike formed parts of one great system; the religious house was an eleemosynary foundation, and the hospital a house of prayer. It was impossible in practice, to those who had the actual working of this system before their eyes, to make the distinction sought to be instituted in later days. The voice of such a one as Latimer was as the voice of the solitary crying in the desert, and only serves to make it more clear how fatal and disastrous was the nature of the current which swept away all, and could sweep away no less than all, monasteries, hospitals, churches, colleges, chantries, into one common vortex of ruin.

APPENDIX

THE following is a summary showing approximately the various sums of money received by the Augmentation Office from the dissolution of the monastic houses, &c.; also roughly how the money thus obtained was spent. To this is added a summary of the accounts of the treasurer of the royal jewel chamber, showing the value of the plate of the religious houses and churches, and the way it was disposed of by the royal orders. The first part is obtained from the Rolls of the Treasurer of the Court of Augmentation, the second from the account of Sir John Williams, keeper of the royal jewels, printed by the Abbotsford Club. The words "approximately" and "roughly" are used because in the troublesome task of dealing with the mass of figures on the Rolls it is possible, even probable, that error may have crept in here or there; but it is believed that such error is not considerable enough to detract in any way from the substantial correctness of the subjoined statement.

Appendix

ACCOUNT OF THE TREASURER OF THE COURT OF AUGMENTATION
From the 24th April, 1536, to Michaelmas, 1547.

Receipts.

	£	s.	d.
Revenue from monastic lands	415,005	6	10½
Paid by religious for royal license to continue	5,948	6	8
Sales of monastic lands by king	855,751	18	5
Sales of woods	634	6	6
Fines paid by tenants for new leases	4,529	9	10½
Sales of ornaments, vestments, lead, bells, furniture, buildings, &c.	26,502	1	0¼
Deductions from religious pensions as a forced loan to the king	9,443	15	6
Loan to king for war purposes from the religious and clergy	12,870	16	8
Payments by collectors and other officers for royal leave to be free from military service	5,776	7	8½
Miscellaneous: Arrears of collectors, &c.	1,979	19	11¼
Total receipts	**1,338,442**	**9**	**2½**

Disbursements.

	£	s.	d.
Fees and wages	14,444	3	4½
Annuities	25,039	6	5¼
Pensions to religious	33,045	5	8¾
Office expenses	11,067	19	3½
Value of plate handed to king	11,393	12	11¼
Purchase of lands	51,749	9	9½
Payment of debts	12,909	1	9¼
Plate purchased for presents	14,619	12	10¼
War expenses:—General	238,078	5	3¼
Foreign	136,631	17	6½
Guns and munitions of war	171,819	17	11
Naval matters: Ships and provisions	27,922	3	5½
Coast fortifications	64,485	4	3½
Spent by king on royal palaces	61,014	11	5
Expenses of Prince Edward of Wales in household matters, &c.	23,000	0	0
Royal household expenses and money for king's use	274,086	19	8¾
To secure the surrender of the abbey of Abingdon	600	0	0
Various expenses, chiefly military and naval	57,135	3	2
Total disbursements	**1,229,042**	**14**	**11¾**
Balance[1]	109,399	14	2¼
	1,338,442	9	2½

---

[1] Of this £109,399, 14s. 2¾d. no less than £76,141, 8s. 3d. was still due for lands which had been sold.

Account of Sir John Williams for Plate Received in Royal Jewel House.

Receipts.

	£	s	d
Gold plate, 14,531¾ ounces, worth	19,016	2	6
Gilt plate, 129,520 ounces, worth	21,258	15	6¼
Parcel gilt plate, 73,774¾ ounces,[1] worth	11,942	10	2¼
Parcel gilt and white plate, 4341¼ ounces, worth	795	17	11
Silver plate, 67,600⅜ ounces, worth	10,518	8	11½
Total value of plate [2]	63,531	15	1
In money from spoils, &c.	15,156	7	2½
” ” ”	393	14	1
Total receipts	79,081	16	4½

Disbursements.

	£	s	d
Plate bought for the king	4,849	6	6¾
"New trimming images of gold"	6,015	15	7¼
Expenses of Anne of Cleves	3,078	7	7
Money coined and sent to Ireland	10,285	8	4
King's parks	441	7	0
Purchase of manor of Ashill	1,000	0	0
Coast fortifications	9,933	6	8
Office expenses and sundries	1,023	10	0
Given to the king's "own hand" in plate and money [3]	41,913	17	10½
Total disbursements	78,540	19	7½
Balance	540	16	9
	79,081	16	4½

[1] The value, £6942, 10s. 1¼d., given in the print of the Abbotsford Club is obviously wrong in this item.
[2] Large deductions are made from the values for the weights of the precious stones set in the metal, and also for the wax, paper and cement found in the process of melting.
[3] This item is given as £46,636, 1s. 1¼d., but the total of £78,540, 19s. 7½d. makes the account inaccurate, and this item is diminished so as to secure the total. The treasurer pleads that when the keeper's house in London was burnt down he lost £2000 at least.

INDEX

ABBOTS, attitude of, 107
Abingdon, surrender of abbey of, 340
Addington, parish priest of, 36
Agatha's, St., monastery, Yorkshire, 267; suppression of, 269
Alane, Alexander, Scot., cited, 141, *note*
Albans, St., convent of Pre annexed to, 27; granted to Wolsey, 6, 16; reports of, 115, 349; abbot of, replaced, 349–350; surrender of, 350
Allegiance to Anne Boleyn, oath of, 51
Allen, Dr., complaints of, 20, 22; exactions of, 21, 83
Ambresbury, Wiltshire, convent of, 303
"Amicable grant," 19; difficulty in raising, 24
Andrew's, St., Northampton, confession of monks of, 122
Ap Rice, John, visitor, authority of, 79; letters from, 80, 82, 84, 168; reports from, 114, *note*, 115, 119, 168; dependence on Crumwell, 168; history of, 167; requests reward for services, 167; abbot Mackarel examined before, 216
Aristocracy of the revolution, 3
Aske, Robert, leader of the "Pilgrimage of Grace," history of, 231; statement of the causes of the movement, 224–229; assumes command, 232; enters York, 232–233; letter to Henry, 236; persuades the people to accept pardon, 239; visits the king, 246; report on the people's impatience for fulfilment of royal promises, 247; Norfolk's attempt to trap him, 249; trial and execution of, 263
Athelney, surrender of abbey of, 346–348

Attainder, forfeit of property by, 269, 374, 387, 395
Audley, Sir Thomas, chancellor, pleads for abbeys of St. John's, Colchester, and St. Osyth's, 390
Augmentations, Court of, 179; amounts received by, for houses refounded, 186; feeling against, 203; amount received from suppressions, 397; accounts of, 426, 428, 433
Avecourte, Warwick, priory of, 185
Avery, Thomas, steward to Crumwell, 148
Axholme, prior of, 64
Aylesbury, friars of, 319, 324, 326

BALE, testimony of, concerning monks, 114, 117; cited, 311, 312, *note*
Barclay, Alexander, 145, *note*
Bardney, monastery of, 218–219
Barking, abbey of, 307; treasures of, 308
Barlings, monastery of, 215–219, 271
Barlow, William, Bishop of St. David's, 193, 337
Barnes, Master, 36
Barnwell priory, Layton at, 332
Bartlett (*alias* Bartelot), clerk, 81; letters to Crumwell, 126
Bartley, friar, 144, *note*
Barton, Elizabeth, *see* Kent, Maid of
Bath, present of hawks sent to Crumwell from, 150
Battle Abbey, visitation of, 88
Beaulieu, complaint of abbot of, 27; surrender of, 437, *note*
Beche, Abbot, *see* Marshall, Thomas
Beckett, *see* Thomas, St.
Beckwith, Leonard, royal receiver, 402, *note*

Index

Bedyll, Thomas, 53; sent to the Carthusians, 54, 61; authority of, 79; reports of the Carthusians, 62; death of, 403; appropriations of, 403, *note*

Beigham abbey, 20; sales of, 138, *note*

Bellasis, Richard, destruction at Bridlington and Jervaulx, 272-273

Bells, broken up, 420, 421, *note*; claimed by people, 422, *note*

Belun, bishop of, 31

Benedictines, abbey of nuns at Pollesworth, 184, 297; abbey refounded at Bisham, 193; number of convents for women, 291-292; revenues of convents, 297; fall of Glastonbury abbey, 362 *et seq.*, and of Reading, 378 *et seq.*, and Colchester, 388 *et seq.*; temporary restoration at Westminster under Mary, 456

Bere, D. Richard, imprisonment of, 72; history of, 72, *note*

Beverley, Grey Friars at, 251

Bigod, Sir Francis, 248-250

Bilsington, Kent, monastery of, 190

Bisham, priory of, 193; abbey founded at, by Henry, 193, 337, 338, *note*

Bishops, general character of, 5; often foreigners, 5; non-residence of, 6; hostility of the nobles to, 6; visitations of, 10, *note*, 11, 116; suffragans often Irish, 6; attitude towards Henry, 77; suspension of authority of, 78, 79; instructions from Crumwell to, 132; northern "Pilgrims'" opinion of them, 229; new bishoprics created, 431, *note*

"Black Book," 97; doubt as to its presentation to Parliament, 101, 102, *note*, 104, and as to its ever having existed, 102, *note*, 104; alleged destruction of, 102, 103, *note*

"Black Death," terrible visitation of, 1, 2; effect on the Church, 2

Bocking, Dr., monk of Christchurch, Canterbury, 36; arrest, 39; public penance, 40; execution, 44

Boleyn, Anne, 23; hostility to the "Holy Maid," 39; attitude to Rome, 78, 85; execution, 95, 176

Boleyn, Sir Thomas, created Viscount Rochfort, 364

Books, service, destruction of, 418, *note*

Booth, Dr., bishop of Hereford, 130

Boreman, Richard, made abbot of St. Albans, 349-350

Borodale, Gawin, charge against, 280; receives abbotship of Holm Cultram, 281; pension of, 281

Borough, Lord, escape of, from the Lincolnshire rioters, 208

Bourchier, Henry, Earl of Essex, 49

Bourchier, Father Thomas, testimony of, 44, *note*

Boxgrave, monastery of, 191

Bradewaye, Charles, prior of Alcester, 185

Bradley, Marmaduke, bribe offered by, for abbotship of Fountains, 162, 257

Bradshaw, Augustine, prior of St. Gregory's, 454

Bradstock, priory of, 82, 164

Brereton, Randal, 221, *note*

Brereton, Sir William, 221, *note*

Bribery, prevalence of, 4, 22; probable cause of the refounding of suppressed houses, 187, *note*

Bridlington, Yorkshire, priory of, 260, 271; destruction of shrine of St. John of, 405

Brigittines, prior of, 62

Brinklow, Henry, author of "Complaint of Roderyck Mors," cited on the corruptness of the law, 4, *note*; on the prison system, 4; testimony to the life of the monks, 9

Broke, William, monk of Charterhouse, 63

Brown, Anthony, trial and execution of, 315-317

Brown, Dr. George, appointed "grand visitor," 51, *note*; proceedings against the Richmond friars, 53

Bruton, Legh's treatment of the abbot of, 82, 164

Buildings, destruction of, 422, 423, *note*

Bulkeley, Katherine, abbess of Godstow, 171, 172, 305-306

Burgoyn, Bartholomew, monk of Charterhouse, 63

Burnham, convent of, 297, *note*

Bury St. Edmunds, visitation of, 119; report of, 119

Byrkhed, Thomas, appointed abbot of Norton, 221, *note*

CALWICH, Staffordshire, cell at, 194
Campeggio, Cardinal, 13
Canons regular, *statuta* for, 15
Canterbury, connection of the monks of Christchurch with the "Holy Maid," 39, 43; character of the monks, 133; fire at, 89; St. Thomas's shrine at, 89, 407, 408, *note;* convent of St. Sepulchre's near, 36; visitation of Austin friars at, 320-321; execution of Friar Stone at, 321, *note;* appeal of monks of, to be allowed to retain their habits, 344; inventory of spoils from, 409, *note,* 410, *note*
Cantwell, Sir Thomas, 144
"Capacities" of friars, Ingworth's plea for, 329-330; sought after by expelled monks, 448-449
Capon, John, or Salcot, abbot of Hyde, 40; preaching of, 40; receives Elizabeth Barton's form of confession, 41; receives see of Salisbury for surrender of Hyde, 348
Carey, Dame Elinor, 23
Carmarthen priory, reasons pleaded for its continuance, 192
Carter, Thomas, abbot of Holm Cultram, 279
Carthusians, attitude of those of Sheen towards the Observants, 53, and of those of the Charterhouse towards the king, 59, 60; religious life of the Charterhouse monks, 60; yielding of, to the oath of supremacy, 62, 72; influence of the prior of the Brigittines upon, 62; preparation for death, 64; imprisonment and execution of the three priors, 65-68; reception of Crumwell's visitors at the Charterhouse, 66; restrictions exercised at, 70; cruelties practised upon the monks, 61, 70, 73; removed to other houses, 71; surrender of, 74; adherence to old faith, 62; pensions granted to, 74; refounding of St. Anne's monastery at Coventry, 186; later history of, 457, *note*
Cartmell, priory of, 245
Casali, agent of Henry and Wolsey at Rome, 29; letters from, 29
Casali, Gregorio, 29; Wolsey's letter to, 32; evidence concerning the pope's desire for reconciliation, 177

Castello, Cardinal Hadrian de, 14
Catesby, report of convent of, 124; bribe offered by prioress of, 149, 295; commissioners' appeal on its behalf, 295; Crumwell's inflexibility, 295-296; pension granted to prioress, 296
Cathedrals, proposed erection of, 30, 32
Catherine of Arragon, divorce of, 25, 38; sentence of the Holy See against it, 46; attitude of the Observants concerning it, 47; her death, 95, 176
Catton, abbot of, St. Albans, 349-350
Caversham, image of Our Lady at, 170
Cells, suppression of those belonging to foreign houses, 27, 28; method of dealing with small houses claiming to be cells of larger, 183-184
Chapuys, Imperial ambassador, his letters concerning the "Holy Maid," 40, 42; the parliament of 1534, 45; the Observant friars, 56; the separation from Rome, 63, and the king's refusal to allow visitation of houses of the order of Cisteaux, 105, *note;* anecdote of Henry at a stage play ridiculing the clergy, 108; opinion of Cranmer, 108-189; account of Crumwell, 136, *note;* on the number deprived of a living by suppression, 194
Charterhouse, *see* Carthusians
Chaucer, cited on the life of the nuns, 298, 299
Chauncy, Maurice, testimony to the Charterhouse monks, 60; his pension, 74; later history of, 457
Chertsey, reports of the abbey of, 115, 117; surrender of, 193, 337
Chichester, destruction of shrine of St. Richard of, 406, *note*
Chiksand, visitation of convent at, 120
Choral song, love of, 418, *note*
Church, effects of the "Black Death" upon, 1, 2; appointments made by the king, 5; condition of, prior to the Reformation, 4-6
Churches, desecration of, 199-201; churches of the friaries, 311; purchased by the people, 425, *note*
Cisteaux, the king's refusal to allow visitation of houses of the order of, 105, *note*

Clement VII., bulls of, 30, 32; coerced by Wolsey, 17, 18, 26; petitions of the Grey Friars and Franciscan Observants to, 20; poverty of, 26; Henry's attitude towards, 28; illness of, 31; recovery, 31; desire for reconciliation with Henry, 177

Clement, Mother Margaret, 72

Clementhorpe convent, suppression of, 182

Clergy, position of, prior to the Reformation, 4, 5; liability of, under the statute of "præmunire," 140; livings in the gift of monks, 9; examination of, by order of Crumwell, 200; articles drawn up by the Pomfret meeting, 238

Cobb, Thomas, master of the "Holy Maid," 35

Cockerel, James, prior of Gisborough, 263

Colchester, abbey of St. John's at, 388; complaints against monks of, 389-390; oath of supremacy taken by abbot and monks, 390; pleaded for by Audley, 390; arrest of abbot, 391, *note*; execution of abbot, 394; pillage of, 395

Colyns, William, bailiff of Kendal, 244, 246

Combe abbey, 443

Commissioners, royal, work of, 78, 93-94; complaints of one another, 81-84; number of, before the meeting of parliament, 98; reports of, 94, 124; articles of inquiry framed for, 79; charges of, 83; motives and characters of, 115-116, 158 *et seq.*; commission appointed for the taking over of the lesser houses, 180-181; different nature of reports of, to those of previous visitors, 183-184, *note*; adventure of, with the Louth rioters, 207-208; proceedings of, at Chester, 221-222; visit of, to Holm Cultram to receive its surrender, 281; suppression of convents of women, 293 *et seq.*; testimony to good work done by the convents, 299; appointment of, for visitation of friaries, 313; powers of, 313, *note*; reports of, 318 *et seq.*; resumption of work after northern risings, 331; instructions regarding surrenders, 331-332; attempt to check report of general suppression, 332-334; various suppressions, 337 *et seq.*; suppression of Glastonbury, 372 *et seq.*, and of Reading, 387, and Colchester, 395; inquiry into methods of, 401 *et seq.*; self-appropriations of, 401 *et seq.*

Commons, House of, servility of, 98, 111; Henry's method of coercing, 107, 111

Commoners, their grievances and hardships, 225-229

Commonwealth, benefit of the monasteries to, 227-228, 462-464

Comperta, 100; value of, 96, 120; doubt as to their having been laid before parliament, 101; commission of inquiry into, 102; documentary evidence for, 113-114, *note*; dishonest use made of, 117-118; not to be regarded as confessions, 123; comparison of, with reports of 1536, 124; form of, 115; date of, 116-117

"Confessions," doubt as to the existence of, 121, 122; unreliable nature of those, so-called, obtained by Dr. London, 326-327

Conished, priory of, 20

Constable, Sir Robert, 233, 235, 248, 262, *note*, 263

Convents, suppressions of, 293 *et seq.*; number of, before dissolutions, 291; number of, which purchased temporary exemption, 294; revenue of, 297; method of life in, 298; instructions to commissioners regarding final suppression of, 301

Cook or Faringdon, Hugh, abbot of Reading, history of, 379, *note*; opinions of, 380, *note*; charges against, 381, 382, *note*; examined in the Tower, 384; trial and execution of, at Reading, 385-386

Cooke, Robert, friar of Rye, 50

Cordrey, John, abbot of Chertsey, 193, 337

Cornworthy, Devonshire, convent of, 191

Cortesi, Gregorio, letter to Cardinal Contarini, 178, *note*

Court of Street, chapel of, 35-36

Coventry, reports from, 114, 442; destruction of Grey Friars' house

Index

at, 171; vain attempt to save cathedral at, 424

Coventry, William, religious of Wombridge, 183

Crabhouse, report of nunnery of, 115

Cranmer, examines the "Holy Maid," 39; licenses of the preaching clergy revoked by, 108–109; mediates for the Canterbury monks, 43; opinion of their conduct, 133; yearly payment by him to Crumwell, 148; friendship with Crumwell, 154; Chapuy's opinion of, 108–109; censure of Dr. London, 173; presides over trial of Friar Forest, 58; opinion of the king's marriage with Anne Boleyn, 176; popular opinion of his divorcement of Catherine, 228, 229

Crossed Friars, story of the prior's depravity examined, 125, 126

Croyland abbey, sends a present to Crumwell, 149; story of plate of, 335

Crumwell, Thomas, complaints against, as Wolsey's visitor, 20, 22, 137–138; defence of Wolsey, 138; accessibility to bribes, 22, 78, 138, 147–151; reign of terror under, 142, 146; policy towards Anne Boleyn, 38–39, 95; power of, 141, 144, 151–153; history of, 136, *note*, 137; wealth of, 138, 147–152, 156, *note;* unpopularity of, 139, 142–143, 154; infidel principles of, 137, 154; rise in Henry's favour, 129–141, *note;* policy of, 137–144; arbitrary actions of, 146; dealings with the religious, 80; persecutions under, 146; danger of, at Wolsey's fall, 138–139; expenditure of, 151–152; estates purchased by, 150, 151, *note;* fall of, 152–154; accusations against, 153–156; confession of, 155; execution, 156; testimony to his supremacy over the prelates as Vicar-General, 141, *note;* petitions to, for houses to be spared, 190, 193; bitter feeling against, 203, 225; letter on the Northern rising, 242–243; Norfolk's letter to, on selection of juries, 262; letter to Norfolk concerning Bridlington priory, 272; dealings with abbots of Holm Cultram, 279, 280, and with prior of Lenton, 282–283; abbess of Catesby's plea to, 295; other appeals to, 305, 306, 307; rebukes Ingworth for leniency, 322; reassures monasteries as to report of general suppression, 334; abbot of Abingdon's remonstrance with, 341; presides at trial of Abbot Harwood, 343; orders abandonment of religious habits, 344; his illegal trial of Abbot Whiting, 374 *et seq.*

Crumwell, Sir Richard, crown grants to, 150, *note;* searches Bedyll's house, 403

Crutched Friars, *see* Crossed Friars

Cubley, Richard, canon of Wigmore, 132

Curwin, Dr., sermon of, 48, *note*

DARCY, Lord, 230, *note*, 233, 235, 248, 263

Darcy, Sir Arthur, 273

Dare, William, abbot of Langdon, 128; recommended for a pension, 128

Darvel Gadarn, image, 58, *note*

Davy, John, imprisonment of, 72

Delapray, Cistercian convent of, 297

De la Ware, Lord, 191

Denny, abbey of, 80

Dennys, Mary, prioress of Kington, 301, *note*

Derby, Earl of, 234–235

Derby, Dominican house at, 314

Dering, John, public penance of, 40

Dispensations, granted by Henry, 58, *note*

Dissolutions, *see* Suppressions

Dissolution of houses by attainder of abbots, 269

Doncaster, "Pilgrims of Grace" at, 233

Dover, report of monastery of, 128; report of suffragan of, 133 (*see* Ingworth); illegal suppression of, covered by the Act, 189

Droitwich, Ingworth's visitation of friars at, 321; attempt to spare church at, 322

Durford, visitation of abbey of, 87

Durham, bribe offered by prior of, 149

Dutton, Sir Piers, 149, 221–223

Dymmoke, sheriff of Lincolnshire, 209, 210, 215

ECCLESIASTICAL appointments of Henry distasteful to the people, 199, 229-230
Edgecombe, Sir Piers, letter to Crumwell, 190-191
Education of women, existing only in convents, 298-299; effect of dissolution of monasteries on, 472
Edward VI., progress of spoliation under, 476; death of, 476
Elizabeth, Princess, declared illegitimate, 176
Elstow, Friar, reported by Lyst, 47; rebukes Curwin, 49, *note;* examined before the council, 49
Emaus, Thomas, of Worcester, 145
Episcopal registers, 10
Erasmus, cited, 418 *note*
Esholt, convent of, 183
Evesham, abbot of, replaced, 351; surrender of, 352
Exeter, Marchioness of, connection with the "Holy Maid," 41
Exmew, imprisonment of, 69, 70; execution of, 70
Eynon or Oynyon, John, priest of Reading, connection of with northern rebels, 381; execution of, 386, *note*

FAENZA, Bishop, letters of, 69
Faringdon, *see* Cook, Hugh
Farley, visitation of, 88
Feckenham, Dr., abbot of Westminster, 456
Finch, William, cellarer of St. Bartholomew's, 22
"First fruits,' statute of, 210, 213, 228
Fish, Simon, author of the Supplication of Beggars, 8
Fisher, Bishop, opinion of the "Holy Maid's" virtues, 37; fine imposed on him, 43; execution, 75
Fletcher, Bernard, evidence of, against Dr. Mackarel, 217
Folkestone, report of monastery of, 128; illegal suppression of, covered by the Act, 189
Forest, Friar, confessor to Queen Catherine, 47; conduct of, reported by Lyst, 47; imprisonment of, 49, *note*, 50, 57; condemnation of, 57-58; martyrdom of, 58, *note*, 59
Foster, John, steward of Romsey, 352, 353, *note*

Fountains, visitation of abbey of, 117; election of abbot of, by bribery, 162; implication of the quondam abbot in northern risings, 257; purchase of lands of, 399, *note*
Foxe, Edward, Wolsey's agent, 26; injunctions for the visitation of Wigmore, 131
Foxe, John, monk of Charterhouse, 63
Franciscan Observants, history of, 46, *note*, 56, *note*, 57; house of, at Greenwich, 46, 54; defence of Queen Catherine, 47; petition to the pope, 20; attitude to Henry, 46; house of, at Richmond, 53; steadfastness of, 52, 53, 55; suppression of the order, 56; sufferings of, 56, 57; dispersal in other countries, 57; accusations against in connection with northern rising, 251; house of in Guernsey dispersed, 313-314; temporary restoration of, at Southampton and Greenwich, under Mary, 456, *note*
Franke, John, registrar of the bishop of Lincoln, 206
Freeman, John, royal receiver, 194, 199
Friars, remonstrance of, concerning Wolsey's powers, 20; Simon Fish's condemnation of, 8-9; popular affection for, 20; difficulty of overcoming opposition of, 46; general of mendicant orders appointed by Henry, 51, *note;* "grand visitors" commissioned, 51; steadfastness of, to ancient faith, 53, 55; refusal of the Richmond friars to take the oath, 54; important part taken by, in religious life of the country, 310; work of, 310-311; popularity of, 311; number of friaries before the dissolution, 311, and number of friars, 312; suppression of the friaries, 312 *et seq.;* oath rejected by, 313; trials and executions of, 315-316, 321, *note;* dependence of on alms, 317; poverty of, at time of visitation, 318; endeavours to secure surrender of, 319, 327; severity of measures employed against, 323; London's charges against, 324-325, 326-327; royal spoils from suppression of, 327-328; hardships of, 329-330

Index   487

Frideswide's, St., Oxford, dissolution of, 17, 18
Froude, historian, cited, 103, *note*, 126, 129, 209, *note*, 215, 405
Furness, Lancashire, abbey of, charges against abbot and monks, 274; surrender of, 276; paltry compensation to the monks of, 277; destruction of, 278; effect of suppression of, 278
Fyllol, Jasper, gaoler at Charterhouse, 70

GARDINER, bishop of Winchester, Wolsey's agent, 26; in danger of being sent to the Tower, 170, *note*
Garendon, report from, 124
George, Friar John, letter of the mother of, 53
Ghiberto, pope's official, 17
Gigliis, Silvester de, Wolsey's letter to, 13; letters from, 14
Gisborough, election at, 149
Glastonbury, episcopal visitation of, 10, *note*; Layton's report of, 161; history of, 362-363; Abbot Whiting, 363; his position, *ibid.*; takes oath of supremacy with his monks, 364; reasons for subscribing, 365, *note*; visited by Layton, 367; reasons for suppression of, 370-372; arrival of royal commissioners, 372; their proceedings, 373; trial of abbot, 374 *et seq.*; execution of abbot, 378
Gloucester, surrender of friaries at, 319-320
Godstow abbey, Dr. London's treatment of abbess of, 171, 305; suppression of, 306
Gold, Henry, 40; execution of, 44
Goldstone, Prior, his plea to Crumwell, 344
Goldwell, Thomas, prior of Christ Church, Canterbury, 391, 449-451
Gostwyke, John, Crumwell's secretary, letter to the king, 156, *note*; money transactions with Crumwell, 151, *note*
Gracedieu, reports of convent of, 124, 292; suppression of, 293; pensions to nuns, 293
Grants of property of suppressed houses, 398 *et seq.*
Grants to expelled monks, 436, 438, 440

Gratuities, monks dismissed with trifling, 438
Green, Dom John, imprisonment of, 72
Greenwich, Observants at, *see* Franciscans
Greenwood, William, imprisonment of, 72
Gregory, Crumwell's son, 151; enriched by Henry, 155, *note*; education of, 91
Guardianships entrusted to abbots, 227, *note*
Guernsey, friars of, 313
Gyffard, George, commissioner, 124

HADLEIGH or Hadley, monk of Canterbury Cathedral, 36; arrested, 39
Hadrian de Castello, Cardinal, 14
Hailes, abbot of, 93
Hale, John, execution of, 67
Hales, Christopher, attorney-general, 39
Hall, Robert, abbot of Norton, 221-223
Hall, historian, 58, *note*
Hallynrakes, Dame Johanna, 183
Harpsfield, Nicholas, account of Cranmer's preaching, 110
Harrison, groom of King's privy chamber, story of, 276, *note*
Harwood, John, abbot of Vale Royal, 342; denies truth of surrender, 342-343; trial of, 343; pension of, 344
Hayfield, Thomas, arrest of, 52
Henry VIII., despotic power of, 3; complaints to, concerning Wolsey, 20; condemnation of Wolsey's visitors, 22, and of Wolsey's methods, 23, 24, 25; opposition of the friars, 46; divorced from Catherine, 25; sentence of the Holy See against the divorce, 46; severance from Rome, 45, 46, 51; title of "Supreme Head" assumed, 51, 52, 58, *note*, 63; popular feeling towards, 63, 75, 77; bill of, for suppression of smaller houses, 99; coercion of the Commons, 107, 111; declaration to the Lincolnshire rebels, 121; dealings with Crumwell, 139; policy towards those about to be condemned, 155, *note*; declarations with regard to suppression,

147; avarice of, 45, 77; revenue of, 77; granted power by Parliament to deal with lesser monasteries, 176; hopes for his reconciliation with Rome, 176–177; determination of, not to effect a reconciliation, 178–179; rebuked by Pole, 178, *note*; number and value of lesser houses taken possession of by, 188, *note*; replies to the demands of the Lincolnshire rebels, 211; orders hanging of abbot and canons of Norton, 223; letter to Duke of Norfolk concerning "Pilgrims of Grace," 233–234; dealings with the Pilgrims, 235–236; further instructions to Norfolk, 236–237; pardon read to the insurgents, 239; writes to his ambassadors to discount effect of Northern rising, 241; instructions to the herald concerning proclaiming of the pardon, 244; delay in fulfilling promises, 247; endeavours to trap Northern leaders, 250; breaks from the Doncaster convention, 250; examines evidence against accused, 252, *note*; recommences work of suppression, 265; instructions to Norfolk, 265–267; introduces law of confiscation by attainder, 269; letters to Earl of Sussex, 267, 270, 275; trifling amount gained from suppression of the friaries, 327–328; methods of obtaining possession of the houses not granted by Parliament, 331–334; denies intention of general suppression, 332–334; proceeds of the suppression, 397 *et seq.*; proceeds of destruction of shrines and relics, 409–410, 412–413; entire proceeds from dissolution, 427–427; periods of his attacks on ecclesiastical property, 428; method of spending the proceeds of spoils, 432, *note*, 433

Herbert, Lord, cited on Wolsey, 33, and on the spoils of the religious houses, 189

Hethe, Nicolas, prior of Lenton, 282–283

Hexham, Northumberland, resistance of the canons to its suppression, 194

Hillyard, Dr. Richard, 353–355

Hilsey, John, made "grand visitor," 51; report from Exeter, 52

Hinton, Carthusian priory of, 344, 345, *note*

Hobbes, Richard, abbot of Woburn, 284; charges against, 284–286; confession, 286; execution, 290

Holm Cultram, abbey of, 279; charges against abbot of, 279–280; surrender of, 281; gratuity to monks of, 281

Hook, Dean, cited on Crumwell, 142–143

Horde, Prior, of Hinton, letter of, 344

Hornby, Lancashire, priory of, 190

Horncastle, rising at, 208–210; demands to the king, 210

Horne, Brother William, 73

Hospitality of the monks, 9, 226–228; cessation of after the suppression, 106–107, 226

Houghton, prior of Charterhouse, early life, 60; committed to the Tower, 61; imprisonment of, 65; execution, 67; signing of the act of supremacy, 62; exhorts his penitents to refuse to abjure papal supremacy, 59–60

Howard, William, letter to Crumwell, 143

Hussey, Sir William, 220

IMMORALITY, charges of, against monks, 96

Income tax, levied by Parliament, 200

Ingworth, Richard, reports of, 159, 312, 318; assistance of, to Crumwell, 133; consecrated suffragan bishop of Dover, 313; commissioned for visitation of friaries, 313; rebuked by Crumwell for his leniency, 322; pleads for the expelled friars' "capacities," 329

Ipswich, suppression of St. Peter's at, 26; Wolsey's college at, 26

JAY, prior of Hexham, 197

Jennings, Richard, prior of Maiden Bradley, 129

Jervaulx, abbey of, 254–257, 271, 273

Johnson, D. Thomas, imprisonment of, 72

Johnson, Elizabeth, nun of Arden, 183

Index   489

Jordayn, Dame Isabel, 23
Juries, coercion of, 261, *note*; selection of, by Norfolk, 261-262

KENILWORTH, Augustinian monastery of, 194
Kent, "Holy Maid" of, 35; history of, 35; influence of, 37, *note*, 38; examined by Cranmer, 39, and by the Star Chamber, 40; public penance of, 40; confession of, 41; bill of attainder against, 42, 43; injustice of proceedings against, 44; execution of, 44; Fisher's opinion of, 37
Keveran's, St., Cornwall, 27
King's colleges at Cambridge and Windsor, endowment of, 28
Kirksted, monastery of, 219, 271
Knight, Bishop, 22

LAND, monopoly of, created by Henry's policy, 471, *note*
Lane, Ralph, junior, Crumwell's agent, 144
Langdon, surrender of monastery of, 128; story of the abbot of, 126; illegal suppression of, covered by the Act, 189
Langley, priory of Benedictine nuns at, 293; suppression of, 293
Latimer, Bishop, hostility of, to Friar Forest, 57; sermon of, 59; evidence regarding the *comperta*, 101; endeavours to persuade the king to save some monasteries, 133; presides at trial of Thomas Emaus, 145; denunciation of Clement Litchfield, 351; on education after the dissolution, 472-473
Latimer, Lord, 233
Launde, priory of, 151, *note*, 335, 399
Laurence, Prior Robert, 64
Layton, commissioner, 79; subservience to Crumwell, 79, 161; instructions to, and methods of, 79-80, 162; visits the North of England, 95; *comperta* of, 117; reports of, to Crumwell, 87, 122, 144, 147, 161, 337, 340; character of, 160; history and preferments of, 160; money transactions with Crumwell, 162; popular opinion of, 166; Abbot Mackarel examined before, 216; efforts to counteract report of general suppression, 332-334; visits Glastonbury, 367; revisits Glastonbury for its suppression, 372
Lead, melted down for profit, 419, 420, *note*
Lee, Dr. Edward, archbishop of York, visits Houghton and Middlemore in Tower, 61; takes the oath of the "Pilgrimage," 233; convenes a meeting at Pomfret, 237-238
Lee, John, canon of Wigmore, 129
Lee, Roland, bishop of Coventry and Lichfield, 53, 61, 148, 424
Legbourne, convent of, 201
Legh, commissioner, 79; subservience to Crumwell, 79; instructions to, and powers of, 79; complaints of, concerning Layton, 81; visitation in the North of England, 95; reports of, 115; *comperta* of, 117, 119; history and character of, 163-166; made Master of Sherburn hospital, 166-167; complains of Ap Rice, 168; demand of Yorkshire "Pilgrims of Grace" concerning, 166; Abbot Mackarel examined before, 216; visits abbey of Holm Cultram, 281; suppresses convent of White nuns of Grace Dieu, 293; charge against, 301; employed in suppression of Vale Royal, 342; visits St. Albans, 349
Leicester Abbey, report on, 120; bribe paid by the abbot, 149
Lenton, priory of, 282
Lewes Priory, visitation of, 88; granted to Crumwell, 151; surrender of, 338, *note*; destruction of church, 338-339
Lewis, Father, Observant, 36
Libraries, ransacked, 143; destruction of, 417
Lilborne, Thomas, subprior of Louthpark, 205
Lincolnshire rising, its causes, 198-201; outbreak at Louth, 204-208, and at Horncastle, 208-210; demands of the people sent to the king, 210; royal forces collected, 211; the king's reply to the demands of the people, 211-213; reading of the royal proclamation, 213;

surrender of the people, 213;
Henry's action to counteract effect
of rising abroad, 214; insurgents
pardoned, 215; punishment of
leaders, 219; Robert Aske's part
in, 231
Litchfield, Clement, abbot of Evesham, 351
Little Marlow, priory of, 91
Livings, granting of, to expelled monks,
442, 447-449
London, Dr., commissioner, 79;
history and preferments of, 169;
destructive methods of, 170, 324
et seq.; accusations against, 171-172; his false account of William
of Wykeham, 173; relations with
Gardiner and Cranmer, 173; public
penance of, 172; punishment and
death of, 174; advocates pensions
for nuns, 297; employed in suppression of convents, 304, *note,*
and in visitation of friaries, 319-324; on pensions, 442, 443
Louth, Lincolnshire, rising at, in
consequence of suppressions, 201
et seq.
Louth-park, dissolution of monastery
of, 201
Lumley, Lord, 233
Lyst, Richard, lay brother of Greenwich, 47
Lyttleton, William, of Evesham, 454

MACAULAY, cited, 1.
Machiavelli, principles of, recommended by Crumwell, 137
Mackarel, Dr., abbot of Barlings,
215, *note;* charges against, in connection with Lincolnshire rising,
209, *note,* 215; examined in the
Tower, 215; condemned to death,
219; executed, 271
Maiden Bradley, prior of, 89, 129
Malpas, priory of, 185
Man, Henry, Carthusian monk, letter
concerning the "Holy Maid," 37
Marham nunnery, Norfolk, 191
Marillac, French ambassador, account of Crumwell's fall, 153; on
the people's attachment to old religion, 411
Marshall, Thomas, abbot of St. John's,
Colchester, 388, *note;* early history
of, 389, *note;* arrest of, and imprisonment in Tower, 391, *note;*
accusations against, 391-394; execution of, 394
Marton, York, priory of, 190
Mary's, St., Winchester, convent of,
186; destruction of, 424; last
prioress of, 452, *note*
Mary, Queen, temporary restoration
of monasteries under, 456; death
of, 457
Masters, Richard, priest of Addington, 36, 40, 42, 43, 44
Melford, Abbot, of Bury St. Edmund,
119-220
Michael's, St., convent at Stamford,
183
Middlemore, Humphrey, 61, 70
Missenden, Mary, new prioress of
Stixwold, 192
Monasteries, dissolution of the lesser,
by Henry, 176 *et seq.;* refounding
of some by the king, 185, *note;*
Robert Aske's testimony to their
good work and the popular estimation for, 226-228; return to, during
"Pilgrimage of Grace," 232, 244;
severities practised against, on account of Northern risings, 267;
dissolution of, on attainder of abbots,
269; resumption of suppression of,
after Northern risings, 331
Monks, livings in patronage of, 9;
alleged to be responsible for Lincolnshire rising, 215-219; and for
"Pilgrimage of Grace," 251, 267;
bishoprics given to, 448, *note*
Montague, John, prior of Malpas, 185
Moore, William, blind harper, 382,
383, *note*
More, Sir Thomas, answer of, to
Simon Fish, 8; complains to
Wolsey of visitors, 20; signs impeachment of Wolsey, 32; execution of, 75; speech at trial, 367,
note
Moreland, William, monk of Louthpark, 204; condemned, 219
Mountgrace, monastery of, 354, 355,
note, 411
Moyle, Thomas, royal commissioner,
372, 387

NETLEY Abbey, 437, *note*
Newcastle, Black Friars of, 317
Newdigate, Sebastian, 69, 70

Index 491

Newminster, suppression of monastery of, 268

Nobles, destruction of power of, 3; jealous opposition to ecclesiastics, 6; Henry's favours to, 99, *note;* join the "Pilgrimage of Grace," 233

Norfolk, Duke of, 233, 235, 238-239, 249, 261, *note,* 263, 265, 315-316

Northampton, confession of monks of St. Andrew's, 122, *note;* plea in favour of monasteries at, 124

Northumberland, Henry, Earl of, 23

Norton, Cheshire, abbey of, suppression of, 221; opposition to suppression, 222

Norwich, reports from, 114; trial of Walsingham men at, 315

Nucius, Nicander, Greek traveller, his version of Henry's speech to Parliament, 100, *note*

Nuns, sufferings of, 85; plead to remain in their convents, 90; visitor's reports of, 123; contrasted with later commissioner's reports, 192; treatment of, on dissolution of lesser monasteries, 182-184; terribleness of dissolution to, 291; number of convents at dissolution, 291-292; regularity of, 292; various suppressions, 292 *et seq.;* the only teachers of women, 298-299; occupations of, 301; number turned adrift after dissolution, 309

OATH of supremacy, tendered to religious, 62, 72, 76, 284, 313

Observants, *see* Franciscans

"Official" class, created by Tudor policy, 4

Ortiz, Dr., letters concerning the nuns, 85, 301

Osyth's, St., grant of, 150, *note*

Oxford university, 18; Wolsey's colleges at, 16, 17, 22, 24, 30; London's visitation of friaries of, 325; state of learning at, after dissolution, 472-473

PARKYNS, John, offer of bribe by, 149

Parliament of 1529, 99; session of 1534, 45, 49, and of 1536, 97; obsequiousness of, to Henry, 98-99, 111, 176-177; grants the lesser monasteries to the king, 176; Act of 1539 to legalise suppressions already made, 429

Parochial tithes, converted to secular purposes at dissolution, 473, 474, *note*

Parr, Sir William, 216, 219

Paul's, St., Cross, 40

Payn, Friar Hugh, 52

Pecock, Friar, 50

Pearson, Walter, 72

Pensions to religious, instances of granting, 91, *note,* 123, 269, 329, 341, 346, 348, 355, *note,* 357, *note,* 436; granted to superiors only, 181, 281, 435-436; omitted, 283; granted to nuns, 293, 296, 297, 304, *note,* 436, 441; probability of fair payment, 435, 443; monks commonly expelled without compensation, 436, 440; pensions conditional on long residence in a house, 437; reasons for granting of, 439; refused by some, 439; amount of pension paid to superiors, 440-441; total number of patents for, 440, *note;* houses or privileges added to pensions, 441; livings in lieu of pensions, 442, *note;* generous pensions pleaded for by Dr. London, 442-443; place of payment of, 443, *note,* 444; abuses in payment of, 444, *note;* deductions from for the king, 445; commission appointed to inquire into, 446; sales of, 445-447

Pentney, monastery, plea on behalf of, 191

Peterborough, abbot of, 22; first dean of, 123; bribe offered from, 149

Peto, Friar, 47, 48, 49

Petre, William, royal commissioner, receives surrender of Lewes priory, 338; destruction of, at Lewes, 338-339; dissolves Hinton priory, 345; visits St. Albans, 349; replaces abbot of Evesham, 351

"Pilgrimage of Grace," demand of, 166; causes of the rising, 224-230; rapid spread of the outbreak, 231-233; meets the king's forces, 233; demands sent to the king, 234; meeting of leaders at York, 236, and at Pomfret, 237; receives the

royal pardon and disperses, 239; measures taken by the king to discount effect of rising abroad, 241; instructions to herald concerning proclaiming of royal pardon, 244; the second rising, 250; evidence of witnesses, 251-260; trials and executions, 261-264
Pipwell, bribe offered by abbot of, 149; destruction of abbey of, 423
Placidus, Dan, monk of Winchcombe, 92
Plate of the monasteries, 404
Plays, religious, 108
Pole, Cardinal, 7, *note*, 6, 138, 178, 451-452
Pollard, commissioner, 161, 372, 374, 375, 378, 387, 406
Pollesworth, abbey of, 184, 297, 299
Pomfret Castle, surrenders to the "Pilgrims," 233
Poor, spoliation of, 107, 134, 468; relief of, by the monks, 32, 226-228, 463; effect of suppression on, 464-467, 475
Pope, Sir Thomas, 180, 186, 189, 269, 342
Præmunire, use of statute of, made by Henry, 140, 364
Pre, convent of, dissolved, 27
Premonstratensian nuns, site of Stixwold granted to, 192; monks of the order accused of fomenting Lincolnshire rising, 215
Prisons, condition of, 4, 61, 146
Property, rights of, 111; confiscation of, on attainder, 269
Public opinion, power of, 108
Pudsey, Elizabeth, prioress of Eshott, 183
Pulpit, use made of, 46, 109
Purchase of monastic lands, 399 *et seq.*
Purgatory, doctrine of, 133
Pursglove, Robert, prior of Gisburne, 348, 349, *note*
Pyle, Roger, abbot of Furness, 274

QUATUOR, Sanctorum, cardinal, 26, 29

RAMBRIDGE, abbot of St. Albans, 16
Ramsey Abbey, sale of, 399

Rastall, Mr., sent to the Charterhouse, 67
Raynes, Dr., 201; murder of, 208, 209, *note*
Raynes, John, bookseller, 403, *note*
Raynscroftys, Brother, Observant, 47
Reading, Grey Friars of, 325, 328
Reading Abbey, destruction at, 170-171; connection of with Northern rebels, 381; charges against the abbot, 381, 382, *note*; trial and execution of the abbot at Reading, 385-386; forfeiture of, by attainder of the abbot, 387; work of royal commissioners at, 387, *note*
Reding, Thomas, imprisonment of, 72
Reformation, causes of, 1
"Reign of Terror," under Crumwell, 142, 146
Relics, royal crusade against, 404-405
Religious, condition of, prior to the Reformation, 7, 10, 11; discipline of, 92-93; charges against, of incontinence, 118-121; oath of supremacy tendered to, 76; charges against, in the "Black Book," 101-102; difficulty of disproving charges, 113; relative number accused, 123; current calumnies concerning, 125-132; absence of supposed confessions of, 121, *note*; right to appeal to Crumwell, 80; distress and poverty of, 89-91; bribes offered by, 22, 93, 148-149; number desirous to abandon religious life, 123; dismissal of young religious, 80, 90, 106; popular veneration for, 76, 134; charity of, 9, 463; present opinion concerning, 97; pensions of, 91; scattering of, at dissolution of lesser houses, 181-182; number deprived of a living, 190, 194; instances of harsh treatment of, 283; number expelled during general suppression, 359, 360, *note*; anticipate royal spoliation, 334-336; employments of, after expulsion, 447 *et seq.*; bishoprics given to, 448, *note*; scattering of, after dissolution, 451; conformance of, to new religion, 454; rapid dying out of, 455; temporary restoration of houses under Mary, 456; consequence of the suppression of, 460-462; good work of, 462-464

Index

Reynolds, Father Richard, imprisonment of, 65; history of, 65, *note;* execution of, 67
Rich, Hugh, of Richmond, 40, 44, 50, 53
Rich, Richard, chancellor of Court of Augmentations, 180, 402
Richmond, Observants of, 53-54
Risby, Father, 40, 44, 50, 53
Robert, friar of Knaresborough, 252, *note*
Rochester, monk of Charterhouse, 74
Roche Abbey, suppression of, 356-359
Romburgh Priory, seizure of, 28
Rome, separation from, 45, 63, 78; temporary hopes of reconciliation with, 176-179
Romsey, Hampshire, convent of, 352
Rowse, Robert, examination of, at trial of Abbot Marshall, 392-393
Russell, Sir John, 211, 290, 322
Rutland, Lady, letter concerning "Holy Maid," 40

SAGAR, Stephen, abbot of Hayles, 349
Salt, Robert, imprisonment of, 72
Salviati, Jacobo, letter to Campeggio, 31
Saunder, Anthony, lecturer, 93
Savage, Isabel, prioress of St. Michael's, Stamford, 183
Sawley, abbey of, 232, 235, 260, *note,* 270
Scryven, Thomas, imprisonment of, 237
Sedbar, Adam, abbot of Jervaulx, 255-257, 263
Selby, grant of monastery of, 402
Seymour, Sir Thomas, 352, 353, *note*
Sheen, Carthusian house at, 53-54
Shelley, Dame Elizabeth, last abbess of St. Mary's, Winchester, 452, *note*
Shewsbury, Earl of, 233
Shrines, demolition of, 405
Smarte, John, made abbot of Wigmore, 130
Smithfield, priory of St. Bartholomew's at, 22
Somerset, destruction of buildings in, 419

Sopham, Layton's report of prioress of, 166
Southampton, Observant friary at, 50
Southwell, Richard, 191
Spalding, prior of, 22
Spelman, Sir Henry, 107
Spoils of the monasteries, value of, 397 *et seq.;* and of shrines and relics, 409-410, 412-413
Spying employed, 142-143
Staines, Brian, account of the murder of Dr. Raynes, 209, *note*
Stable, suggested employment of abbey as, 273
Stamford, destruction at, 171
Stapleton, William, 251
"Statute of Uses," 203
Staveley, Ninian, 254
Stixwold, Lincolnshire, convent of, petition of, 187
Stokesley, Bishop of London, letter to Houghton, 61; opinion of early suppression, 107-108; imprisoned, 308
Stone, Friar, execution of, at Canterbury, 321, *note*
Stratford, convent at, 307
Stretham, Edmund, prior of Crossed Friars, 125-126, *note*
Suffolk, Duke of, 20, 211, 235, 247, 249
"Supplication of beggars," 8
"Supplication of Poor Souls," 8
Suppression, by Wolsey, 17-19, 26-29; causes for Henry's suppression, 75-76; monasteries suppressed before the passing of the Act, 106; meeting of Parliament of 1536 to pass the Act of, 97, 99, 104; unpopularity of, 20, 78; opposition to the Bill for, 107; passing of the Act, 111, 176-177; sermons employed to break down public opposition to, 109; petition against, from Parliament, 134; denial of the king's intention of, 147, *note,* 332-334; social result of, 9-10; the king's suppression of the lesser monasteries, 179 *et seq.;* time occupied in the work, 182; number and value of houses suppressed, 188, *note;* number of persons who lost their livings by, 190; suppression of Lincolnshire monasteries, 199-201, of Norton abbey, 221, and of Yorkshire monasteries, 224,

note; grievances and hardships of the commoners consequent upon, 225–229; the work of, resumed on the conclusion of Northern risings, 265 *et seq.*; suppression of convents of women, 293 *et seq.*, and of friaries, 312 *et seq.*; progress of general suppression, 331 *et seq.*; number of houses suppressed from 1538 to 1540, 359; suppression of Benedictine abbeys of Glastonbury, Reading, and Colchester, 362 *et seq.*; Act of 1539 to legalise suppressions already made, 429; consequences of, 460 *et seq.*

Supremacy, royal, 45, 51–52, 58, 63–64, 76, 202, 228, 254, 263, 284, 317, *note*, 321, 364, 365, *note*, 387, *note*

Supremacy, papal, adherence to, 55, 57–59, 62, 66, 70, 77, 144, 199, 315, 321, 323, 346, 380

Sussex, Earl of, 265, 267, 270, 275

Swithin's, St., payment extorted from prior of, 164; shrine of, at Winchester, destroyed, 406

Syon, Bridgettine house of, 308, 441, 451, 453, *note*, 456

TEMPEST, Nicholas, 259, 260

Thetford, report from priory of, 120, *note*

Thomas, St., shrine of, at Canterbury, testimony to its magnificence, 407, 408, *note*; its destruction, 408–410; erasure of the name of, 144, 408

Thirsk, William, quondam abbot of Fountains, 257, *note*, 258, 263

Thwaites, Edward, his "Miraculous Work at Court of Street," 35, *note*

Tiltey, Essex, monastery of, 190

Totnes, priory of, 191

Townsend, Sir Roger, Crumwell's agent, 145, 339

Trafford, William, prior of Charterhouse, 71; pension of, 74

Trafford, William, last abbot of Sawley, 260, *note*, 270

Tregonwell, John, royal commissioner, 341, 345

Tunbridge, objection to dissolution of monastery at, 19

Tunstal, Bishop, of Durham, 45, *note*; servant of, 411

Twynham, destruction of priory at, 171

Typlady, Thomas, citizen and broderer of London, 414, *note*

VAGRANTS, Acts passed to deal with, 470, *note*

Vale Royal, bribe offered for abbotship of, 149; dissolution of, 342

Verbal treason, severe punishments for, 315, 321, *note*, 323, *note*

Vernon, Margaret, prioress of Little Marlow, 91; becomes governess to Crumwell's son, 91

Vestments, reserved from spoils for the king's use, 414, *note*, 415, *note*; sales of, 415; used for secular purposes, 416

Visitations, episcopal, 10; powers of visitation obtained by Wolsey, 14, 15

Visitors, Wolsey's, 20–24, *note*, 28

Visitors, royal, *see* Commissioners

"Voluntary surrenders," so-called, 326, 331, 336

WADHAM, Sir Nicholas, 352, 353, *note*

Waldegrave, William, informer, 144

Walden Abbey, *comperta* of, 115; report from, 169

Walle, Thomas, of Canterbury, 39

Walsingham, chapel of Our Lady at, 144–145; popular discontent at, 314

Walstroppe, report of monastery of, 124–125

Walwercke, James, execution of, 74

Ward, Isabel, prioress of Clementhorpe, 183

Wardeboys, John Lawrence de, abbot of Ramsey, 440

Warham, Archbishop of Canterbury, 19, 36

Warwick, destruction at, 171

Watton Priory, 235, 252

Waverly, visitation of abbey of, 87; letter of abbot to Crumwell, 193

Webster, Augustine, prior of Axholme, 64–65, 67

Wells, trial and death of Abbot Whiting at, 377–378

Westminster Abbey, 456, 457

Westacre, reports from, 115, 122, 333; surrender of, 339, 340, *note*

Whalley, abbey of, 259, 270, 271
Whalley, John, commissioner, 67
Wharton, Robert, Abbot of Bermondsey, 441
Whitehead, Dame Isabel, 458-459
Whiting, Richard, abbot of Glastonbury, position and influence of, 363; difficulties of the times, 364; takes oath of royal supremacy, 364; reasons for subscribing, 365, *note*, 366, *note;* visited by Layton, 367; character of, 368; arrival of commissioners, 372; examination of, 373; sent to the Tower, 373; illegal trial of, 374 *et seq.;* execution of, 378
Wigmore, accusation against abbot of, 129; Bishop Fox's report on, 131
Wilson, John, prior of Mountgrace, 354, 355, *note*
Wilson, Nicholas, 355, *note*
Wilton, appointment of abbess to, 23; complaint of prioress of, 306; abbesses of, 307, *note*
Winchcombe, information against abbot of, 92; lecturer appointed at, 93
Winchester, jewelled cross at priory of, 105; amount paid by prior of, to Crumwell, 148
Woburn Abbey, 283
Wolsey, holding of pluralities by, 6; rise of, 12; dealings of, with Rome, 12-18; suppressions of, 17-19, 26-29; power of, 12, 15, 16; opposition to, 16, 19; given the abbey of St. Albans, 16-17; revenues of, 21; agents of, 20, 22; obtains powers of visitation, 14-15; endows colleges, 16, 23, 27; charges against, 23-24; treaties with French king, 25; attempt to be elected pope, 31; proposes to be made vicar-general of the pope, 25; court of, 137; impeachment of, 32, 138-140; death of, 377, *note*
Wombridge Priory, 183
Wood, William, prior of Bridlington, 260, 263
Worcester, foreign bishop of, 5, 14; sale of property of friars to the town, 328
Wriothesley, friend of the Observants, 57
Wykeham, William of, London's false report on, 173

YNGWORTH, *see* Ingworth
York, visitation of, 96, 114; entry of Robert Aske into, 232-233; meeting of insurgent leaders at, 236; commission at, for trial of Northern insurgents, 263

THE END

CHISWICK PRESS: PRINTED BY CHARLES WHITTINGHAM AND CO.
TOOKS COURT, CHANCERY LANE, LONDON.